Don Green

1395

A HISTORY OF THE ROMANS

A History of the Romans

FRANK C. BOURNE *Princeton University*

D. C. HEATH AND COMPANY
Lexington, Massachusetts Toronto London

The maps in this book were drawn
by Donald T. Pitcher.
Chapter illustrations by Aldren A. Watson.

Library of Congress Catalog Card Number: 66–11588

Preface

It is the purpose of this book to present an account of the Romans that will make them intelligible to college students, and to trace their experiences in such fashion that their rise, maturity, and decline will be credible and instructive. While Roman history falls naturally into great divisions of unequal length, which are indicated by the Parts of this book, a constant effort has been made to emphasize the continuity of the Romans' experience and the effects of the triumphs and failures of one age on the problems of the next. The chapters within each Part treat shorter periods or particular aspects of Roman civilization with sufficient brevity to make one or more of them reasonable assignments for weekly classroom discussions.

Many of the events of history are tied to geographical sites, and it is annoying to be unable to locate these without making long excursions from the study of the text. The maps liberally distributed throughout the book furnish the student with a good idea of the location of the areas mentioned close to the places in the text where they are discussed. Moreover, the index indicates specific maps on which most of the geographical locations discussed in the text may be found.

Students invariably find genealogical and chronological tables, such as those in the Appendix, useful; but it is hoped that a greater use will be made by students and teachers of the other two appendices. With minor exceptions, in the text I have avoided transforming ancient monetary values into contemporary terms, for such attempts are always unsatisfactory and often alarmingly inaccurate in days of inflation and monetary manipulation. It is hoped that the brief account in Appendix III of the coinage in three major periods of Roman history and the list of selected prices will lead the reader to reflect seriously on the interrelations of metallic coinage, public confidence, and the prices of various articles and services. He may thus become better able to compare the standard of living among the Romans and that of his own world.

With the exception of a few areas of intensive research of his own, the writer of a Roman history must lean heavily on the work of others. The knowledgeable reader will quickly discern the debt that this book owes to such established greats as Gibbon and Mommsen and also to such competent contemporaries or near-contemporaries as Rostovtzeff, Frank, De Martino, Tibiletti, De Sanctis, Magie, L. R. Taylor, Homo, Carcopino, A. H. M. Jones, and many more. He will also see the results of the study of many articles and monographs, whose number forbids listing, though it cannot erase the gratitude for the unselfish labor that these works represent. From a standpoint of practicality, I have decided to include as Appendix IV a bibliography, not of these useful modern works, but rather of those ancient texts, translated into English and readily available in inexpensive editions, that can be used by teachers to sharpen and deepen the appreciation of their students for the problems of Roman history at every turn.

Finally, I wish to express my gratitude to Princeton University for its generous policy in respect to leaves wherein some of the research and writing of this book could be done, and I am especially grateful to my students, who for twenty years have annually made Roman history a new and exciting experience for me.

Princeton, New Jersey   *Frank C. Bourne*

Table of Contents

Maps

PART

One

Pre-Roman Italy

Chapter 1

PREHISTORIC ITALY

The difficulties of writing even a moderately satisfactory account of peoples that flourished before written documentation are very great. Those difficulties are heightened by the air of authority sometimes assumed by specialists presenting quite inconsistent evidence. Nearly every sentence needs to be qualified by "possibly," "perhaps," or "probably"; but these words are tiresome, and therefore most of us yield to the desire to say something positive. It is therefore necessary to state briefly what are the sources for our knowledge of very early history in Italy, and what are the limitations and virtues of each source.

ANCIENT SOURCES FOR PREHISTORY. There were numerous ancient Roman historians who treated their own most ancient past, and the works of some of these writers still are extant. These give an appearance of great value, for they present a relatively consistent chronology and a wealth of detail. Livy devotes one full book of the *Ab Urbe Condita* ("From the Foundation of the City") to the prehistory of the Latins and to the regal period of the Romans (traditionally 753–509 B.C.), and it took Dionysius of Halicarnassus four books to cover the same periods. Both of these men, however, composed their histories in the first century B.C., more than five hundred years after the events that they described; and other sources for early history—Plutarch, Appian, Dio Cassius—are even later. These writers sometimes state their sources of information, which frequently prove to be the works of annalists, who recorded the events of the past in

1

chronological order, each event under its proper year. The earliest of the annalists, however, lived no earlier than the late third century B.C., and therefore they also composed their works several hundred years after the events that they described. Where did they get their information? Some of it came from the writings of the neighboring peoples that were civilized and literate before the Latins were—the Etruscans to the north or the Greeks of southern Italy and Sicily; but such information was bound to be casual and fragmentary, since Rome and the Latins were not the primary interest of these other peoples. There were also the oral traditions of the Latins themselves handed down from father to son, and at least some written records, both public and private. Writing probably was not used in Latium, however, before the sixth century B.C., and surely was not extensively used before the fifth. Furthermore, the city of Rome was captured by the Gauls and sacked in 390 B.C., and the Roman historians themselves assert that many, though not all, of the records were thereby destroyed. Such public documents as did survive included treaties, laws, decrees of the Senate, and the lists, chants, and ritual handbooks kept by religious officials. The pontiffs, for instance, each year kept a calendar on which the lucky and unlucky days were indicated and which ultimately contained the names of the consuls and the most important events of each year. These calendars were collected around 123 B.C. and are known as the *Annales Maximi* ("Greatest Annals"), but their information must have been meager and arid. Some private documents could be found in the archives of the great families of Rome, and these contained helpful information about past civil and military careers; but the ancients themselves viewed some of these with suspicion, for family pride often prompted exaggerated or completely false claims.

The ancient Roman historians were faced with a problem. Their country had become the most powerful in the ancient world and it must have a history. Flattering song and story soon connected the Romans with the fall of Troy and the wandering Trojan refugees (*ca.* 1200 B.C.), yet continuously dependable information about the Romans was scarce before 390 B.C. Somehow 800 years had to be accounted for, and the chroniclers went to work as best they could with such documents, records, stories, and lists as they had. Some of the material was quite good—it appears, for example, that Roman schoolboys learned by heart their early and great codification of law, *The Twelve Tables* (451–0 B.C.), and records of its text can be regarded as fairly dependable; but the detailed circumstantial accounts of a Livy or a Dionysius must be treated with great care.

MODERN DISCIPLINES.   Fortunately for the modern historian of Rome, there have developed a number of ancillary disciplines, which help to verify or refute the ancient historians, and which often provide us with new information of which the ancients themselves had not the slightest knowledge. One of these disciplines is anthropology, which, strictly speaking, is the science of man. Anthropologists however, generally limit themselves to a study of the emergence and relations of races, physical types, and so-called primitive cultures. Specialists in this field have come to recognize certain characteristics that tend to be common to different peoples at an early stage in their cultural development. The insights developed by such scholars are helpful in suggesting plausible explanations for enigmatic evidence found in art objects, the oral traditions of ballad, epic, and myth, religious rites including burial customs, and the petrified fragments of primitive law embedded in historical legal practices.

Students of linguistics have compared the vocabularies and morphology of historical languages in order to investigate the habits, habitat, government, law, and general cultural progress of the speakers of prehistoric tongues. This is a singularly treacherous milieu. It is possible for a competent scholar to demonstrate relations between languages and dialects, but it is not so easy to demonstrate the relations between their speakers, as the English-speaking peoples of Minnesota and Liberia would testify. When used carefully and sensibly, however, linguistics is an important tool.

A related area is toponymy, the study of place names. This study frequently has been used to trace the supposed migrations of various peoples. It does indeed tell us that a given people has at some time influenced a given area. However, there is a singular lack of unanimity among linguists as to the linguistic identification of some Italian place names; and the appearance of Utica (Carthaginian) and Syracuse (Sicilian Greek), as well as Harlem (Dutch), Albany (English), and Keuka (American Indian) in New York should emphasize the need for caution.

The pride of place goes to ARCHAEOLOGY. Here the careful study of the physical remains of ancient peoples is constantly being refined by techniques ensuring more accurate dating and a more accurate picture of the relations of one people and of one culture with another. By studying the decay of a radioactive isotope called Carbon 14 chemists are able to establish the date of archaeological materials with an accuracy of plus or minus 350 years. For very early dates this is a great step forward. Aerial photography is another modern technique that has done much to advance our knowledge by locating important evidence or sites that would not be apparent from the ground level.

The findings of the archaeologist, directed and interpreted by new techniques, the insights of the anthropologists, the patient investigations of the linguists—all these must be combined with a careful yet imaginative use of the ancient literature in order to create credible accounts of the early Italian world. There also is the factor of physical environment, which has remained sufficiently constant since classical times that historians can use modern data to illuminate the ancient experience. This factor, which consists of geography, climate, and natural resources, is of great importance, for it has both an immediate and a long-range effect on men. By "immediate" we mean that a man is not likely to become a fisherman or a farmer in the Sahara or a refrigerator salesman in the Arctic, nor will he develop the practices and ethos peculiar to those pursuits. By "long-range" we refer to the biological processes of natural selection whereby some peoples, such as the Eskimos, have acquired certain physical characteristics, including a stocky stature, especially beneficial in their habitat. These long-range effects are hard to demonstrate, partly because of the long periods of time necessary for productive observation and partly because of mankind's mobility. Yet in the area of the world that we are about to study historians, archaeologists, and anthropologists have discovered a physical type, "Mediterranean Man," so pervasive and so durable for 4000 years, despite constant intrusions of other types, that we may suppose this particular strain better adapted to the Mediterranean environment than the many intruders have been. Therefore, though they will not be tiresomely repeated, the facts about geography, climate, and natural resources here enumerated should be kept constantly in mind.

GEOGRAPHY.   The familiar Italian boot in the middle of the Mediterranean, with the large island of Sicily at its toe and Sardinia and Corsica off its knee, is about 650 miles long and generally not over 125 miles wide; though in the north, where Italy is part of the continent, the country is more than twice as wide. Sicily contains a little less than 10,000 square miles;

Sardinia is a little smaller; and Corsica has over 3000 square miles. More important than Italy's size is its site, for its position astride the central Mediterranean basin gave its inhabitants a commanding situation in a world tied together by that sea.

The lofty Alps, forming a great crescent along the northern frontier, have a number of good passes and have never been a serious barrier to invasion. The Appenines, which meander down the spine of the peninsula, lowered the quality of much of the area for farming, while in ancient times the numerous spurs extending toward the coasts tended to fragment the land into mutually suspicious political units. On the credit side, however, we must admit that a people that could face and resolve the challenges of this perverse environment might well develop the techniques needed to withstand and unify an even more obstinate world.

The coast of Italy is blessed with few good harbors, and the land has almost no navigable rivers. Such good harbors as exist are largely on the western coast, and this tended to orient Italy more toward the west than toward the east. The Po is the only large river, and its watershed played no part in early Roman history. The Tiber is Italy's most famous river, but it is shallow and treacherous and some difficulty was experienced even in antiquity in towing provisions up it to imperial Rome. Perhaps because of these physical limitations, Romans did not in the beginning adopt the sharp practices and cosmopolitan views of the commercial Greeks and Phoenicians. Their disregard for these matters is signified by the control of the great offshore islands by non-Italians for 250 years after the establishment of the Roman Republic.

NATURAL RESOURCES. In antiquity the soil of Italy was fertile, though shallow. It encouraged the Italians to be farmers and to develop the strengths and weaknesses characteristic of farmers. Furthermore, the alternation of mountain and plain led the Italians to discover the advantages of separate summer and winter pastures at different elevations. This resulted in a need for public pasture lands for the small landowners, free movement between mountains and lowland, and the practice of communal cooperation and forbearance. The land was not well endowed with natural resources, but such as were known were put to good use. The excellent timber that graced the mountains was early sought by foreign traders. The mountains also yielded beautiful building stone that ultimately glorified Italian towns. Some tin is to be found in central Italy, and this made possible the fine bronze work of the second millennium B.C., while the iron of Tuscany and of its island Elba was important in stimulating the Villanovan and Etruscan cultures of the early first millennium. Of some importance too, especially to intrapeninsular trade, were the salt mines of Sicily and the salt pans near the mouth of the Tiber.

CLIMATE. There has been considerable speculation as to the optimum climate for man. One recent investigator has specified temperatures ranging from 38° to 64° Fahrenheit with frequent weather changes and many cyclonic storms. The climates of northern and central Italy are not far removed from these desiderata (at Rome the mean temperature in January is 46°, in July 76°), while southern Italy and Sicily are somewhat warmer. One must add to these factors the salubrious effects of the neighboring seas, the sun, the limpid air, and the clearly etched landscape to understand what has made outdoor living in Italy a joy.

PALAEOLITHIC MAN IN ITALY. While it is believed that the climate of Italy during the classical period was not far different from that of today, Italy, like the rest of the world, has undergone long-term periods of cooling and warming associated with the advance and retreat of glaciers as well as the lesser fluctuations of temperature and of rainfall that characterize interglacial periods. Probably in one of these interglacial periods some 500,000 years ago the genus *Homo* first developed. Specimens that used pebble tools appeared throughout Africa and Eurasia at that time. But *Homo sapiens* perhaps appeared only as recently as 50,000 years ago during a warmer period between two extremes of cold during the last (Wisconsin) glaciation period. Remains of this palaeolithic (Old Stone Age) man, consisting of a few skeletal fragments and flaked instruments of flint and quartzite, are found in northern Italy and in Sicily. Palaeolithic man seems normally to have hunted only smaller game and to have depended largely on nuts, berries, and edible plants. Some probable remains of palaeolithic man are found in Italy even after the appearance of neolithic (New Stone Age) culture, but certainty cannot be attained, since anthropologists must demonstrate racial differences, at least for palaeolithic man, by such meager remains as a few skulls found by chance.

NEOLITHIC MAN IN ITALY. – (*ca.* 5000 – *post* 2000 B.C.).
It is believed that with the retreat of the last glaciers, men enjoying a common culture, known as neolithic culture, spread throughout the Mediterranean basin and into central Europe.

NEOLITHIC
ITALY

The Alps

Po River

LIGURIA

Ligurian
Sea

The Apennines

Elba

TUSCANY

Tiber R.

Corsica

Adriatic
Sea

TAVOLIERE
DISTRICT OF
APULIA

Sardinia

Tyrrhenian Sea

Sicily

AFRICA

Malta

Mediterranean Sea

This does not necessarily mean in every case migration; there are some areas where there appears to have been a steady development from palaeolithic to neolithic. The sources of neolithic culture are uncertain. It may have developed independently in several places; but the great antiquity of cultural finds in the Near and Middle East make these areas likely candidates.

Italy shared in the general neolithic culture, and with it there appeared there the physical type called by anthropologists "Mediterranean Man," a type that has dominated the area ever since despite repeated invasions. How the neolithic people first came to Italy is disputed, but the best opinion is that there was a general expansion northward from the savannahs of the Asian and African steppes when the rainfall there decreased markedly as the glaciers of Europe receded. Some adventurous souls could have crossed the seas from Africa to Italy using the islands of Malta and Sicily as stepping stones; others could have crossed from Africa to Spain at Gibraltar and made their way along the Spanish and French coasts to Liguria and northern Italy.

Neolithic man was able to perfect tools of stone, jadeite, and flint, which were ground and polished. His remains also include glazed pottery and indications that he could manufacture cloth. While still very dependent on hunting, he was also a herder and domesticated the ox, sheep, goat, ass, and perhaps the horse. He collected and ate various wild berries, nuts, and seeds, as palaeolithic man had done, but there are also indications that he cultivated a few varieties of grain.

Some neolithic men lived in caves, but others lived in round or elliptical huts. These were frequently built over a sunken floor with the walls and roof of plaited branches, or withes, meeting at the top and covered with skins, straw, or mud. A smoke-hole in the center is perhaps prophetic of the impluvium (skylight to admit rainwater and light) in the atrium (main room) of the later Roman house. Some neolithic sites suggest an active communal life. The Tavoliere district of Apulia in southeastern Italy, for example, has revealed over 200 neolithic settlements from *ca.* 2500 B.C., and it is the largest known neolithic site in Europe. The settlements consisted of roughly circular areas up to 800 yards across surrounded by ditches averaging twelve feet in width. Sometimes there were several concentric ditches, in one case as many as eight. Within these enclosures there often are found a number of smaller circular enclosures from 40 to 150 feet in diameter and limited by ditches from four to ten feet wide. The purpose of these settlements is not ascertained with certainty, but they have the appearance of furnishing stockades for the domesticated animals of related families or of fellow clansmen. They do not seem to have been military establishments; at least, weapons have not been found in connection with them.

Neolithic men inhumed their dead, who are frequently found buried in a squatting or foetal position. With the dead were buried implements and personal effects. Frequently the skeletons of the dead were painted with red ochre, perhaps because red was considered the color of living health. The burial of artifacts in the graves certainly suggests a belief in some sort of an afterlife.

"Mediterranean Man" absorbed and submerged numerous later arrivals: the speakers of various Italic dialects, Celts, Orientals, Greeks, Teutons, and Goths. It is noteworthy that the characteristic neolithic inhumation persisted in central and southern Italy, despite the adoption of linguistic and other cultural practices that are linked with people with different burial behavior. Also, the survival into historical times of rites and religious practices involving the use of neolithic tools suggests that the neolithic inhabitants had a considerable unacknowledged influence on later arrivals. To appreciate this influence fully one needs only reflect on the tremendous effect in recent history of the established neolithic culture of the Red Indians of North America on the technically far superior European immigrants. In America, before the natives were largely eliminated, constant contact, both friendly and hostile, over several centuries was one of the most important factors in changing the ethos of the immigrants, creating Americans out of Europeans. In prehistoric Italy there was not nearly so great a technical advantage on the part of the bronze-using immigrants; and it appears that the industrious neolithic peasants, especially in southern Italy, gave to the invaders as much as they received from them and furnished much of the manpower, customs, and character to the Italy of the future.

Chapter 2

THE EMERGENCE OF THE ITALIC PEOPLES

We have seen that anthropologists and archaeologists have found evidence of an industrious pastoral and partly agricultural neolithic population in Italy in the third millennium B.C., one that enjoyed a homogeneous culture, though this does not necessarily mean that all its members spoke the same language. By the middle of the first millennium B.C. (500 B.C.), however, there is no question of the heterogeneous nature of the Italian peoples in respect to both language and culture. Because Italian man was illiterate until just before that date we must depend on the disciplines ancillary to history to chart his development. These cannot speak with complete accuracy, and they often are equivocal, yet they do give us some insights.

ITALIC PEOPLES AT THE BEGINNING OF ROMAN HISTORY. By 500 B.C. the picture was somewhat as follows: in the north were the Ligurians and the Raetians, whose languages were possibly of the Indo-European family, but with an earlier substratum; the Venetians and the Messapians on the eastern coast spoke Indo-European tongues allied to that of the peoples on the other side of the Adriatic, though Venetian also shares certain features with Latin. The Picentines on the central eastern coast were themselves not homogeneous: some seem to have spoken an Indo-European tongue, but others did not. The peoples of the Apennine mountain chain spoke a group of closely related Indo-European dialects called Osco-Umbrian or Sabellian; on the western coast were the more distantly related Latins; and farther south were the Sicels, whose tongue shows resemblances both to Latin and also to the language of the Messapians. In addition, there were members of Greek-speaking colonies dotting the southern coasts of Italy and Sicily; there were Semites in far-western Sicily; and the northwestern coast of Italy was held by a people speaking a tongue not yet deciphered or classified, the Etruscans, who were the strongest single group in the peninsula.

How did this heterogeneity arise? In the first place, despite recent advances in knowledge, our information about the neolithic Italians still is meager. It is true that there is a close similarity in their implements, artifacts, and burial practices from site to site, which indicates that they shared a common culture, but we do not know anything of their language, or if they all spoke the same language. It does seem clear, however, that they did not speak tongues related to the Indo-European family of languages. If they did speak different though related Mediterranean dialects, the effect of these different dialects on the Indo-European tongue or tongues that they adapted would partially explain the different Indo-European dialects found in Italy in historical times.

THE INDO-EUROPEANS.   It is natural to be curious about the source of those Indo-European languages that ultimately pervaded Italy, about their speakers, and about the means whereby they spread into distant territories. However, statements about those proto-Indo-Europeans are based upon inferences drawn from their daughter tongues and are quite inexact. Attempts to establish their homeland and to describe their government and ethos from such evidence is full of pitfalls. The best that we can say is that in neolithic times (*ca.* 3500–2000 B.C.) the speakers of the parent Indo-European tongue or tongues must have lived somewhere roughly midway between their points of extreme expansion in antiquity, Ireland and India, and also somewhere north of the Mediterranean and Near Eastern lands, whose inhabitants we know did not speak Indo-European tongues. It is entirely possible that at some very early date they occupied a relatively small and compact area, but attempts to identify the area exactly through a study in the daughter languages of words for physical features, such as trees or fishes, are dangerous. They are dangerous because there is reason to believe that there have been changes in climatic conditions in Eurasia in the period under discussion, thus changing the flora and fauna. There is also a tendency for men to give an old familiar name to some new similar object when the old object disappears. Perhaps the best that we can venture is that the parent Indo-European language (or dialects) was spoken by the late fourth millennium B.C. Its speakers did some farming and they had domesticated the horse and the goat. Unlike their Egyptian and Mesopotamian contemporaries, however, they were illiterate. Our oldest documents in daughter tongues (in Asia Minor and

India) are 1000 to 1500 years later in the second millennium
B.C., and this is ample time for very distinctive differences
among the daughter languages to have arisen.

How did the speakers of Indo-European tongues arrive in
Italy? If, as we believe, they were semi-pastoral, semi-agricul-
tural peoples of central Eurasia, they would have been especially susceptible to changes of climate, particularly to long
periods of drought. Under such a natural pressure, related
groups, often probably of no great size, would have drifted away
from the center toward the west, east, or south, seeking better
opportunities for their flocks and families. As they moved in the
sparsely settled neolithic world, some superiority of those
Indo-European speakers — in organization, language, numbers,
or technology — might have led tribes among whom they moved
to adopt their tongue. Intermarriage and constant modifications
of the language by the new speakers, repeated over long periods of time, may explain the marked divergencies in the
Indo-European dialects by historical times, even in as restricted
an area as Italy.

THE BRONZE AGE; THE LAKE DWELLERS (*ca.* 2000 B.C.).
Somewhere before they entered Italy the speakers of Indo-European tongues learned the use of metals, either discovering it
by themselves or learning it by commercial or other contacts
with the more advanced peoples of the Near East. Sometime
around 2000 B.C. probably the first Indo-European speaking
people appeared in the lake district of northwestern Italy. Of
course we cannot say with certainty what language these arrivals spoke, but the later linguistic history of the area makes this a
plausible hypothesis. They are distinguished by the fact that
they erected pile dwellings in the lakes of the district and that
they knew the use of copper, though stone implements continued to be used also. The lake dwellers were hunters and fish-
ermen, but they had also begun to cultivate some grains and to
domesticate a few animals. Unlike the neolithic inhabitants of
Italy, they seem to have cremated their dead. They must have
come in sufficient numbers, then, to retain rites peculiar to
themselves. It is likely that the prestige of their technical superiority caused neighboring peoples that had contact with them
to adopt or adapt their speech. This would explain the traits of
Ligurian, a tongue that exhibits archaic Indo-European features
but also has traces of a non-Indo-European substratum. The
Indo-European nature of Raetic (if it is Indo-European) might
be similarly explained, with a different substratum or substrata.
The large quantity of amber found at lake dwelling sites indi-

cates that the inhabitants maintained trade routes across the Alps, for amber is a product of northern latitudes. In time the lake dwellers undoubtedly were absorbed physically by their more numerous neighbors, but evidence of their peculiar culture is found well into the Bronze Age.

THE TERRAMARA PEOPLE (*ca.* 1500 B.C.).   About five hundred years later, in the middle of the second millennium B.C., there appeared in the Po valley another people that resembled in some respects the lake dwellers, but that do not seem to be directly descended from them, for their pottery and other art objects connect them with central Europe across the eastern Alps. These immigrants built whole villages on pile-supported platforms above the surrounding plain. The villages seem to have been laid out in a fairly regular form and to have been surrounded by a moat. These settlements have been given the name of *terramara* (rich earth) from the local designation of the sites by Italian farmers, who find the decomposed debris of these areas a rich fertilizer for their crops. While the form of such villages may reflect purely local circumstances, such as a perennial danger of flooding, the culture that we find there is more important. The inhabitants were advanced in both agriculture and metallurgy. They had flax, wheat, and beans, at least wild varieties of fruits and nuts, and had domesticated horses, dogs, oxen, pigs, sheep, goats, and fowl. They probably used carts, and they had learned to make full use of bronze, manufacturing both the instruments of war and those of peace, such as sickles and pins.

Objects similar to those found on the *terramara* sites are found all the way down the peninsula. While they are unmistakeably of the same culture, they show a number of differences due to local factors. This related Bronze Age culture that spread throughout Italy, of which the *terramara* settlements were one part, is sometimes called Apenninic Culture. Probably all the peoples that shared this culture did not speak the same tongue—many probably still were speaking dialects of the earliest Mediterranean language; but probably the bearers of this first Bronze Age culture into Italy did speak an Indo-European dialect. Further, it may be that the ancestors of some of the peoples of historic Italy, the Latins, the Sicels, and the Venetians derived their languages, or some elements of their languages, from the *terramara* folk; for linguists find not only archaic features in these three tongues, but also certain resemblances between them. In any case, the *terramara* folk practiced cremation, placing the ashes of their dead in jars closely packed

13

together in cemeteries and with a minimum of funereal furniture. This would seem to imply a certain disregard for, or disbelief in, life after death, in contrast to the precautions taken by the neolithic peoples among whom they had settled.

MYCENAEAN CULTURE (*ca.* 1500–1100 B.C.).   Meanwhile another culture of the Bronze Age, that of the Aegean, Minoan, and Mycenaean peoples, made but little impact on the Italian mainland; but Sicily and Sardinia were strongly influenced from this direction both in the Copper and Bronze Ages. In Sardinia small groups of herdsmen and farmers felt a need to build as a defensive measure strange conical towers of stone called *nuraghi*. These dot the countryside in great numbers and bear a strong resemblance to medieval castles. The objects discovered in the islands indicate both that they had a busy trade with the eastern Mediterranean and that native cultural development was under stimuli from that direction. Probably the *nuraghi* were built because the residents had good reason to guard against piratical forays that went hand-in-hand with affluent trade.

THE IRON AGE.   Transition from the Bronze Age to the Iron Age was relatively late and gradual in Italy (*ca.* 1000 B.C.). Knowledge of the use of iron originated in the Near East and spread to Italy along a northern route through the Balkans and also along a southern route by sea. Presumably this new technique was brought into the peninsula by later immigrants from the north, people that also spoke Indo-European tongues and cremated their dead. They need not have arrived in great numbers, however, or in the role of conquerors. While their technology, language, and culture spread westward and southward, other arts and techniques came by the sea route from the south and moved northward; and the two prongs of Iron Age culture met and interpenetrated one another in central and north central Italy.

VILLANOVAN CULTURE (*ca.* 1000–750 B.C.).   There were a number of different centers of early Iron Age culture in Italy, each with distinguishing features, yet each also showing certain common elements. There was a Comacine-Golassecan culture around the lakes of northwestern Italy; Atestine in Venetia; while the Apenninic peoples moved from the Bronze to the Iron Age partly under the influence of their northern neighbors and partly under that of the Greek colonies that had begun to dot the southern and southwestern shores of Italy. The best

THE PEOPLES
AND CULTURES OF
EARLY ITALY
2000-500 B.C.

RAETIA

LAKE
DISTRICT
COMACINE-GOLASECCAN
CULTURE

VENETIA

ATESTINE
CULTURE

Illyrians

LIGURIA

Terramara
Settlements

Elba

Etruscans

VILLANOVAN CULTURE

PICENUM

UMBRIA

APENNINIC CULTURE

Corsica

Sabines

Aequi

Vestini

Rome

LATIUM

Volsci

Sabellians

CAMPANIA

Iapygians

Messapians

Sardinia

Oscans

Greeks

Phoenicians

Sicily

Sicels

Greeks

AFRICA

Malta

Mediterranean Sea

attested is the Villanovan culture, named from a village near Bologna where early archaeological evidences were discovered. This culture is found in a broad diagonal from northeast to southwest across the northern half of Italy, and it approximates the modern areas of Emilia, Tuscany, and part of Latium. Even within this area there are noticeable regional differences, and Villanovan culture is therefore sometimes divided into Northern and Southern Villanovan. The culture of the north was probably brought by Indo-European speaking immigrants who cremated their dead, while the inhabitants of the southern section were affected not by immigrants but only by their culture which spread both from the north and by sea from the south and east.

In the early part of the Iron Age (*ca.* 1000 B.C.) the use of iron itself was still rather rare, but other articles found in Villanovan graves are unmistakeably different from earlier Bronze Age objects. In the north, the ashes of the dead now were placed in biconical vases decorated with geometrical designs. In the graves were finely executed bronze ornaments and elaborately worked pins. Articles of hammered bronze, decorated with *repoussé* technique, included vases, bowls, tray-tables, cups, and girdles. However, as new sources of iron were discovered and developed we find greater use of it. Even chariots were made with iron wheels. The appearance of fine work in gold and silver and articles from abroad, such as amber from the North and glass paste from the East, suggests an increasingly important trade by land and sea, perhaps because iron was found and worked in sufficient quantities to become a feasible article of exchange.

The inhabitants of the southern section of the Villanovan area shared many features of this early Iron Age culture, but there were some differences. In the South, techniques were not quite so advanced; cremation did not completely replace inhumation; and the receptacles of the ashes of the dead were not the rather impersonal biconical jars of the North, but urns made to resemble the huts in which the earthly life had been spent. In this area probably there had been fewer immigrants; penetration had been only cultural, and therefore the burial practices that the inhabitants adopted were modified by the older neolithic traditions of inhumation and by the concern for the afterlife that is implied in the burial practices of Aegean and other Mediterranean cultures.

So far we have perhaps accounted for a part of the patchwork of peoples that are found in Italy at the beginning of history: we have supposed that the peculiarities of the Raetians and Ligurians in the North were due to early and imperfect contacts with one of the earliest penetrations of Indo-European culture. We have further noted the possibility that the Venetians, Sicels, and Latins owe common archaic features of their languages to the influence of another early cultural penetration, perhaps that of the *terramara* people. Furthermore, the Latins and the Venetians enjoyed a share, at least, in the related Iron Age cultures, the Villanovan in central Italy and the Atestine in Venetia. Finally, we have found that the Latins were settled in the southern part of the areas penetrated by Villanovan culture, where they also were under the strong influence of older native, as well as other Mediterranean, influences.

These same Latins, with Rome as their center, were the dynamic nucleus, the template, the mould upon which a homogeneous Roman Italy was at length fashioned. However, we must still account for four other great peoples that were present at the beginning of history and that were directly influential in the formative years. These are the Italic peoples of the Apennines, the Etruscans, the Greeks, and the Phoenicians. Of these, the Etruscans were so important at so early a date that they deserve a separate chapter; and there we shall also examine, briefly, the Greeks and the Phoenicians. However, the Italic peoples, the non-Latin Indo-European speaking peoples of central and southern Italy, exclusive of the Greeks, furnished a major portion of the material from which Roman Italy was forged. The Romans were in constant contact with them, frequently in conflict and sometimes in alliance; and ultimately while absorbing them the Romans inevitably absorbed many of their institutions and characteristics.

THE SABELLIANS.   While Iron Age culture radiated out from the Villanovan area to affect the peoples both north and south, and while much emanated from the Greek colonies along the southern shores of Italy, there were also at indeterminate dates groups of people speaking Indo-European tongues who sifted down through the mountainous regions of central and southern Italy. It is not clear whether their immediate source was the north, or whether they came from across the Adriatic to the east, or both. In any case, they imposed their Indo-European languages on the peoples that they found already resident in those areas, although the earlier inhabitants probably modified these languages in adopting them. The most important of these languages was Sabellian, of which there was a northern branch, Umbrian, and a southern one, Oscan. To one or other of these languages the tongues of most of the minor peoples, such as the

Aequi, Sabines, Vestini, and Volscians appear to belong. By historical times the languages and influence of these people were rapidly and effectively spread by a custom called the *ver sacrum* (sacred spring). By this practice, apparently to counteract perennial overpopulation, the young people in certain years were dedicated to a deity, and when of age were sent out to find new homes for themselves. Through this custom the Sabellians rapidly spread down to the sole and the toe of the Italian boot and into the rich lands of Campania; and one branch, the Volscians, pressed to the sea between Latium and Campania.

The Italic inhabitants of central and southern Italy did not develop a city culture, nor were they a nation. Their effective organization was the tribe and the canton, their largest settlements villages. In time of danger they formed federations to wage war, but such unions were not permanent. Unlike their Latin neighbors, we find practically no trace of a government by kings. Their leaders were democratically elected officials, in most cases consisting of councils ranging from two to ten members. Various members of these councils had specialized functions, but whether there are cases where the members were of equal rank, as at Rome, is not clear; in some places, especially among the Oscans, they certainly were not.

In religious practices the Italic peoples bore many resemblances to the Latins. Many of the local Italian deities were disembodied spirits that were important to fertility; anthropomorphism (the creation of gods in Man's image) did not develop for several centuries. Some communities had special colleges of priests appointed to maintain the cult practices and to direct religious rites, for an extremely cautious observance of ritual was characteristic of these early people.

Although for many years numerous Italic peoples were enemies of the Romans, they became their allies and fellow soldiers for centuries. Ultimately they constituted a major portion of the citizen body of Roman Italy.

Chapter 3

PHOENICIANS, GREEKS, AND ETRUSCANS IN THE WEST

We have briefly examined the origins or the prehistoric condition of the Italic peoples that were to furnish the bulk of the human resources of the early Roman State. Our account of them has been constantly obscured because they left no written records, and their literate neighbors seldom mentioned them. There also appeared in pre-Roman Italy or Sicily three peoples whose importance is not in their numbers, but in their great influence in the formative years of the Roman nation. These peoples were the Phoenicians, the Greeks, and the Etruscans. While a number of obscurities also surround these peoples, records and other evidence about them are fuller and firmer and with them we approach the bounds of conventional history.

THE PHOENICIANS.   The Phoenicians lived along a strip of coast of the eastern Mediterranean between the sea and the mountains of Lebanon and Galilee. Their chief cities were Akko, Tyre, Sidon, Berytus, and Byblos. The narrowness of their agricultural resources, the pressures of fierce neighbors to their rear, and undoubtedly a native talent for commerce led them to seek a livelihood on the sea as traders. They were further favored by their situation on the Mediterranean at a terminus for caravan routes from Mesopotamia, and they were in the path of others from Egypt to Asia Minor. For trade they commanded the cedars of Lebanon, which were used in their own ships and were needed by treeless Egypt; they discovered and developed the production of glass from their fine native sand; and they produced a highly prized purple dye derived from offshore shellfish. They learned at an early date not only to distribute their own wares, but also to barter the goods of other people at a profit. They ventured far afield in the late Bronze Age, and already by the time of Homer's *Odyssey* (eighth cen-

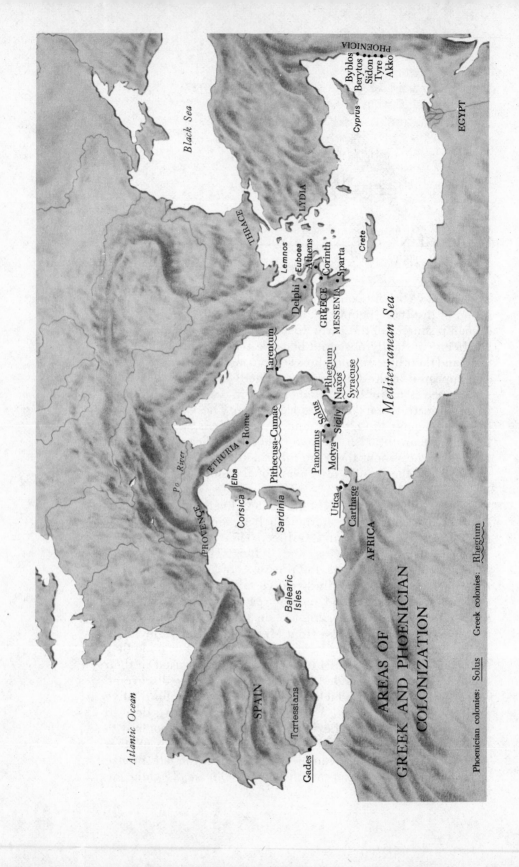

AREAS OF
GREEK AND PHOENICIAN
COLONIZATION

Phoenician colonies: <u>Solus</u>   Greek colonies: <u>Rhegium</u>

Atlantic Ocean

Black Sea

Mediterranean Sea

PHOENICIA
Byblos
Berytos
Sidon
Tyre
Akko

Cyprus

EGYPT

LYDIA

THRACE

Crete

Lemnos
Euboea
Athens
Corinth
Sparta
Delphi
GREECE
MESSENIA

Tarentum

Rhegium
Naxos
Syracuse

Panormus Solus
Sicily
Motya

Utica
Carthage

AFRICA

Pithecusa-Cumae

ETRURIA • Rome

Po River

PROVENCE

Elba
Corsica
Sardinia

Balearic
Isles

SPAIN
Tartessians

Gades

tury B.C.?) were well known as wily traders. To the Orient they brought treasures celebrated in the Old Testament: gold, silver, iron, tin, and lead from Tarshish, according to passages in Ezekiel (eighth century B.C.) and I Kings (seventh century B.C.). (Tarshish is generally taken to refer to Tartessos in southern Spain.) Other sources tell us that Phoenicians had established a trading post at Gades, near Gibraltar, at a very early date, and they undoubtedly had done so by the ninth century B.C. Ancient seamen tended to stay close to land wherever possible, and the Phoenicians skirted the North African coast on their trips and ultimately established colonies at suitable anchorages along the route. Utica was one of the earliest of these, but Carthage, traditionally founded in 814 B.C., is the most famous. During the colonizing period the preeminent Phoenician city was Tyre, and it was the mother city of these stations. No earlier than the eighth century B.C., establishments were made in the extreme west and north of Sicily at Motya and Panormus, while a third colony, Solus, probably dates from the sixth century B.C. These, with small posts on the coast of Sardinia, served to guard routes of trade to Italy, especially to the Etruscans. The Etruscans were important to Phoenician traders, for they were exploiting the iron of Elba, which was in great demand in the East.

None of the Phoenician colonies was large, nor did any consider itself an independent establishment. The colonies originally served only to protect and maintain Tyre's trade lines to the West. It was only when the mother city was no longer able to defend her outposts that they began to take independent action. From 585 to 572 B.C. Tyre had been besieged by Nebuchadnezzar of Babylon and finally had to recognize Babylonian suzerainty. At the same time the Greek cities of Sicily had launched an attack on the Phoenician stations of western Sicily. This the residents themselves with the aid of native allies were able to beat off, but Tyre had proved unable to help. Apparently soon thereafter Carthage, the most affluent of Tyre's colonies, undertook the leadership of the western Phoenicians. She thereupon embarked on 350 years of activity and wealth that made her one of the great Mediterranean powers.

While the Carthaginians learned to exploit fully the rich agricultural resources around their city, they were not land-hungry in the sense that the Italic peoples or even the Greeks were. They clearly recognized the need to maintain their stations on the narrows between Sicily and Africa in order to protect routes of trade to the north and west. When these were threatened they fought bitterly. It was just such a challenge that brought them ultimately into fatal conflict with the Romans. The Romans, in turn, were influenced by the Carthaginians and copied their technical superiorities. They adopted, for example, Carthaginian scientific agriculture and transformed the Italian countryside from small peasant holdings to large estates, which with the labor of slaves could be scientifically and economically cultivated. Most important, however, the bitterness and barbarity of the military conflicts between Carthage and Rome hardened and brutalized the Romans past recognition.

THE GREEKS.   Greek colonization in Italy and Sicily was far more extensive than that of the Phoenicians, and it was of quite a different character. It was not initiated primarily because of commercial needs. Rather, there were demographic, economic, political, social, and even religious factors involved. There appears to have been a vigorous increase in population throughout Greece starting in the eighth century B.C. Even small cities managed to send out colonies in remarkable numbers; and these at length dotted the shores of the Black Sea, Thrace, Egypt, North Africa, Italy, Sicily, Corsica, Provençe, and Spain. Lack of sufficient arable land in Greece to feed or employ the population was an important factor behind this colonization. Sparta, whose conquest of the neighboring Messenians in the eighth and seventh centuries furnished room for expansion near home, did little colonizing. In some states landless peoples resulted from the overthrow of kings, who generally had been the people's protectors, for these revolutions led to the establishment of oligarchies, which monopolized the land for themselves. Even the Oracle at Delphi played a part in stimulating the emigration from Greece and is said to have been the advocate of the colonies at Cumae, Rhegium, Syracuse, Croton, and Tarentum.

The oldest of the Greek colonies was Pithecusa on the island of Ischia in the Bay of Naples. This was founded between 775 and 770 B.C. by emigrants from the island of Euboea. About twenty years later they moved to the mainland opposite Ischia and established themselves at Cumae. Here they had a rocky hill on the shore for a citadel and a rich surrounding plain for their sustenance. At about the same time that Cumae was established other Euboeans founded Rhegium. Still other Euboeans founded Naxos in Sicily *ca.* 757, Catania and Leontini in 752, and Zancle on the Straits of Messina *ca.* 750; while Megaraeans founded Megara Hyblaea at about the same time. Syracuse, ultimately the most powerful of the Greek colonies, was established in 733 by Corinthians. Toward the end of the eighth century B.C. Peloponnesians founded cities that were to be famous around the Gulf of Tarentum: Sybaris, Croton, and Tarentum. To the first quarter of the seventh century belong Locri, founded by the Cretans, and Siris, established by Ionians from Asia Minor.

Each of these cities became an independent self-governing unit, rather than an "empire" of the mother city. It is true that each city owed her parent city respect and naturally was inclined to trade with her. The bent of the colonies, however, was not commercial but agricultural. Very few of them had good harbors, some of them nothing but sand beaches. What they were interested in and did exploit was farmland; and even Syracuse, which had a good harbor, based its wealth on agriculture. Ultimately the Corinthians came to monopolize most of the carrying trade between Greece proper and the western Greeks of "Great Greece" or Magna Graecia, as it was called.

In the seventh century, as the older colonies prospered, some of the more ambitious founded new colonies. Hence Posidonia (Paestum) was founded by the Sybarites; the Syracusans established Acrae, Casmenae, and Camarina in Sicily; Gela founded Agrigentum around 580 and it soon outstripped its parent in fame and wealth. A little earlier Megara Hyblaea had founded Selinunte in western Sicily, and Zancle established Himera on the northern coast.

It is interesting to note that the Greeks brought all their particularism and all their dissensions with them from their homeland, and that imperialistic or fusionist sentiments among them are not clearly to be discerned until both Syracuse and Athens tried to establish empires in the late fifth and the fourth centuries. Before that time the colonists were chiefly occupied in exploiting fertile land. In Sicily they managed to overrun a great deal of the valleys and plains, for they found the Siculans too weak to ward them off. In Italy, however, they found their match in the vigorous Italic peoples. Still, their affluence supported the cultivation of Hellenic arts and crafts, literature, and philosophy; and their influence radiated throughout the peninsula. First through the Etruscans and later by direct contact, the Greeks of Italy and Sicily became the teachers of the Romans; and later still, as allies or citizens with a knack for business, they became the Romans' fellow exploiters of the Mediterranean world.

THE ETRUSCANS: ORIGINS AND LANGUAGE. The people that had the most immediate and perhaps the most pervasive influence on the future Romans, however, were the Etruscans. The

Etruscans have fascinated scholars and laymen for generations, partly because we have found so many attractive and impressive remains of their culture and partly because an aura of mystery hovers over them, since we have so very few explanations to attach to those remains.

The enigmatic nature of the Etruscans is heightened by the fact that they spoke a language not yet deciphered, and that there has been a good deal of argument, even in ancient times, as to their racial origin. They themselves stated that they were from Asia Minor, naming Lydia as their ancient homeland; and some later Greek writers supported this view. Certainly there is much in Etruscan art and culture that indicates Oriental connections of some sort. There also was, however, an ancient opinion that the Etruscans were natives of Italy that had developed their peculiar culture while basking in an affluence drawn from the exploitation of natural resources, native talent, and foreign trade. To support this view, archaeologists point out that there is no sudden break in culture, no signs of wholesale destructive invasion, between the peoples that display the Villanovan culture (*ca.* 1000–750 B.C.) in Tuscany in the very early Iron Age and the Etruscans (*ca.* 750–100 B.C.). Their sites often are the same or are contiguous.

While the Etruscan language does not seem to be of the Indo-European family, it has not been clearly connected with other language groups. There are about ten thousand Etruscan inscriptions preserved; and, though we cannot claim to have deciphered the language, we can understand with some certainty a good deal of the content of many of these documents and much about the structure of their language. One long inscription from the island of Lemnos in the Aegean shows many similarities to Etruscan, perhaps strengthening the theory of an Asiatic origin for the Etruscans; but, on the other hand, numerous parallels of vocabulary and structure between Etruscan and the Italic languages can be found. These trouble the honest investigator. He must admit the possibility that there were related "Mediterranean" languages widely dispersed in the lands surrounding that sea before speakers of the Indo-European tongues arrived on the scene. In that case adventurers from the Orient could have found peoples in Italy whose tongues were sufficiently closely related to their own to make assimilation relatively easy.

It is most likely that Etruscan culture is the product of an amalgamation of peoples. There were undoubtedly numerous inhabitants of Etruria whose forebears had dwelt there from the Neolithic (3500–2000 B.C.) and Bronze (2000–1000 B.C.) Ages.

Others were descended from those people, however few, that had brought to the area the culture known as Villanovan, which flowered in the early Iron Age (1000–750 B.C.), when the Tuscan mineral deposits began to be exploited and affluence and craftsmanship progressed hand in hand. An increase in attractive material possessions naturally led to an expanding trade and brought central Italy and its people to the attention of the traders of the older, richer, culturally more mature peoples of the eastern Mediterranean. Traders were naturally followed by settlers, colonists, and entrepreneurs. There need not have been great numbers of immigrants, but superiorities in arts, crafts, and religious science soon established for them commanding positions in various settlements. In a world uncursed by nationalistic disposition, capable newcomers could be treated with unfeigned interest, awe, and respect. Etruscan culture was unmistakably the product of some such combination of cultures. It was not something imported whole from north or east, nor yet something developed locally without any external influence.

When we speak of the Etruscans, we speak of a people that shared a language, certain religious beliefs, and a culture, though the latter showed local variations. Etruria was not a nation in the modern sense of the word in the sixth century B.C. any more than was Greece. The Etruscan cities were independent and individualistic, and they often differed with one another in both internal and external policies.

ETRUSCAN RELIGION.   The Etruscan cities did appear, however, to have religious cohesion. It was their specialized knowledge in matters of religion that impressed their neighbors, especially the Romans: "a people," Livy says, "that above all others was devoted to religious practices because it excelled all others in the art of cultivating these." The Etruscan was enveloped by a sense of religious awe, with a feeling for inseparable relations between heaven, earth, and Hades. To lay out the streets of his cities he projected the paths of heavenly bodies upon the earth. Their intersections were also portals through which infernal spirits could rise. Just beyond his walls, which were carefully constructed according to divine instructions, he could see laid out by similar rules cities for his dead. He strode through a vibrant and meaningful world. The colorful painted birds flitting about a pensive dancing piper on the walls of an Etruscan tomb should not be interpreted as merely gay decorations—they were involuntary but sure signs of the divine will. In the Etruscan mind all things were so involved with one

25

another that in the vital organs of beasts they could find the imprint of events past and future. The interpretation of those imprints became an art valued by the Romans long after the Etruscan people had been submerged. The art of interpreting and carrying out the divine will in earthly affairs, the *disciplina Etrusca,* was taught to the Etruscans by a gray-haired child named Tages, who had been found in a field at Tarquinii. So impressive was this discipline that even the Romans, who later portrayed themselves historically as natural enemies of the Etruscans, sent their young men to Tuscan cities to learn. Little wonder that so few held so much of Italy so long spellbound.

ETRUSCAN POLITICAL STRUCTURE.   Thus religion furnished such national unity as there was for the Etruscans. There were twelve great Etruscan gods, and there were twelve Etruscan cities banded together in a league. Representatives of the league met in the Grove of Voltumna (Etruscan *Veltune*). Voltumna was the great god of the Etruscans and patron of one of the league cities, Bolsena. When delegates of the twelve Etruscan cities met at the grove near Bolsena they might discuss matters of mutual interest, just as the Greeks did at the festivals of Olympia or Delphi; but their main object was joint religious activity. Centuries after the Etruscans had lost such national identity as they ever had had, as late as Constantine (fourth century A.D.), they still were meeting to perform their sacred functions.

Etruscan cities were originally kingdoms, as was the semi-Etruscan city of Rome. It is interesting that Rome's first Etruscan king is said to have been named Lucumo in Etruria, which name at Rome he changed to Lucius, for the royal title in Etruria seems to have been *lucumo*. During the sixth and fifth centuries B.C., however, the Etruscan cities joined many other parts of the Mediterranean in replacing their primitive monarchies with aristocratic republics. Rome did this at the end of the sixth century B.C. Her arch-rival, Veii, however, retained a king, and the disapproval of her sister Etruscan cities in the league cost her their political support when Rome threatened her destruction. The *lucumones* were replaced by annually elected officials who seem to have formed a board of magistrates of differing rank and function. At the head of the administration stood a *zilath*; and there also was a *maru* and a *camthi*, who were probably lesser magistrates, though organization surely differed from city to city. The later history of many cities leads one to suppose that they also had councils of elders drawn from the aristocratic families, and that these assisted the magistrates, while the general population did not play an important role in the government. The *zilaths* retained the power and prerogatives of the kings. Much of the paraphernalia surrounding the highest magistracies in Rome, as well as the powers given to them, were derived from the Etruscans. From them came the purple robe for the king or the triumphal general, the throne, the twelve lictors to accompany the chief magistrate (perhaps in imitation of the twelve attendants of the head of the Etruscan league, each symbolizing one of the member cities), and the *fasces*, the bundle of rods with an axe, symbolizing civil and military power. It is likely that not just these outward symbols, but also the idea of *imperium,* the power of a magistrate, who represents the authority of the state, came from the Etruscans.[1]

ETRUSCAN EXPANSION (SEVENTH-SIXTH CENTURIES B.C.).
To trace what little we can of Etruscan history we must depend on the evidence of archaeology and on the observations of other peoples, since we can make little use of their own documents. We know from the Greek historian Herodotus that in 540 B.C. sixty Etruscan ships from Caere cooperated with sixty Carthaginian ones in a battle against the Greek colonists from Phocaea at Alalia in Corsica. The Greeks of Alalia had only sixty ships, but they won the battle. They were so weakened in victory, however, that they had to abandon their Corsican settlement. There are several interesting conclusions that one may draw from this event, for it helps correct a common misconception that the Etruscans formed an empire in Italy. First, this was not a case of united Etruscans defending their commercial empire: only one commercial city, Caere, was involved. Furthermore, Caere could put to sea a fleet no larger than one manned by a recently founded and weak Greek colony, Alalia; and, even though Caere's ships were doubled by allies, this combination was not sufficient to prevail. Finally, as the Greeks themselves admitted, the Etruscans and the Carthaginians attacked the Phocaeans of Alalia in order to curb their acts of piracy. These two notoriously commercial peoples, the Carthaginians and the Etruscans (though here only one Etruscan city) had to protect their trade. Their success in driving away the Greeks did not increase any "Etruscan Empire" in Corsica and Sardinia, both of which were in the Carthaginian sphere of influence three hundred years later, in the third century B.C. This incident

---

[1]   For a full description of *imperium,* see p. 53.

PHOENICIAN, GREEK
AND ETRUSCAN SITES
IN ITALY

Phoenician sites: Panormus
Greek sites: Leontini
Etruscan sites: Caere

CISALPINE
GAUL
VENETIA
Cremona
Po R.
Mantua
Placentia
Mutina
Spina
LIGURIA
Parma
Marzabotto
Felsina
Faesulae

Volterrae
ETRURIA
Populonia
Perusia
Elba
Clusium
Vetulonia
Bolsena
Corsica
Vulci
Tuscania
Tarquinii
Veii
Alalia
Caere
Rome
LATIUM
Volsci
Samnites

Capua
Cumae
CAMPANIA
Tarentum
Pithecusa
Sele R.
Paestum
Siris

Sardinia
Sybaris

Croton

Zancle
Panormus
Locri
Himera
Motya
Solus
Rhegium
Selinunte
Sicily
Naxos
Leontini
Catania
Agrigentum
Acrae
Megara Hyblaea
AFRICA
Gela
Syracuse
Camarina
Casmenae

shows that Etruria was not a nation bent on imperialistic expansion. It was a collection of individual cities interested in commerce. Their wealth did not come from the exploitation of others, but from trade in their own natural resources. The country also enjoyed rich agricultural resources: despite their traditional rivalry, in times of famine the Romans bought grain from Etruria; and grain was the contribution of six of the great cities of the league to Rome as late as the war with Hannibal (late third century B.C.).

At the height of Etruscan affluence during the seventh and sixth centuries B.C. its culture extended north and south to the Po valley and to Latium and Campania. However, this does not indicate a concerted national effort. The cities in these new areas were settled, or conquered and dominated, by surplus populations from the cities of Etruria proper led by roving heroes and freebooters. These men figured in later Roman tales and fables: the Tarquins, Mastarna (or Servius Tullius), the brothers Vibenna, and Lars Porsenna, all were important in the Etruscanization of Rome. The Etruscans moved southward under the leadership of such men as far as the Sele River in the plain of Salerno, just north of Greek Paestum. Nonetheless, their conquests never constituted an empire. Instead, twelve of the cities of Campania organized themselves, on the home model, into a loose confederation, with Capua as the chief city; and in the North, in the Po valley, other cities — somewhat later than in Campania — organized themselves in a similar manner, with Felsina in the leading role. Although there was no concerted effort by the homeland to defend them, the Etruscan cities of Campania felt more secure when they had a lifeline in Latium of Etruscanized cities such as Praeneste, Rome, and Tusculum along the land routes to Etruria proper, and they probably encouraged their fellow countrymen to hold those Latin cities.

DECAY OF THE ETRUSCANS (500–88 B.C.). The Etruscan cities of Campania were subjected to constant pressures. The Greeks at Cumae presented a persistent threat to them. At the end of the sixth century B.C. they helped to engineer the fall of the Etruscan overlords in Latium, including those in Rome; and in 474 B.C. Hiero of Syracuse inflicted a severe naval defeat on the Etruscans off Cumae. Meanwhile, Italic peoples from the hinterland, such as the Aequi and the Volsci, were pressing seaward; and by the fifth century the Volsci had reached the seacoast north of Capua, so that now the Etruscan cities of Campania were effectively cut off from other Etruscan cities by land and by sea. These cities could hold out for only a few decades, and by 430 most of Campania had succumbed to Samnite mountaineers.

A little later the confederacy of the North experienced a similar fate. The late fifth century B.C. was one of the periods of great Celtic migrations. These people, commonly called the Gauls, poured into the Po valley. Little by little the beleaguered Etruscan cities there fell, though strong Etruscan influences remained in some places, such as Mantua. In search of booty the Gauls pressed on into Etruria proper. While most of the cities remained impregnable within their walls, Rome was captured by them and held briefly around 390. Though the Gauls could not hold Etruria proper, they disrupted its economy and hastened its decay. Meanwhile, they took over the rich Po valley between Liguria and Venetia, and it became known thereby as Cisalpine Gaul.

The fourth and third centuries B.C. were periods of progressive decline for the Etruscans. While they were plagued by Gallic incursions, and probably were experiencing some weakening in mineral and agricultural productivity, they were still not a unified people and acted with no unified policy. The Syracusans repeatedly attacked their coast and in the middle of the fifth century were able to conquer and pillage the mineral-rich island of Elba. Some Etruscan cities sent three fifty-oared ships to help the Athenians against the Syracusans in 414–413. In revenge the tyrant of Syracuse in 384 again attacked the coast near Caere and carted off booty valued at 1500 talents from treasures and temples. At the same time, Romans were encroaching on Etruscan lands. Veii, unsupported by her sister cities, fell to Rome in 396; her citizens were sold into slavery and her lands divided among the conquerors. A series of defeats suffered by other cities at Roman hands in the fourth and third centuries brought them all, by 280, into the Roman system of dependent alliances. Meanwhile, the Etruscan cities suffered the same internal conflicts between patricians and plebeians, rich and poor, as Rome. From wars and appropriations the Romans possessed ample land to settle their dissident citizens as colonists, but the Etruscans no longer had such land available. Instead, a civil struggle broke out; and the Romans consistently exploiteded these weaknesses. The Etruscan paintings belonging to this period of despair and decay portray a grisly and morbid concern with death, which replaces the serenity and joyous acceptance of the unity of human experience characteristic of earlier Etruscan art. The Etruscans seem to have been convinced by their own lore that a given number of ages is fated to every people and that they had been allotted eight. So they turned their thoughts to death and to God's will. Interestingly enough, the year in which the eighth age allotted to the Etruscans was completed (88 B.C.) was the year in which their cities received the Roman citizenship and were absorbed into the Roman State, in recompense for their quiescence when other Italian states were fighting for their freedom during the Social War (90–88 B.C.).

ETRUSCAN INFLUENCE. Before the Etruscans lost their freedom and identity, however, years of contact with them had been enjoyed by their conquerors and successors, and in these years the Romans had learned much, although there was much that they were incapable of reproducing. The Etruscan knowledge of drainage had made towns habitable, swamps arable, and gardens flourish. Even though much of the superstructure of their temples was of stucco and timber that has largely disappeared, what is left is rich and colorful. Some of their towns that have been excavated were carefully laid out in city blocks: in the northern confederacy, for example, Marzabotto had streets that crossed each other at right angles at exact intervals, while the famous port of Spina on the Adriatic had canals laid out with the same regularity. The Etruscan metallurgy was extensive, and they showed a wonderful skill in the casting of bronzes of which we possess superb examples. Their sculpture in terracotta was unique. Preserved examples, such as the elegant winged horses of Tarquinii and the Apollos of Veii and Falerii, are monumental yet vivacious and individual. Their jewelry was of a fine and cunning craftsmanship that excites admiration and wonder. Compared with such other ancient painting as we have, their painting is unrivalled for disciplined vivacity and sometimes a disarmingly frank primitivism and naïveté. The Etruscans at first borrowed, imported, and adopted much from Asia Minor; later they fell more and more under the spell of the art and mythology of the mainland Greeks. Always, however, in the days of their assurance their products were stamped with the vigor, optimism, and joy of their own native genius and individuality.

The Etruscans were indeed absorbed, but their influence on the Romans and through them on the Western world is incalculable. From them the Romans not only learned to surround their magistrates with pomp, but they adapted from them the prerogatives and duties with which to endow their highest officials, and these were then handed on to such strong elected executives as the American presidents. The honorable place

31

that women held in their society, as opposed to a nearly Oriental seclusion for some Greek women, is reflected in the prestige and influence of Roman matrons, a power that Western women have generally continued to exercise.

From the Etruscans the Romans apparently also learned the art of surveying and the practice of designing carefully the street patterns in their colonies and military camps. Roman private architecture owed some of its flexibility to them, and temples of the Etruscan type, designed for triads of divinities, became standard on Roman capitols. The Etruscan knack for catching the particular in art was reflected in the famous individualism and veracity of Roman portraiture.

Linguists can cite many a famous Roman name (one scholar has collected twenty pages of them) disclosing Etruscan antecedents. Of course one of the most famous is Maecenas (70?–8 B.C.), intimate of Augustus, scion of Etruscan kings, patron of the arts, and learned in the art of maintaining disinterested friendship in an ambitious world. Vergil of Etruscan Mantua has as a cognomen Maro, recalling the Etruscan magistrate *maru;* and that most Roman of Romans, Marcus Tullius Cicero, not only sports the gentile name of an Etruscan adventurer, Masterna, known in Rome as King Servius Tullius, but the very name Cicero, according to a recent study, would be the Etruscan for "chief" (*cekha*).

And finally, who knows what dark recesses Etruscan religion touched? Many of the names of the great Roman gods are recognizable in the Etruscan pantheon. Etruscan augury and Etruscan concern for the divine order impressed the Romans, was studied by them, and became part of their daily habits. Even the monuments of their decay, their late tomb paintings, obsessed as they were with death and its fiends, were visited and studied by medieval man and found a vehicle for their message in that Tuscan architect of a Christian Hell, Dante Alighieri.

PART
TWO

Survival and Unification

Chapter 4

THE LATIN SETTLEMENT ON THE TIBER

THE LATINS: TERRITORY AND ORGANIZATION.   The territory
of the Latins in earliest times (before 1000 B.C.) was sufficiently restricted and unattractive to make the more surprising
the ultimately worldwide importance of its inhabitants. When
the Latins first emerged as a recognizably distinct people
(eighth century B.C.) their territory (Latium) was bounded
roughly by the Tiber River on the north, across which were the
formidable Etruscans and the Faliscans, who were half-Etrus-
canized and generally hostile relatives of the Latins. On the
west their limit was the sea from the mouth of the Tiber to the
promontory of Circeii, while on the east and south their area
was ringed by foothills and spurs of the Apennines held by
various Sabellian tribes: the Sabines, Aequi, Hernici, and Volsci. The region enclosed by these hostile tribes was not particularly desirable. The coastal area was a pestilential marsh subject
to periodic flooding from the Tiber, uninhabitable without a
brave and intelligent effort. The back country probably experienced severe volcanic action until well into the Bronze Age. In
time, however, the hills thrown up by the eruptions became
healthful sites for Latin villages, and the volcanic ash furnished
a fertile though shallow soil.

   Despite the numerous physical drawbacks of the area,
there are some indications of human occupation of Latium as far
back as neolithic times. Presumably these people were of the
same Mediterranean stock found elsewhere in Italy, and like
the other neolithic peoples they fused with the newcomers,
who spoke an Indo-European tongue, in this case Latin. It
seems likely, from the archaic characteristics of this language,
that the newcomers were the descendants of some of the earliest Bronze Age arrivals in Italy, or at least that they had
learned the language from them.[1] In any case, even in so re-

---

[1]   For the earliest Bronze Age arrivals, see pp. 13, 16–17.

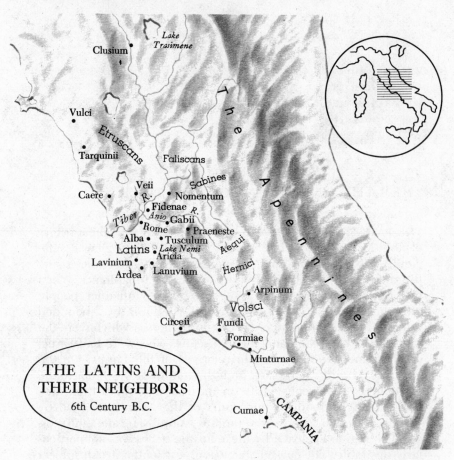

THE LATINS AND
THEIR NEIGHBORS
6th Century B.C.

stricted an area as Latium there were noticeable dialectal differences in the Latin spoken from community to community.
This might have been due either to the influence of neighbors
(as of the Etruscans on the Faliscans), or to the differences in
the number and nature of the earlier neolithic inhabitants absorbed, or merely to the differentiations fostered among the
various Latin communities by relatively small separations in
geography and time. One of the dialects of Latium, that of the
inhabitants of Rome, became the standard Latin for a world
language. This does not mean that it was a better language or
more "Latin," but simply that, as the language of an expanding
and politically adroit people, it became convenient for widespread communication.

The early Latins were largely herdsmen who also practiced agriculture in a small way. They were divided into peoples that as political organizations more closely resembled the
North American Indian tribes than they did separate nations.

Each of these peoples had its own territory or canton (*pagus*). Within that area its town or village (*oppidum*), perched on some inland hill, served both as a shelter from raiders and a refuge from the unhealthy vapors of the marshy lowlands. How small each of these groups was is shown by their number: we are told that forty-seven of them gathered in the sixth century B.C. for joint religious festivals. Originally, then, probably none of them controlled much more than twenty square miles of territory, for all Latium scarcely covered 1500 square miles.

The early Iron Age (after 1000 B.C.) inhabitants of Latium enjoyed the culture called southern Villanovan. Their artifacts found in cemeteries are about of the same quality as those of their near neighbors and no richer than one would expect in a society of peasants. Generally they followed the practice of cremation for their dead, though there were important exceptions; and their regular use of hut urns for the ashes of the dead shows not only the close link that they felt between this life and a next one, but also gives a fair idea of the earliest Latin dwellings.

Each town when first established probably had its own chieftain or king, but at an early date many of them discarded their kings for annually elected officials. There were at least three different traditions of government in this small area. In some villages, such as Aricia, Lanuvium, Nomentum, Fidenae, and sometime at Alba, an annually elected dictator took the place of a king, keeping the king's prerogatives and powers, but exercising them for one year only. Other towns, such as Tusculum, Arpinum, Fundi, Formiae, and Minturnae, had groups of aediles of varying numbers as the chief magistrates. The title and earliest duty of these men probably indicate that they once had oversight of the community's special religious cult (a Latin word for temple is *aedes*), but that, as secular duties expanded, some aediles were endowed with the supervision of the general welfare. Perhaps, however, they had been officials of the palace (*aedes regia*) under the earlier kings and had inherited the latters' administrative tasks when they were expelled. In still other towns there were dual chief magistrates called praetors. This was true at Praeneste and Lavinium, and after the expulsion of the kings at Rome (509 B.C.) the chief magistrates there were at first so called. The mention in equivocal tradition both of a dictator and of praetors at the head of a union, known as the Latin League at Alba, further illustrates that the magistracy in Latium could take a number of different forms.

The Latins had begun to form confederations at an early but uncertain date. Such leagues were loose and precarious in nature and seem to have had largely a religious purpose: one of these, the Latin League, was a joint assembly that met annually on the Alban Mount to worship Jupiter. According to tradition, at such meetings secular matters of general interest also were discussed; and the nearby town of Alba Longa derived some prestige from its proximity to the meeting place, just as Bolsena acquired prestige in the Etruscan League, though one could call neither place a "capital." Another league, smaller but perhaps with greater political significance, centered about the worship of Diana at Lake Nemi near Aricia, while still another honored Venus at Lavinium. Undoubtedly the growing power of the Etruscans to the north and the pressures of the Sabellians to the east and south increased the cohesion and inclination toward cooperation within these groups.

SETTLERS AT THE SITE OF ROME (EIGHTH CENTURY B.C.). On an eminence overlooking a bend in the Tiber River, where there was an island affording an easy crossing, there appeared a new Latin settlement in the middle of the eighth century B.C. This was a village on the Palatine Hill, destined to become the center of imperial Rome. Writers of Roman legends attributed the foundation there in 753 to Romulus and Remus, twin grandsons of the king of Alba Longa. There is no way of proving the identity of its founders, but it is certain that some of the construction on the Palatine dates from about this time. The only earlier dwellings in the vicinity seem to have been in a forlorn neolithic village on the nearby Aventine Hill. Later Latin writers romantically attributed the Palatine settlement to the sentimental attachment of the twins for the scenes of their youthful exploits when they were foster sons of a local shepherd; but archaeologists and historians discover economic and strategic explanations for a Latin interest in the site at that time. The Palatine Hill was defensible, well watered, and accessible to the Latin interior, and commanded the only feasible bridgehead across the lower Tiber. Further, it was the focal point of a number of natural routes to other parts of Italy, which ultimately became the great roads radiating out of Rome. It was astride the route used to convey the salt from the pans at the mouth of the Tiber to the tribes of the interior, and it could command any produce, especially the fine mountain timber, floated down the river for trans-shipment overseas.

During the eighth century B.C. the formidable Etruscans were beginning to develop their unparalleled culture across the Tiber. The Latin countrymen might well have thought it wise to man their best lookouts and most defensible spots. It is notable that even after the Etruscans had established strongholds south of Latium in Campania, they maintained land communications with these settlements in the seventh and early sixth centuries not by the natural and easiest route through Rome, but north along Apennine slopes through Fidenae, Gabii, and Praeneste.

Excavations on the western slopes of the Palatine Hill, called the Germal, reveal an early Latin settlement; the artifacts found there appear to be from the mid-eighth century and show a possible affinity to those of its legendary parent, Alba Longa. To this extent there is archaeological corroboration for the Roman tradition. The dwellings there were nearly rectangular huts approximately twelve by fourteen feet, the floors of which were sunk below the surrounding terrain. The original walls were of wood and mud and the roofs of thatch, and have of course disappeared. However, the general appearance and construction can be imagined from the numerous contemporary hut urns designed to hold the ashes of the dead. The perimeters of the huts' foundations retain the holes where wooden posts were embedded in the ground to support the walls and roof. A post planted in the center of the floor helped support the ridge-pole. This is a feature peculiar to structures found in the area permeated by the Villanovan culture of this time. The hut may have had a window, and it did have a small portico to protect the door from direct downpours. While their porridge and bread, beans and greens were prepared on open hearths or clay stoves in these simple dwellings, the settlers kept an eye on the Tiber crossing and drove their flocks to pasture across the saddle of land connecting the Palatine with the interior.

The earliest Latin settlers had clearly chosen a good site, for in a very few years a cluster of villages crowned the other heights in the neighborhood. The heterogeneous nature of the peoples and customs represented in them faintly presaged the cosmopolitan capital to be. Latin villages appeared on another crest of the Palatine, the Palatual, and also on the Velia, the Caelius (or Querquetual), and on three spurs of the Esquiline: the Cispius, Fagutal, and Oppius. On the eminences of the Quirinal and Viminal, however, were villages that appear to have been founded by Sabines, a mountain people east of Latium whose tongue belonged to the Sabellian family of Indo-European tongues, quite distinct from Latin.

To the north of the Palatine, and skirted also by the Capitol, Quirinal, Viminal, and Esquiline Hills, lay a marshy tract that someday was to become the Roman Forum, center of the Roman world. For the time being, however, since it was outside the limits of the various villages, a part of it served as a cemetery. Burials from the second half of the eighth century are found here and are roughly contemporary with the foundation of the settlements on the heights above. Both cremation and inhumation graves appear, and they are of about the same date. In the cremation graves the ashes were deposited in the typical hut urns at the bottom of pits, while the inhumed were often placed in oak coffins and laid in ditch-like graves. Similar urns, goblets, and bowls with simple Villanovan patterns are found buried in each type of grave. Other burials have been found on the Quirinal (inhumation) and Esquiline (mixed), and there is even one cremation burial found on the Palatine itself between its two villages. Since Roman writers tell of both Latins and Sabines on the scene at the beginning of their history, even of a jointly held throne, it is tempting to see in these graves the relics of cremating Latin peoples and inhumating Sabines. There are, however, enough anomalies—an unexpectedly large number of inhumations on the Esquiline, for example—to urge caution. The divergencies in burial practices perhaps stem not so much from racial distinctions as from the fact that Rome lay on the boundary of two cultural traditions, the Villanovan which favored cremation and the Apenninic which had clung through the ages to inhumation.

By the early seventh century huts were spilling down the sides of the Roman hills and encroaching on the marshy areas below. The graves of the period reveal some improvement in the techniques of locally manufactured pottery, when compared with the earliest remains; while some imported Greek ware, as well as a few examples of glass paste and enamel show that commerce was beginning to develop. During this period contacts with other peoples brought a very important step, the adoption of an alphabet and the first writing in Latin. There should be no illusions, however, as to the size, strength, or culture of these early settlements: they were dusty Italian villages whose chief remains are rough vases, agricultural implements, terracotta stoves, spindles, and safety pins; and they are a far cry from the brilliance then emerging in the nearby Etruscan centers of Caere and Veii, or in the more distant Greek Cumae. Their ties were still with the other Latins, and several of these villages are listed as separate members of the league that met near Alba Longa.

THE SEPTIMONTIUM (SEVENTH CENTURY B.C.). Sometime in the early seventh century the seven Latin villages of the hills of Rome, whether for mutual protection or for cooperation in the exploitation of Latin pastures, formed a loosely-knit league. Traces of this league with the names of the villages participating are found in historical times, for a feast of the Septimontium (the seven hills) continued to be celebrated for centuries. This was not a unification, nor was there yet a town of Rome. If the league was called anything, it would simply have been the Septimontium, and like the Latin League it had a religious basis, which explains the survival of the festival connected with it.

Despite the traditional list of kings of Rome from the first foundation on the Palatine—Romulus, Numa Pompilius, Tullus Hostilius, and Ancus Martius—there was as yet no "king of Rome." Each village probably had its chieftain, who may well have been called the *rex* (Latin "king"). He ruled the people of his village, but he did so with the advice of the chiefs of the village families. Though he had extensive powers, these powers were limited by law—that is, by tradition and by what the people had sworn to do. If he proposed anything new, whether a war or a policy, he had to assemble the men of military age and gain their consent, thus establishing a new law. Ony then did it become binding on the people, for this is the meaning of Roman "law" (*lex*): that which obliges or binds, from *ligare* (to bind or to tie).

The religious inclinations and practices in the villages of the Septimontium, like those of their fellow Latins, were based on a feeling for spiritual forces that lay behind natural phenomena, especially those of garden and pasture. Some of the oldest festivals of the Romans, dating from these early times, reflect attempts to come to terms with these spirits. Thus two festivals peculiar to the Palatine, the Parilia and the Lupercalia, were older than Rome itself and protected the settlers' livestock and homesteads, while the dance of the Salian priests both invoked a martial spirit against enemies and sought to drive away spirits inimical to the prosperity and fertility of crops and flocks. The constant concern for signs and portents later made the inhabitants especially liable to the influence of the Etruscans, who were so adept in these matters. Though the Latins must have seen Greek and Etruscan statues of deities at a fairly early date, they themselves had little feeling for anthropomorphism: to them Jupiter was the spirit of heavenly brightness and Venus the spirit of charm, just as Terminus was the spirit guarding boundary stones and Robigo the one warding mildew or rust off the crops. It was the place of the king as father (*pater*, protector) of his people, to maintain their health by a careful supervision of the dealings with those spirits. It is typical of religious conservatism that even after the monarchy at Rome was abolished there continued to be a king for sacrifices (*rex sacrorum*) who performed the religious duties of the deposed monarchs.

In the days of the league of the Seven Hills foreign contacts must have been seriously limited. Art objects in the graves indicate some exchange with the neighboring Faliscans, Sabines, and possibly Etruscans. It is quite unlikely, however, that the legendary conquest of Sabine towns up the valley of the Anio actually occurred, since on the Palatine's doorstep the villages of the Quirinal and Viminal remained unassimilated. Further, although it is true that Alba Longa seems to have been destroyed during this period, it is improbable that this was the work of the Romans alone, as their later histories boasted. It is more likely that several members of the Alban League, including the several villages on the Tiber, found the leadership of Alba Longa too restrictive and combined to overthrow her. Though not yet redoubtable, the league of the Septimontium was becoming ever more important through its activities; and the obvious tactical and commercial advantages of the site made it a natural target of the adventurous and the ambitious in the superior Etruscan civilization across the Tiber.

Chapter 5

ETRUSCAN ROME

ETRUSCANS IN THE SEPTIMONTIUM (*ca.* 550 B.C.). As early as the seventh century B.C. the Etruscans had achieved a foothold in the rich land of Campania. Latium was not equally attractive, but it was desirable to have a direct overland route through it between Etruria proper and the Campanian cities. Nevertheless, for some time the strong Latin outpost on the site of future Rome forced the Etruscans to use a more roundabout road. The evidence of archaeology indicates that this detour along the foothills of the Apennines, through Fidenae, Gabii, and Praeneste, was open in the middle of the seventh century.

Riches of bronze and gold found in the rock-cut tombs of Praeneste show that by that time Praeneste had an Etruscan ruling class. The antiquity of the Etruscan influence in Praeneste is further indicated by the large numbers of Etruscan features found in the Latin dialect of Praeneste as compared with the Latin of Rome.

The Roman site on the Tiber itself came under Etruscan overlords sometime near the middle of the sixth century. This was not brought about by a concerted Etruscan invasion. Both archaeological evidence and tradition indicate that the Etruscan domination of Rome began with the appearance of adventurers and freebooters with small contingents of supporters. These men gained the ascendancy and chieftainship in the villages of the Septimontium through superiority in arms and perhaps also through the sheer glamour of the more advanced culture that they brought. Roman legends name Lucius Tarquinius as the first Etruscan king, claiming that he was simply a cultured immigrant from Tarquinii who became popular at Rome and was elected by the Romans to succeed his friend, King Ancus Martius, at the latter's death. This undoubtedly glosses over, in the interest of Roman pride, the unpleasant fact of foreign domination; yet in the story there remains a hint that although there were Etruscan overlords, their countrymen did not come in sufficient numbers to inundate the Latin residents.

Roman tradition tells of two Etruscan kings of Rome, Lucius Tarquinius (Tarquin the Elder) and Tarquin the Proud, with Servius Tullius, who bore a Latin name, sandwiched between them. Emperor Claudius, however, who was a scholar of Etruscan history, states that Servius also was an Etruscan and that he originally bore the name of Mastarna (Macstrna). Later Roman historians placed these three reigns between 616 and 509 B.C. This may be fifty years too early for the beginning of the Etruscan hegemony in Rome, which also seems to have extended somewhat later, into the first half of the fifth century. However, Etruscan overlords surely did rule in Rome: there is not only the Roman tradition, but also there are archaeological indications in Rome itself and a certain amount of evidence from other cities. A tomb painting in the Etruscan city of Vulci, for example, shows influence of a foreign tradition on the subject, and it at least does not have the pro-Roman bias of our literary sources. It shows a battle between Mastarna, allied with two brothers named Aulus and Caelius Vibenna (Aule and Caile Vipinas), and one Gnaeus Tarquinius of Rome (Cneve Tarchunies Rumach), who is slain. We know from traditional accounts that the Vibennas were participants in the events of early Rome;

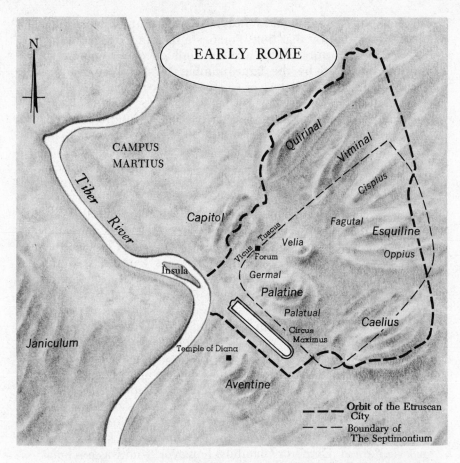

and that they are not merely legendary seems clear from the discovery at Veii of part of a vase dating from the sixth century B.C. bearing the name of Aulus Vibenna (Avile Vipiennas). It would appear, then, that for nearly one hundred years in the sixth and early fifth centuries the site of Rome was dominated by a number of Etruscan adventurers—the Tarquins, Mastarna, the Vibennas, Lars Porsenna of Clusium—seeking to enjoy the benefits that control of its position and trade routes would give.

THE ESTABLISHMENT OF ROME. The Etruscans brought to the villages of the Septimontium unification and organization as a city. The city was the normal political and social unit of the Greek East, and at this very time cities were being planted as colonies along the shores of southern Italy and Sicily. The city was not native, however, to the Italic races nor to their relatives in Spain, Britain, and Gaul; and to the people of Latium it came as a gift of the Etruscans. It would seem, in fact, that it had been through the high development of fortified cities with concen-

44

trated populations that the Etruscans had been able to establish their hegemonies.

The Etruscan kings, who at length replaced the native chieftains, took the scattered villages of the Septimontium and made them a city, probably naming it Rumon (city of the river). This they enclosed with defenses, a few of which still can be seen, though most of the "Servian" (Etruscan) wall of Rome is of a much later date. Further, they drained the marsh that had separated the Latin villages and made of it the Roman Forum, the political and commercial center that was to be the nucleus of empire. These measures immediately enhanced the political and economic stature of the place, and its population increased rapidly with the influx of artisans and traders.

Under Etruscan domination Rome became a bilingual town. The natives were much impressed by the relations of their new overlords with the supernatural. They learned through the agency of Hellenized Etruscans to identify a number of their rustic spirits with Greek deities, though there was no wholesale acceptance of strictly Etruscan gods; and the great Roman trinity on the Capitol, consisting of Jupiter, Juno, and Minerva, copied an Etruscan inclination toward triads. The Latins' belief in the spiritual penetration of the natural world made them especially susceptible to the Etruscan science of augury and divination.

POLITICAL AND MILITARY ORGANIZATION.   Earlier Latin political organization, such as it was, had been largely in natural primitive bodies: the family, the clan, and the tribe; and the other Italic peoples appear to have used these units as well, for there are evidences of them among the Umbrians to the north and the Oscans to the south. Further, there was a grouping of the clans into *curiae* or wards, which probably were geographical units, which gathered for public acts, whether religious or political. Rome of the Septimontium had three tribes composed of thirty such *curiae*. It is uncertain whether or not this tribal division indicates that earlier there had been three separate peoples. Elsewhere the term "tribe" seems to be used as the equivalent of a people (*populus*). In any case, under the Etruscan kings the Quirinal and Viminal Hills were added to Rome. These had not been part of the Septimontium and presumably were peopled largely by Sabine intruders. The whole city was now divided into four new tribes and each was given a geographical designation.

With the Etruscans there also came more formal methods of combat. The old, rather haphazard style of fighting, with groups of supporters formed around a clan leader, was not effective or efficient, as was shown by the easy penetration made by small but disciplined Etruscan units against the earlier inhabitants. According to Roman tradition, one of the Etruscan kings of this period, Servius Tullius, devised a whole new political system based on army organization. As it is described by Livy, however, it would be far too elaborate for the economic and military situation of the time. What Servius probably did was to initiate a military reform by organizing all the residents of Rome for army service, basing the service on their economic capacity to furnish arms, rather than on family connections. Later this basing of the army on wealth was to have constitutional consequences, for it was the germ for a complex legislative assembly of the Republic, the Centuriate Assembly.[1]

For the present, however, the assembly organized along the old lines, by the *curiae* and called the Curiate Assembly, continued to operate as the body that elected a king or ratified his proposals. In this assembly differences of wealth did not count. There continued to be thirty wards, and each ward had one vote, its vote being determined by the majority of the votes within it. While the governing class later had reason to develop its military organization into a more plutocratic legislative body, political or religious conservatism led the Romans to retain this ancient, more democratic, assembly to witness certain acts and to bestow the *imperium* (the right to act for the State) on its elected leaders.[2]

ECONOMIC AND CULTURAL ADVANCE.   The archaeological remains of Etruscan Rome show an increase of imported wares, and there was a great technical advance in locally manufactured goods. Probably to this period is to be attributed the earliest organization of certain basic crafts into guilds, as is reported by Plutarch. These were the bronze-workers, cobblers, dyers, flute-players, gold-workers, leather-workers, potters, and smiths.

Many new temples were constructed, and their dates of dedication extend into the fifth century B.C., indicating that Etruscan domination probably continued into that century. Games were introduced in the area that was to become the Circus Maximus, and in it were established grandstands and other appointments clearly resembling those of Etruscan Tarquinii. For the first time the Roman Forum was made perennially habitable by a drainage system that later, when elaborated and covered, became the famous Cloaca Maxima. The extensive drainage projects in rural areas were also probably due to the

[1]   For the Centuriate Assembly, see pp. 54, 91–93.
[2]   For the *imperium*, see p. 53.

Etruscan lords, for they could be accomplished only with the advent of a highly organized community and of technical proficiency.

In this period Rome became a cosmopolitan city. Famous foreign artists, such as Vulca of Veii, who made statues for the Temple of Jupiter, and the Greeks, Damophilos and Gorgasos, who decorated the Temple of Ceres, were imported. It was at this time that a commercial sector was established in Rome, significantly named the Vicus Tuscus (the Etruscan quarter). Immigrants must have found it difficult to assimilate with the older Latin families and clans. The Etruscan princes probably initiated the guilds for them. The immigrants were also welcomed in the army, which must have given them both status and some influence, while it also helped strengthen the emerging nation. The elaborate program of public works was also probably designed by the kings to assist gifted newcomers by tapping their talents as well as to employ poorer Latins as laborers. All these people would come to owe their allegiance, protection, and well-being to the kings rather than to Latin magnates. These people probably came to form a sizable part of the plebeian population of Republican Rome, as distinguished from the hangers-on or tenants, ex-slaves, and other dependents of noble Latin houses, whom the Romans called "clients."

The Etruscan kings courted popularity in other ways in order to achieve a position of leadership. To them is attributed the foundation of a Temple of Diana on the Aventine, which Varro called "a temple common to all Latins." The cult of Diana at Aricia, the center of one of the most powerful political leagues of Latium, was a stumbling block to Etruscan ambition. By the establishment of a rival worship of the same goddess Etruscan kings tried to attract some Latin allegiance, and to assert for themselves the leadership that this cult implied.

THE ETRUSCANS EXPELLED (EARLY FIFTH CENTURY B.C.).
The period of Etruscan hegemony ended at Rome some time in the early fifth century B.C. Traditionally the last Etruscan king, Tarquin the Proud, was expelled in 509 by the Romans, who were enraged by the arrogance of the ruler and the wanton actions of his family. Actually, there is evidence that the expulsion of Tarquin did not end the Etruscan period, and tales of the activities of an Etruscan warlord, Lars Porsenna of Clusium, probably point to further Etruscan successes in the fifth century. However, the deterioration in the quality of art objects by the middle of that century indicates that a cultural retrogression, incident to the end of the Etruscan monarchy, had set in.

Despite Rome's interest in glorifying her own importance, the expulsion of the Etruscan kings from Rome was not an exclusively internal matter. It has become so befogged, however, by ancient chroniclers and Roman apologists that the causes and order of events can be presented only in a very general way. It is significant that the government in Rome itself did not devolve on all the people after the expulsion, but on the older Latin families there, the patricians. This would indicate that, as the king's natural rivals, the patrician or noble families had taken the initiative.

Rome's neighbors also had good reasons to be fearful of her Etruscan kings. The territory controlled by the Septimontium at the time of the earliest Etruscan occupation can have been little more than fifty square miles, if we can trust the limits implied by the known sites of the nearest free neighbors. The successes of the overlords of Rome with a revamped military organ, even if we make due allowance for exaggeration, gave her by the early fifth century about 350 square miles. This must have alarmed the other Latins, who could always find a ready ally in the Greeks of Cumae. It appears that an Etruscan attack directed from Rome against Aricia, the center of an important Latin league, began the series of events that ended in the establishment of the republican aristocratic government of Rome. The date of the battle around Aricia is vague, but the Latins with the help of Greek Cumae were completely successful. The Etruscan troops fell back in disorder to Rome, and this apparently gave the Latin patricians in Rome itself their opportunity. The newer plebeian elements, though natural supporters of the kings, were wearied by war, resentful of forced labor on ambitious public works, and chastened by the setbacks of their patrons; and they acquiesced in the change of government.

The Etruscan period at Rome was not long enough to Tuscanize the people as, for example, it had the Faliscans. But it was long enough to give them an organization that made theirs the most powerful single town in Latium. Both through their military and through their diplomatic and religious policy the Etruscan overlords of Rome had sought a predominant position in Latium. The Romans had enjoyed that new prosperity and importance, and they were not apt to forget them in the following period.

Chapter 6

FREE ROME AND THE PROBLEMS OF FREEDOM[1]

With the expulsion of the Tarquins (*ca.* 509 B.C.) the history
of Etruscan influence at Rome is by no means ended. There are
many romantic tales of the early Republic and its defense against
Etruscan attack, which undoubtedly betray attempts of the
Tarquins or of the famous Lars Porsenna to acquire or to regain
that lucrative bridgehead. It appears that one of the Etruscan
forays was so successful that the fortifications of Rome, built by
her Etruscan kings, were dismantled. Despite this continuing
hostility, however, the Romans retained many of the trappings
of Etruscan pomp, and they continued to look to the north for
religious instruction. By the middle of the fifth century B.C.,
however, Rome had withdrawn from the affluence and world
markets that had been open to her as a member of the Etruscan
community. The exact dates of these early happenings are uncertain. Most of the traditional dates of earliest republican
history are too early, but none of the modern substitutes for
them are universally accepted. With this warning, it is probably
better to use the conventional dates established for the period
by Varro, a Roman scholar of the first century B.C., with the hope
that there will thus be less confusion when consulting other
works, and that at least the correct order of events can be indicated, even if the absolute dates cannot.

At the time that the Romans established self-government
they were faced with a series of problems. Outside there were
dangerous enemies. The Etruscans were anxious to regain their
rule; Sabines, Aequi, and Volsci were eager to spill their surplus populations out of the mountains of the hinterland onto the
more prosperous plains; and the other Latins continued to be
very suspicious of the Romans. They noted that the Romans had
seemed to enjoy the leadership foisted upon them by their

[1]   For a correlation of external and internal events from 509 to 266 B.C., see the
table on pp. 95–99.

49

volved in a series of campaigns against the Etruscans, especially those of the city of Veii, each jockeying for position along the trade routes of the valley of the Tiber. While there are tales of great victories and great disasters, Rome's position by the middle of the century seems to have been strong enough to win herself a breathing spell.

EARLY CONFLICTS OF PATRICIANS AND PLEBEIANS.
The efficiency of the Romans in dealing with external problems was considerably hampered by a lack of unity at home, for almost immediately after the establishment of the Republic the plebeians found themselves in a perilous civil position. The first families of Rome had been such because they had been the councillors and aides of the kings in guiding and preserving the commonwealth. They were called the *patres* (from the root *pa*, to protect), and the members or descendants of these families were therefore called *patricii*, patricians. As the king's chief advisory body they had developed an *esprit* and pride of their own, and resented bitterly any tyrannical acts of the king. They had been therefore instrumental in organizing the revolt against the Tarquins and, as men of action and of experience in protecting the public interest, they naturally took over the conduct of public affairs (*res publica*) when this revolt succeeded. The power of the patricians was further increased by the support of numerous lesser citizens called clients (hangers-on) who over the years had attached themselves to the fortunes of one or another of the more prosperous or powerful families.[2] These people gave to some magnate their political support in return for sustenance, employment, or perhaps a tenancy.

There were numerous other free persons, however, who had not been chosen as *patres*, and yet had maintained their independence, that is, they did not become clients. These were the commons or plebeians, whose number had been swollen by craftsmen and other immigrants attracted to Rome during the Etruscan period. There were also former clients whose hereditary patrons had disappeared, and there were the commons of conquered and annexed places.[3] Many of these men were sturdy freeholders or townsmen of some means, and since the Servian reorganization (sixth century B.C.) they had been called upon to serve in the army.[4] In return the kings had protected their civil status. Under the new government they found that while they were still expected to serve the State, the patricians,

[2]   For clients, see also p. 47.
[3]   For the origin of the plebeians, see p. 47.
[4]   For the Servian reorganization, see p. 46.

52

on the grounds of their initiative in the establishment of the Republic and their experience in administration, did not propose to allow them a share in the government. Because of this, the plebeians saw the lands that had been conquered through their efforts exploited by the ruling caste; and this was at the very time when the disappearance of Etruscan commerce was bringing an economic depression to the artisans and small people of Rome.

THE EARLY MAGISTRACY.   To rule the newly constituted state the Romans followed Latin rather than Etruscan precedent and set up a plural magistracy: two praetors (*praetores*, those who lead the way) who later were known as the consuls (those who perform together). These two magistrates were elected by the citizens for one-year terms, but during that year they had much of the power and trappings of their royal predecessor. The new magistrates did not retain quite all the regal powers; in matters of religion, conservative fears led to the creation of a *rex sacrorum* (king for sacrifices) to maintain some of the ancient traditional solemnities. With this exception, however, the two elected consuls were the complete executive arm of the government in the earliest Republic. The constitutional history of republican Rome is that of a fragmentation and diminution of those consular powers as they were divided among new officials. Yet, theoretically, the consuls always retained the full powers of the *imperium*, which symbolized their right to act for the State. Specifically, the grant of *imperium* gave the magistrate the following powers: (1) to take the auspices (interpret the divine will from signs) and maintain a general supervision of religious affairs; (2) to represent the State in dealing with individuals or other states; (3) to command the armed forces; (4) to exercise civil and criminal jurisdiction; (5) to punish any who withstood properly constituted authority; (6) to issue proclamations and edicts (these would have the force of law during the term of office of the man that issued them); (7) to convene the assembly or the Senate; and (8) to supervise and administer any matters that pertained to the welfare of the community. While these duties sound rather formidable, actually in a small state with a simple society two men could attend to most of the public business. Further, concern for such great power in the hands of magistrates even for only one year led in the first year of the Republic (509 B.C.) to the passage of a Valerian Law (Roman laws generally were named for their sponsors) which guaranteed each citizen the right to appeal a magistrate's sentence to the assembled people. The duties of the consuls were further curtailed in primitive Rome by the assumption of many responsibilities, later considered public affairs, by families or individuals.

Very early in the Republic, the consuls found it necessary to appoint assistants to carry out investigations. These assistants were called quaestors (from *quaerere*, to seek). Their original duty seems to have been to investigate criminal acts to determine whether they called for public or private action. However, in this uncomplicated society they naturally assumed a variety of tasks. One of the duties that gradually became more complex, especially with the invention of money, was to keep account of the finances of the State. It is as financial officials, therefore, that the quaestors were best known when they ultimately became elected magistrates.

THE CENTURIATE ASSEMBLY.   It was natural that the blessing of the Curiate Assembly (the ancient assembly by wards), which had ratified the selection of the kings, should continue to be invoked to bestow the *imperium* on the king's successors. However, it was equally natural that the men serving in the army should demand the right to select their own leaders and to decide on matters of war and peace. A new primary elective and legislative body for the State therefore evolved, which was called the Centuriate Assembly. It consisted of the citizens organized by the military units called centuries (100 men), in which the right to bear arms was determined by financial competence.

The weight of the vote in the new Centuriate Assembly was with the well-to-do, for they alone could afford the arms necessary for first-class soldiers. There were, therefore, many in Rome without political privilege or an influential vote. The economic suffering and political disabilities of these unprivileged citizens led them to years of protest and political demonstration which ultimately transformed the government of the Roman State. The relatively well-to-do plebeians, who lacked political opportunity, teamed with the poor plebeians, who lacked a livelihood, and in two centuries, through a series of compromises with their patrician opponents, they hammered out a constitution that is a model of what arbitration, tolerance, and patience can do.

PLEBEIAN SECESSION. THE TRIBUNATE FORMED (494 B.C.). Almost all Roman republican history is concerned with agitation for political equality, for the plebeians, for the Latins, and for the Italians. The plebeians were the first to agitate, and the initiative was taken by small landowners. These men, who owned the legal minimum of land for public service (about one and one-third acres), were called upon for almost constant military campaigns. Nevertheless, under the new Republic their right to use some part of the public land to piece out a living became precarious, since the governing patricians tended to monopolize those lands for themselves and their clients. The plebeians might well grumble that most of the public domain came from the conquests in which they had played an important role. Debt from the need to pay the war taxes and to support a family on their meager resources threatened to reduce many plebeians to bondage.

According to tradition, the indignation of the plebeians at their rapidly deteriorating economic condition led them to organize themselves as a sort of state within the State, a movement that culminated in an actual secession of a large number of them to a hill near Rome called the Sacred Mount. This strike against their civic duties was a revolutionary act and it was so regarded by the Romans themselves. However, the weakness of the State in the face of the hostile cities and tribes surrounding it forced the administration to concede to the plebeians in 494 B.C. the right to form a semi-independent body within the State and to elect officials to represent their interests. These officials were originally two or four tribunes of the plebs, a number that soon was increased to ten.

The tribunate was first conceived as a rather negative office: it was the tribune's first task to protect plebeians against unlawful or arbitrary acts by the regular magistrates. This duty quickly led to more positive action; from the simple prevention of acts harmful to a single plebeian, it was an easy step to intercession when plans were discovered that were likely to lead to acts prejudicial to all the plebeians. The tribunes also found it necessary to consult with the body of the plebeians to decide what were their common interests. These activities finally developed for the tribunes the right of general intercession in the acts of the regular officials of the State, and also the right to assemble the plebeians in order to propose "opinions of the plebeians" (plebiscites) and to effect their passage. These plebiscites were not binding on the State, but they served as useful bases for agitation that could lead to legislation in the Centuriate Assembly.

TRIBAL ASSEMBLY ESTABLISHED (471 B.C.).   At first the tribunes were elected by the old Curiate Assembly, but this proved unsatisfactory because the patricians could exert too much influence through their clients, who were, of course, plebeians in status. The Centuriate Assembly was even more unsuitable as a body to elect the tribunes because of the weight given to wealth in it. Ultimately, in 471 B.C., the Romans settled upon an assembly organized by tribes. The weight of the evidence is that the change to a tribal assembly was made because in the fifth century B.C. most clients were not tribal members, since they rented rather than owned land, and only landowners belonged to a tribe. Therefore they would not be eligible to vote for tribunes favored by their patrician patrons and landlords. In any case, from this period on, the assembly that elected the tribunes and over which they presided consisted of all those Roman citizens that were plebeians and that also were eligible for tribal membership. At the beginning of the Republic there seem to have been four urban tribes and fifteen for the rural population. These were increased by additions of territory until, by 241 B.C., there were four urban and thirty-one rural tribes. Though in the earliest Republic tribal membership was based on actual domicile and the possession of land in a given area, by the late Republic tribal membership appears to have become hereditary regardless of place of residence.[5]

To ensure the safety and efficacy of their representative, the plebeians joined in a solemn oath to treat as accursed anyone who withstood the tribune in the execution of his duties. Since such a cursed person could freely be killed, the tribunate actually was supported by lynch law; but the sanctity of the tribunes was a principle so hallowed that over 400 years later a patrician, Julius Caesar, could use a disregard for it by his opponents as his justification for invading the State and overthrowing the Republic.

THE DECEMVIRATE; THE TWELVE TABLES (451–449 B.C.). The tribunes could hardly protect the plebeians from arbitrary action, however, unless they knew what the law was and what was proper juristic procedure. Up to this time the law had been largely a matter of ancestral custom (the *mos maiorum*) and religious taboo, and was in the possession of the patricians alone. Constant pressure and agitation for the "right to know" led in 451 B.C. to an agreement between patricians and plebeians for a temporary suspension both of the regular consular government and of the plebeian officials. In their place there was established a board of ten men called the decemvirs, who were directed to administer the State and at the same time to collect and publish traditional legal practice.

This codification of the law in *The Twelve Tables*, so called because it was published on twelve tablets, was considered by later Romans as the fountainhead of all their law. The preserved portions of this code reveal a rural society, but already one with considerable legal sophistication. There were sections on procedure in civil suits, on theft, private and family property, testaments, religion, and a few matters related to public policy. The decemvirs also included in the code a provision forbidding the intermarriage of patricians and plebeians. No doubt this recognized the social practices of the times, but its public recognition and prescription proved the most unpopular portion of the work. The decemvirate ended in some confusion, apparently with great dissatisfaction among the plebeians. The year 449 saw a restoration of consular government, of the guarantees of civil rights, which had been suspended during the decemvirate, and of the tribunate with its plebeian organization.

The first half century of republican life taught the Romans the lessons of compromise and cooperation both at home and abroad. Their experiences with the Latins and Hernici initiated them in the advantages of foreign alliances; the early and moderate adjustment of some of the differences between patricians and plebeians established a tradition of bargaining and accommodation. These lessons they learned well, and they made them important tools in their attainment of national unity and in the unification of Italy.

[5]   For regal tribal organization, see p. 45.

Chapter 7

CIRCLES OF EXPANSION
IN THE ROMAN CONQUEST OF ITALY[1]

Between the establishment of the Roman Republic (traditionally 509 B.C.) and 266 B.C. this small city-state asserted its authority over all peninsular Italy and at the same time slowly evolved policies which led ultimately to the unification of the Italian peoples. This accomplishment is the more remarkable because most of the first century (the fifth century B.C.) of the infant Republic's existence had been devoted to a struggle simply to survive. From the beginning of the fourth century B.C., however, there were four successive stages of struggle and success which spread Rome's influence in wider and wider circles: (1) the conquest of her immediate neighbors (early fourth century B.C.); (2) the absorption of the Latins (mid-fourth century); (3) the defeat of the Samnites and their confederates (late fourth and early third centuries); and the subordination of the Greeks of southern Italy (early third century).

A great deal of credit for success must go to the Romans' own competence and canniness. There were, however, four external factors in early republican history that were decisive in the final Roman unification of Italy. These four factors were the decline of the Etruscans, the invasions of the Gauls and their continued menacing presence in northern Italy, the explosion of Italic population, and the political folly of the Greeks.

Rome had profited materially from Etruscan occupation and after the expulsion of the kings she was incomparably stronger in relation to the other Latin communities than before. Further, she had acquired experience and a taste for leadership that revealed itself in her first treaty with Carthage (509 B.C.), though it rendered the other Latins uneasy and suspicious.[2]

[1] For a correlation of external and internal events from 509 to 266 B.C., see the table on pp. 95–99.
[2] See pp. 49–50, 108.

58

Danger from the Etruscans to the north and the Sabines, Aequi, and Volsci to the east and south had led the Romans and Latins to a dual alliance.[3] This partnership was made strategically effective by adding as a third member of the alliance the Hernican League, which was situated between and somewhat to the rear of the most dangerous enemies, the Aequi and Volsci. The alliance with the Hernici established a principle that the Romans used consistently in the future, which was to establish friendly relations, alliances if possible, with states to the rear of their potential enemies. This combination was able to contain its enemies and to defeat a joint effort of the Aequi and Volsci near Mt. Algidus in 431. Almost constant nibbling at Volscian territory meant that by 393 the allies had recovered most of the seacoast area all the way to Terracina, a strip that had been Latin in the heyday of Etruscan power.

While the allies assisted Rome against the common danger on the southern front, the danger from the north proved much more specifically her own. The Etruscan city of Veii was almost as large as Rome, undoubtedly of a more advanced culture, and Rome's natural rival. The city was geographically somewhat isolated from the other Etruscan cities, and politically it was isolated by its restoration of a king when the other cities were aristocracies. To survive, it had to maintain a trade route to the sea down the right bank of the Tiber and to keep the bridgehead on the Tiber at Fidenae in friendly hands, in order to trade with the Latins and Sabellians to the south. Stories of conflicts in the thirties and twenties of the fifth century B.C. indicate that Fidenae changed hands several times; but by 425 Fidenae seems to have passed finally under Roman control.

WAR WITH VEII (405–396 B.C.).   By the end of the fifth century B.C., when hostilities with Veii were renewed, the Romans had contrived a friendly arrangement with the Etruscan city of Caere. Caere, which was strategically located on Veii's flank, like Rome had a natural suspicion of Veii's push toward the sea. Through Caere Rome tried to apply on the northern front what she had learned in the Hernican alliance. Caere seems to have furnished free passage through its territory, while its own effort ranged from benevolent neutrality to downright hostility toward its sister Etruscan city. Only two towns rallied to Veii's cause, Etruscanized Latin cities of the upper Tiber valley, Falerii and Capena. Except for these, Rome effectively isolated Veii by playing upon Etruscan jealousies; and after a

---

[3]   See pp. 50–51.

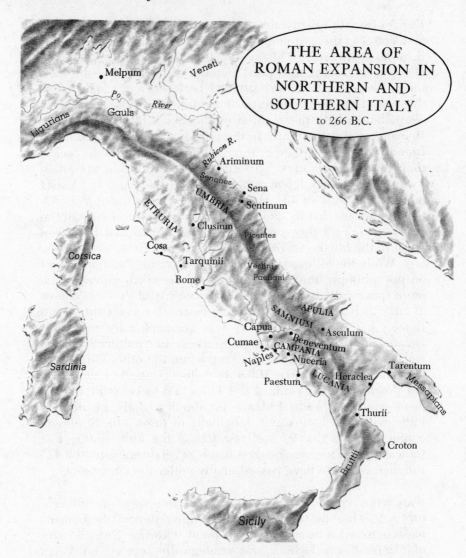

THE AREA OF
ROMAN EXPANSION IN
NORTHERN AND
SOUTHERN ITALY
to 266 B.C.

siege (traditionally of ten years) the city fell (396 B.C.). The town
was sacked, its gods carried off to Rome, and the inhabitants sold
into slavery. In the next two years Capena and Falerii were also
forced to come to terms.

The conquest of Veii was a great landmark in early Roman
history. Rome shared with its Latin allies the settlement of colonies on the northern frontiers of Veii at Sutrium and Nepet a
decade or so after the fall of Veii, retaining the territory of Veii
for its own use. It distributed much of this rich wheatland to its
own citizens and organized there four new tribes, the territorial

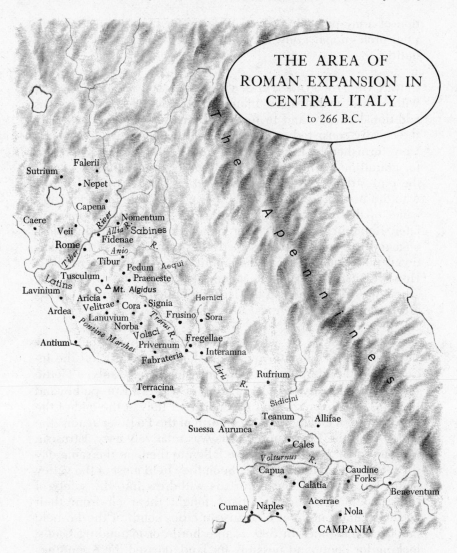

THE AREA OF
ROMAN EXPANSION IN
CENTRAL ITALY
to 266 B.C.

units into which Roman privately owned land was divided. The total number of tribes now became twenty-five. This greatly increased Rome's strength in respect to her Latin allies. Although her territory was smaller (approximately 650 square miles as against 1000 for the League), it was compact and owed its sole allegiance to her. Further, by settling poor plebeians on Veian land the political health and strength of Rome was increased. There were military consequences too. The long siege at Veii had kept the citizens for long periods from making a living on their farms and thus had brought about the introduc-

61

tion of army pay. This paved the way for the organization of a semi-professional army instead of hastily marshalled levies of militia.

ORIGIN OF THE EQUESTRIAN CLASS.   It was during the war with Veii also that more affluent plebeians offered to serve as additional cavalry and to furnish their own horses. Previously the cavalry consisted exclusively of noble youths whose mounts were furnished by the State. The new volunteers set a standard for gratuitious public service. They also formed the nucleus of the equestrian class or knights (*equites*), persons of substance who did not hold public office.[4] It is well to note the origin and name of this class to avoid confusion when they reappear in later Republican history. For generations men of this class engaged in various business activities rather than in the traditional public magistracies monopolized by the higher nobility. However inappropriate the name, they continued to be called "the equestrians"; and in the late Republic they formed a powerful economic and political force.

THE GALLIC SACK OF ROME (390 B.C.).   Upon Rome, now the most powerful state in central Italy, there next fell the incalculable thunderbolt of Gallic invasion. The Gauls, a Celtic people that already held large areas of western Europe beyond the Alps, had been moving into northern Italy at the end of the fifth century B.C. Their advance north of the Po River against the natives and the Etruscan outposts was relatively easy. Etruscan Melpum (Milan) is said to have fallen to them on the same day (in 396) that Veii fell to Rome. Soon they held most of the valley of the Po, although the Ligurians withdrew into the safety of their mountains, the Venetians fought them off from their swamps, and a number of Etruscan cities south of the Po held out for some time. In 390 a large horde of marauding Gauls, looking for booty and possibly for land, crossed the Apennines and attacked the Etruscan city of Clusium. Instead of asking help from the weakening Etruscan League, Clusium appealed to Rome as the strongest state nearby, and the Romans sent an embassy to parley with the Gauls. The Gauls abandoned the siege of Clusium and marched rapidly on Rome, which was only eighty miles away. North of the city, on the River Allia, they crushed a small Roman army. The Romans were not only badly outnumbered (70,000 to 40,000 by one account, though more

4   See also pp. 83–84, 178.

likely 30,000 to 15,000), but they were also thrown into a panic by the huge numbers, wild battle-cries, and masses of cavalry thrown against them. Survivors of the defeat sought refuge in the ruins of Veii, while the inhabitants of Rome, except for a garrison on the Capitol, took to the hills. The city's defenses had largely been leveled during one of the brief Etruscan successes after the expulsion of the kings, and the invaders were therefore easily able to seize and destroy a large part of the city. The garrison on the Capitol, however, withstood a siege of seven months, and ultimately ransomed the city and its territory. Apparently the Gauls were eager to leave, for they found the summer climate unpleasant, and their relatives back in the valley of the Po were being attacked by the Venetians.

The Gallic sack of Rome, which burst the bubble of Roman prestige, seemed to have undone the labors of a century. The Etruscans discussed joint action against her, and the Aequi and Volsci saw the chance to retrieve their losses. Even the members of the alliance, both Latins and Hernici, who for some time had viewed Rome's increasing dominance of their joint affairs with resentment and fear, felt that this was a godsent opportunity to assert their independence of action.

Roman prospects, however, were not as dismal as they first seemed. The Etruscan danger was not as great as it might once have been, for the Etruscans were weakened by civil dissensions and by the continued pressure of the Gauls from the north. Further, Roman manpower had been but little harmed despite the physical destruction of much of the town. It was mainly the State's prestige that had suffered.

Moreover, the citizens showed that same burst of vitality after the disaster that other vigorous peoples have shown under similar circumstances: the Athenians after the Persian sack of Athens, the Romans themselves after Cannae, Carthage after Zama, the Americans after Bunker Hill, and the Germans after Versailles and World War II. First, they sent to the Greeks of Sicily for architects and workmen to help them put a wall around the city that would withstand another attack. Next, they began the reformation of their army to correct weaknesses shown by the recent defeat, working probably under the leadership of Camillus, the conqueror of Veii and their dictator after the Gallic disaster. The phalanx formation, a solid line of fixed spears that the Romans had learned from the Etruscans and Greeks, was modified by the organization of the troops into small units of about 120 men, called maniples. These were arranged on the battlefield so that there were open spaces along their front between each maniple, wide enough to engulf bit by bit an on-rushing Gallic horde and destroy it piecemeal. Moreover, an opposing phalanx, if it tried to engage the manipular force man to man, would be compelled to break its solid front.

A final reason for optimism was the attitude of the Latins, some of whom realized that the Romans were their only bulwark against the Gauls, and in gratitude they were steadfast supporters. These allies furnished the necessary bases for the recovery of the Roman position in Latium itself, a task that took fifty years. When those years were over Rome was in a stronger position than ever before.

THE ROMAN RECOVERY: ABSORPTION OF THE LATINS.
To recover her position Rome at first merely contained the south while recovering her superiority in the north. The Etruscans, immediately taking advantage of Rome's supposed weakness, had attacked; but the speed with which they were reduced by Camillus demonstrates the continuing decay of the Etruscan world. It was probably at the same time that the Latin colonies at Sutrium and Nepet were founded as strongholds in Etruscan territory (*ca.* 383). Long truces were signed with the more important cities of southern Etruria: forty years for Tarquinii and Falerii (351) and one hundred for Caere (353). Relations with the Caeritans had been cordial in the past, as we noted in respect to Veii. Further, they had been declared guest-friends of Rome after they had harbored Roman refugees from the Gallic sack. Some time soon after these events the Romans seem to have bound them even closer, giving them the private rights of Roman citizens—that is, the right of intermarriage and of commercial intercourse protected by law. This act was an important landmark in the development of Roman policy in the unification of Italy, for it signified an attitude contrary to that of other city-states of antiquity, which did not offer to share their citizenship with foreigners.

In Latium there was unrest, and some of the Latin cities had broken away from the alliance and urged others to do so. Ardea, Aricia, Lanuvium, and Lavinium remained loyal, however, and so did three of the old Latin colonies in Volscian territory, Cora, Norba, and Signia. Tusculum also remained faithful, and Roman policy took another significant step in 381 by rewarding the Tusculans with the grant of full Roman citizenship. All these places were invaluable to the Roman recovery, providing assistance and bases from which to convince or coerce the obstinate. The Latin resistance to Rome was led by the ancient cities of Tibur and Praeneste, with the aid of the

Latin colony of Velitrae. The renascent Volscians were enthusiastic allies of this opposition, and the Hernici were occasional ones. At times Rome's opponents even hired Gallic mercenaries. However, the Romans had the advantages of interior lines and undivided policy. They also had a great general in Camillus and an improved military machine, and they chewed away at their opponents. In the earlier phase of the struggle the Latins and Volsci were driven back along the coastline. Antium was forced to reenter the alliance in 377, and soon after the Romans annexed the Pontine Plains south of that city. This land they peopled, and here in 358 they created two new tribes of the Roman State, thus consolidating their gains. In the second phase the Romans turned their attention to interior Latium, and in 358 they forced the old League back into its alliance, while such former non-League cities as Pedum, Nomentum, and Praeneste were forced to enter it by 354.

The Roman-Latin alliance reaffirmed, Rome was immeasurably stronger than before. Her armies were victorious, her people held lands formerly Latin, and she had effectively cut off interior Latin cities from access to the sea. Further, in 354 she concluded a treaty of peace and friendship with the powerful Samnite League, which held the mountains to the Latins' rear; and around 348 she renewed her treaty with Carthage in language that did not veil her claims of hegemony in Latium.

The Latins that had been forced back into alliance with Rome were exasperated and frightened. In 341 they managed to raise supporters among the indefatigable Volscians, the Sidicini, who were threatened by the Samnites, and the Oscans of Campania, who feared both the pressure of the Samnites from the mountains and the spread of Roman influence southward toward their area. Encouraged by their new strength, the members of the Latin League are said thereupon to have demanded citizenship and an equal share in the government from the Romans. When the Romans refused, hostilities broke out. The Romans marched through the land of the Paeligni, whom the Latins had just alienated by attacking them, joined hands with their Samnite allies, and defeated the Latins near Suessa Aurunca. By offering easy terms to the Campanians they speedily detached them from the Latins, and thus in two years (340–338) they were able to force all the Latin cities into subjection. Then Rome dissolved the Latin League. Using her treatment of Caere and Tusculum as a precedent, she admitted a few of the nearer towns to full Roman citizenship, others to half-citizenship, while with still others she entered separate and formal alliances. These alliances were nominally between

65

equals, but there was too much difference now between the power of Rome and that of any other Latin town for real equality to exist; and from now on they were her satellites. The Romans granted to the peoples of these allied Latin towns the rights of trade and marriage with Romans, but not with each other, calculating thus to spike any future dangerous combinations. Since by now nearly half of Latium was Roman, this restriction could not have caused great inconvenience. A Roman colony was sent to troublesome Antium, and Roman settlers were given the lands of even more troublesome Velitrae, both of these being Volscian strongholds.

In consequence of her annexations Rome in 332 added two more tribes to her civic organization. Now she was again the strongest power in central Italy. This position had been won partly through the patriotism and devotion of her leaders and partly through the lessons that she had learned from the Gallic disaster, which were to fortify her city and to improve her army. Also, the Gallic menace had caused a number of states to support her in other times of crisis, for it was Rome that had consistently resisted the Gauls, while others had used or abetted them. The first beginnings of an Italian sentiment may be seen in the rally of diverse peoples around this champion of a common cause. By now her new military tactics were proved, and her diplomatic strategy of "surround and absorb" and "divide and rule" was an established success. A state with such equipment would not long rest satisfied.

THE SAMNITES.   There was another stock of Italians, however, that might have appeared a more likely candidate for the major role in the unification of Italy, for the Sabellian peoples of the central Apennines seemed well on the way to engulfing the peninsula with their sons. The situation created by this dynamic population was a third factor in the story of Rome's unification of Italy. Throughout the fifth and fourth centuries these prolific peoples had sent their surplus population out to seek new homes. The Aequi and the Volsci were Sabellians and had been part of this movement, and the Volsci had pushed all the way to the sea between Latium and Campania. We have seen that the Latins and Romans had managed to contain them by military tactics and the use of their own surplus populations in strategically placed colonies. During the fifth century the Sabellians also overran the Etruscan and Greek cities of Campania. There they absorbed much of the culture of the conquered peoples and settled down to a relatively civilized life in that pleasant land, where they were known as Oscans. Soon they became hostile to their own relatives in the mountains, who tried in succeeding generations to make further descents into the plains. Other Sabellians penetrated the southern coasts of Italy in Lucania, while still others, the Bruttians, pushed out into the toe of the peninsula. Against these peoples the Greek settlements along the coast had to wage constant battle to keep from being pushed into the sea. The Sabellians were fiercely independent and democratic people, and each canton or mountain valley had its own government headed by its *meddix* or *meddix tuticus* (judge of the people). They did form rather loosely federated leagues, however, especially in times of danger. There was a league of Bruttians, one of Lucanians, one of Campanians; and we have seen the Romans early in contact and alliance with another Sabellian league, that of the Hernici. The strongest of these leagues, however, was that of the Samnites, located in the Apennines of south central Italy.

We have already found the Romans and Samnites cooperating during the middle of the fourth century, when they joined in a mutually advantageous alliance against the Gauls. Further, it had proved strategically important to the Romans to have them as cooperating allies in the rear of the Latins during the Latin War; and it was equally beneficial to the Samnites to have friendly Romans at their own rear during their wars with Tarentum and her various Greek mercenaries (340–330). Each people, however, had a special interest in the rich land of Campania, and this consequently led to conflict.

THE SAMNITE WARS (325–321, 316–304, 298–290 B.C.).
With the Latin War the Romans had won a foothold in Campania, and they proceeded to consolidate their position by new conquests, new alliances, and the establishment of strategic Latin colonies. The Campanian League had been given an early and easy peace by the Romans during the Latin War. Partly in fear of their mountain kinsmen the members entered the Roman orbit and very soon accepted partial Roman citizenship, with the promise of protection that this brought. However, the Campanian League did not contain all the cities of Campania, and there were Oscan cities, such as Nola, that still had close ties with the Samnites. There also was one remaining Greek city in Campania, Naples.

The Romans first exerted themselves to remove any challenges to their authority in the area. To contain the Samnites from expansion to the northwest in the valleys of the Trerus and Liris Rivers, the Romans forced Fabrateria and Frusino into alliance (*ca.* 330); Privernum was captured and given partial citizenship (329); and a Latin colony was settled at Fregellae (328). Along the coast connecting Latium with Campania a Roman colony was established at Terracina (329). On the northern Campanian-Samnite frontier Teanum was forced to become a Roman ally (336), and a large Latin colony was established at Cales (334). In Campania itself Acerrae was granted partial citizenship in 332, and in 326 Greek Naples was persuaded to expel its Samnite garrison and accept a Roman alliance. Only Nola was then left outside the Roman system, and the Romans straightway pushed their advantage by taking Rufrium and Allifae on the Samnite frontier. That the Roman activities were not completely innocent or fortuitous is further indicated by treaties of alliance that Rome arranged with the Apulians, who held the plains to the rear of the Samnites on the eastern shore of Italy. Roman strategy, based on experience gained with the Aequi and Volsci, Etruscans, and Latins, now had succeeded in surrounding the Samnites and walling them up.

Active warfare with the Samnites broke out in 325, but the details of the earliest actions are vague. The Romans had some success against the Vestini to the north, attacking them perhaps because they showed Samnite sympathies, while the Samnites attacked the fortress of Fregellae, which they resented as a limitation on their right to expand in the valley of the Liris River. Then in 321 the Roman generals were lured into invasion of central Samnium by false information as to the disposition of Samnite troops. They were thereupon trapped in a closed valley called the Caudine Forks and the whole army was forced to surrender. This was one of Rome's most famous and most stunning defeats, and later writers elaborated the incident and invented numerous revengeful victories following close upon it. In actuality, it appears that the Romans were forced to observe the terms dictated by the Samnites for at least five years. The terms are interesting, for they illustrate the limited and really defensive objectives of the Samnites: the surrender of places on the Samnite frontiers that they considered their own, such as Sora and Fregellae, the promise not to reopen the war, and the granting of hostages.

While observing the literal terms of the treaty, the Romans busied themselves mending fences and improving their position. Ties with cities to the rear of the Samnites in Apulia were strengthened and two new tribes of Romans were settled around Privernum. Probably at this time the number of legions regularly levied by the Romans was raised from two to four. Meanwhile, the Samnites' victory had gained them some adherents, and in 316 a previously neutral Oscan league around Nuceria declared for them.

Fighting was resumed in 316, and a new phase of the conflict dragged on until 304. The Romans slowly but steadily recovered lost ground. The Aurunci were crushed, and a Latin colony was placed at Suessa. Fregellae (313) and Sora (312) were recaptured. Successes steadied Campanian allegiance, and Calatia and Nola were captured and forced into alliance (312). The colony at Fregellae was renewed and another settled at Interamna (312). At about this time some of the Etruscan cities were persuaded to reassert their independence, but their efforts were broken in central Etruria in 310 and they were forced back into alliances. Other Sabellians beside the Samnites had reason to fear the growing Roman domination of central Italy; in 308 the Hernici, and in 305 the Aequi and Paeligni, joined their Samnite kinsmen. The Hernici, however, were not unanimous in their revolt, and those that did revolt were overthrown and given partial Roman citizenship. Thereupon the chief cities of the Aequi and Paeligni were stormed (304). At this point, however, both Romans and Samnites were exhausted, and once more they made peace.

Again Samnium had preserved its own frontiers, but the Romans were stronger than ever. Lost fortresses had been recaptured, more colonies set in strategic locations, the citizenship widened, and new alliances obtained. These gains were perhaps not spectacular, but the other free peoples of Italy found this net of colonies, annexed territories, and alliances drawing ever closer and more uncomfortably around them. For this reason, an invasion of Gauls in 299 encouraged a renewed conflict. The Samnites tried to form a grand combination of themselves, the Gauls, Umbrians, and Etruscans, once and for all to shake off the tentacles of Roman policy. The Roman ability to make good use of their interior lines, however, sped an army northward to defeat a combination of Gauls and Etruscans at Sentinum in Umbria in 295, and this decided the fate of Italy. The Etruscans and Umbrians were speedily brought to heel; and by 290 the Samnites were exhausted and the treaty with them was restored. Among the peoples that had shown sympathy for the insurgents were Rome's close neighbors, the Sabines. In 290 they were annexed and given partial citizenship, which was raised to the full franchise in a few years. The Gauls continued to give sporadic trouble and made incursions south in 284, 283, and 282, but they were finally defeated and driven north of the Apennines, while the land of the Gallic Senones was cleared and annexed. A colony was settled at Sena on the Adriatic to guard the new acquisition.

The Samnite wars point up the great contrast between the Roman will and the Samnite will. In the wars with the Romans the aims of the Samnites were always defensive, focussed on the preservation of independence. Though the Samnites might be repeatedly successful, their successes proved meaningless; but once the Romans were committed, they refused to accept any defeat as final. The early, spectacular, but superficial spread of the Sabellians throughout southern Italy contrasts with the slow steady encroachment of the Romans. By 280 B.C. Rome was the most powerful state in Italy because her leaders knew when to stop, repair, and consolidate, and because they knew the value of concession and of generosity.

PYRRHUS AND THE ᴛARENTINES (281–272 B.C.).   Rome and her allies were now face to face with the Greek cities of southern Italy. These Greeks had imported to Magna Graecia all the curses of jealousy, petty bickering, and undisciplined partisanship that had bedeviled them in the mother country. Although hard pressed by the omnipresent Sabellians (in southern Italy the Bruttians and Lucanians) they still managed to fight with one another. In place of a common effort in their own defense, they had enlisted a series of soldiers of fortune and mercenaries: Archidamus of Sparta (killed in 338), Alexander the Molossian (killed in 330), Cleonymus of Sparta (*ca.* 303), and Agathocles of Syracuse (*ca.* 295). The people of Tarentum, which was the chief Greek city of southern Italy, took the initiative in procuring these forces, and generally had a falling-out both with the generals and with the generals' ambitions before any project for which they were hired ever was finished. They also brought in Pyrrhus of Epirus, the greatest and last of their champions.

On the other hand, Rome's reputation with Greek cities was generally good; she was a longtime friend of Greek Massilia (modern Marseilles) and had deposited an offering to Apollo in Massilia's treasury at Delphi as early as the defeat of Veii. Naples, another Greek city, had received especially favorable treatment from the Romans; and it was clear to others that Rome not only protected them from the Gauls, but also was a more dependable friend than the rough Sabellians or their own fellow Greeks.

It was little wonder, then, that in 285 and again in 282 Thurii, a Greek town of southern Italy, appealed to Rome for aid against the Lucanians. Other cities seconded the appeal, and a Roman garrison was sent to Thurii. A small Roman fleet also visited the area and, while cruising off Tarentum, it was attacked by the Tarentines and some of its ships were sunk or captured. The Tarentines then marched on Thurii and expelled the Roman garrison there. The reason for this surprising action was really Tarentine jealousy at Roman interference in southern Italy; but juridically the reason was an old treaty between Rome and Tarentum whereby Roman ships were not to sail east of Croton, a Greek city of southern Italy. The Romans had indeed broken the treaty during their defense of Thurii, but the treaty seems to have been concluded much earlier with one of Tarentum's Greek mercenaries, and by this time it was considered quite out of date, since Rome now held stations on both coasts of the Italian peninsula. In any case, Rome asked only reparations for damage done by the Tarentines; but negotiations were unproductive. Meanwhile the Tarentines procured the services of the great general Pyrrhus of Epirus for their cause and decided on war.

The war with Pyrrhus has been well embroidered with tales of great daring, bravery, and courtesy. This was indeed the last of an age of chivalry that saw a noble adventurer pitted against Romans not yet brutalized by their conflict with Carthage. The decision was rapid. Despite victories over the Romans at Heraclea in 280 and at Asculum in 279, Pyrrhus own losses made a prolongation of his campaign difficult. Further, only a few Samnites, Lucanians, and Greeks had gone over to Pyrrhus, and it seemed likely in 278 that he would be glad to settle for a negotiated peace with the Romans. At this point, however, the Carthaginians steeled Roman resistance by offering them naval cooperation. The Carthaginian offer was an attempt to keep Pyrrhus from turning his attention to Sicily. In this they were unsuccessful. The Greeks of that island hired Pyrrhus to lead their forces in their interminable conflict with the Carthaginians on the island. Pyrrhus spent two years there, where his victories were accepted with as much suspicion and ingratitude as they were in Italy. He then returned to Tarentum and conducted one more whirlwind campaign in 275, but this also was a failure. Thereupon he left a garrison in Tarentum and embarked for new adventures in Greece.

The Romans then proceeded to complete their system of control. Tarentum fell in 272, and it, as well as the other Greek cities, was given an alliance. A colony was sent to Paestum (273) to keep an eye on the Lucanians, and another to Beneventum to split the Samnite League in two. The Samnites themselves became Roman allies. In the north, a colony at Cosa in

Etruria was established to guard the northwestern coast, and Ariminum was colonized on the Adriatic coast in the *Ager Gallicus* (268). The Picentes were reduced in 268, and in the same year the Sabines were promoted to full citizenship. Half of the forest land of the Bruttians was confiscated, and, finally, in 267–6 the Roman consuls marched through the heel of Italy among the Apulians and Messapians and received the submission of the native tribes.

In less than two and a half centuries one small republican town of central Italy had succeeded in unifying the peninsula. This accomplishment was all the more remarkable because so much of it had been carried out unconsciously or only half-consciously; there had been no ambitious long-range plan, but it had been the product of a steady though unspectacular engagement year after year with immediate problems as they arose. Roman predicaments had included the resentment of cultural superiors, such as the Etruscans and Greeks, the natural jealousy of neighbors and equals, the particularism and fear of domination among independent country peoples, and the strategy of the greatest general of his day, Pyrrhus, the man that Hannibal was to call his teacher. However, Rome built solidly and well as she went, and the war with Pyrrhus showed this clearly. Her policy of encircling alliances had engulfed, one by one, the Latins, Aequi and Volsci, Etruscans, Samnites, Hernici, Campanians, and Greeks. Her judicious bestowal of citizenship and her foundation of colonies in strategic locations had surrounded or divided her enemies. And her willingness to learn from superiors and from adversity had slowly created a formidable military machine. The war with Pyrrhus and the Tarentines not only completed a notable achievement, but it also gave the Romans confidence in the steadiness of their troops before superior tactics and new weapons, and in the correctness of their policy toward their allies and toward the conquered.

Chapter 8

EXTERNAL ADAPTATIONS:
THE ROMAN FEDERATION OF ITALY[1]

From the Rubicon to the Sicilian Straits Rome was now
the mistress of Italy, yet Italy was only about one-fifth Roman.
Rome's allies, satellites, and dependencies represented a whole
spectrum of social and political organization, linguistic background, and cultural progress. In the next two hundred years,
however, she welded that diversity into a cultural and economic
unity so satisfactory to its recipients that they were to demand
that they also should become fully Roman politically. The way
in which this was done is unique, and there is no generic term
that exactly describes it. It is perhaps best to call it the Roman
system, unparalleled before or since.

THE ROMAN FEDERATION OF ITALY.   The Roman system
was not the result of some preconceived and carefully followed
plan. The "plan" is only a discovery of scholars after the event,
and the facts of history connected with the system have suffered
through the devotion of the scholars to their "plan." The Roman
system was the result of trial and error, *ad hoc* adaptation, and
flexibility. However, we can find three fixed principles behind
this system. The Romans always insisted that binding agreements could not be made in the field without ratification in
Rome. This sometimes led to accusations of bad faith, but it
ensured that Roman policy would be decided by cooler and
more experienced heads and not influenced by the immediate,
perhaps unfavorable, situation. Further, treaties once entered
into were considered of perpetual duration; when a people had
bound itself on oath to Rome, she considered any attempt to
dissolve the ties unilaterally a reason for war. Finally, the Roman army played a major role in the system. The troops of

[1]   For a correlation of external and internal events from 509 to 266 B.C., see
the table on pp. 95–99.

Rome's Italian allies were in constant contact with the Roman legionaries and learned to admire and envy them. The military highways constructed by the Roman army were travelled by traders who spread a common culture and language. Roman veterans who settled in colonies inevitably mingled with the natives and influenced them.

After the fall of Tarentum (272 B.C.) and the practical unification of Italy under Roman leadership, there were nearly as many variations in the legal bonds between Rome and the other states as there were states. In this heterogeneity, however, there appears a limited number of types. The differences in the details within each type merely show the tentative and experimental nature of much Roman policy in the early Republic: if a procedure worked satisfactorily, there was a disposition to leave good enough alone, even though later experience might suggest improvements. If we allow for the minor variations that Roman policy permitted, we find five general types of status in Rome's federal union of Italy: (1) There were full Roman citizens, some of whom lived in Rome, some in Roman colonies, some in communities that had been endowed with full citizenship, some scattered through the countryside on individual allotments of conquered soil that had been granted to them, and, finally, some citizens of other states to whom personal grants of full citizenship had been made because of service to the Roman State. (2) There were partial citizens, persons that had been endowed with the private rights and public duties of full citizens, but that did not have the rights of suffrage or office. (3) There were the Latins, who were a special class; the Romans were themselves Latins and they shared together a common language and heritage. The Latins were Rome's earliest allies and colleagues, and they enjoyed special privileges listed below. (4) There were the Latin colonists, who were residents of towns founded in the early Republic jointly by Rome and the Latin League. Rome continued to establish these after the original partnership was dissolved. (5) Finally, there were the Italian allies, some Greek, some Italic, some Gallic, and some Etruscan.

THE LATINS AND LATIN RIGHTS.   By the beginning of the Republic the numerous villages of Latium already had begun to take the form of city-states. These steadily decreased in number as the larger ones, such as Rome, Tibur, and Praeneste, absorbed their smaller neighbors. In her first treaty with Carthage (509 B.C.) Rome had claimed hegemony over a number of Latin towns, a position that she probably had exercised during the

Gauls

Ariminum

Etruscans

Umbrians

Cosa

Sena

Aesis

Spoletium

Picentes

Firmum

Sutrium

Narnia

Nepet

Sabines

Alsium

Fregenae

Rome

Carsioli

Aequi

Alba Fucens

Castrum Novum

Ostia

Ardea

Velitrae

Satricum

Signia

Hernici

Hadria

Antium

Norba

Sora

Setia

Circeii

Fregellae

Volsci

Interamna

Terracina

Aesernia

Pontia

Minturnae

Suessa

Sinuessa

Cales

Saticula

Samnites

Paestum

Benevento — Beneventum

Luceria

Apulians

Venusia

COLONIZATION
AND SOME OF THE
PEOPLES
IT CONTROLLED

Lucanians

Brundisium

Latin colonies: <u>Nepet</u>   Roman colonies: <u>Ostia</u>

Etruscan period. Actually in the earliest Republic she was not able to make good her claim, and the special tone of her relations with the other Latin cities is struck by the treaty, the *foedus Cassianum*, between herself and the Latin League, an association of other Latin states.[2] Rome did not enter the League; the treaty was a defensive alliance between equals, with Rome as one party and the League as the other. Each had every right to participate in other foreign commitments. Rome, indeed, seems to have had special treaties with the Latin cities of Ardea and Lavinium, as well as with non-Latin cities. However, since the members of the League had separate interests and did not always act in common, Rome was stronger than any one member of the League, and progressively gained a preponderant weight in the alliance. The advent of a third member, the Hernican League, tended to confirm this development. The special and close relation between Rome and the other Latins had a number of important results. Their common inheritance and early equality made natural and easy the grant of certain special rights to one another: the right to trade and to have their contracts defended by the laws of either state concerned (*ius commercii*), the right to intermarry and to ensure the legitimacy of resultant offspring under the laws of each state (*ius conubii*), the right to change residence from one state to another (*ius migrationis*), and the parallel right to leave one state in exile and to be accepted in another (*ius exilii*). These rights were the natural products of towns that had been equals in primitive times. Because of their experience with these Latin towns the Romans learned the value of flexibility and of calculated generosity in their dealings with other states, a lesson that continued to have effects even after maturity brought a certain nationalistic exclusiveness. After the Latin War and the dissolution of the Latin League (338 B.C.) the remaining thirteen Latin states were bound to Rome by separate treaties, but their special claims based on their common Latinity continued to be preserved between each of them and Rome.

From the beginning of the alliance between Rome and the Latin League the two allies had cooperated in the foundation of Latin colonies. To these went not only citizens of the various cities of the League, but also Romans who themselves thereby became "Latins" in a political sense. These colonies also had certain "Latin" rights in respect to Rome: the *ius conubii, ius commercii, ius migrationis*, and the right of their residents to vote in Rome if they happened to be there at a time of assem-

[2] See pp. 50–51.

bly. At some date, probably fairly late in the Republic, full Roman citizenship was granted to those citizens of Latin colonies who attained the highest political office in their own local government. This was a new level of thought; citizenship no longer depended wholly upon geographical location. Thereafter "Latinity" began to lose its purely local and racial sense and became instead a term of juristic status or class. It was used ultimately to represent an intermediate class between Roman and non-Roman and to serve as a link between them. A case in the second century B.C. illustrates the point: there was no *ius conubii* between Roman citizens and Spaniards. When in 171 B.C., therefore, 4000 offspring of matches between Roman soldiers and Spanish women petitioned for some regularization of their legal status, they were established as "Latins" in a "Latin" colony at Carteia.

THE EXTENSION OF FULL ROMAN CITIZENSHIP.   At the beginning of the Republic Rome was not strong enough to rule Latium, and we have seen how she came to terms with her Latin cousins. Roman territory and Roman citizenship were also extended, though slowly and steadily, so that the Romans themselves were never inundated by their more numerous allies. The methods of extension differed. In the earliest days the towns of some of her nearest neighbors were demolished as, according to tradition, Alba was destroyed in the days of the kings. Her inhabitants were transferred to Rome and received as citizens, for they were relatives. Veii also was destroyed; but its inhabitants were sold into slavery, for they were considered unassimilable foreigners. The methods used at Alba and Veii soon appeared impracticable, however, on a widespread scale. In later cases where the inhabitants were already somewhat Romanized, whole communities were received into the citizenship, while remaining in their homes and continuing to have at least a modicum of local government. Nearby hamlets such as Crustumerium (499 B.C.?), and later perhaps Tusculum (381 B.C.), were so treated. Again, some land generally was taken from a conquered foe and made Roman territory: all of Veii was taken in this way; but one-third was perhaps nearer the amount normally annexed. Some of this land was rented to the original owners, while some of it was granted to individual Roman farmers. Whole colonies of Roman citizens were settled in other annexed territories. In the early days Roman colonies were founded on strategically important sites. These colonies were small, consisting of only about 300 families. The men were considered to be on detached military service. Roman colonies also tended to be in places where there was not the potential for expansion that is noted at the much larger Latin colonial sites.

PARTIAL ROMAN CITIZENSHIP; MUNICIPIA.   Roman territory was increased in another way, through the grant of partial citizenship (*civitas sine suffragio*, citizenship without the vote) to certain cities or peoples. The nature and intent of this grant changed from time to time. Recipients of *civitas sine suffragio* had the private rights and public duties of full Roman citizens; that is, they had the private *ius commercii* and *ius conubii*, but they did not have the public rights of voting and holding office in Rome. In most cases, however, these people had small interest in or competence for the government in Rome, and their own local governments continued to function with little change. These partial citizens were called *municipes* because they had undertaken the tasks (*munera capere*) of citizens, and from them their towns were called *municipia*. In time these towns became cities with complete citizenship rights, but even then they continued to enjoy a good deal of local self-government.

In this way was born the important municipal system by which Rome ultimately administered the Mediterranean world. The first city to be accorded this treatment was Caere (353 B.C.?). This Etruscan city had long had friendly relations with the Romans, who were grateful because the Caeritans received their refugees during the Gallic sack. The Romans had no expectation of Romanizing this older, more civilized people and accepted them as partial citizens, but left to them their own home rule. The people of Caere were thereafter at a time of census enrolled on a special list, the *Tabulae Caeritum*, and this ultimately became the generic term for the list of all citizens with only partial rights. A little later the Romans also gave this status to Capua and to many Campanians (338). Again they were dealing with a people of another race and culture, and at that time they clearly did not consider this a step toward full citizenship; Volscian Fundi, for example, remained a *civitas sine suffragio* for one and a half centuries. The Sabines, on the other hand, and the country people northeast of Rome were rapidly raised from partial to full enfranchisement (between 290 and 268 B.C.) Here race and circumstances were again decisive. The Sabines had long been in contact with the Romans and were of a closely related stock. Furthermore, their area, consisting of open country, had received many individual Roman settlers, who by intermarriage and other contacts had brought about rapid Romanization.

78

The administrative treatment of the *civitates sine suffragio* differed from people to people. While much was left to home rule, circuit judges (*praefecti*) representing the Roman praetor supplemented the local governments and heard legal cases in various towns. In some places such as Capua, which completely lost its municipal status because of its defection to Hannibal, the circuit judges were the sole rulers. Where populations were sparse and civic organizations embryonic, as in the districts where Roman farmers had received individual allotments of land and were intermingled with people of inferior political status, circuit judges were also important. In such areas they set up court in old country meeting-places (*conciliabula*) or new marketplaces (*fora*). In some cases such rudimentary civic centers eventually developed into municipalities.

The *civitates sine suffragio* were important in establishing and developing the idea of double citizenship that was to be such a factor in the administration of Rome's empire. Although it was at first a special and favorable legal category in which the *municipes* undertook some of the responsibilities of citizens and the Romans gave them protection in private law and from foreign foes, the Romans came to use it also as a punishment both for rebellious allies (the Hernici, 306 B.C.) and for their own unsatisfactory fellow citizens. Furthermore, as external dangers receded for residents of Italy, the Romans tended to stress the civic duties attached to this status, while the *municipes* noted fewer and fewer advantages. By the second century B.C. the Romans abandoned this category when establishing relations with new states, and preferred to use a system of simple alliances, which of course they had also been using all along.

THE ITALIAN ALLIES.   The system of Italian alliances can be described briefly, for it simply is the aggregate of individual treaties between Rome and separate Italian communities. The Romans preferred to treat with cities, but where urbanization was not far advanced they treated with native leagues. Terms differed and could be more or less liberal, but generally the cities would be required to supply Rome with men and money for her wars. While these cities still were legally independent, their freedom in foreign relations was sharply curtailed, and there was a tendency on the part of the Romans to favor aristocratic local governments wherever possible. As time went on and the disparity in power between the parties became ever greater, Rome could also make known sharply her wishes in her allies' internal affairs. With the Etruscan cities long-term truces were more common than treaties of alliance; the Romans seemed both fascinated and repulsed by the Etruscans, and the use of truces implies that they did not feel that they had achieved a final solution for their relations with this remarkable people. Most of the Greek cities received especially favorable treatment and were often asked only to provide naval support.

For the Romans a great strength of this system was the variety of categories within it and the possible variations within each category. Roman foreign relations were not regulated by treaties with the Latins as a group, or the *civitates sine suffragio* as a group, or the Italian allies as a group; there was a separate unique treaty between Rome and each of these cities. Each treaty might contain special privileges or special obligations for the contracting parties. This meant that every city had a unique tie with Rome. This uniqueness fostered jealousies between the cities and discouraged combinations that might be dangerous to Rome. In addition, the judicious grant of Roman citizenship to individual citizens of other states—to ex-magistrates among the Latins and to specially favored "friends of the Roman people" among other allies—ensured the Romans influential partisans almost everywhere.

The efficacy of the Roman system, consisting of full citizens, half citizens, Latin allies, Italian allies, and colonies both Latin and Roman, was given an early test by Pyrrhus and the Tarentines (281–272) who offered the Italians opportunities to break away and reassume their earlier complete and chaotic freedom. It was tested even more severely at the end of the third century by the military brilliance and diplomacy of Hannibal, who offered the Italians the same chance to abandon the Romans. The system withstood these enticements, however, for the Italians recognized their community of interest with the Romans, and they appreciated the peace and security that Rome offered after centuries of continuous friction with their neighbors. Only in the late third and second centuries did that community of interest slowly begin to disappear, as Rome expanded overseas and alone reaped most of the benefits of empire. The Italians then became restive in their inferior role. Years of military and economic association and cultural penetration made them fully aware of the advantages of Roman citizenship, and at length they were to demand at sword's point that they too should be Roman.

Chapter 9

INTERNAL ADAPTATIONS:
THE FLEXIBLE CONSTITUTION[1]

I. THE EVOLUTION OF ROMAN GOVERNMENT
(509–287 B.C.)

The first half century of the Republic (509–449 B.C.) had established a *modus vivendi* for the disparate elements in the Roman State. The patricians held the honors and directed the policy, but the plebeians had their own organization within the State that could defend their interests by agitation, strike, or secession when less drastic measures failed. The consuls led the State with the advice of a largely patrician Senate, but the tribunes could convene a tribal assembly, take counsel in it with their fellow plebeians, and issue its opinions. All male citizens, regardless of social status, met in the Centuriate Assembly to elect the consuls and to make important decisions, such as declarations of war, that were binding on all the people. In the Centuriate Assembly the weight of a man's vote depended on his property, for this determined the amount that he contributed to the State in army service or in other civic duties. Finally, the codification of the previously unwritten law in *The Twelve Tables,* at the end of this first phase of the Republic, had assured for all citizens equal protection in the eyes of the law.

While the plebeians had won some concessions, this did not satisfy the ambition of those plebeians that had become relatively prosperous, nor did it conceal the fact that the patrician magistrates and the senators controlled the disposition of land and booty acquired by war. This was at a time when the power of the Etruscans, whose commercial interests had per-

---

[1] For a correlation of external and internal events from 509 to 266 B.C., see the table on pp. 95–99.

meated and benefited much of the peninsula, was shrinking; and also when the constant border warfare was causing an economic depression. The second fifty years of the Republic saw, therefore, new agitation on the part of the plebeians, both on the politico-social and economic fronts.

THE MILITARY TRIBUNATE WITH CONSULAR POWER.
One provision in *The Twelve Tables,* and one that Cicero characterized as most inhuman, was the prohibition of intermarriage between plebeians and patricians. As with much of the rest of *The Twelve Tables,* this probably merely formalized what had been customary practice. However, there is a good deal of difference between social practice and enforced law, and the plebeians were indignant at the slight. The bitter complaints of the plebeians managed to bring about the repeal of the prohibition in 445 B.C. through the Canuleian Law. Later Roman annalists state that at the same time there was agitation by the plebeians to obtain the right to hold the consulship. These annalists further record that rather than lose their monopoly of the consulship, which elevated its holder to the nobility, the patricians obtained the establishment of a new magistracy, a board of military tribunes with consular power. At the Senate's discretion, this board was to be substituted for the consulship. There could be anywhere from three to six military tribunes on any one board, and both patricians and plebeians were eligible. Election to the office did not bring with it the perquisites of nobility, however, as election to the consulship did. Clearly, then, the military tribunes with consular power were regular army officers (some of whom had been plebeians right along) endowed with the powers of the highest magistracy so that they could perform administrative as well as military duties. Between 444 and 367 the board is said to have replaced the consulship fifty-one times. While accounts of early Roman history by later Roman annalists are often grossly inaccurate, there is little doubt that the board of consular tribunes did exist. There is considerable doubt, however, that the office was founded merely in a pique to checkmate the plebeians. The State was still too young for an aura of veneration to have surrounded the consulship. It was still in a flexible and experimental stage, learning to adapt to changing circumstances. The military boards, therefore, probably reflect merely the ebb and flow of the almost constant border warfare of the day. That the plebeian demand for high office was not the determining factor would seem to be suggested by the fact that no plebeian actually was elected to the office until 400. Whenever the State was in spe-

82

cial danger, the whole command was concentrated for six months in the hands of an emergency leader, the dictator.

THE QUAESTORSHIP.   In keeping with the growth of the State and with the increasingly direct control of the government by the citizens, the quaestorship became an independent magistracy in 447 B.C. Prior to this the quaestors had served as aides to the consuls and had been appointed by them. Now they became elected officials, still under the authority of the heads of state, but subject to the suffrage of the people. Their duties now became almost exclusively financial. In 421 the number of quaestors was raised from two to four and plebeians were made eligible. In 409 all four members of the board were plebeians.

THE CENSORSHIP.   The increasingly heavy demands on the heads of state in the fifth century led to the creation of another magistracy. In order to assign to the citizens their appropriate duties in the army and their proper places in the Centuriate Assembly, periodic censuses had to be taken. However, due to the long period of internal unrest, the rule of the decemvirate (451–450), and the constant external pressures, by 443 no census had been taken by the consuls for seventeen years. The situation was critical, for a whole new generation of youths eligible for army service had come of age since the last census, yet they were still not enrolled. In that year, therefore, two censors were elected. Their duties included taking a census of the numbers and financial status of the citizens and organizing the assembly. Later they also were given the tasks of making up the roll of senators, letting out the state contracts, and performing a religious purification of the State. Using the data collected from the census the consuls could make the annual military levy accurately. A plebeian did not hold the censorship until 351 B.C., and no plebeian performed the lustral purification of the State until 280 B.C.

EFFECTS OF THE SIEGE OF VEII.   The final and bitter struggle with Veii and its long siege that, according to tradition, lasted for ten years (405–396 B.C.) had important effects economically and politically on the internal development of Rome. War no longer consisted of seasonal raids on close neighbors. Since the Roman soldier now had to maintain his siegeworks throughout the year and could not attend to his private affairs, the State was forced to institute army pay. This long war also led to the voluntary enlistment of persons sufficiently well off to provide their own horse and cavalry equipment. These persons were known as *equites equo privato* (knights furnishing their own horse.)[2] While the cavalry could not have played any large part at the siege of Veii itself, this act set an example of public service. More important, this was the beginning of a class of the well-to-do (the equestrian class, or the knights), who were not members of the aristocracy, but who ultimately would command an important place in public and financial affairs. When Veii finally fell, Roman territory was nearly doubled, greatly increasing the public wealth and bringing economic improvement for many plebeians who were settled on Veiian lands on allotments of about five acres each. Four new tribes of citizens were organized on this new territory.

THE LICINIO-SEXTIAN LEGISLATION (367 B.C.). The Romans had barely taken stock of their greatly improved conditions after the defeat of their inveterate enemy, when they suffered a disastrous Gallic invasion and in 390 B.C. the destruction of their city. The Romans had to pay the Gauls to leave and then had to rebuild the city and a strong surrounding wall. The common people were pressed into service under the supervision of architects and engineers imported from overseas. The losses suffered, the expenses of rebuilding, the rising taxes, and the enforced labor led to hard times and to much unrest. The wealthier plebeians, who up to now had failed in their attempts to gain social and political equality with the patricians, found in the clamor and distress of the poor their opportunity. For ten years (376 – 367 B.C.), according to tradition, C. Licinius Stolo and L. Sextius, repeatedly elected as tribunes of the plebs, led an attack on the established government and brought its regular operation to a standstill. Finally in 367 during a military dictatorship they carried their point. The resultant Licinio-Sextian Laws marked another giant step in the resolution of the struggle of the plebeians for political recognition. They won the permanent restoration of the consulship and the abandonment of the military tribunate with consular power. One of the consuls each year thereafter was to be a plebeian. For debtors, they provided that interest already paid on debts should be counted against the principal due, and that the payment of the remainder of the debts could be spread in annual installments over a three-year period. For the landless, they established that no one should rent or hold more than 350 acres of state-owned lands, which implied the release of more land for the poor.

With the reduction of the executive branch once more to two colleagues, steps also were taken to add new officials to

[2] See also pp. 62, 178.

share the increasingly heavy administrative duties. The judicial functions at Rome were taken over by a new magistrate called the praetor. The praetor was created without a colleague, which is unusual for the Roman system. Actually the praetor was looked on as a younger colleague of the two chief magistrates, who formerly also had had as one of their titles "praetor." From this time on they were known by their more familiar name of "consul."

The two plebeian aediles, who had originally been assistants to the plebeian tribunes, had by now taken some of the responsibilities for the care of the city and for public festivals. In 366 B.C. two new aediles, drawn from the patricians, were created. They were called curule aediles because they were entitled to sit on curule chairs, as praetors and consuls did. The curule aedileships were soon opened to plebeians in alternate years, and all four aediles performed similar duties for the remainder of republican history.

PROBLEMS OF DEBT IN THE FOURTH CENTURY B.C.
The use of money increased in the second half of the fifth and in the fourth centuries, which facilitated the charge of interest on loans and increased the economic difficulties of the times. The State now insisted on the payment of taxes and fines in money, rather than in goods, and an early scarcity of metals forced the poor to borrow from the rich when assessments fell on them in years of low yield. Constant military campaigns and an economic depression caused a considerable growth in the amount of debt in Rome. Since ancient practices forbade debtors to put up their family estates for security, by a legal instrument known as *nexum* they instead had to pledge their own bodies to work for their creditors until the debt was satisfied. This led to a condition not far removed from slavery. It was not surprising, then, to find the plebeians acting in behalf of debtors, as they did in 367. Members of this agrarian society felt that they had a legitimate quarrel with usury: their debts were contracted to pay taxes and to furnish themselves with the barest necessities of life. In Rome, by tradition, a loan was not conceived as a financial investment, but was gratuitous; a specified object or objects, or others of the same quantity or quality, had to be returned at the end of a specified period. When interest was charged it had to be entered in a separate agreement; it was not considered a part of the original loan.

There was a good deal of Roman legislation at this time against usury, though such measures were seldom long enforced, for they removed a chief incentive for making loans. In 357 B.C. we hear that the tribunes procured the ratification of a plebiscite reducing the interest rate to eight and one-third percent per year. In 352 the consuls had to appoint a five-man board to cope with extensive debt. At this time they arranged for the State to make loans to debtors to satisfy their creditors. In 347 the tribunes secured the passage of a law cutting the interest rate in half; and in 342 we are told that a law was passed forbidding loans at interest entirely. Finally, in 326, the Paetelio-Papirian Law was passed, which brought gradually to an end the use of *nexum*. Thus one of the chief hardships on debtors was removed, for debt no longer could reduce them to personal servitude. We hear of the conviction of certain usurers in 295, and in 287 unrest because of debt caused a secession of poor plebeians to the Janiculum Hill; but except for these two isolated notes we have evidence of no further debtor agitation until the period after the Second Punic War (218–202 B.C.).

In the period during which Italy was being unified the poorer Roman citizens greatly benefited from the foundation of both Roman and Latin colonies. While the Roman colonies originally were mostly small military establishments (no more than 300 men), in the later Republic they ran to as high as 4000 to 6000 persons. At first, however, the Latin colonies, which included both Romans and Latins, were much the larger. The Roman colonists received a very small allotment of private property (at first the traditional one-and-one-third-acre family plot), but apparently the colony also owned common land subject to the same communal use as the public land of the Roman people. Members of the Latin colonies regularly received much larger private grants but did not have the common lands of the Roman colonists. The number of persons that were benefited by the Roman system of colonization must have been considerable. There is evidence of thirty-three colonies of the Latin type down to 263 B.C., and of six Roman ones to 283 B.C. These perhaps cared for some 80,000 people. Indeed, Livy remarks in his account of 300 B.C. that the large numbers sent into the colonies kept the plebeians quiet.

THE ORDERS OF SOCIETY.   Not all the struggles for equal rights of citizenship show cleanly cut lines of battle. This is because Roman society began to divide, during the fourth and third centuries B.C. into three classes or orders, and sometimes they had ambiguous policies. There were the old die-hard aristocratic patricians, a new patricio-plebeian nobility of office-holders, and the proletariat made up of poor plebeians, including clients and former clients. The ambitions of these classes might lead to combinations that gave surprising results. The public career of Appius Claudius the Censor will serve as an example. He held office in the last phases of the struggle between the orders, and his career seems to have puzzled and infuriated the ancients as much as it has baffled the moderns. As censor in 312 B.C. Appius showed energy and foresight in constructing the first of the great Roman aqueducts to bring a fresh supply of water to the city, and in connecting Rome with Capua during the Samnite Wars by the Appian Way, the "queen of roads." Three of his acts as censor, however, roused resentment and opposition: he refused to resign at the end of his eighteen-month term of office, he included the sons of freedmen in his revision of the roll of senators, and he allowed some persons to register themselves in rural tribes (where their votes would have greater weight) even though they owned no land. Some see in these acts the work of a man of remarkable insight and foresight in an ultraconservative world, but most commentators believe that this arch-aristocrat was marshalling proletarian support to offset the new patricio-plebeian nobility, just as patricians long before had used their clients to swamp the plebeians.

THE TRIUMPH OF THE PLEBEIANS.   Regardless of the machinations of social or political parties, the period between the codification of *The Twelve Tables* and the unification of Italy was characterized by an increasing participation of the plebeians in the government; and it concluded with the irreversible fusion of the separate plebeian government with the government of the whole State. The process was accelerated by the increasing disparity between the number of plebeians and patricians, the need for plebeian participation in ever widening military duties and responsibilities in Italy, the political pride and ambition of more affluent plebeian families, and the judicious exploitation by the plebeians of economic distress among the masses to bring pressure for political reform. The first step had been plebeian admittance to the military tribunate with consular power, which frequently was the chief magistracy in the last part of the fifth and in the fourth century. It was inevitable that soon, in 421, the plebeians should gain the right of election to the quaestorship, for its holders were the first secular assistants of the chief magistrates. The reestablishment of the consulship in 367 as the chief magistracy and the opening of this office to the plebeians signified that scruples could no longer be attached to their competence to represent the State in any capacity, even in dealings with the gods. If at times there were delays before other posts were held by plebeians, it may well have been due as much to the superior qualifications of patrician candidates, the freely expressed will of the electorate, or the political astuteness of magistrates presiding at elections as it was to the need for any enabling legislation. In any case, it was possible for plebeians to be curule aediles soon after 364 B.C.; their first dictator took office in 356, first censor in 351, and first praetor in 337. Beginning in 362 six military tribunes also were elected regularly by the people. In 311 the number was raised to sixteen, and between 291 and 219 to twenty-four, enough to furnish the regular levy of four legions with six officers apiece.

The process of patricio-plebeian assimilation may be considered complete when in 300 the Ogulnian Law provided for an increase in the boards of pontiffs and augurs and required that at least half of the members of these boards should be plebeian. Thereafter only a very few highly specialized but quite unimportant functions were reserved to the patricians alone.

THE HORTENSIAN LAW (287 B.C.).　　The final triumph of the plebeian organization in its drive to power came only a few years later. We have mentioned that there had been at the beginning of the third century B.C. a period of unrest due to economic distress brought about by the long wars with the Samnites. The details are hazy, but apparently senatorial interference blocked an attempt in the Tribal Assembly to pass remedial legislation assisting debtors. Thereupon the plebeians withdrew from Rome to the Janiculum and refused further cooperation with the government. Ultimately, however, the dictator of 287 B.C., Quintus Hortensius, persuaded the secessionists to return, and he effected the passage of a law making the plebiscites enacted in the Tribal Assembly binding on all citizens without consent or ratification by the Senate. With the Hortensian Law more than two centuries of struggle between the orders came to an end: the plebeians' revolutionary state within the State had won the right to rule the whole State if it wished. However, the flexibility, compromise, and tolerance that had led slowly and bloodlessly to this situation also continued to be observed for many years in the actual operation of the government.

II. THE ROMAN REPUBLICAN CONSTITUTION
(287 – 133 B.C.)

The Roman government as it had evolved by 287 B.C. remained essentially unchanged for 150 years. That long period's political stability permits, and its historical importance requires, a thorough understanding of the Roman Republican constitution during that century and a half. The Romans never had a written constitution, nor had they textbooks analyzing the structure of the government or its functions and responsibilities. Despite this, it is convenient for us to describe the Roman government, after the passage of the Hortensian Law, in terms of the conventional modern division of government into executive, administrative, legislative, and judicial branches. This will give us a fair grasp of the way the Roman system worked, but it will also emphasize, because of the exceptions and anomalies that will appear, to what extent the Roman form of government resulted from natural growth, arbitration, timidity, conservatism, or political bargains.

THE EXECUTIVE BRANCH.   The executive branch consisted of elected magistrates. One of the distinctive features of the Roman magistracy was its collegiality: that is, with minor exceptions all magistrates were members of colleges (or boards) of at least two members. All members of a college were of equal rank and could interfere with and veto the acts of other members. Further, higher magistrates could forbid the acts of lower magistrates. This startlingly negative principle suggests the strong Roman fear of tyranny; and the fact that the government operated at all indicates the good sense and forbearance of the men that held elective positions. At the head of the magistracies stood what were once the only, and were almost always the chief, elected officials, the consuls. They led and represented the State both in domestic and in foreign affairs, and they enjoyed the powers of the *imperium* that enabled them to do so.[3] By the third century B.C., however, the consulship was somewhat weakened, both by the loss of some of its powers of action to lesser elected officials and also by the increasing prestige of the Senate, an organ that started as an advisory body of elders to the magistrates and ended by dominating its advisees through the great prestige of its membership and the political and social dangers involved in alienating it.

Among the new magistrates, ranking next below the consuls, was the praetor. His primary function was to direct the administration of civil law in Rome. However, he too had the *imperium* and served as a junior colleague of the consuls. As such, he could either take the place of the consuls at home when they were with the armies, or, if necessary, he too could lead an army in the field.

In addition to these major elected magistrates, there were lesser ones without the *imperium*. These started out as assist-

3   For the *imperium*, see p. 53.

ants to other officials, but little by little they became elective officials with special competences of their own, though they always were subject to the general supervision of the major magistrates. The aediles were in charge of many religious celebrations, temples, the upkeep of the city, and the regulation of the marketplace. The quaestors cared for the treasury, where they not only received and disbursed funds, but also certified and cared for many of the records of the State. Some of them also served in the field as quartermasters and as seconds in command.

After the passage of the Hortensian Law many of the reasons for the tribunate disappeared. Nevertheless the office still continued, though little by little it was largely domesticated. Legally it still was not really part of the constitution, but actually it functioned as such. It retained a little of its original revolutionary character in that its members and its legislative activity, if they showed any special interests at all, focused on the defense of individual rights against the State. The tribunes tended to be young men of good plebeian birth, most of whom looked forward to distinguished public careers. With occasional exceptions, therefore, they might be expected to follow the initiative and wishes of more mature politicians.

THE ADMINISTRATIVE BRANCH.   The nearest approach to an administrative branch in the Roman system was the Senate. Though it was originally conceived only as an advisory body of elders, with the years its influence became greater and greater. Since the magistrates of the State were elected for only one-year terms, the Senate was the only body in the State that could maintain a continuous policy. Since most of the former officials of the State were members, the Senate was also a reservoir of political and administrative wisdom. The Senate retained vestiges of its early advisory nature; it did not have initiative. A magistrate with *imperium* had to convene it and ask its advice (later, as the tribunes became quasi-magistrates, they too could consult it). Once a senator's advice was asked, however, he was free to talk about the subject at hand and anything else that he wished, for as long as he wished. Thus matters of import could be brought emphatically by senators to the attention of the magistrates. Opinions were generally asked of each senator in a set order, the method being to start with the oldest ex-censor and to move through those that had held the censorship, then through the ex-consuls, and so on down the line. The process continued until a proposal was produced that seemed viable to the presiding magistrate. This he then put to a vote. If it passed it was called a senatusconsult (a considered answer of the Senate or, less exactly, a decree of the Senate), and the immense prestige of the body ensured almost certain compliance. Because of their especially complicated nature, matters dealing with foreign affairs and with finance gradually came almost exclusively into the competence of the Senate which ultimately looked upon them as its own responsibility and preserve.

THE LEGISLATIVE BRANCH.   In the legislative branch of the Roman government there were three different assemblies. Each of these consisted of the whole electorate, but their interior organizations were different because of differences in their origins and histories. The differences in organization meant a difference in the weight of the individual citizen's vote, depending on the assembly concerned. This is because in their assemblies the Romans never used a simple count of hands with the majority of the voters deciding. Instead the assemblies were made up of voting units. The single vote of each voting unit was determined by a majority of the voters within that unit. The vote for a proposal could be in three centuries 51–49, 51–49, 3–97; while the popular vote would have been 195 "no" against 105 "aye", under the unit system the measure would carry two to one.

The oldest of the assemblies was the Curiate Assembly, which dated back to primitive Rome, or perhaps even to the pre-Roman villages. Its units of organization were the thirty *curiae* or wards of the early city. As a legislative body it became outdated in early republican Rome, but Roman conservatism retained it for the purposes of endowing elected magistrates with the *imperium* and of witnessing various ceremonies that had a religious significance.

The basic unit of the Centuriate Assembly was the century, and membership in a given century was based on wealth and age.[4] The historical source of this assembly was the army, where at first service was based on the capability to furnish the appropriate arms, and where the men were organized to fight in groups of 100. Such an organization was bound to exert pressures regarding its choice of commanders and their activities. Gradually there evolved a political body to which the chief magistrates, who were also the generals, naturally turned. We do not know what the earliest form of this assembly was, but it probably took the form that we know in historical times sometime early in the fourth century B.C. when the army numbered

[4]   For the Centuriate Assembly, see also p. 54.

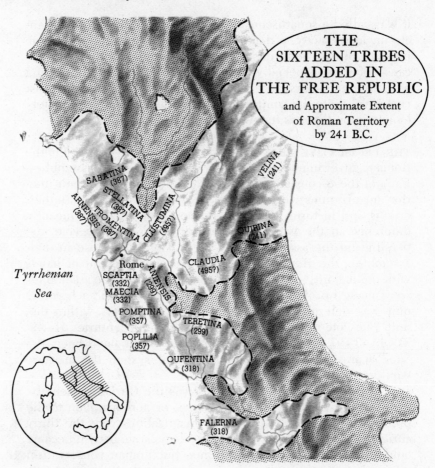

THE
SIXTEEN TRIBES
ADDED IN
THE FREE REPUBLIC
and Approximate Extent
of Roman Territory
by 241 B.C.

SABATINA
(387)
STELLATINA
(387)
ARNENSIS (387?)
TROMENTINA
(387)
CLUSTUMINA (495?)
VELINA
(241)
QUIRINA
(241)
Tyrrhenian
Sea
Rome
CLAUDIA
(495?)
SCAPTIA
(332)
ANIENSIS
(299)
MAECIA
(332)
POMPTINA
(357)
TERETINA
(299)
POPLILIA
(357)
OUFENTINA
(318)
FALERNA
(318)

two legions of 4200 men apiece. As a legislative and electoral body the Centuriate Assembly no longer was composed solely of men in the army. Nearly half its members were seniors (men over forty-six years of age) who were available for only very limited military service. Moreover, the number of centuries, 193, that it had when it finally took shape was not changed with increases of population, and therefore the "centuries" might include far more than 100 men apiece. Of the 193 centuries, 18 were of knights and 80 were of juniors (men under forty-six years of age) and seniors of the highest class of wealth. These constituted more than a majority of the whole, and therefore they could control the vote. The remaining 95 centuries were divided between the four lower propertied classes, with a few centuries reserved for professionals such as trumpeters and armorers, and one century for the *proletarii* or propertyless. It can be seen, then, that a rich man's vote in a century of knights, consisting of only 100 men, would be worth far more than that of a man in the century of *proletarii*, probably with thousands of members. Some of the Assembly's characteristics still betrayed its military origin. Like the army, it could not be convened in the city; it elected the chief magistrates with *imperium*, the consuls and praetors; and it was the proper body to declare war. Its decisions were in a strict sense the laws (*leges*) binding on the people, and it also served as the highest court of appeal in cases involving capital punishment.

The Tribal Assembly also included all male citizens, but here they voted in tribes, units that reflected their places of residence.[5] There were thirty-five of these by 241 B.C., four in Rome and thirty-one outside, which were called the rural or rustic tribes. Here financial considerations had no place, and in this respect the Tribal Assembly was more democratic than the Centuriate Assembly. However, since here too the majority in each tribe determined its one vote, and the vote of each tribe had an equal weight, the conservative small-farmer class of the thirty-one less densely populated rural tribes had a heavy majority over the four populous urban tribes. The Tribal Assembly began as the assembly peculiar to the elections and deliberations of the plebeians, and its enactments were called plebiscites (opinions of the plebeians). As the plebeians swamped the patricians in number there was less and less difference in the composition of the two assemblies. Before the Hortensian Law, assembly by tribes probably was restricted to plebeians, but after it consuls and praetors, as well as tribunes, might well convene the whole people in this manner. The Tribal Assembly elected the tribunes and most of the lesser magistrates. In legislative matters it could be used for all the same purposes as the Centuriate Assembly, except for matters relating to war. Since it was simpler to convene and poll thirty-five tribes than it was 193 centuries, the Tribal Assembly came to be used more frequently for legislation. It also served as the court of appeal in cases that involved heavy fines.

THE JUDICIAL BRANCH.　The chief official of the judicial branch was the praetor. He was in charge of civil litigation, but he was not a judge in the modern sense. He presided during the preliminary stages of a suit when the existence of an issue was determined and its exact nature defined. He then turned the case for actual trial over to private citizens, either to a *judex* (a single judicial delegate of the praetor) or to a board of arbiters,

5　See p. 56.

93

who heard the evidence and rendered the decision. In this way one praetor could supervise a great many cases. Criminal prosecution was in the hands of quaestors (murder and peculation), aediles (commercial offenses), and *duoviri perduellionis* (treason). From such magistrates appeals always could be made to one of the assemblies, the choice of which depended on the nature of the crime and of the penalty.

EXTRAORDINARY OFFICIALS.　There were also a number of extraordinary or irregular officials. There were boards (usually of three men, triumvirs) selected to establish new colonies or to assign the public lands to private individuals. In times of great emergency the consuls could appoint as chief of state a dictator, who then appointed as his chief assistant a master of the horse. Theoretically the dictator led the infantry and his assistant commanded the cavalry. The dictator, being a single magistrate, was not subject to the limitations that rose from having a colleague of equal rank during his tenure; and other officials, such as the tribunes, could not intercede or veto his acts. The term of his office, however, was strictly limited to the duration of the crisis for which he was appointed or to six months, whichever was shorter. By this device, in times of great danger the Romans avoided the paralysis that was potential in their principle of collegiality, while the brevity of the office was their insurance against its tyrannical use.

There were also the censors who, after 443 B.C., were elected approximately every five years to take the census. They collected the data necessary to levy troops, assess taxes, and assign voters to the appropriate centuries and tribes. In caring for the welfare of the State they were apt to rebuke activities that they considered unworthy of good citizens. Their interest in morals was increased in 312 B.C. when the censors were assigned the task of determining the roll of the Senate, for they were authorized to remove any senator whose private or public life did not measure up to the censors' standard for senatorial dignity and integrity. They also had charge of many of the financial affairs of the State—renting out the exploitation of public properties and taxes and letting out the contracts for public works. All these duties together gave the censors great prestige, although they lacked *imperium* and in protocol ranked below the praetors and just above the aediles.

The Roman constitution of the early third century B.C. clearly reflects the many years of trial, bargains, adaptation, and conservatism; and in it there is indeed shown clear suspicion of all government. There were few places where there were not

checks or impingements within or between branches of government. Within the executive branch every higher magistrate had
the right to veto the act of a lower magistrate and to intercede in
the acts of a colleague of the same rank, while the tribunes were
free to intercede against the acts of any magistrate except the
dictator. Again, the executives were elected by the legislative
branch, but the legislative branch could not meet without an
executive taking the initiative. Executives could look forward
to an almost certain lifelong seat in the administrative branch,
and therefore they hesitated to thwart the will of their future
colleagues in the Senate. The judiciary also was elected by the
legislative branch, but acted independently of it after election.
On the other hand, the legislative branch acted as a high court
of appeal from unpopular judgments. All the branches of the
government depended upon, and served to check, one another—except that the Senate held a largely independent position. Even the Senate, however, consisted for the most part of
elected ex-magistrates, and notoriously corrupt members could
be expelled by the censors. As long as it deserved its position of
prestige because of its disinterested activity, all was well; and
this condition seems to have been generally true for well over a
century after the unification of Italy.

The constitution that has here been described is the instrument with which the Romans were to move from the unification of Italy to that of the Mediterranean. It is essentially the
one that was admired by the Greek historian Polybius in the
second century B.C. Further, it was perhaps the most important
single factor in molding the spirit and many striking features of
the American Constitution. It is important, therefore, that we
observe carefully its great successes and great failures in the
two and one-half centuries following the Hortensian Law and
the physical unification of Italy.

TABLE OF EVENTS, 509–266 B.C.

Many of the events discussed in chapters 6–9 are arranged
here chronologically and in parallel columns so that the reader
may comprehend some of the interrelations of the internal and
external affairs of the Romans between 509 and 266 B.C. The
dates used are the traditional ones established by Varro, a
scholar of the first century B.C. Therefore, the earlier ones must
be taken simply as approximations. Where even greater uncertainty exists, *ca.* is prefixed to the date.

Survival and Unification

<table>
<tr><td colspan="2">EXTERNAL RELATIONS</td><td colspan="2">INTERNAL DEVELOPMENT</td></tr>
<tr><td>509</td><td>First treaty with Carthage.</td><td>509</td><td>Establishment of the Republic.
Valerian Law on appeal from sentences.</td></tr>
<tr><td>504–449</td><td>Wars with Sabines.</td><td></td><td></td></tr>
<tr><td>ca. 500–431</td><td>Wars with Aequi and Volsci.</td><td>495?</td><td>20th and 21st tribes established north of Rome: Clustumina, Claudia.</td></tr>
<tr><td>496</td><td>Battle against Latins at Lake Regillus.</td><td></td><td></td></tr>
<tr><td></td><td></td><td>494</td><td>Establishment of plebeian tribunate.</td></tr>
<tr><td>493</td><td>*Foédus Cassianum* with Latin League.</td><td></td><td></td></tr>
<tr><td>486</td><td>Latin colony at Norba (Volscian front).</td><td></td><td></td></tr>
<tr><td>482–474</td><td>War with Veii.</td><td>471</td><td>Establishment of Tribal Assembly.</td></tr>
<tr><td></td><td></td><td>451–450</td><td>The Decemvirate. Codification of *The Twelve Tables*.</td></tr>
<tr><td></td><td></td><td>449</td><td>Restoration of consular government.</td></tr>
<tr><td></td><td></td><td>447</td><td>Establishment of elected quaestorship.</td></tr>
<tr><td></td><td></td><td>445</td><td>Canuleian Law legalizes marriage of patricians and plebeians.</td></tr>
<tr><td></td><td></td><td>444–367</td><td>51 boards of military tribunes with consular power occasionally replace consuls.</td></tr>
<tr><td>438–425</td><td>War with Veii.</td><td>443</td><td>Establishment of censorship.</td></tr>
<tr><td>431</td><td>Battle of Mt. Algidus.</td><td></td><td></td></tr>
<tr><td>405–396</td><td>War with Veii.</td><td>421</td><td>Plebeians eligible for quaestorship.</td></tr>
<tr><td></td><td></td><td>403</td><td>Establishment of knights serving with own horses.</td></tr>
<tr><td>396</td><td>Fall of Veii to Rome.
Fall of Melpum to Gauls.</td><td></td><td></td></tr>
<tr><td>390</td><td>Battle of the Allia.
Sack of Rome by the Gauls.</td><td></td><td></td></tr>
<tr><td>389–358</td><td>Sporadic war with rebellious Latins, Aequi, Volsci, Hernici.</td><td></td><td></td></tr>
<tr><td>389–351</td><td>Uprisings among Etruscans.</td><td></td><td></td></tr>
</table>

EXTERNAL RELATIONS	INTERNAL DEVELOPMENT
	387 22nd–25th tribes established in southern Etruria.
383 Latin colonies at Sutrium and Nepete (Etruscan front), Satricum (Volscian front).	
382 Latin colony at Setia (Volscian front).	381 Tusculum receives full citizenship.
	378 Great "Servian" Wall built around Rome.
	ca. 375 Centuriate Assembly takes traditional form.
	367 Licinio-Sextian Laws on plebeian consulship, public land, debt.
	366 First praetorship, curule aediles.
	364 Plebeians eligible for curule aedileship.
358 Renewal of treaty with Latin League.	357 Reduction of rate of interest. 26th and 27th tribes established in Pontine Plain.
	356 First plebeian dictator.
354 Treaty with Samnites.	
353? Hundred-year truce with Caere.	353? Caere granted partial citizenship.
	352 Committee works on debtor problem at Rome.
351 Forty-year truce with Tarquinii and Falerii.	351 First plebeian censor.
348 Treaty with Carthage renewed.	
340–338 Latin War.	342 Charge of interest abolished.
ca. 340 Alliance with Campanian League.	
338 Dissolution of Latin League; Roman colony at Antium.	338 Campanians, Fundi, Formiae granted partial citizenship.
	337 First plebeian praetor.
336 Teanum forced into Roman alliance (Samnite front).	
334 Latin colony at Cales (Samnite front).	332 28th and 29th tribes established on Latin coast.

EXTERNAL RELATIONS	INTERNAL DEVELOPMENT
	Acerrae (Campania) given partial citizenship.
ca. 330 Fabrateria and Frusino in Trerus and Liris valleys forced into alliance.	
329 Roman colony at Terracina.	329 Privernum (Volscian territory) given partial citizenship.
328 Latin colony at Fregellae (Samnite front).	
326 Capture of Naples.	326 Paetelio-Papirian Law abolishes *nexum*.
ca. 325 Alliances with Apulians.	
325–321 Samnite War, first phase.	
321 Disaster at Caudine Forks.	
	318 30th and 31st tribes established in Volscian and Campanian territory.
316 Nucerian League goes over to Samnites.	
316–304 Samnite War, second phase.	
313 Latin colonies at Pontia (Tyrrhenian island), Suessa (Campania), Saticula (Samnite front).	
312 Calatia and Nola forced into alliance. Latin colony at Fregellae renewed. Colony at Interamna (Samnite front).	312 Appius Claudius censor. Appian Way, Rome to Capua, built.
309–308 War with Etruscans.	
308–304 Revolts by Hernici, Aequi, Paeligni.	306 Revolting Hernican towns captured and given partial citizenship.
304 Latin colonies at Alba Fucens and Sora (N. Samnite frontiers).	
	300 Ogulnian Law opens priesthoods to plebeians.
	299 32nd and 33rd tribes established among Aequi and Hernici.
298–290 Samnite War, third phase.	
295 Defeat of Grand Italian Alliance at Sentinum.	
	290 Sabines annexed and given partial citizenship.
285, 283 Thurii appeals for Roman aid.	287 Hortensian Law: final triumph of plebeians.

EXTERNAL RELATIONS	INTERNAL DEVELOPMENT
283 Invasion by Senones, driven from their country. Roman colony established at Sena.	
281–272 War with Tarentines and Pyrrhus.	
280 Battle of Heraclea.	
279 Battle of Asculum.	
278 Treaty with Carthage.	
273 Latin colonies at Cosa (Etruria), Paestum (Lucania), Beneventum (Samnium).	
272 Fall of Tarentum.	
268 Picentes reduced. Latin colony at Ariminum (*Ager Gallicus*).	268 Sabines receive full citizenship.
267–266 Submission of Apulian and Messapian tribes.	

Chapter 10

THE CREATION OF THE ROMAN CHARACTER

By the third century B.C. the Romans were an established force in the Mediterranean world. And by this time their history and usages had created certain national characteristics. In this they were not like all other ancient peoples. It was difficult in antiquity, and still is today, to characterize the Greeks, because of their vast intellectual range, their variety in politics and literature, and their mercurial temperament. But the phrase "an old Roman" has meaning for almost everyone. Such popular conceptions may appear facile generalizations, but they often contain a good deal of truth. There was indeed a distinctive

Roman character that is demonstrated by their language, literature, and deportment, and its nature had something to do with
the remarkable success of the Romans as soldiers and statesmen. Some ideas and practices that went back to the pre-Roman
world helped form this character, while the experiences and
trials of men in a struggling infant state forged other elements of
it. The evolution of this character was essentially completed by
the time that Italy was unified. We are now at the threshold of
Latin literature, which took for an ideal the early Roman and
made him the standard for later men. It is therefore important
that we set forth his characteristics, wooden and partial and
imprecise though such an analysis must be.

The Roman was devoted to the soil, and he had a peasant's
virtues. The primitive Latins were herdsmen and farmers. Their
roots were deep. Much of their blood must have gone back to
the neolithic men of Italy whose archaeological remains indicate an industrious and peaceful folk. They were the prototype
of the European peasant. In primitive Latin law the familial
plots of land were inalienable, and this focus increased their
owners' devotion. Until well into historical times men sacrificed
their own persons for debt rather than diminish their landed
property. Even in the Romans' grandest days no form of wealth
was considered so desirable and so respectable as the land.
From this attachment thrift developed, and a will to hard work,
and from it also a certain acquisitiveness and exactitude, or
even meanness, in financial dealings. A fierce loyalty to their
land made them equally loyal to its aggregate, their state; and
the farmer-soldier when on the defensive was the best in the
world. The Latin farmer's life was hard. The work was unvary-
ing and laborious: the same tasks had to be performed day after
day, yet the results were never sure. In constant attendance
were drought, flood, hail, and pestilence — all incalculable and
impossible to ward off. Even the most patrician Roman was not
really rich in the early Republic, and under these conditions the
Romans became a people endowed with simplicity, self-reliance, and endurance for routine and hard work.

The Romans were frontiersmen. The first settlements on
the Tiber seem to have been designed to watch and defend the
easiest crossing place against Etruscan invasion. The Roman
site became in turn an Etruscan outpost and stronghold, and
then once more, after the expulsion of the kings, the Romans
resumed their northern watch and held a guard for the Latins
not only against the Etruscans but also against the far more
formidable Gauls. Such a position breeds alertness, vigor, and
instant obedience to authority. Frontiers have not generally

sired cultural advances, but from them repeatedly has sprung vigorous military and political leadership.

The Romans were secular, unemotional, and businesslike. They had a suspicion of specialists in the religious field. The paterfamilias superintended the relations between his own household and the gods, and the elected magistrates performed the same function for the State. There were indeed priests (*flamines*), pontiffs, augurs, and professional religious boards, but generally they served in a consulting capacity, when an individual or a magistrate felt that he needed a specialist's opinion. It is not that the Romans had no sense of the supernatural. These farmers and herdsmen lived in a world of mysterious power. Everywhere they saw both the wonderful and inexplicable workings of fertility and procreation and the equally inscrutable destructive forces that accompanied them. They saw that some vital power, almost an electric force, was involved in every natural phenomenon. *Numina* (spirits) accompanied every facet of their lives. With these they had to live, and experience seemed to show that certain attitudes and routines in respect to those powers ensured a minimum of disaster. This led to an extremely methodical system of ritual and prayer performed by those in places of responsibility to obtain as benign a climate as possible for their acts. It led the heads of the State to ascertain before any official business that no portent indicated opposition by spiritual powers to the contemplated act. Little by little the Romans learned of foreigners' anthropomorphic gods, who were said to preside over various activities and phenomena. Though they might identify some of these with their own native *numina*, they often attached limiting adjectives to them, such as Juno Concordia (the peaceful), Hercules Fidius (the faithful), Venus Victrix (the victorious). To the Romans such abstractions as Honor, Concord, Good Faith, Virtue, Equity, and Victory were actual powers, and they raised temples and monuments to them alone. These religious attitudes led to a number of special Roman characteristics. Their early appreciation of abstractions was important in the rapid development of their disposition for legal concepts; and the impersonal nature of the supernatural led to a formal and contractual relation between responsible citizens and the appropriate powers. However, the local spirits of town, farm, and pasture never lost a special hold that they had on the country people, and an affectionate deference to these has continued to this day, when they masquerade as the patrons of every hamlet in Italy.

The Roman was unswervingly devoted to and ambitious

101

for his family. His sense of the world's mysterious forces extended to the area of human relations. The sequence of father-son-father-son was miraculous and sacred. Strictly speaking, the Roman family (*familia*) consisted not only of the paterfamilias and his wife, their sons with their wives and descendants, and their unmarried daughters, but also it included the family's slaves, many of their farm animals, and their landed estate. To the Roman this family with its own sacred spirit, its genius, was all-important. The family was eternal, the individual merely a fleck on the steady flow of its surface. Nothing was more important than the increase of its prestige by one's acts, nothing more dreadful than its extinction. From this deep identification of self with the whole family came the early inalienability of landed property, from it the tendency to limit the size of the family so that the estate should not be fragmented, from it an unparalleled dependence on adoption lest the family's cult end uncelebrated without a communicant. From it too rose much of the political rivalry of later Roman history. To maintain the family's position Roman society had endowed the head of family, the paterfamilias, with extraordinary autocratic power. This was the *patria potestas* whereby the paterfamilias had supreme authority over the lives and acquisitions of all the members of his *familia*. It was not that he could not be a loving husband, father, and master, or that all these persons and things became his property; but he, like a nineteenth-century ship captain, was endowed with autocratic authority in order that his charge might get safely to port. Such a system bred instant and complete obedience as well as the sublimation of self in a less ephemeral organism.

The Roman was a patriot. He early had ambitions for his State as well as for his family. Under Etruscan chieftains the Latin hamlets on the Tiber got a taste of the advantages in controlling others. They enjoyed the pleasures that accompanied their new position in a capital of trade. Though they threw off the Etruscan yoke, they were loath to relinquish the standard of living that they had obtained from it, and immediately upon the birth of the Republic they began to claim the position that the Etruscans had just relinquished.

The Romans were indulgent of foreign beliefs and practices. They early recognized the virtues of tolerance and of cooperation. The tradition of the various Latin leagues go back into prehistory, and the Romans' experiences with the other Latins and with the Hernici in the early Republic taught them to live with others, to learn from others, to compromise. They never lost this trait, even though with growing power they could and did make greater demands on others. One of the great strengths of their empire was their willingness not only to allow native gods, native administration, and native practices to continue unmolested, but also to borrow and to adapt freely from others whatever they found useful. This made possible the transmission of religions, ideas, and ideals from older cultures, and it helped them to construct for themselves a respectable literature, an efficient military machine, a formidable bureaucracy, and the world's greatest legal system.

The Romans were orderly. A constitutional practice that developed in the Republic emphasized and deepened a tendency that already was part of the Roman character. The Roman willed to do things in a systematic fashion, and so, as the republican government evolved and new officials were needed, the citizen in public life passed through the various offices in a certain order, from the less important to the more important posts. There was no legislation on the matter until the second century B.C., but very early the Romans felt that properly one should, after military service, seek the quaestorship, tribunate (if a plebeian), aedileship, praetorship, and consulship in that order. This was the *cursus honorum* (course of offices). While in protocol the censorship ranked below the praetorship and was not strictly part of the *cursus* at all, its great prestige meant that ultimately it was sought by ex-consuls as the crowning achievement of a public career. The *cursus honorum* not only reflected Roman orderliness, but also ensured that higher magistrates and the members of the Senate were men of some experience in almost all the facets of public life.

Thrifty, acquisitive, self-reliant, vigorous, obedient, secular, loyal, ambitious, adaptable, methodical—the Roman was a dependable ally and a formidable opponent. However, he did not have great intellectual attainments nor deep sensitivity. Indeed, there was also a strain of cruelty in him—or at least of callousness toward suffering—prompted by an environment where lives were easily, almost casually, lost. He was not a particularly charming or attractive person, but one equipped to conquer and to rule the world better than most of his successors have been. He had been steeled by suffering and adversity, but he was tempered by his experience in ruling others. Steadfast and unperturbed, he became the ideal that Horace immortalized as proof against the fury of the mob, the menace of tyrants, the wrath of elements and gods:

> Nay, if the globe itself should split and fall,
> He'd stand serene amidst the crashing ruin.

PART
Three

The Great Rivalry

Chapter 11

THE FIRST PUNIC WAR

The Rome that emerged at the head of an Italian system stretching from the Rubicon to Rhegium could hardly be called a stranger to the arts of survival and success. The Republic itself was nearly two and a half centuries old, and before that there had been the Etruscan kingdom. How the Romans' past influenced them we can discern in their responses to their next great test, their rivalry with Carthage. The principles that they drew from the past and elaborated or augmented during this struggle long and fatally set the character of their empire.

By 265 B.C. Rome and her own territory, the *ager Romanus*, was a rather compact state of central Italy, surrounded by or enlaced with a number of closely related Latin states, and comprising about one fifth of the peninsula's area. North and south of this area were the Italian allies: Etruscans, Greeks, and various Italic peoples, all bound to Rome by special treaties in which Rome promised to defend them in return for their assistance in men or ships. The fidelity of these peoples was bolstered by the numerous Latin or Roman colonies which had been placed among them in strategic positions.

Rome had nearly extended the limits of her system to Italy's natural boundaries, but such an accomplishment did not necessarily mean tranquillity without good will and self-discipline on the frontiers. All of Rome's frontiers bore the potentialities for friction with peoples less familiar to the Romans than their Italian neighbors had been. Beyond the northern frontier in the Po valley were Rome's ancient enemies, the Gauls. They now were settling down to an agricultural existence, but they still were subject to ancient passions and pressures, and to the Romans they were still objects of fear. To the east across the Adriatic, a pirate kingdom held the Illyrian coast. Farther south the Hellenistic cities and states of the Greek cultural zone were bemused by the barbarian upstart that had defeated Pyrrhus and asserted its protection of Greek cities. On the west and southwest, to which Italy was naturally oriented, lay Sicily, half Greek and half a portion of the Carthaginian commercial empire.

CARTHAGINIAN GOVERNMENT AND FOREIGN POLICIES.   Rome and Carthage were old acquaintances. In 509 B.C., upon the establishment of the Republic, Carthage hastened to conclude a treaty with Rome. The treaty indicated that Carthage considered the new government the successor to whatever leadership Etruscan Rome had developed in Latium. The treaty showed no disposition for political involvements or alignments, but was calculated to establish friendship (*amicitia*) so that regular legal commercial contacts could continue. It further stipulated a monopoly for Carthaginian carriers in her vast sphere of influence in the western Mediterranean. Roman traders were limited to the city of Carthage itself and to Sicily. This treaty was renewed and made somewhat more specific in 348 B.C., at the time when Rome was making good its claim of leadership in central Italy.

The nature of these treaties corroborates the observation that Carthage practiced a commercial and not a political imperialism. Phoenician colonies always showed strong ties of respect and duty toward the motherland; and it had been almost reluctantly that Carthage had taken over the leadership of, and later authority over, the Phoenician trading stations of the West when Greek expansionism threatened them in the fifth century. Carthage always preferred peace to war and a negotiated settlement to exasperated victory; and she maintained as far as possible her commercial monopoly in the West by treaties and by threats from her considerable and highly respected navy. Despite frequent altercations with the Greeks of Sicily in the fourth century B.C., especially with Syracuse, Carthage seldom brought her whole weight to bear. In spite of tedious conflicts the Punic territory in Sicily was generally confined to the western third of the island, bounded approximately by the line of the Halycus River.

Carthage was not an aggressive state and certainly did not seek a conflict with Rome. Neither did their enmity rise from grave differences in political ideology. Carthage, like Rome, had an oligarchical (or plutocratic) government with some monarchical and some democratic features. At the head of the government, but (unlike the Roman consuls) with only civil jurisdiction, were two annually elected magistrates, the suffetes. There also was a senate of several hundred members, but a committee of thirty men within it set up agenda for discussion and looked after the day-by-day business. Unlike Roman practice, the generals were not the annually elected magistrates, but enjoyed long-term appointments and therefore had an opportunity to make a science of military tactics and to ingratiate themselves with the troops. However, an elected board of judges, with 104 members, reviewed military events, and very ambitious generals might well be demoted by it, while the very unsuccessful often were crucified. In legislative matters the Carthaginian assembly was not as powerful as its Roman counterparts and it appears to have been consulted only when clearcut disagreement between the suffetes and the Senate made it a court of appeal.

The empire of the Carthaginians was loosely knit. The other Phoenician cities of Africa, the Libyophoenicians, governed themselves with their own laws, issued coinage, and even made treaties. But they owed men and money to Carthage. Also, the nomads of the interior, the Numidians, were required to furnish the mounted troops for which they were famous. Other subject areas furnished men and natural resources, such as minerals. In Sicily at least the yoke was sufficiently light so that many of the natives of the western part preferred a Carthaginian hegemony to either a Greek or Roman one, a preference perhaps confirmed by cruelties that both Romans and Greeks perpetrated on the island. However, Carthage failed to bind the natives of her own Africa in a mutual cause as Rome had the peoples of Italy. Even if she had had the genius for that, unlike the Romans she would have had to work with peoples of very different race and traditions from her own. In any case, the citizens of Carthage early decided to put their wealth to work in their own defense, and for the most part they depended on mercenaries: Libyans, Numidians, Moors, Spaniards, Balearians, Gauls, Campanians, and Greeks, who fought their wars under Punic generals. With good generals such troops were effective, and by using them the Carthaginians kept their empire much longer than, for instance, the Athenians did theirs with citizen troops—and much longer than they could have kept it had they depended on their own relatively small numbers.

Experience with years of Greek aggression in Sicily prompted the Carthaginians to conclude another treaty with Rome in 279 B.C. when the Romans were at war with King Pyrrhus. By promising cooperation and by making a present of silver bullion the Carthaginians hoped to forestall an imminent peace treaty between Rome and Pyrrhus and a threatened attack by Pyrrhus thereafter upon Sicily. The Romans did not conclude peace; but Pyrrhus nevertheless made a whirlwind conquest of the island, which only Carthaginian Lilybaeum and piratical Messana withstood. However, the customary Greek bickerings, jealousies, and particularism soon undid Pyrrhus' work, and by 265 B.C. Carthage once more controlled, or was in alliance with, nearly half of the island.

THE MAMERTINES; CAUSES OF FIRST PUNIC WAR.   The clash between Rome and Carthage was not planned by either city. It came, as so many conflicts do, from meddling in other people's affairs. And it came because of the odd though intelligible policy of the government of Messana. About twenty years earlier, certain Campanian mercenaries of Syracuse had deserted, seized the city of Messana on the straits between Sicily and Italy, killed the men and appropriated the women and children, and maintained constant conflict with the Syracusans. They called themselves the Mamertines, the men of Mamers, the Sabellian god of war.

In 265 B.C. a new and vigorous Syracusan general, Hiero, was so successful against the Mamertines that he was elected king by the Syracusans and very nearly took Messana itself. In despair for their safety the Mamertines appealed to Syracuse's ancient enemies, the Carthaginians, and a Punic garrison was introduced into the town to help defend it. Thereupon, whether because they distrusted their Punic friends or because they saw no inconsistency in calling also on Carthage's recent ally, Rome, they dispatched an embassy to the Roman Senate asking for an alliance similar to those that the cities of southern Italy enjoyed. The Roman Senate was in a quandary. It hesitated, and finally referred the question to a Roman assembly without recommendation. Historians have exercised themselves over the senatorial reluctance. Most think that the senators recognized the likelihood that war would develop overseas with Carthage, a great naval power, while Rome had no fleet at all; some see an unwillingness on the part of the senators to associate themselves with Mamertine brigands; and some suppose reluctance by aristocratic senators to afford another military arena for the development of new plebeian leaders. Philinus of Agrigentum, who wrote a history of the war showing Carthaginian sympathy, asserted, however, that Rome and Carthage had earlier concluded a treaty, in 306 B.C., by which Carthage engaged not to enter Italy and Rome made the same pledge in respect to Sicily. If this was true, the senators knew that intervention in Messana was illegal.

In any case, the Roman people probably had no knowledge of earlier diplomacy and felt no qualms, and they voted the alliance. Why did they do so? Polybius says that their leaders urged the benefits that would accrue to them. It is true that the people were war-weary at the time, but perhaps they looked on this alliance as no more than an extension of their tried and proved policy in southern Italy. After all, Messana was in sight of Rhegium, and many Romans on southern campaigns must have seen it across the straits. The fact that it was on an island was not apt to arouse plebeian sensibilities, for its possession might prove a bulwark against aggression from that direction. Probably the leaders that convinced the people were not so innocent: one consul of the year, and the one who led the expedition to relieve Messana, was Appius Claudius Caudex, probably a cousin of the redoubtable censor, and a member of a family whose member's were always erratic, flamboyant, and sometimes mad. Here were new fields for Claudian glory.

The First Punic War falls into three phases: (1) a period (264 – 255 B.C.) when the Romans took the initiative on land and then on the sea, culminating in an invasion of Africa; (2) a reversion to the Sicilian arena where the Roman efforts were studded by victories on land and by disasters at sea (254 – 249 B.C.); and (3) a period of mutual exhaustion followed by successes of a new Punic general, Hamilcar Barca, until the Romans were spurred to one final naval effort and victory (248 – 241 B.C.).

FIRST PHASE (264 – 255 B.C.).   In 264 B.C. the Carthaginians in Messana, instructed by their government to remain conciliatory, were hoodwinked into allowing the Romans to land and occupy Messana. However, upon reflection the Carthaginian government realized that it could not tolerate the Roman presence in Messana, whether or not this was a violation of a previous treaty of 306, for the Roman practice of making and defending "allies" would constantly menace Carthaginian relations with others of her Sicilian dependents whenever altercation arose. Composing their differences with Hiero of Syracuse, therefore, the Carthaginians set about, though with insufficient forces, to recapture Messana. The Romans around Messana managed to keep the allies separated and during 263 – 262 were able to defeat each of them. Then by offering Hiero of Syracuse favorable terms they detached him from Carthage and concluded a fifteen-year alliance with him. This alliance became a mainstay of the Roman position in Sicily, over the years offering support and supplies that were invaluable.

The Romans then undertook the siege of the Greek city of Agrigentum, which was an important marshalling area for the levies and mercenaries that the Carthaginians now began to

Massilia
ETRURIA
Pyrenees
Ebro R.
SPAIN
Corsica
Saguntum
Balearic Isles
Sardinia
Baecula (208)
Baetis R.
Ilipa (207)
Tartessus
New Carthage (209)
Gades
Carthage
MAURETANIA
AFRICA
NUMIDIA

Luna
Ariminum
ETRURIA
Arretium
Metaurus R.
Elba
Lake Trasimeno (217)
Telamon (225)
ITALY
Corsica
Rome
Arpi
Aecae
SAMNIUM
Casilinum
Cannae (216)
APULIA
Capua (211)
Compsa
Sardinia
LUCANIA
Tarentum (209)

BRUTTIUM
Lipari Is.
Panormus
Tyndaris
Mylae (280)
Drepana (249)
Solus
Locri
Aegates Is.
Emma
Messana
Rhegium
Lilybaeum (241)
Halycus R.
Sicily
Heraclea Minoa
Agrigentum
Leontini
Utica
Carthage
Cape Bon
Cape Ecnomus (256)
Camarina
Syracuse (212)
Bagradas R. Tunis
Aspis
Cape Pachynus
AFRICA
Zama (202)

THE FIRST AND SECOND PUNIC WARS

Dates of important battles shown thus: (256)

gather. A siege of seven months ended after great suffering on both sides. The Punic garrison slipped away and the Romans sacked the town and enslaved the Greek inhabitants. At the time this action brought some hesitant cities to Rome's side, but ultimately the Roman sack of this beautiful town confirmed a sullen hatred among the Sicilians for the barbarians of the north.

Success at Agrigentum convinced the Romans that they could and must settle for nothing less than the complete expulsion of Carthage from Sicily. No attempt on the sea-fortresses of the West could be made, however, without a fleet; and therefore the Romans set about to build a navy with ships patterned on a beached Punic vessel that they had salvaged. Up to this time naval battles had consisted of expert maneuvering leading to the ramming and sinking of the enemy. Rightly realizing their inferiority in such tactics, the Romans proposed to turn their sea battles into land battles by equipping their larger ships with swinging cranes rigged with spikes. These were called crows (*corvi*) by the soldiers. With this equipment enemy vessels could be grappled when they came within range, allowing the redoubtable Roman soldiers to board their opponents' ships and overpower the Punic sailors. After a loss in an early skirmish, a Roman fleet of 143 ships under the consul Duilius was completely victorious in its first major engagement off Mylae in 260. There were further naval victories off Corsica and Sardinia from 259 to 257, though they seemed to decide little, for at the same time the Punic commander in Sicily, Hamilcar, was holding his own, and a long struggle of laborious sieges seemed still in prospect. The Romans therefore decided to change their strategy and to attack the Carthaginian homeland directly, thus cutting off Sicily and forcing its surrender.

To effect the invasion the Romans built an armada of 330 vessels, warships, and transports, and in 256 set sail. After first meeting and defeating a Carthaginian fleet that had been sent to intercept them off Cape Ecnomus, the Romans proceeded to Africa and landed at Aspis on the Cape Bon peninsula. From there the commander, Marcus Atilius Regulus, and a force of 15,000 infantry and 5000 horse plundered the countryside until a Punic force met them on unfavorable ground and was defeated. Encouraged, Regulus proceeded to Tunis where he encamped for the winter. Unfortunately for the Romans, Regulus' obstinacy and prejudice made him a poor choice for commander. When the Carthaginians essayed peace negotiations during the winter he offered terms so harsh that they could not possibly be accepted. Furthermore, he made no effort to encourage the defection of the exploited African natives. In the spring of 255 without waiting for reinforcements and on the worst possible ground for his own forces, he accepted the offer of battle by a Punic army that had been revitalized and trained by an inspired mercenary from Sparta, Xanthippus. In the rout that ensued, Regulus and 500 of his men were captured while 2000 escaped to Aspis. All the rest were killed. The Romans then sent a huge relieving fleet to Africa, which defeated the Carthaginian fleet and embarked the refugees from Regulus' expedition. On the way home a storm overtook the fleet and drove most of it onto the rocks off Camarina. Of 364 ships, only eighty made it to port. The overall Roman loss in this African fiasco must have neared 100,000 men.

SECOND PHASE (254–249 B.C.).   Foiled in Africa by stupidity and natural disasters, the Romans returned to the laborious task of trying to reduce the Sicilian towns. They raised a new navy of 200 ships and in 254 B.C., by combining land and sea attacks, captured the important seaports of Panormus, Tyndaris, and Solus on the northern Sicilian coast. However, since the Carthaginian position in western Sicily remained strong, the Romans made another diversionary attack on the African coast in 253. This new project was abandoned when a number of ships with inexperienced crews foundered on Tunisian shoals. Further, on the return trip the fleet was overtaken by a heavy storm and 150 ships were lost. Once more the Romans grimly redoubled their efforts and managed to construct more ships, ultimately assembling a fleet of 240 vessels.

The severe repulse of a Carthaginian attack on Panormus in 250 gave the Romans the courage to attempt the investment both by land and sea of the great Carthaginian stronghold of western Sicily, Lilybaeum. Thus began a siege that lasted for eight years. The garrison showed constant ingenuity in countering Roman siege methods, and the Carthaginian sailors knew the waters so well that they easily ran the Roman blockade. Moreover, another Claudian, Publius Claudius Pulcher, rashly attacked the Punic fleet at the naval station of Drepana in 249 and sustained a loss of nearly 100 ships. He had undertaken the engagement contrary to the judgment of man and the will of the gods: that morning the sacred chickens, whose eating habits revealed the divine intent, refused their grain. Thereupon the eager consul had retorted, "Well, if they won't eat, let them drink," and had thrown them into the sea. For his defeat Claudius was later fined 12,000 denarii at Rome, an interesting Roman adaptation of the Punic custom of punishing unsuccessful generals. To add to the mortification of this defeat, a fleet of 120 warships and 800 transports proceeding with supplies for the besieging force at Lilybaeum was intercepted in the same year by a skillful Punic admiral, Phintias, as it crept along the southern Sicilian coast. He maneuvered the Romans close to a rocky shore, and then himself taking to the high seas left the Roman fleet to be battered to pieces on the rocks in a storm that he sensed approaching. The Roman commander ultimately made Lilybaeum with only two ships.

THIRD PHASE (248–241 B.C.).   Rome, exhausted, chose to maintain a holding action in Sicily during the next few years. Fortunately Carthage did not press its advantage. For one thing, there seems to have been a change of policies in Carthage at this time. Hanno the Great, who headed an "African" party and later became the outspoken opponent of Carthage's great imperialist family, the Barcids, seems to have been influential in turning the military effort into a greater exploitation of the African territory around Carthage, while giving a minimum of attention to activities overseas.

In 248 B.C., when the fifteen-year treaty with Hiero of Syracuse ran out, the Romans renewed the pact with this most satisfactory ally, this time for perpetuity. In the following year the Carthaginians appointed a young man of great daring and originality to the command in Sicily, a new Hamilcar, Hamilcar Barca. By 244 his forays, harassments, and successes in western Sicily had convinced the Romans once more that they must effect the fall of Lilybaeum by sea blockade. They dared not, however, assess their own citizens or their allies to raise still another fleet. Instead, wealthy members of the State agreed to contribute the necessary funds as a loan to the State, the loan to be repaid in the event of success. A fleet of 200 vessels was prepared during 243–242; personnel was given adequate training; and the fleet was sent to Lilybaeum under the command of Lutatius Catulus. Tardily and in haste the Carthaginians recommissioned their own fleet, but when it arrived in March of 241 it was undermanned and out of practice. The Punic ships were straightway routed, and the fate of the Carthaginians in Sicily sealed. Hamilcar was directed to negotiate with Catulus and get as good conditions as possible. He was an astute and sometimes firm negotiator. He absolutely refused, for example, on pain of reopening the war to surrender any Roman deserters in his ranks. The settlement forwarded to Rome for ratification called for the Carthaginian evacuation of Sicily, the surrender of all prisoners, the levy of an indemnity of 2200 talents payable in twenty annual installments, and a mutual agreement not to attack one another's allies. The Roman assembly did not at first think these terms sufficiently severe and sent an investigating committee. However, the committee was convinced that Hamilcar was willing and able to prolong the conflict if driven too far. It was satisfied by specifying additional terms: the surrender of the Lipari and Aegates Islands, the stipulation that Carthage could recruit no mercenaries in Italy, and the increase of the indemnity by 1000 talents—the additional sum to be paid at once, while the period for paying the remainder was reduced to ten years. The last term probably was dictated by a desire to begin immediately the reimbursement of the creditors that had outfitted the successful navy.

The First Punic War was a remarkable display of tenacity, which is about the best thing that can be said for it. The war developed no great Roman leaders, and seems to have taught the Romans few lessons. They managed to win numerous naval battles, but never learned to cope with the elements, and never set their minds to being sailors. In their harsh conduct toward some of the Greeks of Sicily, such as the Agrigentines, they appear not to have realized that the loyal support of their own Italian allies in this very war was the result of their generally humane treatment of former enemies. Rather, they seemed much more impressed by the short-term effects of the kind of brutality that they had dealt Veii. We shall see that later, when they organized Sicily, they followed an easy but heedless path, heedless because they did not imitate the success of their admirable treatment and organization of the conquered peoples in Italy proper.

The First Punic War tells us a good deal about the Roman people. Their grit and determination during the struggle, the enormous sacrifices of men and money, bespeak the courage of individual Romans and the efficacy of the Italian system. However, the thoughtless way in which the war was entered, the refusal for years to negotiate a peace on equal terms, and at the end of the war the popular insistence on the harshest conditions possible—these were harbingers of national arrogance. The Romans had sometimes lost a campaign, but never a war. Now they began to be unable even to contemplate compromise, to say nothing of defeat. For others to maintain their interests in the face of Roman policy was considered a criminal impropriety; and the Romans insisted on revenge for a war that they had brought on themselves.

The Carthaginians did not show a similar intransigence. When they did have a considerable advantage they did not vigorously pursue it, which was typical of their more peaceable, or at least less truculent, policy. For the Carthaginians, Sicily was only one outpost, though a very important one, and they never turned their full attention to this arena, as their African policy around 250 shows. The failure of Carthage was partly due to strategical errors, and partly to the lack of determination and of human resources. Ultimately, perhaps, in contrast to the Roman success, the failure of Carthage lay in her relations with her subject neighbors.

Nevertheless, Carthage did absorb and seek to take advantage of some of her experiences from the war. She learned to respect the tenacity of the Romans and the strength of the Italian system. She realized that the latter must be shattered before her own resources could support a rivalry with Rome. And Rome's naval victories and occasional military stupidities, reinforced by her annual change of inexperienced generals, suggested that the chances of Carthage on land, Rome's own element, were as good as on the sea, where Punic navies had once ruled, and that, in any case, only on the land would success be decisive.

Chapter 12

RECOVERY AND PREPARATION

CIVIL WAR AT CARTHAGE (241–238 B.C.).   Immediately after the First Punic War the Carthaginians were faced with a bloody conflict at home. During his campaigns in Sicily Hamilcar Barca had been forced to make financial promises to his mercenary troops; but when the army was transported back to Africa, the oligarchical anti-Barcid "peace" party of Hanno the Great began to haggle about the bill. The war had been costly: Sicily was gone, Sardinia and Corsica cut off, and recently most of the Spanish domain with its rich mineral output had been lost to the natives. The government did have financial problems, but the peace party showed considerable stupidity in not dealing with each small unit of soldiers as it disembarked and in allowing the whole army to be reunited in Africa. A bitter and truceless conflict broke out, sparked by the disappointed mercenaries. The exploited natives of Africa rose to join the mercenaries, and even some of the ancient Phoenician towns, such as Utica, supported the revolt. The contestants on each side were so outraged and exasperated that neither could expect mercy from the other; and the cruelties practiced by the mercenaries on their prisoners brought retaliation in kind. Crucifixions were everywhere.

The ungrateful government at Carthage was forced to turn once more to Hamilcar Barca. With considerable magnanimity he cooperated with his political enemies, and after three years of savage fighting in 238 finally quelled the revolt. Carthage was saved, but those three years of pitiless conflict had weakened her as more than twenty years of war with the Romans could not. Her weakness now was palpable and profound.

During Carthage's war with her mercenaries Rome's attitude had been completely correct, even cooperative. Early in the conflict she had spurned a request for assistance from rebellious Carthaginian mercenaries in Sardinia. She had also forbidden the sale of provisions to the rebels in Africa, and had even allowed the Carthaginian government to recruit troops in Italy. This policy may have been prompted by the sanctity of her treaty with Carthage, or by the community of interest felt by the oligarchical government of Rome for the oligarchical peace party now in power in Carthage. However, at the end of the African rebellion when Carthage prepared to recover her rebellious island of Sardinia, the Romans completely reversed their position. In 238–237 a Roman expedition was sent to take over the island, and the protests of Carthage were met by a declaration of war. The unfortunate Carthaginians were far too weak to renew the conflict and were able to ward off another invasion of Africa only by meekly surrendering Sardinia and Corsica and by increasing their payment of indemnity to Rome by 1200 talents.

The reasons for Rome's change of policy are obscure. The strategic advantage of the possession of the offshore islands must have been obvious all along. Perhaps the Romans at length realized just how weakened Carthage was and felt that it was now safe to make outrageous demands. Perhaps the return to authority of their old adversary, Hamilcar Barca, counselled a less friendly policy. Perhaps the possession of Sicily quickly taught the Romans the material advantages of overseas possessions. In any case, her action belied Rome's proud claims of fair dealing and embittered unnecessarily her future relations with Carthage. The act declared to the world the amorality and opportunism of Roman policy, and for that disclosure the Romans paid dearly.

Hanno the Great's niggardly treatment of the mercenaries had brought on their revolt. It also put the aggressive and popular Hamilcar Barca back in a position of some influence. Hamilcar saw that Roman naval success and the loss of Sicily doomed the Carthaginian monopoly of western trade and the prosperity that was based on it. Carthage must turn elsewhere to recover. The party of Hanno favored the exploitation of Africa, but the inhabitants of the interior were intractable and the natural resources meager. Hamilcar therefore determined instead to exploit Spain, where Carthage had had an ancient but small foothold, most of which had been lost during the recent war. Here he hoped to find in minerals and men the means to restore his country's economic and military strength. To enable him to do this the Carthaginian government seems to have given Hamilcar considerable freedom of movement and decision.

ROMAN POSTWAR TREATMENT OF ALLIES AND DEPENDENTS. Rome, as well as Carthage, experienced a revolt at the end of the Punic conflict. Tuscan Falerii, probably because it was tired of contributing to the Roman cause, seems to have tried to avoid renewing its treaty of alliance with Rome at the time of expiration. In 241 B.C. the Romans, acting with characteristic vigor and self-interest, marched on the town, sacked it within six days, and forced the inhabitants to move from their hilltop eyrie to a site on the nearby plain. This despotic act made clear that the Romans would tolerate neither isolationism nor neutralism in Italy.

The problems raised by the administration of the newly acquired possessions overseas were graver ones for the Romans. Sicily contained an independent Syracuse and a few other cities that had been given favorable alliances during the war, thanks to their speedy submission. However, much of the island was conquered territory, and some of it ultimately was confiscated for exclusively Roman use. These areas needed some kind of government. Distance from Rome and the different races involved made the extension of the Italian system of alliances to Sicily difficult. Messana, which contributed a war vessel each year, did fit into the old pattern, while Hiero's Syracuse, as a free and equal ally, owed no contribution at all. But Rome had to deal with more than half the island, which was peopled largely by Greeks or Hellenized Sicilians. It should be observed that Rome made very small military use of Greek manpower even in Italy. Apparently she did not wish, or could not contemplate, such use in Sicily either. Instead of men she resolved to exact money from her new dependents there. She found that both Greeks and Carthaginians had exacted a tithe of the annual produce from the Sicilians, and it was easy to continue this practice. It is doubtful that the Romans formulated any theory concerning this exaction of tribute. If anything, they probably thought of it as payment for the military protection that they must furnish. However, to substitute money for men, who could cooperate in a common defense, was a radical departure from earlier Roman practice. It introduced mercenary motives into foreign affairs, which previously had been largely determined by considerations of security and defense. At first the Romans tried to administer their interests in Sicily directly from Rome, as they always had in Italy, and until 227 B.C. it was considered sufficient to station a quaestor at Lilybaeum to handle their financial and other affairs.

Meanwhile, the Romans spent several campaigning seasons in an effort to reduce Sardinia and Corsica. The Carthaginians had been pretty much satisfied to hold a few coastal markets on these islands and to trade with the natives. The Romans, however, insisted on treaties and clearly defined obligations. The unhappy natives had no notion as to why the Romans were there or what they were about. They fiercely resisted, as they always had, impingements on their liberties, and they took to the inland mountains. The Romans tracked them down with soldiers and specially trained dogs, and found countless opportunities for military triumphs and unlimited supplies of cheap slaves. Here too a tithe system of taxation was imposed on the conquered.

A number of years of experience showed the Romans that a more authoritative and concentrated administration was needed overseas. Inevitably there were legal disputes and situations requiring police action. The quaestor at Lilybaeum was not really equipped to handle these problems efficiently. However, there was another office, the praetorship, which was endowed with the *imperium* and therefore was qualified both to deal with judicial matters and to furnish military leadership.[1] Moreover, as recently as 242 B.C., the Romans had been moved by their increasing legal business with noncitizens to create a second praetor, the *praetor peregrinus*, who was commissioned

---

[1]   For the *imperium*, see p. 53.

to determine and administer just legal principles to be applied in disputes between Romans and aliens or between aliens and aliens. Noting, perhaps, the success of this venture with the problems of foreigners, in about 227 the Romans created two new praetorships. The administration of Sicily became the province of one, Sardinia and Corsica that of the other.

THE REFORMED CENTURIATE ASSEMBLY; GAIUS FLAMINIUS. Besides the new praetorships, there were a number of internal changes at Rome after the First Punic War that had lasting and significant effects. In 241 B.C. the loyal Sabines and Picentes of central and eastern Italy were rewarded by the establishment of two new Roman tribes (numbers thirty-four and thirty-five) in their areas. These were the last tribes the Romans established. Thereafter new citizens or cities newly endowed with citizenship were arbitrarily assigned to one of the existing tribes, which therefore rapidly lost their localized or geographical character. Sometime not long after 241 the Centuriate Assembly underwent a reorganization whereby the classes and centuries were somehow reorganized along tribal lines.[2] Perhaps it was the work of censors, who enjoyed considerable freedom in marshalling the State's resources. Many attribute the change to Gaius Flaminius, the popular leader of the era, who was censor in 220. In the reorganization the eighteen centuries of knights were retained, and there seem to have been seventy centuries for the first class of wealth (thirty-five of seniors, thirty-five of juniors, one of each from each tribe). If there continued to be 193 centuries in all, and this is not certain since the sources are contradictory, then there were perhaps one hundred allotted to the other four classes and five to the supernumeraries. Certainty is impossible.

In one sense such a reorganization would have tended to liberalize the assembly slightly, for the knights and first class would no longer constitute a majority. Because the reorganization was tied to the tribes, however, the conservative farmers of the thirty-one rural tribes could far outvote, even though they might not outnumber, the city residents of the same wealth as themselves, who had only four tribes. In this manner the reorganization may have been calculated to render powerless the more volatile urban vote.

There were, however, other measures in this period that were of a liberal character. When Flaminius was tribune in 232 the poorer classes of Rome were given allotments of land in the

---

[2]   For the earlier organization of the Centuriate Assembly, see p. 91–93.

Ager Gallicus, a region on the eastern coast from which the Romans had driven the Gallic Senones in 283. These allotments were made much against the will of the senators, who had been privately exploiting that land, and their party regularly thereafter cited Flaminius' action as the commencement of demagoguery at Rome. Another measure supported by Flaminius was a Claudian law, passed in 218, forbidding members of the senatorial class to engage in commercial activities. This may have been designed to ensure disinterested public service by the administration, or it may have been prompted by knowledge of the influence that commercial interests had had on the government of Carthage. In any case, it fortified the inclination of the ruling class to accumulate land and to look upon agriculture as the sole respectable source of income, while it widened the differences in ideals and policies between senatorial families and other well-to-do families that did not enter the political arena, but turned to the world of trade and commerce.

FOREIGN INFLUENCE IN ROME.   The growing activity of the Roman commons during this period may have been stimulated by an increasing awareness of the practices of the Hellenistic world. The Roman troops had by now spent years campaigning amid the Greeks of southern Italy and Sicily, and foreigners were beginning to settle in Rome. We hear of a Greek physician practicing there in 219 B.C. Livius Andronicus, a Greek of Tarentum, translated the *Odyssey* and Greek dramas into Latin, while Gnaeus Naevius composed lampoons and also an epic account of the First Punic War in the native Saturnian verse.

RELATIONS WITH THE GAULS (238–218 B.C.).   During the First Punic War the Gauls of the Po valley remained relatively quiet. We hear of successful skirmishes by the Boii in 238 B.C. and of general alarms in 236, but these came to little. Instead of retaliating directly against the Gauls, the Romans from 238 to 236 turned their efforts against the Ligurians, who had filtered down the western coast as far as Pisa. Perhaps the move was prompted by the hope of ultimately taking the Gauls with a flank attack. In any case, Luna and Genoa were captured and the Ligurians were driven back into their mountain strongholds.

The Roman activities in the area alarmed the Gauls, however, and led to a coalition of the Boii, Insubres, Lingones, Taurini, and the mercenary Gesati, which threw an invading force into Etruria in 225. The invasion created popular hysteria because of a prophecy that the Gauls must possess Rome a second time. The authorities allayed the panic by burying alive in the Forum a Gallic man and woman in order to "fulfill" the

122

NORTHERN ITALY
AND THE ADRIATIC
Late 3rd Century B.C.

prophecy. After some initial success the Gauls' huge force was trapped between two Roman armies and destroyed at the Battle of Telamon. A Roman offensive followed. In 224 the Boii and Lingones south of the Po were forced to make peace. In 223 Flaminius crossed the Po and, with the aid of the Gallic Cenomani, defeated the Insubres; and in 222 their strongholds of Acerrae and Milan fell, and the tribe submitted to a Roman alliance. The peninsula of Istria was subdued in 221, and by 220 the Roman lines extended to the foothills of the Julian and Carnic Alps. To consolidate and fortify these advances, two strong Latin colonies were established at Placentia and Cremona in 218. These ensured a foothold on each bank of the Po at important crossing points.

THE ILLYRIAN PIRATES.   Even before she had completely solved her problems on the northern front, Rome was forced to

123

take action on the Adriatic. This she did reluctantly. The Illyrians, whose livelihood was piracy, had extended their territory down the eastern coast of the sea from Dalmatia to Epirus. The Romans received complaints about piracy in the Adriatic, but they took very little action until finally the pirates began to make forays on the Italian coast itself. When Rome sent envoys to protest, the Illyrian queen Teuta not only had the bad judgment to refuse satisfaction, but she allowed one of the envoys to be assassinated on his homeward trip. In 228 the Illyrian forces were speedily defeated and limited to northern Illyria. A Greek adventurer, Demetrius, who had aided the Romans, was set up as ruler of Pharos, while "friendship" (*amicitia*) was granted to Epidamnus, Apollonia, Oricos, Corcyra, Issa, the Parthinians, and the Atintanes.

The Romans' use of the word *amicitia* in international relations was ambiguous. Legally it meant merely a declaration of normal friendly relations between the peoples concerned. However, when she chose, Rome treated the bond as something stronger, as though she were the protector and the *amici* her clients. This second interpretation was soon called into play in the Adriatic theater. Demetrius proved ungrateful and ambitious, and either did not understand or did not take seriously Rome's friendship for the peoples to the south. In 220 he ventured to capture a city of the Parthinians, Dimale, and to defy the Romans. Revenge was swift. Pharos fell in 219 and was made a protectorate. Demetrius fled to the court of young King Philip V of Macedon, where he played upon that monarch's fears of Roman interference in an area the Macedonians considered their natural sphere of influence.

Temporarily at least, by 219 Rome had settled on her three fronts the problems that had faced her in 265 when she assumed the leadership of a united Italy. By her conquest of Sicily, Sardinia and Corsica she commanded the Tyrrhenian Sea to the west. The Gauls to the north had been subdued, and a united Italy extended almost to its natural frontiers in the direction of the Alps. On the Adriatic, diplomatic relations and maritime security had been established. However, the resolution of these problems not only meant the creation of new rivals with new fears, but also betrayed the Romans into moral and strategic errors. Just as they were completing their work in the Adriatic the results of some of these past errors were about to break around the Romans' heads.

CARTHAGE IN SPAIN.   Meanwhile, Carthage's new western policy under the direction of Hamilcar Barca was paying off handsomely. Under the command of Hamilcar himself (237 – 229/8 B.C.), of his son-in-law Hasdrubal (229/8 – 221 B.C.), and then of his own son Hannibal the Carthaginians recovered the old realms of Tartessus in southern Spain, moved slowly up the eastern coast, and made considerable progress against the tribes in the center of the peninsula. The mineral wealth that they exploited brought Carthage several thousands of talents per year; even more important, they found here a warlike people that could be trained to fight loyally and well under inspired leadership.

Hamilcar's active and successful policy in Spain prompted a Roman investigating committee in 231. This was perhaps suggested by Rome's old friend and ally, Massilia, which feared for its Spanish trading posts. However, when Hamilcar replied to the Roman inquiry that he was merely seeking the means with which to pay Carthage's obligation to Rome, the committee seems to have been satisfied. His son-in-law, Hasdrubal, depended more on diplomacy than on arms to increase Carthaginian influence in Spain. He ingratiated himself with many natives by taking a Spanish wife, and his success was so noteworthy that the Romans dispatched another embassy to Spain in 226. This time the concern probably was for themselves: the Gauls of the Po valley were now an immediate menace, and there was a danger that with intelligent assistance the Celts of Spain and of Gaul might compound Rome's difficulties. The embassy was successful in persuading Hasdrubal not to proceed in arms north of the Ebro River in Spain. What Rome conceded to Hasdrubal in return is nowhere stated. If we can judge from accounts of the embassy and from later Carthaginian actions, Hasdrubal must at least have been accorded a free hand south of the Ebro River. Hasdrubal's career was cut short in 221 by an assassin, and he was succeeded by his brother-in-law Hannibal, the son of Hamilcar.

THE SAGUNTINE AFFAIR.   Hannibal reverted to his father's more militaristic policy, and in less than two years he had gained control of the major tribes and territories south of the Ebro River, except for the town of Saguntum. This town seems to have contained a pro-Roman party, and at some unspecified date (Polybius says "several years before Hannibal") had been received into Roman "friendship." This became the immediate cause of the Second Punic War.

Saguntum soon was involved in quarrels with its Spanish neighbors. Since all these neighbors were Carthaginian allies, Hannibal naturally went to their assistance. Much has been written on whether Rome's agreement with Saguntum preceded or followed her agreement with Hasdrubal regarding the line of the Ebro. However, the date of the Saguntine agreement is not actually important; if, as Hannibal's actions indicate, Hasdrubal was given a free hand south of the Ebro, then any prior arrangement between Rome and Saguntum was thereby rescinded. On the other hand, if there was a later engagement with Saguntum after the agreement with Hasdrubal, the Romans must have made it in bad faith. The dilatory action recorded for the Roman Senate after it heard that Hannibal threatened its "friend" Saguntum, and the protestations of later Roman apologists—some of whom even try to locate Saguntum north of the Ebro!—indicate that this was a piece of Roman opportunism and that Roman consciences were troubled. At whatever date the Romans entered into relations with Saguntum, they did so with a knowledge that this town was an enclave in Carthaginian territory that later might be exploited just as Messana had been in Sicily. Hannibal knew, as his predecessors in Sicily had known, that such enclaves could not be allowed to exist, for they were an open invitation for imitation by any disaffected city or tribe among Carthaginian subjects.

By attacking Saguntum Hannibal precipitated the crisis that sparked the Second Punic War, but behind his act were years of Roman provocation: Rome had made the early and arrogant error in the rape of Sardinia; Rome had made the crafty and injudicious treaty with Saguntum. Always suspicious of others' prosperity and intentions, she had set about in Saguntum to stunt the Carthaginian revival with an excuse so palpably contrived that Carthage now was convinced that Rome had always been Machiavellian. And Hannibal, young and confident in his army, his plans, and himself, used Rome's malice to procure his countrymen's backing to avenge the past and insure the future.

Chapter 13

HANNIBAL'S WAR

The recent threat of a Gallic invasion had convinced the Romans in 225 B.C. that they needed to take stock of the Italian military potential that they could command. This was discovered to be approximately 700,000 infantrymen and 70,000 cavalry. To contend with that latent power Hannibal appeared in the Po valley in the autumn of 218 B.C. with 20,000 veteran footsoldiers and 6000 horsemen. He had as well a strategical plan and his own brilliant powers of leadership and tactics, which is the reason why the Second Punic War is so often called "Hannibal's War." It is not that he precipitated the war any more than Rome's murky policy did, but as a man and as a general he was worth myriads of troops. Of course, his tiny force did not represent the Carthaginian potential any more than the first Roman armies to meet him represented Rome's; but Carthage never could match from her empire the number of absolutely reliable soldiers that Rome could raise in the heartland of her system. In the end numbers did resolve the issue, although it took sixteen years for them to do so.

EARLY ROMAN STRATEGY.   From the day that the Romans decided to make Saguntum a cause of war they had a plan of operation. They proposed to attack Carthage itself in order to exploit her well-known unpopularity with her neighbors in Africa and keep her on the defensive. Another army was to be sent to Spain to cut off that source of manpower and wealth. The inconsiderate speed with which Hannibal arrived in Italy foiled half this plan, since the legions in Sicily slated for the African expedition had to be recalled to defend northern Italy. However, a Spanish expedition under the command of the consul for 218, Publius Scipio, was already under way when Hannibal's movements became known, and Publius had the insight to send his legions on to Spain under the command of his brother nevertheless. The following year he joined them, and the successes of the Scipios in Spain for six years prevented the dispatch of reinforcements to Hannibal from that source when they could have been valuable.

HANNIBAL'S ITALIAN POLICY.   Hannibal counted on the elements of speed and surprise, but his long-range plan included much more. He hoped that his march through northern Italy would rally the Gauls to his support, for they had long been Rome's enemies and were but recently subdued. He planned to champion local interests in Italy in order to weaken the Roman system there by detaching dissatisfied allies. He also proposed to form an alliance of extra-Italian states upon whose interests or ambitions Roman expansionism had impinged. As he began his campaigns he had a well-deserved confidence that his tactical superiority would ensure a success in early encounters, and he supposed that this would trigger the long-range developments that he desired. At no time, however, did Hannibal appear to contemplate the destruction of Rome. What he seemed to hope for was her limitation to the *ager Romanus* in central Italy, and the complete independence of her allies, though the resultant chaos might indeed have been the end of Rome. In any case, it was his studied policy to set free Italian prisoners and send them home with assurances of Carthaginian good will. It is not clear whether his consistently chivalrous conduct toward opposing commanders simply reflected a generous character or marked his desire to keep open the avenues of negotiation with the enemy.

EARLY ROMAN DEFEATS. FABIUS CUNCTATOR.
The first phase of Rome's struggle with Hannibal (218–216 B.C.) is characterized by strategical and political experimentation, repeated military disasters for the Romans, and the shattering of the myth of natural Roman superiority, which had been fostered by the outcome of the First Punic War and by a generation of successes against lesser opponents. In 218 Hannibal was victorious in a cavalry skirmish with the consul Publius Scipio on the Ticinus, and a little later he maneuvered the Romans into accepting battle near the Trebia under conditions disadvantageous to Rome. The Romans lost 30,000 men, while another 10,000 broke through to safety. Somehow, by the time the news reached Rome, the reports were ambiguous, and some people considered the breakthrough of the 10,000 a proof that the Romans were really superior and that the defeat was wholly due to unfortunate physical circumstances.

On the whole, the news from the north was interpreted by

the nobles as an indication that the gods were offended, and by the popular party that the leadership of the nobles was inadequate. Along with the patrician Gnaeus Servilius, therefore, the people insisted on electing as consul for 217 their hero, Gaius Flaminius, who had supported the popular cause as tribune in 232, praetor in 227, consul in 223, and censor in 220. Thus began one of the follies that plagued the early stages of the war: the use of political criteria to select military leadership. Flaminius, with an army of from 30,000 to 40,000 men, marched to Arretium in Etruria to watch one of the passes through which Hannibal might advance, and Servilius went to Ariminum on a similar errand. Hannibal actually crossed the Apennines by a third, more difficult, and unguarded route.

Hannibal's intelligence service seems to have been excellent and led him to suspect jealousy between the Roman commanders. He proceeded therefore to tempt the pride and rashness of Flaminius by brushing past Arretium, pillaging the lands of Rome's allies, and then heading in the general direction of Rome. Flaminius followed and was skillfully led into a trap on the northern shore of Lake Trasimene. Here, where the hills approach the beach in two places and a small plain opens up between, Hannibal awaited his prey. His men were posted in the woods on the heights screened by an early morning mist, while a few visible Carthaginians in the forward distance tempted the Romans on. When the Romans were within the valley the exits were closed. From back, front, and side the enemy roared down from the hills. The Romans were practically annihilated, and Flaminius was killed. In addition, 6000 cavalrymen sent by Servilius to investigate were either killed or captured. In keeping with his policy Hannibal ostentatiously freed the Italian prisoners and sent them home, but enslaved the Romans.

News of the disaster convinced the Senate that the unified command of a dictator was needed. But dictators were appointed by the consuls, and now one was dead and the other was absent with the army. The senators therefore requested the assembly to elect a dictator. This was irregular; but even more irregular was the people's action in also electing a master of the horse, who, as the dictator's assistant, was normally appointed by him. Politics had continued to play a part, however, and thus the conservative Quintus Fabius Maximus as dictator was saddled with a popular master of the horse, Marcus Minucius Rufus, who was thoroughly unsympathetic to him.[1]

[1]   For the term "popular" in Roman history, see pp. 207, 240.

The dictator's name has come down through history with the famous epithet "Cunctator," the Delayer. This is derived from the policy that he pursued during his dictatorship, and that he supported, with appropriate modifications, during the remainder of the war. He recognized that Hannibal was a superior tactician and he knew that his own troops were not thoroughly trained. He determined, therefore, to dog Hannibal's steps and give his own men experience, to hamper Hannibal's attempts to take walled places, and to discredit him in the eyes of the allies as nothing more than an adventurous marauder. He was resolved not to subject his men to pitched battle with the Carthaginians until he was sure that they were thoroughly ready to engage with veterans. Meanwhile Hannibal, finding that his successes in the north did not seduce Rome's associates in central Italy, skirted Rome, which he had neither the numbers nor the equipment to attack, and headed south. There he hoped to find not only sufficient supplies to maintain his troops, but also peoples like the Samnites whose ancient love of independence would now lead them to his standard. Fabius followed his own plan of action conscientiously, but Roman pride could not long bear the sight of the burning farms and plundered villages that Fabian strategy had to permit. Feeling ran high. The people's champion, Minucius Rufus, half insubordinate, through his own rashness and perhaps through Hannibal's calculated connivance had achieved a number of minor successes against the invaders. These were magnified in Rome. The Tribal Assembly thereupon produced a new monstrosity in raising Minucius to an illogical "co-dictatorship" with Fabius. Minucius was encouraged by his elevation to initiate military action that nearly resulted in a disastrous encounter with Hannibal, but he was saved by the prompt and ungrudging assistance of Fabius.

THE DISASTER AT CANNAE (216 B.C.) AND ITS RESULTS.
Popular discontent with Fabian tactics continued in 216 B.C., and as one of the consuls for the year the people elected Terentius Varro, a democratic favorite who had supported the election of Minucius to his co-dictatorship in 217. The other consul was the conservative patrician Aemilius Paullus. Aroused public opinion forced the consuls to abandon the policies of Fabius and face the enemy like Romans. The only delay now was in the search for an occasion to engage on ground that would not be too disadvantageous. Maneuvering brought the two armies together on the banks of the Aufidus River, near Cannae, in Apulia in the month of June. Here the Romans were utterly routed and the conservative Aemilius was killed. Uncertainties

as to the actual number of men present explain the diverse reports of Roman casualties, which range from 40,000 to 80,000 men. Hannibal himself lost less than 6000. Cannae was an important though not decisive engagement in the Second Punic War, but its fame has gone down through history because it was Rome's most stunning defeat, and because Hannibal's tactics were so effective. He had arranged his weaker allies in the center of his line, which was formed like a crescent bowing toward the Romans. This center then slowly gave way under the pressure of the heavy-armed legionaries, but it never broke; and as it moved back Hannibal's strong wings gradually closed inward until the Romans were caught and pressed together in a vise with no room to maneuver or fight. Meanwhile the superior Carthaginian cavalry took just the right amount of time to rout the inferior Italian horse, and then appeared at the Romans' rear to complete the work of annihilation. This battle became for tacticians throughout history the model of the envelopment of a larger force by a smaller one.

At first it seemed likely that the victory at Cannae would assure the success of Hannibal's program. Many of the Samnites and Apulians straightway went over to him, not so much in enthusiasm for his policies as in the belief that a new master had arrived in Italy. Lucania and the Bruttians also defected. Most important of all, the second greatest city of Italy, Capua, opened its gates to Hannibal, and a number of her smaller neighbors followed suit. Further, Philip of Macedon now decided that an alliance with Hannibal would serve to end the unwelcome Roman influence on the eastern Adriatic. In addition, the unceremonious execution by the Romans of Tarentine hostages, who were trying to escape custody in Rome, threw Tarentum into Hannibal's arms in 213.

The year 215 held further disaster: Rome's faithful friend, Hiero of Syracuse, died, and he was succeeded by a grandson, Hieronymus, who was pro-Carthaginian and who entered into alliance with Carthage. However, Syracuse had a strong pro-Roman party, and the day seemed to be saved when Hieronymus was assassinated. But the situation in Sicily changed again when in 214 the Roman commander on the island, Claudius Marcellus, stormed and took Leontini, which had continued to sustain Punic sentiments. Besides pillaging the town, he coldbloodedly beheaded 2000 of the troops there because he said that they were deserters. A shudder of repugnance for these northern barbarians swept through the island. The democratic pro-Carthaginian party at Syracuse brushed Rome's partisans out of office and many other towns followed suit.

ROMAN RECOVERY IN ITALY (216–209 B.C.)   The defections from Rome were dismaying, but many of the Greek cities of southern Italy, and all the colonies and the allies of central Italy, stood firm. Roman determination itself seemed steeled by Cannae. After a few religious excesses immediately following the disaster, such as the burial of Greeks and Gauls in the Forum Boarium, the citizens closed ranks and set about the second phase of the struggle with determination. The popular party was chastened and from then on left the Senate largely in control of the war. Partisanship was so muted that even the senators went out to meet Varro, the leader of the popular faction who was a survivor of Cannae, ingenuously or ironically congratulating him "that he had not despaired of the Republic." Rome's new policy combined Fabian strategy (refusal of open combat with Hannibal on the ground of his choosing), diplomatic maneuvering, and the proliferation of armies. Each of the Roman field armies now contained fewer legions, but more such armies could be distributed throughout Italy. Further, there was an appreciable increase in the number of legions. For example, there had been twenty legions in the field in 214, there were twenty-two in 213, and twenty-five in 212 and 211. With these superior numbers the Roman generals could now consistently recover or threaten those places that had gone over to Hannibal, as long as he was not in the vicinity, for he could not spare enough men to provide adequate garrisons for all.

Meanwhile southern Italy suffered. The Romans stripped its farms and destroyed its resources in order to deny provisions to Hannibal, and he swept away whatever was left. The Italians began to find that they really had little in common with the Carthaginian and that any hope of remaining neutral was fanciful. To them Hannibal's use of Gallic troops among them was a constant reminder that in the past it was Rome that had been the bulwark against those unstable marauders.

Without ever offering open battle to Hannibal the multiplied Roman armies slowly and inexorably recovered their lost places. Casilinum, Compsa, and Aecae were retaken in 214, and Arpi in 213. In 212 the Romans began the siege of Capua. The countryside was now stripped so bare that even wealthy Capua could not support Hannibal's army for uninterrupted periods. In his absence the Romans were able to complete entrenchments that the Carthaginians could not penetrate. In 211 a desperate dash by Hannibal to the very gates of Rome failed to draw the Romans away from Capua. In that year Capua surrendered, its leaders were executed, its lands confiscated, and its government dissolved. The district was thereafter administered by a prefect appointed in Rome.[2]

Tarentum held out somewhat longer; but in 209 its garrison of Bruttians betrayed the city to the consul of the year, Quintus Fabius Maximus. Although ancient civilized practice condoned pillage only when a city had been stormed, the exasperated old general allowed the troops to ransack the town, and he sold the 30,000 inhabitants into slavery. Thus in seven years Roman policies had recovered much of the position lost at Cannae. True, Hannibal still moved about southern Italy undefeated, but the numerous Roman armies could maintain their strongholds against him, and there were so many of them that they could even afford the luxury of an occasional defeat at his hands.

THE FALL OF SYRACUSE (212 B.C.) AND RECOVERY OF SICILY (214–210 B.C.).   During 214 B.C. Claudius Marcellus, the Roman commander in Sicily, undertook the investment of Syracuse. The pro-Roman party there had continued its partisan activities by murdering the whole royal family, even the women, and these excesses had driven the city, in nationalistic desperation, to a final and complete break with Rome. The Carthaginians sent a force of nearly 30,000 men into the island, and this expedition managed to take Heraclea Minoa and Agrigentum, the island's second most important city. The Roman effort at Syracuse was hampered by the dangerous presence of these Carthaginians, who might surprise the besiegers and who could slip provisions into the city by sea. The defenses of Syracuse were bolstered by the genius of Archimedes, the great engineer and mathematician. The efficacy of his devices for defense so terrified the Roman troops that they dared not approach so much as a piece of string dangling from the city walls lest it prove to be some devilish contraption.

Also, the anti-Roman feeling throughout the island was well appreciated by Rome's commanders. To inhibit further defections from this quarter, the strong city of Enna in central Sicily was made a valuable lesson. Suspecting its citizens of ill-will, its Roman garrison fell upon the unarmed and credulous inhabitants while in assembly in their theater and massacred them. The success of this measure set the tone for future exploits.

Meanwhile, the pro-Roman party in Syracuse still existed

---

[2]   See also p. 79.

and was active. One Sosis, who had been a party to the assassination of King Hieronymus and the murder of the royal family, in 212 assisted the Romans in discovering weaknesses in the city's defenses during a national festival. The outer walls of the city were thereupon carried and the suburbs pillaged. The rest of the city held out for some months, but the nearby Carthaginian camp was nearly destroyed by fever and the city within was rent by factional anarchy. The control of Syracuse finally fell to foreign mercenaries, who made terms with Marcellus. Once the royal treasures were secured, Marcellus turned the city over to the pillage of his troops. The loyalty of Hiero, the years of service to Rome by the Syracusans, the harsh necessities under which the people had operated, all were forgotten. The accumulated treasures of centuries were destroyed by ignorant soldiers, or they were carted off to Rome as loot. In the midst of it all a Roman soldier slew Archimedes while he was studying a problem in geometry.

The revolt of the island continued even after the fall of Syracuse. It seems that as late as 210 B.C. there were sixty-six towns that still were in arms. The immensely successful forays of Mutines, a cavalry officer that Hannibal had sent to harass the Romans, made their recovery difficult. But again luck was with the Romans. There was a falling-out between Mutines and the commander of the garrison at the main Carthaginian base in Agrigentum, and Mutines offered to betray the city to Marcus Valerius Laevinus, the Roman consul of 210. That astonished general grasped the opportunity and exploited it by executing the leading citizens of the town and selling all the rest of the inhabitants into slavery. The proceeds of this transaction were forwarded to Rome. Thereupon twenty other towns were betrayed, six were stormed, and the rest submitted. Traitors were then rewarded, patriots beheaded, and Sicily was returned to the useful service of the Roman people.

THE EROSION OF HANNIBAL'S POSITION (214–203 B.C.). Hannibal's grand alliance disappointed him at every turn. He had hoped that the free Italians, Macedonians, Gauls, and Carthaginians would unite in a great concerted effort after Cannae. Philip of Macedon, however, failed to grasp vigorously the opportunities offered by Rome's perplexities after her great disaster, and he frittered away his time in attacks on Rome's protectorates in the Balkans. By the winter of 212/211 B.C. the Romans were able to counter Phillip's projected expedition to Italy by taking the diplomatic offensive in Greece. They reached agreements with Philip's Greek rivals, Aetolia, Sparta,

Messene, and Elis, and they maintained friendly relations with the Illyrians and King Attalus of Pergamum. The resultant pressures kept Philip busy and bottled up in the Balkans from then on.

In view of Rome's rapid recovery of Italian towns and of Philip's failure to appear, Hannibal's only hope now to stave off the complete erosion of his program was reinforcements from Gaul or Spain. In 208 Hannibal's brother, Hasdrubal, did indeed slip out of Spain with such a force, and after a circuitous march through the Basque country and Gaul and over the Alps, arrived in Italy in 207. Messages to arrange a rendezvous with his brother were intercepted by the Romans, however, and they now used their interior lines to good effect. With great secrecy southern armies rushed to join northern ones, trapped and defeated Hasdrubal in the valley of the Metaurus River in Umbria, and returned to their stations without Hannibal's knowledge. The sequel contrasts the mental or moral state of the contestants. Hannibal had made it a constant practice to search out the bodies of dead Roman commanders and dispatch with all care the remains to their widows or children. But the Romans, so long as they could not rival Hannibal in tactics, did not try to do so in chivalry. The consul Tiberius Claudius Nero contemptuously announced to Hannibal his brother's arrival in Italy by tossing Hasdrubal's severed head before the ramparts of the Punic camp. Hannibal now recognized the inevitable, collected his remaining forces, and retired into Bruttium. Here he remained for four more years, almost ignored by the Romans, who feared to molest him. Elsewhere they continued their mopping-up operations and prepared a final blow for Carthage itself. Carthage made one more attempt to relieve Hannibal; his brother Mago was dispatched to Italy from the Balearic Isles in 205. He captured Genoa and endeavored to recruit allies in the area. However, the Gauls were now lukewarm to the distant Hannibal and were less sure of his ultimate triumph. It was 203 before Mago could venture southward. He fought one indecisive battle in Etruria, but was himself so badly wounded that, recalled to defend Carthage from the imminent danger of Roman invasion, he expired on the voyage home.

In 205 the desultory war in the Balkans also came to an end. Rome had neglected her allies in Greece once she had procured them, and the Aetolians were forced to make peace with Philip in 206, a development that led to mutual recriminations in later years. In 205 the Romans also came to an understanding with Philip, and the terms were confirmed by the Treaty of Phoenice. Thereby the prewar situation in the Bal-

135

kans was approximately restored. Philip gave up a number of territories that he had taken on the Illyrian coast, but the Romans allowed him to keep the land of their "friends" the Atintanes and some of the territory that he had gained from Pleuratus the Illyrian. This desertion of the Atintanes shows that Rome did not really consider the claims of *amici* quite as obligatory as she averred when she wished to pick a quarrel. By the Treaty of Phoenice another incidental distraction had been cleared away so that slowly the Romans' whole attention could be focussed on the central stage now being prepared in Africa.

Chapter 14

THE ROMAN SUCCESS

In tactics Hannibal had proved himself the Romans' master and teacher, but Rome's superior strategy and superior human resources produced her ultimate triumph. The superior human resources can be attributed to the past wisdom of her treatment of neighbors and relatives, which ensured their loyalty, and to the long experience of her people as freemen and as farmer-soldiers, which made them patient, tenacious, and patriotic. As for Roman strategy, a large part of the credit should go to the Roman Senate for its coolness in the face of disaster, for its decision to increase the number of armies in the field, and for its adoption of the Fabian strategy of destroying the Carthaginians by slow attrition. However, credit should also be given to the family of the Scipios, who helped to accomplish the Senate's strategy and added to it an aggressiveness that carried it to success.

PUBLIUS AND GNAEUS SCIPIO IN SPAIN (218–211 B.C.).
In 218 B.C. the consul Publius Cornelius Scipio, who had started for Spain with an expeditionary force, discovered that Hannibal was already in Gaul. Scipio saw the importance of the original plan, and rightly sent his brother Gnaeus on to Spain

with the troops, while he returned to Italy to organize the resistance there. In the following year he went to Spain as proconsul, and both his and his brother's commands there were annually extended by the Senate until 211. Thus, early in the war the Senate with ever greater regularity used an expedient that they had been forced to adopt during the Samnite Wars: it prolonged the *imperium* of magistrates beyond their year of office, terming these officials proconsuls or propraetors.[1]

From 217 to 211 the joint operations of the Scipios were so successful that none of the Spanish reinforcements on which Hannibal had counted could be spared him. At the time of the Scipios' appearance in Spain the Carthaginians were holding a number of Spanish children in Saguntum as hostages for the loyalty of Carthage's allies in Spain. Fortunately for the Scipios, a disaffected Spaniard betrayed these children into the Romans' hands. By releasing them to their parents the Scipios created a reservoir of good will among the natives not only for Rome but also for their own family. A naval victory off the Ebro in 217 was followed by a crushing land victory in 215 and the capture of Saguntum in 212. The Scipios accomplished much with very little help from Italy.

The Carthaginians, however, had by now put down a revolt by the Numidian king Syphax in Africa and could turn their full attention to Spain. In 211 the Scipios, placing too great confidence in their Spanish allies, overextended their divided forces in southern Spain. The Spaniards proved fickle and melted away. Both Roman armies were defeated by superior Carthaginian forces and the commanders were killed. A remnant escaped north of the Ebro and there was rallied by a courageous Roman knight, Lucius Marcius, whom the troops themselves quite irregularly selected to command them. Thus a foothold in Spain was preserved.

THE YOUNGER SCIPIO IN SPAIN (210–206 B.C.).   The Scipios were dead, but they had done important service in Spain, for they had held back Spanish reinforcements to Hannibal during Rome's most critical hours. When word of the Scipios' defeat arrived in Rome, she was rapidly recovering from the defeat at Cannae and was able to prepare new efforts abroad. After the siege and fall of Capua (211 B.C.), therefore, Gaius Claudius Nero was dispatched to Spain as propraetor with sufficient reinforcements to hold the Roman position.

Rome next decided to put on a full-scale campaign in

[1]   For such extensions of *imperium* for magistrates, see pp. 185–186 below.

Spain and determined to appoint a commander with greater authority than a propraetor. However, since Carthage still had vast resources in Spain and held the greater part of the country, the available Roman commanders had very little enthusiasm for this assignment. At length, only Publius Cornelius Scipio (later known as Scipio Africanus), son of the Publius Scipio recently killed in Spain, came forward as a candidate. He was enthusiastically elected to the new command with the rank of proconsul, although he was only twenty-five years of age and had proceeded in the course of offices only as far as the aedileship.

Concerning the young Scipio, history is equivocal. He is said to have saved his father's life in his first battle at the age of seventeen, yet the act is also attributed to a faithful slave. He intimated that he constantly called on strong spiritual powers for guidance in time of need, but perhaps he was cannily playing on the people's superstitious awe. He was imaginative, cultured, and aloof, respected—even revered—but not really very much liked in a world of devoted, suspicious, and mediocre men. In any case, he was the first private citizen to be endowed with the proconsular *imperium* without first having held the regular *imperium* through the traditional *cursus* of magistracies; and this flouting of tradition by the electorate—for expediency, even if also for a man of superlative qualifications—set a dangerous precedent that lesser men might later follow.

Scipio arrived in Spain in the autumn of 210 and immediately set about training his men and seeking friends among the Spaniards. In early 209 he made a rapid dash on the Carthaginian stronghold of New Carthage. The town itself had been insufficiently garrisoned, and the main Carthaginian armies were divided and distant. Furthermore, Scipio had good intelligence of the vicinity and was able to direct an attack across a shallow lagoon at low tide while the defenders were distracted by a feint over the more obvious land route. The town was taken, and into Scipio's hands came treasures, ships, stores, Carthaginian soldiers, and more Spanish hostages. His kind treatment of the latter bound many a Spanish chieftain to him, and Roman sovereignty in Spain is partly due to his personal popularity.

In 208 Scipio marched against Hasdrubal Barca, brother of Hannibal, and surprised and defeated him at Baecula in the upper Baetis valley. Hasdrubal, however, managed to extricate the better part of his troops after the battle, and eluded all Roman attempts to bottle him up in Spain and prevent his fatal march to Italy.[2] In 207 Scipio defeated the main Carthaginian forces near Ilipa. He drew up his troops with a weak center and strong wings and surrounded and destroyed a larger Carthaginian army, thus showing that he was a successful student of Hannibal's victories in Italy. From then on there were only occasional minor interruptions to a Roman advance that culminated in the surrender of Gades. By the autumn of 206 the dominion and the wealth of Spain were Roman.

Among his final acts in Spain Scipio contrived a meeting with the young Numidian prince Masinissa, who led an African contingent of cavalry for the Carthaginians. This interview was to bring a fine harvest to the Romans for many years, for Masinissa soon became Rome's most useful ally in Africa.

SCIPIO IN SICILY (205–204 B.C.).   In 206 Scipio returned to Italy and straightway was unanimously elected consul for 205. As colleague he was given the pontifex maximus, whose religious duties confined him to service in Italy. This arrangement ensured that the command in Sicily, and any expedition against Africa that might be launched from there, must fall to Scipio's lot.

Many senators, remembering their own years of struggle to reach the highest commands, naturally resented and distrusted Scipio's rapid rise and youthful self-assurance. However, they gave their grudging consent to a Sicilian command for Scipio, with the provision to invade Africa only "if it were in the best interests of the State." Scipio was not authorized to levy new armies, and the legions assigned to him consisted of survivors of Cannae who had been sent to Sicily in disgrace. Still, supplies and materiel flowed in to the new popular favorite as freewill offerings from Etruria, while volunteers from the Umbrians and other Italic peoples swelled his forces and helped construct an invasion fleet. Scipio was especially affable to the Sicilians and, by exempting them from actual military service, he prevailed upon them to equip and train a considerable number of Italian volunteers as cavalry.

Scipio's period of preparation in Sicily was not without harassment, however. One of his lieutenants, Quintus Pleminius, whom he had placed in charge of the recently recovered city of Locri in southern Italy, grossly betrayed his trust by looting the town and its famous Temple of Persephone; and in the ensuing fracas two Roman military tribunes were killed.

[2]   See also p. 135.

News of these outrages reached the Senate, accompanied by unfriendly reports that Scipio was living in the luxurious style of a Greek in Syracuse. The complaints were clearly prompted by the jealousies of Scipio's political enemies, especially old Fabius Maximus, who opposed any African campaign while Hannibal remained in the peninsula, and Marcus Porcius Cato. A senatorial commission punished Pleminius and investigated Scipio's activities in Sicily in order to recall him if necessary. However, the commission was so impressed by the excellence of his military arrangements and by the training and morale of his men that they ordered him to Africa in joyful expectation of success.

THE AFRICAN EXPEDITION (204–202 B.C.).   The first season in Africa (204 B.C.) brought initial successes, but the combined forces of the current Carthaginian commander, Hasdrubal Gisgo, and of the Numidian Syphax forced Scipio into winter quarters near Utica. During the winter Syphax attempted to mediate peace between Rome and Carthage. Scipio entered into prolonged negotiations with him, assuring Syphax frequently that the Romans were nearly ready to confirm terms acceptable to Carthage. However, Scipio was only playing for time while his staff officers, disguised as slaves of the negotiators, accompanied them to the Numidian camp and spied out its appointments. The Romans then rewarded the peacemaking efforts of the credulous barbarians by breaking off negotiations and setting fire at night to their wooden huts. They then massacred the Numidians and their Punic friends who came to help battle what they thought an accidental blaze.

While those who recall Roman tradition might ponder this expression of Roman good faith, this treachery was counted by Scipio's admirers as one of his most brilliant exploits. It seriously weakened the Carthaginians' potential, and a new force that they hastily gathered together was defeated in the plains around the River Bagradas in the spring of 203. Syphax was captured soon afterward. By the autumn of 203 these disasters forced the Carthaginian Senate to seek peace terms. The terms that Scipio proposed were severe, though not catastrophic, and a Carthaginian embassy proceeded to Rome to procure their legal ratification. Carthage was to remain intact, but Masinissa, the princeling whom Scipio had befriended in Spain, was to become king of independent Numidia. Carthage would continue to draw revenues from her coastal settlements, but must respect the autonomy of the Libyan and Cyrenaic tribes of the interior. She must renounce interference in the affairs of Spain,

Gaul, and Italy, pay an indemnity of 5000 talents, and surrender all but twenty of her warships.

While the terms were being discussed in Rome, Hannibal and his brother Mago were recalled from Italy. The arrival of Hannibal seems to have inspired some Carthaginians, probably without the connivance of the government, to attack and plunder a number of Roman transports that had strayed into the Bay of Tunis. The wrongdoers were truculent and, since appropriate reparations were not made, the war was resumed, this time with Hannibal as the Punic commander. Hannibal did what he could, but the Carthaginian loss of Syphax and his Numidians had given the Romans, aided by the rival princeling Masinissa, the superiority in cavalry. At Zama in 202 Hannibal could prolong the maneuvering but not ward off defeat. Thanks to the weakness of the contingents of citizens in the Punic army, the Roman superiority in cavalry, and Scipio's cool application of the tactics that he had learned from Hannibal, the Romans were able to surround and exterminate Hannibal's veterans.

The terms dictated to the Carthaginians were far more oppressive than before. Carthage was restricted to its immediate territory in Africa, approximately modern Tunisia, and it became a dependent ally of Rome. Its fleet was now limited to ten warships and the indemnity was raised to 10,000 talents, payable in fifty years. It was forbidden to wage war outside Africa, and could do so within Africa only with the permission of Rome. On its borders was established a strong Numidian kingdom under Rome's new ally, Masinissa.

ROMAN POLICY TOWARD FALLEN CARTHAGE.   The Carthaginians now were faced with years of effort to pay the Roman indemnity, and they were under constant harassment from the Numidians. There never had been any set boundary between the two peoples. The Numidians were simply the nomads south and west of Carthage, who as allies had once furnished her with cavalry. Now Numidian ambitions led to territorial encroachments. Appeals by Carthage to Rome in the disputes that arose inevitably were decided to the advantage of Rome's favorite. Thus the Roman dispensation meant the ultimate extinction of Carthage, though the combined animosity of Rome and Numidia prolonged her death throes for fifty years.

Scipio admired Hannibal and encouraged him to remain in Carthage to help her meet the obligations of peace, as he had led her in war. Hannibal was elected suffete in 196, but he found himself at once in conflict with a corrupt civil administration. Nevertheless he pressed through ·the Carthaginian

Assembly administrative and fiscal reforms that assured the just and scrupulous observance of the State's obligations. This so enraged the wealthy classes of Carthage that their agents in Rome went to the Senate and accused Hannibal of plotting an anti-Roman conspiracy with Syria. An investigating committee was dispatched by the Senate to Carthage, and Hannibal understood Roman objectivity sufficiently well that he felt it wise to flee the country that he so long had served. He escaped to Antioch where he advised Antiochus the Great for some time, but unrelenting Roman pursuit finally led him to commit suicide at the court of Prusias of Bithynia in 183 B.C.

THE EFFECTS OF THE WAR ON ROME.   For the Romans the Second Punic War held important lessons. Some they learned, some they neglected. Some were too severe, and they neither mastered them nor recovered from the shock. The unfailing loyalty of central Italy showed the wisdom of the generous settlements and alliances that Rome had made there. So did the steadfastness of the Latin colonies and of most of the Greek cities. In retrospect Rome could view with satisfaction the spirit of her citizens in their country's darkest days. Her contractors with patriotic zeal had furnished goods on credit without charge of interest for the Spanish armies in 215; her senatorial class had voted a special tax on the wealthy in 215 to procure rowers; all classes had made voluntary contributions of their wealth in 210; and in 205 volunteers and donations had flocked to Scipio's standard in Sicily from all Italy.

There were, however, faint signs that Rome could not be entirely complacent, and that new social and economic problems should receive sympathetic and imaginative care. In 209 twelve Latin colonies had been forced to suspend their contributions to the Roman cause on the grounds that they no longer had men or money. The era saw the arrival of irresponsible businessmen such as Postumius of Pyrgi, who deliberately sank worthless cargoes on rotten ships and then collected insurance from the government. Relations with the allies also needed attention. Many of the allies who defected after Cannae took that step only because they believed that there was no alternative. While Capua defected in part through jealousy, Tarentum had done so in a frenzy at Roman brutality.

Hannibal and his Spanish veterans had much to teach the Romans about tactics, and most of these lessons the Romans absorbed. The advantages of long-term commands such as Hannibal's over the annually elected Roman generals became very clear to them. Therefore, despite the jealousies of families and factions, which prized the rewards and prestige of command, the Senate more and more kept competent consuls and praetors in the field after their year of elected office by making them proconsuls or propraetors for many further campaigns. The Romans, however, refused to correct their weakness in native cavalry. The Italians simply never learned to fight effectively from horseback, and the Romans neglected the cultivation of this military arm until the very end of their Empire.

The war increased admiration for stolid oligarchical mediocrity. This was the lesson taught by the example of the devoted and determined, but not brilliant, Quintus Fabius Maximus, the "Cunctator." The failures of the popular and impulsive Flaminius, Minucius, and Varro confirmed the portent. Therefore, although he caught the popular imagination and at first seemed destined to dominate the State, Scipio Africanus was to find that he could not crack the prestige that the senatorial class won during the struggle. The oligarchs could proudly demonstrate that it had been the democratic parties in the allied states that had favored Hannibal, while their own aristocratic guest-friends had been the mainstay of the pro-Roman parties and had saved the unity of Italy. The ascendancy of a handful of powerful families during the war was jealously guarded against the unsettling emergence of brilliant individuals for nearly a century.

A brutal war made the Roman leaders and Roman people brutal. Undoubtedly later Roman annalists overly idealized early practices, but the attitude of Rome's early Italian antagonists suggests that most of them had little reason to hate her and much to thank her for. But the age of chivalry and of self-restraint was departing, and humane feelings were still undeveloped among the Romans. At one point in the war nearly half of Rome's allies had fallen away, and defecting allies received dreadful chastisement. It was easy for the Romans to be frightful when they had been thoroughly frightened. The disposition and habits produced and exercised during duress, terrible as they may be, are not straightway laid aside when times of prosperity follow; and a trail of blood, perfidy, and oppression now marked the Roman advance for nearly 200 years.

Four centuries after the Second Punic War a Carthaginian (Septimius Severus) sat on the Roman throne, and one might characterize him as the avenger of Hannibal; but the Barcids actually had their vengeance on Rome for her treacherous rape of Sardinia much sooner. When they left the Mediterranean, they left a Hellenistic world that did not contain a single strong potential Roman enemy. The results were demoralizing. The Roman ruling caste, elevated by its victory over Hannibal, no longer had to display the prudence that is nurtured by rivalry. Without external rivals the Roman nobles lost the self-discipline and selflessness that thrive in times of danger; without vision they would allow the Italy that Hannibal had devastated to lapse into ruin, and without pity they would goad their exploited inferiors to rend the vitals of the State.

PART
Four

The Wages of Success

Chapter 15

THE MILITARY MOMENTUM

The Romans emerged triumphant from the settlement with Carthage with bright prospects and high prestige. They now should have had time to recover, to heal wounds, and to develop Italy's economic potentialities. Instead, Rome plunged into almost constant warfare which lasted for nearly seventy years. Roman wars were fought in the West to consolidate former conquests and in the East to establish Rome's hegemony in the Hellenistic world. We can readily understand the need to keep peace and establish orderly government in Spain, the islands of the western Mediterranean, and Cisalpine Gaul, but the Roman involvement in the East is more complex. It surely was not prompted at first by a desire either for territory or for markets, though such incentives were present later, in the first century B.C. Nor did activity in the East stem from any undue tenderness for the welfare of the Greeks; the Romans admired and adapted Greek culture, but they affected considerable contempt for contemporary "Greeklings." The stimulus for the initial Roman moves in the East was fear rather than ambition, fear which had its roots in the Roman experience during the Hannibalic War and which was aggravated by a desire to revenge the Eastern aid or sympathy for Hannibal. These passions were sharpened by widespread isolationism, which counselled both hastiness and impatience in foreign relations, by a national intransigence fed by pride, stubbornness, and conceit, and by an inclination to opportunism which betrayed the Roman character and blackened its reputation. The ensuing brief account of their conflicts (200–133 B.C.) will clarify this analysis. A study of the Roman experience in other fields of endeavor in the second century B.C. will, in succeeding chapters, show how profound the effects of these military ventures were.

INTERNATIONAL PROBLEMS (EARLY SECOND CENTURY B.C.).
East and West presented quite different problems of foreign

GAUL

The Alps

CISALPINE
GAUL (225)

Gauls

Cremona
Po
Placentia
R.
Parma
Ligurians
Luna
Luca

Mutina
Bononia
Pisaurum

Aquileia

ISTRIA

GALLIA
NARBONENSIS
(121)

Massilia

ILLYRIA
(167)

ITALY
Veii
Rome

Potentia

Adriatic
Sea

Capua

Samnites
Tarentum

EPIRUS
(165)

See Inset

SPAIN

Lusitanians

Vaccaei
Cauca

Celtiberians

Pyrenees

Segeda

FARTHER SPAIN
(206)

Italica
(206)

Gades

Carteia

Numantia

HITHER SPAIN
(206)

Balearic Isles

Corsica
(237)

Sardinia
(237)

MAURETANIA

NUMIDIA

Carthage

AFRICA
(146)

Sicily
(241)

Mediterranean

ILLYRIA
(167)

MACEDONIA
(148)

Pydna

EPIRUS
(165)

THESSALY

Cynoscephalae

Demetrias

THRACE

AETOLIA

Thermopylae

BOEOTIA

Euboea

ACHAEA (146)

Heraclea

Corinth

Athens

Orchomenos

Argos

Aegina

Delos

GREECE

Sparta

Dates when independent states
came under Roman control: (406)

148

ROME
AND HER NEIGHBORS
2nd Century B.C.

Caspian Sea

Black Sea

THRACE

MACEDONIA
(148)

CAPPADOCIA

Aegean-
Sea

Pergamum

Gauls

Taurus Mts.

KINGDOM OF THE SELEUCIDS

Corinth

Magnesia

ASIA
(129)

GREECE

Rhodes

CILICIA
(102)

SYRIA

Crete

Cyprus

PHOENICIA

Sea

Alexandria

Persian
Gulf

EGYPT

Red Sea

policy, and Rome's aims and reactions in the two areas also were quite different. As time wore on, however, the techniques that the Romans used for these two dissimilar problems became more and more alike, and the techniques themselves degenerated along with the men that employed them.

In the West, the Gauls of the Po valley had to be returned to allegiance to ensure the northern frontiers and the safety of Roman settlers in the area. Spain, composed of a multitude of small anarchic tribes, had to be organized so that the rich coastal and mining areas wrested from the Carthaginians could be protected.

In the East there were three major states, the successors of the empire of Alexander, and as far as the Romans could foresee, any one, or at least any combination, of them might prove hostile and dangerous. Macedonia, the smallest of them, was compact, warlike, and devoted to its ruling house. Syria was large and sprawling: it extended from Phoenicia to the Indus, and its ruler, Antiochus III (the Great), was reasserting his control over his semi-independent princes. Egypt was the richest and the weakest state. It was ruled by the Greek descendants of Ptolemy, one of Alexander's generals, and the rulers had never won the support of the people, so that they had to depend on mercenaries hired largely from the Greek world. At the moment an infant on the throne surrounded by corrupt guardians aggravated the dynasty's weaknesses.

In addition to these three states, there were a number of smaller states that had to be taken into consideration in Roman calculations. The mercantile island republic of Rhodes was prosperous and respected and had kept the eastern seas policed since the deterioration of Athens. The kingdom of Pergamum was ruled by a middle-class family called the Attalids, which had gained a title and a good deal of respect by beating back the marauding Gauls in the third century B.C. There were in addition two appreciable leagues of Greek cities, the Aetolian League in northern Greece and the Achaean League in the Peloponnesus, and a scattering of small independent or semi-independent city states, mostly Greek, in Greece proper, in Thrace, along the coast of Asia Minor, and on the Aegean islands.

During the first three-quarters of the second century B.C. Roman efforts were largely concentrated in the East. When one compares Rome's military exploits in the East and West from 200 to 133 B.C., there is a distinct impression that the pacification and settlement of the West were sandwiched in whenever a pause in major Eastern conflicts allowed:

	EAST		WEST
200–196	Second Macedonian War		
		197–191	Recovery of Cisalpine Gaul
		197–198	Sporadic campaigns in Spain
192–189	War with Antiochus and the Aetolians		
		181–163	Sardinia and Corsica
		181–154	Campaigns against Ligurians
171–167	Third Macedonian War		
		154–140	Wars in Spain with Celtiberians and Lusitanians
149–148	Fourth Macedonian War	149–146	Third Punic War
		143–133	Numantine War
146	Achaean War		

THE SECOND WAR WITH MACEDON (200–196 B.C.).

Philip of Macedon's attitude toward the Romans after making peace with them in 205 B.C. was correct if not cordial. He seems to have renounced thoughts of expansion toward the west and turned to the development of his kingdom in the Aegean area, which would be at the expense of Egypt and of some of the lesser states. Philip raised anxieties in many quarters. In the Greek cities he had courted popular favor, which set the ruling oligarchies against him; he had attacked and ruthlessly subdued a number of inoffensive Greek cities in the vicinity of the straits between Europe and Asia. A reported agreement between himself and Antiochus of Syria to divide between them Egypt's outlying possessions caused grave concern among the lesser Eastern powers, and in 201 B.C. Rhodes and Pergamum joined to attack Philip's expeditionary forces in Asia, though their own territories had not yet been violated.

Rome had made but a sorry showing in her recent venture in Greek politics during the Second Punic War and she was not popular. However, now the medium-sized nations thought that pressure from the West might be used to correct the disturbance of equilibrium that Philip and Antiochus threatened. As early as 202 B.C. the Aetolians had complained in Rome of Philip's attacks on their allies in the Aegean, but the Romans had brushed them off. They were offended because the Aetolians had made a separate peace with Philip in 206 B.C. during the First Macedonian War, though the lack of Roman support had then dictated

151

Aetolian policy. Also, in 202 B.C. the Romans were still involved in Africa.

In 200 B.C., however, another embassy waited upon the Roman Senate, this one from Pergamum and Rhodes. These states were not Roman allies—at best they were merely *amici*, friends of the Romans; but already we have noticed that the Romans found this a happily vague term that they could interpret as they wished. It was not contrary to Roman policy to take advantage of Philip's temporary embarrassment in Asia, where he was being harassed by the Pergamenes and Rhodians, and to take advantage also of their own veteran army. Besides, the Romans had a grudge to settle with Philip for his alliance with Hannibal, and they seldom forgot or forgave a bad turn. The senators determined on war, but they had a major obstacle to overcome—the reluctance of both Philip and of the Roman people to go to war. The Centuriate Assembly, weary of conflict, at first flatly refused to declare war; and Philip, though Roman embassies delivered preposterous charges and demands, could not be outraged into taking the initiative. They asserted that he had attacked Roman allies, when in point of fact Pergamum and Rhodes had been the aggressors, and they were *not* Roman allies. They forbade him to attack any Greek state, as though all Greece were their protectorate and he a Roman client and no sovereign. These affronts he cooly ignored. However, a short time later he became embroiled with the Athenians, who in a fit of religious passion had murdered some of his allies; and when he supported his allies against Athens, the senators returned to the Roman assembly with new ammunition and bullied it into war.

The early campaigns were desultory. The Greeks showed little enthusiasm for Rome's professed championship, though finally the Aetolians did join her in her combat against their old enemy. Philip displayed masterful delaying tactics, and after each impasse regularly proposed a negotiated peace; but the Romans always demanded more than he could grant and held out for unconditional surrender. It became clear that they planned to make Macedon a buffer state against northern tribes, as Masinissa's Numidia was in Africa against the Moors and tribes of the Sahara. This aim finally was effected by the consul of 198 B.C., Titus Quinctius Flamininus, a philhellene. By promises, condescension, a quite un-Roman graciousness, and some show of force Flamininus enlisted the aid of other Greek states, notably the Achaeans and ultimately the Achaeans' archenemy, Nabis of Sparta. Then, with his veteran troops and the undoubtedly considerable assistance of the Aetolians in June 197 B.C. Flamininus met and decisively defeated Philip at Cynoscephalae in central Thessaly. Negotiations and settlement followed soon after. It was high time: Antiochus of Syria, unperturbed by his recent ally's misfortunes, was cooly moving into the areas of Asia that Philip was being forced to abandon; and the Romans had been too occupied to intervene.

ROME IMPOSES FREEDOM ON THE GREEKS (196 B.C.).
To the annoyance of the Aetolians, who had repeatedly suffered at his hands, the Romans refused to destroy Philip. His state was too useful for the protection of Greece from northern barbarians, and at present the Romans certainly had no intention of assuming that burden themselves. Further, the Aetolians' protestations of their contributions to Philip's defeat annoyed Flamininus, who was a vain man. Philip was instructed to withdraw within his ancestral boundaries, which was a sufficiently vague directive to guarantee further trouble, and to accept a moderate fine, a limitation in armaments, and a Roman alliance. The Aetolians received far fewer territorial gains than they believed that they deserved and had been allowed to expect, while Thessaly, which they coveted, was organized into independent leagues.

The Greeks now observed that the Romans consulted with them and sought their support when they were needed for a conflict, but imposed their own peace terms when the war was over. Mutterings became louder when Flamininus acquiesced in the assassination of a Boeotian patriot by bravos hired by a pro-Roman party. To quiet increasing Greek uneasiness, Flamininus in 196 B.C. arranged a theatrical announcement at the Isthmian Games. To the delight and complete misunderstanding of the Greeks he proclaimed the imminent withdrawal of all Romans and the freedom of all the Greek city-states. Their patron lingered on with his troops for another two years, however, while he assisted in settling their affairs. He gravely convened his Greek allies and asked their wishes in respect to the control of Argos, which Nabis, the tyrant of Sparta and now also a Roman ally, had acquired by a deal with Philip earlier in the war. However, after the Greeks had agreed to support a war against Nabis to free Argos and he had been defeated, Flamininus disregarded the desire of the Achaeans to destroy this socialistic ruler, whom they considered so dangerous, and instead imposed a Roman peace on all parties. Finally, in 194 B.C., despite Greek suspicion of Roman sincerity and some doubts in Rome itself as to the wisdom of the move, the Roman troops returned home and left the Greeks to enjoy their imposed freedom.

The Romans were gone, but bitter feelings against their settlement remained. The Aetolians felt that their priceless contribution had been unrewarded. The Thessalian leagues were artificial and shaky. Philip's boundaries were uncertain and his neighbors straightway began to come to Rome with complaints for decision. The Achaeans saw the unification of the Peloponnesus foiled by the preservation of Nabis in Sparta. And there were glaring exceptions to the freedom proclaimed for the Greeks; no effort was made, for example, to gain freedom for the Greek island of Aegina from Rome's Asian ally Pergamum. Furthermore, Rome's unilateral declaration of freedom for Greek cities constituted an unprovoked challenge to the *status quo* in Asia Minor, which was dotted with Greek cities previously subject to a number of larger states. Nevertheless, what had appeared to the senators as the worst threat to Roman security now was removed, and they left the complications of the East to seek the settlement of the West.

THE RECOVERY OF CISALPINE GAUL (197–191 B.C.).
A series of campaigns in Cisalpine Gaul between 197 and 191 B.C. returned the region essentially to Roman control. The area south of the Po was given a whole series of municipalities. The populations of Placentia and Cremona were reinforced by new colonists, and colonies were established at Potentia, Pisaurum, Bononia, Mutina, and Parma. Roads linked these posts and extended northward. A Latin colony was established at Aquileia in 181 B.C. to protect the Po valley from invasion from the northeast. While the area south of the Po was rapidly urbanized and Romanized, that north of the Po was left Gallic with its ancient cantonal organization. However, many Roman settlers in the ensuing century appear to have moved into this rich land beyond the frontiers to seek better opportunities than Italy's lagging economy offered.

THE SETTLEMENT IN SPAIN (206–195 B.C.).   Rome's decision to retain Spain after the Second Punic War was probably based more on strategic than on economic grounds, though the Romans secured quantities of booty and precious metals from its mines. Spain was divided into numerous tribes of restless, reckless, chivalrous people still living in their "heroic age." There was no one prince or state that Rome could use as its client or favorite to maintain its interests, and therefore Roman troops had to be used to hold and protect the rich coastal area against the Celtiberians and Lusitanians of the interior. Now for the first time, Roman soldiers had to be retained overseas for long periods of service. The Roman government soon learned how unpopular this was; and the ensuing low morale, political pressure, and threats to desert had much to do with a continuing Roman preference elsewhere to establish protectorates rather than to annex territory. The formal organization of the peninsula by the Romans took place in 197. It was divided into two provinces, Hither and Farther Spain, and two new praetors were elected in Rome as their administrators. The relations of the Spanish chieftains, first with the Carthaginian Barcids and then with the Roman Scipios, had been on a personal and heroic basis. Now with formal provincial organization, the Spaniards felt that their personal ties and obligations were gone. Roman demands soon proved as onerous and humiliating as the Carthaginian ones ever had been. Fighting broke out almost immediately with the new organization, and it became so fierce that in 195 B.C. the consul, Cato the Elder, took charge in the peninsula. He did much to subdue the Hither province, but there was sporadic fighting in succeeding years. The vast amount of booty reported in these early days (130,000 pounds of silver, 4000 pounds of gold between 206 and 197 B.C.), as well as the exploitation of the mines organized there by Cato, indicate that the Romans proceeded to milk Spain as freely as the Spaniards later did Peru.

RELATIONS WITH ANTIOCHUS THE GREAT (196 – 188 B.C.).
Long before the Romans could make any final settlement in the West, however, they were recalled to the East by the deterioration of their arrangements there. The Aetolians were still loudly resentful at their cavalier treatment, and Antiochus the Great was uneasy at the implication that the freedom of Thracian and Asian cities that he considered legally his was being supported by the Romans simply because they had Greek populations. He had no ambitions in the West, but he did wish to resume his ancestral boundaries, both in Asia Minor and in Thrace, and he also wished to regularize his relations with the Romans. They, however, had sulked and hedged ever since 196 B.C. when they had demanded that Antiochus keep hands off the possessions of their "friend" Ptolemy of Egypt, only to find that they had been outmaneuvered and that Ptolemy was about to become Antiochus' son-in-law. There was still in the air their subversive promise of freedom to all Greek cities, even those of Asia Minor, yet the Roman negotiators privately confessed to Antio-

chus' ambassadors in 194/3 that if he would withdraw from his Thracian possessions, they would end their support of the Greek cities in Asia Minor. This clearly showed the cynical nature of Roman policy: their promises to all Greek city-states had been propaganda and now could be modified to remove any threat to their arrangements for the Greek city-states of the West alone. To do this they tried a device that they had used before with an equal rival, the Carthaginian Hasdrubal in Spain: they would accept a clearly defined line of demarcation, the Bosphorus, between their own and Antiochus' sphere.

Antiochus could see no reason for surrendering his rightful possessions anywhere to Roman effrontery, and he determined to play the same game in Greece that the Romans were playing in Asia, encouraging dissatisfaction and unrest. However, he found too willing and too impetuous an ally in the Aetolians. They hustled about, arousing opposition to Roman interference, and gave glowing accounts of Antiochus' intentions. The only immediate result was an ill-timed insurrection by Nabis in 192, which the Romans subdued with Achaean aid. The Aetolians finally precipitated the war that they wanted by calling on Antiochus to free the Greeks and then seizing as a debarkation point for him the fortress of Demetrias in Thessaly. In the fall of 192, Antiochus was rushed into sailing for Greece with insufficient preparations and an army of only about 10,000 troops.

In the late winter of 192/1 a Roman expeditionary force, under Acilius Glabrio, landed in Greece. To Antiochus' surprise, Philip of Macedon adhered to his Roman alliance and assisted the force. The combined allied pressure brought Antiochus to bay at Thermopylae in late April. There he was outflanked when a Roman detachment surprised and defeated the Aetolian troops guarding the mountain paths, and he was forced to abandon his crushed and fleeing troops and escape with a remnant to Asia.

A tragicomedy now ensued in Greece. Aetolian resistance stiffened, and the Romans had to take town after town by laborious siege. The Aetolians steadfastly refused the terms of unconditional surrender "to the faith of the Roman people," for by now they too well understood what this expression really meant. The delay was maddening to the Romans. Not only did it give Antiochus time to regroup his forces in Asia, but it also was proving embarrassingly useful to Philip. He, adhering to the terms of the agreement by which he entered this conflict, was happily conquering and returning to his possession cities on his borders that the Romans previously had taken from him and given to the Aetolians. The situation was intolerable. Finally, Flamininus, the architect of the earlier Greek peace, had a happy inspiration. With the consent of the Roman commander Acilius, he persuaded the Aetolians to accept a truce while sending an embassy to Rome to seek more favorable terms. The Roman flank was thus secured, Philip was barred from further aggrandizement, and the Romans could delay the subjection of the Aetolians until after Antiochus had been dealt with.

A series of naval engagements with Antiochus' adherents in 191 and 190 was necessary, but finally the Roman fleet with the aid of Pergamene and Rhodian contingents cleared the sea and Asia lay open to invasion. In late 190 the Roman forces under the consul Lucius Scipio, assisted by his famous brother Africanus, crossed into Asia, and in January 189 decisively defeated Antiochus' Oriental levy near Magnesia. Later that year Scipio's successor, Manlius Volso, marched through various regions of Asia Minor, and as he went extorted vast sums from the unhappy communities by which they purchased Roman "friendship." His march ended with the punishment of the lawless Galatians, who dwelt in the mountains of Asia Minor and were a constant harassment to their Greek neighbors, and the taking of some 40,000 captives as slaves. By the terms of the peace signed in 188 B.C. Antiochus was barred from territory north of the Taurus Mountain Range and his armaments were limited, though he was still independent and was not treated as a client. However, the Roman treaty, by shutting him off from his Greek possessions, brought about the orientalization and disintegration of his domains. While Rome contemplated no foothold for herself in Asia, her propaganda for the freedom of all Greek cities now came to plague her, for her allies demanded their due. Both Rhodes and Pergamum were suitably rewarded with new territory, regardless of earlier promises to the Greek city-states of Asia Minor. Greek cities that once had belonged to Pergamum or had been slow in embracing the Roman cause were summarily turned over to the Pergamene King Eumenes. His greatly enlarged realm was now the exact counterpart in Asia of Masinissa's Numidia in Africa, and like Masinissa he now busied himself for years in serving Rome's interests.

THE SUBJUGATION OF THE AETOLIANS (191–189 B.C.).
Meanwhile the Aetolians had to be dealt with. In 191 B.C. the Senate had been implacable to the Aetolians' embassy, which Flamininus had craftily advised them to send, and the war had been renewed. In 190 the Scipios also found an Aetolian war inconvenient while fighting in Asia and, taking a page from Flamininus, again persuaded the Aetolians to accept a truce.

The senators were this time no more lenient, and the war recommenced in 189 B.C. However, heroic resistance by the Aetolians, the presentation of gifts to the appropriate Roman generals, and the intercession of other Greek states in behalf of the Aetolians finally won terms for them short of unconditional surrender. At the subsequent settlement the Romans decided that if the Greek states were not willing to play spontaneously the part of dutiful and grateful clients to their Roman patron, they would write it into the treaty. Therefore the Aetolians had to sign a peace in which they promised to preserve "the authority and the majesty of the Roman people." Thus Rome's first Greek ally became her first avowed Greek client.

With the Aetolian and Syrian settlements there was again peace in the eastern world, but all was not completely serene. Many of the boundaries established by the peace treaties were ill-defined, and this would lead to future disputes. Philip was aggrieved: the Roman settlement with the Aetolians curbed his revengeful expansion in that direction, he had not received extensive territorial reward for his aid against Antiochus, and he found his ambitions toward the Aegean and Adriatic foiled by the Roman guarantee of the Greek states. There also was some disenchantment with Rome's interpretation of "freedom" for the Greeks, who interpreted freedom as the right to do precisely as they pleased. And the lower classes of Greece found their economic plight in that moribund land unrelieved, while even their chance to sell their services as mercenaries to the kings of Syria, which for years provided an outlet to a surplus population, was now removed by Roman restrictions on Antiochus' rights to recruit.

SPAIN, GAUL, THE WESTERN ISLANDS (181–154 B.C.).
In the western Mediterranean sporadic fighting in Spain had continued year by year, but the administration of Tiberius Sempronius Gracchus in Hither Spain (180–178 B.C.) finally brought about nearly twenty-five years of peace through military successes and sensible administrative policies. He settled roving and marauding tribes on sites that promised to become flourishing towns, and he concluded with the various tribes just and reasonable treaties. The gratitude of the Spaniards for his justice and forethought extended down to the next generation of his family.

In northern Italy the Gauls had been quickly subdued, but the wild Ligurian highlanders offered a more prolonged and stubborn resistance. Concerted action against them began in 181 B.C. In 180 the area between the Arno and Macra Rivers was cleared and 40,000 inhabitants were transferred to parts of Samnium devastated by the Hannibalic War. The colonies of Luca and Luna were thereupon established on the territory from which the Ligurians had been removed. However, the Ligurians were still not completely pacified, and we have notices of Roman expeditions against them in 175, 172, 166, 158, and 154. In fact, the area became a happy hunting ground for triumphs for ambitious generals, and many of their victories were as exaggerated as their expeditions were unprovoked and unnecessary. We can, perhaps, gain some small understanding of the Romans' impact on the Mediterranean world of the second century B.C. when we reflect upon the pain that they imposed on this one primitive people alone.

Elsewhere, the Sardinians and Corsicans tried sporadically to reassert their traditional independence. From 181 to 176 B.C. there were outbreaks, but in 176 the Sardinians were crushed and the Roman general took captive 80,000 natives. These humans glutted the contemporary slave market, and "cheap as a Sardinian" became a commonplace expression. Operating from the new Roman colony at Aquileia, expeditions into the Istrian Peninsula in 178 and 177 subdued the natives and secured the northeastern frontiers. In 163 Corsica finally was subdued. Meanwhile, Rome's old ally Massilia, charged with the care of the route from Cisalpine Gaul to Spain, sank into the status of a client state, analogous to Numidia in Africa and Pergamum in Asia.

The detailed account of Rome's military activity East and West up to this point shows the direction and the patterns of Roman involvement with the other Mediterranean peoples. Reactions to problems had at first been tentative, but by the end of the first quarter of the second century B.C. Roman experience was sufficiently rich that characteristic aims, methods, and reflexes had begun to appear. In their manipulation and control of their neighbors in ensuing years the solutions became more incisive, drastic, and perfunctory.

THE WAR WITH PERSEUS (171–167 B.C.).   Greece felt a bitter futility at not being able to prevent Roman interference in her affairs, an interference that was calculated to keep the peace and the *status quo*. The Achaeans were constantly foiled in their attempts to unite the Peloponnesus, and Philip nursed his grievances. Though he continued to observe his commitments to the Romans, he built up the military and economic potential of his country. This may have been done without thought of revenge, but the Romans were ever watchful and suspicious, and they tried to undermine Philip's position by seducing Philip's son, Demetrius, to aspire prematurely to his father's throne. This sorry device ended with the accusation and execution of Demetrius for treason, and he soon was followed in death by his sorrowing father.

Another son, Perseus, who succeeded in 179 B.C., inherited his father's dislike of the Romans, and he feared and resented the favor they had shown his brother. He tried to improve his position by dynastic marriages and prudent alliances, by supporting and assisting the poor of Greece, and by avoiding acts overtly hostile to Rome. But all was in vain. Eumenes of Pergamum actively and spitefully pressed his dislike of Perseus by long lists of accusations against him of anti-Roman activities, many of which were trivial rumormongering or fabrications. However, the lists were so long that the Romans were convinced that there must be some truth in them and decided to destroy Perseus. In 172 he received from the Romans demands sufficiently humiliating that he had to reject them. However, Perseus had an army, and the Romans had yet to raise an expeditionary force and integrate their allies' forces. Therefore, the Roman envoy, Marcius Philippus, used the same device that had outwitted the Aetolians, and prevailed on Perseus to send an embassy to Rome, for he deceitfully suggested that more favorable terms might be obtained there. By this subterfuge the Romans won a delay of six months so that they could get ready for war. However, when the fighting began the Romans were repeatedly outmaneuvered since their generals, most of whom had received such training as they had against primitive peoples of the West, were incompetent and their troops were inept. Perseus repeatedly sought terms after each of his victories, but the Romans stubbornly refused to be mollified. Perseus' destruction was determined. Finally, in 168 B.C., a competent disciplinarian and tactician, Aemilius Paullus, early in his command totally defeated Perseus at Pydna.

When peace was restored, the Romans impatiently determined to punish the Greeks for their lack of enthusiastic support of the Roman war against Perseus. Not just defection, but suspicion of any sympathy for Perseus was enough for punishment. Macedonia itself was divided into four "free" republics, each, the Romans thought, with sufficient native troops and income to defend the northern frontiers. However, half the taxes of these free states were to go to Rome, the royal mines and forests became Roman property, and the four republics were forbidden all intercourse with one another. In Macedonia, it appears, the Romans now were determined to set up client states in order here as elsewhere to reap the benefits of conquest without assuming the responsibilities. Illyria was similarly divided into three states. These former enemies fared well, however, when compared to Rome's friends. From the Achaeans, who had been regular, though sometimes critical, supporters of Rome, a thousand of the leading citizens were shipped to Italy—presumably to stand trial for unspecified offenses, though they never were tried. They remained in Italy as hostages until in 151 B.C. 300 aged survivors were contemptuously allowed to return home as now harmless.

With the fall of Perseus, his counterweight Eumenes of Pergamum was no longer needed. The Romans were conscious that their favoritism for this toady had made him and them unpopular in the Greek East. Now they dropped him, and he was even forbidden to visit Italy to plead his cause. Further, a Roman attempt was made to subvert his brother, Attalus, as Prince Demetrius of Macedon had been subverted; but the Attalids proved in this case to have solid middle-class virtues and disappointed the Romans by ignoring the temptation. Eumenes was allowed to hold his kingdom, but attacks and harassments from his neighbors were not discouraged until his death and Attalus' succession in 159 B.C.

Rhodes fared even worse. It had been encouraged to offer mediation between Rome and Perseus after Rome's repeated military blunders in the early years of the war. For such effrontery the island republic barely escaped a Roman declaration of war. As it was, its commercial importance was ruined by the Roman "liberation" of its possessions on the mainland and by the establishment of a free port on the island of Delos by Italian commercial interests, which reduced the revenues of Rhodes by eighty-five per cent. The combined effects of the weakening of Rhodes and of Syria in the East led to a revival of piracy in that area that was to be a problem for the next century.

None of Rome's actions are as unaccountable as the treatment of Epirus: there the Roman general, Aemilius Paullus, on his way home from Macedon, by the order of the Senate distributed his troops through the country on the pretext of levying a heavy fine. He thereupon devastated in one hour all its towns and carried off 150,000 inhabitants to be sold as slaves. To round out the list: in Aetolia, after peace was established, a pro-Roman citizen named Lyciscus had 500 of the leading anti-Roman patriots killed at a meeting of the assembly, and he received a Roman rebuke only because he had used Roman soldiers to accomplish this shocking act.

Neutrals too now felt Rome's curt disdain. At the end of the war with Perseus Roman commissioners were sent to Egypt to bring to an end one of the interminable Syrian-Egyptian conflicts. Antiochus Epiphanes of Syria was besieging Alexandria, and one commissioner, Popillius Laenas, presented him with a Roman directive to withdraw. When Antiochus hesitated, Popillius drew a circle about him in the sand and ordered him to make up his mind before stepping out of the circle. The Syrian god-king thereupon yielded and retired to his Syrian capital. This marked the end in the Mediterranean area to all international relations. Now all countries equally were Roman clients: the Greeks and Pergamum were cowed, Rhodes was ruined, Syria fell straightway into dynastic quarrels, and Rome encouraged fraternal discord in the royal house of Egypt.

RECURRENT WARS IN SPAIN (154–140 B.C.).   In the West Roman arrogance and brutality showed even more rapid development, and the records of the Spanish wars are among the sorriest in Roman history. The region of Farther Spain was rich. In peace it afforded many opportunities for a resourceful governor to line his pockets, while war compounded the opportunities. Incursions by raiding Lusitanians brought a full-scale war there in 154 B.C. The greed of the Roman generals involved was equalled by their incompetence, and their incompetence by their perfidy. Inconsequential successes or frequent setbacks finally led the praetor of 151 B.C., Sulpicius Galba, to come to terms with three tribes, promising them lands upon which to settle if they would lay down their arms. When they had done so, he surrounded and slaughtered them. Treacheries such as these led to regular campaigns against the Romans by the Lusitanians under their great patriot, Viriathus. His war was to last until 139 B.C., and the Roman generals suffered repeated reverses at his hands. At last the consul of 140, Servilius Caepio, after breaking a peace treaty that Rome had signed with Viriathus, procured his assassination and the speedy end of the war.

While these events were taking place in Farther Spain, the Celtiberians of Hither Spain were attacked by Roman forces in 153 B.C. after they had refused to obey a Roman order to cease fortifying the town of Segeda. The first Roman general to attack them sustained a crushing defeat. His successor, Marcus Claudius Marcellus, pursued the war with vigor until he received the enormous sum of 600 talents of silver from the natives, upon which he awarded them a peace treaty. His successor, Lucius Lucullus, finding that his opportunity for glory and gain had thus been foiled, in 151 B.C. attacked the Vaccaei, who were not Roman subjects and who had been on good terms with the Romans. The first town that he captured, Cauca, purchased its safety by a heavy ransom, but despite this the troops marched in and enslaved or slaughtered the 20,000 inhabitants.

162

Finding the natives now less trusting and easy booty therefore scarce, Lucullus marched off to Farther Spain to cooperate with the equally distinguished governor there, Sulpicius Galba, in his war with the Lusitanians. A lull ensued in the Celtiberian War until 143 B.C.

THE DESTRUCTION OF CARTHAGE (150–146 B.C.). Over the years, Masinissa of Numidia had proved a superlative model of a client prince of Rome, while Carthage, which was also an obedient client, was an object of petty Roman suspicion and hatred. The vigor and genius of that mercantile city had made it prosperous, and it had paid off its indemnity to Rome. Further, it had generously contributed supplies to various Roman ventures. But Masinissa was a difficult neighbor. Able and ambitious, he not only effected the cultural and agricultural improvement of his country, but he aimed ultimately to rule his kingdom from the city of Carthage. The Romans had carefully left the boundaries between Numidia and Carthage vague, and yet they had forbidden Carthaginians to venture in arms beyond those boundaries. This encouraged Masinissa to make repeated attacks on Carthage and then refer the "dispute" to Rome for arbitration. In such cases Rome regularly decided for its favorite or, what was equivalent, took no action at all, so that slowly Carthaginian territory had been whittled down to a very narrow area. Finally Carthaginian patience wore thin, and in 150 B.C. the citizens resisted and pursued their Numidian tormentors. Ultimately they again were defeated, but nevertheless in Rome their resistance was deemed a breach of the peace concluded after Zama. The isolationist Cato and his Roman supernationalists had long harbored a pathological hatred for their old rival. Now was their chance, and they decreed Carthage's destruction. It seemed wise to them, however, to spare Roman arms and effort to the utmost, and so a slow and deceptive series of requirements was used to disarm their contrite client and victim. Carthaginian envoys were first told that they might retain freedom, laws, and territory, but must send 300 leading citizens as hostages to Rome. When this had been done and their leadership decimated, they were told that they must surrender their arms. This too was done. Then came the thunderbolt—they must destroy their city and move to a site ten miles inland. Now the wrath and the willpower of the Carthaginians raised and sustained them. Their bravery and resourcefulness, combined with Roman incompetence, preserved them for nearly three years. Finally, in the spring of 146 B.C., Scipio Aemilianus, grandson of Hannibal's conqueror, engineered their investment, starvation, enslavement, the utter destruction of their city, and the cursing of its site. While a number of Carthage's old allies were declared free cities, the administration of her own former territory was now assumed by the Romans themselves. It became the province of Africa.

ANNEXATION OF MACEDON AND DESTRUCTION OF CORINTH. While Carthage was in her death struggle, a pretender to the Macedonian throne named Andriscus appeared and enlisted enough Macedonian support to defeat the militias of the four Macedonian republics. He would have been quickly put down but for the incompetence of the Roman generals sent against him, which lengthened the struggle from 149 to 148 B.C. At its conclusion the Romans determined to end the experiment with client states in Macedon, for here, as in Africa, it had not led to stability. The area was reunited and was given permanent military occupation as the province of a Roman magistrate. The addition of Epirus to Macedon returned it almost to its ancient territorial limits. The Roman governor also was given the general surveillance of the Greek leagues and cities to the south.

In Greece itself discontent now burst into one last passionate flame. The economic distress of the lower classes made them ripe for an uprising, and all of Greece was provoked by the return from Italy of the remaining aged Achaean hostages (151 B.C.) and by the curt Roman interference in the constant quarrels between the Achaean League and Sparta. Sparta, which had been a member of the League for some years, now wished to secede. A Roman commission not only supported the Spartans but announced that the Senate had decided also to detach and "free" from the League Corinth, Argos, Orchomenos, and Heraclea. The Achaeans, clinging to their position as free allies of Rome, refused to accept orders and went to war. In 146 B.C. the Achaean army, though supported by much of Greece, was defeated at Corinth, which had resisted Roman "liberation." That unhappy city was razed to the ground, its treasures of art shipped to Italy, and its inhabitants enslaved. What was good enough for the barbarians of Spain and for African Semites was now also good enough in Roman eyes to teach the Hellenes a lesson. The Greeks, however, must bear some of the blame; they had refused to learn the nature of their situation, and they had managed to egg the Romans into delivering the final blow.

THE NUMANTINE WAR IN SPAIN (143–133 B.C.). In 143 B.C. the struggle by the natives of Hither Spain was renewed, partly in sympathy with Viriathus' war in Farther Spain.

164

This conflict is often called the Numantine War because resistance centered around the town of Numantia. The first two years were spent in preliminaries, but the consul of 141, Quintus Pompeius, could not in two years reduce the Numantines and finally offered them a peace treaty for thirty talents of silver. When his successor, Popillius Laenas, appeared on the scene, Pompeius forswore his agreement and the Roman government backed him up. They did not, however, return the thirty talents. Popillius was no more successful than Pompeius in the next two years, while his successor, Hostilius Mancinus, in 137 B.C. had the supreme humiliation of finding his army of 20,000 men surrounded by and forced to surrender to a Spanish army of less than 8000. A new treaty, which included the release of the 20,000 Roman soldiers, was then agreed to by the general and confirmed by young Tiberius Sempronius Gracchus, who was present as Mancinus' quaestor and whom the Numantines trusted for his father's sake. The Senate, however, abjured the treaty and turned Mancinus over to the Numantines (but not the 20,000 troops), though the Numantines contemptuously dismissed him. Mancinus' successors in 136 and 135 B.C. did better only because they did nothing. Finally, in 134 B.C. the Roman people suspended the law whereby the consulship could not be repeated in order to elect as consul and send to Spain the most eminent general of the day, Scipio Aemilianus.[1] At last, with an army of 60,000, to which he first had to teach discipline, Scipio completely invested the town and in 133 B.C. forced its surrender. The Romans had developed in Spain an unpleasant habit of chopping off the hands of surrendered opponents; and so most of the inhabitants of Numantia—not much more than 4000 men by now—chose to commit suicide, while their town was razed to the ground by the man who had learned to destroy Carthage.

TECHNIQUES DEVELOPED IN FOREIGN AFFAIRS.   Rome's military momentum took her tragically far between the defeat of Hannibal and the fall of Numantia (202–133 B.C.). At the beginning of the second century B.C. Roman aims were not expansionist. The Romans wished only for security, and their actions were based on suspicion and fear that others might follow Hannibal's example. Their policy was to keep other states weak, divided, and, if possible, grateful. This Roman hope was based on the Italian institutions of patronage and clientship, and on the traditions of responsibilities, duties, and gratitude

[1]   This law was passed *ca.* 150 B.C. See also p. 211.

that distinguished them. However, they found no understanding of this principle among eastern foreigners.

We have already seen that the fear and hatred generated by Hannibal's invasion of Italy lowered the morality and the forbearance of the Romans in their dealings with other people. During the wars of the second century B.C. the Romans further experimented with strategy in foreign affairs, and they elaborated techniques and policies that made them the masters of the Mediterranean.

Propaganda was a useful tool: the loudly proclaimed "freedom for the Greeks" (196 B.C.) was observed cynically by the Romans themselves, but was a deterrent for opponents with designs on the Greeks and was a pious cloak for Rome's own interference in the area.

In treaties, a studied vagueness in respect to boundaries was employed. Where Rome truly feared a rival, such as the Barcids in Spain in the third century B.C. and Antiochus the Great in Asia in the second, she favored clear lines of demarcation (the Ebro, the Bosphorus); but if she destined a slow death for a weaker but still troublesome opponent, indefinite boundaries promised countless opportunities for harassment. This technique was used against Carthage after Zama (202 B.C.), against Macedon after Cynoscephalae (197 B.C.), and against Syria after Magnesia (190 B.C.), and effected the ultimate destruction of all three states.

Roman religious law insisted that Rome always had to enter wars as the injured party. She discovered that her treaties of friendship (*amicitia*) were excellently flexible instruments to evade any embarrassment to the Roman conscience: *amici* could be strategically established where friction was bound to lead to war. Saguntum was so used to precipitate the war with Hannibal (219 B.C.), and the same device proved useful to maneuver Philip, Antiochus, and Perseus—all of whom were reluctant—into conflict. On the other hand, the claims of *amici* were not really binding. These "friends" could be abandoned if it appeared expedient, as the Atintanes were to Philip in 205 B.C.

The Romans early learned to favor separatism. They preferred numbers of small, evenly balanced rivals instead of dangerously large neighbors. This explains Rome's early friendship for Rhodes, Pergamum, and the Achaeans rather than for Macedon, Syria, or Egypt. Even these small states she tried to isolate and weaken at the slightest sign of independence of action, as Rhodes discovered in 167 B.C. and the Achaeans in 146 B.C. The Romans also found it wise to develop fifth columns even among their allies, and oligarchic pro-Roman groups were supported in all the Greek cities, regardless of the bad character of some of the adherents thus gained. Similarly, attempts were made to stir up dynastic jealousies in royal houses: Roman officials tried to turn Prince Demetrius of Macedon against his own father Philip and Attalus of Pergamun against his brother King Eumenes; and for generations they cultivated the wrangles among the royal Ptolemies of Egypt.

Roman diplomats soon learned the advantageous use of strategic delay. By illusory promises they thus procured the neutrality of Antiochus while they disposed of Philip (200 – 196 B.C.); they repeatedly used the same tricks to obtain truces from the Aetolians while they pursued Antiochus in Asia (191 – 190 B.C.); and Perseus was similarly beguiled (172 B.C.) when the Romans were simply not yet quite prepared to destroy him. Duplicity took a further step in Rome's deceitful disarming of Carthage before revealing the resolve to annihilate her as well (150 B.C.).

Before the end of the period the Roman secret service had learned to assassinate a heroic opponent, such as the Lusitanian Viriathus (139 B.C.); and commanders repeatedly disavowed sworn engagements with the Spanish natives (with the Lusitanians in 151 and 140 B.C., the Celtiberians in 151, and the Numantines in 141 and 137) and rewarded their credulous opponents with massacre. The enslavement, mutilation, or utter destruction of those that dared withstand Rome's will (Epirus in 167 B.C., Carthage and Corinth in 146, the Numantines, 143 – 133) raised terrorism to the standing of state policy.

Once committed to interference outside Italy, the Romans found that one crisis and its settlement seemed simply to lead to another crisis. The consequent sufferings and complaints of the rest of the world seemed more and more petty to the busy masters of the Mediterranean in the midst of their great undertakings, and their responses became steadily more perfunctory and drastic. The subduing of weaker rivals progressively required less strength—at first physical, later moral. Before the end of the second century B.C. the Roman State had become a calloused bully in a cowering Mediterranean world.

Chapter 16

THE CONSEQUENCES OF WAR IN CITY AND COUNTRY

The tragic consequences of Rome's wars and conquests were evident in almost every phase of second-century life. Perhaps the areas where the effects were immediately and most devastatingly apparent were the Italian countryside and the related urban centers. The whole agricultural economy of Italy changed tremendously in the second century B.C., and the change was reflected in a complete transformation of the urban population.

DECLINE IN POPULATION.   During the third century B.C. Italy had supported a society of peasants holding small plots of land and using common lands for grazing. In such an economy a reasonably good-sized family had been important and necessary for labor, while any human surplus could be drained off into the colonies that had been part of Rome's early strategic policy. This surplus was no longer available. During the Second Punic War the physical losses in manpower had been staggering. The numbers of dead at just three Roman defeats, Trebia, Trasimene, and Cannae, ran to approximately 100,000. The census figures show a decline from 270,213 in 233 B.C. to 214,000 in 204 B.C., and this appears to represent not simply the loss of 56,000 males but of 56,000 complete family units. The other Italians, who shared the military burden and in whose territory most of the campaigns were fought, must have suffered losses proportionately grave. Further, most of these losses were from the farm population, for it was the peasantry that furnished the best soldiers. Instead of allowing for recovery, the policies of the second century B.C. led to further and almost continuous losses. The uneven records of history have left us a few figures for those slain in some of the battles and campaigns (between the years 201 and 151 B.C., approximately 95,000), but they do not account for the men that died outside the major battles, for the casualties in most Roman victories (the Romans preferred to give losses only in their defeats), or for those that succumbed to the diseases compounded by wars and military camps.

Another direct contributor to the decline of population was pestilence. Epidemics ravaged Italy in 187, 181, 180, and 174 B.C., with such high rates of mortality that minimum levies for the armies were raised with difficulty. And, whether from considerations of expediency, comfort, or despair, celibacy came to be practiced in Italy to such extent that the censor of 131 B.C. pleaded with the people to marry for the sake of patriotism and suggested compulsory marriage to ensure a future army. It is true that immediately after the Second Punic War there was a rise in the census figures, which reached 337,452 by 164 B.C.; but thereafter the decline was steady, and by 131 B.C. they had sunk to 318,823.

THE ABANDONMENT OF SMALL FARMS.   The destruction of property during the Hannibalic War had likewise been severe. Hannibal destroyed villages that he could not hold, and each side systematically ravaged the countryside in order to hamper its opponent's efforts. Whenever a district changed hands, the surviving citizens were prey to robbery, violence, and murder both by the departing troops and by the victors, since each side might suspect the residents of sympathy for their opponents. The result was that much land lay idle because the owners simply had disappeared, and much more land was abandoned soon afterward when discharged soldiers returned to find implements, farm animals, and buildings all swept away with nothing to replace them.

The policies of the government in the second century B.C. did much to worsen the situation. Nearly eighty percent of Roman government revenue was used on military adventures, while part of the remainder was allowed to lie unused in the vaults. No attempt was made to apply any of this to the recovery of the countryside. The soldiers were often held overseas for disastrously long periods of time. In 180 B.C., when the Senate bowed to the complaints of troops serving in Spain, they sent 14,000 replacements for the discharged and the dead, specifying that first right of discharge went to those that had served in Spain continuously for seven years. Clearly many of the soldiers' families did not survive such extended absences.

The disappearance of many Italian families during the Hannibalic War, the desertion of the land by the discouraged, and the wholesale confiscations of the property of those that had wavered—all this increased enormously the public domain at the disposal of the government at Rome. This land the senatorial class could exploit as it saw fit. And there was an immediate need to secure an income from it. The State's creditors from the Hannibalic War expected an early settlement, and the wars of the early second century B.C. required financing and were not immediately lucrative. An indication of the quantities of land that the State had available is signified by the transfer of 40,000 Ligurians from northern Italy to the abandoned lands of Samnium in 180 B.C. In such hilly country several hundred thousand acres must have been needed to support so large a settlement.

A whole new set of national and international factors, then, was making itself felt. A growing shortage of men precluded the use of the vacant land for widespread colonial or individual allotments, and we shall soon see that during this century such allotments became less and less economical. Further, by tradition the colonies were founded for strategic rather than economic reasons, and such as were founded in the second century B.C. were designed to hold the northern frontiers against the Ligurians and Gauls, or were placed along the seacoast out of fear that Antiochus the Great and his guest Hannibal might attack by water.

Though most Italians had been impoverished as a result of the Hannibalic War, there were those that had richly profited from furnishing war supplies to the State. Many businessmen saw opportunities for sound investment in the abandoned lands of Italy. There also were nobles that now were becoming wealthy while commanding in foreign lands. These men were not tempted to expand Italy's economic frontiers, for they had been reared in a tradition where only the plough and the sword made respectable professions. In fact, the Claudian Law of 218 B.C., forbidding commercial activity to senators, had forced them to the land to support their family fortunes.

However, the opportunities for making money from the land required different crops than in the past. In the past a small-time farmer could raise grain almost as well as a great entrepreneur, but this crop now was becoming unprofitable. In some places perhaps the soil was becoming eroded and less fertile, and at least in the markets of Rome there was some competition for local produce from the cheap grain that came as tribute from the provinces. True, individual families still could supply themselves, and there still were other municipal markets; but the cultivation of grain never had been enough. Peasants had always had to depend on some outside work to make a living, and the opportunities for this were fast disappearing.

THE RISE OF LATIFUNDIA.   On the other hand, the demand
for dairy and ranch produce for the city and the army, and the
growing popularity of the produce of vines and olive trees
furnished attractive new fields for investment. Investments in
these areas were made even more lucrative by new scientific
developments in agriculture and new sources of cheap labor.
Ironically, the wars, which were siphoning off the peasants and
free day-laborers, were furnishing at the same time quantities of
slaves for such large-scale enterprises. These slaves were cheap
and expendable: we read of 30,000 acquired at Tarentum, 150,-
000 from Epirus, 9500 from a single Spanish campaign; and
Corsicans and Sardinians were a glut on the market. The result
was the development of great estates (*latifundia*) either in the
form of plantations (*fundus*) or ranches (*saltus*). Obviously,
these estates could not be acquired by peasants or returning
veterans. Ranching required vast holdings that would provide
pasture in the mountains in the summer and on the lowlands for
the winter; and vineyards and olive orchards, though more
modest in size (anywhere from 60 to 150 acres), were equally
outside the competence of the poor. Thirteen persons were
necessary to care for an olive grove of 150 acres, sixteen for a
vineyard of sixty acres, and more labor would be needed at
harvest time. Further, vineyards need five years after planting
before they become fully productive, and olive groves need at
least ten. A substantial amount of capital was necessary, therefore, in order to produce these crops.

Soon after the Hannibalic War wealthy Romans began to
establish these large plantations in Latium. Here they accepted
public lands in partial payment of loans that they had made to
the government during the war, and they found it possible to
purchase quantities of private land and to rent even more from
the government. Appian, an historian of the second century
A.D., informs us of the result: "The rich obtained possession of
the greater part of the undistributed land, and, as time passed,
becoming confident that no one would ever dispossess them,
they absorbed the areas adjoining their own and the small
portions of the poor, purchasing some under persuasion and
taking others by force. And so they came to cultivate vast tracts
instead of farms, using slaves on them for laborers and herdsmen."

Latium was not the only area where this acquisitiveness
found expression. After the capture of Capua its territory, the
Ager Campanus, was confiscated and the bulk was rented to
entrepreneurs for exploitation, with the former owners providing the hired labor. This was the most fertile section of Italy,

and the government treasury had found in the rents from it one of its more dependable sources of revenue. Nevertheless, the encroachments of the rich on this public land were so successful that in 173 and 172 B.C. a consul had to conduct an investigation to recover appropriated lands. In 162 a praetor was commissioned for the purpose of buying back these lands for the government from their private usurpers—with public funds! Small freeholders could hardly hold out against the power that such wealth and arrogance commanded.

RANCHES AND OVERGRAZING.   While plantations were a popular investment by the wealthy, they did demand some care and supervision by the owners. Ranches, however, suited both politicians and businessmen better, for here supervision could be at a minimum, and the owners could remain in Rome to care for the affairs of state or their other business enterprises. Cato shrewdly observed that ranching was not only the first, but also the second and third most profitable way of exploiting the land. Vast tracts of the undistributed lands became, as it were, the private domains of the rich. Only one herdsman was needed for each 80 to 100 sheep, yet the number of slave shepherds employed became so great that conspiracies and rebellions soon arose among them. In 185 B.C. for instance, 7000 such culprits were condemned by the praetor. This lends credence to Pliny's assertion that some ranches supported as many as 257,000 sheep.

This exploitation of the land, especially in southern Italy, had a serious and permanent effect. The deforestation of the Italian hills and mountains had been proceeding for some time, and the subsequent cultivation of the hillsides had caused erosion serious enough to make farming less attractive and lucrative. Now the more profitable returns from ranching led the Romans, probably through ignorance, to put far too many animals on the land. In some cases four times the safe maximum were accomodated. The grass was too closely cropped, bushes and even trees were destroyed, root systems were damaged by the burning over of the pastures in the spring, and the sharp hooves of the numberless migrating sheep all hastened the denuding of the hillsides, the erosion in the valleys, and the formation by the siltage of malarial marshes along the coast. Lands once prosperous were speedily and permanently ruined, and such freeholders as may have survived the onslaught of the great landlords withdrew discouraged to search for a livelihood elsewhere.

THE FLIGHT OF THE PEASANTS; URBANIZATION.   Of course all the peasants did not leave the land. The eastern coast and Umbria were less affected by the advent of *latifundia*, and the small farm was still profitable near large centers of population, where truck gardens were in demand. But the pressures in southern Italy, Latium, and Etruria, continued to operate. The small farmer lacked money and materiel to improve his competitive position; the continuing flow of slaves shut him out from employment as a hired hand by which he needed to supplement the income of his small plot; and the army made constant levies for its unending wars. In fact, we now see more clearly one of the best reasons for Rome's reluctance to annex more territory after Spain: it was too difficult and too dangerous to raise and maintain the occupation armies to hold, police, and defend such lands.

Returning veterans often not only found their property encumbered by neglect and debt, but also they found the drudgery of the farm unattractive after the excitements of glory, travel, and pillage. Some of the dispossessed apparently left the country entirely; the area of northern Italy across the Po had been left to the Gauls with their own cantonal organization, yet it was very swiftly Romanized, which probably means that many Romans were willing to seek their fortunes in those richer though foreign lands. However, large numbers headed for Rome for the excitements and opportunities that the capital might offer. These migrants were not only Roman citizens; in 187 B.C. and in 177 the Roman authorities had to return numbers of Latin allies to their homes in response to the complaints of local authorities that they could not raise their required military contingents, because so many of their residents had run away to Rome.

These movements of populations greatly changed the nature of Rome, and undoubtedly lesser Italian states experienced similar changes. The tendency not to raise the status of Italian allies aggravated the situation; in 177 B.C., for instance, the Samnites and Paelignians complained that 4000 of their families had moved to the Latin colony of Fregellae.

The greatly increased wealth of the upper classes prompted them to a higher standard of living, and Hellenistic palaces with interior gardens, colonnades, decorative art, special dining rooms, kitchens, and bathrooms, began to replace the earlier simple structures of wood and stucco. The economic changes also increased the mass of depressingly poor, the proletariat. Construction in Rome could not keep up with this swelling population, which was huddled together in tenement houses that were without sanitation and in constant danger of fire and collapse.

THE NEW CLIENTAGE.   Rome attracted the disinherited, but it had little to offer them constructively. It never found through manufacturing an economic means to employ the growing population, and the throngs of slaves and freedmen monopolized such services for the rich as there were. The proletariat had to depend therefore on minimal employment and on such largesse as the ambitions of the rich dictated. And the rich, caught by the need to retain their status through elective office, found it expedient to furnish a minimum subsistence to many of these poor people in a sort of parody of the ancient patron-client relation.[1] Quantities of persons thronged the doors of the nobles accepting food, money, or invitations to meals. In return they enhanced the prestige of their patron by escorting him daily to the Forum, and strengthened his political power by supporting him at the polls. The nobles developed further popularity by furnishing entertainments by which these unemployed could while away their empty hours: elaborate private shows whenever funerals or weddings gave an excuse, or splendid public spectacles in theater, circus, or arena when as aediles the celebration of national festivals fell to their lot.

While the quarters of the poor in Rome did not keep pace with noble houses, the general appearance and comfort of the city in the second century B.C. was improved. Main streets were paved with hard lava stones, drains were covered, three public law courts were built in the Forum in the first half of the century—a bow to the litigious nature of Roman society—and in 144 B.C. a high-level aqueduct was constructed by the praetor, Marcius Rex. While not yet rivalling them in splendor, Rome was brought a little closer to the great cities of the East, Antioch and Alexandria, which she already outstripped in power.

The direction that Rome took in the second century B.C. in the settlement of agricultural and social problems was dangerous, for it led to developments that it would be increasingly difficult to correct by peaceful methods. Expansion within Italy had ended, but the Romans tried to continue their old habits and did not seek new solutions to the growing problem of poverty. Rich and poor in Rome had long had a tradition of conflict, but in the past the rich had sought to control the poor through loans, and when pressures on debtors became too severe, re-

[1]   For ancient clientage, see p. 47.

medial legislation had found satisfactory solutions before catastrophe could strike. Further, the impoverished had been settled
in colonies or on other allotments of land and started life anew
with a reasonable chance to make good. But now the competition of small farms with large ones was out of the question. A
relatively small group of wealthy men controlled large portions
of Italy, not simply because they alone could afford to exploit
agriculture lucratively, but also because they controlled the
government (they were the Establishment), and as the government they leased the public lands of Italy to themselves. Their
grip on the government constantly tightened, and they were
progressively better equipped to corrupt and control the poor
voters of Rome through bribery. It finally appeared that this
subversion of the interests of the commonwealth could be
corrected by little short of revolution. Further, the demands
made on the pocketbooks of the rulers by the people changed
the rulers' nature. Rome had long had a governing aristocracy,
which had been generally upright and reasonably disinterested.
Now, however, the demands on the governing class for services,
for food, for bribery, and for games — and the sumptuary and
bribery laws of the era attest the reality of these pressures —
changed that class from an aristocracy to a plutocracy with
altered standards of morality, interest, and deportment.

Chapter 17

INDUSTRY AND COMMERCE
AFTER THE HANNIBALIC WAR

NATIONAL REVENUE.   Thanks to the two military successes against Carthage in the third century B.C. and to a whole
series of conquests in the first half of the second century, Rome
and Italy became the recipients of great material wealth in the
forms of booty, tribute, extortion, and opportunities for lucrative
investment. It has been calculated that the government alone
received 610,600,000 denarii in the first half of the second

century B.C., and a great deal more found its way directly into private Roman cash boxes. To understand this amount of money, it is necessary to realize that the silver content of a denarius would be worth between thirteen and twenty cents on the American market in the mid-twentieth century. However, its buying power was enormously greater: one denarius would buy approximately as much wheat in the second century B.C. as fifty cents will in mid-century America.

The government's income, however, was not spent in a constructive way to increase the country's productivity. Instead, an estimated 472,500,000 denarii of the above income were spent on the military, and only about 20,000,000 were devoted to public works. Furthermore, the one-way flow of wealth—from conquered territories to Italy—inhibited the industrialization of Italy and the stimulation of healthy production for export. The very nature of the flow meant that Italy must be a buyer rather than a seller, and it never was able to break away from the economic pattern established in this period.

ROMAN ANTI-COMMERCIAL SENTIMENT.   By long tradition the Latins were farmers and shepherds and could not shake off a national disrespect for industry and trade. They early identified industry with foreigners. Far back in the regal period the Etruscans had brought many arts and crafts and various forms of commercial activity to Rome, and the Vicus Tuscus (Etruscan Quarter) became a center for shops and business activity. The Greeks always had excelled in commerce, and some of their colonies in southern Italy had grown rich while distributing fine manufactured goods in the peninsula. Under the aegis of Rome's Italian federation the Greeks of Italy were now beginning to enjoy especially favorable commercial opportunities throughout the Mediterranean. In the Roman mind the Carthaginians, of course, were associated most closely with mercantile interests. The Romans' equivocal feelings for the Etruscans, Greeks, and Carthaginians seem to have extended to the occupations in which these three peoples were especially skilled.

MANUFACTURING.   While there was some manufacturing in Italy, very little of it was Roman. In his *De Agricultura* Cato listed the places where the best farming equipment could be procured, and many of these were Greek and Oscan cities of Campania. Etruria still was productive, and articles of cloth, wax, iron, and bronze were made there. The mining of iron continued to flourish in Populonia, although the copper mining industry was beginning to decay because of the competition of Spanish copper. In central Italy, arms and implements for agriculture and building were manufactured. The slowness of transport (an ox-cart will travel only ten to fifteen miles a day) dictated the manufacture of cheap household wear and heavy equipment, such as olive presses, fairly close to their markets. Fine bronze ware continued to be produced at Praeneste, and this was a heritage of the long Etruscan occupation of that town. Campania was perhaps the most flourishing section. Capuan industry regained its preeminence after the setback of the Hannibalic War, and Pompeii and Puteoli were also important. All these Campanian towns manufactured cloth, terracotta, and rope; and the area commanded the materials, workmen, and craftsmanship to process iron and copper ore and turn out implements of excellent quality for household and farm.

CONTRACTORS AND INVESTMENT COMPANIES.   It is true that there was some Italian and Roman business life, but the average Roman citizens tended to leave manufacturing to others and found it unprofitable or unattractive to compete in small shops and businesses. Instead, typical Roman development in the commercial world took the peculiar direction of letting out many undertakings to be performed on contract. The State had no civil service or work force and had to contract for any work performed in its behalf, except for tasks undertaken gratis by elected executives and magistrates. Private citizens also frequently used this device, not only for undertakings such as gathering a harvest or erecting a building, but even for such a peculiarly private matter as settling an estate. With imperial expansion, the need for such middlemen increased. During the Second Punic War associations of financiers and boat-owners had been formed to furnish the necessary transport for men and supplies. The public works of the period, such as the new law courts, roads, streets, covered sewers, and aqueducts, were also built by such private associations. After the acquisition of possessions overseas even more elaborate organizations were necessary. Not only did certain taxes, such as port duties, have to be collected—and this required organizations equipped to undertake rather ambitious programs a considerable distance from home—but also some means had to be found to exploit the farms, forests, pastures, and rich mines that fell to the ownership of the Roman State by conquest.

In time, the exploitation of many of these opportunities fell to companies (*societates*) which were elaborately organized, with numerous shareholders. The major investment in these projects was in the hands of the moderately to very well-to-do class of knights (*equites*). By the Second Punic War there were about 12,000 such Romans. Legally these knights were of no different status from the rest of the population, but wealth, social position, and a sense of their special contributions to the State gave them a feeling of superiority.[1] However, the old established families (the Establishment) were very jealous of their claim to nobility, which was gained and sustained by election to the highest magistracies; and generally they managed to exclude men of recent wealth from attaining those offices (the consulship and praetorship). Therefore, in the late third century and throughout the second century B.C. the knights turned their energies to a development of financial enterprises. While the Claudian Law of 218 B.C., which forbade senators to participate in commercial undertakings, may largely have been prompted by a concern for senatorial dignity and impartiality, it also may have been enacted partly to please equestrian interests. It was not until the late second century B.C. that the knights were finally recognized as a special political force in the State, the *equester ordo*.

NEW OPPORTUNITIES IN COMMERCE.   Rome's expansion in the second century B.C. opened tremendous opportunities in trade and commerce for Roman and Italian businessmen. The conquests of Alexander of Macedon had already greatly expanded the contacts of the Aegean with the Near East and Middle East, and now the Roman successes in both East and West facilitated the exchange of goods throughout the known world. In the West the Roman denarius soon became the common means of exchange, and independent states with their own mints tended to alter their coinage sufficiently to make exchange easier, while in the East exchange depended more on the use of gold by weight. The wide involvement of Roman society in investments overseas brought about a spirit of mercantilism that permeated the Roman world.

Although Roman honesty and fairness in business dealings was widely acknowledged, and a Roman's account books were freely used as evidence in law suits, developing financial opportunities produced some less attractive features. Increase of family property was made a chief end in life. Gifts were viewed with distrust as indicating the tendencies of a spendthrift, legacies to nonrelatives were taxed, and everyone squeezed every ounce of advantage from contracts that he legally could. Even

---

[1]   For the knights, see also pp. 62, 83–84.

disputes of fact or honor were settled like commercial transactions by legal procedures borrowed from the world of loans and contracts.

As the empire grew, companies of investors became more and more necessary for handling large-scale business projects. Individuals learned to diversify their investments so that a disaster to a carrier or miscalculation by a contractor would be balanced by profitable returns elsewhere. This method, favored by the elder Cato himself, amounted to a sort of insurance, especially in shipping. While there was a considerable investment with the Roman State itself for its requirements overseas, even more ample was the need of fleets of transports to supply the Eastern states and Greece, which always was short of foodstuffs, and to bring home luxuries to which Italy was becoming accustomed. To supply these markets there were merchants specializing in imports and exports, as well as retailers, shipowners, leaders of caravans, and storehousekeepers. The number of specialized workers employed around docks or at anchorages was noteworthy—several kinds of stevedores or boatmen, depending on their methods of unloading cargo, and even divers, who were employed to recover materials lost overboard at debarkations.

The expansion of trade in the Mediterranean also affected the art of navigation. Lighthouses were built and harbors were improved. Instruments were designed to improve stellar navigation. Handbooks were prepared to guide travellers and businessmen around the harbors and trade routes of the Hellenistic world.

Ease of communication, at least in the eastern Mediterranean, was increased by the prevalence of the Greek language. A version of this language, the *koine,* the dialect in which the Christian New Testament is written, had become the lingua franca of the Levant. Many Italian merchants actually were Greeks from the ancient Greek cities of southern Italy, and the prevalence of their tongue made participation in this commercial world feasible and easy.

BANKING. The activities of businessmen abroad rapidly developed the field of banking, and soon there were houses that maintained connections with each other in many cities. Entrepreneurs could make deposits in any of these and obtain letters of credit on others. Closely connected with the banks and commercial houses were the moneychangers, who facilitated the interplay of international and local trade. The widespread operations of these various specialists in commercial transactions, whom the Romans lumped together in the term *negotia-tores*, led to a system of loans and credits that were available to Roman businessmen all over the Mediterranean. Moneylenders had even more lucrative clients in the governments of provincial municipalities. Many of the provincial cities in years of bad harvests were not able to pay their tribute to the Roman government when due, and they were forced to borrow. The returns on such investments could at times be scandalously high, but, at least in the earlier days of provincial government, the Roman governor exercised some control over the practices of the financiers within his area of jurisdiction.

The charge of high rates of interest on loans made in the provinces attests to a certain change in the Roman character. In an agrarian society, imponderables such as drought or flood had sometimes meant mortgages, foreclosure, and expulsion for the unfortunate, but profits for the lenders. In a closely knit society, repugnance for these consequences long counselled the Romans to establish severe penalties for usurious rates of interest. However, changing sensibilities, the distance of client-victims from their exploiters, and the very magnitude of the operations appear to have somewhat blunted Roman delicacy in this matter.

In the Roman portions of Italy itself, the Roman heritage and agrarian sentiment sought to control the rate of interest by keeping on the books laws that dated back to the fourth century B.C. Nevertheless, usurers had discovered a way of circumventing the law. They did this by making a fictitious transfer of their accounts to members of allied states, who were not legally bound by the Roman restrictions on rates. By 193 B.C. complaints concerning this practice became so great that all creditors in allied states were directed to make a public statement of their dealings with Roman citizens, and the debtors were allowed to choose to be governed by the laws of whichever state they wished in proceedings regarding loans. When the great extent of the practice was revealed, a plebiscitum was passed with the authorization of the Senate, imposing on members of the Italian confederacy the same law regarding the loan of money that applied to Roman citizens.

THE INFLUENCES OF THE BUSINESS WORLD.   How much the foreign policies of the Roman government in the second century B.C. were influenced by economic considerations is a matter of dispute. At times measures were taken which indicated clearly that the Roman government was unfavorable to Roman businessmen. After the conquest of Macedonia in 167 B.C.

the Senate voted to close the Macedonian mines, rather than work them, stating that the mines could not be exploited without the use of Roman contractors (*publicani*) and that wherever they were used the laws were subverted and the rights of the allies ignored. On the other hand, we must note that in one year, 146, Roman policy directed the utter destruction of two of the greatest commercial cities of antiquity: Carthage and Corinth. Some believe that these actions were taken as the result of economic rivalry, and were calculated to create a commercial monopoly for Italian businessmen, although the vindictive animosity of Roman leadership may equally have been the decisive factor. Even more noteworthy is the treatment of the commercial republic of Rhodes after the third Macedonian War (171 – 167 B.C.). The Rhodians had incurred intense Roman displeasure because they had offered to mediate in the dispute with Perseus. At the end of the war the Roman establishment of a free port at Delos quickly and thoroughly ruined Rhodian commerce, while it enriched traders and speculators that used the new facilities. One could reasonably suppose that the senators had some conception of what the effect of their action would be. The suspicion is increased when we learn that many of the Italian freedmen and slaves that controlled the lucrative slave-market on Delos bore the names of old and noble houses of Rome.

With its transformation into a free port Delos became the focal point of trade in the eastern Mediterranean. Much of our information concerning the commerce of the day comes from the archaeological and epigraphical remains found on the island. From Delos Italian bankers directed their international operations. Here goods were received from the East and transshipped to western markets. Slaves were gathered in enormous quantities to supply the demands of western mines, ranches, and other enterprises. One ancient authority stated that the port sometimes received, processed, and exported 10,000 of these unfortunates in one day, though this figure probably is exaggerated, if we can judge from the remains of the harbor's facilities. The benefits of all this activity were not widely shared; not only was Rhodes ruined, but Delos' own titular sovereign, Athens, received little or no benefit from it. Neither were the natives of the island enriched by the activity there: the wealth that passed through the island was chiefly enjoyed by speculators and profiteers.

Indeed, in the long run the acquisition of empire brought very little prosperity to Roman and Italian economy. There was greatly increased wealth for a few, but very greatly increased poverty for the many. Capitalists preferred to invest their money abroad for large returns, rather than in the economic improvement of Italy. The vast import of slaves that accompanied conquest further depressed the position of the freeborn. It has been estimated that a slave's labor for a year, including amortization and interest on the original investment, cost approximately 128 denarii. A freeman and his wife could scarcely support themselves on less than 300 denarii. This meant that the poor were deterred from raising families of a size that would maintain or increase the free population, and that no significant rise in the living standards of the laboring classes could be achieved. The situation that resulted was not completely unlike our own technological unemployment. The riches that poured into Italy, then, did not permeate society. Although the economy showed some aspects of capitalism, the discouragement of mass production and the ubiquity of slavery prevented the expansion and use of a healthy free labor force and a rise in the standards of living for farm people and city proletariat.

Chapter 18

FRIENDS, CLIENTS, AND PROVINCES

By the middle of the second century B.C. most of the Mediterranean world, excepting Mauretania, had entered some kind of relations with the Roman state. These Mediterranean peoples fall roughly into three categories, and each of these categories has an imperfect analogy, or perhaps pattern, in Rome's earlier relations with her Italian neighbors. There were friends and allies (*amici et socii*) of the Roman people; they were presumably the equals of the Romans, just as the Latins or the Samnites or the Carthaginians once had been. Then there were the protectorates or client states; they resembled the bulk of Rome's Italian allies in that they owed Rome various duties without any large compensation. They could, however, generally depend on Roman assistance in case of external aggression. Finally, there were the subject provinces, which consisted of annexed territory, most of it overseas. They were as helpless abroad as the defeated Capuans, Tarentines, or Veiians had been in Italy.

THE ACQUISITION OF PROVINCES.   The earliest subjects outside of Italy were acquired for want of a better solution. Probably the primary consideration both in the annexation of Sicily and of Sardinia-Corsica had been defensive, to see that they did not again become Punic strongholds. Similarly, the Spanish peninsula had been in the third century B.C. a source of wealth and manpower for Carthage, and after its conquest the Romans could not allow it once more to lie open to the enemy. But there followed fifty years of reluctance to add new territory, and various alternatives were tried before the annexation of Macedon (148 B.C.) and of Carthage's immediate environs as the province of Africa (146 B.C.). In the rest of the century there were added only Asia (129 B.C.), formerly the kingdom of Pergamum, willed to the Romans by its sovereign in the hope that his people would thus receive kind treatment; Gallia Narbonnensis (121 B.C.), organized to protect the highway from Italy to Spain; and Cilicia (102 B.C.), a nest of pirates that needed surveillance and correction.

EVOLUTION OF PROVINCIAL ADMINISTRATION.   In the beginning there was no real attempt to Italianize outlying possessions. In Spain, Scipio had given homes to some of his veterans that wished to stay there, and they formed a community which he called Italica. In 171 B.C. veterans with their native concubines were given a colony in Spain at Carteia, which enjoyed Latin rights. Although there was in this period no concerted program of colonization overseas, army camps inevitably affected the economy and habits of the surrounding natives through the channels of trade. Roads, such as the great military highway from the Pyrenees to Gades, encouraged commercial traffic. Further, the pacification of large underdeveloped areas made easier their penetration by Roman traders and businessmen, who inadvertently did much to prepare the Western provincials for later assimilation.

At first, Roman commanders abroad worked largely by trial and error to establish an adequate organization and administration in the new territories. We have already seen that immediately after the First Punic War (264–241 B.C.) the administration in Rome itself tried to govern Sicily from the distance and sent only quaestors to the island to maintain Roman interests there. But soon it had become clear that an official with *im-*

perium was needed, and two new praetors were added for the two provinces of Sicily and Sardinia-Corsica (227 B.C.). "Province" originally meant the sphere of action to which any official was assigned and it always retained that meaning, but it also came to have a geographical significance, referring to the area in which the official's actions were performed, and this is the more common sense in which it is used here.

At the end of the Second Punic War the territory won in Spain was added to the Roman system and organized (197 B.C.) as two new provinces, and two new praetors were elected annually to serve as governors. The rather unhappy experience of the Roman government with its governors overseas, and especially with its Spanish governors (who proved frequently to be irresponsible and venal), led the Senate to make some changes with the acquisition of Macedon in 148 B.C. It sent out to that newly conquered area a senatorial commission to draw up, in cooperation with the military commander, a charter for the province. This was the *lex provinciae*, the constitution of the province. It established the basic regulations for the province and defined the rights and duties of each of its communities. The venture was so successful that it was continued as new provinces were added. Later the governments of the Spains and Sicily were reorganized by similar commissions.

The bulk of the provincials were looked upon as surrendered persons, *dediticii*, at the disposal of their Roman rulers. They often were also referred to as *stipendiarii*—those who must assume the burden of paying the soldiery that had conquered and controlled them. Even as late as the first century B.C. Cicero referred to these provincial lands as *praedia populi Romani*, estates of the Roman people. But actually the Romans had neither the civil service nor the inclination to assume the detailed administration of their conquests. Therefore, wherever the systems or regulations of previous rulers had worked well, the Romans generally maintained them or modified them as little as possible. While the legal status of the subject communities differed, depending on past relations with Rome, the Romans found it wise not to tamper overmuch with local administrations. Only where a people was fragmented into an unmanageably large number of very small communities, as in Spain, did the Romans encourage the union of several of them into somewhat larger and more economical units.

TYPES OF CITY-STATES WITHIN PROVINCES.   In general the provincial communities can be grouped into three categories. There were some that had been allies of the Romans before

the Romans annexed their surroundings, and often they had
assisted the Romans in that annexation. These remained *civ-itates foederatae*, free allied cities, retaining the legal status
they had had before the Romans appeared on the scene. They
really were not part of the province in which they were situated
but were independent enclaves. Then there were cities that did
not have ancient alliances with Rome but whose cooperation
with the Romans merited special consideration. These became
free and immune cities, *civitates liberae et immunes*. Their
freedom and immunity were based not on treaty but on a grant
from the Roman Senate which could be revoked at any time.
The great bulk of the cities, however, were *civitates stipendi-ariae*, tax-paying cities without any legal rights, though in fact
they often enjoyed various privileges — at least the right to order
most of their local affairs. The situation in Sicily will give some
idea of the relative number of each type of community: in that
province there were three *civitates foederatae*, five *civitates
liberae et immunes*, and the remaining fifty-seven city-states
were stipendiary. A majority of this last group paid a tithe on
their land, but the land of at least a dozen was utterly confiscated
and made public property. It was rented by Rome to the former
inhabitants or to wealthy Romans, so that the occupants had
to pay a rent as well as a tithe.

THE ROMAN GOVERNOR.   The governor of a province was
usually an annually elected praetor with *imperium*. The con-stant and perilous conflicts in some areas such as Spain, how-ever, sometimes dictated the use of consuls as governors. As
heads of state they brought additional prestige and experience
to the task, though this also meant the neglect of their executive
duties in the capital. Roman willingness to experiment in these
matters is further indicated by the election of praetors for Spain
for two-year terms in the early second century B.C. because of
the distance of travel, though this experiment was soon
dropped. Instead, in the several new provinces added after the
middle of the second century B.C., administration devolved
more and more upon the promagistracy. This consisted of an
extension by the Senate of a magistrate's *imperium* beyond his
elected year of office. In other words, a praetor in Sicily could
rule the province a second year as propraetor if no one was sent
to replace him at the end of the year for which he was elected.[1]
This practice first developed during the Samnite Wars
(326–290 B.C.), but it had been widely developed in the Han-

---

[1]   See also pp. 143, 204.

nibalic War (218–201 B.C.), when many commanders had to be kept in the field for long periods, as for example the Scipios in Spain. A promagistrate legally was acting "as though he were" or "for" (*pro*) a magistrate, and he was outranked by a magistrate when they were together in the field.

The Roman governor united in himself all the functions of government. He was the chief administrative officer, the military commander, the source of new law, and the chief justice. He could be an unlimited monarch, though most governors had enough sense to take into consideration the restraints of custom and public opinion. Upon entering office the governor issued an edict stating how he proposed to handle the matters not specifically established by the *lex provinciae*. While in his province, as head of the administration, he supervised the relations of the units under his control to one another and to Rome. As commander-in-chief of the military forces he had to keep order within the province and defend it from outside attack. Such assignment could be very demanding, and it regularly was so in Spain. He also had to hear the important legal cases in his province, and all of those that involved Roman citizens. To do this the provinces were divided into circuits or *conventus*, and the governor sat for a period in the chief city of each. The acts of a governor were valid only for his term of office, but governors seldom tried to undo what their predecessors had done, and they often adopted from previous provincial edicts a great deal of the material that appeared in their own. The edict of the urban praetor, who presided in Rome over suits between Roman citizens alone, was also consulted by the governors in preparing their edicts, and thus a cosmopolitan mixture of Roman law and the local law of other Mediterranean peoples developed.

THE GOVERNOR'S STAFF.　　Also on duty in each province was a quaestor, elected annually in Rome. In Sicily there were two. The quaestor was supposed to be in charge of all financial matters, receiving and accounting for all government income and making such expenditures as were necessary. The quaestor could thus be a check on a rapacious governor, but by custom a quaestor was expected to regard the governor much as a son did his father, and this inhibited the quaestors' effective control. A governor also was accompanied by a number of *legati* or aides, appointed by the Senate but generally selected from nominations made by the governor himself. These aides could assist the governor in the performance of his duties or could be deputized to serve for him in his absence. With him travelled also a number of *comites* or companions, young men of good family who were learning the ropes of public life and were simultaneously looking for chances to pick up a bit of provincial cash.

TAXATION.   The provinces were looked upon as producers of revenue, and this attitude increased during the Republic. At first the legal justification for the taxes imposed seems to have been that they were compensation for the expenses of conquest, parallel to the indemnities imposed on Carthage, Macedon, and others after they had been defeated. Later the Romans looked upon provincial territory purely as property of the Roman people and upon the inhabitants as renters. It was not until the Principate that provincial taxes were justified on the grounds that they paid the expenses of each area's administration and defense. Of course, some land did become legally Roman: land that had belonged to the former rulers or had been confiscated from the recalcitrant was made *ager publicus* and was rented out. But the rest of the subject territory (as distinguished from allied or immune cities) paid either an annual fixed tax or a tithe of its produce. In general, the Romans followed the procedures already practiced by the former rulers. In provinces with a fixed tax there was no problem about collections, for each community raised its own share and handed it over to the Roman quaestor. In tithe-producing areas, however, the Romans found themselves with no adequate civil machinery, and they had to depend on contractors (the tax-farmers, *publicani*) to make the collections. These publicans were speculators. They bid for the right to pay to the State a lump sum representing the tithes estimated for a given area, which they expected to recoup by collecting a tenth of the crops actually grown. In years of good harvest they could make a sizeable profit, but in years of poor harvests the publicans were tempted to cut or eliminate their losses by exacting a greater share of the crops than the law specified.

The contracts in Sicily, which had a system of tithes, were let locally in each community and were generally bought up by local entrepreneurs. But large Roman companies of investors (*societates*) were formed to collect the indirect taxes there, such as the customs dues (*portoria*) or the fees for pasturage on public lands (*scriptura*). Other companies were organized to develop natural resources, such as the mines of Spain or the forests of Macedon. These companies of publicans were important and busy in the second century B.C., though they did not begin to make immense profits and to do immense harm until toward the end of that century. During his tribunate (123–122 B.C.)

187

Gaius Gracchus let out the collection of the tithes of the province of Asia for five-year periods. The whole contract was let to only one bidder, and the enormous bids for this monopoly were made in Rome, rather than in the province as in Sicily. The vast size of the sums involved in such a contract ruled out bids by the provincials and left the field to the huge stock companies of Roman businessmen. Thereafter Roman capital became ever more deeply and lucratively involved in provincial affairs.

EXTORTION.   Roman rule was onerous, but this was not because the tax burden was greater than it previously had been, nor because the provincials had lost any real freedom. Few Roman provincials had ever experienced real national freedom; and where freedom counts most, in local affairs, under Roman rule it continued much as before. The provincials suffered more from the misuse of the office of Roman governor. In his office the boasted checks and balances of the Roman constitution had disappeared. Here the only control now was self-control. In Italy, autocratic action by a magistrate was reduced by the right of a colleague to intercede in case of official irresponsibility, but in the provinces governors were almost sovereign. Further, the source of power and of policy, the Roman Senate, was distant and not unsympathetic to the governors' need to make money to recoup their losses in public service. The opportunities to extort, particularly through the control of the courts of justice and through the right to levy and billet, were very great. The opportunities of the Roman governor to do ill, however, were surpassed by those of the publicans. In no one's view were they responsible to the provincials; rather, they were accountable to the members of their *societates*, who expected good returns from their investments. The exploitation by the publicans often was compounded by the activities of bankers and other businessmen, who hurried to the provinces with loans at exorbitant rates of interest for those towns that could not immediately meet their financial obligations to the Roman government. The publicans and other Roman businessmen often used their influence with wealthy senators at Rome, who had hidden interests in their stock companies, to bring pressure to bear on provincial administrations. Hence, detachments of Roman legionaries might be called out to support the "legal rights" of Roman investors against the hapless natives when the gods, nature, and weather had failed them.

It is true that the victimized provincials could appeal. Their appeals sometimes caught the ear of a young tribune seeking political advancement, and he might haul the culprit before the

Tribal Assembly. However, this process was tedious and expensive for the plaintiffs, and the outcome was uncertain. Finally, the number of unsavory cases that stemmed from the consistent maladministration of Spain led in 149 B.C. to the passage of the Calpurnian Law, which established a standing court with a jury of senators to try such cases of provincial extortion. This law was later modified by a Junian Law, and then in 121 B.C. by the Acilian Law. We do not know the terms of the Junian Law, but the Acilian Law reflected a growing dissatisfaction with the frequently prejudiced decisions of senatorial juries in favor of the senatorial governors. The Acilian Law established instead juries composed of equestrians. These juries, it is true, did not spare the governors, but they proved in the long run just as corrupt as senatorial juries, for they conspired with the equestrian businessmen to perpetuate the merciless exploitation of the provincial taxpayers. The control of the standing juries for extortion remained an object of political contention to the end of the Republic.

There were a few other deterrents to completely autocratic behavior by Roman governors. The Senate could refuse to confirm the acts of the governor when he returned to Rome, though of course this was small restraint on a determined malefactor. Roman citizens living in a province often furnished a healthy influence; and for many provinces there were in Rome influential figures that served as hereditary patrons for foreign peoples. These were normally the men that had conquered the areas concerned or their descendants. Such men considered themselves responsible to look out for the provincials whom they had brought into the Roman system. Furthermore, it is inevitable that the names and shocking exploits of the great blackguards should have gone down in history, while we tend to overlook the great majority of administrators under the Roman system, who were really responsible men, or at worst merely innocuous.

It is clear, however, that there were important failures in republican provincial administration. There were three reasons for this: the short terms of the governors, which hindered them from developing any real concern or understanding for their charges; the imposition of an inequitable and unscientific system of taxation and collection; and, finally, an inadequate control of the provincial administration by the central government.

CLIENT STATES.   The development of a system of protectorates, or client states, overseas can perhaps be traced to Rome's experiences with its Italian allies, for while those states had been legally independent, yet they had certain duties or encumbrances in their relations with Rome. One of the chief characteristics of client states was that they were avowedly the inferior members of the treaty that bound them to Rome. The Aetolian League was one of the states legally so bound to Rome at an early date. This the Romans insisted upon after the war with Antiochus, because in their eyes the Aetolians had refused to slip gracefully and gratefully into a subordinate role after Rome freed the Greeks. Instead, the Aetolians had shown a quite un-Roman ingratitude toward their benefactor, and the Romans finally insisted on having in writing what the traditional Italian patron-client relation had led them to expect as natural. Carthage also was a client state by treaty after Zama, and Numidia was long the model one. Pergamum did very well in this role in the second century B.C., and for years Massilia recognized that its future lay in a deferential concern for Roman interests.

In Roman eyes client states had one great advantage over annexed territory. Client states situated on the edge of the Roman sphere of influence insured the protection of Roman interests against potential rivals beyond that sphere without requiring any great outlay of Roman men or money. Of course the success of a client kingdom depended on whether the area concerned already had some centralized and fairly stable government. One of the earliest examples in Roman history of a client state, Illyria, had filled this requirement, as did Massilia in the West, Numidia in North Africa, and also the kingdoms of Pergamum and Cappadocia in Asia. The fragmentation of Spain and the lack of any one strong prince there had made the solution of a client state impossible and was a factor in the Roman decision to annex it. The solution of the client state was tried in various guises in Macedon, first in subordinating Philip and Perseus to Roman purposes, later in the establishment of four free yet tribute-paying republics; but the resurgence of Macedonian nationalism forced the Romans in 148 B.C. to abandon their experiments.

The protectorate was a favorite device of the Senate. It meant that Roman manpower, the peasantry, which was melting away and was more and more reluctant to undertake arduous and ruinous overseas duty, could be conserved. It also meant that the Romans need not move armies into the field heavily weighted with the Italian allies, for there was a danger that increased Italian responsibility might stimulate increased Italian expectations of reward. It meant too that the nobility need not be enlarged by the election of more magistrates with *im-*

perium for administrative duty overseas. Roman businessmen were given special privileges in most of the client states, and were allowed to form special corporations or unions (*conventus*) in foreign cities to promote their special interests. In some client states, such as Numidia, Roman generals found it possible to arrange for the settlement of their army veterans on extremely favorable terms in a kind of irregular Roman colony, thus paving the way for the Romanization and ultimate absorption of whole territories.

Ultimately, the protectorate proved a poor substitute for direct control. Macedon was an early failure (149 – 148 B.C.), and the Achaean League and its allies insisted on unmasking Rome as their master rather than their ally (146 B.C.). Pergamum truckled and grovelled for years and finally immolated itself (133 B.C.). At length even Numidia under Jugurtha was to stir and give trouble (111 – 105 B.C.). All became more abject: some, like the Massilians, gradually sinking until they approached the level of the provincial subjects, others, like the Achaeans, after one burst for freedom, reduced perforce to that status.

However, despite its drawbacks and the lack of enthusiasm among foreigners for it, the Senate valued the solution of the protectorate in foreign relations because of its great economy. Though military ambitions and growing financial interests pressed the State toward annexations, client states were retained in some areas well into the Principate.

INDEPENDENT STATES.   In the early second century B.C. there were in the Mediterranean area a number of states that at least outwardly treated with Rome on equal terms; they were called friends and allies, or just friends. Macedon, Syria, and Egypt were once the foremost of these, but the lesser states of Greece and Asia Minor also held this status for a time. However, the second century saw the demotion of nearly all of them to an inferior class. By 148 B.C. Macedon had tumbled from friend to client to subject. Syria and Egypt were to all purposes helpless client states by the middle of the century. As Rome's power became disparate with her neighbors', her arrogance and impatience with them increased. At length in her eyes there was no difference between the highest and the lowest, so long as they were not Roman. It is a far cry from the declaration of Greek independence by Flamininus in 196 B.C., which showed an appreciation for the dignity of other, though lesser, men, to the destruction of an ally, Corinth (146 B.C.), a client, Carthage (146 B.C.), and a subject, Numantia (133 B.C.), alike in so short a time.

EFFECTS OF ROMAN CONTROL.   What did all this mean to the Roman world, external and internal? To the subject peoples it brought a degradation in status, much poverty, and misery. But it also brought slowly the development of a common culture, a common legal code, and ultimately a widespread and enduring peace. For the Italians it brought added burdens of service without commensurate recompense. Few were raised in status, and from their position of overwhelming strength Roman officials sometimes blandly ignored the treaty rights of the other Italians. However, an Italian sense of community of interest began to be stirred in this era, and this bore fruit in the first century B.C.

Rome's Mediterranean position was most destructive and demoralizing to the Romans themselves. The denizens of the city of Rome learned to expect, to insist on, subsistence and entertainment furnished by their subjects, with little thought for the justice of their demands or for the ill will that their callousness engendered. Roman rural manpower was sapped by the constant military demands upon it, while economic conditions in Italy made it difficult to maintain or reproduce that manpower. The Roman nobility's need for money and its cult of mediocrity consistently put incompetent and venal leaders into the foreign field. The consequent chaos in the administration of the empire was to lead the Roman assemblies to interfere in areas in which they had neither knowledge or competence. By the middle of the second century B.C. the great Roman sympathizer, Polybius, felt that the Roman, who had earlier been incorruptible, was now a declining moral figure. The absolute power that Rome enjoyed abroad corrupted, and its poison pervaded every class of the ruling race.

Chapter 19

INTELLECTUAL FERMENT

The Romans' successful wars against their southern neighbors and against Carthage in the third century B.C., and their rapid domination of the East in the second century B.C. had brought them into constant contact with older and more mature civilizations. The Punic, Greek, and Hellenistic civilizations with which they were in contact had long histories, profound literatures, and social and intellectual graces that silently indicted the rawness of their conquerors. But the conquerors longed for recognition and admiration. The income from their ventures overseas gave the Romans an affluence with which to humor the new tastes and new desires that they now had acquired. They set out, therefore, to seek and to create a history and a culture for themselves from such materials as they could find and such suggestions as others would give them.

SPREAD OF GREEK INFLUENCES IN ITALY.   The Romans had been in contact with the Greeks and with Greek civilization for a long time, both through the Hellenized Etruscans and directly through their neighbor to the south, Greek Cumae. As the Romans moved southward and added Magna Graecia and Sicily to their system, they became even more directly influenced by the Greeks. In the campaigns of the third century B.C. Roman troops had been stationed for long periods in the brilliant Hellenic settings of the southern Italian cities, and their officers had mingled with the local intelligentsias. Greek was rapidly becoming a second language for Roman nobles and, if we can judge from the purely Greek words and Greek derivatives used on the Roman stage, a good deal of Greek vocabulary became a part of the common language. Greek culture was, then, at hand to furnish the means with which the Romans could express their intellectual and emotional yearnings.

While the sights and institutions of the old world of Greece made deep impressions on Roman travellers, residents in Rome itself were also affected. The people could admire the numerous objects of art that arrived as booty, gifts, purchases, or the result of simple pilfering. After the defeat of King Perseus of Macedon in 167 B.C. his complete library was transferred to Rome. Many of the 1000 Achaean hostages that were quartered in Italy shortly after this, including the famous philosophical historian Polybius, were cultured men of affairs. Important philosophers visited Rome, including Crates of Mallos, who gave a series of lectures there in 159 B.C. while serving as envoy for Pergamum. Critolaus the Peripatetic, Diogenes the Stoic, and Carneades the Academic lectured in Rome in 155 B.C. while on an embassy from Athens. Somewhat later the Stoic, Panaetius, joined the circle of literary men around Scipio Aemilianus (the younger Africanus), the man that conquered and destroyed Carthage in 146 B.C. All these men opened Roman eyes to totally new intellectual experiences and new intellectual techniques. Most of the listeners were impressed and eager to participate, though some saw dangers for the ancient Roman ideals and character and vigorously disapproved.

ROMAN EDUCATION.   Roman education had originally been a practical one, and boys and girls received their training mostly at the hands of their mothers and fathers. Boys needed to become adept in military exercises and in the art of farming, and they also needed some knowledge of public affairs and preparation to support their views in debate. Public speaking was, therefore, very important, and much could be learned from the older members of the family or from its prominent friends. The talented Greeks, though, could display far superior rhetorical techniques and far greater cleverness in argument than earlier Roman orators. The Greeks also brought with them the idea of the school, with formal instruction under trained men. Many Romans recognized the advantages in public life that such training would bring, but Rome lacked the literary works and models to serve as vehicles for such instruction. This problem in education elicited diverse reactions. A conservative father such as Cato the Elder taught his children himself. He instructed them in Latin grammar, Roman law, and in the arts of boxing, swimming, riding, and fighting. He also composed a special Roman history for them, to impress them with the great deeds of their forefathers. However, a distinguished internationalist, like Aemilius Paullus, not only instructed his children in the field sports of the Romans, but also procured Greek masters to teach them grammar, logic, rhetoric, modelling, and drawing. One product of this curriculum was his son, Scipio Aemilianus, who was the center of the literary circle mentioned above.

The tastes that the Roman soldiers acquired in the third century B.C. while on service in southern Italy and Sicily soon stimulated at Rome the production of literary works that furnished a beginning for instruction in belles lettres. The troops had seen and enjoyed the performances in tragedy and comedy in the great festivals of towns like Tarentum and Syracuse; and by the mid-third century a former Tarentine, Livius Andronicus, had moved to Rome and set to work to satisfy Roman demand. He translated Homer's *Odyssey* into Latin, using the native Italian Saturnian verse, and this version continued in use as a schoolbook to the end of the Republic. He also translated Greek dramas for presentation at Roman festivals. His younger contemporary, Gnaeus Naevius, continued Livius' work by adapting many Greek tragedies and comedies into Latin. But he did more: he wrote dramas with Roman subjects, and he composed an epic in Saturnians on the First Punic War, in which he had participated. In this work of his old age (he died *ca.* 199 B.C.), as an introduction to his main account, he related the legendary origins of Rome. Thus he was instrumental both in the foundations of Roman historical literature and in the development of a national legend that would give the Romans the respectability that they craved in the family of nations.

LATIN LITERATURE OF THE SECOND CENTURY B.C.

The great impetus in the Hellenization of Rome and the first permanently influential developments in Latin literature took place in the second century B.C. From the first half of the century came our examples of Roman comedy. Twenty-one plays of Plautus (*ca.* 254–184 B.C.) and six of Terence (*ca.* 195–159 B.C.) have survived, and they illustrate the overwhelming influence of the Greeks in plot and characters, though there is considerable that is Italian in many of their allusions, their humor, and some of their situations. For our purposes they are of great importance, for they indicate the level of intellectualism and taste of the general public. A far greater popularity was enjoyed by the more vigorous, often farcical, and even bawdy Plautus than by the more humane, refined, and craftsmanlike Terence.

The greatest and most influential writer of the era, however, was Ennius (239–169 B.C.). He composed tragedies, comedies, historical dramas, and miscellaneous semi-philosophical or critical works. Most important was his account of the

195

Roman people in the *Annales*. In this epic he adapted Greek hexameter verse (the verse to be used by Lucretius and Vergil) to
the Latin tongue and glorified the Romans in an account of their
history from the legendary arrival of Aeneas to the wars of his
own day. He was considered the real father of Latin literature,
and later generations revered him. Ennius was the product of a
small southern Italian town, Rudiae, which was a gathering
place of three cultures, Greek, Oscan, and Latin. Here he absorbed much of Greek culture and was strongly influenced by
the rational and skeptical attitudes of local Greek thinkers and
writers. He was particularly impressed by the theories of Euhemerus, who had written a treatise showing that the gods were
not at all supernatural, but were once mortal men who later
were worshipped because of their beneficial deeds during life.
This work Ennius translated into Latin. The skeptical spirit also
appeared in his other works. As models for his tragedies he
preferred those of the cosmopolitan Euripides, who had
shocked Greek audiences with unconventional and rationalistic
views of god and man. Ennius' tragedies also contained sentiments about the deities that reflected the views of materialistic
philosophers, who denied all divine intervention in earthly
affairs.

EFFECTS OF GREEK LITERATURE ON ITALIAN RELIGION.
The preference on the Roman stage for the strikingly agnostic
tragedies of the Euripidean type was coupled with the popularity of smart and amoral comedies based on the Greek comedies of the day, filled with niggardly or lecherous old men,
wastrel sons, prostitutes, and scheming slaves. Together they
made a considerable impression on the Roman mind. True, the
tragedies generally were given very ancient or mythical settings, and the playwrights of comedies carefully placed their
un-Roman sentiments and situations in equally un-Roman
settings. These were thought to be sufficient precautions to
keep the people from applying the unconventional views and
morals of the Greeks to their own Roman world. Nevertheless,
the ideas presented on the stage soon became commonplaces
and radically changed the religious atmosphere among the
Romans.

There were, moreover, other factors to lead the ordinary
Roman away from a simple religious faith. Admittedly the
animism of the early Romans had led to no mythology and to
little moral commitment. Still, at least in the country, the need
for correct procedures in the presence of unseen powers and
the awe at these all-pervasive influences had strengthened the

feelings of responsibility and self-control. Now, as the State superseded the family, public officials were charged with the care of the "peace of the gods." While once the paterfamilias, surrounded by his women, children, and slaves, had made his peace with the supernatural powers, now the State officials performed rites prescribed by expert scientific theory, and theology laid its chilling hand on religion. At the same time Greek literature encouraged the identification of its anthropomorphic gods with the various Italian spirits, and these gods appeared in the guise of fallible human characters in song and story. In comedy they were even laughable and immoral. So, in Plautus' *Amphitruo*, Jupiter could appear on the Roman stage as a deceptive old lecher, and Mercury as a cunning slave.

The skeptical, rationalistic, or simply flippant views imported by philosophers, literary artists, and theorists were furthered by a growing realization among Roman citizens that State officials were manipulating State cults and religious practices for political purposes. To this period belong the Aelian and Fufian Laws, which allowed any higher magistrate to interfere with political meetings on the grounds that he had observed a bad omen. Further, the continued performance of ancient agricultural rituals as the official State rites alienated the city population, which now found them meaningless. The urban proletariat found little comfort in the propitiation of spirits that controlled mountain springs or vegetable rust, and its members turned increasingly to the emotional excitements of the more personal and sometimes orgiastic Eastern beliefs. One of these was the worship of the Great Mother Goddess, brought from Asia in 204 B.C. This involved colorful and exciting processions and the self-mutilation of devotees. At the same time there was a rapid spread of dark and secret celebrations by worshippers of Bacchus, and these seem to have included frenzied and ecstatic trances that sometimes ended in orgies or even murders. The enthusiasm with which these strange foreign practices were embraced in the first two decades of the second century B.C. denotes the economic, social, and emotional dislocations of the time.

THE HELLENISTIC PHILOSOPHIES AMONG THE ROMANS.
By the end of the first quarter of the second century B.C., a number of Greek philosophers had appeared in Rome as travelling lecturers or as ambassadors for some of the Greek city-states. Their extremely skillful use of the language won the respect of many Roman politicians, though the elder Cato and other conservatives were loudly hostile to the dialectics and

disputations of the various sectarians. Ambitious Romans speedily found attractive and expedient the systematic nature of the various philosophers' teachings, for they could be used to defend logically a number of different political postures. Soon they were listening eagerly to Greek slaves, wandering lecturers, diplomats, visitors, hostages, and members of literary coteries in the great Roman houses. In the second half of the second century B.C. effects of these studies were apparent in the speeches and political activities of a number of influential leaders.

EPICUREANS.   By 173 B.C. the Epicureans already had become sufficiently well known in Rome that the magistrates expelled two of their number from the city for fear of the consequences of their teachings. Gaius Amafinius translated into Latin the works of Epicurus probably around the middle of the century, and his work is said to have made a great impression throughout Italy. The Epicureans were materialists who had based their whole philosophical system on the theory that the universe was totally composed of countless atoms and infinite void. The atoms were conceived of as indescribably tiny; millions of them were required to form the objects of the visible world. These aggregations took place because of the natural affinities of certain types of atoms for each other when they happened to collide. Not only did individual atoms have natural affinities with other atoms, but their aggregates too had affinities for each other. For example, this explained the gregariousness of those great aggregations of atoms called men and the other social beasts. This concept led to a theory of social contract: men developed different social conventions depending on the differences of the circumstances under which they congregated. In each case, however, laws and statutes were established by men in recognition that they must surrender complete freedom of action in order to enjoy protection from the aggression of others. Laws varied with changing circumstances and were determined by a whole people's "pursuit of happiness." This Epicurean criterion of government found its way into the American Declaration of Independence through the influence of Thomas Jefferson, an avowed Epicurean. Some practicing Epicureans among the Romans followed their Greek master by a complete withdrawal from the political arena; but others, such as Sulla, Julius Caesar, and Cassius, were to take drastic, dangerous, and not wholly selfish measures to correct systems that they thought did not properly serve the contemporary situation.

SKEPTICS.   The Academic Skeptics were the liberals of the day. They taught that absolute certainty is nowhere possible, but they believed that constant study and experiment could bring men ever closer to Truth. Laws and institutions, therefore, would be constantly refined and improved as knowledge of society and its needs improved and, further, as the needs of society itself were modified. This sect had numerous distinguished adherents, and it was popular with jurists, for they could see how clarification, interpretation, and the use of legal fictions were actually extending the meaning of ancient legal texts. By these means early legislation, such as *The Twelve Tables*, could be made applicable in the complex business world of the second century. Two famous second-century jurists, Publius Mucius Scaevola and Publius Licinius Crassus, were probably of the Academic persuasion and, significantly, in the last third of the century we will find them supporting the earlier and more temperate legislation of Tiberius Gracchus, who hoped to improve the social and economic condition of the proletariat. In the first century B.C. the great legal orator, Marcus Cicero, claimed to be an Academic.

STOICS.   The school that naturally was most attractive to the Romans, however, was Stoicism. The Stoics believed that the basic substance of the world was fire which, in the burning, assumed the various forms of natural phenomena around them. The world was a great cosmic machine which began in fire and would end in fire as well. It went repeatedly through exactly the same cycles, and these cycles were always exactly the same because they were directed by Natural Law, or Providence, or the Deity, which permeated all things in much the same way that heat permeates a metal. Since this deity permeated all men, in some sense all men were brothers. There was, also, Absolute Law and Absolute Justice, which would be found when mankind conformed perfectly to the Stoic Natural Law. Stoic belief in the brotherhood of man and in a worldwide natural law gave a philosophical basis for Rome's growing empire and for her development of a law that was suitable for all races (the *ius gentium*). The idea of an all-permeating deity, whose purposes right reason must discover and follow, struck a responsive chord with earlier Roman animism. And the idea that the law of this deity was eternal and immutable satisfied a Roman hunger for material certainty. Moreover, the picture of the Stoic sage—virtuous, grave, decorous, imperturbable, and rather grim—was not unlike the idealized primitive Roman.

Devotees of this sect, however, could follow as curiously diverse paths as the Epicureans did. For example, in the mid-second century Laelius the Wise shied away from agrarian reform when opposition developed, for fear that he was upsetting the arrangements of Providence; yet later in the same century the Stoic teachers of Tiberius Gracchus are said to have inculcated in him his revolutionary ideas, which called for a more equitable distribution of national wealth among the citizens. The first century A.D. was to see in the Stoics the great party of the opposition to the Principate. They had no objection to a monarch, but held that he must be the "best man," the sage, rather than a person whose claims were merely hereditary. The second century A.D. finally witnessed in the person of Marcus Aurelius the marvel of a Stoic sage as emperor.

THE EFFECTS OF GREEK IDEAS ON THE ROMANS.   Exactly how deeply Greek culture penetrated at this time is problematical. Some nobles were genuinely well educated according to Hellenistic standards. Flamininus, who proclaimed the freedom of the Greeks in 196 B.C., was greatly admired by the Greeks for his knowledge of the Greek language and of Greek etiquette. Aemilius Paullus exhibited all the marks of a truly cultured man in that he gave his children a thoroughly Greek education; he treated Perseus and the defeated Macedonians with understanding and compassion; and he suffered the most severe personal misfortunes with philosophical equanimity. The young Gracchi, whose political leadership was to dominate the period from 133 to 122 B.C., received thoroughly Greek training also; and this seems to have been influential in the formulation of their unconventional political ideas.

Other examples, however, lead to reasonable doubts about most Romans' understanding of Greek culture. Mummius, the conqueror of Corinth, ordered his workers to replace any lost or mutilated masterpieces from that pillaged city with something just as good, as though superlative excellence could be assayed or reproduced by ignorant Roman soldiers. Lucius Anicius, the victor over the Illyrians in 167 B.C., assembled the most celebrated musical soloists in Greece for his victory games. He clearly preferred a loud noise to technical skill, for he not only made them all play in unison, but when this proved insufficiently amusing he forced them to battle or brawl. This the Roman spectators found pleasant and diverting. As for the commons, they became accustomed to Greek amusements and demanded them, but the more profound reflections found in the Greek originals disappeared or were eschewed. The smart ambiguities of Greek New Comedy about religion and private morals corrupted the ancestral Roman certainties about these matters; the religious and philosophical skepticism of their betters seeped down to them; and the spiritual hungers that rise from life on the pavements led to emotional excesses.

The growth of wealth and power in the second century B.C. also led to a greater concern for the individual than for society as a whole. Both the Hellenistic philosophies and the Oriental religions of the era were personal and egocentric. They concentrated on the questions, What am *I*? How can *I* be happy? How can *I* be saved? rather than on the problems and guidance of larger groups, such as the family or State. The interests of family fortunes were neglected for the sake of individual gratifications. For example, earlier a family's wealth had been carefully conserved for the good of all its members, and the law placed close controls on spendthrifts and the division of estates. Now, various legal subterfuges were discovered whereby women became emancipated from the control of the men of the household and thus could transfer their portions of a family's property to other houses.

Parallel strains appeared in the solidarity of the State—a number of prominent figures appeared to be putting their personal ambitions above the interests of the Republic. As early as 232 B.C. the tribune, Gaius Flaminius, had been thought to display demagogic characteristics when he rose to power by sponsoring such popular measures as the distribution of the Gallic land to the poor of Rome, and he consistently courted the people and challenged senatorial control down to his consulship and death in 217 B.C. In 216 a butcher's son, Gaius Terentius Varro, was believed to show similar tendencies by gaining the consulship through a popular and emotional attack on the delaying tactics of Fabius Maximus. Many persons thought that Lucius Marcius had set a bad precedent for ambitious leaders of the future when in 212 he allowed the soldiers to elect him propraetor in Spain without waiting for a senatorial appointment, even though he thus saved the Roman position in Spain after the defeats of Publius and Gnaeus Scipio. Further, the career of Publius Cornelius Scipio Africanus himself had set an ominous note, for he not only stood for the office of curule aedile before the legal age, but he presented himself for the proconsulship of Spain when barely twenty-four years of age. He was also the first private person to receive the *imperium*.

The precedents of the third century B.C. were followed in the second by an abundance of insubordination and lack of self-discipline. Two examples will suffice. In 173 B.C. the consul Marcus Popillius Laenas without provocation attacked a town of friendly Ligurians and killed or enslaved more than half the population. When the Senate called him to account, he arrogantly insisted on a thanksgiving rather than restitution; and though some recompense finally was made, family connections saved him from punishment. In 171 the Senate was surprised to discover that one of the consuls, Gaius Cassius Longinus, had deserted the post in northern Italy to which he had been assigned and was leading an army through the Balkans without anyone's permission in order to wage the current war in Macedon, which he coveted.

Individualism stimulated remarkable displays by private persons as well. In 179 B.C. the censors collected the funds and made the plans to construct a new aqueduct for Rome, but one Marcus Licinius Crassus would not allow the conduit to run across his property, and the project had to be abandoned. The examples set by leading men in Rome were bound to be reflected in the opinions and attitudes of the rest of the citizenry. The lessons taught by the nobles were reinforced by those shown on the stage. In the *Miles Gloriosus* of Plautus, one of the most sympathetic characters is an old bachelor who consistently argued that men should aim for pleasant lives of moderation and personal gratification, untrammelled by demanding wives and civic duties. Although this play portrayed an intrigue attributed to the city of Ephesus in Asia Minor, its message did not fall on deaf Roman ears. Cato the Elder saw the dangers for the State in excess of individualism, and his reaction appears to have taken the interesting turn of writing a history of Rome in which he failed to give the names of any generals in the wars that he described lest he glorify the individual, though he did record the exploits of Surus, the bravest of the Carthaginian war elephants.

ITALIAN ELEMENTS IN ROMAN CULTURAL DEVELOPMENT.
The intellectual developments in Italy were not entirely due to Greek influence or reactions to it. Latin was rapidly becoming the common language of Italy. While the early Roman historians, beginning around 200 B.C., wrote in Greek, partly to command and impress a wider audience, Cato composed his history, or *Origines*, in Latin; and he included in it an account of the development of other Italian states besides Rome. He also wrote a book on agriculture, which survives and which includes much native and practical wisdom. In the second half of the second century there were numerous histories, pamphlets, memoirs, and collected letters in Latin. At the same time there

also began the publications in jurisprudence that became an outstanding achievement of Roman culture. These included interpretations, commentaries, and the establishment of general principles from individual cases. In the plays of Plautus, although they were adapted from Greek originals, there was much of the native Italian wit and raillery that are clearly Plautus' own contribution. These same Italian traits were transformed by Lucilius (180–102 B.C.) in the last third of the second century B.C. into a new and distinct genre of literature, satire. It is characteristic of a people as it becomes more powerful and more self-confident also to become more self-critical. This often gives rise to a satirical spirit in literature, and at Rome Lucilius created a special form of poetry with which to unmask the crimes, follies, and deceptions of the day. His social and economic position as a Roman knight and his friendship for the Scipios gave him considerable personal protection, and he needed this protection as he lambasted the cultural pretensions and the serious political and moral shortcomings of his day.

The second century B.C. must have seemed to many, at least to those who were not hungry, a wonderful time, with its great clutter of new and exciting thoughts and things. There were dangers in these intellectual excitements, but probably very few Romans were conscious of them. It can be demoralizing for a young and immature culture to adopt wholesale the products, ideas, and practices of an older, mature, fully-developed society. The recipients tend to discard or discredit their own native customs and principles, yet the borrowed ones in their new environment do not carry the conviction, the feeling of "rightness," that comes with roots. In their wide acceptance of things Greek, the Romans neglected or suppressed many of the virtues that had been especially Roman. Few any longer possessed firm standards for either public or private deportment; and appeals to self-interest, partisanship, and violence threatened to replace the ancient sense of civic responsibility.

Chapter 20

THE POLITICAL AFTERMATH

THE SENATE IN ASCENDANCE. The Roman government emerged from the Hannibalic War (218–202 B.C.) with far less constitutional balance between its branches than there had been in the third century. The Senate's prestige and power had grown far out of proportion to its theoretical role as an advisory body. This was partly due to a need, during a long and hazardous war, for some compact and efficient body to make important decisions quickly. This task fell to the Senate, for the magistrates were absent in the field much of the time and could not see the whole strategic picture from their camps, and the assemblies were scattered in the armies all over Italy and Spain. This situation held true for so many years that it established patterns of conduct. The Senate also gained power because of the conspicuous success of senatorial policies and senatorial champions during the conflict, in contrast to the misfortunes of leaders of a more popular or independent bent, such as Gaius Flaminius, Terentius Varro, and Minucius Rufus. Part of the Senate's power was gained, then, through the grateful surrender by other branches of the State, and part was gently usurped in the face of continued crises and disasters.

The Senate's control over the magistrates was strengthened by its gradual assumption of the right to prolong the magistrates' terms of office. The expedient of the promagistracy had been initiated as early as 326 B.C. at the siege of Naples in order to keep the commanding consul in the field for another year.[1] The crises of the Hannibalic War extended the practice, and the prolonged campaigns overseas in the second century B.C. increased its value. As more and more administrators with *imperium* were needed in the provinces, it was natural to use more and more promagistrates. Since provincial governorships

[1]   See also pp. 143, 185.

could be made highly lucrative, the control of these posts gave the Senate a powerful tool of patronage. Through the subservience or long absence of many magistrates on duties of state, the Senate also slowly acquired most of the control in financial matters, which really belonged to the consuls and censors.

Moreover, the people steadily relinquished more and more of its constitutional prerogatives in the field of foreign affairs to senatorial direction. This was dictated by the increased complications in this field, as the government had to deal with scores of friends, allies, client states, and princelings all over the Mediterranean; and the Senate already had proved so successful in foreign affairs that the people's confidence in it was natural. When the assemblies did take an independent line, as they did when they at first refused to declare war against Philip (200 B.C.), they generally could be cajoled or frightened into submission. It is true that occasionally the Senate seems to have bowed against its better judgment to the people's appetite, as in the rape of Epirus (167 B.C.), which furnished the landowners of Italy with 150,000 slaves and netted the soldiers about two dollars apiece in booty, or in the sack of Corinth (146 B.C.), which benefited only the commercial class of Italy. However, the people did not venture to reassert itself in matters of high policy until there had been decades of mismanagement of foreign affairs, as in the case of Spain. The hegemony of the Senate rested firmly, then, on three activities: the control of the extension of magistracies, the supervision of finances, and the direction of the State's foreign affairs.

THE SENATORIAL ESTABLISHMENT.   The vehicle by which these senatorial powers were applied may be sufficiently described as the senatorial machine, the Establishment. The Senate was composed of most of the Romans with political experience, and its members were endowed with traditional prestige and privileges. With their prerogatives they could effectively direct and control the will of the people. This was because the people's assemblies had no initiative of their own, but could be convened only by magistrates or tribunes; and the magistrates were all "senatorial" men (or at least they could be played off against one another), while the college of tribunes was so large (ten men) that at least one member always could be found that could be persuaded to veto an offensive measure or to present one that the senators desired. Senatorial domination of officials meant, therefore, that almost invariably legislative proposals would be discussed in the Senate before they were brought to the people. Thus, even after the Hortensian Law of

287 B.C., the Senate had effective control over most legislation by the assemblies.

Senatorial control of electoral procedure was equally effective. The nonsenatorial wealthy, usually found it to their interest to vote with the senatorial class, and since the two groups accounted for nearly half the centuries in the Centuriate Assembly, the senators could almost always be sure of a compliant slate of officials. The rich could also use their wealth to good effect to influence doubtful tribes, as the passage of several anti-bribery laws in the early second century B.C. attests. They also made use of a less specious form of bribery in providing elaborate public and private entertainments, which gained great popularity for the generous when they were candidates. This practice also engaged the sincere but ineffective attention of reform legislators of the day. Candidates could check on the "honesty" of their voters too, for it was not until the thirties of the second century that the secret ballot was introduced, which first allowed the proletariat to sell their votes, but not deliver.

For the governing class the censorship proved an important prop, for its power of patronage was immense. The censors were generally elected from among the most distinguished representatives of the senatorial Establishment, and they controlled the letting of huge contracts for public works and for the tax-farming overseas, while their decisions were not subject to popular review. Any danger of tyranny or of the use of censorial power against the Senate's political interests, however, was obviated by the collegiality of the office, for the censors had to agree before making any important change in a citizen's status.

Not only did the Senate control most legislation by its domination of the magistrates, who introduced the bills to the assemblies, and by a thorough discussion of most bills before they were introduced; but also the decrees of the Senate itself (the senatusconsults) came to be regarded almost as legislation. Technically, of course, a senatusconsult was only the advice of the Senate to a magistrate. It seems, however, that the presence of the plebeian tribunes at the Senate's meetings after 287 B.C. increased the authority of senatorial decrees. It was presumed that if an opinion was expressed in the Senate which appeared to be contrary to public interest, one of the tribunes would veto it. The lack of such veto, therefore, was taken to imply public approval. As a result, senatusconsults were allowed to hold in areas where only measures by the assemblies had been considered valid. Further, the people were given the illusion that they controlled legislation, because ambitious tribunes always could be found to present government measures to the people for their ratification.

The people's self-esteem was further increased by the Porcian laws of this era, which extended the ancient right of appeal. Romans in Rome had enjoyed the right to appeal to the assemblies against harsh sentences by magistrates ever since the beginning of the Republic. Now this right was granted to Romans in the provinces against governors, and apparently even to Roman soldiers. However, if democratic action in the assemblies should get out of hand, the Aelian and Fufian Laws of the mid-second century B.C. provided for interested interference. These laws allowed any magistrate to suspend a Tribal Assembly if he observed unfavorable omens, and unfavorable omens were not hard to find when the interests of the Establishment were threatened.

NOBLE FACTIONS.   While it is possible to speak of a senatorial machine, this term does not apply to all the senators. There were cliques and factions within the Senate itself, wheels within wheels, that dominated and directed that body over the years. The Romans never had political parties in the same sense that we do, and even the terms "popular" and "conservative" were not used in any exact sense. At the center of the Roman factions were the great families, which for reasons of patronage and pride were anxious to control the elections and the government. Some of the families concerned were the old patrician ones that had been active since the earliest Republic, but others were those great plebeian houses that had benefited by the attainment of the highest magistracies since 367 B.C. This was the new nobility of office, a patricio-plebeian nobility, which could be attained only by a person that had been elected to a higher magistracy, and it could then be passed on to his descendants. It had arrogated for itself distinguishing dress and jewelry, the right to display portraits of the family's ancestors (*ius imaginum*), and reserved special seats for its members at public functions. Its families intermarried, and became more exclusive with the years. Between the years 232 and 133 B.C. fifty-eight families accounted for the 200 consuls; 159 of them came from only twenty-six families; and 99 of them from only ten families.

Important blocs or alliances of these great families had begun to emerge in the third century B.C. Most noteworthy among these was one which was a combination of Claudii, Sempronii, and Fulvii; there was another of Aemilii, Livii, and Cornelii; and a third centered around the Fabii, who cooperated with a number of other families, including some prominent Italo-Roman ones. Such familial factions attempted to control the higher offices of State, partly because of the prestige and dignity that resulted for their houses, partly because control of the business of the State offered opportunities to improve the family's financial position after years of unpaid public service. Though there might be rivalry among these great families, generally they all would unite against newcomers and the dilution of the spoils of office.

To control the electorate each faction had a nucleus of support in its own clients, freedmen, and fellow tribesmen. In the second century B.C. the migration of many impoverished rural tribesmen to Rome meant that important blocs of voters in the small but numerous rural tribes were always present, available for meetings, and susceptible to generous public banquets and handouts, to elaborate games, and to judicious bribery. The great families of Rome enjoyed an immense advantage with tribesmen that hailed from the areas where their ancestral estates were located.

No clearly defined programs can be confidently assigned to the factions. True, the Fabii tended to be isolationists, but the family of Flamininus, the great Hellenist, was a member of that group. The reformers and independents of Cato's following also pursued the isolationist line. On the other hand, the Cornelius Scipios tended to be internationalists. None of the groups, however, clung to the slogans of their factions if the demands of expediency or of national interest dictated caution.

Even during the national emergency of the Hannibalic War dynastic rivalry had its place. The Cornelii were prominent in the earliest years of the war; the ill-fated popular bid of Flaminius and Minucius came next; and the Fabii and Claudii dominated the slow recovery of the State after Cannae. The Cornelii, with Scipio Africanus at their head, bid fair to be Rome's preponderant family in the late third and early second century B.C. Still, Scipio was an indifferent politician and he was unwilling to use his unexampled popularity to attain an unconstitutional position. Nevertheless, his already unorthodox public career caused concern, and a combination of the frightened, led by Cato the Elder, and of the jealous rival houses made life in Rome miserable for this extraordinary man, and he was forced into retirement after the war with Antiochus.

For a long time there was little opposition by the people to factional control. As long as the government was efficient, successful, and not blatantly corrupt there were few murmurs. This was especially true when the appeal to the people at elections gave them the comfortable feeling that they were in control. Further, the appearance and reappearance of many of the same old names as candidates for high office was not so much a cause for dissatisfaction as for a feeling of security and pride. The illusion of popular control was heightened by the use of complaisant tribunes to introduce to the Tribal Assembly for ratification measures that had been initiated by senatorial debate. We have evidence for twenty-two bills passed by the Tribal Assembly between 200 and 133 B.C. that seem to have been introduced *ex auctoritate Senatus* (with the Senate's prior approval). Though the presiding officers at the passage of these bills might be tribunes, the highly legal and technical nature of many of them indicates that older senatorial heads were the prime movers. Indeed, tribunes became so devoted to senatorial authority that in 188 B.C. four tribunes actually vetoed a measure because it lacked the senatorial *auctoritas*. This bill had been introduced by another tribune, and it granted citizenship to three Latin towns. Their tribunician veto was not withdrawn until it was explained to the four docile officials that the grant of citizenship always had been a prerogative of the people, not of the Senate, and that senatorial authorization would be improper. We know of four other tribal bills during this period that failed to pass just because they lacked senatorial backing. The only anti-senatorial plebiscites of which we have record during the first two-thirds of the second century (and this includes the two providing for the secret ballot at elections and on juries) had the strong support of the Scipionic faction and clearly reflect the jousts of that ambitious and exceptional family with the other, more conventional senatorials.

DECAY UNDER THE ESTABLISHMENT.   The first restlessness against the Senate started with the farmers, on whom the burdens of warfare fell and whose economic position grew ever more precarious. Cato the Elder was their hero, and the archaism and isolationism exhibited by the measures taken under his guidance—the blue laws, the laws against bribery and luxury, the extension of the laws of appeal, and the censure of egregious wealth or ambition—reflect his and their ideals. However, these early suspicions and doubts of the Senate were as nothing compared to the disillusionment with the upper classes that was to come. As all effective Mediterranean rivalry collapsed, the Roman State and Roman leaders were left with no manifest need for self-control. This seems to be the reason why Scipio Nasica always countered Cato's famous "Carthage must be destroyed" with "In my opinion Carthage must be preserved." More prescient than Cato, Nasica felt that the Romans needed a rival to save themselves from their own uninhibited ambition. Already the third decade of the century had seen the reckless selfishness of Popillius Laenas, who attacked inoffensive Ligurians for glory and loot, and the insubordination of Cassius Longinus for the same reasons regardless of public policy. Many Roman families, riding high at home and unfettered abroad, felt free to exploit and plunder, and squabbled with each other only over the spoils. Those that pondered the heritage of unselfish patriotism among ancient Roman heroes were troubled by what they now saw around them.

Meanwhile the economic distress of the Italian peasants forced more and more of them to increase the impoverished rabble of the city, and freedmen swelled the tide. Many joined as "clients" the factions of the great families. They supported their patrons with their votes, but they too had wants that must be filled. In foreign affairs the reaction to those wants may be seen in the demands for brutal expansionism, for the unconditional surrender and the extermination of foes. In the world of diplomacy and war, where they had absolutely nothing to venture, the proletariat could take the vicarious satisfaction of being an imperial people; and from the arrogant exactions that Rome made overseas came their parties, pageants, and bribes.

The economic, social, military, and political developments of the early second century B.C. created a demoralized citizenry led, at the best, by mediocre men—and, at the worst, by scoundrels. The Centuriate Assembly, which elected to the highest offices and determined war and peace, was dominated by the two upper financial classes, senators and knights. Both groups developed increasingly strong interests in opportunities to plunder overseas. The Tribal Assembly, the body more frequently used for legislation, found that under ordinary circumstances the majority of the voters present in each of its component tribes were members of an urban proletariat. They were the disinherited and displaced onetime farmers of Italy, and their votes more and more reflected hungry irresponsibility. The mediocrity of leadership was furthered by the mutual suspicions and jealousies of factional rivalry. The oligarchs of the Senate deflated war heroes by refusing them triumphs, withholding extensions of command, and finding legal harassments for any that evinced independence, initiative, or superiority. The dictatorship was abandoned after 202 B.C., partly because the people had insisted as early as 217 to a right to interfere in what had once been the purely senatorial prerogative of appointment, and partly because the next seventy years saw no crises that demanded it. When later such a crisis did arise, the Senate showed its fear of great men by voting extraordinary powers (by the *senatus consultum ultimum*) to the consuls, its regularly elected presiding officers, whom it completely dominated, instead of reviving the dictatorship. The suspicion and fear of individual excellence and of any disturbance of the equlibrium between the family factions led to the passage of the Villian Law on minimum age requirements (180 B.C.), which blocked early or rapid advancement in the course of offices, even in the case of outstanding ability, national interest, or popularity. Similarly, around 150 B.C. legislation was obtained completely forbidding reelection to the consulship. Indeed, a special law had to be passed to exempt Scipio Aemilianus from the provisions of this bill so that the popular executioner of Carthage (146 B.C.) could carry out the same assignment at Numantia (133 B.C.).

Sallust, a historian living in the first century B.C., called the first two-thirds of the second century B.C. a period of political harmony. And so it was, at least on the surface. The satisfaction of appetites, the income from war and subjects, the complacency of success, and the astute manipulation of electoral and legislative machinery kept most criticism silent. It is probably true that the clumsy apparatus of the small-town constitution of Rome needed some kind of authoritarianism to handle the multiplied problems of empire, and this was furnished by the Senate. However, the senatorial Establishment was not simply efficient; it also blocked all attempts to reform and improve that constitution, because reform threatened its prerogatives. Improvement certainly was needed, for the uninhibited exploitation of the conquered and the plundering of the inoffensive were demoralizing an appreciable portion of the leaders and of the people with whom they shared the spoils, and were scandalizing the rest. Yet the reactionary reformers, such as Cato, by their nationalistic fervor carried their hatred of a Carthage or Corinth to such an extreme that their heartless actions equally undermined moral authority. The thoughtless and undisciplined political and economic exploitation of success in the seventy years after the Hannibalic War took the Roman Republic a giant step toward ruin.

PART
Five

The Disintegration of the Republic

Chapter 21

THE GRACCHAN EXPERIMENTS IN REFORM

THE PROBLEMS.   The period in Roman history dominated by the political careers of Tiberius Sempronius Gracchus and his brother Gaius (133–122 B.C.) was decisive in the destruction of traditional Roman government and character. The social, political, and economic developments during the second century B.C. had created a number of dangerous and mutually aggravating problems: the free peasantry of Italy was in decline; the armies, which depended on the peasantry, lacked recruits; the slums of Rome were swollen; and the great estates which depended on slave labor were on the increase. Committments abroad demanded more and larger armies, and their successes intensified Italy's economic and social problems, for they rendered more and more slaves available and furnished the wealthy with greater fortunes with which to exploit them. There was little prospect for reform as long as the republican government was dominated by senatorial families unwilling to surrender their economic and political advantages, while their constitutional position seemed impregnable. The problems were involved and volatile, and any attempt to resolve them seemed destined to promote strife.

The efforts of the Gracchi to cope with these problems were strenuous, but they proved a disastrous failure. The gap between the privileged and the exploited in Italy was already wide and rapidly widening, and the Gracchi did little to heal the breach. Their programs and the countermoves of their opponents did, however, set precedents in political methods and objectives that were to dominate and madden the Roman world for the next 100 years. Their efforts perhaps hastened the substitution of a nondemocratic government based on power for a government based on prestige and tradition.

AGRARIAN AND MILITARY DECLINE.   Rome's successes in the second century B.C. had led to a rapid decline of the free peasantry. The agricultural economy of Italy, developing along the most profitable lines, now had small room for the family farm. Military adventures had forced away, lured away, or decimated the peasants of the small farms, while countless slaves had replaced them as the laborers of Italy. As the country folk melted away, a hungry urban proletariat increased—hungry because industrialization did not accompany urbanization, and such employment as the city offered also fell largely to the large numbers of slaves and freedmen. Since the Romans believed that only citizens with property should be asked to undertake military duty, they now saw the fountainhead of their armies drying up. And armies were constantly needed, if not for war, at least for the police actions that empire demands. The problems, then, were military, economic, and social, and all these were aggravated by the increase in slavery. All these problems needed attention, but the problem of slavery presented instant and insistent danger.

SLAVE UPRISINGS.   The second century had been a great century of slave-taking and it had been repeatedly shaken by slave uprisings. In 198 Setia in Latium was the center of a conspiracy by African slaves; in 196 a legion was required to quell outbreaks on the great Etruscan plantations; and ten years later 7000 slaves were condemned to death in Apulia. Right after the middle of the century 450 slaves were crucified at Minturnae, and troops had to be called out to crush a revolt of 4000 slaves at Sinuessa. Residence and travel in remote areas became more and more dangerous. Although laborers on plantations frequently worked in chain gangs and were confined in underground barracks at night, the herdsmen had to be left free to tend their flocks, and they were thus able to avenge themselves on lone Romans. Nor was this always discouraged; in one case, at least, a Sicilian nabob, whose slaves showed him their rags, asked them if travellers in their districts didn't wear coats.

It was at Enna in Sicily in 135 B.C. that one of the most dangerous slave revolts broke out. A small initial outbreak of only 400 men spread rapidly. Workhouses were opened and shackles removed; and at length 20,000 under their slave generals disputed with Roman armies for Sicily, until the consul of 132, Publius Rupilius, finally wiped them out. This war was in full career during the tribunate of Tiberius Gracchus (133 B.C.) and was a constant reminder to the government of the gravity of the slave problem.

EARLY MOVEMENTS TOWARD REFORM.   The teachings of Greek historians and philosophers led many prominent Romans

216

to observe their own dilemmas with a critical eye. As they became more conscious of the world around them they saw warnings of disaster everywhere. They knew that in their rise to power they themselves had taken advantage of the slave-oriented governments of Etruria. In their struggles with Carthage they had conclusive proof of the superiority of a free patriotic peasantry in the formation of a national army. Polybius, the teacher and confidant of the great in this era, consistently pointed out to them the important part that depopulation had played in the decline of Greece during the third and second centuries.

A number of eminent men believed that corrective action must come soon. These included Appius Claudius Pulcher, the *princeps senatus,* and the jurists Publius Mucius Scaevola and Publius Licinius Crassus. Some of these men had been influenced by the teachings of Carneades and the Skeptics,[1] and even had heard Carneades' lectures, and they were committed to a program of moderate reform carried out by constitutional processes. Some of their political opponents, men who were moderate conservatives, such as Gaius Laelius, Scipio Aemilianus, and the censor of 131 B.C. Caecilius Metellus, also recognized these pressing problems. As praetor in 145, or perhaps as consul in 140, Laelius had proposed to the Senate that some action should be taken to return the Italian countryside to health. We do not know the details of his proposal, but the harsh criticism of it by the moneyed classes taught that Stoic worthy to recognize the workings of Providence,[2] and he prudently withdrew his suggestion.

After the middle of the century liberals moved in other ways to emancipate the voters from the grasp of the vested Establishment. In 145 they presented a bill to replace cooptation to the priesthoods by popular election. This was defeated, but it revealed an understanding of the importance of religious interests in maintaining the conservative position. In 139 a Gabinian bill was successfully passed establishing the secret ballot at elections, and in 137 a Cassian law extended this to trials. Here a blow was struck to free the poor voters from the menaces of their betters. Furthermore, as early as 149 B.C. a Calpurnian Law had established courts to try errant governors, which showed a growing sense of responsibility toward the empire's subjects.

THE GRACCHI. FAMILY HERITAGE AND EDUCATION.
The first organized attack on Rome's economic and political problems, however, came in 133 B.C. under the leadership of

---

[1] For the political views of the Skeptics, see p. 199.
[2] For the curious inconsistencies of Stoic political thought, see pp. 199–200.

Tiberius Sempronius Gracchus. Both on his father's and on his mother's side (she was Cornelia, daughter of the great Scipio Africanus) there were ancient traditions of high principles and of service to the State. A great-uncle, Tiberius, as consul and general had treated the slaves that volunteered after Cannae with a wisdom far above the average of his nation. Tiberius' great-grandfather, also named Tiberius, had achieved fame as the defender of the common man when he fined a haughty patrician lady, a member of the Claudian *gens,* 25,000 pounds of bronze for speaking disparagingly of the plebs during the First Punic War. Tiberius' uncle Publius had collaborated with the elder Cato in attacks on dishonesty in public life. Tiberius' father, still another Tiberius, had demanded such high standards of conduct from his fellow citizens, showed such magnanimity and good faith to his colleagues, and displayed such kindness and honesty to the conquered Spaniards that he was regarded as the friend and protector of citizen and alien alike.

The eminence of the Sempronii was more than equalled by the Scipios. Cornelia loved to reminisce about the great deeds of her father. Scipio Africanus had indeed been a great and patriotic man, although his attitude throughout his life toward the nobility and consitutional custom was highly unorthodox. Not only did he enjoy special dispensations from the people in respect to age and the *cursus honorum,* but also personal popularity and fame allowed him to depend on volunteers and free contributions in order to make his invasion of Africa. Close to the end of his life, probably in 187 B.C., when he and his brother Lucius were called to account in regard to booty taken from Antiochus, he was so outraged by the inquiry that he took the rolls of accounts which he had intended to deposit in the treasury and tore them to pieces before the senators' eyes, saying that he, the man to whom Rome owed its salvation, would not so degrade himself. Such actions were of heroic proportions, but they also were rich and heady fare for young, impressionable minds.

Formal education, too, may have had something to do with Tiberius' way of thinking. Cornelia had procured the services of Diophanes, known as the most learned Greek of his day, and of Blossius of Cumae, a Stoic philosopher, to educate her sons. Blossius' influence on Tiberius and later his relations with a communistic slave-rising in Asia lead us to place him among those thinkers that drew communistic, or at least socialistic, inferences from the Stoic theory of the "brotherhood of man."

EARLY EXPERIENCES OF TIBERIUS. Tiberius had been a young companion of his cousin and brother-in-law, Scipio

Aemilianus, at the siege of Carthage. He could have observed the strength and weaknesses of that unhappy land and seen that Carthage had grown rich from well-kept farms and commerce but had been weakened by its dependence on slaves and mercenaries. Thereafter Tiberius had become quaestor for the unfortunate Mancinus before Numantia in 137 B.C.; and his father's great reputation in Spain had enabled Tiberius to secure the release of the Roman troops captured there.[3] But his peace treaty had been abjured by the Senate, and only his popularity with the grateful people had saved him from being surrendered to the Numantines along with Mancinus, naked and bound. Such an experience did not inspire his confidence in the nobility. Further, his initial trip to Spain had taken him through Etruria, and he had taken special note of the disappearance of free laborers there and had pondered on its importance; and upon his return anonymous placards appeared on the city walls, calling on him to remember his family's traditional service to the people.

THE TRIBUNATE AS THE INSTRUMENT OF REFORM.
Tiberius was not yet thirty when he ran for the tribunate. For a young and enthusiastic reformer the tribunate had certain advantages over other offices with which to inaugurate a program of land reform.[4] A tribune could initiate legislation by convening the tribal assembly, and he did not have to undergo first the years of political activity that the praetorship and consulship required. Also, the tribunate had developed in its early days as the office that defended the oppressed and dealt with early agrarian problems and therefore its ancient traditions recommended its use. To a young Roman with a Greek education the glamour of Periclean democracy also was great. In Athens a popular official elected annually (such as Pericles had been) had contrived to lead and control the government by his prestige with the assembly of citizens. At Rome the tribunate must have appeared the office that could be made to approximate the civil aspects of Pericles' position in Athens.

INITIAL AGRARIAN PROPOSALS.   Soon after his induction into the tribunate in December 134 B.C. Tiberius took counsel with those outstanding liberals that were concerned with the decline in the small farmer class and the rise of an economically unstable urban proletariat. From their assessment of the situation there emerged a program than which, says Plutarch, "no

[3]   For Mancinus' surrender at Numantia and the elder Tiberius Gracchus' exploits in Spain, see pp. 158, 165.
[4]   For the early history of the tribunate, see pp. 55, 90.

milder or gentler was ever devised in the face of such injustice and greed." There was already on the books the ancient Licinian-Sextian Law of 367 B.C., which had limited the exploitation of public lands to no more than 500 *jugera* per person (approximately 300 acres), but it had not provided for allotments of surplus public land to the poor. Tiberius' proposal called for the surrender of all state-owned lands above the limit of 500 *jugera*. Estates up to this limit, however, were to be retained as the permanent property of the former possessors, and in addition these possessors were to be allowed 250 *jugera* apiece for each of their sons. Further, the former possessors were to be paid a just valuation for all improvements that they had made on surplus lands now to be recovered by the State. Needy citizens then were to be settled on the recovered properties. The offer to reimburse the possessors for lands that they held illegally may appear unusual, but we must recall that the State had found large leases desirable and had encouraged them right after the Second Punic War, and also that precedent for reimbursement existed in the payments made in 162 B.C. to recover Campanian lands.

THE SECOND AGRARIAN BILL.   The wealthy immediately began a campaign of vituperative propaganda, accusing Tiberius of revolutionary tendencies and threatening to block the passage of any such measure by the use of the veto. For this purpose they secured the assistance of another tribune, Marcus Octavius. Tiberius delivered speeches in defense of his views and used public and private persuasion to gain the Senate's cooperation. But the opposition was adamant. Tiberius therefore dropped his first proposal and brought in a bill that merely reaffirmed the Licinian-Sextian Law, stating that this would be enforced. To it was added a provision to allot to the poor lands now illegally held by the rich. For individual allotments there were numerous precedents in Roman history going back at least to the early fourth century B.C. and to the annexation of Veii. The new bill was far less liberal to the former possessors than Tiberius' first suggestion, for it contained no provision for reimbursement by the State. Naturally, Octavius also promised a veto for this bill. While legally the great landholders had a poor case, in equity there was something to be said for them. In the early second century the government had encouraged their occupation of abandoned lands, for it then had needed an income from them. The law had developed interdicts to protect their possession of those lands, so that they felt that they had certain proprietary rights to them. They had with assurance bought farms adjoining their leaseholds or even enclaves within their holdings, and these had often lost their identity. Such property now held ancestral graves, and had been used as dowries and as security, so that in this respect subversion of credit was threatened. Although a strict interpretation of the established law, then, was against the great landholders, one can understand their distress and can see why Cicero constantly refers to the proposed legislation as revolutionary, almost as confiscatory, which it certainly was not.

Since argument and entreaty failed to move the nobles and their champion Octavius, and since each time an attempt was made to read the new bill to the assembly Octavius forbade proceedings, Tiberius tried a different approach. He proposed to the Tribal Assembly that Octavius be deposed from office on the grounds that he was not fulfilling the historic purpose of a tribune, protecting the interests of the plebeians. The deposition was thereupon effected. Although Tiberius' action may not have been strictly unconstitutional, it certainly signified a new conception of the relation of the people and their elected officials, who had always been treated as invulnerable during their terms of office. It had features that puzzled the ancients as they do us. It is curious that Octavius did not use his veto in this matter that so conspicuously concerned himself, or that other tribunes of anti-Gracchan sentiment did not do so. Apparently Tiberius' contemporaries, lacking precedent, did not know what to do.

With a new and friendly tribune replacing Octavius the agrarian bill was passed and became law. A commission of three members was elected to supervise the recovery of the surplus possessed lands, to act as judges in disputes about boundaries and titles or the actual legal status of properties, and to superintend the allotments. The first board elected consisted of Tiberius, his younger brother Gaius, and his father-in-law Appius Claudius. To ward off early discouragement among the settlers or attempts by the rich to resume their possession, this time by legal purchase, the allotments were made inalienable, at least for the moment.

The commission's activities entailed considerable expense for surveyors, investigators, and clerks. However, the Senate, which controlled the purse-strings, resolved to hamper the work as far as possible by allowing a mere pittance for expenses. It was, therefore, fortunate for the commission that Attalus III of Pergamum died at about this time and left his kingdom by will to Rome. Tiberius thereupon threatened not only to use the income from the bequest to facilitate the work of settlement, but also to refer to the assembly the whole matter of the organization of the new acquisition, which the Romans called the province of Asia. The threat to interfere with the Senate's monopoly of foreign affairs and finance appears to have effected a change in the Senate's attitude, for the work of the commission went ahead, though a revolt in Asia under the leadership of Aristonicus interrupted the organization of the province and the receipt of any income from that quarter for several years.

DEATH OF TIBERIUS GRACCHUS.   In view of the intense hatred that his activities had engendered, Tiberius decided that he must stand for a second tribunate in order to enjoy the personal security needed to carry out his duties. This was not unconstitutional because the tribune, as a plebeian official, did not come under the law forbidding the repetition of magistracies. But it was contrary to recent custom, and a barrage of rumors and innuendoes concerning Tiberius' tyrannical aspirations whipped the conservatives into such a frenzy that, under the leadership of Publius Scipio Nasica, they clubbed to death Tiberius and 300 of his supporters on election day. Thus for the first time in republican history blood was shed in an internal dispute. Shortly afterward the consuls of 132 B.C., Popillius Laenas and Publius Rupilius, were authorized by the Senate to investigate Tiberius' "conspiracy," and they self-righteously executed, fined, or exiled a number of citizens, apparently without allowing their victims the right of appeal guaranteed to all citizens. The excitement and frustrations of political partisanship might lend some slight justification for the massacre on election day, but further senatorial persecution of Tiberius' supporters after there had been time for calm deliberation was an appeal to lynch law that was an evil precedent for future political action.

THE WORK OF THE AGRARIAN COMMISSION.   Tiberius' opponents preferred to maintain that their dispute was with his political aims and methods and not with the people that his program benefited. The agrarian commission was allowed to function, and vacancies on it were filled by persons sympathetic to its purposes. We do not know just how much land was recovered nor how many people were settled, but there are indications that a considerable amount was done. Some of the boundary markers put up by the commission still exist and ancient writers on surveying indicate that they once were very frequent and very useful. Literary evidence also indicates considerable activity. There was a rise in the census between 131 and 125 B.C. by 76,000 family units, though for decades the figures had been stagnant or declining. This rise could have been caused by the emancipation of their sons by patresfamilias so that they would be eligible for the allotments contemplated by the commissioners.

The complaints of the Latin and Italian allies at this time also indicate that the commission was very active. What worried the allies were the suits initiated to determine the boundaries between Roman public land and their own allied territory and the danger that they might lose the use of that surplus Roman public land that they had been allowed to farm or otherwise exploit for a very small fee. They appealed for help to Scipio Aemilianus, who knew well the importance of the allied troops in the Roman army. He contrived the transfer of judgments in cases involving allies to a consul, probably on the grounds that such matters involved treaties and foreign relations and were outside the competence of the commission. This transfer severely limited the amount of land available for recovery, for the consul assigned, Sempronius Tuditanus (consul 129 B.C.), preferred to march off to war in Illyria as soon as he saw the difficulty of his task, and the suits and acquisition of land from the allies ceased.

All liberal and popular sentiment was not dead with Tiberius, however. The people's anger turned on Scipio Aemilianus, their former darling, because he condoned Tiberius' death; and the mystery of his own sudden death in 129 B.C. has never been solved. Scipio Nasica, though made pontifex maximus, was hurried out of the country on an embassy and died in Pergamum. Papirius Carbo, a tribune of 130 B.C., continued the work of the previous decade by extending the use of the secret ballot to the legislative assemblies. He did not succeed, however, in passing legislation for the right of reelection to the tribunate, which would have vindicated Tiberius' second candidacy.

DISCONTENT AMONG THE ALLIES.   The decade after Tiberius' death saw an abortive but important attempt to improve the lot of the allies. Some action in this area was long overdue. As the empire had expanded and Rome's own eligible soldiers had decreased, the burdens placed on the allies had increased; yet at the same time the increased value and prestige of Roman citizenship made both nobles and people less and less willing to share it. No advances in status had been enjoyed by allied states since 188 B.C., and it also was becoming more and more difficult for individuals to advance. Increasing signs of Roman arrogance were especially irritating to the other Italians. Instances were noted of a smaller share of the booty for allied troops, of smaller allotments of land for Latin settlers, and of high-handed treatment of natives by Roman officials passing through their towns. The nervousness of the allies was increased when the agrarian commission began to scrutinize their lands. In view of Italian complaints, the consul Fulvius Flaccus, who was also a member of the agrarian commission, suggested an improvement in the status of both Latins (to Roman citizenship) and Italians (to Latin rights), or the grant of the right of appeal to any communities that preferred to remain free and allied rather than accept a change in status. By this provision Flaccus recognized the need for protection of all Italians against the outrages of irresponsible Roman magistrates. But the whole proposal was coldly received by the people, and the Senate intervened and diverted Flaccus by sending him off to Gaul to protect the allied city of Massilia. The allies were disappointed, and one Latin town, Fregellae, noted in the past for its fidelity to the Roman cause, broke into open revolt. Fortunately for Rome, the town was betrayed before the rebellion spread, and the place was destroyed by the praetor Lucius Opimius as an example to others. But the warning to Rome was also clear and was disregarded only by the willfully blind.

Meanwhile conflict had raged for some time in Asia, where a pretender to the throne of Pergamum, Aristonicus, had appeared before the Romans could fully organize their bequest from Attalus III as a province. While the Greek commercial cities of the coast were cool to revolution and preferred the Romans, the serfs and slaves of the interior rallied to Aristonicus and under his standard created a communistic state. Interestingly enough, in his retinue was Blossius of Cumae, who had been Tiberius Gracchus' tutor and who had escaped the senatorial vengeance after Tiberius' fall. So enthusiastic were the insurgents and so unprepared the Romans for any resistance anywhere that it took from 132 to 129 B.C. to reduce their new possession. Campaigns were also launched to quell unrest among the Illyrians (129 B.C.), in Sardinia (126 B.C.), and in the Balearic Isles (123 B.C.).

GAIUS GRACCHUS, TRIBUNE (124–122 B.C.).   Gaius Gracchus, Tiberius' younger brother, had gone out with the governor to Sardinia in 126 B.C. as his quaestor; but by 124 he was convinced that he was being kept abroad deliberately by political opponents. In that year, therefore, he returned to stand for the tribunate, although his superior, the governor, remained at his post. After fending off investigations regarding his premature return to Rome and the suggestion that he had a sympathetic involvement with revolted Fregellae, he was successful in his campaign for office.

Gaius was more intelligent than his brother and more dangerous to the established order. His experience with the agrarian commission and his early political career, which had been spent in the glare of his brother's tragedy, led him to analyze and plan as Tiberius never had. No certain chronological account of the legislation of his two terms of office (December 124—December 122) can be constructed, but his laws reveal a consistent program: to continue the improvement of the economic and social health of town and country, to create a dependable political front that could successfully contest supremacy with the senatorial Establishment, and to secure a satisfactory solution to the problem of the allies.

First, however, there was need to vindicate his brother's career. One of Gaius' earliest measures reaffirmed the right of Roman citizens in capital cases to appeal to the assembly and, unlike the earlier laws on the subject, Gaius' law now specified the penalties to magistrates that denied such right. The consuls of 132 B.C. recognized the portent and went into exile. Another bill of Gaius would have denied to any official removed from office by the people the right to seek another elective position. Such a law would have affirmed the constitutionality of Tiberius' deposition of Octavius and would have validated the completely new concept that an unpopular tribune could be deposed by an accuser and an aroused Tribal Assembly. However, since the bill appeared to be directed against a single man it was withdrawn before a vote.

Another early measure of Gaius provided that the State furnish troops with their military clothing and forbade the enlistment of youths under seventeen years of age. These provisions reveal the lowered qualifications for the army in property and age that the decline in rural population and average wealth had forced upon the authorities.

THE GRAIN LAW.   The grain law of Gaius Gracchus was one of his most important accomplishments, for it aimed to transfer to the State from rich patrons and political aspirants the responsibility for keeping grain on the market at a fair and steady price. The law provided that a stated amount of grain, approximately five pecks, should be made available to every Roman each month at an established price. This price was set at six and one-third *asses* per peck.[5] All male citizens appear to have been

5   For the buying power of Roman coinage, see Appendix.

equally eligible regardless of property qualification. Political opponents, and later writers have tried to label this program a dole or, at best, the charge of only a nominal fee. This probably is not so. Records for prices of grain in this era are scanty, but such as there are indicate that this was a fair market value. Further, it must be remembered that much free grain came into Roman hands through tribute. Some of this would be needed by the armies, but a part would have been sold to entrepreneurs who then made a profit on the resale. The State now proposed to pass along a saving to the consumers. Gaius had before him numerous examples in Hellenistic states where the care for an orderly market was a duty of the government; and in Roman history examples of governmental intervention and purchase of foreign grain in times of dearth went back to the fifth century. Now, by the construction of large granaries along the Tiber, grain could be procured in great quantities in years of good harvest and stored against disappointing harvests.

What Gaius aimed for was a steady supply of grain at small expense to the State. At the same time, however, the measure had a grave political purpose. Despite the popularity of Tiberius' activities and despite the laws instituting the secret ballot, Tiberius had had to depend for support on rural, rather than urban, voters; the nobles still controlled the proletariat's stomach. So great was this power that in 124 Gaius, despite his family's reputation, was elected only to fourth place among the ten tribunes. "But by this one measure," Appian (a Roman historian of the second century A.D.) tells us, "he quickly gained control of the people." By this law Gaius proposed to ensure henceforward an independent urban electorate. The abuses to which the program later was put cannot be wholly charged to Gaius—they develop in any government service where the rulers and ruled are both corrupt.

AGRARIAN AND COLONIAL LAWS.   Gaius also was responsible for a new agrarian law. This may seem odd, since he was himself an administrator of his brother's still operative measure, but the Romans frequently brought in a new measure when modification was needed in a previous bill. Such had been Tiberius' own agrarian law, which merely extended the Licinian-Sextian Law of 367 B.C.. What was new in his agrarian law is not clear, though we have frequent references to it in later legislation; but it may well have regularized the position of allied possessors of Roman public land and permitted continuation of the work of the agrarian commission, while still protecting various special, and especially allied, interests.

Gaius also followed precedent in establishing colonies.

Earlier colonies had been largely strategic, though they were bound also to have social and economic effects. Now Gaius proposed to establish them simply for these secondary effects. In Italy colonists were dispatched to Tarentum, Scolacium, and Capua, sites that once had been important industrial and commercial centers. These did not contain just drainings from the proletariat; some members of moderate wealth also were enrolled so that the new colonies would have the advantage of their investments and business experience.

Even more unusual was the decision to establish a colony on the site of Carthage. The site had contained one of antiquity's most prosperous trading centers, and its choice dramatizes the commercial aspect of Gaius' plans. He was conscious that Carthage had grown great through a combination of strong commercial and agricultural components, and the colonists there were granted estates of 200 *jugera* to be held with the same full legal rights as in Italy. For this establishment Gaius enrolled 6000 colonists, not only from Rome, but from all Italy. This implied the recognition of Italian as well as Roman problems in economy and population and, perhaps, constituted some recompense to the Italians for the resumption of state domain and for their disappointment that their legal status as allies remained unimproved.

THE EQUESTRIANS BECOME A POLITICAL FORCE. Despite his reelection to the tribunate for 122, for which constitutionally no new or special law had been necessary—only a complacent presiding officer—Gaius needed firmer support than the urban mob. The wealthy, if they voted together, still had tremendous influence in the tribes and could control the Centuriate Assembly. He determined to break this solid front while providing efficient solutions to administrative problems by detaching the wealthy equestrian businessmen from their community of interest with the senatorial nobility.

The organization of the province of Asia offered an opportunity. Because the will of Attalus had specified freedom for many of his former cities, the taxation of Asia had been haphazard and irregular. Now Gaius imposed a regular system of tithes on the whole area. He also specified that all the tithes of Asia for a five-year period were to be auctioned and sold at Rome at one time. Clearly provincial business associations were not financially able to compete in such an enormous undertaking. This put unlimited means for expansion in the hands of the businessmen of Rome. The equestrians were, of course, grateful to their benefactor for these new opportunities for investment.

A number of recent scandalous decisions by senatorial

juries in trying cases of extortion by provincial governors furnished a further opportunity to honor Rome's wealthy equestrian class. At first it had appeared to Gaius that a sufficient remedy for corrupt senatorial juries was to make the members liable to prosecution for bribery. Later, however, it seemed expedient to transfer the membership in juries entirely to the equestrian class. Since these men could be considered disinterested, the antibribery clause was not included in the new arrangement. Perhaps Gaius could not be expected to foresee that the knights might use their control of the courts to persecute any senatorial governors that threatened equestrian business interests in their provinces, but he knew well that he had irrevocably separated the senators and knights and created in the latter a community of interest that was to make them a third force in the State.

OPPOSITION TO GAIUS TRIUMPHANT (122–121 B.C.).
Gaius was now the most important man in Rome and his continuing leadership seemed assured. But he had to seek a solution for the problem of the Latin and Italian allies, and on that issue his great coalition foundered. All of his support was, in fact, selfish support, and herein the senatorials descried his weakness. Two could play at the game of detaching supporters from the opposition by adroit legislative programs, and the Senate found a clever agent in Livius Drusus the Elder, one of the tribunes of 122 B.C., and an unblushing spokesman in Gaius Fannius, the consul and a renegade Gracchan. With the Senate's blessing Livius set out to cap Gaius' proposals with measures that would be more appealing to the proletariat. He countered Gaius' three commercial colonies in Italy with a proposal for twelve colonies for which there would be no financial means test and which would receive exclusively 3000 of Rome's poorest citizens. The allotments of land made under the Gracchan land laws still commanded a small rental. These Livius would wholly remove. Livius also vetoed Gaius' proposal to give Roman citizenship to the Latin allies and Latin rights to the other Italians, merely offering Latin soldiers immunity from scourging by Roman officers. But Fannius surpassed Livius in demagoguery by delivering a speech in which he warned the city folk that an increase in the number of Roman citizens would jeopardize their good seats at shows and festivals. The Roman equestrians too could see nothing but danger for their own interests in the grant of civic rights to their Italian competitors who were numerous and prosperous. And the colony at Carthage, the establishment of which Gaius was himself then

supervising, offered plentiful opportunities for denunciation, rumor, and innuendo. Gaius' enemies asserted that citizen colonies outside of Italy were contrary to custom, and they pointed out that the number of Greek daughter colonies that ultimately outshone the mother was frightening! They were shocked at the idea of a settlement on the accursed site of Carthage: reliable witnesses there had seen wolves tear up Gracchus' boundary stones with their teeth and lug them away! They whispered too that the inclusion of Italians in the foundation of the colony was but a surreptitious way of awarding to them Roman citizenship.

By the time that Gaius returned he could not recover lost ground. The people were indifferent to his political objectives and downright antagonistic to the bill for the Italians. And so Gaius was defeated in his bid in the fall of 122 B.C. for a third term in the tribunate. At the same time Lucius Opimius, the cutthroat that had wiped out Fregellae, was elected to the consulship. The new year of 121 B.C. found the Establishment busy repealing Gracchus' laws. At one session a fracas took place in which an attendant of the consul was killed. Overjoyed at the opportunity to wipe out the Gracchans, the senators directed the consul to "provide that the State shall receive no harm." The Gracchans hurriedly armed themselves and took up defensive positions on the Aventine Hill. The Senate's decree, which later was frequently used and received the technical description of a *senatus consultum ultimum* (ultimate decree of the Senate), legally did no more than assure the consul of the Senate's moral backing. But the senatorial party henceforth claimed that it amounted to a declaration of martial law and a suspension of the civic right of appeal in the face of avowed enemies of the State. In this case, Opimius organized a posse and hunted out and killed up to 3000 Gracchan supporters. Gaius himself fell by the hand of one of his faithful slaves. The Senate thereupon directed Opimius to construct a Temple of Concord to celebrate the return of harmony to the State.

THE PLACE OF THE GRACCHI IN ROMAN HISTORY.
The Gracchi have received radically divergent judgments throughout history, judgments that frequently more clearly reveal the ideological persuasion of the judges than the actual significance of the Gracchi for the future of the Romans. There is no question as to the patriotism of the Gracchi or as to their complete dedication to their country's health. Dispute arises over the wisdom of their programs and the methods that they chose to effect their aims.

ARCHAISM.   Tiberius Gracchus idealized the past. He saw the social and economic conditions of an earlier age through a golden haze and he tried to impose them on his world. There is no question that the earlier conditions were the heathier and more vital, but it also is certain that social and economic man of the late second century B.C. was far removed from his predecessor of the early Republic. To impose an antique mould on modern man was dangerous. We shall see Sulla trying to do the same thing in the political field a half century later with equally explosive and unsatisfactory results. No matter how many Romans Tiberius put back on the land, as long as there were military demands on the peasantry and the economic conditions of the Mediterranean world stayed the same, Italy would quickly return to the state in which he had found it—differing only in having experienced the frustrations that come from unnatural change.

IMMATURITY.   Tiberius' agrarian law shows that a long and patient process of education and propaganda was needed. But Tiberius was so carried away by the utility of his project that he paid small heed to the difficulties with which it was surrounded. If both the Gracchi had paid as much attention to the successful methods of earlier Roman statesmen as they did to their social and economic ideals, they would have found that perseverance, self-control, and forbearance were of the greatest importance. They would have realized how shocking to the average citizen is departure from precedent and established custom, even when such departure is not illegal or unconstitutional. Youthful impatience and arrogance led them to neglect the expedients that their predecessors had shown to be most effective.

LOSS OF CHECKS AND BALANCES.   Theoretically Rome had lacked for a century and a half any constitutional check whereby the rights of minorities or the long-term policies of the State could be protected from the precipitate whims of the plebs. In practice, however, such a check had been present in the control that the administrative body, the Senate, could usually exercise over some of the tribunes. This does not mean that popular measures never could be passed, but if they clashed with senatorial interests or with senatorial perspicacity, the electorate had to be firm enough to ensure the election of a board of tribunes completely sympathetic to its wishes. The business of government did not, therefore, depend on the changing passions of a city mob. Tiberius Gracchus shocked and eroded the public morale by rejecting the painfully patient Roman system of controls.

SUBVERSION OF TRADITIONAL PATRON-CLIENT RELATIONS. Gaius also broke with tradition. We have already noted that in the second century B.C. the relations between many individual members of the proletariat and of the nobility appear to have been vicious and corrupt. However, this relationship, whereby patrons fed their "clients" for their votes, had developed naturally from the needs of both parties. Even in appreciating the cogency of Gaius' desire to bring that relation to an end, we must admit that his grain law weakened the sense of individual responsibility in both patrons and clients by transferring the obligation to furnish cheap food from the patron to the State.

MOB-RULE FOR AN EMPIRE CREATED. The combined effect of the deposition of Octavius by Tiberius, the introduction of the secret ballot, and the assumption of the responsibility by the State to furnish a steady supply of cheap grain was to reduce all chances of conservative control by an enormous degree. However much the Gracchi may have been influenced by the example of Periclean Athens, and whatever the successes of Athenian democracy may have been, it is clear that by the time of the Gracchi Rome was an empire, not a city-state, and a city-state's machinery was ineffectual in the face of its peculiar problems. The creation, or resurrection, of the tribunate-tribal assembly machine was, therefore, monstrous, and its ineptitude was destined to devour the vitals of the State for decades to come.

THE GRAIN LAW AND PUBLIC MORALITY. While legislation such as the grain law of Gaius Gracchus had been introduced with the best intentions, it could become especially dangerous when invoked by the form of government that the Gracchi introduced. In the beginning the State might expect only to furnish grain at cost. But in a world of political realities, when the recipients of such benefits are unhampered in their legislative capacity and are without the self-control that may come from a profound education, the only direction in which this situation can develop is toward a constant increase in the obligations of the State by further reductions in price, and a constant increase in the "rights" of the people. The grain legislation of Gaius combined with the political policy initiated by Tiberius embarked the Roman State on the assumption of obligations and the Roman people on the assumption of rights that appear to have demoralized them both. And by their violent and bloody reaction to these Gracchan efforts the conservatives little by little taught the people to wield the weapons of violence and assassination that would destroy the Republic.

Chapter 22

IN THE SHADOW OF THE GRACCHI

The use made by the Gracchi of dubious constitutional procedures in the passage of their bills, the creation by Gaius Gracchus of the equestrian businessmen as a political force dominated by pecuniary considerations, the sense of power briefly enjoyed by the proletariat, and the violent reaction of the senatorial class to the Gracchan dispensation joined to lower the morals of the rulers and the morale of the whole country. During the next thirty years the Jugurthine War in Africa, the rise of the great popular leader Marius, and the outbreak of the Social War in Italy copiously illustrate the unfortunate effects of the Gracchan episode on the Roman people.

THE FATE OF GRACCHAN LEGISLATION.   With the death of Gaius Gracchus the senators appeared momentarily to have reasserted themselves as the State's ruling force, but they did not dare to hazard their position by an immediate and complete abrogation of the Gracchan laws. While the law establishing the citizen colony at Carthage was indeed repealed before Gaius' death in 121 B.C., those that had received allotments there could keep them with full legal rights. The State continued to be responsible for a steady grain supply in the Roman market, though a law passed in 120 B.C. probably raised the price so that the treasury would suffer no losses. It would have been foolhardy for the senators to endanger relations with the knights; therefore they did not venture to take away from them control of the juries of the extortion courts which Gaius Gracchus had given to them.

Even the agrarian commission was allowed to continue its existence for a time, and it took ten years of whittling away at the Gracchan legislation for the disposal of public lands before the government contrived a settlement that it thought suitable. Probably as early as 121 a law was passed permitting possessors of Gracchan allotments to sell them. It is reported that the rich began to buy them up or even to seize them by force. But legally these plots still were considered public domain, and the limitation to 500 *jugera* for any one possessor still held. In 118, however, a new law not only abolished the agrarian commission, but also specified that public property now in the hands of possessors should be deemed private property. Owners were to pay rent to the State and the income from this source was to be applied in some unspecified manner to the relief of the poor. By this political bargain the rich now were free to acquire any amount of the formerly public land that they wished, while the application of the rent to the welfare of the proletariat served as a recompense for ceasing further allotments to the poor. The money may have been used for the grain program. The settlement of the land question was essentially completed by 111 B.C., when a new agrarian law confirmed as completely private and unencumbered not only the estates of 500 *jugera* that had been left to the old possessors, but also the allotments made to individuals by the Gracchans, and lands irregularly possessed by individuals since 133 B.C.

The measures taken since 133 B.C. had seriously curtailed the amount of public property in Italy. There still remained certain rich properties, such as the Campanian lands, that were leased out and on which the government depended heavily for income. There were other lands that were still legally public but were entailed to certain individuals or families for past or current services to the State. There were common lands that had been specifically assigned to groups of colonists; and there was still some unallocated land, largely pasture, which the general public was allowed to use, with a limit set to the number of animals that each owner could graze on it. This meant that any further proposals for allotments of land in Italy must either deplete the revenues of the State, assign land of inferior quality, or acquire land by purchase or confiscation. Whatever disposition of public land might be made in the future, the development of the land laws from 121 to 111 B.C. buttressed the rich with a new legality in the control of old public lands and encouraged the further development of great estates. An early consequence of the change of legal status effected by these land laws can perhaps be seen in the speech of a tribune in 104 B.C., in which he stated that in his day not 2000 persons in Italy had possessions of any consequence. Cicero called this assertion "words of terrible significance aimed at a levelling of property," but he did not deny its truth.

EQUESTRIAN INTERESTS EXPANDED. Retention of control of the extortion courts permitted the knights to exploit the provincials without serious fear of intervention by senatorial governors. In the three decades after Gaius Gracchus gave them this powerful tool, they found ways to further their business interests in a number of areas. Strong senatorial opposition to colonies overseas had wrecked the Gracchan settlement at Carthage in 121 B.C., and opposition to such settlements bitterly continued; yet in 118 with the assistance of young Lucius Licinius Crassus, member of a family with a long tradition of liberalism, a bill was passed establishing a permanent citizen colony outside Italy at Narbo in southern Gaul. This created a fine depot from which Roman businessmen could trade with the natives of the Gallic interior and even extend their activities beyond to Britain. The construction of the Via Domitia, which linked Italy with Spain and passed through Narbo, further improved the value of the colony for the mercantile interests. The energy with which the Balearic Isles, which had been a refuge for pirates, were conquered and settled with Roman or Italian residents of Spain around 121 B.C. also reflects the determination of the commercial interests to keep the western seas open.

A FRUSTRATED PROLETARIAT. The first decade after Gaius Gracchus' death was not without discontent among the plebeian poor, but their animosity was muffled by poor leadership and by the general solidarity of upperclass interests. However, a proletarian tradition rapidly grew up around the Gracchi, and the people kept alive their deeds and aspirations by devotions and memorials at the spots where they had been killed. A tribune in 120 B.C. dared to try Opimius, the consul of 121, for his condemnation of Gracchan supporters without allowing them the right of appeal, but the attempt was unsuccessful. The acquittal of Opimius at that time became a strong legal argument of future senators that by the passage of a *senatus consultum ultimum* they could legally declare martial law and suspend civic rights. What was worse, the successful defense of Opimius encouraged the recall from exile of Popillius Laenas. He had headed the court that condemned Tiberian sympathizers in 132 B.C. without appeal, at a time when there was neither the excuse of insurrection nor of senatorial decree. In 119 B.C. there was some agitation

234

to restore the Gracchan provisions of the grain program, but this was blocked by Gaius Marius, who then was tribune, on grounds of public economy.

Since the people were generally unsuccessful in retaining the central position that they had enjoyed under the Gracchi, their resentments against the ruling Establishment found emotional release in other directions. Rome was suddenly astonished with the news that the young daughter of a Roman knight had been killed by a thunderbolt. The people took this prodigy to mean that the sacred national purity had been besmirched. Sinners against the sacred national interest were not hard to find, and the populace followed with morbid interest the pontifical trial in 114 B.C. of three Vestal Virgins, daughters of the highest nobility, accused of immoral relations with a number of young men of high social position. The people were indignant when only one of the ladies was found guilty and were satisfied only with a new trial, a new court, and a notoriously severe judge. The burial alive of the other two maidens in 113 still was not enough to atone for the suspected corruption of the aristocracy. Evil portents were seen everywhere, and the popular demand for expiation was not satisfied until two Greeks and two Gauls had been sacrificed in the Forum Boarium.

THE JUGURTHINE WAR (111 – 105 B.C.).   Even after the popular excesses connected with the trial of the Vestal Virgins, the people saw portents everywhere, and these portents seemed to be confirmed by the outrageous conduct of a petty war in North Africa. In this conflict the people saw their suspicions of aristocratic competence and honesty justified, the knights saw the sacred rights of their investments undermined, and patriots felt that the good name of their country had been betrayed. All this started with a dynastic dispute in the client state of Numidia. As king of Numidia from 201 to 149 B.C., Masinissa had been a faithful and useful ally. Under his direction the boundaries had been extended, and agriculture and commerce were greatly improved. His peaceable successor, Micipsa, continued the economic improvement of the country. Roman traders and investors abounded. But on his deathbed in 118 B.C. Micipsa was faced with a dilemma: his two sons Hiempsal and Adherbal were neither mature nor astute, while his nephew Jugurtha was both. He decided to leave the throne to their joint rule. The result was as rapid as it was predictable: the more volatile brother, Hiempsal, was straightway eliminated by Jugurtha, and the weaker Adherbal soon found himself a fugitive in Rome. Jugurtha, now that he had secured all Numidia, also sent representatives to Rome, and they were usefully supplied with generous portions of the royal treasures with which to win senatorial favor. Jugurtha had served with Scipio's army before Numantia (134–133 B.C.), and his personal charm, intelligence, and vigor had recommended him to many Roman nobles. For his part he had found a growing tendency among many Romans to consider past favors in making important decisions. His attempts to secure recognition might easily have been successful, for the system of client states such as Numidia had been developed by the Romans to relieve themselves from burdens of administration and defense, not to embroil them in internal or dynastic issues. Rome would be inclined, therefore, to recognize any stable and friendly regime.

PARTITION OF NUMIDIA (116 B.C.). FALL OF CIRTA (112 B.C.). Adherbal's pleas for justice, however, caught the ear of the patrician consul-elect, Marcus Aemilius Scaurus. This man, by his venerable and imposing appearance, his ostentatious support of virtue, and his cunning as a politician became the symbol to many Romans of the ideal aristocrat, and for years he was enrolled as the first man of the Senate. Scaurus had risen from poverty to great wealth and had many business interests. The gentler Adherbal seemed less of a risk to the commercial world of Aemilius Scaurus than the impetuous Jugurtha, and Adherbal's gratitude for being restored surely would produce complaisance for Roman business interests in Numidia. Scaurus' influence therefore led the Senate to appoint a commission of ten to proceed to Numidia under the presidency of Lucius Opimius, the senator that had engineered Gaius Gracchus' destruction, to settle the dispute. The commission decided to partition the country. Adherbal was awarded the richer and more developed eastern section, Jugurtha, the larger but wilder west. However, the cousins soon were at war again, and Jugurtha's superior force at length shut Adherbal up in his capital at Cirta. Frantic appeals to his sponsors in Rome for help were answered by two more commissions, one of which was headed by Scaurus. The commissioners expostulated with Jugurtha, who was polite but noncommittal. As soon as they departed in 112 B.C. he forced the surrender of Cirta, executed Adherbal, and in the tumult massacred a large number of Italian and Roman businessmen, who had been enjoying the special privileges exacted from Adherbal and who had assisted in the city's defense.

BESTIA'S CAMPAIGN; SUBMISSION OF JUGURTHA (111 B.C.). A howl arose in Rome. The knights complained because their

business interests had been undermined, and they blamed the
government for not having taken vigorous action in Numidia.
The proletarians joined the clamor mostly through patriotic
ignorance. They had no idea of the difficulty, the dangers, the
expense, or the manpower that effective interference in North
Africa entailed. They themselves had no substance, and since
they were ineligible for military service they had no personal
involvement at all; but these lords of the slums felt that their
national dignity had been affronted by a rascally African. Thus
self-interest and emotion conspired to revive the Gracchan
alliance of proletariat and businessmen and to exert pressure on
the Senate to undertake a war that was unwise and unnecessary.

The Senate declared Numidia a consular province for 111,
and it fell to the lot of Lucius Calpurnius Bestia. He set out with
an army and a staff composed of the highest nobility, including
the egregious Scaurus. Some progresses with an air of success
about them were made up and down the country; but it soon became clear that the nature of the land, which favored irregular or
guerrilla tactics, the people's devotion to their king, and the
lack of vital urban areas would demand a determined and massive Roman effort. Jugurtha, however, had no desire to quarrel
with Rome; he merely wanted to keep Numidia. A truce was
therefore arranged, secret parleys begun, and a treaty of peace
negotiated after Jugurtha showed his submission to Rome's
majesty by surrendering to her thirty elephants and some other
treasure. The consul and his staff then headed for Rome to
secure ratification for the arrangement. They had reason to be
pleased. Roman honor, though a little tarnished, had been
vindicated, and peace had been restored with a minimum of
effort and expense.

However, there had been rumors of bribes, and Bestia was
greeted in Rome with grave suspicions both as to his treaty and
as to his personal conduct. A tribune, Gaius Memmius, had the
brilliant idea of summoning this newly subdued king to Rome
under a safe-conduct to give evidence as to his relations with
Bestia and his staff. Jugurtha duly arrived in Rome, but somehow another tribune was persuaded to veto every effort to take
the king's testimony. The matter took a new turn, however,
when one of Jugurtha's retinue secured the assassination in
Rome itself of a cousin of the king, Massiva. The consul-elect
for 110 B.C., Spurius Postumius Albinus, had suggested Massiva
as an alternative candidate for the Numidian throne in case it
was proved that Jugurtha's submission was a sham and that he
had bribed Bestia. Postumius obviously hoped that to him
would fall the glorious and lucrative task of placing Massiva on

the Numidian throne. Jugurtha's audacious reaction to the suggestion was too much even for the senators. The king was hustled back to Numidia, and the war was resumed. As he left Rome, Jugurtha is said to have looked back at the city from a rise on the Appian Way and thoughtfully summed up his experience of Rome and Romans with, "a city for sale and ready for destruction if it but find a buyer."

WAR RESUMED; DEFEAT OF AULUS POSTUMIUS. METELLUS. Spurius Postumius' campaign in Numidia was far less successful than Bestia's. He marched up and down the country without ever catching Jugurtha. His attempts to negotiate craftily against a man far his superior ended only with suspicions in Rome that he was guilty of collusion. Finally, in frustration he put his army into winter quarters and went to Rome for elections. In his absence his brother and lieutenant Aulus led the army out to attack Jugurtha's distant teasure-city of Suthul — whether for personal glory, the public purse, or his own cupidity has never been determined. Jugurtha surrounded the army, forced its capitulation, marched it under a yoke of spears, and concluded a treaty with Aulus calling for immediate Roman evacuation of Numidia. Back in Rome the populace was outraged. Aulus' treaty was rejected, though no one seemed to think it any longer necessary to Roman honor that the rejected commander should be turned over to the enemy, as Mancinus had been to the Numantines only a quarter of a century earlier. Further, a bill sponsored by the tribune Gaius Mamilius established special courts to try those who had cooperated with Jugurtha against the interests of Rome. Oddly enough the unsinkable Scaurus, who was not entirely free from suspicion himself, contrived to acquire the presidency of one of the courts. The jurors were knights, and the procedure was inquisitorial and indignant. To the people's joy not only the nobles Postumius and Bestia suffered; Lucius Opimius, the hated consul of 121 B.C. who had killed Gaius Gracchus, was also driven into exile. The Mamilian Commission may have been unfair, but the wholesale suspicion of the governing order that now permeated society was a damning indictment of the whole Roman State.

The new consul and general of 109 B.C. commanded universal respect and raised the people's hopes. Not only was his personal integrity unquestioned, but his very name, Quintus Caecilius Metellus, inspired confidence. His father, a brother, and four cousins all had recently been consuls. He took with him to Africa as aides two new men of proved military competence, Rutilius Rufus and Gaius Marius. With them he whipped a demoralized army into shape and began a series of battles hoping to force a showdown with Jugurtha. For two years he captured towns and could report successful engagements to Rome, but an army of nomadic people on their own wild terrain could disintegrate into harmless shepherds and farmers in a moment, while a new army could rise like magic from the same elements. Jugurtha himself was just as elusive and still held his people's loyalty. Metellus in despair tried to buy the king's assassination, for even this model Roman now found the ancient contempt for such practices old-fashioned and unrealistic.

THE GRACCHAN POLITICAL FRONT RENEWED; MARIUS.
Meanwhile the proletariat of Rome was becoming restive and the equestrians were equally vexed at the extended interruption of their business activities in Numidia. They now found in Gaius Marius the leader they needed to wrest the initiative from the nobility's hands and to reassert the alliance of proletariat and knights that had flourished under Gaius Gracchus. Marius had been tribune in 119 and praetor in 115. He was a farm boy from the Volscian town of Arpinum, an unlettered man with no strong political convictions. As a man of no family he should have expected no further advancement. But he had been granted a marriage with a daughter of the ancient and now reviving patrician house of the Julii, and he believed that an opportunity had come to seek the highest office. Further, he was galled by the condescension of his superior, Metellus, who repeatedly assured him that his hopes were foolish. Metellus had long delayed Marius' departure from Africa to stand as candidate for the consulship of 107 B.C. Marius had therefore proceeded to undermine Metellus' own position in Numidia by inspiring letters from the Roman army in Africa and even more influential ones from the businessmen who were poised in nearby Utica, hungrily expecting to return to the markets of Numidia. These letters assured the Romans that Metellus was prolonging the war because of his aristocratic love of unlimited power, and that Gaius Marius, if he were general, would soon have Jugurtha in hand and the war at an end. A week's whirlwind campaign by Marius in Rome solidified the alliance of people and knights. They thought that here surely they had found a rugged, old-time Roman, and that with him they would be able to reassert their glories and their interests against increasing senatorial arrogance and incompetence.

The Senate already had extended Metellus' command for another year. However, the tribunes rushed to the people a bill transferring Numidia to Marius, and it was triumphantly passed.

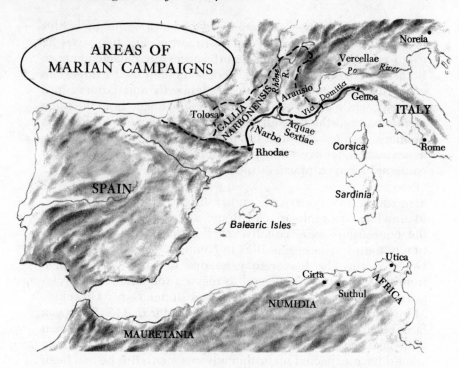

Thus the great *popularis* came to power. For Marius was a *popularis* in a way that the Gracchi never could be. This term has little to do with democratic or popular aspirations; it signifies the belief that high leadership should go to the competent, whatever their station or origin. It is in this sense that Julius Caesar, a great aristocrat, was a *popularis* and Marius' successor.

MARIUS' SUCCESS AGAINST JUGURTHA (107–106 B.C.).

In preparing to return to Numidia Marius raised a new army, and though his change in recruiting seemed small at the time, it had large consequences. For some time the State had been lowering property qualifications in order to meet the need for troops from a poverty-stricken populace. Now Marius waived all requirements, merely by asking for volunteers rather than for a draft. Multitudes flocked to the great name both from the urban proletariat and from the impoverished rustics. All looked to the commander to lead them to profitable victories and thereafter a fresh start in life. Marius welded this mob into an efficient fighting machine by patient and thorough training and then by the conquest of Numidian towns that offered increasing difficulty in the taking. His aim was to capture and destroy or (now that he had more troops than the Romans normally had been able to raise) to garrison all the strongholds that might serve as

240

rallying points. This strategy entailed a swing through difficult country all the way to the Moroccan frontier. Although Jugurtha was not cornered, confidence in his final survival was shaken, and in 106 his father-in-law, King Bocchus of Mauretania, opened negotiations with the Romans. Marius wisely delegated the tasks of diplomacy to his far more subtle aristocratic aide, Lucius Cornelius Sulla. By his mixture of personal charm, candour, and firmness Sulla convinced the old king that the future was with Rome, and Jugurtha was betrayed into Roman hands. Thereupon this exciting and competent barbarian was killed in a Roman prison. Rome did not venture to add to her territories or assets by this war, and a Prince Gauda, whom Marius had befriended, was placed on the throne. Marius personally acquired liberal grants of land in Numidia where his veterans could be settled in irregular but specially privileged colonies, safe from any possible future senatorial harassment. The grateful Gauda ensured the safety of Numidia for investment and exploitation. The businessmen had insisted on this war and had reaped their rewards; but the havoc wrought in the national political structure, security, and confidence raises some doubt as to the wisdom of their guidance in foreign affairs.

MIGRATIONS OF CIMBRI AND TEUTONS (120–102 B.C.). SENATORIAL INCOMPETENCE ON THE NORTHERN FRONT.

When Marius returned to Rome for his triumph in 105 B.C. he found himself, despite a law forbidding reelection to the consulship, again selected for that post for 104. He was needed because of the continued demonstration of mediocrity and incompetence by senatorial commanders on the vulnerable northern frontiers. Since about 120 B.C. great nations of people, the Cimbri and the Teutons, had been on the move in central Europe seeking new homes. They seem to have originated in lowlands near the North or Baltic Seas and to have been driven forth by a slow advance of the waters upon their homeland. They appear to have been Germans, the first wave of the vigorous people that was to erode Rome's empire. When they first arrived near the Roman frontiers they requested lands for settlement; but when their request was brusquely denied by the Roman command, they turned peaceably aside. However, a Roman commander could enjoy the distinction of a triumphal procession in Rome only if he could certify that a Roman victory under his command had produced at least 5000 dead among the defeated; and in 113 B.C. the proximity of so many potential corpses was too great a temptation for the consul Papirius Carbo. He therefore laid an ambush for the migrants near Noreia beyond the northeastern frontier, but he suffered a severe defeat. For this he was prosecuted at Rome and anticipated conviction by taking poison. Undisturbed by this example, in 109 the consul Silanus also attacked the Germans, who had moved north of the Alps toward Gaul, and was likewise soundly beaten. The Germans still did not turn upon Italy; but the Roman reverses at German hands caused some of the tribes of Gaul to become disaffected, and the consul of 107 by sheer incompetence managed to lose his own life and all but a remnant of his army to a Gallic insurrection. His successor in 106, Quintus Servilius Caepio, was more successful. He contrived the return to allegiance of the dissident Gallic tribes, and he grasped the opportunity to confiscate the fabulous treasures of their temples in Tolosa. Interestingly enough, the whole cargo, while being expressed to Massilia for shipment to the treasury in Rome, completely disappeared and was never heard of again.

The pretended loss of the treasures of Tolosa in 106 cannot compare with Caepio's exploits in 105. He remained at his post as proconsul, but was joined by a new consul, Mallius Maximus, like Marius a new man. Mallius was in command of a second army and outranked Caepio, but the latter refused to obey or to cooperate with his superior. Fortunately for the Romans, the Germans had not pressed their advantage after the defeat of Silanus in 109, but had sought homes in Spain and Gaul. Now they reappeared in southern Gaul still searching for a place to settle. Here in 105 at Arausio the combined jealousies and madnesses of Caepio and Maximus brought the destruction first of a Roman supporting force and then of the army of each Roman commander separately. It is said that 80,000 fell, a disaster rivalling Cannae in numbers and morally far worse, for it was brought about not by national unpreparedness nor by the tactics of an able enemy, but by incompetence, internal bickering, and greed. At home the people's anger was fortified by honest fright. Even the senators could not but concur in the need to draft Marius, the hero of Numidia. Indeed, their confessed bankruptcy is certified by the five successive consulships to which Marius now was elected from 104 to 100 B.C. The knights were beside themselves and also insisted on Marius' command. Not only were their carefully husbanded business interests in Gaul imperilled, but the culprit Caepio had somehow managed during his consulship to wrest the jury courts from them. Marius could serve them in more ways than one.

MARIUS VICTORIOUS IN THE NORTH (104–101 B.C.).
Fortunately the Germans again did not immediately follow up

their victories over the Roman commanders, and Marius was given time to prepare. He was able to raise and train an army, using his new form of recruiting. He also developed the use of the cohort, a unit of from 500 to 600 men which he found preferable to the smaller maniple that was formerly the basic tactical unit. The cohorts provided greater striking power, yet were still small enough to be flexible. Weapons also were improved, and the men received instruction in individual gladiatorial-type combat developed for military use by Marius' old colleague in Africa, Rutilius Rufus. Morale was sustained by a constant state of alert, and physical condition by the construction of a canal to improve shipping facilities at the mouth of the Rhone. Such a use of the military was a harbinger of the great public works that in the Principate were regularly undertaken by the standing armies.

At length the Germans decided to move into Italy in two divisions. The first was met and annihilated by Marius' smaller but disciplined force near Aquae Sextiae in 102. Nearly 100,000 of the enemy are said to have died or to have been captured. Marius then hurried to Cisalpine Gaul where in 101 B.C. he joined the proconsul Lutatius Catulus at Vercellae in destroying the other German horde, which had crossed the eastern Alps. Thus Italy was saved, and the two commanders returned to Rome for a joint triumph.

SLAVE WAR IN SICILY (104–99 B.C.).   At this time the great Mediterranean plague, piracy and the sale of victims into slavery, was the cause of a Second Slave War in Sicily.[1] In preparation for his campaigns against the Germans Marius had requested contingents from various client kings to assist him. When some of them replied that they could not supply them because so many of their men had been captured by pirates, it was decided in Rome that these captives must be sought out and returned to their homes. The governor of Sicily, Licinius Nerva, thereupon freed a few hundred, but the angry pressure of the great business interests on the island, which depended on slave labor, forced him to desist. The disappointed slaves, in turn, rose and overran the island. The commanding generals in Sicily for the next two years were so ineffective against the slaves and so frenetic in their jealousies and accusations of one another that ultimately they both ended up in exile. It was not until 101 that a former aide and now the consular colleague of Marius, Manius Aquillius, could be spared for the island, which

[1]   For the First Slave War, see p. 216.

243

was completely returned to order by 99 B.C. Here again generals of the senatorial class had proved selfish and inept.

SIXTH CONSULSHIP OF MARIUS (100 B.C.). ALLIANCE WITH GLAUCIA AND SATURNINUS.   When Marius entered upon his sixth consulship in 100 B.C., the State was at his feet. He had all the power that Gaius Gracchus had lacked. However, he was no reformer; he had no program, no ideals, and no political competence—he merely wished to be great and to care for his veterans. But to ensure the veterans' interests he had to maintain the coalition of knights and proletariat that had gained him his commands. To do this he depended on two men who had learned to stay in power by every device, legal and illegal, used by Gracchans and by their opponents for a quarter century. These men were a praetor, Servilius Glaucia, and Lucius Appuleius Saturninus, tribune for the second time. They already had been of service to the people, to Marius, and to the knights. In his first tribunate in 103 B.C. Saturninus had acquired African lands for veterans of the Jugurthine Wars, which pleased the plebs; and he sponsored a measure that made it a crime to "diminish the majesty of the Roman people." Under this vague indictment a number of the absurd predecessors of Marius in the northern command were driven into exile, which pleased the knights. In 101 Glaucia had effected the restoration of the juries in the extortion courts to the equestrians, which strengthened the political power of the alliance between knights and people; and he contrived, perhaps by murder, the election of Saturninus to his second tribunate.

REVIVAL OF POPULAR GRACCHAN PROGRAMS.   With the great Marius now at their side Saturninus and Glaucia expected to carry all before them. But at this point senatorial opposition began to strengthen. The nobles no longer feared the Germans, who were gone, and they sensed that Marius was politically naive. As Saturninus brought forward his measures, therefore, tribunes friendly to the Senate exercised their vetoes. Senatorial partisans reported the sound of thunderclaps, an omen considered sufficiently grave to require the adjournment of an assembly. The quaestor Caepio, son of the now exiled hero of Tolosa, even broke up proceedings with a gang of ruffians. But Saturninus also had learned the violent tactics of the Gracchan era and enlisted the help of Marian veterans. Their show of force procured the passage of a number of bills, which could not please equally all the members of Marius' alliance. The people were gratified by a grain law that probably restored the provisions of Gaius Gracchus' program, although this worried the monied classes, which for two decades had held that the State could not afford these terms. A colonial law provided the establishment of Roman army veterans in Sicily, Achaea, and Macedonia. This pleased the Roman troops; but Marius, like Scipio Aemilianus, knew that the Italian veterans also deserved well of him. He already had drawn censure for granting citizenship because of bravery to two cohorts of allies after the defeat of the Germans at Vercellae, and now he had made provision for Italians in the colonies and was even given the right to grant some of them citizenship. This offended the Roman proletariat, which continued to have no notion of diluting the advantages of Roman citizenship by sharing it. And the nobility was infuriated by an agrarian measure, which accorded individual allotments of land in Gaul to veterans, because it contained a clause directing all senators to take an oath to uphold it on pain of fine, expulsion, and exile. This measure also was passed under unfavorable auspices and by force.

FAILURE OF MARIUS' NEW POPULAR FRONT.   Marius was a true *popularis*, but he was no democrat or hoodlum and he began to have some doubts about the objectives and methods of Saturninus and Glaucia. When the question of the oath to support the agrarian law arose, he took it, but with the qualifying phrase, "to the extent that the measure is valid." The doubt implied in his statement was embraced, and his example was happily followed by all the senators except Marius' great predecessor and personal enemy, Quintus Metellus, who stiffly went into exile rather than so demean his dignity. Saturninus and Glaucia were alarmed at Marius' implied criticism. They realized that once out of office they surely would be prosecuted for their illegal use of force and disregard of omens and portents. They proposed therefore to perpetuate their position of immunity from prosecution, Saturninus by running for a third tribunate and Glaucia by standing for the consulship. The latter was clearly illegal, for the Villian Law explicitly required an interval between the end of one magistracy and the entrance upon the next higher. The pair finally decided to improve their chances by the assassination of Glaucia's chief rival for the consulship. At this outrage they lost almost all their backing. The knights long had been withdrawing support from them because their violence and appeals to the mob threatened the stability of business, and the Senate now felt strong enough again to pass a *senatus consultum ultimum* and call upon Marius to restore order. He arrested Saturninus and his followers and shut them up in the senate house for safe-keeping, but partisans climbed onto the roof, tore off the tiles, and stoned the prisoners to death.

Reaction was immediate and complete, and the combination of equestrians and proletariat again seemed broken. Metellus was recalled from.exile. The legislation of 100 B.C. was all declared invalid on the grounds that it was passed by force and contrary to the auspices. One tribune sympathetic to Saturninus was even convicted because he kept a portrait bust of the dead man in his house. Marius' sixth consulship had indeed proved inglorious and clearly revealed his lack of political sagacity or leadership. To escape the scorn of all he left for an extended tour of Asia, hoping that he might stir up enough trouble there amongst Rome's neighbors that the State would soon again require his services as its preeminent general.

MODERATE SENATORIALS SEEK REFORM (100–91 B.C.).
During the decade after the fall of Saturninus and Glaucia a number of moderate senators tried to correct some of the abuses that the recent disorders and scandals had brought to light. Since the Gracchi, the practice of tacking distasteful clauses onto popular measures in order to ensure their passage had apparently been frequently used by legislators. In 98 B.C. a law sponsored by the two consuls forbade such omnibus bills. The law further specified that all bills must be posted publicly through three market days before they came to a vote. Thus measures could not be secretly prepared and passed by surprise, which had been a tactic favored by popular leaders. In 96 B.C. the King of Cyrene left his realm to Rome, but the Senate decided not to extend its responsibilities, for which it already had proved inadequate, and left the cities of the kingdom to care for themselves. It did, however, contract for the exploitation of the king's own private estates, and this no doubt pleased and benefited the equestrians to whom this duty would fall. In 95 B.C. the consuls passed a law forcing all Italians resident in Rome to return to their home places. This was probably prompted by the disorders in which Marius' Italian veterans had participated during the heyday of Saturninus and Glaucia, but it was a gratuitous insult to a long-suffering people.

Some senators felt that they should assume greater responsibility for the well-being of the provincials committed to their care. One promoter of this attitude was the distinguished jurist Quintus Mucius Scaevola, governor of Asia in 97 B.C. In concert with his friend and assistant Rutilius Rufus, he dispensed justice in his province with so firm and steady a hand that the equestrians found their profits from that unhappy country sharply reduced. Scaevola was too influential for attack, but Rutilius was a new man without popular or noble following. The businessmen therefore had him arraigned in 92 B.C. on a palpably false charge of extortion while in Asia. He was condemned by an equestrian court and exiled to Asia, where his alleged victims entertained him for the rest of his life as their honored guest. By this event the senators were sharply reminded that they did not have independence of action and that the political forces evoked by the Gracchi still were determined and powerful.

LIVIUS DRUSUS THE YOUNGER, TRIBUNE (91 B.C.).
In 91 B.C. there came to the tribunate a partisan of the Senate and a reformer, who thought that by compromise he could resolve the two most dangerous national issues: the abuse of the juries by selfish interests and the status of the Italian allies. The man was Livius Drusus the Younger, son of Gaius Gracchus' old antagonist. Drusus was a conscientious man. He also was a self-satisfied and unattractive prig who could not rouse a devoted following. His aim was to reform the courts by creating juries of both senators and knights, and ultimately to raise the Italians to full Roman citizenship. Since the fall of Fregellae thirty-five years earlier the allies had faithfully assisted Rome in her imperialistic wars in Africa as well as in her wars of survival against the Germans. Their burdens were heavy, yet their rewards were niggardly. Yet the Romans no longer could point to differing customs, language, or interest as barriers to union; 200 years of joint action had moved the Italians far along the road toward becoming a nation. Drusus hoped that he could make enough concessions to the various Roman interests that all Romans would unite in the support of his resolution of the Italian question. This was a vain hope. Each class freely accepted favors, but not one was willing to make any sacrifice for the common good. Drusus first tried to win proletarian support by a grain law. This must have lowered the Gracchan requirements, and we are told that he debased the currency to finance it. He also revived the colonial schemes of his father,[2] which had been dropped at Gaius' death, and he promised to dispense lands in Italy so liberally that his Italian friends became concerned for their own holdings. Indeed, he himself was led to remark that he was leaving nothing but mud and sky for future statesmen to distribute. To gain the senators' favor he proposed giving them

[2]   For the colonial bill of Livius Drusus the Elder, see p. 228.

half of the seats on the juries; and to compensate the knights for this concession to the senators, 300 of the most prominent equestrians were to be added to the Senate. But the senators resented the dilution of their order, the knights had no mind to surrender their commanding position on the juries for the benefit of a handful of their number that would be elevated to senatorial rank, and all three orders were united in their opposition to sharing their citizenship with the Italian allies. And so, as Drusus' commitment to the Italians became ever clearer to the Roman public, the conservative senators, with the backing of the knights and proletariat, declared all of his laws illegal on the grounds either that they controverted the law against omnibus bills or that they had been passed when the auspices were unfavorable. Though he knew full well that growing Italian discontent might break forth in open revolt at his failure, Drusus resigned himself to this frustration. Even so, before the end of his term he fell at the hands of an assassin, plaintively inquiring on his deathbed where the Romans would find another such as he.

Where indeed? Whatever his faults, Drusus had tried to solve Rome's problems. But the Gracchan episode and the three decades that followed had brought the Romans to the brink of impotent frustration at home and mortal peril abroad. The distrust of national senatorial leadership planted by the Gracchi had been strengthend by the Jugurthine and German campaigns. The selfish business and proletarian interests that had been given a taste of power under the Gracchi denied to the Italians the fair treatment that they deserved. And the mutual distrusts of the intransigent interests that had risen in Rome since Tiberius Gracchus became tribune (133 B.C.) portended no solution for the country's growing problems short of an appeal to force.

Chapter   23

THE REVOLT OF THE ALLIES

The assassination of Livius Drusus and collapse of his program was followed almost immediately by the revolt of Rome's Italian allies. This conflict (90–88 B.C.) is commonly called the "Social War" because the Latin word for ally is *socius*. Its outbreak comes to the student of Roman history, as it did to the Romans themselves, as a considerable surprise. It was generated by grievances and resentments that were of long standing, but Rome's organization of Italy was such that it was difficult for the discontented to dare to express themselves.[1] From the beginning Rome made bilateral and perpetual agreements with each of the other states of Italy, binding them all to come to her aid if any one of them tried to break away. Furthermore, the Latin colonies had been so strategically located throughout the peninsula that they hampered hostile combinations in many areas. Moreover, within the various allied states themselves there were influential elements friendly to Rome. The noble houses of other Italian cities maintained guest-friendships with great Roman houses, and many of them had actually been granted Roman citizenship. This was a common reward of ex-magistrates in Latin cities, and in others it often went to individuals for outstanding service to Rome.

THE SOURCES OF ITALIAN DISCONTENT.   There was no real deterioration in the legal position of the Italian allies over the years, but Rome's wealth and power had so far advanced that the allies could no longer view her as merely the first among equals. Just as the Italian noble houses found that their guest-friendships with Roman families were sliding slowly into client-age, so the allied states insensibly accepted treatment more befitting subjects than allies. During the second century B.C.

---

[1]   For the Italian system, see Chapter 8.

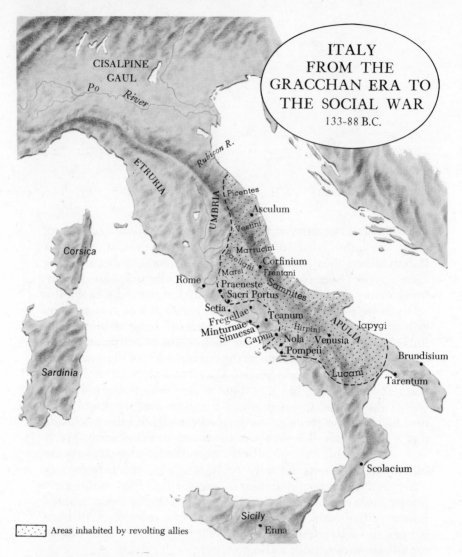

ITALY
FROM THE
GRACCHAN ERA TO
THE SOCIAL WAR
133-88 B.C.

CISALPINE GAUL

Po River

Rubicon R.

ETRURIA

UMBRIA

Picentes

Asculum

Vestini

Corsica

Marrucini

Paeligni

Corfinium

Marsi

Frentani

Rome

Praeneste

Samnites

Sacri Portus

Setia

Fregellae

Teanum

Minturnae

Hirpini

Sinuessa

Capua

Nola

Venusia

Pompeii

APULIA

Iapygi

Brundisium

Sardinia

Lucani

Tarentum

Scolacium

Sicily

Enna

Areas inhabited by revolting allies

Rome's own manpower had become less and less adequate for her far-flung wars, and the allies were required to carry a greater share of the burden. However, there had been no corresponding increase in rewards for them. There is no indication, for instance, that they received any of the Carthaginian indemnity, though their lands and peoples had borne the full measure of Hannibal's occupation. In one case at least, though perhaps this was exceptional, allied soldiers received portions of booty only half as large as those that the Roman troops received. Furthermore, in the Latin colonies founded during the second decade of the second century B.C. at various Italian sites allied participants regularly received smaller allotments of land than the Romans did; and the same was true in 173 B.C., when individual allotments of land in Liguria and Gaul were made both to Romans and to allies. Land and booty were not the only rewards of empire in which the allies received a miserly share: in 184 B.C. a Porcian Law protected Roman soldiers from summary execution by their officers, but the Italians did not enjoy the same protection. By 167 B.C. the income from conquests effected jointly by the Romans and their Italian allies was so great that Roman landowners were henceforth relieved from the land tax, but the Italian municipalities received no share of this income. Their citizen-soldiers still had to support their individual city-states with taxes as well as with arms. This continuing financial support of armies dedicated to Roman ambition was galling; but probably even more galling were the effrontery of travelling Roman citizens and the imperious attitudes of visiting Roman officials. Their outrages were scandalous, and attempts by the central Roman government to control them were meager. Even more frightening to the Italians, perhaps, were the impingements that were made or threatened by the Gracchan agrarian laws in the name of the Roman proletariat upon lands that had been left for centuries to Italian exploitation. These lands the Italians considered rightfully their own, and they were as indignant at the Gracchan challenge to their titles as the great Roman possessors had been. They could not accept that they, the defenders of Italy, should surrender their source of livelihood to the imperious and useless inhabitants of Rome.

Liberal and moderate elements in the Senate long had recognized the injustice and danger of Roman policy toward the Italians and were prepared to support measures that would be corrective. In 129 B.C. Scipio Aemilianus had briefly defended the Italians' possession of some Roman public land; and the consul of 125, Fulvius Flaccus, had tried to procure citizenship, or at least the right of appeal, for them.[2] He had been foiled by reactionary senators and by those that deplored the prospect of their Italian clients becoming their political equals and competitors. At that time, however, the people were clearly not yet strongly anti-Italian; despite his devotion to the Italian cause Flaccus was retained on the commission for distributing public lands, and the people elected him tribune with Gaius Gracchus for 122 B.C. But when Gaius in that year again proposed to raise the Italians' status, the counterarguments of the consul Fannius—that the special privileges of Roman citizens would be

[2]   For the efforts of Scipio Aemilianus and Fulvius Flaccus, see pp. 223–224.

dangerously diluted by being shared—were so convincing to the plebs that no one who thereafter championed the Italians ever received steadfast popular support. Perhaps more than anything else, the specious and demagogic arguments of Fannius had made a peaceful solution of the Italian problem almost impossible.

After the Gracchan episode the perplexities of the Italians continued, while their devoted assistance in the wars with Jugurtha and with the Germans showed their continued worth. Marius knew their value full well, and he had tried in 100 B.C. to reward his Italian veterans by including them in the colonies of his Roman troops. This subterfuge the people resented, and their resentment contributed to Saturninus' downfall. In 97 B.C. the censors also appear to have been sympathetic to the Italian cause. They were either liberal or lax in registering as Romans Italians that professed to be citizens. This pro-Italian venture, however, brought about the Licinio-Mucian Law of 95 B.C., which instituted a rigorous investigation of such claims. Further, the consuls of that year in the interests of orderly government expelled the allies living in Rome. This was a bitter blow to the Italians who thereby lost their only means of bringing pressure upon the Roman government.

THE IMMEDIATE CAUSES OF REVOLT.   Unfortunately, since the Gracchi the Italian problem had been tied up with the intricacies and selfishnesses of Roman internal politics. Marius was known and trusted by many of the Italians who had served under him, and the complacent censors of 97 had been friends of his. On the other hand, the Licinio-Mucian Law of 95 had been to some extent designed to destroy the prestige and power of this Marian and pro-Italian group; and Marius got revenge for the conservative attack on him and his policies by supporting the knights in their successful attack on the senators in 93 B.C. when they convicted the blameless legate Rutilius Rufus.[3] The ruthless power that that famous conviction revealed thoroughly frightened even the most moderate and liberal of the senatorials, and it appears that the younger Livius Drusus was sponsored for the tribunate by them in order to launch an attack on that power: as his father had split the parties supporting Gaius Gracchus in 122 B.C.,[4] so now the son was detailed to win as many supporters as possible to destroy the alliance of the popular Marius and the knights and to attain senatorial objectives. Livius hoped that Roman citizenship would be granted to the

[3]   For conviction of Rutilius, see pp. 246–247.
[4]   For the programs of the Drusi, see pp. 228, 247–248.

Italians by the Senate and that the Senate would thus gain new and powerful support. As his year of office progressed (91 B.C.), he became increasingly convinced that to assist the Italians was not only expedient but also just, and apparently he became more and more deeply committed to them. On this point, however, his whole program foundered: the plebs reasserted their devotion to their exclusive privileges of cheap grain and frequent festivals; the knights balked at the prospect that Italian businessmen now could compete with them on equal terms, and the reactionary wing of the Senate, led by the consul Philippus, added its discontent. Word of Livius' failure and subsequent assassination sped through Italy, where the postures of the different political rivals in Rome surely were not understood. To the Italians, however, it now seemed certain that they no longer could hope for any relief at Rome or with the Romans in order to rise from their inferior position.

Rumors soon sifted into Rome that conspiracy was afoot in Italy, that there had been a marked increase in communications between the allies, and that they had exchanged hostages with one another as an insurance of good faith. The Romans reacted with typical blind self-confidence. In late 91 B.C. officials hustled to various key points to spy, to recriminate, and to denounce. One such representative, the praetor Quintus Servilius, was so outrageously abusive at Asculum that the enraged inhabitants straightway tore him and his aides to pieces, closed the gates, and massacred the Romans residing there. This proved to be the spark that ignited Italy. Yet for a time at Rome internal bickering still took precedence over external danger. Against his fellow tribunes' vetoes and with equestrian assistance the tribune Varius Hybrida procured a law establishing a court to try on the charge of high treason those persons suspected of encouraging the Italians to revolt. This was aimed at those senatorial liberals that had backed Livius Drusus, some of whom were driven into exile before the rapid advance of the Italian organization and preparations for war made it clear that it was high time for the Romans to turn from recriminations to mobilization.

THE ITALIAN ORGANIZATION. ITALIA.   In central Italy the Marsi, Paeligni, Vestini, Marrucini, Picentes and Frentani arose. They were joined in southern Italy by the Hirpini, Iapygi, Lucani, and Samnites. The inhabitants of the important Campanian town of Pompeii and of the strategically located colony of Venusia also rebelled. For the moment, however, the Latin allies and most Latin colonies, the Greek cities of the coast, and Etruscans and Umbrians of northern and north central Italy stood firm for Rome. The rebels established a capital at Corfinium in the central Apennines and called it Italia. A senate was established and coinage was issued, which carried Latin inscriptions for the northern or Marsic confederates and Oscan lettering for the southern or Samnite ones. Two generals were elected to exercise the supreme command, and there also were twelve praetors or field-commanders, each commanding one of the confederate contingents.

The Italians had almost as many troops as the Romans, and they had been trained on the same fields and with the same tactics. They were hardy, well led, and inspired with righteous indignation. The Romans, however, had the advantages of interior lines with good roads, control of the sea, and in time they could call upon the immense resources of their empire. However, recent political developments in Rome had not encouraged the training of great generals. Their only capable and experienced general, Marius, was shunted by the jealousy of the nobles into subordinate commands throughout the conflict. At first the Romans suffered a series of reverses against both the central and the southern Italians. In the central sector two generals and three armies were lost, but the competence of Marius, though serving in a subordinate command, warded off complete disaster. In the south the allies launched a drive into Campania and acquired adherents there, threatened the rich *Ager Campanus*, and cut off the Roman armies in the southeast. Here, as in the central sector, the most promising Roman general was a subordinate commander, young Lucius Sulla, who had been Marius' aide against Jugurtha.

ITALIAN SUCCESSES. ROMAN CONCESSIONS (90–89 B.C.).
It began to appear that the Romans would be well advised to yield to Italian force what they had refused to concede to Italian worth. When the consul Lucius Julius Caesar returned to Rome in late 90 B.C. to hold the elections for 89, he found Umbria and Etruria, hitherto steadfast, becoming restive. The loss of these not only would multiply the military fronts, but would entail a severe loss of men and supplies and would open to the insurgents the great recruiting grounds of Gaul. Before he left office in 90, therefore, Caesar secured passage of the Julian Law, which conferred citizenship on all Latin and Italian communities that had remained loyal. This restrained any further spread of the revolt. Now that the first step had been taken, it was easier in the following year (89) to be astutely generous. A Calpurnian Law promised citizenship for bravery to individual non-Roman soldiers fighting on the Roman side, and the crea-

tion of two new tribes was also contemplated. These probably were designed to contain the new citizens from Etruria and Umbria, but events at the end of the war led ultimately to a different form of registration. A Plautio-Papirian Law held out citizenship to all citizens of allied states, whether or not their states were in revolt, if they would report to a Roman praetor within sixty days. And a Pompeian Law regularized the status of the inhabitants of northern Italy by reaffirming the Roman citizenship to the municipalities south of the Po and by granting Latin rights to the towns north of the Po. The reversal in Roman sentiment concerning the Italians was reflected in a new attitude toward those Romans that had favored the allied cause. The tribune Plautius, one of the sponsors of the Plautio-Papirian Law, also sponsored a law whereby the courts set up in 90 to try cases of treasonable support of the Italian cause now received jurymen elected by the thirty-five tribes and from all three orders of citizens. Its first victim was Varius Hybrida himself, the man that had originally sponsored the creation of that court.

The citizenship laws of 89 B.C. limited the spread of the conflict and ensured Rome's continued access to her sources of men and supplies. Further, now that the original objective of the allies had been procured, many of them appear to have deserted the confederacy; and during 89 B.C. Roman victories began to outnumber Roman defeats. In the north Gnaeus Pompeius Strabo beat down the last desperate effort of the allies to relieve Asculum, which had been under siege since early in the war. We are told that 75,000 Romans here faced 60,000 Italians. Only a handful of the latter seem to have survived. Asculum fell and was brutally punished by Strabo, who owned huge estates in the neighborhood, for the part that it had played in kindling the war. In the south Sulla successfully cleared most of Campania and carried the war into the territory of the Hirpini and of the Samnites themselves. He was rewarded for his success by election to the consulship of 88 B.C. By the end of 89 only pockets of resistance were left, chiefly in Samnium, and even these districts were soon to receive the citizenship, for their arms and their potential votes were to become pawns once more in the morass of Roman internal politics.

FINANCIAL RESULTS OF THE WAR.   Without considering the long-term problems, the immediate ones generated by the war were devastating. Debts became widespread during the conflict, while the uncertainties at home and abroad led financiers to refuse to extend further loans. Hard pressed by their credi-

255

tors, in 89 B.C. the debtors appealed to the urban praetor Sempronius Asellio for relief, stating that they were willing to pay their debts, if given time. Meanwhile, they invoked ancient Roman laws that forbade the practice of usury,[5] and Asellio granted a hearing on those grounds. The financial interests were so infuriated at the threat that an obsolete statute would be used to control their affairs that, while he was conducting a sacrifice in the Forum, the praetor was mobbed and his throat was cut. The Senate launched an investigation and offered rewards, but the influence of the businessmen was sufficiently great that no one offered evidence.

MITHRIDATES INVADES ASIA (88 B.C.). Abroad, Mithridates, the king of Pontus in Asia Minor, had taken the opportunity offered by Italy's civil discord to further his own interests by the occupation of Bithynia, which Rome considered a protectorate. He had withdrawn to his own realm at the insistence of a Roman commission sent out in 89; but when the commissioners incited Nicomedes of Bithynia to raid Pontic cities in order to pay the commissioners for helping to restore him, and when Mithridates' diplomatic protests were answered only with threatening preparations, hostilities commenced. During 88 two Roman commanders in Asia were killed and a third fled to Rhodes. Most of the cities of Asia were overrun by Mithridates, or themselves took the opportunity to be rid of the Romans. Some 80,000 Roman or Italian businessmen are said to have been massacred. Investors in Rome were in an uproar at the loss of this lucrative province, to say nothing of the loss of their agents and representatives. The command of the province for 87 B.C. fell to the lot of Sulla, the consul of 88. However, since he was a senator and a patrician, the business interests viewed him with some suspicion since they blamed senatorial policy for the debacle in Asia. Moreover, Marius, though now very old, was extremely angry at this assignment, for he was jealous of Sulla and long had eyed and coveted a command in Asia, where he might regain his former greatness. Marius and the knights therefore began to search for an excuse to overturn Sulla's assignment.

THE REGISTRATION OF THE ITALIANS. Meanwhile, the various factions in Rome were considering how the new citizens should be registered in a way that would least inconvenience already established interests. The two new tribes sug-

---

[5] For these ancient laws on usury, see pp. 85–86.

gested by the Calpurnian Law of 89 B.C. pointed the way. It was now determined to create ten new tribes, apparently one for each of the major peoples of Italy to be added to the Roman State. This was the senatorial policy, a conservative one that harked back to the practice that was followed before 241 B.C. Before that date any significant addition of citizens was accompanied by the creation of new tribes to accommodate them. But this practice had long been abandoned and new citizens had simply been added to the existing tribes. It was suspected that the present resurrection of the ancient practice was simply a mean subterfuge to minimize the power of the new voters (who should nearly equal in numbers the old ones) by giving them only ten tribal votes, while the older citizens retained thirty-five.

One of the tribunes of 88 B.C., Sulpicius Rufus, had been a friend of the younger Livius Drusus and like him was a member of the moderate reform wing of the Senate. He felt it an injustice that the Italian vote should be sequestered in a minority of ten tribes and he hoped to enlist the new voters on the Senate's side. He proposed to bring home the members of his own party that had been exiled for pro-Italian sentiments in 90 B.C., to control senatorial venality by the expulsion of all members with more than 2000 denarii in debts, and to distribute and enroll both the Italians and the freedmen in the old established thirty-five tribes. Both the consuls and an appreciable portion of the aristocracy were bitterly opposed to these measures, however, and used every device to prevent a vote upon them. Sulpicius thereupon turned to Marius and the equestrians. In return for their support he promised to procure a law transferring the Asiatic command from Sulla to Marius. The bargain was closed and the laws were passed, though force had to be used to procure their passage in the assembly. The apparently inconsistent policy of the knights, who had been most violently opposed to any enfranchisement of the Italians at all before the Social War, is perfectly consistent in terms of selfishness. Now that the Italians were citizens anyway, the knights were not averse to gaining their gratitude in the political field, and in the bargain they would acquire their own candidate to reestablish their interests in Asia.

SULLA'S FIRST CAPTURE OF ROME (88 B.C.).   Sulla and his troops, who were at the time besieging Nola as part of the mopping up of the Social War, had no intention of surrendering the glory and the profits of an Asian campaign. The hearts and consciences of these men had now been hardened by the many years of factional rioting since the Gracchan era and by the horrors of fraternal conflict experienced during the Social War. The callousness of the soldiers toward the suffering of their fellow countrymen, toward national tradition and the government's authority, was reinforced by the increasing personal ambition of their commanders and by the selfish exhortations of the business world. They turned on Rome itself, took the city, and had their political enemies declared outlaws. Marius thus became the victim of his own creation, the army loyal to its general rather than to the State, and he sought sanctuary as an exile in Africa. Sulpicius was captured and put to death.

With the cooperation of his consular colleague, Pompeius Rufus, Sulla proceeded as rapidly as possible to return the government to the principles of the early Republic. Sulpicius' laws were declared invalid because they had been passed with the use of force. Legislation became a prerogative of the Centuriate Assembly alone, and all bills presented to it had to have the prior consent of the Senate. The latter provision returned Rome legally to the situation before the Hortensian Law of 287, though this had continued to be the actual practice in most cases down to Tiberius Gracchus. The tribunes were to be reduced to their old function as defenders of the plebs, and the Tribal Assembly apparently became only the organ to elect them.

Sulla's fellow-consul Pompeius Rufus now attempted to take over the army that had been commanded during the Social War by Pompeius Strabo. Once again, the troops demonstrated the new type of military loyalty and murdered Rufus. Thereupon Strabo quietly resumed his former position. This act was further warning that governmental authority was collapsing and that war lords might soon replace it; but Sulla apparently thought it inexpedient to challenge Strabo, and busied himself with the elections for 87 B.C. One of the men elected to the consulship, Gnaeus Octavius, was a confirmed senatorial and a sympathizer of Sulla's conservative government, but the other, Lucius Cornelius Cinna, was not. Sulla, however, exhibited that somewhat cool and sporty detachment that characterized his career; he accepted Cinna's election, but caused him to swear that he would not try to subvert the new political arrangement. Thereupon he embarked his troops for the East.

CINNA AND MARIUS MARCH ON ROME (87 B.C.).   Sulla no sooner had left than Cinna tried to introduce measures that would recall Marius and other popular exiles and once again would undertake the enrollment of the new citizens in the old thirty-five tribes. In the ensuing altercations Cinna was deprived of his consulship by the pro-Sullan Senate, and Octavius took as a new colleague Cornelius Merula. This was a remarkable choice in this age of outrage and bloodshed, for Merula was a priest, the *flamen Dialis*,[6] and as such was forbidden to look upon a corpse. The choice in effect made Octavius sole consul. But, in any event, the deposed Cinna hastened to the troops that were still besieging Nola, convinced them that his deposition had been illegal, raised support among the Italians by advertising that he favored the more liberal method of registration for the new citizens, and called on Marius to return and join him in a march on Rome. Marius landed in Etruria and raised an army of Etruscan and Umbrian supporters, and the two confederates besieged the city. The beleaguered Senate called upon Pompeius Strabo and his army to relieve the city. It also tried to raise troops by offering the citizenship to the Samnites, who were still rebellious and in arms and who therefore had not yet received the promise of enfranchisement that the other Italians had received. But most of the Samnites preferred the equally hospitable and more notoriously liberal ranks of Cinna; and though Strabo marched to Rome, his attitude was equivocal, and he died before taking any decisive action.

CINNA SUPREME AT ROME (86–84 B.C.).   After a blockade by troops under Marius the city once more fell. Octavius was killed and Merula committed suicide. Marius proceeded to wreak vengeance on those senators that had most offended him, and he had them murdered by a band of liberated slaves. In January of 86 B.C. Marius entered upon his seventh and Cinna upon his second consulship, but Marius died in his first month of office and was replaced by Lucius Valerius Flaccus. For three years (86–84 B.C.) the government at Rome was effectually in the hands of Cinna, or of Cinna and his consular colleague of 85 and 84, Papirius Carbo. Sulla, who was pursuing the reconquest of Asia, was unnecessarily and permanently estranged by this government which declared him a public enemy and confiscated his property. Attempts also were made to replace him in his command overseas. The consul Valerius Flaccus set out in 86 for that purpose, but he was incompetent and unpopular and was killed by his own men, who elevated his legate Flavius Fimbria to the command. Fimbria's troops, however, refused to combat Sulla's army. After some successful actions against Mithridatic forces in Asia they went over to Sulla in 85. In 84 Cinna himself set out to convey troops to Epirus in order to combat Sulla, but his troops mutinied before embarkation and killed their commander.

---

[6]   The *flamen Dialis* was a priest of Jupiter. His post was extremely ancient and was surrounded by taboos.

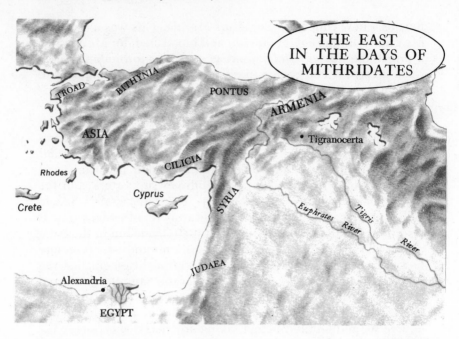

THE EAST
IN THE DAYS OF
MITHRIDATES

TROAD

BITHYNIA

PONTUS

ARMENIA

ASIA

Tigranocerta

Rhodes

CILICIA

Crete

Cyprus

SYRIA

Euphrates River

Tigris River

JUDAEA

Alexandria

EGYPT

SULLA'S CAMPAIGNS IN THE EAST (86–84 B.C.).

Meanwhile Sulla's steady successes in the East were inexorably
pointing toward a day of reckoning in Italy. In 86 he captured
Athens, which had gone over to Mithridates and had encouraged
that king to launch an expedition into Greece. However, in two
brilliant engagements Sulla scattered and destroyed Mithridates' invading forces. Then in 85 Sulla opened diplomatic
negotiations with him to seek an early settlement. Mithridates'
position in Asia itself was deteriorating: a number of the Greek
cities found his rule as noxious as Roman rule had been and
were becoming restive; Licinius Lucullus, a lieutenant of Sulla,
had raised a fleet which in cooperation with the Rhodians
effected the recovery from Mithridates of some Aegean islands and coastal points in Asia; and Fimbria's army, which
had been dispatched from Rome in 86, was waging a successful
campaign in northern Asia Minor. In a personal interview
with Sulla in the Troad, Mithridates therefore agreed to
Sulla's terms: to withdraw into Pontus, give up all conquered
territories, pay an indemnity of 2000 talents, and surrender
part of his fleet. The terms were lenient because Sulla had
other urgent matters to settle and wanted an honorable but
expeditious peace in Asia. Sulla settled the affairs of Asia by
restoring the various satellite kings expelled by Mithridates,
by punishing prominent adherents of Mithridates in the Greek
cities of the province of Asia, and by placing an indemnity of

260

20,000 talents on the province to cover the cost of the war and the amount of taxes lost during it. After billeting the troops upon the Asians during the winter of 85/4, in the spring of 84 Sulla embarked his men for a leisurely return to Italy.

THE END OF THE ITALIAN QUESTION.   In Rome the news of Sulla's exploits had a mixed reception. Many senators did their best to placate Sulla and to arrange a peaceful settlement. At the same time, however, the consuls made hectic attempts to shore up the defenses of Italy against Sulla's return. They depended heavily on the gratitude of the new citizens of Italian extraction, both because they had granted citizenship to the Samnites, who were formidable soldiers, and because they had supported the liberal policy of registration in the old thirty-five tribes rather than adopting the conservative plan to register the Italians in new tribes. However, when Sulla returned to Italy he made known his determination to respect the commitments made to the new citizens regardless of the circumstances of the grants. This completely cut the ground from under the Marians, and it signalled the end of Italy's struggle to become a nation. Now at length both camps were agreed that the vote of old and new citizens alike should have an equal weight in the assemblies.

Rome's war with her allies and the settlement, though grudging and calculated, that followed it laid the foundation for a united Italy from the Alps to the Straits of Messina. It assured the cultural assimilation of all Italy to Latium and the consequent Latinization of western Europe. Further, it established the idea of dual citizenship: of a vigorous municipal government and life within a larger national framework. The new citizens were finally enrolled in thirty of the old tribes. (They were naturally not included in the four urban tribes, which still contained freedmen and the citizen residents of Rome; and the rural tribe Pollia already was so large that it received no additions at this time.) This was a giant step toward the creation of a Mediterranean citizenship. But the cost was dreadful. These years accustomed Italy to the bitterest and bloodiest kind of conflict, fraternal conflict; and the pitifully small rise in the census after the accession of most of the Italians (394,336 reported in 115 B.C. and only 463,000 in 86) reflects the severe losses in manpower both among the Romans and the Italians due to economic decay and fierce military struggle. Its foolish and needless waste stands as a monument to the vanity, selfishness, and greed that imperial success had bred in the Romans of the later Republic.

Chapter 24

SULLA AND ARCHAISTIC REVIVAL

SULLA GATHERS STRENGTH IN ITALY (83 B.C.).
Sulla's army of about 40,000 men landed unopposed at Brundisium in the spring of 83 B.C. Before they started their march up the Italian peninsula the men swore an oath to one another to maintain discipline and not to pillage the countryside. They maintained that their only object was their commander's enemies in Rome, for his enemies were also their enemies. In Campania near Capua they met and routed the army of one of the consuls of the year, Norbanus. Upon approaching the second consular army under Lucius Scipio near Teanum, the commanders decided to establish a truce while terms of peace were being discussed. However, the truce was broken by one of Scipio's aides, and thereafter Sulla treated all hostile action by the Marians as outside the law. The loyalty of Scipio's army meanwhile was subverted by Sulla's veterans, and Scipio saw his men desert to Sulla en masse.

Sulla's army spent the winter of 83/2 in Campanian quarters. During the winter Sulla's statements of policy weakened the influence that the popular government in Rome had over the new citizens. He made it clear that he would observe the promises made to them in regard to tribal registration and that he too would support their distribution throughout the old tribes. Campania, Picenum, and Apulia were secured to him, and his ranks were gradually increased by returning exiled or fugitive oligarchs and by some new adherents. From Africa by way of Liguria came Caecilius Metellus, who had been a promagistrate in Italy during the Social War. As a member of the senatorial party, he had retired to Africa when the Marians came to power in 86 B.C. Since Metellus did not recognize the right of the Marians to rescind his *imperium*, there was perhaps some legality in Metellus' arrival with a military force. However, there could be no constitutional justification for young

Marcus Crassus, who had been evading the Marians in Spain and now also showed up with a band of recruits. This is an example of how the provinces were beginning to be used by the great families not only to enhance their prestige as the influential patrons of the provincials, but also as spawning grounds for personal armies. Perhaps even more remarkable than the army recruited by Crassus was the arrival of young Gnaeus Pompey, son of Pompeius Strabo, who had raised a private army of three legions from his father's veterans and clients in Picenum and who, on his way to join Sulla, destroyed a number of contingents of troops loyal to the central government. Sulla expressed his gratification at Pompey's arrival and regularized the proceeding by gravely greeting the young upstart as "imperator," that is, "general."

SULLA TRIUMPHANT (82–80 B.C.).   In 82 Sulla headed for Rome. To withstand him the central government sent out the younger Gaius Marius, who at the age of twenty-six had been made consul, not for his eligibility or capability, but for the magic of his name. Marius was soundly defeated at Sacriportus and had to seek refuge in Praeneste, while Sulla proceeded to occupy the city of Rome. Campaigns on behalf of Sulla in Etruria and Cisalpine Gaul by Crassus, Pompey, and Metellus were largely successful. However, Carbo, the other consul of the popular party, still maintained a considerable anti-Sullan force in Etruria. The close investment of Marius in Praeneste, however, brought about the denouement. Several vain attempts were made in 82 to pierce Sulla's lines encircling the town. At length the Samnites tried. They had remained loyal to the Marian party because the lax government of the *populares* left them in effect free, as long as they fought. After their attempt to relieve the town of Praeneste also proved abortive, they turned and dashed for Rome in hopes that if they seized and pillaged the city Sulla would abandon the siege of Praeneste. Taking part of his troops, Sulla hurried after them. The battle before the Colline Gate was fierce and bloody, but the Samnites at last were defeated and three or four thousand of them were captured. At word of this, Praeneste surrendered and Marius killed himself. Carbo in Etruria then lost his nerve and fled the country. Except for a few strongholds all Italy was now fallen to Sulla. Meanwhile, in 82 B.C. Marcius Philippus occupied Sardinia for Sulla, and in 81 Spain was at least temporarily recovered. Pompey was sent to Sicily and, after its fall in 82, proceeded to Africa where in 81 and 80 he disposed of Marian resistance there. In Asia Sulla's successor, Licinius Murena, was bold enough to invade Pontus contrary to Sulla's treaty with Mithridates and was sharply repulsed. A complaint from Mithridates to Sulla brought a reprimand for Murena and a recall to Rome. With this frivolous and irresponsible adventure at an end, the Roman world was once more united and at peace.

SULLA REFORMS THE STATE ON ANCIENT LINES.
Although peace was reestablished at home and abroad, it was a peace that held no promise unless firm measures were taken to maintain it. Sulla felt that first of all he must scotch the popular party—the alliance of Marians, equestrians, and urban rabble—so that it could not again dominate the State. He himself had not been in his early days a doctrinaire conservative, but the Marians had tried in 88 to ruin his public career, and after his departure for Greece they had victimized his family and friends. He was perfectly aware of the shortcomings of the current oligarchs, but he had been forced into their camp, and now he remained true to them even while trying to revive the ancient and more attractive image that they had displayed in the early Republic. Sulla was faced, however, with more serious problems than simple punishment and revenge: he had to bring peace to Italy; he had to see to it that the city's proletariat no longer could try to run an empire. He also had to reorganize the magistracies so that another Marius would not arise, and the provincial commands so that no more generals like himself would return from abroad to impose their will on the State.

In the late autumn of 82 B.C. Sulla sent word to the Senate that an extraordinary magistracy was needed to reconstruct the State, and he added that he felt equal to such a task. Valerius Flaccus, the *princeps senatus*, was thereupon appointed *interrex*, to preside during the interregnum caused by the loss of the two consuls. He in turn got passed by the Centuriate Assembly the Valerian Law, whereby Sulla's previous arrangements were confirmed and he was appointed a dictator without term, authorized to take such steps and issue such laws without veto or appeal as were necessary to reform the State. This dictatorship was to be the medium for his work, but it was not the old republican dictatorship, which had been abandoned since the Hannibalic War. The authorization by the people, the elimination of the right of appeal, the lack of a terminal date, the very task essayed looked back to the Decemvirate that drew up *The Twelve Tables* in the fifth century B.C. rather than to the constantly more restricted dictatorship of the third century.[1] There

---

[1]   For the rules governing the conventional republican dictatorship, see p. 94. For the Decemvirate, see pp. 56–57.

were indeed precedents for each of the features of this new dictatorship, but not for the whole. However, since Tiberius Gracchus the Roman constitution had been gradually disregarded, especially by the popular or Marian party.

THE PROSCRIPTIONS.   The elimination of Sulla's personal and political enemies had begun with the occupation of Rome. On the third day after the Battle of the Colline Gate the three or four thousand Samnite prisoners were rounded up in the Campus Martius, and those implacable foes of Rome were killed to a man. But individual murders of prominent Romans also proceeded in such numbers that Sulla agreed to remove some of the uncertainties surrounding his opponents' fate, and he began to publish lists of those condemned. These persons were to be destroyed and their property confiscated, and any assistance to them was to be severely punished. The first proscription list contained the names of forty senators and 1600 knights, and the list swelled until, by June 1st, 81 B.C., and the official end of proscriptions, perhaps 4700 persons had been killed. Naturally the equestrians were the hardest hit, but all classes suffered, for Sulla offered liberal rewards to informers and executioners. Unfortunately the proscriptions sometimes served as a cover for the private enmities or the greed of Sullan henchmen. Over the whole operation Sulla presided with cool detachment, adding to the lists the names of men that he did not hate, that he did not even know. Rome never forgot or forgave that cold nonchalance. By this act, however, Sulla aimed to destroy the leadership of any future attempts to revive the popular pretensions, and by it he also was provided with the lands and monies to effect the settlement of his loyal veterans.

Outside of Rome Sulla kept his word to the Italians and did not seek to change the civil status that they had acquired, whether the grant had come from the Senate or from the Marians. But he did punish severely those towns that had held out against him, and many lost part or all of their territory, with their residents demoted to the status of Latins. He was particularly bitter at the Samnites, who had adhered to the popular cause to the end and finally had tried to sack Rome. In requittal he not only massacred the remnant of their army, but he also had their countryside thoroughly devastated, rendering it a wilderness.

THE SULLAN COLONIES.   The proscriptions had at length furnished both land and money with which to reward and settle the veterans. Some of them were given individual allotments, but in many cases they were settled in colonies strategically situated among the peoples of Italy, and especially close to areas that had favored the popular cause. There were 120,000 of these veterans; and they were loyal to Sulla and bound to defend his arrangements, for only thus could their grants be validated. Sulla's grants of land to his veterans carried the Gracchan provision that the lots might not be alienated, which indicates that Sulla also looked for his country's salvation in a strengthened peasantry; but, unlike the Gracchan colonies, Sulla's resembled those of the early Republic in that they also had military value.

SULLA'S ECONOMIC MEASURES.   The abundance of property thrown upon the market by the proscriptions and the uncertainties connected with the period brought about an economic crisis with a disastrous fall in prices. Great fortunes apparently were made by those that had the money and opportunity to invest at the time. Debtors, however, were ruined, for the market value of their landed estates fell so drastically that they would no longer cover the debts for which they were pledged. Sulla attempted to alleviate the distress by reestablishing the rate of interest at 8 1/3 percent, the fifth century B.C. rate sanctioned by *The Twelve Tables;* and he forbade the ostentatious use and display of wealth. The cheap distribution of grain was brought to an end, a move designed not only to assist the treasury, but also to encourage the emigration of some of those persons that depended on it. An elaborate building program both at Rome and in the municipalities, consisting of walls, theaters, temples, and administrative buildings, furnished work to the poor and increased the beauty of many sites.

POLITICAL MEASURES.   With Italy secured and the veterans settled, Sulla turned to Rome. Never again must the city mob presume to exercise the sovereignty, especially now that Roman citizens no longer were concentrated near Rome, but were distributed throughout the peninsula. The power of the urban proletariat had been exercised through their tribunes, who had acquired legislative initiative. Now Sulla returned the tribunate chiefly to its ancient function—to protect individual citizens from magisterial trespass. However, since the office had proved useful to control errant magistrates or to introduce approved legislation, its right of veto and of convening the Tribal Assembly were not wholly removed, but they required the prior sanction of the Senate. To deter ambitious men from using the office of tribune as a stepping-stone to an advanced career of demagoguery, Sulla forbade ex-tribunes to hold the higher magistracies. To strengthen his following Sulla chose 10,000 of the slaves of persons that he had proscribed, freed them, and allowed them to assume his own gentile name. These Cornelii became a select corps upon whom he and the Senate could depend to curb urban disturbances and attempts to subvert his reorganization of the State.

The Senate, upon which so much of the Roman future depended, was at a low ebb in numbers and ability. It was clear that from magistrates sitting in that body had come leaders even more dangerous to the State than the tribunes. To infuse new blood Sulla added 300 men of equestrian rank to the Senate.[2] "Equestrian" here is an ambiguous term. Many of these men must actually have been young members of the senatorial families, who were enrolled in the eighteen centuries of the *equites equo publico;* others would be men of lower social, but equal financial rank who had proved their worth in Sulla's army, *equites equo privato;* and still others were Sullan adherents that had been raised to the financial level of the equestrian census by acquiring the great estates of the proscribed at bargain prices. When all these new senators were added to the approximately 150 senators who had stayed in Rome and to the exiled and fugitive oligarchs that now filtered back to Rome, the Senate seems to have risen to nearly 600 persons. Sulla wished to keep the Senate at approximately this size. He had set the number of quaestors, who handled the increasing financial administration of the empire, at twenty, and he now caused persons elected to the quaestorship automatically to be added to the Senate. He calculated that thus the Senate would become self-perpetuating without the censors making their traditional reviews of and additions to the senatorial rolls. He also increased the number of praetors to eight so that they could cope with increased court activity. He revived and revised the ancient rules of office-holding to ensure that magistrates would be mature and responsible and would not be tempted to self-aggrandizement. The quaestorship must be held before the praetorship, and the praetorship before the consulship. A quaestor must be at least thirty years old, a praetor thirty-nine, and a consul forty-two. No office could be repeated without an interval of ten years between the tenures. By these measures Sulla hoped to eliminate the abuses that the Romans had suffered during the repeated consulships of a Marius, Cinna, or Carbo.

Sulla took his reforms seriously. When his trusted lieuten-

[2] For earlier discussions of the knights, see pp. 62, 83–84, 177–178.

ant Lucretius Ofella, who had reduced Praeneste, wished to stand for the consulship of 81, Sulla forbade him, for he had not yet been either praetor or quaestor. Nevertheless Ofella persisted, and Sulla ordered one of his centurions to cut him down in the Forum while he was canvassing for office.

Sulla did not abolish the censorship, but its services were little needed for the moment. There were no land taxes in Italy, the army was raised by enlistment, entrance to the Senate was automatic, and the censors' financial duties were performed by the consuls. For the time being at least, he seemed to wish to disregard this prestigious office.

The Sullan organization of the State brought to an end the popular democratic type of constitution initiated by the Gracchi. It was a reversion to the idealized fifth and fourth centuries B.C., although Sulla made some allowances for the new problems that had come with empire and with an expanded citizenry. Gone was the tribune's grip on public life through his wide powers of intercession, and gone was the independence of the tribune's plebeian assembly that could legislate for the Mediterranean world, though it actually represented only the citizen residents of Rome. Sulla also eliminated the third basis of the popular power established by Gaius Gracchus—the equestrian jury. He now established seven permanent courts to handle seven specific criminal matters: extortion, murder and poisoning, forgery and fraud, embezzlement of public funds, bribery at elections, treason, and assault. This was the first solid organization of criminal law and criminal courts at home. The juries for these courts were to be drawn from the newly enlarged Senate, each jury under the presidency of a praetor or an ex-aedile. His regularization of the criminal courts was one of Sulla's greatest and most lasting contributions to Rome. Interestingly enough, by transferring the trial for treason and other political crimes from the people to a jury court, Sulla in effect abolished capital punishment for such crimes, for the principle was still observed that only the people, and not a jury court, could condemn to death.

PROVINCIAL ADMINISTRATION.   There remained the task of regularizing provincial administration and providing that governors should not again pose to the State the same dangers that Sulla himself had posed. He proposed an arrangement whereby the eight praetors and two consuls annually elected should spend their year of office carrying out administrative duties in Italy. Prorogation, however, should become a regular part of the official career, and praetors and consuls should spend the year after they held office in Italy as promagistrates governing the provinces. Though military command was not forbidden during the first year of office, it would seldom be necessary for a magistrate to command an army in unified Italy. To ensure the elimination of armies from Italy, Cisalpine Gaul was organized as a regular province. It probably was at this time that the Rubicon River was set as Italy's northern boundary. While Cisalpine Gaul was now highly Latinized, a military force was still needed there to cope with the occasional attacks on the plains by still barbarous mountain tribes. There were now ten provinces — Sicily, Sardinia and Corsica, the two Spains, Macedonia, Africa, Asia, Narbonese Gaul, Cilicia, and Cisalpine Gaul — and the eight ex-praetors and two ex-consuls would ordinarily suffice for the regular administration of these. The Sullan plan was not rigid, however, so that magisterial terms could extend longer than two years if death created vacancies that regular elections would not fill. It was left to the Senate to decide which provinces were consular and which praetorian, and it thus could reward the more obedient magistrates with the more desirable assignments overseas. A further control over governors was furnished by Sulla's new treason law, for which he established a special court. This court was designed to arraign governors that began unauthorized conflicts, those that did not leave their provinces within thirty days after the arrival of their successors, and those that crossed their provincial boundaries under arms. It was the last provision, of course, that Caesar was to break when he crossed the Rubicon from his Cisalpine province in 49 B.C.

Such was the Sullan reconstruction of Rome. He used tyrannical methods to avoid a tyranny, for he realized that the country was not yet emotionally ready to accept an undisguisedly autocratic government. He idealized the past as much as Tiberius Gracchus had, and he tried to restore a government that would emulate the revered early republican model. But his design ignored the irreversability of human experience. To stand the slightest chance of success so idealistic a project required capable and dedicated citizens, lieutenants, followers, and successors. The degrading effects of the two generations since Tiberius Gracchus had trained almost no such men. Sulla had been forced to turn for his aides, not to confirmed or die-hard oligarchs, but largely to men that might be considered moderates, some of them men that had served on the other side. Their past training and past attacks on established government would make it easy for them to subvert Sulla's constitution too, as his closest lieutenants, Crassus and Pompey, were soon to show. It is true that the Sullan reorganization in itself had certain bad features: it was not wise to displace competent farmers with indifferent ones, and Sulla's confiscations in Italy in order to give land to his veterans did exactly that. Each group soon became the center of discontent and intrigue. Sulla's suspension of the censorship would have meant chaos in the assemblies sooner or later, and the elimination of the censor's additions to the Senate meant that older men that had proved their competence in other fields than politics could not be elected to that body. These were pertinent criticisms of Sulla's program, but the criticisms cannot obscure the fact that his was a vigorous attempt to put Rome's past to work in order to reform her chaotic present.

SULLA THE EPICUREAN.   The surprised world applauded, and wondered when in 79 B.C. Sulla resigned all his powers and stood without attendants or guards, a private citizen in the Forum. He said that he held himself accountable for his acts as a magistrate and that he would explain and defend them to any man that might ask; but all were in awe of him, and no one challenged him. After a few days in Rome he retired to his country estate in Campania and devoted himself to rural pleasures. The act was in keeping with the man. It is true that before retirement he had shored up his own and his constitution's future as best he could; but he would have been startled at the world's surprise that he should put aside his extraordinary position once his task was done. To us his dictatorship seems to have been of a modern mold, looking toward the Caesarism of the future, but to him it was of an antique cast and looked to the past; he was still a general of republican stamp and ideals.

Sulla Felix, Sulla the Blessed, was one of Rome's most enigmatic figures. He was one of the handful of Roman Epicureans,[3] who felt that they could not enjoy the peace of mind that their philosophy dictated until their warped and faulty environment was righted. They were also the early existentialists; they believed that what was, was and that what must be done must be done dispassionately. So it was with Sulla. When his task of reconstruction was finished, he could seek retirement without regret among the rural pleasures that the contemporary Epicurean poet Lucretius idealized. His whole life echoes Epicurean theology: from his early career Sulla was convinced that he was blessed by the gods and especially by Fortune, Fortuna, whose name when she is always beneficent is Felicitas. Hence his cog-

---

[3]   For the political consequences of Epicureanism, see p. 198.

nomen, Sulla Felix. This goddess shares her feast days and her functions with the Latin spirit of charm, Venus (Greek Aphrodite)—Venus, the Roman name for the highest throw of the dice, Venus, the mother of the Romans, the goddess of love and of the generative force, and the patroness of Lucretius' great poem on Nature and Epicurean philosophy. This is the reason that in Greek inscriptions Sulla Felix is rendered Sulla Epaphroditus. To the true Epicurean the person that really had faith in the gods opened his heart to them so that their grace fell upon him voluntary and unforced. Such was Sulla Felix; and Felicitas stood by him to the end to ensure a quick and painless death for him (78 B.C.) in the height of blessedness.

Chapter 25

THE SENATE'S LAST FAILURE:
THE PRINCIPATE OF POMPEY

The thirty years between the death of Sulla (78 B.C.) and the Battle of Pharsalus (48 B.C.) are among the most tumultuous, involved, and best documented in Roman history. They are often viewed as especially significant on the grounds that they spelled the end of the Republic. Spell it they did, but their significance does not lie here. The end of the Republic was already determined by mistakes that had been made in the previous half-century, and by the customs, practices, and ideals that had developed during those fifty years and had shaped men far different from their republican ancestors. In the period from 78 to 48 B.C. the reactions of these men to constitutional and psychological problems presaged and set precedents for the coming authoritarian government.

DISSATISFACTIONS WITH THE SULLAN CONSTITUTION.
Sulla's attempt to reconstitute the State satisfied very few Romans. His work clearly showed that no law-giver, no matter how well intentioned, can resurrect for his people their past, no

matter how superior, if the people do not wish it, are not made to wish it, or are no longer good enough for it. Tiberius Gracchus could not do it; Sulla could not do it. The passions and sufferings and piddling contrivances of generations had come between and done their work. The Marians and other *populares* and liberals resented the loss of their wealth, of their confiscated lands, and of the constitutional leverage provided by the Gracchan tribunate. The Sullan veterans, who had been given much of the confiscated land, found farming far less satisfactory than battle and plunder. The proletariat longed to recover the distribution of cheap grain; and the business class deplored its diminished profits and the political power that Sulla had taken from it. Internal discord encouraged challenge within and without the empire. Mithridates prepared to resume his expansionist policy in the East; Sertorius, the ousted Marian governor of Nearer Spain, returned in the West; while slaves and the destitute all around the Mediterranean sought revenge in revolt and piracy. The one group that should have given full support to Sulla's dispensation was the Senate. But the vast majority of the nobles seemed to think, now that the reins of government were returned to them, that they could resume their family squabbles, their games for position, and their rivalries to be first in enjoying the empire's plunder. What is worse, as the leading figure of the era there was produced a man who had just enough ability, just enough plausibility, to fool almost everybody including himself. For thirty years the great man Pompey and the senatorial oligarchs hurtled from dilemma to dilemma and from crisis to crisis; and when they finished the Republic had expired.

THE REVOLT OF LEPIDUS (78–77 B.C.).   The government embarked on a comedy of errors at once. One of the consuls of 78 B.C., Aemilius Lepidus, had been supported for election by Sulla's young lieutenant, Gnaeus Pompey, despite some objections from Sulla. In office, Lepidus decided that he stood to gain political profit by supporting the dissatisfied elements in the State. He straightway raised a cry for a restoration of the power of the tribunate, a renewed program for the distribution of cheap grain, and a restoration of the estates confiscated by Sulla. Such proposals coming from a head of government of course roused the dissatisfied, and an insurrection broke out among the displaced persons of Etruria, where the Marians had been strong and Sulla's settlement severe. The Senate thereupon unwisely armed Lepidus and his fellow consul Catulus and sent them north against the insurgents. The rebels naturally flocked to the radical consul Lepidus as though he were their champion. The senators then desperately elicited an oath from both consuls not to start a civil war, an oath that Lepidus conveniently discovered was good only during the year of his consulship. At the end of the year he marched on Rome. However, he was checked by Catulus; he retreated to Etruria and sailed to Sardinia, where he soon died.

THE RISE OF POMPEY.   During their attempts to cope with Lepidus and his supporters, the senatorial guardians of Sulla's constitution managed even greater folly. Marcus Junius Brutus, a lieutenant of Lepidus, was holding Cisalpine Gaul for his chief. The senators decided to commission Gnaeus Pompey to dislodge him, for Pompey's family had influence in Gaul. Pompey's father was the hated Pompeius Strabo, who had sacked Asculum and played so ambiguous a role when Marius and Cinna took Rome.[1] However, young Pompey was handsome and athletic and had brought three legions from his family's district in Picenum to Sulla in 83 B.C. Sulla then had appointed him his lieutenant to pacify Sicily and Africa where, by executing such prominent ex-magistrates as Carbo and Domitius Ahenobarbus, he earned the unenviable title of "that stripling executioner." Thereupon, always protesting that he was only the reluctant and modest representative of his troops, he blackmailed Sulla, half-outraged and half-amused, into granting him a triumph, despite the fact that he held no constitutional magistracy. It was Sulla who greeted him ironically as *Magnus*, "The Great." The young man upon reflection decided that the epithet did indeed best describe his genius, and he adopted it as his cognomen. Thenceforth he was Pompeius Magnus, Pompey the Great. Now in 77 his cup was full: in his eyes the Senate had confirmed Sulla's judgment—he was indispensable. He hurried to Cisalpine Gaul and to Mutina, shut Brutus up there, accepted his surrender on terms, and then had him killed. Thereupon, despite the commands of his superior, the proconsul Catulus, Pompey found countless reasons not to disband his troops and sat waiting not very patiently for his next assignment.

SERTORIUS AND POMPEY IN SPAIN.   The opportunity was at hand and was urgent. Sertorius, who had been governor in Nearer Spain (83–2 B.C.) and a partisan of the popular party, had been driven from the Iberian peninsula in 81, but was recalled by the Lusitanians in 80 to be their leader against the

---

[1]   See pp. 255, 259.

oppression of his successors. He was signally successful from 80 to 77 both as an administrator and as a general. He taught the Spaniards to combine Roman discipline with their own guerrilla warfare. His troops were so successful that he controlled most of Spain at the expense of the senatorial governor of Farther Spain, Metellus Pius. As an administrator Sertorius had studied the character and won the trust of the natives. He established a school for chieftains' sons so that, endowed with a Graeco-Roman education, they might become effective future leaders of their country; he set up a Roman administration in exile consisting of fugitive *populares;* and he harassed the Sullan government by maintaining an understanding with Mithridates of Pontus in the East and with the ubiquitous and powerful Mediterranean pirates. In 77 B.C. he received a considerable reinforcement under the command of Marcus Perperna from the survivors of Lepidus' venture in northern Italy. The Senate, now faced with the ineffectiveness of its own generals, the increasing power of Sertorius in Spain, and the blatant and menacing presence of Pompey and his troops near Rome, compounded its unconstitutional follies and gave Pompey a proconsular command in Spain.

From 76 to 74 B.C. Sertorius more than held his own against the new commander, although the other senatorial commander, Metellus, had significant and, to Pompey, invidious success against Sertorius' lieutenants. Finally Pompey threatened the Senate that he would withdraw from Spain, army and all, unless he were sent more men and supplies. The senators, who had no desire to see him back in Rome, complied; and little by little the superior resources that Pompey now commanded began to tell. In 73 B.C. Pompey scored some victories; and in 72, still undefeated, Sertorius was assassinated through the machinations of his jealous lieutenant, Perperna. Pompey had little difficulty thereafter in dealing with Perperna. The latter was defeated and executed, and his papers, including letters that might incriminate leading figures at Rome sympathetic to the popular cause, were judiciously burned by Pompey. Metellus had continued his command of Farther Spain from 79 to 71, and actually he had had more uniform success against the Sertorians than Pompey had; but his career and his character were more orthodox than Pompey's, and he dismissed his troops upon crossing the Alps in 71 B.C. and proceeded for Rome for the inevitable triumph.

SPARTACUS' REVOLT (73–71 B.C.) AND CRASSUS.   In 73 B.C. another folly of the Roman system was forcibly demonstrated.

Occupants of a gladiatorial barracks in Capua revolted, gathered servile support, and defended themselves against the government's forces by taking up a position on Mt. Vesuvius. A band of seventy-four men under a Thracian leader named Spartacus quickly grew to seventy thousand. Indifferent troops with inadequate commanders were sent by Rome to cope with the problem, and Spartacus defeated five praetors and both the consuls of 72 B.C. Soon large portions of southern Italy were at the insurgents' mercy. It was apparently the original design of the rebels to break out of Italy and to return to their homelands in the north or in the Balkans. But success and opportunities for revenge held them in Italy. Finally in late 72 the Senate appointed to the command another Sullan lieutenant, Licinius Crassus, who was a praetor in 73, and gave him eight legions. By early 71 B.C. he had rounded up and defeated most of the rebels. Crassus did not return all the runaway slaves that he captured to their owners. Instead, he decided to improve the morale of the Roman citizens by crucifying 6000 of them along the Appian Way between Capua and Rome.

Earlier in 71 panic had led the senators to urge Pompey to speed his forces returning from Spain in order to assist in quelling the slave revolt. While marching back through northern Italy he encountered and defeated 5000 fugitives from Crassus; and this happy accident bolstered another of his claims to eminence. Unlike the conventional Metellus, Pompey was thus able to enter Italy with troops still under arms.

FIRST CONSULSHIP OF CRASSUS AND POMPEY (70 B.C.).
The two heroes, Crassus and Pompey, now sat with armies before Rome ostensibly awaiting the triumphal recognition of their services. Crassus was a candidate, and probably a legal one, for the consulship of 70 B.C., but Pompey had no intention of allowing political precedence to his lesser rival and announced his candidacy also. The Senate demurred, for Pompey was clearly ineligible: he was six years younger than the minimum age established by Sulla's laws and he had not held the praetorship, or even the quaestorship. But Pompey, like Lepidus, suddenly found virtues in the ancient power of the tribunate. He promised the people that he would support a full restoration of the powers of the tribune if he were elected consul. In the face of the popular enthusiasm that Pompey's promises aroused the Senate was helpless. Its mistake had been made six years earlier in creating that extraordinary command for Pompey. At this point one really could not expect a man that had held the *imperium* so long to start at the bottom of the

ladder as quaestor. Therefore the Senate found it possible to waive the constitutional impediments, and Pompey and Crassus were duly elected consuls for the year 70 B.C.

Pompey now proceeded to fill his commitments to the popular party. Agitation for the restoration of the pre-Sullan tribunate had continued since Lepidus. Tribunes had sought complete restoration in 76, 74, and 73 B.C., and in 75 the consul Aurelius Cotta carried a law that permitted tribunes to seek higher office. It appears that a revival of the Gracchan grain law by Lepidus also had been allowed to stand; and in 73 B.C. a consular law, the Terentian-Cassian Law, provided for the purchase of Sicilian grain above and beyond the annual tithe in order to supply the program's needs. These two ex-lieutenants of Sulla now delivered the final blow to their patron's constitution, and the political rights of the Gracchan tribunate were fully restored.

A significant change was made in the jury courts also. A number of cases of notorious corruption in senatorial juries during the previous decade had been capped in 70 B.C. by the case of Verres, the governor of Sicily. During his three years in the province he had stolen or extorted 40,000,000 sesterces. He had sold justice and favors with an equal hand, planted false suits in order to accept bribes for dropping them, and scourged and murdered both provincials and Romans. His guilt was manifest, but his friends and money went to work in Rome. He might have escaped had not the provincials' advocate been young Marcus Tullius Cicero, who had served as a quaestor among them. He adroitly countered the legal obstructions and presented the evidence so forcefully that Verres went quietly into exile before the case was finished. The unscrupulous activities of leading Romans in behalf of Verres, however, was damning. Before the end of the year an Aurelian Law transferred the courts to a mixed jury: one-third senators, one-third knights, and one-third *tribuni aerarii*, who seem to have been of a financial class just below the knights. The censorship also was revived in this year, and the censors purged the Senate of sixty-four members and counted 910,000 citizens.

LUCULLUS DEFEATS MITHRIDATES (74–67 B.C.). After their year as consuls, during which Pompey's inexperience and awkwardness led Varro to write for him a handbook on proper senatorial procedure, neither Crassus nor Pompey accepted a provincial assignment. Crassus was busied with his constantly increasing wealth, and no opening was at hand commensurate with Pompey's self-esteem. The one really desirable command, that in Asia, was for the moment successfully held by a staunch senatorial, Lucius Licinius Lucullus, the man to whom Sulla had dedicated his *Memoirs* and a man not unlike the dictator in philosophical persuasion and tactical brilliance. To him had come the command in a new war with Mithridates of Pontus in 74 B.C. The Senate had procrastinated for years in respect to Sulla's settlement in Asia and never had ratified his treaty with Mithridates. When the king of nearby Bithynia died, in his effects there was discovered a will leaving his realm to Rome. This will was commonly considered a Roman forgery, and Mithridates feared that Bithynia would offer to the Romans a splendid base from which to attack Pontus. He took counter-measures in 74 B.C. by supporting an alleged son of the dead king in his claim to the Bithynian throne. Between 74 and 72 B.C., despite a scanty supply of men and materiel from Rome, in a series of brilliant campaigns the Roman general Lucullus drove Mithridates from his kingdom and forced him to seek sanctuary with his son-in-law, Tigranes of Armenia.

In 71 and 70 B.C. Lucullus turned his attention to the unhappy province of Asia, which had served as his base of operations against Mithridates. Sulla had imposed a fine of 20,000 talents on Asia in 85 B.C. for its part in the first war with Mithridates, and the provincial towns had had to finance the payment of this fine by floating loans with Roman bankers. The high rate of the compound interest charged by the Roman financiers meant that in less than fifteen years the total debt of the Asians had risen to 120,000 talents; many had had to sell their children into slavery to meet their quotas, and the towns were bankrupt. Lucullus took drastic action. He scaled down the debt to 40,000 talents, reduced interest to twelve percent, and helped the provincials pay the interest by alloting to that purpose the income from a temporary tax of twenty-five percent on the Asians' property. The provincials were grateful for this drastic but effective measure, but the financial circles in Rome were furious. In 69 B.C. Lucullus attacked Armenia in an attempt to force the surrender of Mithridates and routed Tigranes at his capital of Tigranocerta, though he was outnumbered six to one. In Rome, however, equestrian circles went to work to make his position in the East more and more difficult. Asia was withdrawn from his authority in 69 B.C. and Cilicia in 68. His command against Mithridates and Tigranes was transferred to the consul Glabrio in 67, and agents from Rome were at work tampering with the loyalty of his staff and troops.

POMPEY AND THE PIRATES (67 B.C.).   The activities of Pompey and Crassus as consuls in 70 B.C. had given heart to the popular party, and by 67 it had elected a board of tribunes prepared to exploit fully the powers that had been returned to the office. Gaius Cornelius carried a law forcing praetors to observe their own annual edicts, thus protecting the people from arbitrary legal actions. He sponsored another measure providing that personal exemptions to laws could be voted by the Senate only when there was a quorum of 200 members. The tribune Aulus Gabinius revenged Roman financial interests in Asia by stripping Lucullus of his command in Bithynia and Pontus and giving it to Glabrio. Roscius Otho further pleased the businessmen by reserving fourteen rows of seats in the theater next to the orchestra for the knights.

The great triumph of the year for the popular party was the Gabinian Law, which created an extraordinary command over the whole Mediterranean against pirates. As the champion of the tribunate Pompey was chosen for this command. Piracy had made trade on the seas and life on the seacoast extremely hazardous. The pirates were organized into what amounted to a great maritime republic. They dealt with kings, supported Sertorius and Mithridates, sailed unmolested into important harbors such as Syracuse, carried off two Roman praetors in their robes of office, pillaged Delos, and so interfered with the transport of grain that supplies in Rome fell short. Between 78 and 74 B.C. Servilius Isauricus had rooted out some of them along the Asian coast; but a special command against them for the praetor of 74 B.C., Marcus Antonius, was distinguished mostly by his exactions from the provincials and his complete defeat by the pirates in 71. In the limited area of Crete the proconsul Caecilius Metellus slowly but steadily was reducing piratical strongholds during 68 and 67 B.C. Now Pompey was to control all the Mediterranean and fifty miles of coast around it; he was to be assisted by fifteen senatorial legates; and he would command a fleet of 200 ships, enlist as many men as he needed, and have 6000 talents to spend on the project. The senatorial party fought the measure with all its resources—not that it objected to an extraordinary command, for it had just granted one to Antonius—but it feared this great power in the hands of a man such as Pompey. The senators did not understand that Pompey would never be a danger to them as long as they flattered and magnified him. The only senator sufficiently perceptive to see this and to support the bill was the quaestorian Gaius Julius Caesar.

Pompey set about this task efficiently. He divided the

Mediterranean into districts with a commander and fleet for each district, sealed off the Dardanelles, the straits at Gibraltar, and those between Sicily and Africa. Then, scouring the seas and driving the pirates into the hands of one or another of his subalterns, he swept clear the western Mediterranean in forty days. The campaign in the eastern Mediterranean was crowned by a great sea victory off Cilicia. Pompey was able to announce a successful resolution of the whole pirate problem in only about three months. Efficient organization combined with overpowering resources had quickly and easily eliminated a dangerous nuisance that the Roman government had tolerated for years. Further, Pompey used his victory in a moderate and sensible manner: instead of crucifixions and enslavements he used the captive pirates to repopulate areas where there was an economic future. Here was the ideal of popular statesmanship at its best, and this is perhaps the reason why Julius Caesar, who had an eye for talents of all sorts, had supported Pompey's command.

THE MANILIAN LAW. POMPEY IN THE EAST (66–62 B.C.).
The *populares* now felt sure that Pompey was their man, and they hastened to use him. They had seen to it that Lucullus, who had shaved their profits in Asia, sat helpless with a mutinous army, while Mithridates recovered most of the kingdom that Lucullus had taken from him. As a final indignity to Lucullus, one of the tribunes of 66, Gaius Manilius, brought in a bill extending Pompey's command over the whole Near East and the war with Mithridates. Caesar and Cicero were among the active supporters of the measure. Cicero's oration in its favor is unashamed in its recognition of the financial interests involved and in its adulation of Pompey. Mithridates and Tigranes both had been so weakened by Lucullus' campaigns that they offered little resistance to Pompey's overwhelmingly superior forces. Mithridates escaped to the Crimea, where ultimately he fell a victim to a rebellion while he was still scheming against Rome. Pompey also quickly contrived an agreement with the Parthians, and it soon was followed by the collapse of Armenia, which became a client state. He organized the new provinces of Bithynia and Pontus, subdued the Jews, added Syria to the empire, and by 62 B.C. had given most of the Near East a permanent organization, extending frontiers, rewarding faithful friends, and establishing around Rome's eastern periphery a ring of client buffer states, which could furnish the empire material assistance and which were attached to himself by personal ties of gratitude.

POMPEY'S RIVALS GIRD THEMSELVES (65–62 B.C.).
Pompey's successes left the oligarchs frustrated and beaten, but the *populares* also began to have second thoughts about their champion. Had they created a monster? Pompey had started as a Sullan lieutenant; would he return like Sulla to impose his own settlement on the State? Pompey's old rival Crassus, a leader of Roman business interests, saw the weakness of his own and of his party's position if Pompey returned in force. He therefore set out to shore up his defenses. As censor in 65 B.C. he tried to enroll the Transpadane Gauls as citizens in order to gain influence in an important recruiting ground, but his colleague in the censorship vetoed the action. He attempted to make the kingdom of Egypt tributary on the grounds that the late king of Egypt had willed his realm to Rome. This would have opened a rich field for businessmen's activities and room for a new army as a counterweight to Pompey, but again he was foiled by the senatorials, who questioned the authenticity of the will, and by Cicero, who saw that the claim was directed against his hero Pompey. Crassus next plunged into the murky politics of 65 B.C. Both of the elected candidates for the consulship of that year had been convicted of bribery and the election was set aside. There seems to have been a conspiracy thereafter to kill the substitute and duly inaugurated consuls and to set up a new government. The plan is known as the First Catilinarian Conspiracy and was the creation of another discontented politician named Sergius Catiline. The conspiracy totally misfired, but Crassus was thought to have been sympathetic, for he appeared to support Catiline's unsuccessful bid for the consulship in 64 B.C. and perhaps again in 63. After Catiline was defeated at the polls in 63, however, Crassus divorced himself from Catiline's radical program and resigned himself to whatever fate Pompey's return to Italy might bring.

CATILINE AND CICERO (63 B.C.).   Catiline did not give up as easily as Crassus. He was the scion of an old though decayed patrician family, and he resented his repeated frustrations at the hands of the Establishment and of the electorate. After his defeat in the elections of 63 B.C. he collected a coterie of the discontented—debtors, Sullan veterans, displaced Marians, and adventurers—and planned a coup that would eliminate the present government, destroy the city, and establish a new deal for the have-nots. Catiline was a nuisance and his scheme never could have gone far as long as there was a victorious Pompey ready at any time to save a grateful fatherland. But his measures could have brought destruction and suffering to Rome, and the city was saved from an unpleasant experience by the vigilance of Cicero, one of the consuls of 63. He watched and discovered the culprits, trapped those that remained in the city, and with Cato's help received a senatorial blessing for the summary execution without trial of the confessed conspirators. For his efforts the senators and the tenement dwellers acclaimed him father of his country.

JULIUS CAESAR EMERGES AS A POPULAR CHAMPION.
In the senatorial debate concerning the disposition of those Catilinarians that had been apprehended in Rome, the praetor-elect, Julius Caesar, had spoken strongly against the majority of the senators, who favored immediate execution. The conspirators had not been under arms, and Caesar held that by law such persons could be condemned to death only after trial before the people. This was the gist of the ancient right of appeal guaranteed to all citizens, but it was a courageous stand for Caesar to make at this point, for he himself was suspected for past radical associations, though even Cicero had to admit that during the conspiracy both Caesar and Crassus had furnished him with important information. In any case, Caesar's stand increased his popularity, a popularity that already had taken root when he defied Sulla by refusing to divorce his second wife, though she was the daughter of Sulla's enemy Cinna. The people were even more pleased by the lavish games of his aedileship in 65 B.C., for which he contracted enormous debts, and by his restoration of the monuments of Marius, which the Sullans had thrown down. The popularity began to pay off in 63, when he was elected pontifex maximus over the superior claims of older and more distinguished rivals. Caesar had learned early not to alienate rivals unnecessarily or irremediably. As praetor in 62 B.C. he supported a measure that would have recalled Pompey to deal with the army of Catiline. Fortunately this proved unnecessary, but his good will toward Pompey was noted. Further, he refused to appear in court against the dissolute young aristocrat, Publius Clodius Pulcher, on trial for desecration, though the crime closely touched Caesar's own household and official position as the head of the State religion. Clodius, disguised as a young girl, had broken into Caesar's residence in 62 in an attempt to debauch Caesar's third wife, Pompeia, during the women's ceremonial worship of the Bona Dea. Caesar divorced Pompeia, on the ground that his wife must be above suspicion, but he apparently saw possibilities in the dashing and unprincipled Clodius and kept his friendship. At the end of 62, with Pompey about to reappear in Rome,

Caesar borrowed enough money from Crassus so that his creditors would let him out of the city. He then left to assume the governorship of Farther Spain with its opportunities for military and administrative experience and for recouping a fortune.

POMPEY, CRASSUS, AND CAESAR ANTAGONIZED (62–60 B.C.). Pompey came home in 62 B.C. with the unimaginative expectation of plaudits from the crowd and the grateful deference of the Senate. He had done much to deserve these: the menace of the pirates was gone, Mithridates was no more, Roman revenues had been raised from fifty to eighty-five million denarii per year, three new provinces had been organized, and a ring of client kingdoms around Rome's frontiers served as a buffer against her foes. To crown his excellence Pompey belied his critics by disbanding his troops as soon as he landed in Italy and, now posing as a strict observer of the constitution, he proceeded to Rome for his triumph and reward. The worried *populares* such as Crassus breathed a sigh of relief and then watched the ensuing events with bemused interest. The senators were enchanted to have Pompey unarmed and at their mercy. Now was the opportunity to get even with this renegade upstart. He was, of course, greeted with all respect, and his triumph was a brilliant affair. But the Senate could not forget his resurrection of the tribunate when he and Crassus were consuls (70 B.C.); Lucullus resented the way Pompey's victories had been built on his own earlier campaigns without giving him credit; and Cato, the incorruptible descendant of the Censor, haggled over every item in Pompey's eastern settlement, which he had presented to the Senate for ratification. Naturally, the State should have examined closely so important a matter before ratifying it, but the petty and obstructive tactics of Cato and his associates were unproductive and infuriating. Pompey had no greater success in obtaining a settlement for his troops. By now enlisted armies looked to their generals for land when they were discharged, and Pompey quite properly had expected the Senate to help him keep faith with his veterans. But through 61 and 60 B.C. constant hindrances were raised to his efforts to use public lands left over from the Gracchan and Sullan allotments, lands which he proposed to supplement with purchases financed by the income from his new conquests in the East.

Pompey was not the only object of the harassments by the righteous Cato and his circle. The great stock companies of tax-farmers had bid too much in 61 for the privilege of collecting the taxes of Asia. In 60 when they discovered that their collections from the province would not cover their pledge to the government, they tried to avoid bankruptcy by obtaining some remission of their contracts. Crassus represented the interests of the financiers, but the oligarchs maintained that the contracts were inviolable and refused to take action.

The senators miscalculated, however, in dealing with Caesar, whom they feared for his great popularity and for his championship of Marius' memory. He returned in 60 B.C. from Spain after accomplishing the seemingly incompatible feats of successful warfare over the Callaeci and Lusitani, an excellent and fair administration of his province, and the acquisition of enough wealth to pay much of his enormous debts. He was eligible for a triumph, but he also wished to stand for the consulship of 59. The senators dallied over the grant of a triumph while at the same time refusing permission for Caesar to stand for the consulship in absentia. They expected that they thus would keep him from getting the consulship for it was illegal for generals to enter the city while awaiting a triumph under arms. But Caesar was an Epicurean and knew the value of empty honors. He therefore waived his right to a triumph and entered the city to canvass. Since there was no doubt that he would be elected, the senators set about to make his regime as innocuous as possible. They cheerfully and virtuously raised enough money to bribe the voters into providing Caesar with the most conservative of colleagues, Calpurnius Bibulus; and they thought that they had ensured the destruction of any ambitions that Caesar might have by voting to these future consuls as their provinces the care of the forests and sheepwalks of Italy.

THE FOUNDATION OF THE FIRST TRIUMVIRATE.   Caesar's friendly relations with Crassus and complacency toward Pompey now became politically productive. In return for their united and firm support he engaged to procure the legislation needed by Pompey and to satisfy the request of Crassus' tax-farming friends. Thus senatorial folly brought into existence the secret agreement or cabal that is known as the First Triumvirate. Once consul (59 B.C.), Caesar fulfilled his engagements without hesitation. Bibulus and obstructionist tribunes were driven from the Forum. One of Caesar's laws ratified Pompey's Eastern settlement; another lowered by one-third the amount that the tax-farmers of Asia must pay to the central government; and by two other laws the remaining public lands of Italy, including the rich *Ager Campanus*, were turned over to Pompey's veterans and to the poor of Rome. Constitutionalists protested, and Bibulus sought to make the whole program technically illegal by

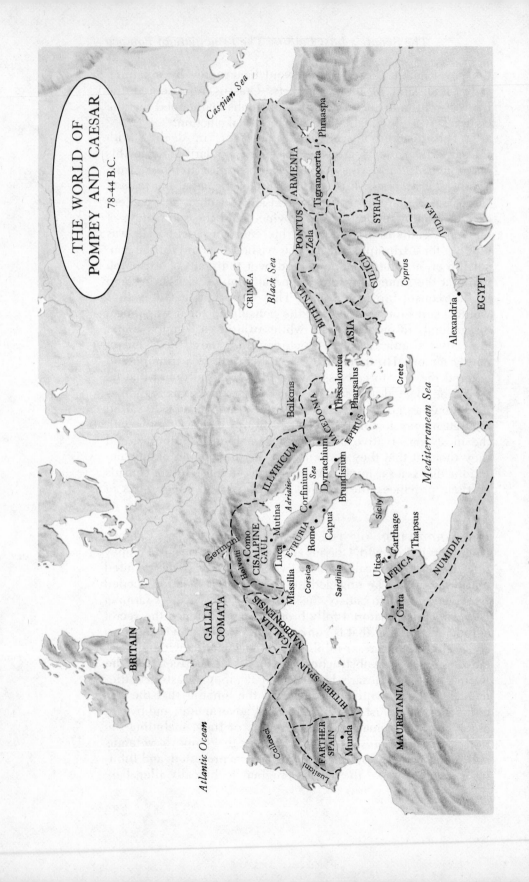

THE WORLD OF
POMPEY AND CAESAR

78-44 B.C.

Caspian Sea

ARMENIA
Phraaspa
Tigranocerta
PONTUS
Zela
SYRIA
BITHYNIA
JUDAEA
CILICIA
CRIMEA
Black Sea
ASIA
Cyprus
EGYPT
Alexandria

Mediterranean Sea
Crete

Balkans
Thessalonica
MACEDONIA
Pharsalus
Dyrrachium
EPIRUS
ILLYRICUM
Brundisium
Adriatic
Sea
Mutina
Corfinium
Luca
ETRURIA
Capua
Como
CISALPINE
GAUL
Rome
Sicily
Carthage
Thapsus
Germani
Helvetii
Corsica
Utica
AFRICA
Massilia
Sardinia
NUMIDIA
GALLIA
COMATA
GALLIA
NARBONENSIS
Cirta

BRITAIN

Atlantic Ocean

MAURETANIA

HITHER SPAIN
FARTHER
SPAIN
Munda
Lusitani
Callaeci

stating that he saw inauspicious omens each day. But the very irregularity of Caesar's procedure bound his partners firmly to him, for they feared that any attack on his methods of obtaining legislation would actually screen an attack on their programs. Thus Pompey, who had returned to Italy ready to be the Senate's champion and *princeps*, was once more, though reluctantly, forced into the popular camp. Caesar further bound Pompey to himself by giving him his daughter Julia in marriage, a dynastic match that proved a political and romantic success. Caesar also did not neglect to provide for his own future safety. A friendly tribune, Publius Vatinius, procured a law setting aside the Senate's plan to shunt Caesar off into an innocuous administrative job after his consulship. Instead, the new law granted Caesar the command in Cisalpine Gaul and Illyricum for five years. Shortly after this the governorship of Transalpine Gaul also fell vacant and was added to the others.

THE TRIBUNATE OF CLODIUS (58 B.C.).   Cicero and Cato threatened that once Caesar was in his provinces they would question the legality of all of his legislation of 59 B.C. To prevent this, Caesar used the talents of Publius Clodius. Clodius was a patrician by birth and therefore was ineligible for the plebeian tribunate, but Caesar as pontifex maximus arranged for Clodius to be adopted into a plebeian family, had him elected to the tribunate, and commissioned him to silence the offending pair. Clodius devised an honorable exile for Cato by carrying a bill to annex Cyprus and naming Cato as the executor. This was an appeal to Cato's sense of patriotic and Stoic duty and it was effective. For Cicero, who had testified against Clodius in the famous desecration trial (61 B.C.), there was a harder fate. Clodius brought a bill to outlaw anyone that had condemned Roman citizens without trial. The measure was clearly aimed at Cicero for his hasty execution of the unarmed Catilinarian conspirators in 63 B.C. After pitiful and fruitless appeals to an embarrassed Pompey, whom he so long had supported and magnified, Cicero went tearfully to exile in the East.

Clodius was not just a toady of Caesar, however. He had a good many projects of his own and he proceeded to them enthusiastically. One measure forestalled the right of magistrates to cripple political activity by watching for inauspicious omens as Bibulus had tried to do. Clodius' measure allowed the observation of omens only to augurs and tribunes. Another law completed the natural demagogic direction of grain legislation by providing for the distribution of grain completely free of charge to the people. A third measure rescinded an earlier ban on political clubs, which had been springing up on the model of the old artisans' clubs, and were now used in pressure politics. With Clodius' revival of these clubs or *collegia* the hooliganism of organized bravoes became a regular factor in Rome's politics. Clodius' own group was soon put to work on Pompey himself, for the uncomfortably conscience-stricken general began during the year to show sympathy for the restoration of Cicero. It was one of Clodius' jobs to keep Pompey in line, however, and this he did by so dismaying the great man with insults and threats that Pompey avoided Rome for the rest of Clodius' year of office. Other gangs, however, were pressed into service, especially by the Pompeian tribune Milo in 57; and Caesar's approval for Cicero's return was procured, provided the orator hereafter would support the triumvirs. The return of Cicero was finally effected during the summer of 57 B.C. and he was restored to his properties and rights.

THE TEMPTATION OF POMPEY.   Pompey's cooperation in the recall of Cicero raised senatorial hopes. The senators' only chance to regain control of the government was to split the triumvirate, and it now appeared possible that Pompey could be tempted. A sudden dearth of grain on the market in 57 B.C. led the senators to sponsor a measure giving Pompey proconsular *imperium* for five years in order to deal with the grain supply. Forty million sesterces were appropriated for this project. The appointment pleased Pompey, who was becoming uneasy at the news of Caesar's successes in Gaul. Caesar had moved outside the limits of his transalpine province in 58 B.C. to return the migrant Helvetians to their home and to drive invading Germans under Ariovistus back across the Rhine. Resulting involvements with various Gallic tribes led to Roman domination of central and coastal Gaul in 57, and most of the rest of the country appeared obedient by 56. Pompey's jealousy even led him to listen to renewed attacks on Caesar's legislation of 59 B.C., though tampering with Caesar's laws of that year could well cause difficulties to both Crassus and Pompey, who had profited from them. Crassus therefore sped to Cisalpine Gaul, where Caesar was wintering in early 56, and Pompey was soon prevailed upon to join them at Luca.

REAFFIRMATION OF THE TRIUMVIRATE.   The conference at Luca returned Pompey to his colleagues and to the *populares*. He was genuinely fond of his wife Julia and was not yet prepared to break faith with her father. Then too, for the present Caesar and Crassus could offer greater inducements to him than the senators. It was agreed that Crassus and Pompey were to hold the consulship together again in 55 B.C.; Crassus was then to indulge his fancy for military glory with a command for five years in Asia, while Pompey was to receive the command of the two Spains for an equal period. Caesar knew that much work still remained in Gaul, and Crassus and Pompey were to procure an extension of his command there for five more years. As soon as Pompey and Crassus were installed in their consulship, they procured for themselves through a complacent tribune, and despite violent opposition by other tribunes, the provinces decided on at Luca. Then the two consuls in effect extended Caesar's command by pushing through a law that forbade the discussion of a successor to Caesar before March 1, 50 B.C.

CAESAR IN GAUL (56–51 B.C.).   After Luca, Caesar returned to his work in Transalpine Gaul. In 55 B.C. the Germans again were chastised; and Roman prestige and pride were enhanced by expeditions into Britain in 55 and 54. However, Gaul itself was not yet truly subdued. There were local revolts in 54 and 53, and these culminated in a great national uprising in 52 under the formidable Vercingetorix. The revolt brought Caesar to the brink of disaster, but brilliant strategy, tireless effort, and magnificent leadership pulled him through. Thereupon his organization of all Gaul in 51 B.C. was so tactful, so fair, and so generous that the Gauls became his most dependable supporters, and the area began its development as one of the happiest and most prosperous parts of the empire.

DISORDERS MAKE POMPEY PRINCEPS OF ROME.   Gaul during the years of Caesar's conquests was scarcely more dangerous or confused than Rome. Crassus departed in the fall of 55 B.C. for his eastern command, publicly cursed by his political opponents. Pompey elected to remain in Rome on the plea of his supervision of the grain supply, and he sent legates to Spain to administer his provinces there in his name. During the elections for 53, all four candidates for the consulship as well as the presiding consuls of 54 were involved in corruption. There was such a scandal that the year ended with no election at all. In September of 54 Julia, Pompey's wife, died; but the ties between the partners were not at once broken, and in the autumn Pompey lent Caesar one of his own Spanish legions. Consuls for 53 finally were elected in July of that year, just a year late. At this juncture ominous news arrived that Crassus had been defeated and killed in June by the Parthians near Carrhae with a loss of almost 35,000 men. Now, with the counterweight of Julia and Crassus gone, there was good reason for foreboding among those who were worried about the rivalry between Caesar and Pompey; but there was high hope among Caesar's enemies that they could make Pompey their man and destroy their antagonist.

Disorders surrounding the elections for 52 B.C. outdid those of 53. The gangs of Milo, who was contending for the consulship, and those of Clodius, who was seeking the praetorship, kept Rome in a turmoil and made life there unsafe. Even the consuls were wounded in the rioting. Since he still had the proconsular imperium for his work with the grain supply, Pompey had remained outside the city and sat watching the confusion within and waiting for the people to demand him as their savior. The first of January 52 passed, again without new consuls. Riots and street fighting reached a climax when on January 18th some of Milo's ruffians killed Clodius. The latter's infuriated partisans then carried the body to the Forum and used the Senate House as a pyre in which to cremate their dead hero. Street fighting and murders raged for days, and the *interreges*, who were appointed in the absence of consuls to hold the elections, found it impossible to convene an elective assembly. Finally the Senate, with Bibulus and Cato in the forefront, decreed to Pompey a sole consulship and the power to raise troops and restore order. The appointment was unexampled and illegal, but Sulla's tenure of the dictatorship without legal or temporal restrictions had rendered the office suspect, and at least Pompey would be subject to the temporal restrictions of the consulship. As Cato drily explained, "any government is better than none at all."

Pompey's vigor, firmness, and impartiality in restoring order and in trying the culprits of the recent reign of violence impressed even the most suspicious of the senatorials. He was sole consul, enjoyed the right to raise troops and support them from the public treasury, he had control of the vital grain supply of Italy, and he maintained armies in two provinces which he administered through his lieutenants. He was now indeed the *princeps*, the first man of the State, and was so viewed by his contemporaries. By the late summer of 52 B.C. he was sure enough of himself to restore a more normal government by making his new father-in-law, Caecilius Metellus, his colleague in the consulship.

POMPEY'S POLICIES WEAKEN CAESAR'S LEGAL POSITION.
As Pompey's relations with the Senate became closer, his actions toward Caesar became ambiguous. He had already rejected Caesar's suggestion for a new marriage alliance after

Julia's death, but in early 52 B.C. he supported a bill brought in by all ten tribunes allowing Caesar to stand in absentia for the consulship. This would presumably be for 48 B.C., when ten years had elapsed since the completion of Caesar's first consulship. By the summer of 52, however, Pompey appeared to have nullified his earlier action by carrying a law that required the presence of all candidates canvassing for office. When the effect of this on Caesar was pointed out to him, he protested that it was an oversight, and on his own authority he attached a codicil to his bill in which he exempted Caesar, although the measure already had been passed. To tamper in this way with bills already filed was, of course, high-handed and of dubious legality. More ominous to Caesar than Pompey's "oversight" in this matter was Pompey's new law which provided that magistrates were not to proceed immediately to their provinces after a year of office in Italy, but were to undergo a waiting period of five years. This was a good law on its face, for it discouraged the expenditure of a great deal of money in buying office with the expectation of a speedy recovery in the provinces. But it could be disastrous for Caesar. He knew that if he allowed himself to return to Rome as a private citizen, his enemies, led by Cato, would immediately attack. The earlier arrangement whereby a successor for himself could not be discussed before March 1, 50, sufficiently protected him. His successor would then be one of the consuls elected in the summer of 50 B.C. for the year 49 and would not be ready to replace Caesar in Gaul until January 1, 48. Meanwhile, if Caesar could legally stand in absentia for the consulship in 49 and be ready to take office on January 1, 48, he would be constantly in office and thus protected from indictment. Now all this was changed; a past magistrate could at any time replace Caesar when his term in Gaul expired, and this appears to have been sometime in the late fall of 50. Against these new dangers his sole defense was to gain control each year of at least one tribune who could veto any attempt to replace him in Gaul until his prospective consulship.

THE SENATE SPARS WITH CAESAR (51–50 B.C.). The senators sensed that Pompey was nearly theirs. From now on, while Caesar and Pompey tried to maneuver each other into a flagrant breach of the law, the extremists among the oligarchs made no pretense of disinterest or constitutionalism, but waged a campaign that led relentlessly to civil war. While Caesar was completing the organization of Gaul in 51 B.C. there was no open break, but the rabidly anti-Caesarian consul Marcus Marcellus already was trying to promote the replacement of Caesar on the grounds that his work in Gaul was finished. Marcellus was opposed, however, by his colleague in the consulship and by Pompey himself, who stated that it would be improper to discuss the subject until March 1, 50, in accord with the earlier commitment to Caesar. Marcellus showed his scorn for all of Caesar's laws, however, by having a citizen of New Como, to which Caesar had given Roman citizenship, scourged in Rome. Since the man was a Transpadane of Cisalpine Gaul and would have had Latin rights at the very least, if not the citizenship, this arrogant act did not endear the senatorial factions to the liberals or Italians. However, Caesar had used some of his Gallic wealth to secure the interest of at least four tribunes and of other influential voices in his behalf, and thus no irremediable steps could be taken against him by the oligarchs during 51 B.C.

Prospects for Caesar at the beginning of 50 B.C. looked no brighter. One of the consuls, Claudius Marcellus, was violently opposed to Caesar, and one of the censors of the year, Appius Claudius Pulcher, set about to remove from the Senate as many of Caesar's supporters as possible. A Parthian scare in the East led Pompey to propose reinforcements there, and the Senate voted that Pompey and Caesar each should contribute one legion. Pompey contributed the one that he had lent to Caesar in 54 B.C., so that both legions would really come from Caesar's army. But Caesar rewarded the soldiers liberally and sent them off to Rome, though it was noted that the Parthian danger suddenly vanished and the troops were not sent abroad at all, but were kept under arms in Italy. Caesar's great tactical triumph of the year, however, was in politics, for he procured the services of the tribune Scribonius Curio. Curio had been his enemy, and at the beginning of the year he gave the appearance that he continued to be so. But soon Curio's speeches did not so much attack Caesar as make a plea for peace, the common good, and fair dealing. He said that both Caesar and Pompey were dangers to the State; both must put down their arms, or neither must; otherwise to disarm one would throw the State into the tyranny of the other. He vowed that he, Curio, would veto any other arrangement. The comedy was excruciating. Cicero, who as an eligible ex-magistrate had been forced to go to be governor of Cilicia, was furious at missing it. Curio vetoed all senatorial actions that were aimed at Caesar alone, and his vetoes were greeted with rage by the Establishment and with joy and relief by the people and by a large bloc of the senators, both of whom wanted peace. Curio's alleged neutrality was very plausible, and

Pompey's capricious changes of party had not increased his popularity.

POMPEY FINALLY WON BY THE OLIGARCHS.   The elections of 50 B.C. for the year 49 again returned consuls unfriendly to Caesar, but Caesar did succeed in having his trusted and valiant lieutenant, Mark Antony, elected to the tribunate. Matters came to a head before the end of the year 50, however. On December 1st the consul Claudius Marcellus submitted to the Senate the proposal that Caesar should be replaced. This was passed; but when Curio made a counterproposal that both Caesar and Pompey be required to resign, it received the overwhelming support of 370 members, while only 22 voted against it. Such a small number was the hard core of the Establishment that would destroy Caesar and would destroy the State if need be, but would not tolerate a loss of its control of the government. Curio was the hero of the Forum, and the consul Marcellus was beside himself. The next day the latter caught at rumors that Caesar was preparing to march on Rome and called on the Senate to begin mobilization. At a meeting of the Senate Curio denied the rumor and vetoed the proposal. Marcellus then proposed a vote of censure on Curio, but the motion was rejected by the senators. In a passion at his pacific Senate, Marcellus rushed off to Pompey, handed him a sword, and on his own authority commissioned Pompey to defend the State. The great man gravely accepted the burden. Caesar, however, did not even then surrender his hope for an accommodation. Couriers made trips to Rome offering to give up all his command except two legions and Cisalpine Gaul until his consulship. He even offered to relinquish his command entirely if Pompey would do the same. But Pompey was now convinced that he should operate in politics as he had in warfare, only with irresistibly superior forces. Caesar must surrender all, while he would give up nothing. The vetoes of the tribunes Antony and Cassius were in vain; the consuls warned them that they would no longer vouch for their safety in Rome; and as soon as they had escaped the city and headed north to Caesar, the Senate passed the ultimate decree and directed all officials to join in eliminating their public enemy, Caesar.

RIVAL POLICIES, PLANS, AND TACTICS (49–48 B.C.).
Pompey had a plan of operation which appeared logical. He would withdraw from Italy, if necessary all the way to the Near East, where his great personal credit and enormous resources in

men and materials could be marshalled into an overpowering force. Pompey believed that his armies in the East, combined with his complete control of the sea, would then act with his forces in Spain to catch Caesar in a pincers and either starve him into submission or crush him in the field. Caesar's plan was action, swift and decisive. Starting with only one legion, but with men that were trained, resolute, and devoted, he swept from Cisalpine Gaul across the Rubicon River, and down the Italian peninsula. As other troops from Gaul caught up with him and Italians joined his ranks, he took the army of his archenemy Domitius Ahenobarbus away from him at Corfinium, and then sped on to Brundisium in an attempt to prevent the embarkation for the East of Pompey's legions and levies. This he could not stop. However, in sixty-five days he was master of all Italy. Everywhere there had been friendliness for him and his cause, indicating that the Roman citizens of Italy did not conceive that they had fought the Social War to perpetuate the intrigues of the Roman Establishment. And everywhere Caesar had shown clemency and a lack of bitterness. He had offered friendship to opponents and had spared the lives and goods of his most fanatic foes. In Pompey's camp, in contrast, the talk was of revenge, confiscations, proscriptions, and the division of the spoils from the property of Caesar's friends. Even Cicero was shocked at the vindictive greed of his allies.

When he arrived in Rome Caesar found confusion. The oligarchs had left in so precipitous a panic that they had even forgotten to empty the treasury. Caesar collected for consultation a few senators that had remained in Rome, left Marcus Aemilius Lepidus, one of the praetors that also had remained, in charge of the city, and gave Mark Antony charge of Italy. Curio was sent off with the troops that had gone over to Caesar at Corfinium to secure Sicily and its grain supply, and Valerius was sent to Sardinia, which expelled its oligarchical governors even before he arrived. Caesar himself hurried off to Spain where, in a whirlwind campaign of forty days, he disposed of the generals and five legions of Hither Spain. Shortly thereafter Varro, the governor of Farther Spain, surrendered his two legions. The troops were disbanded and their officers allowed to depart and to join Pompey if they wished. On his way back to Italy Caesar accepted the surrender of Massilia, which his men had been besieging; and then he set about to resolve Italy's most pressing problems before venturing upon an eastern campaign. He had been named dictator before arriving back in Rome, and under this authority he effected debtor relief by establishing a board to assess property at the values prevailing before he invaded Italy and to force creditors to accept this property in fulfillment of debts. He restored exiles and the sons of the proscribed; presided over elections for 48 B.C., in which he himself was elected consul; and abdicated his dictatorship after holding it only eleven days. He then prepared to invade the East. So far his only disappointment, though a bitter one, was news that Curio, who had secured Sicily for him, had moved on to Africa and had been overpowered and defeated there by the Numidian Juba and the Pompeians.

A great deal of Caesar's success was due to his own brilliance, unquestioned authority, clemency to opponents and neutrals, and devoted assistants—Curio died rather than return in defeat to face a commander whom he loved and had failed. Things were different in Pompey's camp. It took time to assemble and train the masses of troops that came pouring in. The senators settled down in Thessalonica and fretted at delays, squabbled over future honors, and criticized Pompey. Why had he abandoned Italy? Why did he delay crushing his opponent? Where was his vaunted overwhelming strength? Was he delaying merely to enjoy his supreme command indefinitely? The senators and Pompey disdained each other, and each had grounds. Early in the war Cicero had written to Atticus that Pompey's military strategy was as inadequate as his political tactics always had been inept. Cicero was not a good judge, but such constant carping was distracting and irritating to the commander.

After Caesar had evaded Pompey's naval patrols in the winter of 49/8 B.C. and had gotten half his army across the Adriatic to Epirus, Pompey raced him to the important port of Dyrrachium and established himself there. Then, when Mark Antony had joined Caesar with his remaining forces, Caesar tried to bottle Pompey up in Dyrrachium. However, after several months Pompey's forces discovered a weakness in Caesar's lines which permitted a breakthrough, and Caesar was forced to withdraw his main force to Thessaly and to regroup there.

PHARSALUS (48 B.C.).   Pompey's camp was gleeful. Caesar was on the run, and Pompey was persuaded to follow him in order to bring this tedious war to a close. At Pharsalus on a sultry summer morning in 48 B.C. he offered Caesar the pitched battle that Caesar had wished. Pompey had about 45,000 infantrymen to Caesar's 22,000, and 7000 cavalry to Caesar's 1000. He depended on the crushing superiority of the latter to turn Caesar's right flank. But Caesar placed veterans at an oblique angle behind his right wing facing the expected flank attack. He armed them with spears and instructed them to stand firm and to use their spears to jab the young Pompeian horsemen in the face. At this unorthodox procedure Pompey's cavalry broke and fled. Now it was the turn of Caesar's reserves and cavalry to outflank the enemy, whereupon the Pompeians were thrown into confusion and driven from the field. When Pompey saw his cavalry break he went into his tent. Plutarch tells us that he sat there for a little while with his thoughts of thirty years of grandeur. Then as he heard the enemy piling across his ramparts, he started up with, "What? Right into my camp?" and, divesting himself of his insignia, he fled to the coast. Of all the kings and the rulers that he had countenanced and patronized he chose to seek refuge and assistance with young Ptolemy XII of Egypt. However, the king's advisers found him a dangerous guest, and had him stabbed and buried on the shore, though they embalmed his head as a present for Caesar. Of Pompey's troops 24,000 surrendered after Pharsalus. The rest were dead or scattered. To their leaders Caesar offered pardon. Some accepted; some retired to Africa to fight another day.

POMPEY THE GREAT. Pompey was a great organizer, and he seems to have been personally an attractive man. His military success was not based so much on tactical brilliance as on planning backed by an overwhelming superiority of force. He also was graced with luck — to reap where others had labored — and he made the most of it. But given a problem of organization Pompey was supreme, as the efficient handling of the problems of piracy and of grain shortage showed. He also was a supreme egoist — even his vainest supporter, Cicero, thought him vain, and in his private letters referred to him as Sampsiceramus, a petty Asian despot with a large name. He was unprincipled, humorless, and deceptive. But these very traits gave him *dignitas*, and success gave him *auctoritas* (prestige), and these impressed almost everyone, even himself. Caesar, however, was not fooled, nor was Clodius, nor was Caelius Rufus, who wrote to Cicero, "he generally thinks one thing and says another, but really doesn't have the wit to hide what he wants." Still, these comments should not obscure the importance of Pompey the Great. His constitutional innovations and subterfuges, far more than the work of his great rival, became the precedents and patterns for another arch dissimulator, Octavian, who in the next generation would have to appease the past while creating the future.

Chapter 26

THE DICTATORSHIP OF CAESAR

THE RANGE OF CAESAR'S PROBLEMS.   The victory at Pharsalus convinced many Romans that the issue was finally decided, and some of the more moderate followers of Pompey returned to Italy to make their peace with Caesar, Cicero among them. But for Caesar there remained a mass of problems that was staggering. There still were many intransigent republicans and they were gathering in Africa around Cato the Younger, Attius Varus, and Metellus Scipio. There also were the client kings that had followed Pompey, and their status had to be reviewed. Caesar's legions, now swollen by Pompeian defections, had seen many years of service and had to be regulated, rewarded, and in part disbanded. The years of political uncertainty had created economic and social dislocations in the forms of debt and crowded slums. More complicated was the provision for the prosperity and safety of thousands of communities that now lay sprawled around the Mediterranean as parts of Rome's empire. And most difficult of all was the establishment of some stable and efficient central government that could direct and protect the whole.

CAESAR SETTLES THE EAST (48–47 B.C.).   Caesar apparently overestimated Pompey's strength and therefore followed him to Egypt. The pursuit proved unnecessary, but as soon as Caesar discovered this and had made his decent regrets for his dead rival, typically he seized the opportunity to settle the somewhat confusing affairs of Egypt. The late king of Egypt, Ptolemy Auletes, had named the Roman people as guardians of his heirs, and Caesar as consul proposed to perform the duties that guardianship imposed. He was still owed enormous sums of money that had been promised to him and Pompey for saving Ptolemy's throne in 59 B.C., and Ptolemy had never completed these payments. Auletes' eldest son, Ptolemy XII, and his eldest daughter, Cleopatra, had been married, in accordance with Egyptian practice, and jointly promoted to the throne. When Caesar arrived in Egypt the royal couple was at odds, and Caesar as their guardian and creditor was the natural arbiter. Ptolemy XII spurned Caesar's judgment that his sister and wife should have her royal rights restored; but Cleopatra found great favor in Caesar's eyes and he insisted. The residents of Alexandria, however, in a fashion made familiar by many bankrupt states resented Caesar's claim to debts and his inclination to act the arbiter and to display the symbols of Roman power in their "sovereign" state. The offended rabble, supported by Egyptian troops of young Ptolemy, pressed Caesar's small force in a series of street battles and naval conflicts in and around the harbor of Alexandria. These skirmishes proved extremely dangerous, and Caesar's own life was several times imperiled. However, the timely arrival of reinforcements under Mithridates of Pergamum and Antipater, minister of the high priest of Jerusalem, at length enabled him to overwhelm Ptolemy's troops, and the king was drowned in the scuffle (spring 47 B.C.).

Despite the wealth of problems that now faced him in the West, Caesar did not immediately return to the capital. He had again been named dictator at Rome soon after Pharsalus, but for a while he left the administration of Italy to Antony, his master of the horse. For the two months following the Alexandrian War Caesar inspected the assets of Egypt, which someday would be Rome's, in the company of the vivacious and astute Queen Cleopatra. At length, in the early summer, when the queen was well gotten with child, he secured the future of Egypt by marrying Cleopatra to her still younger brother, Ptolemy XIII, a lad of thirteen, and by leaving a Roman garrison to protect the royal couple. Its captain was a freedman's son, a man of sufficiently low social station that an army command even amid the wealth of Egypt would not too much tempt his ambition.

Caesar's dalliance in Egypt was partly cut short by dangers that had arisen to his rear in Asia Minor during the early months of 47 B.C. The dangers came from Pharnaces, son and successor of the great Mithridates of Pontus. Pharnaces' inheritance had consisted of his father's possessions in the southern Ukraine, but he had taken advantage of the Roman civil wars to recover part of his father's Pontic kingdom in Asia Minor as well. Here he had defeated Caesar's lieutenant, Domitius Calvinus. Caesar now moved into Syria, rewarded those that had recently assisted him in Alexandria, and then hurried to Pontus with so nondescript a force that Pharnaces was seduced at Zela into attacking the Romans uphill. The rout of Pharnaces was complete, and the celerity of Caesar's movements and success has been immortalized in his own characteristic dispatch from this campaign: *veni, vidi, vici.*

Caesar returned to Rome in the autumn of 47 B.C., but he stayed only long enough to settle temporarily the havoc caused by two of his supporters. Caelius Rufus and Cornelius Dolabella, as praetor and tribune respectively, had curried popular favor through the introduction of legislation greatly favoring debtors. This was diametrically opposed to the policy clearly laid down by Caesar in 49,[1] and his presence restored order. There was trouble also with the veterans, some of whom had been brought to Italy after Pharsalus and had grown restive and mutinous while awaiting Caesar's orders. They demanded rewards and discharge; but to their dismay their general immediately acquiesced, addressed them as "citizens" instead of his usual "fellow soldiers," and turned on his heel. The episode illustrates better than volumes Caesar's sense of the dramatic and his understanding of men's hearts. Struck to the quick by his implied scorn, his legionaries utterly recanted and clamored to continue in his service. And there was need of them, for by now the hard core of republican resistance had settled in Africa and had had time to organize.

THE CAMPAIGN IN AFRICA (47–46 B.C.).   The Pompeian Attius Varus, who had held Africa against Curio's invasion in 49, was joined after Pharsalus by oligarchical partisans from all over the Mediterranean. These were headed by Cato the Younger and by the ex-consul Metellus Scipio. Scipio's rank gave him the command, but probably the republicans' greatest assets were the tactical brilliance of the legate Labienus and the cavalry and light armed troops of King Juba of Numidia. Labienus had been Caesar's chief lieutenant in Gaul, but had gone over to Pompey at the beginning of the civil war, and Caesar was more than once brought to the edge of disaster when his old aide and pupil directed an opposing force. Juba was in many ways a less happy addition. He was vain, arrogant, and barbarically cruel. There was considerable sentiment in Africa for the cause of the *populares* because there were in Africa and Numidia many descendants of Marius' veterans who had been settled in those lands after the Jugurthine War (111–105 B.C.). However, the republicans made no attempt to conciliate these people, but rather under Juba's initiative whole communities that were suspected of popular sympathies were

---

[1]   See above, pp. 292–293.

utterly destroyed. Among the Roman residents of Africa, therefore, the republican cause began to be identified with barbarians and barbarism, and Caesar profited from this.

Caesar had difficulties in transporting his troops to Africa, and the campaign dragged out for seven months until he could collect a force large enough to venture a pitched battle with the republicans. During the time, however, he won many adherents through his unwavering kindness to the natives, and he also secured the services of a Campanian freebooting adventurer, Publius Sittius, an old supporter of Catiline. Sittius teamed up with King Bocchus of Mauretania to take some of the pressure off Caesar by harassing Juba and his Numidians from the west. When Caesar's army was at last at hand and ready for combat, the republicans long and skillfully evaded open battle, both from respect for Caesar and because they expected to benefit from his great difficulty in procuring supplies from Europe. At length, in the spring of 46, Caesar attacked the city of Thapsus, a move that forced Scipio to take action lest he completely lose the confidence of the Africans. The battle was on a spot judiciously chosen by Caesar to favor his veterans while denying room to maneuver to the greater republican numbers and cavalry. The rout was complete. This battle essentially marked the end of republican resistance — the remnants of anti-Caesarians that thereafter gathered in Spain were not republicans, but supporters of the dynast Pompey. Here in Africa, in the city of Utica, Cato the Younger, the man around whom the ruling clique of Rome had rallied because he was the very incarnation of their republicanism, committed suicide rather than come to terms with Caesar or accept his clemency. By some curious perversion of the human mind, this act of intransigence and cowardice was glorified by later republicans as that of a great patriot. By his obstructionist policies Cato, more than any other man, had encompassed the fall of the Roman Republic; and incalculable harm was done in subsequent history by this foolish sanctification.

THE SPANISH CAMPAIGN AND MUNDA (45 B.C.).

Some of Caesar's opponents, including Labienus, escaped after Thapsus and joined a growing movement of resistance in Spain under the leadership of Pompey's elder son, Gnaeus Pompey. The movement in Spain was not sparked by enthusiasm for the moribund Republic, however, but by the name of Pompey the Great, because his generous settlement of that land after the defeat of Sertorius (72 B.C.) as well as his long governorship of both Spains (54–49 B.C.) had created a strong clientage there for him and his family. The inclination of the Spaniards to favor the Pompeians had been increased by the exactions of Cassius Longinus, Caesar's governor of Farther Spain (49–47 B.C.); and though the offending magistrate was replaced in 47, the harm was done. Caesar was needed in Italy, but his lieutenants made inadequate progress against the desperate Pompeians who felt, perhaps justifiably, that their long resistance had placed them beyond the pale of reconciliation. The remaining republicans could take little comfort in their leader, the young and brutal Gnaeus Pompey, who had tried to murder Cicero when the elderly statesman decided after Pharsalus to return to Italy; but the Pompeian army was formidable, for it consisted of thirteen legions and enjoyed the superior counsel of Labienus. Caesar set out to engage his opponents' force with only eight legions, but for weeks he was unable to bring Pompey to battle. Finally, in the spring of 45 B.C., the two armies confronted each other under the walls of Munda. Caesar and his troops were now sufficiently exasperated by this seemingly endless struggle that, when finally brought face to face, the Caesarians were willing to charge uphill against a larger force. The conflict was long, bitter, and without pity. When finally the superiority of Caesar's line, combined with a flank attack by the Moorish horse, turned the scales, no quarter was given, and 33,000 of the Pompeians are said to have fallen. Of their leaders only Pompey's younger son, Sextus, survived to disturb the peace in later years. In Spain as elsewhere, Caesar rewarded faithful communities, but the stubborn support of Pompey there led him to more widespread confiscations and penalties than he had exacted before, and the income from these went to the support of a needy exchequer.

CIVIL PROBLEMS FACING CAESAR.   The time given to Caesar between the day that he crossed the Rubicon and his assassination (49–44 B.C.) was terribly short for a man that needed to remodel an empire. It was necessary to establish peace and unity before attempting many constructive civil measures, and Caesar was battling the Pompeians at Munda in Spain as late as March 45 B.C., less than a year before his death. However, Caesar's genius allowed him to cope with some of his civilian problems between and even during his military campaigns. These efforts, combined with such progress as he had time to make after Munda, give us some concept of his plans for the Roman world.

We can see that Caesar's work for the rehabilitation of the empire had to be done on three levels. There were problems of poverty, debt, and administrative anarchy that admitted direct and immediate correction. There was a need for an effective and just disposition of the various components of the empire so that they could provide efficient and happy government to their residents while also providing health to the whole Roman State. For this there already was considerable machinery at hand in the current but not standardized provincial governments and in the multitude of municipal governments that Rome had spared during its expansion. Finally, a central government had to be devised that would direct and coordinate the efforts of all its parts. In the time remaining to him Caesar did a great deal to correct the nuisances of the first category, and he made significant advances or suggestions in the second field, but how the State ultimately would have been administered and ruled had Caesar longer survived is simply speculation. In any case, he decided to use the dictatorship as his administrative vehicle. After Thapsus he was given this office annually, and in early 44 B.C. he received it for life. This choice freed him from the obstructions and annoyances that young and ambitious tribunes could offer to other magistrates; and by qualifying his dictatorship with the phrase "for the administration of public affairs," Caesar showed that he expected that it would take him longer to assess and correct Rome's problems than Sulla's relatively brief (82–79 B.C.) dictatorship "for the reorganization of the State."

DEBT.   One of the immediate and recurring problems was that of the debtors. It appears that many debtors had supported Caesar in the hope that his revolution would cancel their past mistakes. But Caesar was not a radical in economics. He had no intention of subverting the rights of private property. On the other hand, he did recognize the hardships resulting from war, and as early as 49 B.C. he had insisted that a fair valuation be given to debtors' property when used to satisfy creditors. This measure was repeated in 47; and at that time he also allowed a remission of interest on all debts for the duration of the war and of rents in those price ranges that indicated the extreme privation of the renters. At the same time, his stern exaction from his own intimates of full payment for confiscated properties indicated that there would be none of the widespread profiteering that Sulla had tolerated. By these measures Caesar succeeded in allaying economic distress without alienating the propertied classes, which appreciated the stability of his government and thought it worthwhile to make a few temporary sacrifices.

THE URBAN PROLETARIAT.   Another intolerable nuisance
was the mob of Rome. Caesar was convinced that the urban
proletariat should not carry any special political weight or play
the world's sovereign. A rigorous census was taken of the tenements of Rome, and the number of persons currently receiving
a dole of grain was reduced from 320,000 to 150,000. To discourage further immigration in search of such benefits, the
number of 150,000 was then set as the maximum number to be
supported by the State with free grain. All future petitioners
had to wait for a vacancy on the rolls. Some of the persons
removed from the rolls were undoubtedly dissemblers; others
were transferred to Caesar's extensive colonial program.

The political clubs (*collegia*) that had set the rabble to
work terrorizing the streets of Rome and paralyzing the government in the days of Clodius and Milo were forbidden. Only the
traditional associations of craftsmen were allowed to continue,
for they were ancient and were centered around the worship of
a patron deity appropriate to each craft.

THE CALENDAR.   One of Caesar's most durable improvements was the reform of the calendar. The Roman year was
based on lunar months, and this meant that the board of pontiffs, in whose care the calendar was placed, had to add interca-
lary months frequently in order that lunar year and solar year
would approximate one another. By 46 B.C. political confusion
had interfered with the interpolation of added months for so
long that there was more than two months' difference between
the calendar and the sun. Caesar added sixty-seven days to the
year 46 B.C., and he then instituted a calendar of 365¼ days,
which was based on the researches of Alexandrian astronomers,
and this calendar has been in constant use ever since except for
minor improvements adopted in 1582 A.D.

CAESAR'S ITALIAN PROGRAM.   For the improvement of Italy
itself Caesar proceeded to use whatever lands still were available for the settlement of the surplus population of Rome. He
recognized that it was important that there should be many
Italians, for a surplus Italian population could carry its homogeneous culture abroad to help unify the empire. Political
preferment, as well as prizes, were given to fathers that raised
large families. By a law directing ranchers to hire at least one-
third free labor Caesar provided greater security from the dangerous slave gangs for those travelling in Italy, and he also
increased the opportunities of employment for free-born citi-

zens and their families. Charters or samples of charters were drawn up for the municipalities of Italy, though towns were not forbidden distinctive practices based on local tradition ąnd prejudice. The municipal officials were enlisted to perform at local levels duties that would supplement and lighten the tasks of the central government: at the time of the census, for example, local officials gathered the vital data and forwarded them to the censor in Rome, thus eliminating the need of a large bureaucratic staff. Clearly many of Caesar's measures for municipal government were in a half-finished state of preparation when he was assassinated. Mark Antony—it is uncertain whether from loyalty or impetuosity—had Caesar's legislative drafts collected and ratified without having them edited first, and our remains, therefore, are striking and suggestive, but are not organized or complete.

PLANS FOR PROVINCIAL WELFARE. Caesar did not plan only for the health of the Italian heartland. He also directed veterans and the surplus proletariat of Rome to the numerous colonies in the provinces. These were scattered all the way from Spain to Pontus and from Achaea to Africa. We have long continuous fragments from the charters for new settlements in the provinces, and they show detailed care for municipal well-being. They again illustrate that Caesar was not radical: his concern for a responsible civic leadership is consistently accentuated, and persons whose professional or moral background might testify against the cities' dignity were specifically forbidden the magistracies in them. Freedmen, however, were with equal care included among those eligible for civic honors. Caesar as a *popularis* still believed that the endowments of capable men must be enlisted for the commonwealth regardless of racial or civic past.

A very special situation prevailed in Africa, and this may indicate the tenor and gist of Caesar's thinking. Marius had settled some of his veterans outside the boundaries of the province of Africa in the client kingdom of Numidia, and these soldiers had successfully Italianized their territory. Caesar now constituted this area as the province of Africa Nova, and it soon was incorporated into the old province of Africa proper. Next, on the analogy of Marius' irregular colonies, Caesar allowed the adventurer Sittius, both as a reward for his help against King Juba[2] and as a stroke of political policy, to establish colonies in Numidia around Cirta and to endow the settlers with Roman

[2]   See above, p. 298.

citizenship. These settlements were destined, like those of Marius, to be absorbed into the empire by Augustus when they had done their job of Romanizing their surroundings. In his African policy, then, Caesar had adapted his arrangements to the circumstances of the time, while his plans were also oriented to the future development of the area. By these veteran settlements he signified that he was in the tradition of Marius; and by his undismayed establishment of a colony at Carthage and by his inclusion of at least 80,000 of Rome's proletariat in his overseas colonies he declared himself sympathetic to the social and economic aims of Gaius Gracchus. Furthermore, Caesar included both native blood and native talent in his foundations and by this policy he intimated that he envisioned a Mediterranean state based on a common code and culture. The location of his new colonies in Africa at good harbors or at strategic crossroads indicates that he had an eye for the future prosperity of the area and that he hoped that the increased commercial activity of northern Africa would help the whole fabric of the state by opening up new markets to Italian manufacture.

Caesar limited governors' terms of office to one or two years, probably to obviate dangerous challenges to the central government from such officials. He also tended to abandon the use of tax-farmers in favor of the local collection of taxes by the natives themselves. Here we find further evidence that he was determined to protect the provincials from exploitation and that he desired to enlist them in their own and in the national government.

THE PROBLEM OF CENTRAL GOVERNMENT.   It is more difficult to deduce Caesar's long-term plans for the government of the whole Mediterranean world. At his death Caesar already had gone far beyond the expectations and customary platforms of his own party, the *populares*: he had forbidden them to imitate the followers of Sulla and feed on the misfortunes of their political opponents; and he had shown no tendency to revive the Gracchan democracy and depend on the tribunate and city mob to direct the Roman State. Hence, it is not surprising to find some of his own partisans among the conspirators against him, some of whom honestly believed in that kind of a nationalistic democracy that he abjured. Caesar was no patron of a narrowly Roman government for the world. He kept working for a circumstance in which the able would be allowed to contribute to the commonwealth regardless of their own pasts. Hence his clemency and lack of prejudice: he knew that the senatorial party included administrative talents that Rome must not ignore, and he knew from personal experience that the empire had thousands of capable men to be exploited.

The partisans of the old Republic resented his clemency as though it were arrogant condescension. Caesar knew this, but as an Epicurean he also knew that no life was worthwhile if lived in constant dread. His central government, whatever it might prove to be, must not be propped up by a bodyguard or by a detachment of the legions, and he dismissed the escort that adulation had voted for him. His personal ascendancy over and his discipline of his troops were notorious, yet he knew that provision must be made for future discipline and control. This is not easy with a professional army. How can one be sure that the established government and the object of such an army's loyalty will be identical? The Senate had proved unsatisfactory in controlling the army; it had abjured its claim on the day that it irresponsibly refused to provide for Pompey's victorious eastern troops.[3] Yet the Senate was tradition, the Senate was old Rome, the Senate had the trained men that imperial administration needed. The Senate then, had to become the council, the tie with the past and the receptacle of national concentration and sentiment—but it would not please the families of the Roman Establishment that their Senate should become the handmaiden instead of the head of the central government.

A responsible Roman leader needed to look to the solidity and security of his empire: strong frontiers, an integrated and self-respecting population, and a capital to which men's eyes and imagination would turn. Rome had to become the city of the world, beautiful, well-appointed, a cultural center free from poverty. Caesar's colonial policy had begun the reduction of the number of destitute citizens in the capital; the learned Varro had been put in charge of a library system; a new Forum of Caesar enhanced the utility and beauty of the business districts of the city; and new temples, theaters, and improved harbor facilities were in the planning stage. Other projects for the commercial and economic improvement of the rest of the empire were contemplated, and they were as widely diverse as a canal at Corinth to facilitate transshipments at the new colony there and the draining of the Pontine Marshes south of Rome to eliminate a pesthole while providing new and fertile agricultural opportunities. More important were Caesar's plans for political health: the grant of Latin rights as an incentive to progressive provincial cities, the endowment of full citizenship as a

---

[3]   See p. 282.

reward for military service, the widespread colonial program around the Mediterranean to foster a homogeneous Italianized culture, and the enlistment for the Roman Senate not only of prominent citizens of Italian towns—many with pedigrees as long and distinguished as any Roman's—but also of distinguished provincials, such as his senators from Gaul, whom Roman snobs and dandies loved to lampoon. Little by little, then, the empire would evolve out of rulers and ruled into a partnership in which Rome as capital would furnish guidance and leadership. For such a commonwealth economy, prudence, and responsible leadership called for easily defended frontiers. The Atlantic and Rhine were adequate in the west and northwest, the Sahara for the south. But the Balkans and the Near East were unstable, and Caesar had nearly completed his preparations for an expedition to deal with those areas when he was assassinated on the Ides of March (March 15), 44 B.C., by a band of devoted republicans and admirers of the younger Cato, a band led by men that Caesar had raised to positions of high trust and authority, Marcus Junius Brutus, Decimus Brutus, and Gaius Cassius Longinus.

CAESAR THE MAN. Julius Caesar was perhaps Rome's greatest mind; certainly he was its most versatile. He stood so far above his contemporaries in so many fields that it is hard to imagine how there could be a true partnership between him and them. He was a writer of clear, direct prose of the purest Latinity and of great vigor; he was greatly admired as an orator, even by Cicero; and his talents were equally distinguished whether he took the role of a political thinker, organizer, administrator, general, or lover. But Caesar's philosophical persuasion led him to an attitude of indifference to personal safety that perhaps cut short his service to the Roman people. Like Sulla he was a Roman Epicurean, but he was of a more serious turn of mind than Sulla, and in the Epicurean calculus of good and ill he found that his continued existence was of advantage, if to anything, only to the State. "I have lived long enough," he said, and he made clear that his own life had been filled and complete and that he had nothing further to ask for it. He abhorred the ennui that comes with the constant protection of the self, and he willfully dispensed with his bodyguard. One wonders if he was sanguine enough to trust the oath freely taken by the senators, including his assassins, that they would protect his life with theirs, or if he really relied on the sanctity of the tribunician immunity that had been voted to him, when he knew that his opponents were the spiritual descendants of the murderers of the tribunes Tiberius and Gaius Gracchus. In any case, his every motion had the arbitrary air that settles upon those that live without fear; and, in keeping with that fearless and impatient reckoning, the very night before his death he had commented that when death came he hoped that it would be swift. His wish was granted. Caesar's enemies feared his coolness dreadfully, but the people worshipped it. Ancient political theory allowed and condoned the murder of any man that allied himself with the people to subvert the established order. The republican conspirators thought that their act would incite a surge of rededication to the Republic; but neither from the rabble, the army, nor the Italians was there a sympathetic spark. The conspirators could not and would not see that their own class had killed the Republic long before they killed Caesar.

The pity is the waste of talent: that one who had proved himself superb in so many fields in so short a career was not given the time—and time was essential, as the experiences of Sulla and Caesar showed and those of Augustus were to show—to work out a complete settlement for the Romans. Perhaps his settlement, like the others, would have been imperfect; as it was, however, the empire had yet to suffer another dreadful war that it could ill afford, and decades of experimentation were to follow before a reasonable social and political stability was achieved. And the weaknesses of the dispensation that the Romans ultimately received sharpen the regret that we do not know what resolution this superb mind might have conceived and accomplished; for here, as in so much that he did accomplish, the results might well have appeared transparent and inevitable.

Chapter 27

THE SECOND TRIUMVIRATE

THE FOLLY OF THE ASSASSINS. The republican conspirators that gathered around Brutus and Cassius had planned nothing before the Ides of March except to assassinate Caesar. They had no constructive program. In their blind childishness they seemed to believe that the Roman world had been waiting for their desperate act in order to acclaim a beloved and revived Republic. They expected that, once the dictator was dead, the oligarchical government of Sulla would straightway recommence to function. They sought the moral justification for their murder of Caesar in the example of famous tyrannicides in ancient Greek city-states, but they little noted that for generations Rome had no longer been a city-state where all citizens were intimately involved in the government. They also failed to realize that the population of Rome itself had had little reason to be loyal to senatorial government for many years, and that they were reaping the results of years of senatorial indifference and mismanagement both in and outside the capital. Italy had experienced only suffering at the oligarchs' hands, and so had the provinces. Further, the conspirators had not even reflected that in many cases their own magistracies and positions of authority, both present and promised, which they were far from willing to surrender, were the gifts of the very man that they had just killed. Nor had they taken any thought of Caesar's veterans now waiting outside the city for the rewards that the dictator had promised. They were under the command of Caesar's master of the horse, Aemilius Lepidus, and certainly they had no reason to love the Senate.

ANTONY SEEKS A COMPROMISE WITH THE CONSPIRATORS. Little wonder that none of the expected demonstrations of enthusiasm materialized; but nevertheless the assassins with shouts of liberty hurried through the silent or sullen mob and

the stunned soldiery to occupy the Capitol. The partisans of
Caesar at first were thunderstruck and stayed securely indoors
to wait upon events. At length, on the 17th of March, Mark
Antony, who had been a loyal and trusted officer of Caesar and
his colleague in the consulship, called a meeting of the Senate.
Antony was a good Caesarian, but he was not fanatic, and he
recognized that neither the Caesarians nor the conspirators
could at present feel certain of undisputed control of the government. In his career after Caesar's death Antony was never to
prove himself a first-rate general or a first-rate statesman, but he
was often sensible, politic, and adroit. Now, during the weeks
immediately following the assassination, he proved a skillful
player who might well have forged a government acceptable to
both parties. He quickly gained the cooperation of Lepidus
with the promise of Caesar's post as pontifex maximus, and he
next turned to the conspirators and their senatorial admirers.
Antony made them see that a complete revocation of Caesar's
far-reaching plans would lead to anarchy; and fear of this led
both sides to agree quite illogically that they would treat Caesar's death as though it had been a natural event and that they
would confirm both his past acts and his future plans. This
decision not only confirmed the conspirators in the offices that
Caesar had promised them, but it also greatly increased Antony's authority, for Caesar's widow had intrusted Caesar's
papers and war funds to him. Now he could feel free to carry on
Caesar's program in his own and Caesar's names. He effected
Caesar's projects for colonies and for the distribution of lands to
the veterans, and he published the drafts of much of Caesar's
legislation, which is of so rough and unfinished a nature that it
clearly came from plans only partially completed at Caesar's
death. These papers were probably authentic, but contemporaries suspected that some of the foreign dispensations, especially those in which a client prince would show his gratitude to
the Roman government by generous donations, were forgeries
by Antony to line his own pocket. In any case, in early 44 B.C.
Antony seemed well on his way to becoming the arbiter of
Rome.

Antony's position in Rome was further strengthened by the
attitude of the mob. The senators' ambiguous treatment of
Caesar's death forced them to permit a public funeral for him,
and Antony, as the surviving consul, pronounced the eulogy.
The sight of the dead man's blood-spattered robe, a recital of
his honors and of the senators' oath to protect him, and the
revelation that his will left gardens and monies to the Roman
people drove the mob into a frenzy, and it was not safe for the

conspirators to remain in Rome. Antony, however, was all reason and cooperation and was solicitous to find substitutes to perform the public duties of Junius Brutus and Cassius, who were praetors and should have been presiding over courts in Rome. They were sent off to the East to collect grain, while the other prominent conspirator, Decimus Brutus, went to Cisalpine Gaul as its proconsular governor, a post to which Caesar had appointed him.

THE RISE OF OCTAVIUS.   Antony was the most powerful man in Rome, but there was a cloud on his horizon. Young Gaius Octavius, a great-nephew of Caesar, by the terms of Caesar's will had been adopted by Caesar and made his chief heir. During the spring of 44 B.C. he arrived in Italy and applied for his patrimony and for the civil and religious steps that would legalize his adoption. This was embarrassing to Antony. He had found his control of Caesar's wealth useful, and it was no easy task to differentiate between what actually was Caesar's and what was the State's. It was further disconcerting that Octavius, as Caesar's titular heir, could rally those who thought Antony's conciliatory policy toward the assassins traitorous. There is no reason to suppose, and there would be no constitutional ground even to suspect, that Caesar intended Octavius to inherit anything except his name and his civil estate; but the young man put great store by the name, which was confirmed during the summer, and busily courted popularity by elaborate games, the payment of bequests to the people, and tampering with the veterans. Antony found himself steadily weakened, therefore, not only by the criticism of the conspirators, who thought him too powerful, but also by the desertion of many Caesarians, who began to cultivate Octavius because they thought Antony too tolerant. Finally these two pressures forced Antony to seek greater personal security through a law whereby he was given the governorship of Cisalpine Gaul and of Gallia Comata, the area recently added to the empire by Caesar, as a substitution for the more distant and isolated province of Macedonia, for which he had been slated earlier. With an army in nearby Gaul, Antony believed that he could dominate Roman politics as Caesar once did.

By the autumn of 44 B.C. the bickerings, recriminations, and conspiracies of Rome convinced Antony that he should go to his provinces. His preparations were both hampered and hastened by the ominous activities of Octavian. (After his adoption was legitimatized, Octavius' name was Gaius Julius Caesar Octavianus. He preferred to be called simply Gaius Julius Caesar, but to avoid confusion it is customary to call him Octavian.) In the early autumn he had gone to Campania and there, with plentiful funds and even greater promises, he raised an army, completely without constitutional or moral justification. An immediate march on Rome with his new recruits proved a fiasco, but this completely illegal action showed that the young man was ambitious and unprincipled. Soon the glamour of the name "Caesar," which he flaunted as his greatest asset, and the liberality of his promises enticed even more of the Caesarians into his ranks, and he obtained a following which included deserters from Antony's own army. His faction increased with surprising speed. He had a hard core of childhood friends, but his own family was not distinguished, and earlier in 44 B.C. most Caesarians had supported Antony. Caesar's veterans, however, took to him wonderfully, and Caesar's wealthy freedmen were bound to offer considerable support to the adopted heir of their benefactor. And, above all, the desperate and adventurous, disappointed in Caesar's conservatism, now saw a true revolutionary in the adopted son.

OCTAVIAN SUPPORTED BY THE SENATE.   Further support for Octavian came from an unexpected and foolish source. Led by Cicero the majority of the Senate now conceived that it could use Octavian to encompass the ruin of Antony, for whom it nursed a suspicious antagonism. When first he came to Italy Octavian had courted and flattered Cicero, who thought once more that perhaps he had found a pupil whom he could mold and pilot in the affairs of state. And so the senators compounded constitutional irregularity on irregularity and not only gave Octavian propraetorian rank over his freebooting army, but even enrolled him, contrary to all precedent, in the Senate. Meanwhile Cicero burned his bridges behind him by launching an attack on Antony in a series of virulent orations that no one, no matter how conciliatory, could likely forget. For those who worried that Octavian might be as dangerous for the Republic as Antony had been, Cicero reassuringly counselled, "We will praise and honor the young man, and then discard him." And indeed things did seem to go well at first. Decimus Brutus, the republican governor of Cisalpine Gaul and one of the assassins of Caesar, refused to give way to Antony, his duly appointed successor, when he arrived, and Antony was forced to besiege him in the city of Mutina. Thereupon, the consuls of 43 B.C., Hirtius and Pansa, who were moderate Caesarians, were directed by the Senate to cooperate with Octavian and to relieve Brutus. Antony was worsted and forced to withdraw across the Alps.

310

For the moment Cicero and his allies were triumphant. Antony was on the run; Lepidus, the proconsul of Narbonese Gaul, wrote letters assuring the Senate of his good will; and rumors that the East had fallen into republican hands now were confirmed. The conspirators Marcus Brutus and Cassius had been praetors for the year 44 B.C., but Antony and the Senate had sent them to the Orient as grain commissioners because their part in the assassination of Caesar had made them dangerously unpopular in Rome. Later in the year they were allotted the provinces of Crete and Cyrene as their regular assignments. However, with a high-handed appeal to a "higher authority" than the law, a policy which Cicero and his followers in Rome also were now affecting, these two patriots paid no attention to the tasks to which the government had assigned them, but rather set to work to wrest from the constituted authorities the whole East stretching from Macedonia to Syria. By the time that this news reached Rome, they were busy abusing the provincials for the benefit of a senatorial war chest. This bit of audacity the Senate straightway approved. As a crowning piece of good luck, the senators found that both of the Caesarian consuls, Hirtius and Pansa, had perished during the battles around Mutina. Now there was nothing to do to reassert the complete triumph of the old oligarchical Establishment except to turn the legions over to Decimus Brutus, honor young Octavian with an ovation — and retire him.

Octavian, however, would not be discarded. He refused to surrender his troops to Decimus Brutus. Instead, he marched on Rome with his army and demanded a share in the consulship emptied by the deaths of Hirtius and Pansa. The Senate had to accede to this show of force, and Octavian was elected consul, with an obscure relative, Quintus Pedius, as his colleague. It was clear that Octavian's interest was not and never had been with the senators, and while still in Rome he pushed through a measure outlawing the conspirators. Next he once more headed for the north, and this time he not only was backed by an army, but he also had the prestige of being an elected magistrate. Thus in a scant eighteen months since Caesar's death Octavian's boldness and complete disregard of the constitution, aided by the folly of the Senate, had made him the most formidable leader of the Caesarians.

FORMATION OF THE SECOND TRIUMVIRATE (43 B.C.).
One of the curious features of this epoch is the role of the army. Despite the almost constant civil conflict the number of great battles was few. This was largely due to the reluctance of the troops to fight and to the conciliations that they forced upon

their leaders. Many of the legions were veterans of Caesar's wars and had no incentive for fraternal conflict, particularly when the disputants were Caesar's own generals or relatives. And those that were more recent recruits were not eager to face Caesar's veteran fighters in battle. The fluidity of the soldiers' loyalty already had hampered incisive confrontations between Antony and Octavian when Octavian was making his earlier bids for power in Italy in 44 B.C. More recently the troops of Antony retreating from the Battle of Mutina and the legions of Lepidus in Narbonese Gaul fraternized instead of fighting and forced their commanders to pool resources. The other armies of Spain and Gaul soon followed suit. In November of 43 B.C. once again the soldiers' wishes were felt. In full view of their armies Antony, Lepidus, and Octavian met in conference on a small island in the river Lavino near Bononia and decided to join forces and reconstitute the Roman State. This combination is known as the Second Triumvirate. The First Triumvirate had been merely a private working agreement between Caesar, Pompey, and Crassus. But the Second Triumvirate was given the full sanction of law, the Titian Law, voted soon after the meeting. Thereby the three members were given the full consular *imperium* for five years and the right to use that power to reorganize and administer the Roman State. With this act the Roman Republic came formally to an end.

PROSCRIPTIONS.   The new government inaugurated its regime with the proscription of many prominent Romans. The triumvirs noted the perils of Caesar's clemency and proposed to root out at once future conspirators. Even more, they needed the money that the estates of the proscribed would provide to satisfy their legions with wages and settlements of land. Unlike Caesar's, theirs was a revolutionary government; it looked toward a new social and economic order which in Roman terms meant a redistribution of wealth. The triumvirs set ruthlessly to work: personal enemies and political irreconcilables were at the top of the list, but large numbers, especially of the equestrian class, undoubtedly were proscribed only because of their wealth. Song and story later abounded with tales of both loyalty and treachery connected with the proscriptions. There were up to 300 senators' names on the lists, and perhaps 2000 equestrians'. But probably only a small number actually was killed. The triumvirs were more interested in estates than in heads; and most of the proscribed seem to have received sufficient warning that they could escape either to Brutus and Cassius in the East or to young Sextus Pompey, who had survived Caesar's victory in Spain and was freebooting in the western Mediterranean. Only one man of consular rank actually lost his life, old Marcus Tullius Cicero. Cicero's whole life had been plagued by anguished indecision, and when he found himself proscribed he lingered too long among his beloved Italian possessions. The proscriptions cleared Italy of the triumvirs' enemies, but financially they were not especially successful, for the confiscated estates were a glut on the market and prices fell alarmingly.

Meanwhile, in the East, Brutus and Cassius were no less brutally active than the triumvirs. It is true that their victims were not Roman citizens; but cities that insisted on their treaty rights with Rome were razed, temples were looted, and the tribute normally due from a period of ten years was exacted at once from the provincials of Asia. Then, after bolstering the morale of their nineteen legions of liberators with the proceeds of this financial gouging, Brutus and Cassius proceeded into Macedonia to meet a Caesarian army under Antony and Octavian that had been similarly lavished with funds derived from the proscriptions in Italy.

PHILIPPI (42 B.C.); BRUTUS.   The two forces met near Philippi in Macedonia in October of 42 B.C. In an early encounter Brutus defeated Octavian's forces, but Antony was successful against Cassius. Cassius in too early despair took his own life; and three weeks later Brutus also was beaten and committed suicide. Brutus has had a good press in history, and he has more than once been sentimentally regretted as the last of the true Romans. Whether or not the sentiment and the regret are justly lavished on him, surely he did represent one of the better Roman senators of the Republic's later days. He was loyal to his class and he could come to terms with an Antonius, whose family and traditions were as ancient as his own. However, he was enough of a snob to refuse to treat with the *nouveau* Italian, Octavian, and he even condescended to Cicero. While Brutus demurred at Roman's slaying Roman and would have sought a compromise with Antony and the moderate Caesarians, during his last two years he did not scruple to squeeze the poor provincials of Asia in order to play the Roman political game with trumps. In his earlier days he had not hesitated to lend his money to bankrupt provincials at criminally exorbitant rates in order that he might pursue his Stoic fate without material discomfort.[1] With Brutus there perished the righteous type of Roman doctrinaire who called himself republican but had forgotten to

---

[1]   For Brutus' loans on Cyprus at 48 percent interest, see p. 325.

practice the flexibility and tolerance that had preserved the early Republic.

OCTAVIAN IN ITALY AND THE WEST.   After Philippi Octavian returned to Italy to superintend the triumvirs' duties of reconstruction, while Antony remained in the East. The control of the East appeared by far the more attractive and lucrative assignment, for Italy was full of pitfalls. But the struggles, often nearly fatal, that Octavian suffered in the West during the next decade went far toward giving him the Roman world. At the beginning Octavian by no means controlled the whole of the West. Antony still maintained his administration of the Gauls through a legate, while Octavian assumed responsibility for Spain and the islands, and Lepidus ultimately was allowed Africa. Cisalpine Gaul was added to Italy and all three triumvirs theoretically had authority in that combined area, although Octavian was actually there and his presence and activity in the peninsula gave him a considerable advantage. Octavian's pre-eminent position in Italy did not necessarily lead to popularity, however. As soon as he began the settlement of the triumvirs' discharged veterans on confiscated lands (41 B.C.), there were disorders among the Italians whom the veterans were replacing. One of the consuls of the year, Lucius Antony, brother of the triumvir, was incited by Mark Antony's wife, Fulvia, to harass Octavian in his work. At first Lucius pretended that Octavian was taking all the credit with the veterans, while he, Lucius, was protecting his brother's interests in the settlement; but later he sought popularity by appearing to champion the rights of the various municipalities that had suffered confiscation. In the East Mark Antony learned of these events, but did not interfere. He could hardly disavow the actions of his wife and brother; neither could he disavow his commitments to the veterans and to his fellow triumvir. In 40 B.C. after Octavian had besieged them and their adherents in Perusia, Lucius and Fulvia were forced to surrender. They were spared, but many of their republican followers were mercilessly killed by Octavian's forces and the town was sacked.

The problems of Octavian in Italy were compounded by the continuing presence of Sextus Pompey in the western Mediterranean. Many republicans had fled to him during the proscriptions, and his fleet was a constant threat to Italy's grain supply. Sicily was in his hands, and he soon won Sardinia and Corsica as well. However, Octavian did have one considerable accession of strength: Fufius, Antony's deputy commander in Gaul, died, and his son turned over the eleven legions there to

314

Octavian. Further, diplomacy as well as good fortune was at work for Octavian, and in 40 B.C. he was able to arrange a marriage with Scribonia, a relative of Sextus Pompey, in an effort to reach a rapprochement with that magnate.

PEACE OF BRUNDISIUM (40 B.C.). The news of the siege of his wife and brother at Perusia, of the loss of the Gallic legions and of Octavian's other activities were enough to alarm Antony. Moreover, when he tried to land his forces at Brundisium in southern Italy in 40 B.C., that city inexplicably closed its gates to him. Stung by this abrogation of his equal rights in Italy, Antony threatened an invasion of the peninsula with his eastern forces, which had been considerably strengthened by the remnant of the old republican fleet. Once more, however, the veterans intervened, fraternized, and made easier the efforts of mediators to arrange an accommodation. By this so-called Peace of Brundisium (October 40 B.C.) Octavian retained the West; Antony took the East; and Lepidus was left Africa. The pact was sealed by a dynastic marriage; Fulvia had fortuitously died, and Octavian now gave his sister Octavia to Antony.

THE WAR WITH SEXTUS POMPEY (39–36 B.C.). In the West Sextus Pompey was still a problem, and in the spring of 39 B.C. Antony and Octavian met with him in Italy near Misenum and agreed to give him proconsular authority over Sicily, Sardinia, Corsica, and the Peloponnese, while in return Pompey was to guard the freedom of the high seas. But Pompey soon resumed his piratical activities on the grounds that Antony had collected the current revenues from the Peloponnese for himself. His renewed interference with the grain ships headed for Italy soon forced Octavian to a resumption of hostilities. Octavian enjoyed an early success when Sardinia defected to him, but his forces suffered a succession of disasters at sea, and this dictated a period of retrenchment and rebuilding. Octavian's ablest lieutenant, Marcus Vipsanius Agrippa, created naval arsenals in Lakes Lucrinus and Avernus near Misenum that would be safe from piratical forays, and he trained new fleets there that would contend with Sextus (38–37 B.C.). After a conference between Octavian and Antony at Tarentum in the spring of 37 B.C., Antony agreed to contribute 140 ships for the campaign, while Octavian in return promised to recruit 20,000 Italian legionaries for Antony's projected eastern campaign against the Parthians. At the same time the colleagues agreed to renew the triumvirate for five more years, which should continue until the end of 33 B.C. Thereafter the combined efforts of Octavian and Agrippa

315

and of Lepidus, who led an expedition from Africa, resulted in 36 B.C. in the defeat of Sextus in Sicily and his flight to the East, where he ultimately was put to death. Octavian's share in the victory was not heroic; most of the credit was due to Agrippa's preparations and tactics at sea, and some also belonged to Lepidus' land forces. But Lepidus then presumed on his own importance and dared challenge Octavian's right to control Sicily. Once more the magic of the name "Caesar" and the willful legionaries took a hand. Lepidus' troops all went over to Octavian, and he was left the sole arbiter of the West.

OCTAVIAN SECURES THE WEST.   With Sextus Pompey defeated and Lepidus eliminated, Octavian could solidify the advantages of his position over Antony. He and his advisers proved adroit politicians and propagandists. No longer were political enemies treated with the cold cruelty that had distinguished Octavian's earlier victories. Lepidus was indeed stripped of power, but by a revival of Julian clemency he was allowed to retire to a small Italian village and to live out his life there with the empty title of pontifex maximus. Italy began to breathe easier; its grain supply was secured, its veterans were grateful, and peace brought some prosperity or hope for it even to the vanquished.

Octavian had made progress on other fronts as well. When hostilities had broken out again with Pompey in 39 B.C., he had divorced Scribonia on the grounds that she was a nag, though she had just borne him a daughter, who proved to be the redoubtable Julia. Then he had fallen violently in love (or said that he had) with Livia. She was the young and beautiful wife of Tiberius Claudius Nero, and her complaisant husband was persuaded to resign his wife and his two sons by her to Octavian. The wedding took place in January of 38 B.C. From this time Octavian no longer stood on the prestige of Julius Caesar's name alone, nor on the nondescript support that the Octavii afforded. Now he could count on the support of two of the greatest Roman houses, the Livii and the Claudii, who formed the nucleus of a powerful and noble faction for him. The municipal origin of his own family, the Octavii, also had its advantages. Little by little the gibes of his opponents concerning his lowly origin backfired, and Octavian's Italian support was strengthened by the feeling that he truly represented all the people of the peninsula. Octavian returned from his campaign against Sextus Pompey with increased prestige and popularity. For his victories he was granted an ovation, and at this time he also received the sacrosanctity of a tribune (36 B.C.).

316

Octavian's lieutenant, Vipsanius Agrippa, up to this time had far outshone his chief on the field of battle. Fortunately Agrippa was devoted and discreet. Octavian could see, however, that he must bolster his reputation on the military score, and he therefore decided to undertake campaigns against the tribes of Illyria. Between 35 and 33 B.C. he subdued the peoples of northern and coastal Jugoslavia, an area that was notoriously difficult. After these successful campaigns he returned to Italy considerably increased both in military capacity and in military prestige.

ANTONY IN THE EAST (42–31 B.C.).　　When in 42 B.C. Antony was awarded the East as his sphere of operations, it appeared that he had the most attractive assignment of the triumvirs; but ultimately his award proved a quagmire. Antony was enough of a Roman noble to desire prominence and honors, but he also was enough of a sensualist to crave periods of complete relaxation and irresponsibility, and he was enough of a realist to accept a workable compromise instead of clinging fanatically to any unilateral program. In the old-fashioned pragmatic Roman world Antony would have done well, but in a world that was neither sane nor tolerant Antony's kind of balance had little chance. At first, his efforts in Asia were moderately successful. In 41 B.C. he had proceeded to Asia where he raised some money, though the land was prostrate from Cassius' exactions; and he arranged the future of many local princelings and client kings so sensibly that his organization was in large degree wisely followed by his successors. He had an eye for talent from whatever source, as Caesar had had; for example, the elevation of the useful Herod to the throne of Judaea was his work. While engaged in the settlement of the East Antony spent the winter of 41/0 B.C. with Cleopatra, Rome's client queen of Egypt. He was careful to treat the country more courteously than Caesar had, and he assumed the role of a guest there, dispensing with the Roman magistrate's lictors whom Caesar had used and who had so offended the Alexandrians in 48 B.C. The queen, however, was made none the less pregnant by this triumvir than by his predecessor, and within a year she had borne Antony twins.

During the winter of 41/0 Syria and Asia Minor were overrun by a whirlwind invasion of Parthians led by the renegade republican Labienus, son of Caesar's old lieutenant. Asia and Syria soon were cleared by Antony's able lieutenant Ventidius Bassus, but Antony was hampered for several years from a projected invasion of Parthia, which would try to effect Caesar's projected unification of the civilized world, while at the

317

same time increasing Antony's own prestige. The enigmatic behavior of Octavian in Italy and his frequent predicaments there often delayed Antony's plans. He had had to rush to Brundisium in 40 B.C. after Octavian had engaged in civil war with Antony's family and had comandeered the troops from Antony's own province of Gaul. Moreover, when Antony arrived at Brundisium he had found himself shut out from that port, though it legally was the common property of all the triumvirs. Though that predicament ultimately was resolved peacefully, soon thereafter Octavian's troubles with Pompey had required Antony's presence at Misenum (39 B.C.) and at Tarentum (37 B.C.). Furthermore, each time that Antony rushed to the rescue, Octavian's cool and ambiguous attitudes required the tactful interference of friends, self-restraint by Antony, and above all the intercession of the admirable Octavia, Octavian's sister and Antony's wife. She played for some years for Antony and Octavian the role that Julia had played for Pompey and Caesar. But even she must have delayed Antony's preparations for his venture in the East somewhat. She was indeed a remarkably good woman, and it must have taken time for the husband of Fulvia and Cleopatra to get used to this new experience.

ANTONY'S PARTHIAN EXPEDITION.   By 36 B.C. Antony was at length ready. However, his expedition was doomed early in its career; it lost much of its baggage and siege equipment on its way into Parthia through the treachery of the client king of Armenia, who was supposed to be supporting the Roman forces. Antony penetrated Parthia as far as the fortress Phraaspa, but the lack of materiel and the approach of winter forced his retreat. This he executed in a masterful manner through difficult terrain and constant harassment. His army was not broken, but its losses were severe—probably more than one third of its number, which originally totalled nearly 100,000. This setback, coming in the very year when Octavian defeated Sextus Pompey and secured unquestioned control of the West, made Antony's position the more grave. When he reflected soberly on the recent policies of Octavian toward himself and his family, and when he listened to the interested arguments of the Egyptian queen, Antony felt himself forced into various postures of self-defense that he would not otherwise have taken.

CLEOPATRA AND ANTONY.   Cleopatra was a Graeco-Macedonian princess whose ancestors had ruled Egypt since Alexander the Great, and she had steadfastly used her intelligence, her charm, her money, and her body to maintain her ancestral

318

kingdom. The royal house of the Ptolemies, to which she belonged, was foreign to Egypt and depended upon Greek mercenaries to maintain itself there. But the Roman domination of the East had dried up the recruiting grounds upon which her house depended, and she had endeavored to maintain her popularity in Egypt by speaking the native tongue and by seriously identifying herself with the Egyptian great goddess Isis. She now believed that in Antony's political and military perplexity might be her kingdom's safety. If the carefully husbanded treasures of Egypt were combined with Antony's army and authority, there was a chance that she could attain at least an honorable partnership in the Mediterranean world for her kingdom. Her arguments for an alliance between herself and Antony were strengthened in Antony's eyes by Octavian's policy toward him, which continued to be ambiguous and irksome. The 20,000 troops that Octavian promised to Antony at Tarentum in return for the ships that Antony had loaned to him never appeared. Instead, in the spring of 35 B.C. a battered remnant of Antony's fleet was returned to him, and soon thereafter his wife Octavia arrived at Athens with a paltry force of 2000 from her brother. Antony accepted the contingent, small as it was, but sent Octavia back to Rome; he was finished with allowing their marital connection to make him Octavian's dupe—too late.

Before Antony could attempt a settlement with Octavian, however, he had to restore his authority in the East. In 35 and 34 B.C. with the aid of the Median king, he defeated and captured the treacherous king of Armenia, who graced a Roman triumph in Alexandria. Soon afterward, in 34 B.C., at a brilliant ceremony in Alexandria Antony signified his consent to an alliance with Cleopatra by the so-called Donations of Alexandria. By this act he reorganized Rome's client kingdoms and dependencies in the East, with Cleopatra's family the unifying principle. Cleopatra's oldest child, Ptolemy Caesarion, was acknowledged as Julius Caesar's legitimate son and was made joint ruler of Egypt and Cyprus with his mother. For Antony's own children by Cleopatra there was the overlordship of the client kings of Asia Minor or the ancient Ptolemaic possession of Cyrenaica. These donations were relatively harmless and not far different from the arrangements that other Roman generals had made in the East at various times. Antony by no means surrendered all to Cleopatra—despite her hatred for Herod and her ambition to annex Palestine, he refused to let her have her way there. But Antony's eastern policy and its beneficiary, Cleopatra, were seized upon by Octavian's camp as the worthy objects of a campaign of vituperative propaganda. The venture was so successful that it ultimately estranged the people of Italy from Antony.

THE END OF THE SECOND TRIUMVIRATE. The triumvirate legally expired at the end of 33 B.C. and was not renewed. The consuls of 32 were both partisans of Antony, but the suspicions that Octavian's propaganda had aroused against Antony made the consuls reluctant to seek senatorial confirmation of his eastern arrangements. The strained relations between Octavian and the consuls finally led Octavian to enter the Senate, backed by troops, and to speak in so threatening a manner that the consuls and 300 of the senators left Rome to join Antony in the East. During this same spring Antony finally sent a bill of divorcement to Octavia. With the legal end of the triumvirate and the consulship in other hands, Octavian no longer had a constitutional position. His troops and his propaganda, however, were sufficiently effective without constitutional props. Like his would-be mentor Cicero, Octavian pretended that he was following some higher authority when submission to the constitution proved inconvenient. Not only had he defied the consuls in full view of the Senate, but he exacted Antony's will from the safekeeping of the Vestal Virgins and published it. The will confirmed Antony's concern for his children by Cleopatra and stated that in case of death he wished to be buried with Cleopatra in Alexandria. Octavian's propagandists made the most of that: Antony was a traitorous renegade. Stimulated by these revelations about Antony and by Octavian's numerous agents, a fashion spread through Italy of taking an oath of allegiance to Octavian. This oath was as revolutionary as the oath that the plebs had taken many centuries before on the Sacred Mount at the beginning of the Republic, and it was equally effective.[2] Octavian became Italy's sacred leader against the bestial gods of Egypt. Formal war was declared on Cleopatra and an armada was prepared to invade the East.

ACTIUM. The decision between Octavian and Antony took place at Actium on the Gulf of Ambracia in western Greece in September of 31 B.C. Considering the preparations and propaganda that had come beforehand, the battle itself was a sorry affair. Agrippa had cut Antony's supply lines, and the latter thereupon decided to risk a naval battle in the hope that a victory would allow him to cut off Octavian's land forces in Greece and starve them out. However, there was dissension in Antony's

[2] For the secession of the plebs to the Sacred Mount, the oath, and its revolutionary character, see pp. 54–56.

own ranks. Many of his partisans resented the presence of Cleopatra, for they feared that they might appear to be fighting to satisfy her ambitions. Cleopatra, however, was footing the bills for Antony's armada, and so she remained. When at length battle was joined in open water and Antony's fleet grappled with Agrippa's, Antony's center squadrons suddenly and inexplicably turned and made for their harbor. Thus deserted, there seemed nothing for Antony to do but signal to Cleopatra's squadrons to join him in flight; and, hoisting sail, their ships broke through the enemy and made for Egypt. The army that Antony left behind him in Greece soon surrendered.

Octavian did not hurry. It was the summer of 30 B.C. before he reached Egypt. Antony defended himself with such scanty forces as he could muster, but he was defeated and committed suicide. Cleopatra made one final effort to conciliate Octavian and thus to save her kingdom for her children. But Octavian was noncommittal to the queen, while the surveillance of her activities was suggestively lax. When she suspected that he was preserving her only so that she could be made to march in his triumph, she committed suicide. Her oldest child, Ptolemy Caesarion, the natural son of Julius Caesar, was a dangerous rival for Caesar's adopted son and he was murdered, but Antony's twins by Cleopatra walked in Octavian's triumph, and the boy thereupon disappeared from history. The girl ultimately became Juba of Mauretania's queen. His rivals all humbled or exterminated, Octavian at length stood alone, the unchallenged master of the world, with a shattered Roman republic at his feet.

Chapter 28

A CENTURY'S IMPRESS ON THE ROMAN PEOPLE

We have seen Rome emerge in the second century B.C. as
the dominant state of the Mediterranean world; and it was clear
that the social, economic, and intellectual factors of the first two
generations of that century, from the Second Punic War to the
Gracchi (202 – 133 B.C.), drastically changed the Roman people.[1]
The extent of the change in the Romans is attested by the problems of dire poverty, scandalous wealth, depleted agriculture,
inadequate military manpower, and selfish leadership that the
Gracchan episode brought fully to light. The Gracchan dispensation, however, tended to sharpen rather than to correct (as it
had intended) the worst features that had developed in the
second century; and the values that were promoted in the post-
Gracchan century led to the vulgarization of an already vulgar
world. We cannot comprehend the Romans' final acceptance of
authoritarian government, which was signalized by the triumph
of Octavian, unless we review the evidence that the literature
and the social practices of the post-Gracchan period offer concerning the further transformation of Roman taste and Roman
character.

DRAMA SUBMITS TO PROLETARIAN TASTE. The glorification of Rome's urban mob as the empire's ruling element inevitably affected all cultural expression. Those calloused by dire
poverty and a brutal existence required shockingly brutal stimuli. Already with the city's audiences of the mid-second century
B.C. bear-baiting had outdrawn Terence's polished comedies of
manners. When the citizens became accustomed to the sight of
blood spreading on the sands of the arena, or had seen their
own names posted for slaughter in the Forum, or had gaped at

[1]   See above, Chapters 19 and 20.

322

the disembodied head of a favorite displayed above the speakers' platform, then the tragedians' attempts to touch the heart with the human dilemma seemed feeble and unreal. The Age of Roman Tragedy in the third and early second centuries B.C. had been a foreign import from Greek lands, but it had been sustained by the interest, professed or real, of the nobility.[2] Accius, who died *ca.* 86 B.C., was the last writer that could hold the public interest with adaptations of conventional Greek themes of tragedy and with dramas based on Rome's early history. Few audiences now wished to linger over problems of blood guilt or family curses, or over the heroics of an ancient Brutus in conflict with the tyrannical Tarquins, especially when they could watch the old buffoon of Atellan farce being thwacked across the stage. Romans seriously supposed that the homely mimes, which were skits giving true slices of life itself, were far more instructive for modern man. Here was realism, a realism so true to life that condemned criminals could be substituted for the actors at the end so that they could actually be slaughtered as the villains of the piece or crucified as the Prometheus in a bloody denouement. It seemed foolish to listen to a tragic declamation about sin or to a sly and comic allusion to adultery, when the dancers of the pantomine could so skillfully posture and gesture that the very acts themselves could be seen—to the ecstatic satisfaction of the matrons of Rome.[3]

SATIRE.   The brutalization of the masses was only one characteristic of urbanized Rome that laid itself open to criticism; and men were now becoming sufficiently self-conscious that they could discern and criticize the dislocations and incongruities of their advanced society. Even by the time of the Gracchi, Lucilius (180–102 B.C.), the knight of Suessa Aurunca, had created the genre "satire."[4] Lucilius had social position and powerful friends, and he dared to attack not only the Romans' callousness, wealth, fraud, and mismanagement, but also their political immorality. "Old Lucilius attacked the people's leaders and the people too, tribe by tribe," said the poet Horace, and there was much room for it. Lucilius saw not only the elemental passions to which the slums of Rome had been reduced; he also saw the extremities of vice to which greed and political ambition had driven the upper classes. He flayed them all.

[2]   For earlier Latin drama, see above pp. 195–196.
[3]   The mimes were homely skits with dialogue; pantomimes conveyed their messages without words, but by interpretive gestures and dancing.
[4]   See above, p. 203.

THE NEED FOR GREAT WEALTH.   Lucilius was well warranted in his attack on the unscrupulous race for wealth, but in
all fairness we must acknowledge the dilemma of Rome's noble
families. It had been difficult enough before the Gracchan Age
for the great families to maintain their political position by the
judicious outlay of money. They had ensured the steady support
at the polls by their families' clients by giving them some financial support, and they had bribed a sufficient number of voters
in each of the thirty-five tribes that they could count on a majority vote in most of them. This had been possible because
many tribes had very few members permanently resident in
Rome and actually present for meetings of the assembly. With
the introduction of the secret ballot,[5] however, and with the provision of cheap grain to the people by the State, it was practically necessary for a serious candidate to buy the whole populace. A family's complete fortune also could easily disappear
simply in paying the expenses entailed by the aedile's public
games and shows. These had to be lavish in order to acquire the
good will of the electorate in future campaigns for the higher
offices, and in these bids for popularity many men went nearly
bankrupt early in their careers, as Julius Caesar did.

THE SOURCES OF WEALTH.   There was indeed wealth
available for the Roman upper classes, but one could not be too
squeamish about its source. Industry was not a dignified nor an
especially lucrative investment. Manufacturing had been too
long in the hands of freedmen and slaves to attract the interest
of the nobility; and, in any case, an industrialized Italy could
not find flourishing markets overseas. This was because the
provinces had to sell to Italy rather than buy from her, in order
to pay their tribute to the Roman government. Such Italian
industry as there was, then, catered largely to the local markets.
There was considerable work in bronze and iron in Etruria,
Puteoli, and Capua, for in Italy itself there was a steady demand
for utensils and farm equipment. War contracts for military gear
were dependable. There also was developing a healthy industry
in ceramics, especially around Arretium, and its Italian dish-
ware was soon found widely distributed in the ancient world as
far as India.

A far more lucrative source of revenue, however, could be
found in the provinces in various forms of extortion. Verres[6] and
many other Roman governors made great fortunes and reputa-

---

[5]   For the introduction of the secret ballot between 139 and 130 B.C., see pp.
209, 217, 223.
[6]   For the infamous case of Verres, see p. 276.

tions for themselves by their notorious abuse of the provincials. The young and ambitious politicians of Rome never lacked for corrupt governors that they could haul into court—and young men thus put themselves into the public eye, launching themselves on a public career that would end with them holding the same high offices and having the same opportunities to gouge the provincials.

Besides extortion, the most popular means for amassing fortunes were banking, moneylending, and usury. Theoretically these pursuits, as well as the engagement in trade and commerce, were not open to the senatorial class; but the senators could find convenient agents (such as their freedmen) to provide the necessary front and to make for them the forbidden investments in the world of finance or the ventures in the exchange of goods, which sometimes could be very profitable. The result was that not only countless equestrians reaped generous profits from exchanging goods with and making loans to the provincials, but a man of senatorial rank such as the reputedly blameless Brutus was revealed to enjoy the income from a loan that he had made to the poor people of Salamis in Cyprus at an interest rate of forty-eight percent! While the triumvir Crassus had heavy investments in the tenements of the Roman slums, he also profited from the exploitation of enforced labor in the Spanish mines. Both of these investments were lucrative sources of revenue and both exploited the depths of human degradation and misery, but from them Crassus was able to increase his family's fortune from 300 to more than 7000 talents. Even for the only moderately well-to-do there were investments in the companies that contracted to perform state services, particularly to collect the taxes from the provincials. The Romans rapidly learned to become leeches on the rest of the world and to take their privileged position for granted; and there was hardly a citizen with any money at all to invest, who did not put it into the syndicates that despoiled the provincials and who did not judge the opportunities that Rome's empire afforded the greatest of blessings.

THE USES OF WEALTH; THE LAND.   Much of Rome's ill-gotten wealth was poured into the abyss of political bribery. Much more was squandered on conspicuous spending—villas, fishponds, and imported luxuries. Much also was reinvested in the great corporations that undertook public works, exploited natural resources, and farmed the taxes, while the constant crises abroad created ever new opportunities for moneylending. Above all, however, there was a passion to acquire land for vineyards, olive orchards, and livestock. Land in Italy was desirable, but land abroad was more plentiful and often could be equally profitable. The great Pomponius Atticus, special friend of Cicero but on good terms with almost everyone, had estates across the Adriatic in Epirus, and their very remoteness from Italy and its revolutionary confiscations contributed to the stability of Atticus' fortune. It is true that some of the drain on the small farmers of Italy was removed by the new enlisted army, which enrolled many of the landless and of the proletariat instead of conscripting the peasants; but when these new soldiers were discharged, they greatly preferred to be settled in Italy instead of in the provinces, and this made them dangerous to both great and small landowners in Italy. If all else failed, their leaders would practice proscription and confiscation to get Italian land for them. After all, Italy was still the heartland of the empire, and ambitious politicians were pleased to see their supporters settled near at hand. At the beginning of the Republic's last century the Gracchan commission broke up the estates of the great possessors with an eye to restoring an idealized social condition of the early Republic. It did so with some show of legality, but it also set a pattern for the first century B.C. whereby the law and the rights of ownership were completely disregarded in order to satisfy the demands of partisans and veterans. Sulla garrisoned Italy with his supporters; and Pompey, and then Octavian, depended on keeping their discharged veterans close to Rome and grateful for their allotments. The troops had to be rewarded; and after the horrors of revolution and civil war, it was a trifling thing to spill the blood of a great landowner in order to recompense the useful legions.

CAPITALISTIC IMPERIALISM.   The need for wealth promoted aggressive imperialism. It was the Roman commercial interests that pushed the war against Jugurtha (111 – 105 B.C.) in Numidia at the end of the second century.[7] The commercial world brought strong pressure to bear on the Senate when numerous Italian businessmen were lost in the fall of Cirta; and there was much impatience when the lucrative exploitation of Numidia had to mark time during the bungling of the earlier senatorial generals and the deliberate campaigns of Metellus. At length it was the pressure of the business interests in Africa that led to Marius' election to the command, the renascence of the alliance between the equestrians and the *populares*, and the conduct of

[7]   For the details of the Jugurthine War, see pp. 235 – 241.

the war to its bitter end. However, the pain of the businessmen in Africa was as nothing compared to the outrage of the Italian bankers of Asia when Lucullus brought to an end their shameless impoverishment of that province's cities by forbidding them to charge fantastic rates of compound interest (71–70 B.C.).[8] Their enmity encompassed the downfall of Lucullus, and their political influence in Rome procured the eastern command for Pompey, the darling of the business interests (66 B.C.). His expansionism was unbridled and undisguised, and the satisfaction of the population was wholehearted and sincere. "The tribute forms the sinews of our State," reports Cicero, "and the tax collectors are the chief supports of the rest of society: in the retention of our possessions overseas lies our glorious honor, our pledge, the State's exchequer, and the financial interest of a large section of our citizenry!"

The provincials suffered dreadfully. The subdued were the prey of governors and publicans, while the semi-independent or peripheral tribes furnished countless opportunities to those military men who were ambitious for an easy triumph. Subjugation by no means always assured a settled peace. Though Spain had peace for a little while after the fall of Numantia (133 B.C.), in the first century it was wracked by the campaigns of Sertorius and his opponents, and then by Caesar and the younger Pompeys. Gaul was for years a battleground, both during the Germanic invasions (109–102 B.C.) and later under the First Triumvirate (58–51 B.C.). There were numerous disaffections in the Balkans, not just the incursions of peripheral Danubian and Thracian tribes; Greece itself was invaded and Athens sacked during the Mithridatic Wars (86 B.C.). The Asian provinces were so consistently invaded, punished, and milked that this rich land lay prostrate by the time that Antony settled the East. It is true that a few bright spots stood out. Cicero was a conscientious governor of Cilicia; Caesar's propraetorship in Spain was considered unusually responsible; and Mucius Scaevola, Rutilius Rufus, and Lucullus did their best during their brief tenures of office in Asia (97, 71–70 B.C.) to assist the unfortunate provincials. But these were exceptional enough to be a matter for special comment in their own day. Cicero assured his Roman contemporaries that they could little imagine how they were hated by their subjects; and the occasional outbursts of impotent rage, from the massacre of Asculum in Italy (91 B.C.) to that in Asia during the invasion of Mithridates (88 B.C.), bear him out.

---

[8]   For Lucullus and the bankers of Asia, see p. 277.

THE POOR PEOPLE OF ROME.   The Gracchan utilization of the Tribal Assembly as the empire's ruling power briefly elevated the inhabitants of Rome to the control of the Mediterranean world. But these supposed lords of the world for the most part lived in flamboyant poverty. The great grain-producing provinces furnished them a minimum of cheap food, and the provincials contributed the money, the animals, and the gladiators to cheer their hearts at frequent holidays. However, their quarters in the tenements of the Suburra were flimsy, and their livelihood was insecure. There must have been some market for free labor in Rome in the small shops, trades, and services, though slaves appear to have monopolized a good many of such opportunities as there were. Certainly, since slaves were cheap to procure, to maintain, and to replace, it would be difficult for a freeman with a family to compete with them. The public works of Gaius Gracchus were perhaps partly calculated to give work to the proletariat and thus to furnish them some relief; Sulla, Caesar, and Pompey all supported extensive building programs; and lesser statesmen also frequently undertook isolated projects that would call for the employment of the poor. It is also clear from the fragments of the Sullan constitution that a number of small salaried positions existed for aides attached to the ever increasing number of magistracies. Here also there was room for some free labor. The grain law of Gaius Gracchus, with its assurance of the sale of grain on the market at a fair price, probably did not remove all chance that the poor would find this supply supplemented by largesse from the great political houses in return for support at the polls, and the sale of votes clearly remained a dependable source of income for many impoverished citizens. Some joined the army, now recruited from destitute volunteers, in order to improve their place in the world. While actually in service they would receive food, pay, and booty; and the lands that they expected when they were discharged often sufficed to make the recipients prominent citizens of the municipalities in which their allotments were situated. While still in the army these irresponsible new recruits began to learn to impose their will on the empire. They demanded lands, largesse, and compacts between their commanders.[9] This power of the army was selfish and irrational, but it probably was just as democratic as the rule of the urban mob had been.

Despite the drains to colonies or to the armies, however, the destitute of Rome continued to grow in numbers, and by the

[9]   Compare above, pp. 311–312, 315, 316.

time of Caesar they totalled 320,000 persons. These poor people were divorced from economic and emotional stability by their life on the pavements, and they were divorced from the Roman heritage of independence and self-reliance by their very composition. The Romans were liberal in their grant of freedom to slaves, and the city slaves were those whose education, good looks, and proximity to their masters would most often recommend them for manumission. However, many of the Hellenized Orientals who had the advantages of education and charm came from areas that had suffered centuries of tyranny, and these men won their freedom through their excellence as submissive slaves. But the virtues of submissive slaves are not those of responsible free citizens, and these additions to Rome's proletariat were, therefore, peculiarly unfit to participate in the attempts to foster a people's democracy at Rome.

THE PERVERSION OF RELIGION.   For the Italian-born residents of Rome the separation from the soil took them away from their native gods. The homely spirits of hearth and garden had little meaning in a dingy tenement; and the feelings of piety and awe which come to country people from their daily familiarity with the mysterious and wonderful powers of generation and growth soon disappeared in an urban environment of hunger, riots, spectacles, and filth. The poor people of Rome of course knew the names of the famous Hellenic deities and perhaps some of the Greek myths connected with them, but these carried no conviction or comfort. The State religion furnished them with festivals, but these were spectacular rather than intimate—the magistrates performed the sacrifices and put on the show, but there was no involvement or participation by the populace. However, the souls of the city dwellers would not be denied some emotional satisfaction, and the Oriental cults of Cybele and Bacchus appeared early in the second century B.C., bringing with them frenzied orgiastic practices. The cult of Egypt's Isis soon followed and introduced the Romans to initiation, penance, the rites of baptism, and charlatan priests. Mystical and irrational cults such as these possessed the same stimulants to titillate the senses and the same impact to engulf the soul that the arena did, and they therefore attained wide popularity with great rapidity. The literature of the period and the tablets of lead inscribed with curses and dropped down the wells of the city attest the dark practices of sorcery and magic that flourished in the slums in the very days when Cicero and Lucretius were insisting that superstition was dead.

If the poor people of Rome turned away from their tradi-

329

tional deities of woods and field and disregarded the official cult of the State, the upper classes had paved the way. The insistence of the plebeians as early as the fourth century B.C. that they should share in the priesthoods had begun the secularization of the religion of the State and the cheapness in which it was held in the public view. In the late second and early first centuries the manipulation of that religion for political purposes had become more and more blatant. Priesthoods were held only for the prestige that they brought the holder. The observation of signs and portents, which once revealed the will of the gods, now was used only to invalidate the political activities of the opposing parties. Privately the nobles that held the priesthoods gibed at their own pretensions, but publicly they appealed to the people to respect religion's sanctity. This policy was admired and described by those that it did not deceive. In the second century Polybius had said, "What the rest of mankind derides is the foundation of Roman greatness, namely superstition. The element has been introduced into every aspect of their private and public life in a degree that could not be improved upon. Many may be at a loss to understand this; but my view is that it has been done to control the masses." Cicero's old teacher, the pontifex Scaevola, taught, "It is expedient that states should be deceived in the matter of religion." And years later Augustine, asked why the Roman governors had pursued these practices, replied, "It was done, of course, for no other reason than that it was the business of these prudent and philosophic gentlemen to deceive the people in the matter of religion. . . . They persuaded the people to accept as true what they knew to be false, thus binding them the more tightly to their form of society -so that they might subdue and possess them." Especially astute in this practice was Octavian. The fortuitous appearance of a comet after Caesar's assassination facilitated the adoption of the notion that he had become a god, and Octavian exploited to the limit his position as the son of the deified Julius. This policy proved so successful that Octavian did not fail to cultivate the fertile field of religious manipulation in his later years as Roman chief of state.

While the proletariat was embracing new, exciting, and highly emotional religions, the upper classes turned for consolation, such as it was, to philosophy. A Hellenic education at home for all noble or ambitious youths was often supplemented by study in Athens or Ephesus or Rhodes, but the message of the Hellenistic philosophers was also brought directly to Italy and the Italians. Cicero says that a Latin prose version of the Epicurean system had great currency throughout Italy from the second century B.C. onward.[10] However, the greatest Epicurean argument for sanity in an increasingly mad world was made in this period by the poet Lucretius (99–55 B.C.). His *De Rerum Natura* ("On the Nature of Things") is an earnest plea to his contemporaries to stand aside from foolish and empty pursuits and to become spectators of the great cosmic tragedy in which they were also actors. The ethical effects of his work are incalculable. A number of great Romans believed in his thesis, and we have seen some of the effects on public life made by such Epicureans as Sulla, Julius Caesar, and Cassius. Epicureanism, however, generally was frowned upon by the ruling minority because the Epicureans did not believe that the gods meddled in men's affairs, and thus they removed the important control over men's minds of superstition, on which the Roman governing class depended. The astrological nonsense grafted onto Stoicism was more conducive to good order among the masses, and the period produced two hardheaded specimens of this sect in Cato and Brutus.[11] Cicero claimed to be a Skeptic. Actually he was an eclectic, and he performed a magnificent task for western civilization by creating a Latin vocabulary for philosophical thought in the adaptations of Greek thinking in his own numerous philosophical treatises. These were not so much original works as acclimitizations of the heritage of Greece to the Roman mind and situation. They repeatedly testify to the skeptical but pragmatic attitude toward religion among Rome's upper classes.

THE EGOISM OF THE LATE REPUBLIC.   The notable characteristic that is shared by one aspect after another of the late republican world is self-centeredness. The new Oriental religions that attracted the poor were mainly concerned with the salvation of the individual: How can I be saved? And the Hellenistic philosophies also were interested in the questions, Who am I? and How can I be happy? rather than in a rational inquiry into the nature of the universe.

In politics, too, individualism had made its unmistakeable appearance in the cases of Flaminius and of Scipio as early as the Hannibalic War. The examples of those that broke the traditional rules of conduct in public life increased in the second century. The Gracchi may have "gone it alone" and sought a novel political eminence for society's sake, but many followed their example without their social aims. It suffices to point out that each of the marches on Rome, by Sulla, Cinna, Marius,

10   For the Epicureans and their political views, see p. 198.
11   For the Stoics, see pp. 199–200.

Lepidus, Caesar, and finally Octavian, was prompted more by personal ambition and concern for the leader's *dignitas* than it was by a concern for the public welfare. Economic individualism during this age took the form of colossal fortunes, and those of Marius, Lucullus, Atticus, and Crassus have become legendary.

In literature the spirit of the age led historians to turn from the annals and chronicles of the second century B.C. and to compose monographs and memoirs. As examples of the monographs of the period, Sallust's *Conspiracy of Catiline* and *Jugurthine War* are absorbing presentations of the causes and effects of Roman moral decline as viewed by a member of the *populares*, and they were written with some show of impartiality. Sulla's memoirs are unfortunately lost; but Caesar's accounts of his campaigns in Gaul and in the civil wars are adornments of Western literature. Their directness, lucidity, and apparent simplicity have never been rivalled in the historical field. In them art is so well concealed that it hardly occurs to the reader to wonder if here as elsewhere in the literature of the day we have special pleading for the writer's own interests. Caesar came well by his craft, for he was the second orator of the times. This was the age when the art of persuasion through oratory reached its peak, and Cicero was its glorious leader. Even in the case of Cicero, however, too often it was simply fortuitous if the speech were actually calculated for the common good, and was not composed instead in order to cement a political alliance, repay a debt, or conform to a triumvir's policy. This age is damned by the fraudulent casuistry of its catchwords and slogans, whether in the speeches of Cicero or on the lips of the dying. When its speakers used the term "the good" it turned out that they meant "the propertied"; "liberty" was the license of the oligarchs to exploit the world; and "piety" meant revenge by blood-feud. And, with the notable exception of Lucretius, poetry conformed to the general character of the epoch. The *neoteroi*—"the new poets"—found their inspiration in the extravagancies of the contemporary Greek poetry of Alexandria, in the learned, the subtle, the precious, in that which is composed for the initiated alone. If one of the *neoteroi*, Catullus, did break away from this pattern of preciosity and bare his soul to his contemporaries:

> I loathe yet love—no hows, no whys:
> Here my torn heart tormented lies—

all the more did he attest the egoistic character of his age in verses of passion, tenderness, scurrilous invective, but most especially, of himself.

HIGH SOCIETY.   The society of Catullus, in the middle of the first century B.C., was a gay society, dashing and worldly. Some old families indeed still maintained a staid or dignified mien; but the paths to the maintenance of prestige and the acquisition of power, to the luxurious villa, the seaside resort, and the lovely *objects d'art* led through vast outlays to debts and bankruptcy. While the men were freeing themselves from the trammels of traditional Roman frugality, the women were even more active in loosening the ancient restrictions. The Roman matron always had had an importance far beyond her legal status and had played a formative role in many a distinguished career. Now, by the last century B.C., legal subterfuges left Roman heiresses in unfettered command of their considerable fortunes; and in an age of emancipation and great vulgarity the ladies of society are not slow to adopt the habits of the ladies of the stage and back stairway. Clodia, an ornament of the great and patrician family of the Claudii, counted her lovers by the dozen and was involved in a bewildering assortment of intrigues, poisonings, and assassinations. The amours of Servilia, the step-sister of Cato the Younger, were sufficiently notorious to cast doubts on the paternity of Marcus Junius Brutus, her famous son. Women like Clodia and Servilia abounded, using their bodies for their own pleasure and to further their families' political intrigues; and they did this with less excuse than their contemporary Cleopatra, who had a kingdom to save. Yet, when the men so callously married and divorced them as pawns in the game of family politics, is one to wonder that the women soon warmed to the sport?

THE LAW.   Developments in the law kept pace with the changes in society. It was not just the great ladies of Rome that profited from innovations by the jurists and from liberal interpretations or evasions of the law. The legal profession itself began to be self-conscious and introspective. As the Romans' experience with other peoples and with Greek philosophy increased, they examined the rationale of their own legal history and studied the extent to which the principles of their system were shared with others. From these studies there developed the idea that there were basic legal principles common to all peoples, a law of nations, and that this came close to being a kind of natural law. Legal monographs and commentaries began to appear and jurisprudence flourished. The edicts of the foreign praetors,[12] which drew so much from the law of

[12]   For the praetorship and its importance, see pp. 85, 89, 93–94, 120–121.

other peoples and from philosophy, little by little softened the strictness of Rome's own civil law and led to a rule of equity, which applied the universal principles of justice that legal students were discovering. To this age belong the earliest expounders of the Roman legal system. Quintus Mucius Scaevola wrote a systematic treatise on Rome's own civil law; while Aquillius Gallus and Sulpicius Rufus sought in their commentaries to modernize the law through innovation and liberal interpretation. It should further be noted that serious Roman scholars did not confine their research to their law and its antecedents, though this is perhaps their greatest contribution. Their interest in themselves also led to antiquarian investigations of Roman customs and of Latin grammar. The greatest name in this field of research was Marcus Terentius Varro, and the widespread interest in his work perhaps reflects a basic hunger for an earlier simpler world, which we also saw in the political ideals of Tiberius Gracchus and Cornelius Sulla.

THE ADVANTAGES OF ROMAN EGOISM.   The self-centeredness of the Romans had some recompense for their subjects. The Romans could have made themselves much greater nuisances in the Mediterranean world than they did. Once their basic demands for money or auxiliaries had been met by their subjects or allies, they tended to leave them alone as much as was consistent with public order. Many communities, at least in Italy, became sufficiently prosperous to support extensive building programs. Like Rome, they had aqueducts, municipal centers, theaters, arenas and baths, and fine houses. The expanding system of Roman roads served to speed goods and news to and from the municipalities, even though the Romans may have had a largely military purpose in building them. And most important of all, even after towns received the Roman citizenship they continued to govern themselves. Self-government flourished on the level where it means the most to people, on the local level. From this circumstance, whether the result of Rome's tolerance or indifference, the people of the municipalities far more easily bowed to an authoritarian central government than they might otherwise have done. True, edicts and burdens were handed down from Rome, but they seldom were more demanding than those imposed by the gods from Olympus, and they were far more calculable and practical.

This was the conglomerate structure that lay crushed and shattered at the feet of Octavian in 30 B.C., shattered in its own frenetic attempts at self-destruction. It was bankrupt politically, socially, morally, and economically; but it still had some assets, and there was still a spark of life in it. The question was, what would this shrewd young Italian, who already had shown a cunning in politics that chilled the hearts of observers, do with it?

PART
Six

The Augustan Dispensation

Chapter 29

THE POLITICAL AND MILITARY ARRANGEMENTS OF AUGUSTUS

OCTAVIAN. It was a frail but determined young man in his thirties that undertook the task of rebuilding the Roman world. Octavian's qualifications did not at first compel admiration. But the ruthlessness and stubbornness that he showed in his early years would mature into objectivity and tenacity. Good fortune had given him the right to claim the name of Gaius Julius Caesar. He had a few devoted friends; and now, with the Julian name and a marriage alliance with the Livii and the Claudii, he was the head of a formidable political faction. He was, further, the product of an Italian municipality, Velitrae, and he had the caution and conservatism of an Italian peasant. With this heritage he appreciated the sensibilities of the Italians as Caesar never did.

OCTAVIAN'S POWERS (31–27 B.C.). To achieve political stability the Roman leadership required years of experiment and adaptation. The recent past taught the dangers of autocracy, and the past century taught the folly of an unfettered restoration either of the oligarchical government of the Senate or of the demagogic rule of tribune and assembly. Octavian had renounced the title of triumvir, and for the first year after Actium, during which he settled the affairs of the East and returned to Rome (29 B.C.), his authority rested on his annual election to the consulship with an appropriate colleague. His position was also bolstered by the oath, the *consensus Italiae*, that had been taken by a majority of the Italians in 31 B.C. when he set out to destroy Antony and Cleopatra.[1] During these years the Senate loaded Octavian with honors and privileges that threatened to be as invidious as those which had been heaped upon Cae-

---

[1]   See above, p. 320.

sar—and thus destroyed him. Octavian could see that such adulation could lead to disaster. On January 13, 27 B.C., therefore, Octavian announced his relinquishment of all his special and extraordinary powers and the restoration of the normal constitutional government.

OCTAVIAN BECOMES AUGUSTUS (27 B.C.).   The reaction to Octavian's resignation was immediate and strong. Just as the British nobility could tolerate the rule of the middle-class German house of Hanover, for which it felt considerable contempt, so the Roman *nobiles* found it far easier to tolerate the rule of this *nouveau* from the country than the pretensions of any one of their own number. Octavian was persuaded to undertake a ten-year *imperium* over the provinces of Spain, Gaul, and Syria—the areas that had been held by Crassus, Pompey, and Caesar together—and he was also to keep Egypt. A few days later his moderation was rewarded by more honors: a laurel wreath, a shield commemorating his clemency, valor, justice, and piety, and a new appellation, "Augustus," the revered one, the man of more than mortal stature.

So vast a province had to be governed by Augustus' legates, but there was precedent for this in Pompey's extended government in absentia of the Spains from 54 to 49 B.C. The Senate was left with numerous older, more Romanized areas to administer, although some of them, such as Africa and Macedonia, required the presence of troops. But the great majority of the legions would be in the hands of Augustus and his own lieutenants, and he saw to it that all of these commanders were men of small distinction in family or office. Augustus continued to be elected to the consulship from 27 to 23 B.C., and while this partial resurrection of republican government was receiving its trial, so to speak, he went to Spain to direct an attack on the unsubdued mountain tribes that were a danger to the old settlements of the east and south. In 24 B.C. Augustus was forced by illness to return to Rome, and soon thereafter a conspiracy was discovered, contrived by nobles jealous of his monopoly of the consulship, which was considered the birthright of all Roman nobles. The leaders were caught and executed, but it was disquieting to find among them Varro Murena, Augustus' fellow-consul for 23 B.C. and a long-time supporter.

THE BIRTH OF THE PRINCIPATE (23 B.C.).   It was clear to Augustus that he must find some new accommodation with the forces of tradition in Roman government. In 23 B.C., therefore, he himself stepped down from the consulship and thereafter held that post only briefly, when there was some especially significant event to be celebrated. In his and Murena's places he appointed as consuls two men of strong republican sympathies, thus trying to confirm his restoration of the Republic. With the consulship gone, Augustus had to find some other office through which he could continue to guide public affairs. To do this he decided to use the tribunate. As a member of the patrician Julian family, Augustus was of course not eligible to become a plebeian tribune; but in 36 B.C. and again in 30 he had been granted some of the privileges of the tribunate. Apparently he found the rights that came with these honorific grants suggestive of great usefulness, and on July 1, 23 B.C., he began to base his position as the preeminent figure in Roman politics on the grant to him of all the prerogatives of a Roman tribune — the tribunician power — though he did not hold the office itself. With the tribunician power Augustus was able to convoke, and preside at, meetings of the Senate and of the assemblies, initiate legislation, veto unwelcome actions, enjoy personal sacrosanctity, and withal pose in the tribune's traditional role as defender of the people.[2] At the same time he also assumed an *imperium* that was superior to other magistrates' (*maius imperium*), and this in effect gave him authority not only over his own lieutenants, who represented him in his own provinces, but also over the governors of the senatorial provinces. Augustus learned to use his powers adroitly and diplomatically, and much of his future control stemmed from his *auctoritas*, his immense personal prestige, which he had won through successful war, unequalled honors (he was consul for the eleventh time in 23 B.C.), and his proved devotion to affairs of state. He put great stock, too, in the title of *princeps* (prince, first citizen of the State) because it emphasized his civil status. It was his emphasis on this title that ultimately gave the name of "the Principate" to the form of government that he evolved.

AUGUSTUS AND THE SENATE.   As Augustus modified and speciously curtailed his powers, he tried to enlist in the direction of affairs the cooperation of the other traditional arms of government, the Senate and the people. Augustus had all the deference for the old senatorial nobility that his own humbler origin dictated. By three revisions of the senatorial rolls (in 28, 18, and 13 B.C.) he reduced the Senate's size from 1000 to 600 and removed less worthy members who had entered under Caesar's regime or during the disturbances of the Triumvirate.

[2]   For the traditional prerogatives and duties of plebeian tribunes, see pp. 54–55, 90, 219, 230.

He tried repeatedly in other ways to maintain the Senate's distinctive and elevated nature. Only members of senatorial families could stand for the magistracies that led to seats in the Senate. By 13 B.C. the property qualification of a senator was set at one million sesterces. Members of the senatorial order might not marry freedwomen. The prince felt free, however, to bestow the rights of the order, and even the necessary funds, on worthy young men from outside it, and it did not therefore become a closed caste. The Senate was constantly consulted on important affairs of state, and a committee, consisting of the two consuls, one member of each of the other colleges of magistrates, and fifteen senators selected by lot, met regularly with the prince to discuss and prepare legislation. This committee not only served as a liaison between the prince and the Senate, but also by changing each six months it could furnish the prince with a continuous and broad indication of senatorial opinion. Augustus was careful to provide for the appearance of the abbreviation *EX S.C.* (in accordance with a decree of the Senate) on public works and coinage to indicate that in Italy such matters were the Senate's right and responsibility. Further, while he took his most important legislation to the traditional assemblies of the people, many important administrative matters were regulated by senatorial decree. Also, toward the end of Augustus' principate, the Senate began to serve as a court, especially in cases involving its own members or in cases of treason. All in all, probably the weakness of the Senate in contrast with the prince was not so blatantly evident to contemporaries as it is to us; and to many senators of the day Augustus appeared their advocate and defender when they reflected upon the indignities that they had suffered from the Gracchi, Marius, the Triumvirates, and Caesar.

AUGUSTUS AND THE PEOPLE.   Augustus was less successful in enlisting the cooperation of the people. He not only submitted his more important legislation to them for popular approval, but he hoped to make them responsible for the election of candidates to high office, although he presented them with a list of candidates that already had been screened. This was because the elected magistrates furnished the core of the imperial administration, and the prince had to be certain, therefore, that the people would elect capable men. To ensure this he resorted to a variety of devices. The number of petty magistracies at the bottom of the *cursus honorum* was reduced from twenty-six to twenty; thus, by an initial screening, he lessened both the numbers eligible for higher office and the chances for factional dispute. To emphasize the importance of elections he

342

himself descended to the Campus Martius to canvass, as any other noble might, for his favorite candidates. And at some early date he apparently established committees of senators to select nominees. In 5 A.D. ten special centuries of senators and knights from the jury courts were formed to nominate praetors and consuls. The inclusion of knights in these centuries emphasizes Augustus' concern for all Italy and not simply for Rome, for the knights often were drawn from the nobility of the Italian municipalities. Candidates chosen by the special nominating centuries entered the regular lists with great prestige and with ten votes already ensured. Further, Augustus even made arrangements for municipal senators to vote in Roman elections by forwarding absentee ballots in sealed boxes.

But all this was largely in vain. The weak link in Augustus' arrangement proved to be the people themselves. They refused to accept the responsibility that his plans demanded and they insisted that their master make known his wishes. Tumults took place at elections in 22 B.C., at which time Augustus studiously refrained from interference; but others in 19 B.C. were so severe that he was forced to intervene and appoint a consul; and in both 7 and 8 A.D. factional outbreaks forced the prince to interfere. The Romans as subjects were unwilling to act as citizens, and it became clear to Augustus that his hope for collaboration was vain. He himself never admitted his failure, but he left to his successor Tiberius the suggestion that the people's participation in elections should become merely formal.

AUGUSTUS AND THE ARMY.   When the prince returned from the East in 29 B.C. he had attained the control of more than sixty legions. The substance of the Roman world had been sapped in order to support these troops. It was very clear that some settlement must be found for them before any tranquillity and material recovery for the empire could be devised. It would be necessary, of course, to retain some of them under arms to ensure imperial security, but the majority had to be discharged and at the same time rendered grateful and loyal to the established government. By 13 B.C., at least, the number of legions had been reduced to twenty-eight; and main bases for the fleet had been established at Misenum and Ravenna, with auxiliary bases at various strategic points. The confiscations of lands from Antonian sympathizers in Italy, and later the purchase of appropriate areas both in Italy and in the provinces, cared for the settlement of the veterans. Augustus' colonies, unlike Caesar's, were almost completely devoted to his soldiers, instead of having a mixed population. We have evidence of at least twenty-eight of these in Italy, five in Sicily, one in Sardinia, fourteen in Spain, eight in Gaul, fourteen in the Balkans, eleven in Asia and the East, and seventeen in Africa. Augustus records that he spent from his own funds 860 million sesterces to accomplish these settlements, and he was rewarded with loyal adherents at strategic points all over the empire. Moreover, the purpose of the colonies was not wholly partisan; many were deliberately placed on sites where they would ensure the security of seaports and trade routes, or of settled areas, against recently subdued barbarians. They served not merely as pockets of support or defense, for they also were instrumental in the Italianization of large areas of the Mediterranean world.

The army was clearly devoted to the Julian house. But Augustus saw that his own personal ascendancy was not a sufficient guarantee for permanent tranquillity. As early as 13 B.C. he began to furnish many discharged men with gratuities, instead of with land, after they had served their stated terms; and by 5 A.D. the term of service was set at sixteen years for praetorians and twenty years for the veterans of the legions. Then in 6 A.D. he established a special treasury, the *aerarium militare*, to handle severance payments. Thus soldiers might learn to look to the State, rather than to one man, as the guarantor of their future. This treasury was supported by a five percent tax on inheritances, a four percent tax on slaves, and a one percent sales tax.

THE SECURITY AND COMFORT OF THE CITY OF ROME. There was not only a need for protection in the provinces from swollen and irresponsible armies; security within the capital also had often been jeopardized because of the lack of the services vital for safety in a highly urbanized area. Here again Augustus moved cautiously and discreetly, for Rome was the Senate's responsibility, even though a neglected one. A pressing need was for fire protection. In 26 B.C. an aedile, Egnatius Rufus, had used his own slaves to protect the city and had won great popularity thereby, a popularity which the Augustan government at length found so dangerous that Rufus was executed on a charge of conspiracy (19 B.C.). Augustus was stung by Rufus' show of initiative into lending to the State 600 slaves to serve as firefighters in 21 B.C. However, by 7 B.C. the prince had decided that the city government should be completely reorganized, and this led to further changes in fire protection. The city was divided into fourteen regions, each under the supervision of a tribune, aedile, or praetor chosen by lot. The regions were further divided into 265 neighborhoods (*vici*), for each of which the neighbors of the area elected a *vicomagister*, who was to be in charge of local administration and of arrangements for firefighting. By this device Augustus seems to have hoped to develop even in Rome the local participation that was so vigorous in the municipalities. A series of severe fires, however, ultimately stressed the need for a more formal organization; and in 6 A.D. a Prefecture of the Watch was established, with an equestrian at its head. The prefect of the Watch commanded seven cohorts of one thousand freedmen apiece, and these served both as a fire department and as a night watch.

In 22 B.C. Augustus was prevailed upon to undertake the care of the grain supply of Rome (*cura annonae*). Ultimately he administered this trust through an equestrian prefect, and a law was passed providing a heavy fine for any interference with the transport of grain to Rome. In 22 B.C. he also placed two senators, chosen from among the ex-praetors, in charge of the free distribution of grain to the city's proletariat. This service was considered, therefore, a responsibility of the Senate and was paid for from the public treasury. The number of those receiving free grain once more had risen since Caesar's census, and Augustus was forced to revise the rolls again. The number of recipients was now set at 200,000, and each man had to prove that his *origo* (source, ancestral home) was the city of Rome. The low birthrate of the city kept the number of recipients thereafter reasonably stable.

During his lifetime Agrippa, Augustus' best general and close adviser, took a special interest in the water supply of Rome. He built two new aqueducts for the city and repaired three others; and, at his death in 12 B.C., he left to the emperor a trained staff of maintenance men. Augustus turned over the supervision of the water supply to a senatorial board of three curators under the jurisdiction of the Senate; and a similar commission saw to it that the temples and other public buildings of Rome were kept in good repair.

Toward the end of his life Augustus further provided for the safety of the city by establishing there three urban cohorts, of 1000 men each, under the command of the prefect of the city, who was a senator of consular rank. This force was considered a part of the Roman army, but it served as the city's police force. The famous praetorian guard, a body of nine cohorts, was derived from a guard of honor enjoyed by holders of the *imperium* in republican days. Now it was the prince's own personal guard, but it also was responsible for the tranquillity of Italy. Under Augustus only three of its cohorts were stationed at Rome, and the remainder were distributed in the municipalities of Italy.

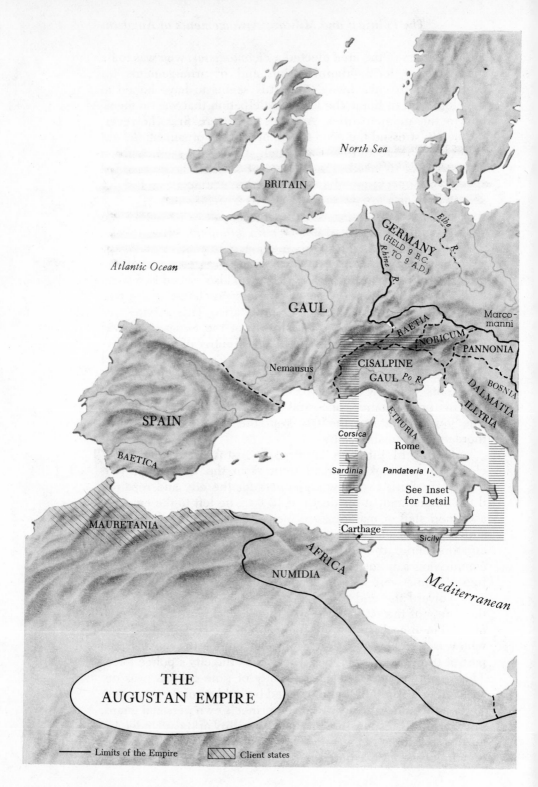

North Sea

BRITAIN

Atlantic Ocean

GERMANY
(HELD 9 B.C.
TO 9 A.D.)

Elbe R.

Rhine R.

GAUL

RAETIA

NORICUM

Marco-
manni

PANNONIA

Nemausus

CISALPINE
GAUL

Po R.

BOSNIA

DALMATIA

ILLYRIA

SPAIN

ETRURIA

BAETICA

Corsica

Rome

Sardinia

Pandateria I.

See Inset
for Detail

MAURETANIA

Carthage

Sicily

AFRICA

NUMIDIA

Mediterranean

THE
AUGUSTAN EMPIRE

———— Limits of the Empire   ▨ Client states

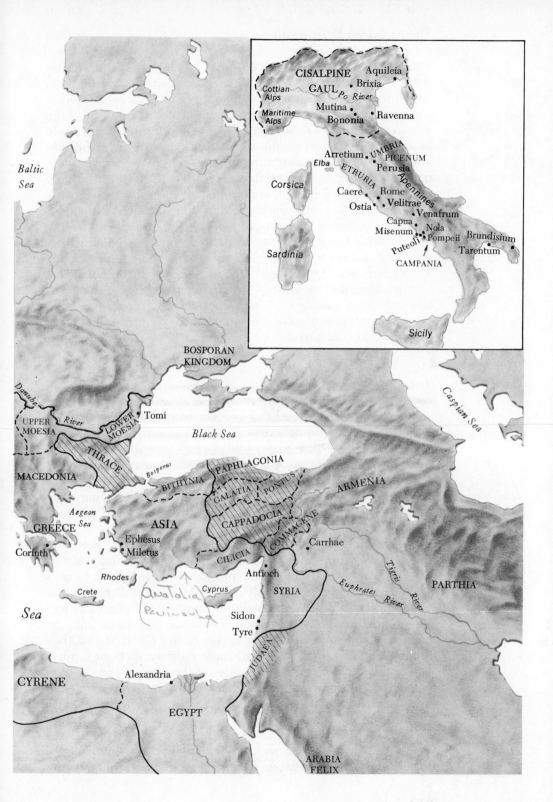

Baltic
Sea

CISALPINE
GAUL

Aquileia
Brixia

Cottian
Alps

Po River

Maritime
Alps

Mutina
Bononia

Ravenna

Corsica

Arretium
UMBRIA
PICENUM

Elba
ETRURIA
Perusia
Apennines

Caere
Rome
Velitrae

Sardinia
Ostia
Venafrum

Capua
Nola
Brundisium

Misenum
Pompeii

Puteoli
Tarentum

CAMPANIA

Sicily

BOSPORAN
KINGDOM

Caspian
Sea

Danube
River
LOWER
MOESIA
Tomi

UPPER
MOESIA

Black Sea

THRACE

Bosporus

MACEDONIA

PAPHLAGONIA

BITHYNIA

GALATIA
PONTUS

ARMENIA

Aegean
Sea

GREECE

ASIA
CAPPADOCIA

Ephesus
COMMAGENE

Corinth
Miletus
CILICIA
Carrhae

Rhodes

Crete
Anatolia
(Peninsula)
Cyprus

Antioch

Tigris
River

Sea
SYRIA
PARTHIA

Euphrates
River

Sidon

Tyre

JUDAEA

CYRENE
Alexandria

EGYPT

ARABIA
FELIX

347

THE SYSTEM OF DEFENSE: EGYPT.   There were foreign as
well as internal dangers to the national security, and they engaged the emperor's care throughout his long career. Republican expansion had in a general way indicated the outline of the
empire, but some of the periphery needed frontiers that could
be defended more economically, and there still were significant
enclaves within the present boundaries where the natives were
constant threats to their settled neighbors. In the East military
campaigns were kept at a minimum, and Augustus relied heavily on diplomacy and on the old system of client kingdoms.
Early a number of expeditions against the Ethiopians (29, 25,
and 22 B.C.) were necessary to defend Egypt's southern frontiers; but in 21/0 B.C. a peace treaty established a buffer state at
Philae between the first and second cataracts of the Nile. This
area was guarded by military installations, and Egypt remained
immune from invasion for two centuries. The region was so
important to the empire's economy that Augustus left three
legions plus auxiliary troops there, and he established a fleet
headquarters at Alexandria as well.

THE ORIENT.   Syria was the mainstay of imperial defense in
Asia, but there probably were no more than four legions regularly stationed there, and this reflects Augustus' resolution not
to squander the empire's resources in the bottomless pit of the
East. The Roman provinces of the Levant were buttressed by a
whole line of client states—Pontus, Paphlagonia, Galatia, Cappadocia, Commagene, and Judaea. In these areas native princes
did good service in defending the frontiers, and in some cases
furnished valuable auxiliaries to the Roman army and administered peoples not yet ready for direct Roman rule. When internal development or casual circumstances dictated, however,
these areas were transformed into provinces, as Galatia was in
25 B.C., Paphlagonia in 6 B.C., and much of Herod the Great's
realm in 6 A.D. There was only one frankly imperialistic venture
in the area, the ill-fated expedition into Arabia Felix in 24 B.C.
The object was the proverbial wealth of the Arabs and the
control of the important trade routes to the Far East that they
dominated. The expedition had some military successes, but it
had to fall back under the severities of the climate and country.
Apparently the natives were sufficiently impressed, however,
that thereafter they entered into friendly trade relations with
the Romans.

The chief problem in the East was relations with the
Parthians. There was no real problem about the maintenance of
the natural frontier between the two powers, the Euphrates. But

Roman pride had been stung by Parthian successes against Crassus and Antony. A more basic difficulty was the suzerainty of Armenia, which controlled invasion routes for either of the great powers against the other, while it remained basically Parthian in racial and cultural orientation. Happily the Parthian rulers were not particularly strong or self-assured during the principate of Augustus. In 20 B.C. Augustus' own presence in Syria, while his stepson Tiberius was moving toward Armenia, was sufficient to move the Parthian king, Phraates, to restore the Roman standards lost at Carrhae by Crassus as well as such Roman prisoners as were still alive. This was sufficient to vindicate Roman honor and allay jingoist sentiment in Rome, and it was followed by the coronation of a pro-Roman candidate for the Armenian throne. This did not end the struggle for that pivotal and unhappy land, however. A Parthian resurgence there led to an expedition by the emperor's grandson, Gaius Caesar (1–4 A.D.), which was again successful in placing a Roman nominee on the throne, but it ended dismally in Gaius' death. Before the death of Augustus (14 A.D.) the country was completely without a king and in a state of anarchy. To round out the eastern picture, Agrippa in 14 B.C. arranged to include in the Roman system of client kingdoms the Bosporan Kingdom, which was situated approximately in the Russian Crimea. Thus an important source of grain was assured to Rome's eastern provinces and armies, and the policing of the Black Sea was made easier.

AFRICA.   The enlarged province of Africa fell to the Senate's lot; yet it, along with Cyrene, needed at least one legion and sometimes more to keep the tribes of the hinterland in line. The necessity of campaigns in that area is indicated by the triumphs celebrated by senatorial governors of Africa in 21 and 19 B.C. Mauretania also fell into Roman hands, but Augustus in 25 B.C. conferred it on the Numidian prince Juba II to administer as a client kingdom, and he was also charged with the protection of the Roman provinces in Africa from the south and west. Augustus followed the precedent of Marius and Caesar, however, in planting colonies in Mauretania outside the formal limits of the empire. These seem to have been under the general supervision of the governors of Baetic (southern) Spain.

THE OCCIDENT.   In the West, Spain called for early attention. The freedom-loving peoples in the northwestern part of the peninsula had been almost untouched by Roman occupation, and in the years of Roman civil conflict and anarchy they

349

had wreaked havoc on the Romanized sections. Augustus himself took the field in 26 B.C., but he was forced by illness to leave his command to subordinates, and the struggle dragged on until 19 B.C., when a policy of ruthless enslavements and massacres by the Roman generals Publius Carisius and Marcus Agrippa brought desolation and peace to the land.

Nearer to home and also troublesome were some Alpine peoples whom history and conquest had passed by. Campaigns against them in 25 B.C. and from 17 through 15 B.C. subdued or exterminated them. Some of the conquered territories were attached for administrative purposes to colonies in the area; some (Raetia, Noricum, the Maritime Alps) became minor provinces under equestrian procurators; and in one case at least, the Cottian Alps, a native prince continued to rule as a Roman prefect.

THE NORTHERN FRONTIERS.   The most formidable military task facing Augustus, however, was the establishment of a suitable northern frontier, especially for the Balkans. Here there had been constant pressure on Macedonia and Thrace, and farther to the west the Romans held only a relatively narrow strip inland from Dalmatia. The country was rugged and trackless and the people brave, yet here was the area that should firmly cement the eastern and western halves of the empire. Campaigns were started against the Pannonians and Bosnians in 13 B.C. by Marcus Vinicius, and were continued first by Agrippa and then by Tiberius, until by 8 B.C. most of the natives had submitted, though later events proved that they had not really been subdued. Sometime after this the area along the southern bank of the Lower Danube, Moesia, was occupied and held by an imperial legate, and the army that had been stationed in Macedonia was transferred to his care.

Meanwhile, beginning in 12 B.C., a general attack was made in Germany under the command of Drusus, Tiberius' younger brother. The reason seems to have been twofold: to eliminate a likely breeding ground for future invasions of Gaul, but perhaps even more to establish a frontier on the Elbe River. The Elbe along with the Danube, which was even now being reached by Tiberius, would have furnished a much shorter and more economical line of defense from the North Sea to the Black Sea than the Rhine-Danube line did. From 12 through 9 B.C. Drusus made sweeping marches through the country and reached the Elbe; but a fall from horseback in 9 proved fatal, and his task was taken up by Tiberius who by 7 B.C. met no organized resistance among the Germans and returned to Rome.

350

Conquest was claimed by the Romans, but the Germans were not really reduced and they were to prove far less tractable or ready for assimilation than the Gauls had been.

From 7 B.C. to 4 A.D. there were a number of obscure expeditions by Roman legions across the Danube or into Germany. These seem in part to have been punitive, in retaliation for desultory raids by Germans into Roman lands; but they were partly dictated by a need to isolate or subdue the neighbors of the Marcomanni before an attempt was made by the Romans on that important people themselves. Under a great national leader, Maroboduus, the Marcomanni had established a formidable empire in Bohemia astride the very line of the Elbe and Danube that the Romans coveted. For the Romans to hold that line, the Marcomanni had to be reduced. This was to be the great final effort in rounding out the empire's frontiers. In 4 A.D. Tiberius returned to the scene and began operations in Germany; and during that year and the next preparatory campaigns were carried out. However, just as the climactic attack approached, news came of a rebellion in the rear. The insufficiently subdued peoples of Illyria and Pannonia rose, massacred Roman garrisons and businessmen, and spread panic all the way to Rome. Tiberius quickly came to terms with Maroboduus and returned to defend Italy against a possible attack by the insurgents and to stamp out their revolt. He was none too soon. The economies in the military budget practiced by Augustus, plus a growing disinclination among Roman citizens (especially those of Italy) to perform military service, meant that there were no reserves and few recruits. Veterans had to be recalled to arms, and even freed slaves were enlisted.

No sooner was the rebellion finally and systematically quelled by Tiberius in 9 A.D. than even more dreadful news arrived: Quinctilius Varus, the Roman governor of Germany, and three irreplaceable legions had been destroyed in an ambush by a German patriot named Arminius. Varus seems to have made the same mistake that other Romans made concerning the German barbarians—he presumed too much on the actual extent of Roman control and had attempted to treat these barbarians as he would treat Asians or even Gauls. In any case, the aging emperor could not replace his lost legions, and except for a few punitive raids the defensive frontier was pulled back to the Rhine.

Regardless of occasional failures and disappointments, Augustus gave the Mediterranean world a political stability and a tranquillity such as it never had known. But the task demanded more than the predominance of one man, whatever his capabilities and good will. The prince had a superhuman task, and he had to use his relatives, intimates, private household, and the knights who, despite all their competencies, had so long been excluded from the direction of public affairs. With these pawns Augustus began the development of an administrative system sufficiently efficient to carry on even under quite inferior princes.

THE PROBLEM OF THE SUCCESSION.   Augustus knew that the future of the State depended on a continuing guiding hand. He also realized that his successor must be a member of his house; to look elsewhere ran the risk once more of ambition and civil war. To construct the appropriate family connections and to provide suitable heirs he directed a maze of dynastic marriages. Since he had only one child of his own, Julia, he arranged the marriages and divorces of even his most remote kinswomen with a master hand. While his use of Julia was the most flagrant, a number of the dynastic marriages that he designed had serious repercussions; for one example, Quinctilius Varus seems to have been entrusted with the important and delicate German command because he was married to Augustus' grandniece. The unhappy Julia first was married to her own cousin, Augustus' nephew Marcus Marcellus, in 25 B.C. Marcellus was voted special dispensations so that he could hold magistracies earlier than the legal age-limit , and it was clear that Augustus hoped that the young man, doubly connected with himself, might prove a suitable successor. But Marcellus died in the autumn of 23 B.C. Next, in 21 B.C., Augustus' closest friend and best general, Agrippa, was called upon to divorce his wife and marry Julia, who was half his age. The marriage was blessed with two sons, both of whom were adopted by Augustus, while their father was associated with Augustus in the tribunician power and in the *maius imperium*. Agrippa died in 12 B.C., however, before his sons, Gaius and Lucius Caesar, had reached maturity. Augustus had depended on Agrippa to watch over and supervise Gaius and Lucius until they were old enough to assume the burden of empire. With Agrippa's premature death, he was forced to turn to his stepsons, Tiberius and Drusus, Livia's sons by her first marriage. Tiberius was asked to divorce his wife in order to marry the somewhat shopworn Julia, while Drusus received Augustus' niece Antonia. Drusus died in 9 B.C., however, and although Tiberius was granted the tribunician power in 6 B.C., he soon quitted Rome and became a semi-exile in the East, partly because of the emperor's marked favor for and promotion of his grandsons Gaius and Lucius, and partly because of his notorious incompatibility with the gay and worldly Julia. The aging emperor was angered by Tiberius' withdrawal; and he was even more furious when at last he learned (what the world already knew) of his own daughter's infidelities to her husband. He exiled her to the island of Pandateria. He still had his grandsons as his props and hopes, and he advanced them rapidly in public life. However, Lucius died in 2 A.D. and Gaius in 4; and the old man finally had to recall Tiberius in that year from his self-imposed exile, adopt him, and once more extend to him the tribunician power as well as the *imperium*. He did this so that at his own death there would be no question as to who the State's *princeps* was and the transmission of power to his successor would be without incident.

THE POLICY-MAKERS.   While Augustus kept in touch with senatorial opinion through his special committee,[3] this was not a true cabinet to cope with the problems of empire or to establish policy. For decisions on basic policy Augustus turned to his most intimate friends. Livia, Agrippa, and Maecenas were his closest advisers, though there were others to be consulted on specialized problems. Thus the ancient Roman custom that a paterfamilias consult his friends before making any important decision became the foundation of an imperial cabinet. The empress Livia was a life-long force, and she and Agrippa were sometimes hard and frank with the emperor. Amusingly enough, it is reported that Augustus never answered a query from Livia without writing it down first to see how it looked. Slaves and freedmen of the household put special skills to work serving as secretaries for the imperial government, and thus they became the nucleus of a bureaucracy. In this area also, the development found its roots in ancient practice, for magistrates long had furnished from their own households such confidential aides as were needed during their annual terms of office.

EQUESTRIANS IN GOVERNMENT.   The knights also were used throughout the empire for diverse administrative and financial tasks. They had special training in money matters; they were the emperor's own Italians; and they were loyal and grateful. As procurators they were placed in the imperial provinces to administer various tax programs, and sometimes an equestrian procurator was the highest official in the smaller provinces. Even in senatorial provinces imperial procurators of equestrian rank were assigned to supervise the emperor's pri-

---

[3]   For the senatorial committee, see above p. 342.

vate estates, and they were thus easily available to observe and to report to the emperor concerning the government in the provinces that were not directly under his jurisdiction. Parallel to the old *cursus honorum* for men of senatorial rank,[4] therefore, there now was growing up a *cursus* for members of the equestrian class, in the army, in the procuratorships, and finally in the great prefectures of Egypt, of the Praetorian Guard, or of the *Annona* (grain supply). The old senatorial *cursus* remained, and the old posts of prestige both at home and abroad were eagerly sought; but the new equestrian *cursus* began to develop posts with more power than the senators enjoyed, although with less prestige because they did not have ancient traditions behind them and they were patently subordinate to the prince. However, the men of the equestrian order whom Augustus pressed into the service of the State did much to ensure the prosperity and success of the whole Augustan dispensation, for they were appropriately placed throughout the empire to see to it that there was more equitable taxation, a more just and efficient collection of it, speedy hearings for the wronged, and speedy reprisal for delinquents.

Chapter 30

THE ECONOMIC CONSEQUENCES
OF THE AUGUSTAN PEACE

STABILITY AND CONFIDENCE.   The establishment of peace in the Mediterranean Basin and the belief that it would continue led at once to an increased prosperity. After Actium a resurgence of confidence in the government brought money out of hiding. It became so plentiful in Rome that rates of interest dropped to one-third of the normal amount. There was a fantastic growth in the number and wealth of Italian capitalists. Many of these men were of the freedman class, men who had learned

[4]   For the course of offices normally followed by men of senatorial rank, see pp. 103, 211, 267–268.

354

to amass great profits from Roman needs for goods and services, yet whose humble origins exempted them from the political suspicion and jealousy of the upper classes. Of course one of the greatest capitalists was the emperor himself, and his fortune, whether inherited from Caesar, wrested from Cleopatra, or the fruit of bequests of grateful friends and subjects, so outshone that of his noble peers that he could inaugurate great public programs from his private resources. Little by little it became very easy for the servants that managed his private fortune to confuse it with the affairs of the imperial provinces, which they also handled. But Augustus carefully supervised the whole financial structure, and he showed himself in his care for the balance sheets of empire to be a very good bourgeois indeed. A standardization of the currency fairly early in the principate was a further stimulus to financial stability: cities were still allowed to issue local bronze, but an imperial standard for gold and silver was established so that commercial exchange was much facilitated.

TAXATION.   Part of the economic distress of the Late Republic had been due to the inequities and uncertainties connected with taxation. The Italians still looked upon the empire as their property for exploitation and they were not inclined to assume part of the burden that public works and defense entailed. Augustus was enough of an Italian to agree with them that the heartland of the empire should keep a preferred position. However, a more careful assessment of provincial assets could do much to correct distress in the rest of the empire. Therefore, a census of population, wealth, and resources was taken periodically in each of the provinces. In the older provinces the census could easily be ascertained by municipal authorities and forwarded to the governor's office and thence to Rome. There was greater difficulty in the new areas, but we know of censuses in Gaul in 27 and 12 B.C., and one was in progress at Augustus' death. Such surveys not only revealed the size of the population, but also the amount and types of agricultural land (whether plowland, vineyard, grove, or pasture), of flocks and herds, and of shops and businesses.

Taxes were based on the data gathered from the census. Italy continued to enjoy freedom from property taxes, but residents did pay a five percent tax on the value of slaves manumitted, and ultimately a five percent tax on bequests, which supported the payments made to army veterans at discharge (the military *aerarium*). Most of the Senate's income was from the provinces. There the land tax was based on the land's productivity, and there also were taxes on personal property and on the trades. There were customs duties too between various parts of the empire, but these seldom exceeded two and one-half percent of the value of the goods in transit. The collection of these taxes was careful and just, and irregularities by collectors brought prompt punishment. The system proved more equitable and more efficient than that of the Republic, and the amounts levied probably did not exceed those exacted by earlier governments, though it must also be remembered that provincials had local municipal taxes to pay as well.

Theoretically the old senatorial treasury (the *aerarium*) was the repository of the collected taxes, and ex-praetors were placed in its charge. Actually, for each of the imperial provinces Augustus set up a local treasury (*fiscus*) which would save paperwork by making disbursements for any given area from its own income. Thus only an account of the balances would pass between each *fiscus* and the *aerarium*. Even with increased efficiency and conscientious economy the treasuries still were often in difficulties. But the emperor's immense personal fortune, the *patrimonium*, was constantly at the service of the State. Augustus thus proved to be the financial as well as the military pillar of the government.

ITALIAN AGRICULTURE.   With financial and political stability Italy made immediate and marked economic recovery, outstripping the provinces both because of its favored status and because it already had enjoyed a decade of peace under Octavian while the rest of the empire was in a turmoil. Farming continued to be its major occupation, and the tendencies of the previous two centuries continued. Ranching in the south and in the Apennines and Etruria still was profitable, and there is evidence that single flocks of as many as 250,000 sheep existed. The more moderate estates of from fifty to two hundred acres specialized in wines and oil, for which there developed a strong foreign as well as local market. Many great owners acquired estates in different areas and diversified their produce in order to insure themselves against poor crops or poor markets for any single area or item. Grain was cultivated everywhere for local use, and enough of it was grown in the Po Valley that it could be exported. Truck gardens thrived near the towns, and there was some development of the poultry industry, especially for the luxury trade (pheasants and peacocks). Dairy produce also was in demand.

The elimination of piracy and the decrease in foreign wars cut off the large supply of new slaves that had characterized the Republic, but some owners fostered the breeding of slaves on their estates with rewards for prolific females; and slaves still furnished a major portion of the labor on large plantations dealing in specialized production. The small farmer still held his own in some places, however, such as the Po Valley, Picenum, and Umbria; and in some places it was becoming expedient to use tenant farmers (*coloni*), a practice that was to prove more and more necessary during the Empire. Horace, for example, had five tenant farmers on his Sabine estate, although he also cultivated a portion of it himself, using a labor force of eight slaves under the supervision of a steward.

ITALIAN INDUSTRY.   Industry also made progress in Italy during the Augustan Age. The emperor favored the bourgeoisie of the peninsula as a counterpoise to the jealous nobility, and the *nouveau riche* in industry and trade became stock objects of patronizing scorn in the works of aristocratic writers. Etruria and Campania led in the production of manufactured goods. The glass industry flourished in Campania and Aquileia under Augustus and challenged the Syrian producers. The beautiful Arretine pottery was at its height during this period, and pieces of it have been found all the way from Britain to eastern India. Some of the pottery factories were large-scale affairs. One at Arretium, for instance, had a mixing-basin for the clays with a capacity of 10,000 gallons.

The metal industry also approached a factory system, with specialists for the various steps in production. Important examples can be found in the iron foundries at Puteoli, which drew their ore from Elba, or those of Aquileia, which imported ore from the famous mines of Noricum. Silver and bronze ware were finished at Capua, and silver ware also at Tarentum.

Much spinning and weaving continued to be done at home, but the goods were finished and distributed by the important guilds of fullers. The wools of northern Italy were particularly famous; and the wool mart of Pompeii was one of the most impressive features of the town. A small town such as Pompeii well illustrates how much of its production was meant for local consumption; the streets are lined with small shops and bakeries where goods were prepared on the spot before the customer's eyes. Even in Pompeii, however, wool, oil, and wine obviously found a wider market, as did a famous fish sauce, *garum*, bottles of which went far afield.

Building materials were produced near every urban market, and there was a good profit in bricks, tiles, lead pipe, cement, marble, and other building stones. The building activity

357

in towns all over Italy during this period indicates widespread stability and prosperity in an industrious and civic-minded middle class. It was during this time that Vitruvius found it worthwhile to compose his influential work on architecture, which treated not only its history, but also its public and private application.

THE EASTERN ECONOMY.   The East, after nearly a century of exploitation, invasions, disorders, and capital levies recovered more slowly. Egypt made the fastest revival. It was in the emperor's special care, and he gave a good deal of attention to the maintenance of its system of canals. Its wheat was an important factor on the world market, furnishing one third of the supply for the city of Rome. There was also its monopoly of papyrus, and it produced a particularly fine linen. Native building stones and gems also were quarried and prepared there, and a fine sand made possible the manufacture of glass products of high quality. Early in the Augustan era imperial protection fostered the revival of the great workshops of Alexandria, which received the raw materials of the Orient and processed them for the western market. Alexandria soon prospered as it never had before, and it became the second metropolis of the empire.

Syria was at the terminus of overland trade routes from the Orient and had its share of processing luxury items for the Mediterranean world. It also produced its own dates, figs, and plums, and an excellent wine; and the asphalt from the Dead Sea was in demand. But perhaps its two most famous products were Sidonian glass and Tyrian purple dye, and in the Augustan Age a market for these developed all over the empire and far beyond its borders.

The provinces of Asia Minor produced wines, figs, minerals, drugs, and shellfish, but their greatest fame came from such celebrated textiles as Milesian wool and Coan silks. Greece proper alone continued in the economic decline that it had suffered for centuries. There was a demand abroad for the famous Greek marbles, however, and the popularity of Greek art furnished employment for artists and copyists.

THE WESTERN ECONOMY.   Many of the western provinces included much virgin territory that had not yet been fully developed, and another half-century would be needed before they furnished serious economic competition to Italy. The old provinces of Sardinia-Corsica and Sicily, however, still raised cattle, grain, drugs, and hemp. Africa continued to be as rich as it had been under the Carthaginians, and its biggest produce was grain, which came to rival Egypt's on the Roman market. It also furnished fruit, oil, dyes, marble, and medicines. Spain was rich in minerals; it yielded 20,000 pounds of gold annually, perhaps eight tons of silver, and lead, tin, and iron were exported in quantities. The pots on the rubbish piles of Italy testify to the export from Spain also of wine, oil, wax, honey, and fish sauce. Spain also furnished fine linens and beautiful wools. Gaul's prosperity increased rapidly during the period. Augustus did not press the urbanization of the land, but little by little the Celts descended from the hilltops and established towns in the valleys, and this made the administration of the country easier. The Gauls were great imitators, and they not only produced grain and livestock, metals, wool, and flax, but they soon attempted the manufacture of glass and pottery in a bid for the northern market. Even the wilder Danubian lands produced some wine, oil, dairy products, and fish, and the iron of Noricum was famous and supplied the factories of Aquileia. As the legions were stationed for considerable periods in permanent or semi-permanent camps along the frontiers, another stimulus to industrial and commercial life was given by the settlement of tradesmen, service people, and prostitutes in shacktowns (*canabae*) nearby. These in time frequently became flourishing markets and contributed to the economic development of backward areas.

TRADE WITHIN THE EMPIRE.   With the pacification of its shores the Mediterranean served not to separate but to join the lands around it. Improvement in navigational aids increased the safety of sea transport; and the establishment of permanent naval bases at Misenum and Ravenna, with subsidiary bases elsewhere, prevented any renascence of piracy. Freightage by water was inexpensive and customs barriers between the various sections of the empire were sufficiently low that they offered no real restraint of trade. A stable and uniform currency, the construction of good roads, a laissez-faire policy on the part of the government, and the revival of great trading cities such as Corinth and Carthage were added stimulants for a healthy expansion in commercial activity. Much cargo was carried by businessmen of modest means, little better than pedlars, who picked up goods in one port and moved on to another where there was a chance for profitable sale. But there also were great import and export firms with large warehouses in important ports such as Alexandria, Puteoli, and Ostia, and these companies commanded ships that could carry at least a thousand tons.

Some shipping companies specialized to such an extent in the transport of provisions to Italy, especially of wheat, that almost regular sailings were developed and a fairly dependable passenger service became available. Luxury items were popular and they made profitable cargoes, but the great bulk of the empire's trade lay in the exchange of foodstuffs and other necessary staples between the various districts within the empire, such as grain, wine, olive oil, metals, lumber, pitch, tar, and hemp.

The newly opened provinces of the north and west offered expanding markets during the Augustan period, but probably Italy itself was the greatest market of all at this time. The appetite of the peninsula for materials of all sorts was enormous, and the archaeological and literary remains indicate a significant consumption of goods from all over the world. Part of the wealth that was necessary in order to buy so heavily in the whole world market came, of course, from Italy's especially privileged position as the ruling element in the empire. But during the Augustan Age Italy's role was not wholly parasitic. A great many of its imports were financed by the heavy volume of exports. The provinces had not yet reached productive levels that could challenge Italy's position; thus her wines were in great demand throughout the world—Pliny says that two-thirds of the Mediterranean's vintage wines came from the peninsula—and her manufactured goods were found in quantities from Britain to India and from Finland to the Sahara.

FOREIGN TRADE.   Foreign trade began to thrive in the Augustan Age. The commercial ventures to distant places certainly are interesting, but probably they were not of critical importance economically. Capuan bronze and glass found its way up through the rivers of central Europe to Poland and Norway, while quantities of Arretine pottery, typical of the period, are found in Britain. In return came tin from Britain; from northern Europe the Romans received furs, skins, slaves, dried fish, and the highly desirable amber; and the Crimea furnished grain to the cities and armies of Asia Minor. Up the East Coast of Africa came ivory, palm oil, tortoise shell, spices, and slaves; while in return the residents of the empire sent them the liquors, gewgaws, and weapons that in time became the regular European reward for Africans. Some time in the late first century B.C. it was discovered that the monsoon winds facilitated a direct passage for ships across the Indian Ocean from Egyptian ports to India. After this discovery merchants could avoid the dangerous route that skirted the coast of Arabia

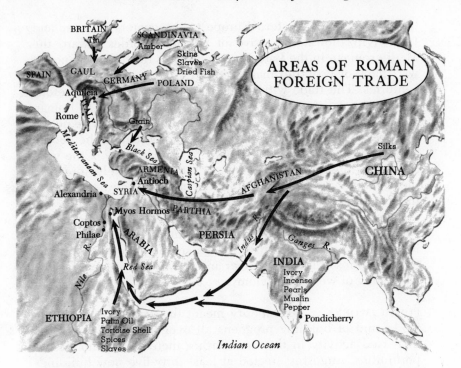

and Persia. The trip out could be completed in forty days, and soon as many as 120 ships were making the trip annually. The rapidity of commercial expansion to the Far East is testified by the appearance of large amounts of Arretine ware on the eastern shore of India near Pondicherry, by the hoards of Augustan coins that have been discovered in India, and by the Indian embassies to Augustus reported in the literary sources of the period. Some of the imported goods originated in India itself, including ivory, incense, pearls, rare stones, muslin, tortoise shell, and especially pepper, for which the Romans acquired a fantastic taste and for the storage of which they built great barns on the Tiber. Overland from China through Afghanistan and down the Indus came silks, which Romans soon would not be denied, regardless of war, calamity, or cost. On the trip out Roman ships took wine, copper, lead, coral, cheap cloths, and gold; and in the first century A.D. the trade is said to have been valued at 50,000,000 sesterces a year, the profit to traders being worth one hundredfold their investment.

While the foreign trade of the empire may seem a small and inconsequential fragment of its economy, its exports across the Rhine and Danube advertised to the northern barbarians the road to a land of untold wealth and allure, just as centuries later a few precious objects and word-of-mouth reports attracted

361

the barbarians of Western Europe to the centers of Aztec and Inca civilizations. The drive of northern hordes toward the Mediterranean in the Late Empire, then, is related to the northward flow of beautiful manufactured articles in the preceding centuries. The trade with the Far East appears less dangerous to Roman security, and the supply of luxurious silks to Roman effeminates may seem of no great importance. It must be noted, however, that this trade was dreadfully important to the people that lived along the caravan routes to China. Many of the wars and mass migrations of Central Asia that ultimately spread to the Danubian and Rhenish frontiers of Rome can be linked to the interruptions of that commercial traffic upon which the natives depended for a livelihood. A more immediate danger was postulated by the Roman economists of the time, who feared that this trade in luxuries was creating a serious drain on their supplies of gold and silver and thus was instrumental in a worsening of western economy.

PUBLIC WORKS.   Prosperity meant the expansion of public works and of building programs all over the empire, and the increased activity in this area further increased economic opportunities. Augustus erected at least forty-five new buildings and restored at least eighty-six more in Rome and Italy, and he urged other wealthy Romans to immortalize themselves by similar activity. There is no province that does not testify to the munificence of the emperor and his friends in the construction of some public edifice. With growing urban populations everywhere, the problem of an adequate water-supply increased. Rome's supply had been the special care of Agrippa. After Agrippa's death Augustus built one more aqueduct for the city of Rome, extended another, and repaired them all. And we have evidence for work by either Augustus or Agrippa on aqueducts for Brixia, Caere, Capua, and Venafrum in Italy, Nemausus in Gaul, Alexandria in Egypt, Ephesus in Asia, and Antioch in Syria.

The construction and repair of roads, harbors, and other aids to commercial enterprise were a special concern of Augustus. Italy now consisted of more than 450 separate communities, and the prince was anxious to improve the communications between them. At the same time he was reluctant to trespass in an area that traditionally was the Senate's. At first he tried to interest other nobles in undertaking road construction in Italy, for this was in the tradition of republican magistrates. In the later part of his life, however, he initiated a good many road-building projects himself, though he repeatedly catered to

362

senatorial sensitivities by associating the Senate with himself in the inscriptions that appeared on Italian milestones. Elsewhere he planned and began great networks of roads to open up Spain and Gaul. These projects were elaborated and carried out by his successors. Canals and harbor projects were completed at the mouth of the Po nearest Ravenna, canals were cleared in Egypt, and cisterns were established along the caravan route from Myos Hormos on the Red Sea to Coptos on the Nile in order to service the traffic of goods from India on its way to the factories of Alexandria. All of these projects not only expedited commercial and military movements throughout the empire, but also made possible the efficient dispatch of the empire's civil servants and thus were the necessary preliminaries to the establishment of an imperial postal service (the *cursus publicus*).

There was, of course, poverty during the Augustan period. There was unemployment, and slavery laid its dead hand on the industrial future. Nevertheless, the maintenance of internal peace, the economical conduct of the military establishment, the equitable distribution of the tax load, the government's concern for the well-being and employment of the population, and the free and easy movement of goods throughout the Mediterranean Basin made the early principate the most prosperous epoch contrived under the economic system of the ancient world.

Chapter 31

THE CONSTRUCTION OF AN AUGUSTAN IMAGE

The Romans of the Augustan Age were prosperous and they were grateful. The memory of one hundred years of chaos led most citizens to count any loss of political freedom as small when compared to the blessings of security. Augustus, however, faced the future with misgivings. For a century the Romans had proved themselves politically and socially irresponsible, dedicated to greed, pride, and ambition. The emperor believed that continued Roman prosperity and the stability of the Mediterranean world depended on a rededication of the Italians, the people of the heartland, to their ancient ideals. Somehow he must evoke the traditional image of the honest, sober, and honorable Roman of the early Republic and convince his contemporaries to conform to it. To assist him Augustus could call upon an obedient legislative branch, his control of the religious establishment, and a keen eye for propaganda. He used them all; but he did more — he gave himself to the program. Augustus did not simply offer himself as a guide to the Romans; he tried to make his own life a pattern, an image, of the devoted, hardworking patriot.

LEGACY-HUNTING.   Greed for wealth lay at the root of many of Rome's ills. It rose from the need of the members of the upper classes to have enough money to make the large financial outlays necessary for a successful public career.[1] By the Augustan Age, however, the search for wealth had ceased to be merely an accessory to political advance and had become an end in itself. This aberration might have seemed relatively harmless, if it had not brought about a serious drop in the birthrate in Italy at the very time when the emperor wanted a vigorous Italian population with which to dominate and unify the Mediterra-

See above pp. 323–327, 333.

nean world. The simple fact was that members of the upper classes in Rome found the possession of children a significant hindrance in the search for, and enjoyment of, money; and children especially interfered with the peculiarly Roman game of legacy-hunting. The vigor and scope of this pastime among the Romans is too well attested for there to be doubts as to its gravity. All Romans felt that it was a matter of courtesy to remember their friends in their wills by legacies, but ultimately a passion developed among upperclass citizens to court an increase in the size and number of such bequests. Wealthy people with no natural heirs of their own became the objects of the most consummate flattery and gifts in the hope that their wills would contain handsome rewards for the attentions that they had received while living. Cicero received legacies amounting to twenty million sesterces, and Augustus to one billion four hundred million. To receive such attentions was, of course, extremely pleasant and made the childless state very desirable, since men with children were ignored on the grounds that they were not likely to diminish the inheritance of their natural heirs. Even as discreet a man as Seneca tried to console a bereaved mother by reminding her that in spite of her grief she should get some satisfaction in reflecting on the solicitous attentions that she now would receive. Indeed, legacy-hunting would be comical if its implications were not so tragic; it rapidly and notoriously emasculated the leading families of Rome. To compound the problem, the countryfolk soon followed the example of the rich. In 4 B.C. Augustus paraded in Rome a villager with eight children almost as a prodigy; yet families of that size in the second century B.C. had been recorded without surprise or special comment.

LAWS ON MARRIAGE.   Augustus turned his authority as a legislator to encourage and sanctify the revival of fruitful marriage. The Julian Laws of 18 B.C. and the Papian-Poppaean Law of 9 A.D. dealt with almost all aspects of the subject. Sections of the laws on adultery set up public tribunals to try cases of marital infidelity and established severe penalties for those convicted. Previously adultery had been punished only in family councils of the parties concerned; but Augustus wished to emphasize that the State had a strong interest in the moral tone of society. The laws encouraged marriage in all sections of the populace. Citizens, with the exception of men of senatorial rank, were now specifically permitted to marry freedwomen, a custom which social prejudice previously had inhibited. The exception in the case of senatorials stemmed from the emperor's wish to preserve their purity of caste as a part of Roman tradition.[2] The emperor established penalties for celibacy and childlessness and rewards for large families; and in the rewards and penalties that he chose Augustus showed that he thoroughly understood the Roman madness for wealth, wills, and high office. Marriage between persons beyond the normal age of childbearing was penalized by confiscation of dowry; celibates, spinsters, and the married but childless could accept legacies only from close relatives; and single women were subjected to a special tax in the bargain. For those that entered into fruitful matches, however, there were commensurate rewards. Fathers received preference at the polls when they ran for public office. Free citizens that were the parents of three children (four for freedmen) could receive legacies from anyone (the so-called *ius trium liberorum*), and this privilege was naturally highly prized. Most of these punishments and rewards applied in any practical way only to the upper classes, of course, but Augustus had great faith in the importance of the example that they set to the rest of the population. He believed that an improvement in their habits might raise the moral tone of the whole society and return the large family to fashion.

It would be unjust to label Augustus' legislation on marriage as totally ineffective. It is true that many Romans showed great recalcitrance and invented many interesting subterfuges to escape the laws' provisions; but the program was celebrated by contemporary poets as marking the renascence of the family virtues. It was certainly held in high esteem by later writers, and its provisions received elaboration and commentary in the later law.

LAWS ON MANUMISSION.   Augustus not only needed an increase in men, but they needed to be Italian men, if Italians were to be the agents for unifying and Romanizing the world. Here again contemporary Roman practice and the potlatch spirit of the times raised difficulties. Roman magnates were liberal in the manumission of slaves during their own lifetimes, and such freedmen became Roman citizens. But on their deathbeds slave-owners outdid themselves, often liberating hundreds, to the disgruntlement of their heirs, ensuring themselves a tremendous funeral and undying gratitude and fame with their freedmen. Augustus was an Italian countryman who idealized the Roman past and hoped to revive its vigor and virtues; yet these new freedman-citizens, with their un-Roman traditions

[2]   See below, p. 367.

and their experience in servility, were the antithesis of his wishes and needs.

The emperor therefore introduced a legislative program that was designed to prevent the mongrelization of Italy by the too ready admission of new citizens who affected to despise her ancient traditions. Laws in 2 B.C. and 4 A.D. limited the percentages of a Roman citizen's slaves that he could free, with an upper limit of no more than one hundred by any one owner; and other provisions restricted further the volume and irresponsibility of manumission by insisting that masters who freed slaves be at least twenty years of age, that slaves be at least thirty and of good reputation, and that there be a formal ceremony before a praetor or some other competent magistrate or board.

THE ESTABLISHMENT OF CLASSES.   Augustus was nearly as interested in the morale of his contemporaries as he was in their morals. He believed that carefully distinguished classes, each with its own ideals and duties, would have a higher *esprit* than an undifferentiated or completely fluid society. His own admiration for the ancient nobility, and his belief that respect for it would give the population an obvious standard, led him to establish for members of the senatorial class especially rigid rules of conduct, wealth, birth, and service of the State,[3] while they in turn enjoyed the distinction of wearing a broad purple band on their togas and had a monopoly of the ancient and eminent republican magistracies. The knights also received special consideration. During the civil wars all sorts of parvenus had claimed this station, depending on their wealth alone. Now the emperor revived the annual review of the knights of Rome and inspected their qualifications; and apparently the same rite was performed in the municipalities of the empire. The property qualification of knights was set at 400,000 sesterces, their dress was distinguished by the addition of a narrow purple stripe, and they were allowed to wear golden rings. Men of this class served on juries, were the military tribunes of the army, and held the posts of procurators and prefects in the imperial administration.[4] For the more humble citizen there were the food and entertainments of the city and the chance for prestige by election as a *vicomagister*. There was also a possible career in the army, where the well-paid centurionate offered excellent opportunities for advancement to the capable. Even the lowly freedmen could achieve status by appointment or election to

[3]   See above, pp. 341–342, 365–366.
[4]   See above, pp. 353–354.

the board of Augustales, who celebrated the worship of the emperor's genius (spiritual personality).

Though Augustus placed a good deal of emphasis on class, and a great deal of amusing snobbery existed in the Roman system, the lines were not rigid. The emperor felt free to promote deserving knights to the senatorial class. Army veterans often became members of local aristocracies. Men that had gone to the highest ranks of the centurionate might, after discharge, embark on equestrian careers. Even the imperial freedmen sometimes held posts of the highest confidence and importance in the administration. The use of freedmen in sensitive positions perhaps in part reflects official educational policy; it was presumed that members of the upper classes received a traditional education, but the only training for them that was compulsory was physical and military. However, skills and insights that come from a more liberal education were needed, and so, as in other civilizations, a despised minority attained positions of wealth and power because they prized and cultivated the intellect more than their social superiors did.

RELIGIOUS REVIVAL. It had been the function of the magistrates and pontiffs, who represented the State in matters of religion, to preserve the *pax deorum* (peace of the gods)—to assure the good will of the deities, or at least to neutralize any bad will that they might have—by appropriate and highly formal rites and ceremonies. If things did not go well with the State, then, it was not difficult to discover that ritualistic mistakes had been made. There had been, however, an unabashed use of religion for political purposes in the first century B.C., and this had led the public to cynicism and considerable neglect both of ancient rites and of the temples. Some patriots, such as Varro, Sulla, and Caesar, had been concerned for a religious revival. Augustus too felt that a religious restoration must be at the core of moral regeneration and that he must lead the way back to the old gods, back to their compact with the Romans, back to a restoration of ancient piety. He not only restored the temples—eighty-two of them he tells us—but he resurrected ancient offices, such as taboo-ridden priest of Jupiter, the *flamen Dialis*, ancient deities, such as Dea Dia, a primitive agricultural goddess, and ancient brotherhoods, such as the *Fratres Arvales*, who performed highly formal ceremonies on behalf of the State. The men chosen for these functions were men of the highest station in an attempt to convince the people that they were returning to ancient ways under the leadership of a responsible nobility.

Certain of the Greek gods that by now had long been adopted by the Romans were given special attention. For example, Mars Ultor, Mars the Avenger, was the patron of the Julian family, and it was astutely suggested that he had presided over Augustus' revenge of Julius Caesar at the Battle of Philippi. However, it was in Apollo that Augustus found his most valuable ally. It was he, the god of the sunlight, and of intellect, of decency, and of civilization who had put the dark, bestial gods of Egypt to flight at Actium; and poetry, art, and the coinage, as well as the erection of a temple to the god next to the prince's own residence on the Palatine, were made to suggest the close association of the god and the man.

THE IMPERIAL CULT.   The Hellenistic peoples long had expressed their gratitude to their rulers by lavishing divine honors upon them. Such practices were foreign to the Romans, but the translation of Euhemerus by Ennius in the second century B.C. had familiarized them with the theory that the gods were once men whose deeds had been especially beneficent to mankind. Further, Roman proconsuls in the Orient often found themselves treated in the same fashion, for in the eyes of the provincials they simply replaced their Greek rulers. The deification of Julius Caesar (42 B.C.), therefore, was not a revolutionary novelty—his own ancient relative, Romulus, was supposed to have been translated to heaven as the god Quirinus. A special aura thereafter hovered over Octavian-Augustus, for he now was the "son of the deified Caesar." In the East he too was soon accorded divine honors, and altars and temples were raised. The worship of Augustus at these centers was generally not maintained by itself, but was associated with the worship of the goddess Roma. As early as 29 B.C. religious confederacies of Eastern cities were permitted to meet annually at a central point to celebrate the rites for Roma and Augustus. The propaganda value of this institution was soon apparent, for it focussed the gratitude of the provincials on the capital and on its prince, distant, stately, but benign; and the practice was soon introduced into the West, with altars at Lyons in 12 B.C., on the Elbe in 2 B.C., and at other provincial centers.

In Italy the sensibilities of the Italian nobility would not permit the worship of a living contemporary, though the proletariat so adored Augustus that it probably was willing, and the poets made arch allusions in their writings to the emperor's divine associations. In Rome, however, the *vicomagistri* of the various neighborhoods presided over the local worship of the spirits of the crossroads and also of the genius (spiritual personality) or Lares (household gods) of Augustus; while in the municipalities the Augustales celebrated rites and gave feasts and pageants in honor of the *Lares Augusti.* Thus the humble of Italy as well as the provincials found a focus for religious expression in the person of Augustus.

Augustus' prestige was further advanced, though his actual power was not altered, by his election as pontifex maximus in 12 B.C., after the death of Lepidus. This post always was held thereafter by succeeding princes as titular heads of the State religion. More important was the celebration in 17 B.C. of the Secular Games. These, based on an ancient Etruscan age (*saeculum*) of 110 years, signified the end of one epoch, the purification of the people, and the inauguration of a new age. People flocked from all over Italy to witness this palpable evidence of a rededication to Rome's great traditions; and a high point in the festivities was the rendition by a choir of fifty-four boys and girls of an ode especially written for the occasion by the poet Horace. Its stanzas reflect the spirit of confidence and tranquillity, the aspirations for property and increase, and the image of success that the emperor wished expressed.

THE BEAUTIFICATION OF ROME.   The building that Augustus undertook in Rome fortified the ideals, the program, and the repute that he wished his government to have in the eyes of the empire. A new Forum of Augustus was a splendid backdrop for statues and memorials of Rome's great heroes and, of course, of famous ancestors of the Julian house. Temples of Mars Ultor and Apollo emphasized the deities most closely associated with the Julii and with Augustus. Two constructions illustrate especially well how Augustus used his building program to dramatize his program of reform and revival. The Altar of the Augustan Peace in the Campus Martius near the Tiber masterfully combines the art of the Greeks and the spirit of the Romans. It was adorned with Rome's greatest frieze, which depicted in a procession the imperial family together with members of the Senate and a happy populace. Idealized and united, they signified the relation that Augustus' social and political legislation sought. Also in the Campus Martius he erected his mausoleum. This too reflected his ability to recall the past in the interest of men's hopes for the future, for he chose a great cylinder piled high with earth and planted with cypress trees, a form that descended from the great tumulus tombs of the ancient Etruscans. Before the mausoleum's doors on tables of bronze was inscribed a text, the "Deeds of Augustus," composed by the emperor himself. By the very simplicity of the account of his public career Augustus contrived to give credence to the image of himself and of the principate that he wished men to act upon.

AUGUSTAN LITERATURE.   Augustan Rome attracted men of learning and genius from all over the world. Dionysius of Halicarnassus wrote in Greek critical works on Greek authors and a fulsome and rhetorical account of early Roman history. From Spain came the elder Seneca, who illustrated the techniques of rhetorical exercises. Diodorus of Sicily compiled a universal history of uneven quality. Strabo came from Pontus to write a geography filled with learning about the lands of the Mediterranean Basin. And in the philosopher and universal historian Nicolaus of Damascus, Augustus found a man to compile a friendly account of his own youth and education.

Italy itself reaped in this tranquil era a rich literary harvest unparalleled in Roman history, though it sprang from the seeds of blood and chaos sown in the Late Republic. A number of the notables of the era, such as Valerius Messalla and Asinius Pollio, were patrons of the arts; but Maecenas, the lavish minister and tactful friend of Augustus, outdid them all. The great names of classical Latin—Vergil, Horace, Tibullus, Propertius, and Livy—were gathered into Augustus' orbit. If they were not all complete monarchists, at least they all were grateful for the Augustan Peace and wholeheartedly approved the emperor's emphasis on the ancient virtues and the Roman tradition. All these men paid and repaid the emperor for his efforts on behalf of their country. Without the great authors of the era the Augustan Age would have been synonymous only with Philistinism. In his youth Vergil (70–19 B.C.) had expressed his love for the Italian countryside in his pastoral poems, the *Eclogues*; and in the *Georgics*, perhaps the world's most perfect didactic poem, he taught the beauty and dignity of the land, while teaching the agricultural arts of Italy. These poems reinforced Augustus' emphasis on the virtues and values of Italy's simple agrarian past. In his great epic, the *Aeneid*, Vergil intimated that the travels and trials of Aeneas and of his Trojan band from captured Troy to a new home in Latium paralleled the labor and self-sacrifice of the Romans in conquering the world. He thus glorified the legendary past of the Romans as an incentive for idealism among his contemporaries. The labors required to effect the union of Trojan and Italian reflected the difficulties that must accompany the creation of a unified world. But Vergil was more than a propagandist. He transcended the particular by revealing for all men the suffering and the steadfastness, the duty and honor, the moral as well as the physical bravery of

371

those who will turn the barbaric, chaotic, and selfish into order and light.

In the *Satires* Vergil's younger friend Horace (65–8 B.C.) made smiling comment on the foibles of his world and of himself, and gently insinuated suggestions for improvement. The artful simplicity of his *Odes* have made him the despair of translators and imitators. While love and laughter, wine and contentment, were often Horace's themes, the *Odes* also contain a frank appreciation of the new order and a celebration of those Roman virtues that an agrarian society had developed and that Augustus sought to revive. Tibullus (ca. 55–19 B.C.) and Propertius (ca. 50–16 B.C.) were essentially poets of peace and love, but they too at times frankly stated Augustan themes; and in all these poets ran the strong Italian spirit, the passion for the concrete, for commonsense, and for the land, qualities that animated the emperor.

But nowhere was the glorification of Italy and its people stronger than in Livy of Padua (59 B.C.–17 A.D.). His history of Rome, *From the Foundation of the City*, is a monument to Rome and to the Italian people. They were his center, they his theme, and their virtues had proved themselves through centuries of trial. This might be a romantic and moral view of history, but it coincided with Augustus' own inclination to glorify the past while building the future, and the emperor could afford to smile at what he considered Livy's republicanism, for it conformed to his own policy to mask the Principate as a republican renaissance.

There is, however, something a little pathetic in this Golden Age, for it found its gold largely in a glorification of the past. All of the adornments of Augustan literature were really the products of pre-Augustan chaos. Augustus had the good fortune to inherit the talents of an earlier day, and the promise of his regime gave hope for the future to sensitive men who were sick of bloodshed. These men produced with good will; but Augustus' own epoch does not seem to have generated the stimuli for future creativity, and there is a distinct ebb in the literary work toward the end of his principate.

Only one able poet is almost completely the product of the early Principate, the facile Ovid (43 B.C.–18 A.D.). No one else could make the Latin hexameter so supple, so deceptively simple. His poetry was graceful, witty, and outrageously impudent. Augustus had allowed this bright young Italian knight to embark on a political career, for he thought that he could make yet another public servant out of him. But Ovid preferred the composition of verse and the fast social set of Rome to a career of service. With him the age's taste for didactic poetry found novel expression in a handbook on seduction, the *Ars Amatoria* (The Art of Love). This was not the use of talent that Augustus, the restorer of ancient virtue, could appreciate. Even Ovid's less offensive productions, such as the *Heroides, Amores,* and *Metamorphoses,* contained society's witty scoffing at the virtues sponsored by the government. The emperor had little sense of humor, and he resented irresponsibility and evasion of duty. Therefore, when in 8 A.D. some involvement of Ovid in a court scandal gave Augustus an opportunity, the emperor's implacable anger banished the poet to Tomi on the Black Sea, and no contrite or pitiful verses could appease disappointed majesty. Ovid remained in exile until his death.

THE IMAGE OF AUGUSTUS.   The Augustan dispensation was a success. Everywhere Romans were reminded of the benefits that the prince had brought to them. The poets wrote of his excellence; his inscriptions on public works and on the ubiquitous milestones were constantly before their eyes; and his portraits and slogans adorned the coinage. There were oaths of allegiance to be taken, celebrations and festivals to be enjoyed, and everywhere were the more substantial blessings of peace. As Augustus' yacht cruised past Puteoli in 14 A.D. on that last voyage that ended with his death in Nola, the sailors on a ship from Alexandria burned incense to him and declared that through him alone did they live and sail the seas in security, enjoy the blessings of liberty and the fruits of their labors.

His life was so long that by the time of his death mankind could not contemplate another solution than the Principate. The advantages of a strict but just administration were clear to the provincials; the proletariat kept the liberty of a saucy tongue, but was monarchical at heart; the knights had never been so prosperous and petted. A whole new generation of nobles had grown up, many created by the prince himself, and few of the old ones survived to recall or regret the despotic hegemony that they had enjoyed before Caesar. It is true that cases of civic irresponsibility in the epoch boded ill for the future. The loyal troops were far away on the frontiers, and there slowly developed a gulf between the civilians and the military, for the people of the Italian heartland shunned service in the army while valuing its protection. It is also true that the people quickly renounced political activity, and that the greater efficiency of the prince's establishment meant a gradual impingement on the activities of the Senate. But the deterioration was slow, and Augustus' rule furnished the standard against which future reigns were measured both by the princes themselves and by their subjects.

When Augustus came to Italy in 44 B.C. he was an ambitious youth. He was cold, calculating, and ruthless. He was also an Italian countryman, who believed in the worth of Rome and Italy and cared deeply for his land. With these native endowments, with his adoptive father's name, and with the supreme follies of his opponents, in thirteen years he contrived to win the world. Once he had arrived at supreme power he found himself a sickly young man with a coterie of strong-willed supporters who knew that he alone could hold their world together. Augustus never completely lost his unattractive characteristics; but once he was at the top, with death always a hovering probability, the forces within him were channelled from care for himself to care for the State; he willed to regulate that most irregular structure. Despite his willfulness, he was cautious with all the caution of an Italian peasant. He did not make foolish and heroic ventures where prudent experiment and patience would do. His favorite admonition to subordinates was to "hurry slowly." This policy he pursued at home and abroad, whether dealing with the Parthians or piecing out a viable government with Senate and people. Probably no point is more significant than the provincial worship of Rome and Augustus together; he made himself Rome. This was, perhaps, like his constitution a bit of fraudulent facade; but what the people thought of him was of utmost importance to the State, and his official portrait is handsome and pensive, showing the weight of responsibility.

Augustus was Rome's slave as well as her master. He loved his family, but gradually its members fell away or were sacrificed: the favorite nephew Marcellus, the favorite stepson Drusus, the beloved grandsons Gaius and Lucius, all died when the prince had placed the greatest hopes in them. The other stepson, Tiberius, was unsympathetic; and the two Julias, daughter and granddaughter, by leading immoral lives were traitors to the responsibilities and respectabilities of their station. When all were gone, the emperor lived on, still devoted, still determined, still an actor. His success can partly be measured by the decree, passed in 2 A.D. on the motion of an old republican opponent, that he be declared *pater patriae*, father of his country. Those on whom he depended and who failed him felt the implacable wrath of a being that had lost himself and had become his role—the State. The poet Ovid learned this among the frosts of Tomi; Tiberius, too proud to play a subordinate though useful part, reflected on it as a semi-exile in

Rhodes; and the Julias, whose high station made their adulteries treason, remembered it on barren Mediterranean islands. Augustus lost himself in his country, and in his devotion became one of the greatest servants of Western man. His life was public, sad, and useful. And finally, on his deathbed in Nola he called for a mirror, arranged his hair and expression, examined his image there, and then to his attendants directed the poignant question, "In this comedy have I played my part well?"

PART

Seven

The Principate: Tiberius Through The Severi

Chapter 32

THE JULIO-CLAUDIANS

THE SUCCESSION. The line of princes called the Julio-Claudians (14–68 A.D.) was so called because its members were descended either from the Julian family of Augustus or from the children of the empress Livia by her first marriage, to Tiberius Claudius Nero. Some of them carried the blood of both families in their veins. During the Julio-Claudian period the general shape of a new form of Roman government began to emerge. The principate of Augustus (23 B.C.–14 A.D.) was a personal relationship between him and the State. It was buttressed by precedents set in the earlier Republic by leading citizens who were called *principes,* and it depended much on Augustus' own tact and personal prestige. During his whole life the principate was a tentative and exploratory solution to Rome's problems, and the direction that it would take was uncertain. But Augustus' authority lived after him, fostered both by gratitude for the benefits of his government and by his position after death as a god. Augustus believed that the Roman State must continue to be directed by some first citizen, a kind of paterfamilias for the whole country. His belief in this solution was widely shared by his contemporaries, at least partly because of his undoubted success. Clearly members of his own family, and especially his own designated associate, were preferred candidates for this position, for thus the country would be spared the results of ambitious rivalry that it once had suffered. Indeed, only when there were no Julio-Claudians left did the disaster of civil war once more strike. Moderns have much criticized ancient Roman historians because their works so often amount to biographies of the emperors and the scandals of Rome. This disapproval is largely unwarranted; one-man government had been in the air for at least a century before the end of the Republic, and the nature and manner of the ruler was indeed the directive force of Rome. His policies would ultimately affect every walk of life; he was indeed the "soul of the empire."

TIBERIUS (14–37 A.D.).   It was the policy of Augustus always to have an associate with sufficient power and prestige that there would be no embarrassing interregnum at his death. This policy proved a success. When the emperor died in 14 A.D., there was no opposition to the elevation of Tiberius to his position. Tiberius was both the stepson and adopted son of Augustus, and he already had been endowed with the tribunician power and the *imperium*. In 14 A.D. the Senate conferred on him these same powers for life, while it enrolled the dead emperor among the gods as the deified Augustus.

Tiberius, however, assumed the leadership of the State with some reluctance. He was not a popular man, and he knew it. He was fifty-five years old and he knew precisely the burdens and loneliness of great authority. Further, the clear preference of Augustus for other relatives—for Marcellus, for Gaius and Lucius Caesar, and even for Tiberius' own brother Drusus—had hurt him and perhaps made him somewhat resentful. In the very hour of accession he had to hear publicly read from the will of Augustus the phrase, "since harsh fortune has taken my sons Gaius and Lucius from me, Tiberius Caesar shall be my heir. . . ." But he was a well-educated man with a long career as a general and as an administrator, and he had the solid tradition of the Claudian family behind him. He also had a strong sense of responsibility, which had been considerably strengthened by his close association with Augustus in his later and more conservative years. He therefore took up his duties, though he earnestly beseeched the cooperation and assistance of the senators in the government in order somewhat to lighten his work in his declining years.

GERMANICUS.   Tiberius' position was made more difficult than it needed to be because Augustus had tried to arrange for the succession even beyond Tiberius' lifetime. While the old emperor had reluctantly adopted Tiberius and made him his heir, he had stipulated that Tiberius adopt as his son an Augustan favorite, Germanicus. Germanicus was Augustus' own great-nephew and he was married to Augustus' granddaughter, Agrippina the Elder. Clearly the emperor planned that ultimately Germanicus would be his successor. Tiberius dutifully fostered Germanicus' public image in preference to that of his own son, Drusus the Younger, and this was not easy. Germanicus was handsome and popular and had considerable dash about him, but he was not entirely dependable. After the death of Augustus unrest broke out among the troops both on the Rhine and in Illyria, sparked by grievances connected with the

380

tyrannies of petty officers and by Augustan economies that had lengthened the terms of service. At the time, Germanicus was in command on the Rhine, and Drusus was in Illyria. Drusus handled the Illyrian army correctly and firmly and obtained its submission without making embarrassing concessions, but Germanicus allowed matters to get quite out of control. He forged a letter from Tiberius promising improvements, paraded his weeping family, threatened suicide, and finally instigated the massacre of the ringleaders by their own fellow soldiers. These exploits he followed up with a series of ineffectual forays into Germany to restore discipline among his demoralized troops. Despite his disapproval of Germanicus' conduct and of the policy of expansion in Germany that Germanicus favored, Tiberius allowed him to remain there until the spring of 17 A.D. Then he granted him a triumph and sent him to the East to learn the difficulties of empire in that area and to supervise the settlement of a number of problems in the provinces and in the client states.

In the East Germanicus performed his official duties satisfactorily. However, he made an unauthorized trip into Egypt, a domain so important that Augustus had forbidden all persons of senatorial rank access to it without the prince's express permission. He also became involved in a dispute with the governor of Syria, Gnaeus Piso, who was a trusted friend of Tiberius and who was clearly expected to counter any mistakes or excesses on Germanicus' part. The quarrel culminated in the expulsion of Piso from his province, and this development soon was followed by the illness and death of Germanicus in the early autumn of 19 A.D. Before he died, Germanicus and his wife Agrippina became convinced that somehow he had been poisoned either by Piso or by Piso's wife. This was demonstrably ridiculous; but the popular clamor of the mob, the quarrels, and the innuendoes of partisans that accompanied and followed the trial of Piso, who ultimately committed suicide, led many Romans to interpret Tiberius' just and temperate treatment of the affair as proof that he was criminally sympathetic to Piso. The gossip and bitter feeling engendered by this episode were terribly important, for they warped the rest of Tiberius' reign and clouded with suspicion thereafter the reception of even the most salutary measures that the prince might attempt. The follies of partisanship increased the unhealthy state of affairs. Drusus and Germanicus had been devoted to each other; but among those that could not believe that Tiberius was sincere in his advancement of Germanicus there had risen a semblance of party strife. The partisans of Drusus expected that if he suc-

381

ceeded they could hope for a more republican government and greater favor for the aristocracy. The party of Germanicus hoped that if he succeeded there would be a reversion to the more liberal and expansionist policies of Julius Caesar. The death of Germanicus did not dim the hopes of his party, which now centered its attentions on the widow Agrippina and her brood of three boys and three girls.

THE CONSPIRACY OF SEJANUS. Drusus was now the heir apparent, but he sickened and died in the autumn of 23 A.D. as unexpectedly as Germanicus had. Once more Tiberius, who now was sixty-four, had to seek an appropriate successor. He therefore commended to the Senate the two oldest sons of Germanicus and Agrippina, Nero and Drusus. At this point, however, a new and sinister figure appeared upon the scene in the person of the praetorian prefect Aelius Sejanus. Sejanus was an equestrian whose strength, bravery, and efficiency had strongly recommended him to Tiberius, and the prince depended on him as a trustworthy and disinterested adviser. But Sejanus was ambitious and he appears to have abused the emperor's confidence consistently. On the pretext of effecting greater efficiency and better discipline, Sejanus had prevailed upon Tiberius to concentrate the nine cohorts of the praetorian guard, which he commanded, in a camp at Rome. He thus controlled a formidable body of troops where they could exert maximum pressure on the public. Apparently he had long been intimate with Livilla, the wife and now the widow of Drusus, and through her he hoped to gain greater power. He asked the emperor for her hand in marriage, probably with the thought that in time he could become regent for her infant son by Drusus and exclude the line of Germanicus from the succession. For the time being, his request was refused, and he was forced to try another tack.

Sejanus was fortunate in that Germanicus' widow Agrippina was of an imperious and suspicious nature and that her sons were often foolish and indiscreet. Sejanus played upon these shortcomings and finally drove Agrippina and her sons to such desperate measures that he managed to convince Tiberius that they were unbearable, if not dangerous, to himself. Sejanus' schemes were furthered in 29 A.D. by the death of Livia, widow of Augustus and mother of Tiberius, for she had been a restraining influence on friction within the family. Thereafter Tiberius was prevailed upon to relegate Agrippina and her eldest son Nero to islands, on the grounds that they were enemies of the State. Nero committed suicide in 30 A.D., and his brother Drusus was imprisoned in Rome on a charge of treason.

Meanwhile Tiberius had left Rome and taken up residence and semi-retirement on the island of Capri in 27 A.D. With the emperor thus isolated, it was easier to control the information that reached his ears and to influence his decisions to a marked degree. The subservient Senate believed that a new master had been found and began to heap adulatory honors upon the prefect. Sejanus' success seemed certain, but in 31 Antonia, the mother of Germanicus, managed to smuggle a confidential message to the emperor revealing the machinations and intentions of his prefect. Tiberius thereupon acted swiftly and warily. Gaius, Germanicus' surviving son, was kept under the emperor's eye on Capri, and a safe man, Sertorius Macro, was dispatched to Rome with a long letter to the Senate and a secret commission to gain control of the praetorian guard. The timing was perfect: Sejanus was lulled into a sense of security by a false report that the emperor's letter would recommend him for the tribunician power and thus confirm his partnership in the Empire. While the long and at first ambiguous epistle was being read, Macro had time to secure the praetorians and substitute for the regular guard at the Senate House the soldiers of the Watch, whose commander disliked Sejanus. A denunciation of the prefect at the end of the emperor's letter found him helpless, and he and his family were straightway executed. Even his divorced wife committed suicide, but before doing so she wrote to the prince to reveal that Sejanus and Drusus' widow Livilla had been confederates for years, and that they had contrived Drusus' death by poison. This series of disasters further weakened the emperor's position, for he now had no mature and dependable person, as Augustus had had, upon whom he could call as an obvious colleague and successor. His loneliness and disillusion at Sejanus' betrayal embittered Tiberius' later years even more and strengthened his inclination to become a recluse.

THE SENATE UNDER TIBERIUS.   From the beginning of his principate Tiberius indicated a desire to cooperate closely with the Senate. This not only was in keeping with Augustan example, but it was in the tradition of the aristocratic and republican Claudian family. As long as he lived in Rome, Tiberius attended the meetings of the Senate regularly, asked its advice and consent, and enlarged its powers as an elective, legislative, and judicial body. On the recommendation of Augustus, who was disappointed at the irresponsibility of the electorate, Tiberius gave to the nominating committees, composed largely of senators, the right to select all the candidates for high office. Thereafter election by the people became simply the ratification of the selection made by the nominators. Decrees of the Senate were frequently solicited, particularly for administrative matters, and to the Senate he generally referred all cases of high national importance for trial. Here were tried the cases of treason (*majestas*), a charge that was to cause great trouble in many imperial administrations. As early as 103 B.C. there had been a law to punish those that "lessened the majesty of the Roman people"; and a Julian law in 8 B.C. brought exile and confiscation of goods to those who lowered the esteem of the State by reflecting on the person or name of its prince. The charge was terribly vague, and the danger that it would be abused by tyrannical or greedy rulers was increased by the fact that the State had no secret service or bureau of investigation of its own. Rather, the government depended on its private citizens to watch for any threats to the public welfare, and the practice led to the rise of professional informers, who were encouraged in their trade by receiving as a reward a share of the estate confiscated from those convicted. Under Tiberius, however, the trials were open, petty charges were dismissed out of hand, and the emperor himself occasionally defended the accused or appeared as a witness in his behalf. Abuses of the law of treason by other princes led some later historians to suppose a reign of terror under Tiberius, but this does not actually seem to have occurred despite the provocations of Agrippina and her supporters and the shocking revelations of the conspiracy of Sejanus.

ADMINISTRATION OF THE EMPIRE.   Tiberius' administration of the provinces was notable for the excellence of the men that he chose to serve. Poor officials were promptly suspended and punished, while good administrators were kept at their posts for many years—a policy that seems to have puzzled and annoyed his aristocratic contemporaries, who still looked upon public offices as rights to be shared by all of them fully and frequently. The emperor was equally firm in his control of his own slaves and freedmen. These men were used in handling the masses of paperwork involved in administrative and financial matters, but Tiberius did not allow them to take advantage of their confidential positions, as many later emperors did.

The excellence of Tiberius' administration was appreciated by the provincials and was rewarded by peaceful conditions, broken only by minor disturbances. In Africa the Musulamii held out for several years (17–24 A.D.) under a local leader,

Tacfarinas; but this was an area under senatorial control, and the Senate's handling of the affair was dilatory until Tiberius prodded it into action. There also was a brief revolt in Gaul in 21 A.D. under two local patriots, Julius Florus and Julius Sacrovir. This movement was perhaps connected with the suppression of Druidism, which the Romans considered cruel and dangerously nationalistic. The rising, however, was quickly controlled by the legions on the Rhine.

FINANCES.   In financial affairs Tiberius observed the strictest economy, yet he was just to the tax-paying public and even generous in times of disaster. When one of his governors forwarded more money from taxes than was expected, Tiberius tartly informed him that he "should shear his sheep, not skin them." Residents of Rome received assistance after fires and floods; and Tiberius' treasury helped the cities of Asia to rebuild after disastrous earthquakes. During a financial panic in 33 A.D. he aided the hard-pressed by advancing loans that were interest-free for three years. However, his disinclination to waste money, especially on the popular spectacles of the circus and arena, brought more adverse comment from the people than his benefactions brought gratitude. In any case, on his death he proved to have run the Empire so well that he left a surplus of 2,700,000,000 sesterces in the treasury.

One of Tiberius' economies was in the construction of new edifices in Rome. His self-restraint in this matter probably increased his unpopularity, for it reduced the amount of work available to the laboring class. However, he was very active in construction that would increase the commercial health of the country. In Spain he made vast additions to the Augustan system of roads and thus opened to commerce the central part of the peninsula. He repaired the roads of Gaul, and he recognized the need to develop the recently rebellious Balkans by constructing there an extensive system of highways, for which he used military labor. In Rome itself he established a senatorial board to supervise the care of the Tiber and to provide for its even flow; and the public buildings and aqueducts of the city were carefully kept in repair.

FOREIGN POLICY.   Abroad Tiberius' policy was conservative and sometimes firm. Client kingdoms that continued to be useful were retained, but where they appeared to be sufficiently Romanized, they were assimilated to the Empire as provinces. Thus, Cappadocia became a province under the rule of an equestrian procurator, and Commagene and Cilicia appear to have been placed in the jurisdiction of the governor of Syria during Germanicus' trip to the East. At the same time a Pontic prince, Zeno, was placed on the throne of Armenia, and ruled there successfully until his death in 34 A.D. Zeno's success was partially due to the fact that Tiberius had sensibly chosen for the Armenians a candidate educated in the Armenian manner of living. When, after Zeno's death, the Parthian king attempted to place his own son on the Armenian throne, Tiberius took vigorous action. He aided the seizure of the throne by an Iberian prince, Mithridates; and as a counterstroke he supported a revolution in Parthia itself with sufficient effect that the Parthian king was glad to acquiesce in his Armenian settlement. On the German frontier, after the withdrawal of Germanicus, Tiberius encouraged dissension among the German tribes, and this policy was so successful that little overt Roman action was needed there during his long reign.

Later Roman writers created a portrait of Tiberius as a crafty dissimulator and cruel tyrant. Only in modern times have historians learned to appreciate the excellence of his government. The records of the period document his conscientious effort to give the Roman world a good administration and to retain as much of the republican procedure and spirit as he reasonably could. The records are equally explicit that the law was administered with justice, that there was general foreign and domestic tranquillity, and that the economy thrived. The adverse picture of the reign has arisen partly because later writers ascribed to Tiberius practices that actually belonged to some of his successors, and partly because of the tragedies of his personal life. Already disappointed in his reliance on Germanicus, Drusus, and then on Germanicus' children, the final blow was his realization of the nature and extent of the conspiracy of Sejanus. This man upon whom he had placed all his trust not only had proved traitorous, but, what was worse, had despoiled him of nearly all his family. Age, weariness, and disgust with the flatteries and falsities of Rome led him to remain in semi-retirement on Capri. While there, he continued to direct policy and attend to the Empire's needs, but he did not show the vigor and determination that Augustus had had in his later years. His greatest failure was to provide and train a capable successor to rule an ungrateful populace, and this failure was destined to prove calamitous to the Roman people.

GAIUS CALIGULA (37–41 A.D.).   By Tiberius' will Gaius, the surviving son of Germanicus, and Tiberius Gemellus, Tiberius' grandson, were appointed co-heirs of the emperor's private estate. Gaius had the favor of the praetorian prefect, Macro, and Macro's influence led the Senate after a few days to vote to Gaius, who was only twenty-five years of age, the tribunician power and those other honors that marked him as *princeps*. The Romans were deliriously happy to be rid of the dreary old recluse of Capri. Gaius was young and Gaius was present. He was the son of their hero, Germanicus. He rescinded unpopular taxes, adopted his cousin Gemellus, prosecuted the professional informers, was deferential to the Senate, ordered the return of popular elections to the assemblies, brought his awkward and neglected uncle Claudius out of retirement to be his colleague in the consulship, and showed a quite un-Tiberian favor for the theater, circus, and arena. But the holiday was brief. Tiberius had given the young man almost no preparation for an understanding of Roman government and its responsibilities. The highest office that he had held was only the quaestorship. Further, he had spent the past few years on Capri in constant and genuine fear for his life, for he had seen the fate of his mother and elder brothers during the conspiracy of Sejanus. Now he was catapulted to the most powerful position in the world, and the sudden change of fortune seems to have been too much for him. The stability of his antecedents was not promising; after all, he was directly descended from Julia and from Mark Antony. Furthermore, he had been brought up as a small child on the Rhenish frontier where he had been idolized and spoiled by the troops. They called him Caligula, Little Bootsie, because his ambitious mother dressed him in a small version of the soldiers' garb, and this is the name by which he is best known today. His youth was spent in the house of his grandmother, Antonia, where his companions were his distant cousins, the Oriental princes of Thrace. They were despots and had considerable influence on his thinking, and their influence was intensified by his intimate, the Jewish prince Herod Agrippa, who well knew how to be an Oriental autocrat. About six months after his accession a severe illness fell upon him and it appears to have magnified his native weaknesses. He emerged mad, and his madness took the form of a special interest in the significance of absolute power: what are the limits, if any, on a creature endowed with it?

The scandals of Gaius' reign were accompanied by a fear of the emperor's unpredictable actions. This fear stifled independence of action by senators and administrators alike. His lavish expenditures soon required money, and he found the institution of professional informers an easy way to bring to his treasury the estates of wealthy persons. He encouraged the informers to denounce all persons that had been enemies of his mother and brothers or had been flatterers of Sejanus — and they had been legion. Their confiscated wealth he then shared with the denouncers. With cold logic he pursued the thesis that he was divine by descent (from Julius Caesar and Augustus) and by his appointment to the principate, and that such an extraordinary creature as he could not reasonably have limitations placed upon him. His cousin Gemellus was soon murdered. His relations with his sisters were, in the manner of Oriental despots, incestuous; and after her death the favorite, Drusilla, was deified. The two surviving sisters turned against him and were exiled. His excesses included the construction of a bridge across the bay between Baiae and Puteoli, and of another from his palace on the Palatine to the Capitoline, so that he could consult with his colleague Jupiter in his temple. It is alleged that he planned to give the consulship to his favorite horse, Incitatus, which he already had made a patrician.

Yet there were some constructive measures taken during Caligula's principate. He initiated road repairs in Spain, built a lighthouse at Boulogne to guide British traders, prosecuted Italian road contractors that had neglected their duties, and began the construction of two new aqueducts for Rome, which were completed by Claudius. These activities indicate that Augustus and Tiberius had built so well that there was considerable momentum to carry on constructive work in the Empire even under a madman. Actually, it was the members of Caligula's court and family that suffered most, though he once was heard to regret that the whole Roman people did not have a single neck so that he could sever it.

Abroad Gaius reversed the tendencies under Tiberius and reestablished a number of client kingdoms. He found realms in Pontus, Lesser Armenia, and Thrace for his three boyhood cronies, the Thracian princes. Commagene was given back to its royal house; a prince was bestowed on the Iturean Arabs; and his intimate, the astute Jew Herod Agrippa, was also given a principality. But, inconsistently, Mithridates of Armenia was removed and exiled, and the useful Ptolemy of Mauretania was forced to commit suicide and his kingdom was thus thrown into turmoil and war. Gaius visited the Rhine, but his purposes are uncertain — whether to appease the troops or actually to invade Britain, as he for a time proposed. In any case, nothing came of the expedition except anecdotes, probably false, about his whimsical or outrageous actions on the trip. He was extremely sensitive about his godhead, and Jewish reluctance to recognize it threatened to set the East on fire, for he was determined to have his statue placed in the Temple in Jerusalem. Catastrophe there was probably averted, however, by the governor of Syria, who delayed carrying out the emperor's orders, and by the emperor's timely assassination in January 41 A.D. by a tribune that he had grossly insulted.

CLAUDIUS (41–54 A.D.).   At the death of Caligula one of the praetorians had found the emperor's frightened old uncle Claudius hiding in the palace and hauled him off to the praetorian camp. Here, perhaps at first in jest, he was proclaimed emperor, but the idea soon caught on and was clinched by the new emperor's promise of a gift of money to each praetorian, a promise that established an unhappy and binding precedent for future princes. Until he had been made consul by Caligula (and also the butt of the prince's perverse humor) Claudius had been shunted out of public life because of his physical disabilities, which had resulted perhaps from an injury at birth or from some form of paralysis. He stammered and slobbered and limped and belched in a world that idealized the human form. He had a good mind, however, and he had received training and encouragement in historical studies from the great Livy. His early researches in history, biography, and antiquities—he had written a long study of Augustus and histories of the Carthaginians and Etruscans—gave him broad perspectives in social and political tendencies that his predecessors had lacked. He greatly admired Augustus and tried to return to that emperor's close cooperation with the Senate, but in his liberalism and passion for efficiency he went far beyond the first prince, and some of his activities are more reminiscent of the pioneering spirit of Julius Caesar.

CLAUDIAN ADMINISTRATION. BIRTH OF BUREAUCRACY.
Hitherto emperors had used their slaves and freedmen to assist with the details of empire in much the spirit and manner of the old republican magistrates. Under Claudius the various functions were organized into administrative bureaus—there were bureaus for finance, correspondence, petitions, legal decisions, and records—and these were directed by freedmen of the emperor, whose centralized position and close contact with the emperor gave them great influence. Their power and superior efficiency inevitably impinged on the authority of the senators and aroused their jealousy. The senators were distressed to see these freedman-bureaucrats, whom they despised for their low social status, commanding such great patronage. The senators also were irritated because Claudius assumed the censorship in

47–8 A.D. True, this was an ancient republican office, and he took a colleague in proper fashion, but the post involved the right to add or subtract members of the Senate, and the control that this right implied was resented.

PUBLIC WORKS.   Claudius' public works were extensive and sensible. He completed the aqueducts begun by Caligula, repaired others, appointed a procurator to care for the water supply, and increased the staff of maintenance men to service it. Aqueducts in Asia, Africa, and Gaul are attributed to him. He also had a great interest in the promotion of commerce. Probably no emperor did so much road-building all over the Empire, and he designed and built a huge new harbor at Ostia capable of handling 200 ships and connected to the Tiber by a canal. This ensured a more expeditious and less expensive delivery of supplies to Rome. He saw, however, that adequate port facilities alone were not enough to ensure sufficient provisions for the city. He therefore encouraged shipowners to enter into the transport of grain to the city, which was less lucrative than other commercial ventures, by offering them government insurance and special privileges and exemptions in regard to taxes. He improved the system of canals in Gaul to speed traffic by water between the Mediterranean and North Sea, and he improved the harbor at Boulogne. He entered upon a ten-year project to drain the Fucine Lake in Italy in order to eliminate a pesthole of malaria, provide additional arable land, and improve the navigability of the Liris River.

FOREIGN AFFAIRS UNDER CLAUDIUS.   In foreign affairs Claudius abandoned the more conservative and cautious policies of Augustus and Tiberius and more closely approached the adventurous and expansionist spirit of Julius Caesar. Most of Gaius' client kingdoms were allowed to continue, but that of Herod Agrippa, which came to include almost all of Herod the Great's kingdom, became a province under the administration of a procurator after Agrippa's death in 44 A.D. Mauretania was added as two provinces when in 42 A.D. the rebellion inspired by Gaius' attacks on the ruling house of that land had been put down. Dynastic quarrels in Thrace led finally to its annexation as a province in 46 A.D.; and close relations established with the Bosporan kingdom in the Russian Crimea meant that the Black Sea was practically a Roman lake and was well policed against piracy. The most ambitious scheme of the reign, however, was the conquest of Britain and its addition as a province. The major expedition was completed in 43 A.D. with the emperor himself in attendance, and by 47 A.D. all of southern England had been conquered to a line approximately from Lincoln to southern Devon. A number of friendly client princes were included in the system devised for the newly acquired province. In the treatment of provincials Claudius is also reminiscent of Caesar. He not only was liberal in the grant of Latin rights or citizenship in provincial communities, but as censor he also was firm in insisting that provincial citizens had as much right to stand for the highest offices in Rome as the older Italian citizens did.

THE CLAUDIAN COURT.   The chief criticism levelled at Claudius has centered around the influence upon him of his freedmen and of his wives. This has been somewhat exaggerated, because the writers of the period were largely aristocrats, who resented the influences of the palace on the emperor. Yet there were indeed unhealthy influences at court. Claudius was very indulgent toward his wives. He had four of them in his career, and they all were bad women. His third wife, Messallina, bore him a son and a daughter, Britannicus and Octavia, but this lusty lady was not satisfied with the emperor, and finally, while still empress, she actually engaged in a public wedding ceremony with another man at a time when the emperor was absent from Rome on an inspection tour at Ostia. Her successor was the younger Agrippina, daughter of Germanicus and Agrippina the Elder. She was thus a sister of Caligula and Claudius' own niece, and this marriage in Roman law was incestuous. However, Agrippina used her charms to good advantage and prevailed upon the emperor to have special legislation passed to legalize such matches. Both Messallina and Agrippina were avaricious and they, in cooperation with the imperial freedmen of the court, contrived to amass immense fortunes. They did this in part by playing on the fears of Claudius, who was a rather timid man, accusing many persons of wealth and standing of treasonous activities. The most frightening aspect of the matter was that many of the subsequent trials were held in the secrecy of the palace, in direct contrast to the open trials of the principate of Tiberius. Agrippina was an ambitious and ruthless woman. She had a son, Nero, by her earlier marriage to Gnaeus Domitius Ahenobarbus and she was resolved that he should be Claudius' successor, although Claudius already had a son, Britannicus, by Messallina. When she had maneuvered Nero into a commanding position—he was adopted by Claudius and married to Octavia,

Claudius' daughter—according to ancient writers she had her husband poisoned; and there is nothing in her life either before or after his death to make this unlikely.

NERO (54–68 A.D.). Nero was only sixteen years old when he entered upon the principate. He had been an impulsive child with marked aesthetic tastes, and he carried in his veins not only the blood of Julians, Claudians, and Mark Antony, but also that of his paternal family, the brutal Ahenobarbi—his father was considered one of the cruelest and most despicable men of his day. However, the new reign opened auspiciously. The young man deferred to his mother, to his tutor, the Stoic philosopher Seneca, and to his praetorian prefect, a sensible old soldier named Burrus. The first five years equalled men's hopes that a new golden age of tranquillity and justice had arrived. But Agrippina's thirst for power was insatiable. She so insisted on the centerstage that a struggle between herself and Seneca and Burrus soon developed. The two men disapproved of a female ruler. They seem to have envisioned a new type of government, in which the principles of the republican system were protected as far as possible and the prince was assisted and advised by a duumvirate of wisdom (Seneca) and experience (Burrus). In any case, Nero's counsellors and his mother competed for the prince's allegiance by catering both to his passion for the stage and recital hall and to his taste for livelier women than his wife Octavia; and in so doing they hastened the destruction both of themselves and of Nero.

The republican ideals that were mouthed by Seneca and Burrus masked the continued trend toward monarchy. The very refusal by Nero of a perennial consulship, which was advertised as a sign of his modesty, actually underscored the detachment of the prince from the republican machinery of government. More and more the protection of the legal rights of Romans became a kindly indulgence of the prince rather than an undisputed prerogative of citizenship. For the time being, however, the Romans were sufficiently contented with their prosperity to ignore their changed condition. They enjoyed the advantages that came from the government's continued care and expansion of the system of roads and the improvements of the facilities along them. There was a special interest in the waterways, including both improvements in harbors in Italy and the provinces and work on canals and navigable rivers. Nero also took an active interest in the reconstruction of Rome after the destructive fire of 64 A.D. These works, however, combined with the extravagances that marked the later years of his reign, were a considerable drain on the treasury. Fiscal control therefore came more and more into the hands of the emperor, with the senatorial treasury now under prefects of praetorian rank. To Nero's reign also belongs an appreciable debasement of the coinage, a move that was dictated in part by the emperor's ambitious building programs.

The crimes of Nero's reign were infamous and patent. They were the more dreadful because Nero himself was a physical and moral coward. His adoptive brother Britannicus was poisoned early in the reign because he might prove a rival. His mother's ambition and her disapproval of his unstatesman-like devotion to the arts and to his mistresses caused him to have her murdered in 59 A.D. Octavia was divorced and murdered in 64 A.D. at the prompting of his mistress Poppaea, who aspired to be empress. His timidity at signs and portents, combined with an increasing need for money, led him to revive the fraudulent trials for treason by 62 A.D. In that year the death of Burrus, who was succeeded by an unprincipled Sicilian named Tigellinus, opened the way for a reign of terror against those whose wealth roused the cupidity, or whose birth raised the jealous fears, of Nero and his court.

He lost all sense of proportion or propriety in his love of the arts. He was genuinely concerned about his vocal training, and his worry concerning the competence of his rivals at musical and poetic competitions reveals a real pathological condition. Of course he won all contests, whatever his blunders, and he knew that he would, yet his fears kept him in a constant emotional uproar. This undignified public behavior led to the alienation of most of the nobility, and his crimes hastened it.

In 64 A.D. a dreadful fire swept Rome. Nero was eager to rebuild the city and to erect an enormous system of palaces for himself on land now cleared by the disaster, and his eagerness led to the suspicion that he was responsible for the fire. Popular suspicion of the emperor was, of course, heightened by his previous crimes, but in this instance it probably was unfounded. In any case, Nero's natural cowardice led him to accuse the Christians as the causes of the disaster. The charge was perhaps assisted by the enmity for the Christians of the Jews, in whom Poppaea seems to have been interested. There also may well have been some indiscreet hallelujahs uttered by the Christians during the holocaust, since they were expecting an early end of the world by fire; and this may have lent substance to suspicion of them.

Nero's growing unpopularity with many elements in the State culminated in conspiracies against him in 65 and 66 A.D., and upon discovery these led to the deaths of such worthies as Nero's old tutor, Seneca, the poet Lucan, and the inimitable playboy and literary maverick Petronius. The discovery of each conspiracy increased Nero's fears, the power of the informers, and the sycophancy of the surviving senators.

The emperor made a grand tour of Greece in 66 and 67 A.D., in which he garnered 1808 crowns of victory at the various great Hellenic games, though at one point he fell out of his chariot. This period also saw the execution of some of his best generals, including Corbulo the hero of the Armenian War, because he suspected their loyalty. By the end of his Greek tour indignation at his cruelty and contempt for his way of life began to spread even to the armies and to undermine the devotion of the troops to the Julio-Claudian house.

THE PROVINCES UNDER NERO.   There was also a steady deterioration in the administration of the provinces and in relations with client kingdoms. True, Nero was popular with the Greeks; and during his grand tour, in an act reminiscent of the decree of Flamininus in 196 B.C.,[1] he declared the Greeks free, though of course this meant little more than local autonomy and the alleviation of taxes. In Britain the mishandling of the client states, the greed of money-lenders, and an arrogant miscalculation of the independent spirit of the British led in 61 A.D. to a great revolt under the direction of the Icenian queen, Boudicca; and 70,000 Romans were slaughtered before the revolt was quelled and the country recovered. In the East, the important kingdom of Armenia was the center of vigorous activity. This region was of strategic value both to Parthia and to Rome, for neither would dare an offensive against the other if Armenia were in unfriendly hands, and each was fearful when Armenia's king was a dependent of the other. Since the Late Republic the Romans had claimed some kind of suzerainty over Armenia; but when Nero came to the throne Tiridates, the brother of the Parthian king, was on the Armenian throne and refused to recognize the Roman claims. Vigorous campaigns by the great Roman general Corbulo (57–60 A.D.) drove Tiridates from the country, but an incompetent Roman puppet, followed by an incompetent Roman administration, put Tiridates back in Armenia by 62 A.D. Finally Corbulo was sent back to Armenia, and through diplomacy and a show of force he effected a compromise. Tiridates retained the Armenian throne, but he came to Rome in 66 A.D. to receive his diadem from Nero's hands.

[1]   See above, p. 153.

Considering the racial connections of the Armenians with the Parthians, perhaps this was as good a solution as could be found, but it certainly was not the great victory for the Romans that Nero tried to make Tiridates' visit to Rome imply. Meanwhile, the harsh and untactful policies of the emperor's governors and troops in Judaea by 66 A.D. had all Palestine in flaming revolt.

THE REVOLTS AGAINST NERO (68 A.D.).   At length Nero's crimes, his flaunting of the Roman sense of propriety, and most of all his failure to spend some time with the army sealed his downfall. In early 68 A.D. a revolt broke out in Gaul, headed by Julius Vindex, the governor of one of its sections. This revolt was at least tacitly supported in Spain by Sulpicius Galba, the governor of the hither province. Galba was ultimately joined by Otho, the governor of Lusitania and an earlier husband of the empress Poppaea. However, the Roman troops on the Rhine looked upon this movement simply as a nationalistic Gallic uprising, and Vindex was defeated by the Rhenish commander, Verginius Rufus. Verginius' troops were thereupon prepared to declare him emperor, but Verginius demurred and instead put himself at the service of the Senate. That body, encouraged by the praetorian guard and by Nero's cowardice, dismay, and lack of action, declared the emperor a public enemy. When Nero received word of this, he lamented that the world should lose such an artist as he and then cut his throat, though even for this he needed the assistance of a faithful freedman. Thus ended the Julio-Claudian house that had been founded a century earlier by Augustus and Livia.

THE CONSEQUENCES OF THE JULIO-CLAUDIAN PRINCIPATE. The long and generally prosperous reign of Tiberius confirmed the efficiency of Augustus' new form of government. By Tiberius' death the Romans had accepted and enjoyed its benefits for two long generations (23 B.C.–37 A.D.). However, in spite of Tiberius' own sympathy for the republican traditions and his own preferences, the successes of the two reigns directed the Principate toward monarchy. This was partly due to the early and almost complete renunciation of political responsibility by the people—Caligula's attempt to revive popular elections was sheer demagoguery and he himself soon abandoned it. It was partly due also to a growing disinclination for initiative or independence of action among the senators, many of whom represented new families or were men who realized that political advancement depended on the good opinion of the prince. The actual inequality of the partnership between Senate and prince was made abundantly clear by the hesitation of the senators to take any important action during Tiberius' long retirement on Capri until that all-important letter from the emperor arrived indicating his wishes. Further, the brutal and treacherous abuse of the prince's latent power by a minister like Sejanus gave a lesson not soon forgotten.

The Senate found that more and more it was becoming a vehicle to approve the prince's policies and the high court to try cases that affected his interests. The madness of Caligula and the excesses of Nero might indeed be brought to an end; but the fact that they had taken place at all emphasized to the senators that there was the constant possibility of autocracy. This contingency wreathed even the kindliest prince with an aura of silent fear. Further, actions that had originally been taken by princes merely as experimental or emergency measures, and that had been based purely on the prince's personal authority, now came to have legal sanctions. For example, Augustus had personally campaigned for candidates that he preferred—he gave them his commendation (*commendatio*), and they were almost certain to be elected because of his prestige. But as Augustus grew older he tended to submit such candidate's names in writing, instead of actually electioneering for them, and by the time of the Flavians (69–96 A.D.) the right of such commendation with unopposed election had been written into positive law. The magistracies were thus being transformed from areas of political initiative to positions of administrative activity in the sprawling business of the Roman State, under the direction of the prince.

Also in the Julio-Claudian period there was a slow revelation of the power of the army, which had been camouflaged by Augustus. Claudius admitted it when he granted a donative of money to the praetorian guard for its support. Nero furthered it when he followed Claudius' example. And in 68 A.D. it burst openly on the scene, when the armies of the frontiers felt themselves neglected by the central government.

THE INTELLECTUAL CLIMATE. RHETORIC.   The change in Roman government meant a gradual change in the intellectual life and manner of Roman society. The Roman higher educational system continued to emphasize rhetoric. Rhetoric was no longer needed for the great political debates that had characterized the Late Republic, but for some people it still provided the necessary training to become advocates in the law courts of

Rome. The increasing complexity of Roman law also meant that specialists (jurisprudents) in the field of civil law increased, and they offered advice on technical points to the rhetorically trained advocates who did the actual pleading. Much of the rhetorical training involved practice in the composition of speeches on highly artificial and unrealistic cases. These compositions required subtlety and they were safe from dangerous political allusions, though their fantastic subjects might raise doubts as to their propriety in the educational system. However, centuries of capable administrators were trained in this manner, and this may indicate that such an education did help prepare a public servant to make logical or plausible decisions in the novel or puzzling situations that constantly faced Roman public servants.

LITERATURE.   The effect of a rhetorical education on literary men was less happy. The distinguished literary patron and historian of the Late Republic, Asinius Pollio, had started the fashion of public literary readings. In writing for such performances there was a great temptation for authors to seek a spontaneous flurry of applause by clever turns, bold conceits, and quotable phrases. These are the weakness and the adornment of much of the literature of the so-called Silver Age. In addition to the perils of rhetoric, the Principate itself seems to have exerted a bad influence. Those who were actually born or brought up under the new government felt neither that flush of gratitude for the present nor hope for a golden future that had inspired Augustan writers.[2] They took a great many of their comforts for granted. No longer feeling the inspiration that came from the hopes and the birthpangs of a new society, they turned to craftsmanship instead, and much of the literature was highly polished, precious, sententious, and blasé. The authoritarianism of the Principate that had begun to appear even under Augustus in the exile of Ovid[3] also made itself felt, especially in the field of history. There were historians, but most of their works have disappeared, many suppressed by a government sensitive to criticism. Only the writings of the adulatory Velleius Paterculus survive—we have a considerable portion of his history of Rome down to Tiberius' principate—but his work is sketchy and his political career under Tiberius led to an uncritical treatment of that prince and of Sejanus.

The works of Seneca, the tutor of Nero, reflect the un-

[2]   See above, pp. 371–372.
[3]   See above, pp. 372–373.

happy influences both of the Principate and of rhetorical training. Seneca composed numerous moral essays on uncontrover-
sial topics, and he also has left us nine tragedies. These plays
painfully exhibit the taste of the day for the declamatory.
Though Seneca was considered a Stoic philosopher, Epicurean
sentiments are often found in the choruses of his plays — which
marks the syncretic tendencies and the lack of profound beliefs
in his age: people borrowed and adapted all manner of things
that pleased them, with little regard for logical consistency. The
scenes in Seneca's plays are sometimes outrageously lurid and
bloody, and this has led most scholars to suppose that the plays
are "closet dramas," composed for the lecture hall rather than
for the theater. Seneca also may have been the author of an
ungrateful and tasteless satirical sketch on the deification of
Claudius, the *Apocolocyntosis*. This piece was perhaps written
to please the empress, who had had Claudius murdered, or Nero,
who had benefitted from the act. Since these two insisted on
making Claudius a god, however, both the authorship of the
satire and its purposes are something of a puzzle. In any case,
the work is interesting as a commentary on contemporary
thought, constitutional practice, and the hardness of the Roman
heart.

The poets of the period are somewhat more attractive. The
Spanish epigrammatist, Martial, began his composition of smart
verses during the reign of Nero, though he really belongs to the
Flavian period. Lucan, the nephew of Seneca, composed a
poem on Caesar and the civil wars, which was still unfinished at
the time that he became involved in a conspiracy against Nero
in 65 A.D. This work, commonly called the *Pharsalia*, is vigorous, and some of its scenes are gripping; but here again is a
striving for the epigrammatic, the startling, even the repulsive,
in order to move the listener. Lucan had talent, but it had not
yet subdued contemporary taste. There is a greater ring of
sincerity in the six satires of a young Stoic poet named Persius.
His satires were published after his death (62 A.D.) and they
castigated the literary aberrations of his day, which he described as frothy nerveless stuff that floated on the surface of
reality like spittle or dried cork. However, Persius' own style
was so crabbed, precious, and filled with learned allusions that
scholarly commentaries on his poems outweigh his actual literary output many times.

Major prose works of the Julio-Claudian era reflect
scientific and technical advances and considerable interest in
the noncontroversial scholarship of the day. Columella wrote an
up-to-date work on farming, the *De Re Rustica*, which illustrated

the growing knowledge of improved methods of agriculture and of agrarian management. The *Natural History* of the elder Pliny is a tremendous hodge-podge of information and misinformation about the world. It is a goldmine for specialists interested in anything from the asphalt of the Dead Sea to the vital statistics of Italian towns.

In a special category is the *Satiricon* of Gaius Petronius. We possess only a portion of three books of what was perhaps as many as twenty. But there is enough to show that it was a work of prose fiction, liberally intermixed with verse, recounting the adventures of three completely unprincipled rascals of some education, ready wit, and high sexuality. The work is not only a brilliant and sparkling account of life in southern Italy among freedmen, slaves, travelling scholars, quacks, *nouveau riches*, perverts, and fortune-hunters, but it is also our most valuable source for the spoken Latin of the day and the interests, ambitions, complaints, and petty triumphs of the poor. Furthermore, the poetry that is put in the mouths of fantastic rogues is quite as good as anything contrived by Lucan or by Nero himself. The *Satiricon* is the only literary product of the Julio-Claudian age that can be counted among the great books of world literature.

RELIGIOUS DEVELOPMENTS. While the population might view the deified Augustus or the deified Claudius with some satisfaction, and the freedmen might appreciate the social importance of their position as Augustales,[4] the official Roman religion really had little that was solidly comforting for the ordinary citizens. Many of the records of the Arval Brethren, one of the religious orders revived by Augustus, have survived, but by the time of Nero they were largely concerned with sacrifices for the birthdays or other anniversaries of the imperial family. Undoubtedly the countryfolk continued to worship the ancient deities of the soil as they did down to the very end of the Empire; but in the city the intellectuals were attracted to the cold reason and world brotherhood of Stoicism, or to the somewhat spiritualized system of the Neo-Pythagoreans, who presented their devotees with a mixture of mathematics, initiations, and release from earthly dross. Large numbers of the population abandoned themselves frankly and utterly to the more spiritual, exotic, and exciting sects, such as the followers of the Egyptian Isis, of Judaism, or of Christ, the new man-god who had appeared in Palestine during the principate of Tiberius and whom local jealousies and fanaticism had martyred,

---

[4]   See above, pp. 368, 370.

despite the justice, or at worst the massive indifference, of the Roman government.[5]

If one were to examine only the emperors and the imperial government at Rome, the Julio-Claudian period might well appear to portray a world governed by irresponsible neurotics seconded by nerveless poltroons. But the immediate effects of even the worst prince were felt only by his family and a coterie of aristocrats, or at the worst by the residents of Rome and the hugely rich. As a whole, the Mediterranean Basin was beginning to enjoy a peace and prosperity that is unexampled before and after, and men were grateful.[6] Italy itself was especially prosperous, as its archaeological record shows. This prosperity brought dangers. It was for the Italians a period of decadent extravagance. There was foolish splendor and foolish spending, and there was a retreat from the Roman virtues revived by Augustus and from the sense of confidence and hope that animated the Augustans. Prosperity and pleasure seemed endless, the frontiers and the problems of empire far away. This very prosperity, however, and this sense of security made it more and more difficult to procure Italian volunteers to guard and insure the benefits of the new Roman government. The blessed inhabitants of Italy seemed little to note or to care that at the very time that they had achieved a comfortable peace, the army on the frontiers was discovering that it was the final authority in the State.

[5]   For a fuller discussion of Christians and the Roman State, see Chapter 43.
[6]   For a further elaboration of these aspects of the Principate, see Chapters 37–40.

Chapter 33

THE YEAR OF THE FOUR EMPERORS

The events of the years 68 and 69 A.D., following the assassination of Nero, reveal that the Augustan Principate, as developed by Augustus' Julio-Claudian successors, had by no means become a perfect solution for the Mediterranean world. The Romans were faced with three major problems: Could the integrity of the Empire be maintained? What should be the constitutional basis of the principate? How were the Empire's armies to be kept loyal to the central government and essentially Roman? The events that forcibly made these problems clear during these two years were revolts by Jews, Gauls, and Batavians; the consecutive accession of four princes to the throne between June 68 and December 69 A.D.; and the high-handed part taken by the armies of the Rhine, Spain, the Danube, and the East, and by the praetorian guard in elevating the princes.

THE JEWISH REVOLT. 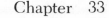 The Romans had made good progress in the assimilation of the Mediterranean's diverse peoples. But it was still far from complete, and there was one people that remained largely outside assimilation because it was essentially unassimilable, the Jews. The Jews were difficult because their philosophy of the relations of church and state so differed from the Romans'; the Jewish system subordinated temporal affairs to religion, while the Roman ideal placed religion in the service of the state. Julius Caesar had established a *modus vivendi* with the Jews with a series of edicts and laws that recognized Jewish peculiarities and granted them various exemptions and immunities from the services that they found especially repugnant. Thereafter, Augustus' good friend, the harsh but capable Herod the Great, had kept his countrymen in line. But with Herod's death in 6 A.D. Judaea had become a procuratorial province under the general oversight of the governor of Syria, and its

401

procurators at the best often had been inept. The threat of Gaius to establish his personal cult in the Temple clearly brought home to many Jews the uncertainties of their future. There had been some comfort for them in the restoration of the kingdom under Herod Agrippa I in 41 A.D., but the return to provincial status in 44 at Herod's death was a further aggravation. The country's own internal quarrels increased the dangers of the situation. There were constant frictions between the Jews and the gentiles that inhabited the Hellenized cities of Palestine; between the rich and the poor among the Jews themselves; between the Hellenizing upper classes, who had come to terms with the Romans, and the Pharisees, who represented a strict submission to ancient law; and between Roman officials and soldiers, who found Jewish manners and customs repulsive, and the mass of the Jews, who found the Roman rule ungodly and outrageous. These circumstances were made worse by the deteriorating economic conditions in that barren country.

At length in 66 A.D. a series of riots broke out in the cities of Palestine. There were a number in Caesarea, the residence of the procurator, where the Jews were demanding equal political rights with the gentiles, and others in Jerusalem, where the governor had confiscated seventeen talents from the Temple's treasury, presumably to make up for arrears in taxes. The Romans did not take firm steps at once, and soon the disorders were nationwide and had become an organized rebellion under the rather reluctant leadership of the high priest's party. In February 67 A.D. Nero had dispatched the capable general, Flavius Vespasian, a man of sufficiently low birth that Nero did not fear him as a rival, to cope with the situation. Vespasian's careful strategy, plus the continued dissensions among the rebels themselves, had cleared most of the country by the time news of Nero's assassination had arrived. Jerusalem, however, was still in rebel hands, and its besiegement was left until there was a clearer picture of the new situation and possibly of new policies in Rome.

THE GALLIC REVOLT.   In the West relations between the Romans and most provincials were far different. The Gauls had been quickly Romanized, the country was prosperous, and Gallic senators graced the benches in Rome. Such nationalistic movements as there had so far been, such as the brief rising under Julius Florus and Julius Sacrovir in the days of Tiberius, were weak and very limited in extent.[1] The Roman treatment of

1.   See above, p. 385.

the Germans along the banks of the Rhine followed the same tolerant policies that had won the Gauls: they were left their own tribal systems, individuals were attached to Rome's interest by the grant of Roman citizenship, rivalries between tribes were permitted in order to discourage dangerous combinations, and German auxiliaries served in the Roman army under native chieftains. These auxiliary troops played an important role in the defense of the frontiers against their own kinsmen of the German interior.

The Gallic rising against Nero in 68 A.D. led by Julius Vindex clearly was not nationalistic. Vindex was a Romanized Gaul and the governor of Gallia Lugdunensis, and he straightway appealed to the reputable governor of Hither Spain, Sulpicius Galba, to put himself at the head of a movement "to save the human race." The Roman armies stationed on the Rhine, however, recalled the nationalistic risings in Gaul under Tiberius and decided that it was their duty to ensure the tranquillity of the interior as well as to defend the frontier. Under the governor of Upper Germany, Verginius Rufus, the revolt of Vindex was quickly crushed. It appears, however that Verginius' troops were as disgusted with Nero as the Gauls had been, for they thereupon offered to support their own commander as a replacement for Nero, an offer which he repeatedly refused.

GALBA (68–69 A.D.).   Meanwhile, on April 2, 68 A.D., Galba had accepted the invitation of Vindex for support and had put himself at the service of the Senate and the Roman people. As an incentive he had before him Nero's recent sentences of death for the successful general Corbulo and for the governors of Upper and Lower Germany; he had been warned that a similar fate awaited himself. At the defeat of Vindex he was in despair, for his own forces were scanty; although Otho, the governor of Lusitania, supported him. Soon, however, word arrived that Nero had been deserted by the praetorians and by Nymphidius, their prefect, and that the latter had promised the troops a liberal donative of money to support Galba. The Senate concurred, for Galba's family was ancient and his life and public career had been honorable and correct.

During his short reign Galba made nearly every mistake possible to lose public esteem and to alienate almost everyone. An emperor may be firm and he may work for reform, but he must have tact. This Augustus had had and Tiberius had not. Now Galba appeared even less astute in winning friends and handling public opinion than Tiberius had been. When the

403

governors of Africa and Lower Germany showed ambiguous attitudes toward the new prince, he had the former assassinated, and he condoned the murder of the latter by one of the governor's own aides, Fabius Valens. He then made the mistake, however, of not treating Valens with the gratitude that the assassin expected for his crime. The praetorian prefect Nymphidius, who had bought the praetorians for Galba, was displaced by Galba's own friend Laco, and was thereby piqued into an insurrection. Galba's stock with the praetorians also was not aided when he refused to pay the promised donative to them. The excellent Verginius Rufus was recalled from Upper Germany, where his prestige and authority were immense. He was replaced in Germany by a nonentity, and he was treated with great coolness when he arrived in Rome. There was a bustling but inefficient hunt for the monies that had been squandered by Nero, but the recoveries nowhere equalled the uncertainties and fears that the investigations raised. Notorious malefactors such as Tigellinus were left untouched, and Galba's own supporters were said to be lining their pockets.

Word of Galba's unpopularity soon reached the Rhenish legions. They were discontented because of the treatment of Verginius and the obvious favor that Galba showed the followers of the Gallic Vindex, whom they had defeated. On January 1, 69 A.D., they refused to take the oath of allegiance to the emperor. When the news reached Galba, he realized that he should strengthen his position by adopting an associate and successor. However, instead of choosing the popular and strong Verginius or Marcus Salvius Otho, who as governor of Lusitania had supported him and whose high favor at court had led to the greatest expectations on his part, he named Marcus Piso Licinianus. Piso was of high birth and of blameless character, but he had neither experience nor following. But the troops of Germany had not waited for this move of the emperor. Spurred on by Fabius Valens, still resentful that his crime had not been rewarded, the soldiers declared the new governor of Lower Germany, the amiable and completely incompetent Aulus Vitellius, their candidate for the throne.

OTHO (69 A.D.).   In Rome, where the appearance of a new claimant on the Rhine was still unknown, Otho, disappointed in his hope that he would be Galba's choice, managed to subvert the praetorian guard. He made himself popular with those troops by his pleasant presence and ready purse, in notable contrast to Galba. He sent a contingent of troops to seek out and dispatch the old man and his heir on January 15th. No one seemed to care, except for the senators, who regretted one of their own kind; and the debasement and helplessness of the senatorial order are emphasized by the speed with which it granted the tribunician power to Otho.

Otho was of a good but not ancient family. He had proved a conscientious and capable governor of Lusitania for ten years, a post to which he was assigned by Nero, although he had held only quaestorian rank theretofore. Nero had made the appointment solely so that he could monopolize Otho's wife, Poppaea, and later acquire her. After the murder of Galba, Otho set out to make his peace with the Senate and to correct some of the discontents generated in Galba's brief reign. His time, however, was short. The Rhenish troops already were on the move toward Italy. Vitellius himself showed little enthusiasm for his own elevation, but his ambitious lieutenants, Valens and Alienus Caecina, had no intention of allowing the praetorian guard once again to impose its candidate on the nation. They accomplished a brilliant passage of the still wintry Alps and arrived in the Po Valley by March of 69 A.D. Otho had secured the allegiance of a large part of the Empire, but his legions were scattered and far away, and he had been too slow to defend the passes of the Alps with such forces as he had at hand. Now, without delaying events and awaiting reinforcements from the Danube, he insisted on meeting the German forces near Cremona in April 69 A.D., where his greatly outnumbered troops were defeated. Although urged by his supporters that he still had numerous legions in the loyal provinces with which to reverse the decision, Otho decided to commit suicide rather than continue the slaughter and hazard further months of uncertainty.

VITELLIUS (69 A.D.).   Peace was reestablished, but there existed a number of sources of future trouble. The legions arriving from the Danube to assist Otho were sent back to their posts, and they left in bad humor. One legion was detached to build an amphitheater for Cremona, a menial task which it resented and for which it was to exact a dreadful payment. There was also much resentment at the disbandment of Otho's proud praetorian guard and its replacement by troops from the German legions. Furthermore, the Rhenish legions had pillaged and mutinied as they had passed through Gaul, and they had pilfered in the towns of Italy. Now their insolence and hooliganism in Rome itself brought home to Romans once more, after a century without civil war (31 B.C.–68 A.D.), how perilous were the forces that faction could unloose.

405

Vitellius was a well-meaning man and a somewhat reluctant emperor, the tool of his abler subordinates. His father had been a capable and trusted associate of Claudius, and Vitellius had thrived on his father's reputation—his own capabilities were largely gustatorial. At first the Senate and all the legions acquiesced in his elevation, but soon the leaders in the East took a second look. The moving spirits of discontent there were Licinius Mucianus, the governor of Syria, and Tiberius Alexander, the prefect of Egypt. As their candidate they supported Vespasian, the commander in the war against the Jews. After convincing Vespasian himself, these kingmakers succeeded by the middle of July 69 A.D. in securing the support of the troops of Egypt, Judaea, and Syria.

THE ELEVATION OF VESPASIAN.   With a reasonable force of supporters now assured, Vespasian turned over the command in Judaea to his son Titus and proceeded to Egypt in order to secure the granaries there in case a lengthy war required him to bring pressure on the Roman stomach. Mucianus meanwhile started out with a moderate force to march to Italy through Asia and the Balkans, hoping to pick up support on the road. Before his arrival, however, the troops along the Danube, still smarting from their failure to assist Otho and from their treatment by Vitellius, declared for Vespasian and headed for Italy under the leadership of a subordinate commander, Antonius Primus. The issue was once more determined near Cremona in late October 69 A.D. in a battle that lasted throughout a night. The Vitellians were demoralized by a lazy summer in Italy and even more by their leadership, whose loyalty to Vitellius was rightly suspect. After a bitter struggle the Danubian legions were victorious over the Vitellians and at length stood before the walls of Cremona and the new amphitheater that they had been forced to construct the previous spring. The city was sacked and burned to the ground in recompense, and the troops swept on to Rome. There the unhappy Vitellius had entered into negotiations with Flavius Sabinus, Vespasian's brother and the prefect of the city, for a peaceful solution through his own abdication and retirement on a pension. Agreement had been reached, but the soldiers of the Rhenish legions in Rome were not about to allow their emperor to desert them. Vitellius was forced back to his palace and Sabinus was besieged in the Capitol and ultimately slain. Then at length the troops of Antonius Primus reached the city and fought through the streets killing the Vitellians to a man. Vitellius himself was publicly executed on the 20th of December. Again the city was the plaything of victorious troops, whose appetite for pillage had been whetted by Cremona. Fortunately, Mucianus arrived in January of 70 A.D. to restore order and to rule the city for Vespasian until the new emperor's arrival there in the late summer.

THE REVOLT OF BATAVIANS AND GAULS.   The civil wars of 68–69 A.D. ended, as they had begun, with disturbances in Gaul. There, on the Rhenish frontier, a Romanized chief of the Batavian auxiliaries, Julius Civilis, decided that it was time to throw off allegiance to the empire entirely. The Batavians were Germans who inhabited approximately the area of the modern Netherlands, and they long had been trusted allies. At first the aims of Civilis were hidden, because both Antonius Primus and Flaccus, the governor of Upper Germany, had approached him with the suggestion that he rise against Vitellius in Vespasian's behalf. This he did; but as Vespasian's armies proved successful, it became clear that Civilis was rising not against Vitellius, but against Rome. He made overtures to various Gallic leaders to cooperate with him, and these at first were coldly received. However, his early successes against the Romans led two Gallic peoples, the Treveri and Lingones, also to rise and to threaten the creation of a separate empire of the Gauls. Upon his arrival in Rome Mucianus took early and firm action. An adequate expedition was sent to the area, and the revolt collapsed, with the Batavians holding out until the end of 70 A.D. The weakness of the uprising proved the success of Roman policy in most of Gaul; and the punishment of the insurgents, even of the German Batavians, was not severe. All were allowed to return to their former legal status, although one change of policy was made: thereafter auxiliary troops, such as the Batavians, generally were not stationed near their homelands, where separatism might arise, and henceforth their military commanders were less often chosen from their own chieftains.

LESSONS AND WARNINGS.   The civil wars of 68–69 A.D. brought clearly and brutally before the Roman people three basic problems about their government that had been camouflaged or ignored by Augustus and his Julio-Claudian successors: the constitutional basis of the office of *princeps*, the loyalty of the Mediterranean community of peoples to the Roman government, and the role of the Roman army in that government. Final answers were not immediately found, but some of the policies now adopted ultimately led to a considerable improvement in the Roman situation.

One of the difficulties with the office of *princeps* was the irregularity of succession. Tiberius had succeeded to the throne because he was adopted by Augustus and had been associated with him in the tribunician power. Gaius had had the favor of the praetorian guard, and so did Claudius, who had strengthened his claims by a payment of money to them. Nero had been elevated through adoption and murder. The one constant factor had been some relation to the Julio-Claudian family founded by Augustus and Livia. Vespasian proposed to end uncertainties and divisive rivalries by openly governing the succession by primogeniture. He had two sons, and he trained them to succeed him. Furthermore, he clarified the rights and duties of the prince, which had insensibly expanded under the Julio-Claudians, by having them spelled out in a special law at the beginning of his principate and ratified by a vote of the people. This is the famous Law on Vespasian's *Imperium,* a portion of which still survives because in the fourteenth century the Italian patriot Cola di Rienzi had a copy of it set up in Rome to assist him in his struggle with the autocratic papacy. He did this because he believed that it showed that in ancient Rome even the power of the prince ultimately was derived from the people.

In regard to the peoples of the Empire, there were problems, but also heartening signs. Even in a time of civil war the integrity of the Empire had been maintained because the revolts had been localized and relatively weak. This seemed to show that Roman policy toward the peoples of the polyglot Empire had been focussed in the right direction, and the gentle treatment of the Gauls and Germans at the end of their rebellion showed that the new administration understood the efficacy of the tolerant imperial policy of the recent past. It is true that after their defeat by Titus in 70 A.D., the Jews suffered the destruction of their Temple and the abolition of their Sanhedrim (national council) and high priesthood. But even they, who had given so much trouble, were still permitted their special immunities from various imperial duties in return for the payment of a poll tax, a tax which once went to their Temple, but now was diverted to Jupiter Capitolinus.

The famous statement of Tacitus that during the Year of the Four Emperors the secret of empire was revealed, that its control depended on the legions, is of course true. But these legions were still sufficiently Roman that they could sicken of fratricidal conduct and they still could be made to listen to an able commander. The resurrection of the same passions and pillage in 68–69 A.D. that had marked the last days of the Republic one hundred years before led the soldiers to avoid such extremes again for over a century — until after the assassination of Pertinax in 193 A.D. Emperors now learned that they must pay more attention to the troops, and most of them did so. Tangentially, however, the problem of the army raised a new and graver problem—the problem of population. The present army still had many Italian soldiers in it, and they would indeed take pity on their civilian sons and brothers. Given the declining birthrate in Italy, however, how long could the Roman army be kept loyal by being kept largely Roman? Could Italy furnish enough Italians that the process of assimilation throughout the Empire would continue, reaching, for instance, to the vigorous Germans? Already by the middle of the century some private persons sufficiently recognized the need that they were establishing foundations in their home towns for the support of the poor children of Italy.[2] The show of force by the army in 68–69 A.D. made suddenly and brutally clear that the maintenance of adequate Italian replacements might one day be a matter of life and death.

Chapter 34

THE FLAVIANS

VESPASIAN (69–79 A.D.).   Titus Flavius Vespasianus has been called the second founder of the Principate, and there is some justice in that judgment. When he was elevated by the troops he found himself faced with many of the same problems that had confronted Augustus: the country had been rent by rival generals and factious armies, the government was bankrupt, and, what was worse, men's faith in the inevitability of the Roman Empire had been shaken. To meet these problems Vespasian did not enjoy all the advantages that Augustus had exploited to such good effect. Unlike Augustus, he did not have the aura of divine parentage, the youthfulness, or the claims of manifest destiny. However, like Augustus he was of municipal

[2]   For the government's support of poor Italian children and its private antecedents, see below, Chapter 40.

stock, from the Sabine town of Reate. His grandfather and father before him had been publicans and moneylenders, and partly due to this heritage and training he brought to his task good sense, a respect for property, a willingness to work, an earthy sense of humor, and the canniness of a peasant. His sober virtues remained with him. From now on the court turned away from the gaiety and extravagances of the Julio-Claudians and, despite lapses, generally exhibited the quiet respectability of Vespasian's bourgeois origin.

EMPHASIS ON PEACE. As the founder of a dynasty, Vespasian realized that invidious comparisons of himself with Augustus might be made. To bolster the belief that he too had divine favor, even before he left the Orient for Rome reports reached the capital of wonderful prodigies and of miraculous cures effected by the new emperor. When he arrived in Rome, and the civil strife in both East and West had been ended, he further recalled Augustus' emphasis on the blessings of peace by closing the Temple of Janus, which signified the end of strife and return of normalcy. Two of his principal public works were a Temple of Peace and his new forum, which he named significantly the Forum of Peace. He saw that prosperity could only return with the reestablishment of confidence in the stability of the State. The mutinous legions of the Rhine, which had lost that confidence and gone over to Civilis and his separatist rebellion, were at once disbanded and replaced. Thereafter the Flavians seem to have favored the recruitment of soldiers from the middle classes of the Romanized provinces rather than from the dregs of the Italian proletariat, which had proved unstable and unruly as early as the military disorders at the accession of Tiberius (14 A.D.). The dangers from native auxiliaries were lessened by the combination of various ethnic groups in these units and their assignment to areas of duty distant from their home places. The praetorian guard also was reformed: it was reduced in size and its command given to the emperor's elder son, Titus.

THE SUCCESSION AND STOIC OPPOSITION. Vespasian was determined that Rome should be spared ambitious strife for the principate, and to effect this he frankly prepared his sons to be his successors. This was probably an important cause for the intermittent opposition to the Flavians that emanated from the two popular Roman philosophical sects, the Cynics and the Stoics. The Cynics, by arguing for a life lived according to nature, often ended up as anarchists, and their itinerant lectur-

410

ers were a source of widespread and sometimes dangerous entertainment for the masses. They clearly contested any suggestion that a man's sons were his appropriate successors. Stoicism was more popular with the upper classes. It was no longer arrantly republican, as it had been in the days of the younger Cato, but it supported the thesis that the Roman ruler should also be the "best man," and presumably that he should be chosen by that collection of sages that the Roman Stoics idealized, the Roman Senate. But Vespasian knew the Senate and its shortcomings very well, and he wryly retorted to criticism that he would be succeeded by his sons or by no one. A number of the more vociferous philosophical critics were exiled and one was killed, though this was against the emperor's wish. Meanwhile, he gave his elder son Titus thorough training and his complete confidence—Vespasian shared the consulship with him seven times, took him as his colleague in the censorship, gave him the tribunician power and proconsular *imperium* in 71 A.D., and made him praetorian prefect. The younger son, Domitian, was consul six times and held the title of prince of the youth.

FINANCIAL REFORM.   The civil wars and the excesses of Nero had left the government in a serious financial condition. Vespasian set about to correct this, and his family's tradition in banking and tax-collecting stood him in good stead. New taxes were devised and old ones were collected rigorously. The emperor's assumption of the censorship (73–74 A.D.) led to the revaluation of all the property in the Empire, and certainly the growing prosperity of the Empire since the Republic justified an increase in revenue. Public property and the imperial estates also were given a centralized and efficient administration, and much public land that lax supervision had allowed to be occupied by squatters was recovered for the treasury. Greece was returned to the status of a taxpaying province; and Rhodes, Byzantium, and Samos lost their status as free states and became sources of revenue for the provinces to which they were assigned. Even the statesmanlike grant of Latin rights to all Spaniards meant that there was now created a larger group of Roman citizens eligible to pay the inheritance taxes, for which citizens alone were liable. And the emperor's own frugal manner of life—Nero's palaces were abandoned—assured the people that the funds that he raised would be wisely spent.

PUBLIC WORKS.   The restoration and repair of buildings and streets in Rome were badly needed, and work was begun immediately. Other areas that had been sacked or destroyed in the civil wars also were soon reconstructed. In Rome the Capitol and numerous temples were rebuilt, the channel of the Tiber was dredged and its banks strengthened, and aqueducts were repaired. On the frontiers permanent army camps were built or restored; and there was much work performed on the system of roads, especially in the East, where they had great strategic value. Much of the work on the roads and on the defenses was performed by the soldiers, and Vespasian set a good example to his subjects, shouldering baskets of rubble in clearing away the debris that war and fire had left in Rome. He recognized also the importance of a generous public works program as a palliative to the chronic unemployment of Rome; and when an inventor offered him a device whereby building materials could be more cheaply transported in the city, he rewarded the man, but he refused the device with the protest, "Suffer me to feed the poor."

EDUCATION.   Middle-class though. he might be, Vespasian recognized the importance of the Romanization of the Mediterranean world and the role that education would play in effecting it. Secondary school teachers were encouraged by an exemption from various local taxes throughout the empire; and this canny bourgeois was the first to establish and support professorial chairs of rhetoric at Rome.

VESPASIAN AND THE SENATE.   By his assumption of the censorship in 73 A.D. Vepasian was able to replenish a Senate that was depleted by war, conspiracy, and natural causes. For his new senators he went to the municipalities throughout the empire and chose men who, as members of the equestrian class, already had done the State good service in administrative positions. The majority still were drawn from the Western provinces; despite their long service in the East, the Flavians were still Latins and promoted the Latin-speaking part of the Empire. The Senate was treated by Vespasian with all respect, but he did not defer to it; and it was clear that he looked upon it as a reservoir of administrative talent rather than as a partner in power. This is apparent from his decision to date the beginning of his reign from his acclamation by his troops, not from his recognition by the Senate.

VESPASIAN THE MAN.   Vespasian was a hard and conscientious worker. By rising before dawn to begin his duties he set an example that his aides and administrators found difficult to follow. Many of his reforms might have been far more unpopular, but his own devotion to duty proved his sincerity, and his sense of humor tided him over a number of difficult spots. The more fastidious Titus complained to his father of the indelicacy of taxing the public toilets, but the old man waved a copper under his son's nose with the comment that the money from that source had no odor. And his humor stayed with him to the end. During the progress of his final illness he observed, "Alas, I'm afraid that I am becoming a god"; and then, more poignantly and more like an ancient Roman, he struggled out of bed with the words, "An emperor should die on his feet," and expired there in the arms of his attendants. As was the Roman custom, a well-known actor wore the emperor's death mask and all his paraphernalia of office and marched directly behind the bier in the funeral procession, imitating Vespasian's words and manner. The affectionate amusement of the people at the old man's thrift and wit is reflected in the actor's query of the officials as to how much this funeral was costing him. When they replied, "Ten million sesterces," the wag cried out, "Give me a hundred thousand and throw me into the Tiber!" In any case, after the funeral they made him a god, and he undoubtedly made a better one than most.

TITUS (79–81 A.D.).   Titus had been his father's active, trusted, and devoted associate throughout Vespasian's reign. As praetorian prefect he had protected his father from conspiracy with such zeal that he had acquired a reputation for cruelty; and a passionate love affair with Berenice, sister of the Jewish king Julius Agrippa II, had raised a popular clamor against a second Cleopatra. Suspicions as to his character probably, then, had been an important factor in the philosophical opposition to Vespasian's plan of succession. However, once on the throne Titus allayed all fears. He dismissed Berenice, maintained his father's modest establishment, and showed himself kindly, open, and solicitous for the welfare of his people. Handsome, well-educated, and a proved warrior as well as administrator, Titus became the pattern for the ideal prince, the "darling of the human race." His affability is illustrated by a remark made when at dinner he could remember no benefit conferred on anyone since morning, "Friends, I have lost a day." But his generosity was not prodigal. He continued his father's strict financial policies, restored more sections of the Roman aqueducts, and expanded the work on the system of roads all over the Empire. In Rome he dedicated the nearly completed Colosseum and the famous Baths of Titus. He also took upon himself most of the repairs, rebuilding, and relief of the victims from two great disasters that marred his reign, a terrible fire that swept Rome in 80 A.D., and the eruption of Vesuvius in 79 A.D. that buried Herculaneum, Pompeii, and Stabiae. Titus suddenly died of a fever after a little more than two years of rule, and he was straightway deified by a sorrowing Senate and people.

DOMITIAN (81–96 A.D.) AND DESPOTISM.   At the death of his brother, Domitian hurried to the praetorian barracks and had himself acclaimed emperor before the Senate was even consulted. This set the constitutional tone of the reign. He had a passion for power that was flagrant. Earlier, as the family's representative in Rome during the months after Vespasian's accession, but before the emperor had reached the city, Domitian had had a youthful taste of power and he had enjoyed it. Until his accession, however, his ambition had been stifled by his elders, who had apparently gauged his character well. He had been given consulships and marked out as a successor by father and brother; but he was not given military assignments or a real association in power by either Vespasian or Titus, and he had been forced instead to spend much time in study and in literary pursuits. From the beginning he made no secret of his autocratic attitude. His treatment of the Senate was cavalier, and it was capped by his assumption of the censorship in 85 A.D. This was not the useful revival of a republican office as in the case of Augustus, Claudius, and Vespasian. Instead, Domitian became *censor perpetuus,* which indicated that he would have life-long supervision of the roll and persons of the senators. Furthermore, after 83 A.D. he regularly wore the garb of the triumphator even in the Senate House, which flaunted his military superiority to the senators' civilian weakness.

DOMITIAN'S ADMINISTRATIVE POLICIES.   Although Domitian's theory of government was autocratic, it certainly was efficient. The building programs of his predecessors were pressed forward on an even greater scale—"mad about building," his contemporaries judged. He finished works that his father and brother had begun, and adorned Rome with stadia, music halls, temples, and in his own behalf a magnificent palace on the Palatine. Libraries were restocked, storehouses repaired; there was a vigorous continuation of road construction, especially in the East; and the water system of Rome was given far more efficient care by the appointment of curators who served for long terms. A great many of Domitian's public works were prompted by political rather than by economic considera-

414

tions, however. In some cases it was simply for ostentatious propaganda—he put his name on buildings that he merely repaired as well as those that he initiated—but it also was calculated to earn the gratitude and support of the masses in his resolve to dominate the State. He inherited the Flavian canniness in financial affairs, but in some respects he was more generous than his predecessors. For example, he gave full title to squatters on unassigned pieces of public land, though Vespasian and Titus had been reclaiming such property for the treasury. The governors that he chose served long and well, and the excellence of his choices is shown by the number that were retained by later and happier administrations. The people of Rome were kept contented by elaborate shows. He ensured the army's loyalty by visiting it, and sometimes by leading it on the more important frontiers. He clinched his popularity with the troops by raising the legionaries' pay from 900 to 1200 sesterces a year. He took a keen interest in agriculture and, observing an imbalance between the production of wheat and wine, he passed legislation to limit the spread of vineyards and called for the actual reduction of them in the provinces, although this measure apparently was not very effective.

THE OPPOSITION TO DOMITIAN.   Domitian's administrative policies proved so excellently sensible that few could seriously object to them. Opposition to the Flavian dynasty revived, however, because of the high-handed manner in which Domitian put his policies into effect. People feared that there was another Caligula in the making when they discovered that the emperor forced his personal aides to address him as "master and god." As the monarchical tendencies of his reign became unmistakable, philosophers and astrologers again became vocal in their derision of autocrats, and once more they suffered a decree of banishment. Domitian's popularity was not increased by an attempt to restore and enforce Augustan laws on morality. He revived the ancient punishment of burying alive Vestal Virgins that had broken their vows. This punishment shocked the sensibilities of a more tolerant age, especially when the emperor that enforced it felt no moral compunction at using his own niece as his mistress. Equally offensive to Romans was his promotion of athletic and literary contests of the Greek type and the erection of handsome edifices to house them; to a people inured to the bloody arena, Greek footraces and literary contests were un-Roman and perverted.

One upshot of the unrest at Domitian's tyrannical manner was a conspiracy in early 89 A.D. headed by the legate of Upper

415

Germany, Antonius Saturninus. This military uprising was quashed by the loyal governor of Lower Germany. By the time that Domitian had hurried to the scene order had been restored, but also all the incriminating letters written to Saturninus by sympathizers had been destroyed. Domitian, however, knew that the sympathizers existed, and from then on he saw conspiracy everywhere. He continued to administer the empire conscientiously and well, but he also lavished calculated cruelty on a terrible hydra of suspicion and hatred: the more men that he suspected and condemned, the more potential assassins appeared to be created. It was a badly frightened autocrat that lived in rooms with walls so beautifully polished that he could detect any suspicious move at his back, and a sorry prince that had to sleep with a dagger under his pillow. When at length even his notoriously indolent cousin, Flavius Clemens, became a victim, and when even the riffraff of Rome found agents of the prince trying to discover disaffection among them, no one felt safe. The final and successful conspiracy was headed by Domitia, the emperor's wife, and by the praetorian prefects, and they were joined by numerous officials of the palace who lived in constant dread. The conspirators secured the consent of an aged jurist and senator, Marcus Cocceius Nerva, to take the throne if the plot succeeded, and they then effected the assassination of the tyrant in September 96 A.D.

THE FLAVIAN ACHIEVEMENT. Despite the differences in personality in the three Flavians, there is a continuity and unity to their work. Domitian was essentially carrying out the strong policy of his father both in increasing the power of the executive at home and in improving the defenses and administration abroad, but he lacked Vespasian's discernment and humor and Titus' amiability for the task. Among them, however, the Flavians gave organization, direction, body, and method to the Principate, and these had a lasting influence.

FLAVIAN DEFENSE AND FOREIGN AFFAIRS. The Flavians were not expansionists, but they saw that the army must be occupied and kept in line. To do this they initiated three important improvements in military policy. They gave the troops judicious exercise in the construction of public works and in a kind of defensive offense on the frontiers in Africa, Britain, Germany, and along the Danube, all areas that needed to be secured. They recruited new soldiers from the stable middle classes of the provincial municipalities. And they were careful to station the legions in widely separated camps and thus avoid concentrations of power that might tempt ambitious generals. Furthermore, all three men were well known to the troops and commanded their support.

The defensive system of the Empire was improved by the establishment of more clearly defined boundaries that would be economical to supervise and hold and that were calculated to protect the provinces from unruly elements within the Empire or from surprise incursions from without. It was recognized that Nero's compromise in Armenia had essentially put that kingdom in Parthia's orbit. An enlarged and much stronger Cappadocia was therefore established to anchor the eastern frontier, Syria's boundaries were extended, and a system of roads was straightway constructed to ensure rapid communication among the six legions assigned to the East. These roads were also designed to facilitate the transfer of troops to the eastern frontiers from the West if need arose. In Numidia and Mauretania there was a constant pressure on the nomads to settle down or be eradicated; and the government's efforts in that area were rewarded by a remarkable agricultural development there in the next epoch. In Britain, the centers of constant nationalist unrest in Mona and Wales were taken; in the north a reasonable frontier was established between Solway Firth and the Tyne; and there were advanced posts established as far north as Inchtuthill on the Tay. However, Domitian wisely discouraged unprofitable invasions of Ireland and the Scottish Highlands.

THE GERMAN FRONTIER.   In their upper reaches both the Rhine and the Danube, which rivers generally approximated Rome's northern frontier on the continent, turn southward, and they thus created a dangerous salient, a sort of arrow, that pointed directly into the heart of Gaul. As early as 73–4 A.D. Vespasian began to penetrate the area, seeking to secure it by roads and forts. Vespasian's efforts were continued by Domitian, who initiated campaigns against the Chatti in 83 A.D. and again in 89; and these campaigns led to the establishment of a string of watchtowers and auxiliary forts that protected the rich valley of the Neckar River and shortened the line of imperial defense by many miles. Domitian also regularized the government of Upper and Lower Germany along the Rhine, giving those areas, which previously had been merely military districts, their own financial administration and thus making them conventional provinces.

THE DANUBIAN FRONTIER.   On the Danube danger arose for the first time since the days of Augustus, and it came from

417

the Dacians. Dacian tribes now were united under a young, vigorous, and ambitious king, Decebalus; and the problem that this emerging nation presented was compounded by activity on the part of its neighbors, the Sarmatians near the mouth of the Danube, and the Marcomanni, Quadi, and Iazyges farther up the river opposite the provinces of Pannonia and Noricum. The Dacians invaded the province of Moesia in 85 A.D., and the invasion was repelled by Domitian himself; but a retaliatory expedition into Dacia under one of his generals proved a disaster. A more successful attempt to punish the raiders in 88 A.D. presaged an early settlement; but Roman plans were interrupted by the conspiracy of Saturninus in 89 A.D. and by new wars with the Marcomanni, Quadi, and Iazyges in that year and again in 92. The costs in men and materiel that the Roman government was suffering in order to stabilize the Danubian frontier convinced Domitian that it would be wise to reach a compromise with King Decebalus. A treaty was therefore made with the king whereby one of his relatives accepted for him a diadem from Domitian, thus signifying Rome's nominal suzerainty over the area. In return for this nominal submission, the Romans promised the loan of engineers and the grant of an annual subsidy to Decebalus to assist him in the development of his country. Considering the problems that Domitian faced, this probably was a sensible as well as economical solution, but the Romans derided it as being a surrender to barbarian recalcitrance. However, the concentration of nine legions along the Danube, the largest aggregation of troops in the Empire, presaged the importance that this sector was to have in the next century.

FLAVIAN ADMINISTRATIVE POLICY.   The excellence of the administrators chosen by the Flavians is witnessed by their distinguished careers even after the Flavians had disappeared. The list included men such as Agricola, Fronto, Frontinus, Pliny, and even Tacitus. It is perhaps to Domitian that we owe the initiation of the professional specialization in administration that the office of *juridicus* implies. The *juridicus* was appointed to supervise the legal activities of civilians in the larger provinces, and thus he marks the beginning of the separation of the military and civilian competences in provincial staffs.

Beginning with Augustus the equestrian class, the middle class of Italy, had been the natural ally of the prince, for the emperor had provided for the advance of the knights in the face of the exclusiveness of the senatorial nobility. Under the Flavians the knights were especially devoted to this new middle-class dynasty. Little by little its members began to replace the imperial freedmen, who had flourished under the Julio-Claudians, in the great bureaus and household posts. The censorship of the Flavian princes also facilitated the promotion of many proved members of the equestrian class to the Senate.

The principles of thrift, good husbandry, and respect for property and property-rights, which was a Flavian tradition and a tradition of the equestrian class, were reflected in the growing feeling that the prince was the servant of the State, the man whose virtues included providence and solicitude for the welfare of the citizens. Even the most autocratic princes began to feel this; and their success as heads of government was measured by their treatment after death — whether they were deified, damned, or ignored. In the next century the standards of conduct for a prince that the Flavians had sketched were accepted as the basic principles of rule.

INTELLECTUAL AND RELIGIOUS LIFE.   The self-conscious resurrection by the Flavians of Augustan principles in public life is paralleled by developments in the intellectual life. Of the Flavian epic poets, Silius Italicus, who wrote a poem on the Second Punic War, worshipped the Augustan Vergil. The *Argonautica* of Valerius Flaccus owed much of its delineation of character to Ovid; and Statius reworked ancient themes in his *Thebais* and *Achilleis*. Somewhat better are the impromptu verses of Statius, the *Silvae*; but all these works show the unfortunate devotion of the age to displays of erudition and rhetoric. More attractive is Martial, whose chief work was composed during this period. His witty and often satirical epigrams bring to our scrutiny every facet of Roman society, and they do so with terseness, vivacity, and a felicity of expression that have made Martial's name synonymous with the epigrammatic form. The great and successful rhetorician, critic, and teacher, Quintilian, spent much effort trying to recall Ciceronian Latin as the standard for the day. His *Institutes of Oratory* is especially interesting, for it gives a complete course of instruction in rhetoric, and from it we derive much of our knowledge of ancient pedagogy.

Cosmopolitan Rome still produced no literary figures of note. Silius Italicus, Martial, and Quintilian were provincials from Spain, as Seneca and Lucan had been in the preceding era, and they showed the conservatism and the deference to an earlier Rome that characterized provincial thinking. All of these men benefited from the Flavians' patronage of literature and education — Silius and Quintilian even received consular sta-

419

tus—but the literary record of the Flavian age is nonetheless not brilliant. The culture of the period was trite and conventional, though it surely still made an impression on all classes, and not simply on the nobility. For the permeation of the liberal arts to the masses not only do we have some testimony in Petronius' *Satiricon*, but also there is abundant evidence in the art and graffiti found at Pompeii, which was destroyed at this time. Everywhere in Pompeii, in the decoration of public places, the scratchings on the walls, and the adornments of private dining rooms and gardens, there was a smattering of the poets, both ancient and contemporary, and a love of pretty, graceful things.

This widespread diffusion of art objects and of cultural knowledge, shallow though it might be, conformed with the religious developments of the day. It is interesting that between a violent earthquake at Pompeii in 62 A.D. and the final destruction of the city in 79, the residents had not bothered to repair a number of the temples dedicated to conventional deities, but the Temple of the Oriental Isis was immediately restored. It is clear that the purely ritualistic practices of the State cults were continuing to lose the interest of the citizens. They now demanded the systematic and emotional religions of the East, which were keyed to their appetites. Here they could "lose themselves," just as they could lose themselves in the sensuous rhetorical flourishes of the Flavian poets and in the security assured by hard-working and conscientious autocrats.

Chapter 35

THE ADOPTIVE EMPERORS

With the assassination of Domitian and the end of the
Flavian dynasty, the Romans seem to have sensed that there
was need of further modification in their method of acquiring a
prince. The Flavian dependence on primogeniture had given
the succession a regularity that had been an improvement on
the haphazard methods of the Julio-Claudians; but Domitian
died without an heir, and Domitian's autocratic tendencies
suggested that primogeniture was not a completely successful
answer to the problem. At this point, whether by design or by
chance, a form of succession was devised that combined the
virtues of regularity with an assurance of the personal and
administrative qualifications of the princes elevated. Four
emperors in succession now were followed on the throne by
"sons," but these sons were men whose competence for high
office had first been demonstrated and who then were legally
adopted by the ruling prince and designated as his successor to
the throne. This solution could satisfy the criticisms that the
Cynic and Stoic philosophers had levelled at the Flavians, and
during the experiment the empire flourished in an atmosphere
of internal harmony and material prosperity. Certainly there
was poverty during the period, there were uprisings, and there
were wars made more grievous by pestilence; but under the
adoptive emperors the Roman Empire reached its greatest
geographical extent, and peace and contentment were more
widespread over the Mediterranean world than ever before or
since.

NERVA (96–98 A.D.).   Marcus Cocceius Nerva, the man
chosen by the conspirators and by the Senate to succeed Domitian, was sixty-six years of age when he was called to the
throne. He came from a family of jurists and officials that had
been of moderate importance for a century; and his own gentle-

Caledonians

Inchtuthill

ANTONINUS' WALL

HADRIAN'S WALL

IRELAND

Mona

York

North Sea

Atlantic Ocean

WALES

Lincoln

BRITAIN
(43-7 A.D.)

DEVON

English Channel

Boulogne

Batavians

Elbe R.

Germans

Rhine R.

Chatti

Alamanni

LOWER GERMANY

BELGICA

LUGDUNENSIS

GAUL

UPPER GERMANY

(ADDED
74-89 A.D.)

Marcomanni

Sudeten
Mts.

Quadi

AQUITANIA

Lugdunum

BAETIA

The Alps

NORICUM

PANNONIA

NARBONENSIS

Po River

Aquileia

ILLYRICUM

LUSITANIA

(HITHER SPAIN)
TARRACONENSIS

Nemausus

Cremona

Forum
Julii

Corsica

Ravenna

DALMATIA

SPAIN

ITALY

Italica

BAETICA

Rome

Sardinia

Ostia

Misenum

Capri

Sicily

MAURETANIA
(42 A.D.)

Lambaesis

AFRICA

NUMIDIA

Mediterranean

Leptis Magna

——— Extent of the Empire

422

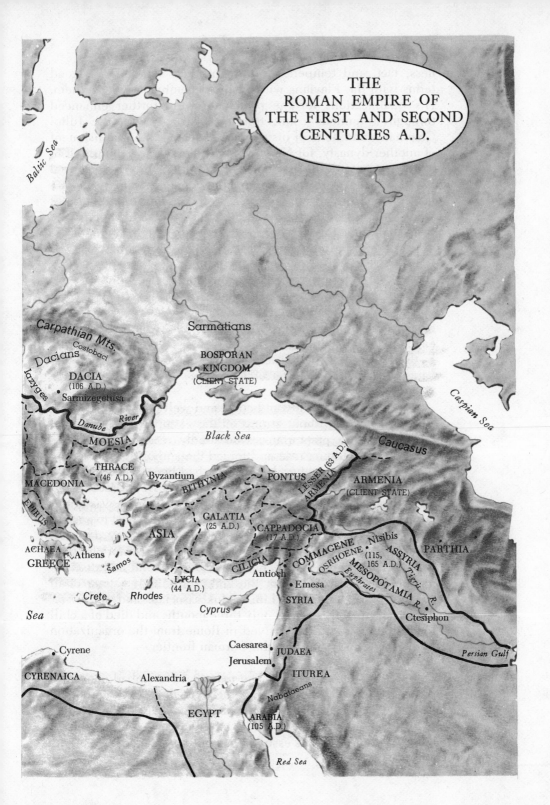

THE
ROMAN EMPIRE OF
THE FIRST AND SECOND
CENTURIES A.D.

Baltic Sea

Carpathian Mts.
Costobaci
Dacians
DACIA
(106 A.D.)
Sarmizegetusa
Iazyges
Danube River
MOESIA

Sarmatians

BOSPORAN
KINGDOM
(CLIENT STATE)

Caspian Sea

Black Sea

Caucasus

THRACE
(46 A.D.)
Byzantium
BITHYNIA
PONTUS
LESSER (63 A.D.)
ARMENIA
ARMENIA
(CLIENT STATE)

MACEDONIA
EPIRUS

GALATIA
(25 A.D.)
ASIA
CAPPADOCIA
(17 A.D.)
PARTHIA

ACHAEA
GREECE
Athens
Samos
Crete
Rhodes

CILICIA
LYCIA
(44 A.D.)
Antioch
Emesa
Cyprus
SYRIA
COMMAGENE
Nisibis
OSRHOENE
ASSYRIA
(115,
165 A.D.)
MESOPOTAMIA R.
Euphrates
Tigris R.
Ctesiphon

Sea

Cyrene
CYRENAICA
Alexandria

Caesarea
Jerusalem
JUDAEA
ITUREA
Nabataeans
EGYPT
ARABIA
(105 A.D.)

Persian Gulf

Red Sea

423

ness, tact, and temperate sentiments had kept him on good terms with the Flavians without his becoming servile to them. His qualifications for the principate were further enhanced through a tenuous connection by marriage with the Julio-Claudians; and none of his supporters feared the establishment of another dynasty, for Nerva was childless. Once confirmed in office Nerva, with the assistance of a group of elderly senatorial advisers, tried to restore the confidence and morale of the Roman people. He arranged for the purchase and distribution of lands for the poor of Rome. He initiated a program whereby the State undertook to assist in providing food and education for the poor children of Italian municipalities. This program, which the Romans called the alimentary institution, supplemented widespread efforts by private charity, and under succeeding emperors it expanded into one of the Empire's most distinctive services.[1] Nerva also saw to it that citizens now legally could leave legacies to municipalities throughout the Empire, and this encouraged the affluent to remember their home towns liberally in their wills. Furthermore, the new emperor discouraged any harassment or persecution of Domitian's toadies that revenge might prompt.

Nerva was certainly an honest and well-meaning man, but his regime was without strong military support. This became clear when the praetorians, who fondly recalled Domitian's liberality to soldiers, rose and forced the authorities to execute their own former prefect because he had been a leader in the conspiracy against Domitian. In this mutiny Nerva recognized the danger and the weakness of his position, and he was determined not to make the mistake of Galba. He decided to answer the challenge of the soldiers with an act that they dare not rebut. He straightway adopted as his son the governor of Upper Germany, Marcus Ulpius Trajan, a strong general and disciplinarian, and he arranged for the grant to the new Caesar of all the powers that marked him as his associate and successor. Nerva survived this act by only three months and died of a chill before his new son had arrived in Rome from the organization of the roads and camps on the German frontier.

TRAJAN (98–117 A.D.).   The man that Nerva had chosen to succeed him was the first provincial to come to the Roman throne. Trajan came from Italica in Spain, where his family had lived for generations, though its members had long held high office in Rome. He was essentially a military man, direct, metic-

[1]   For a more detailed description of the alimentary institution, see below, Chapter 40.

ulous, and efficient. But the deep sense of responsibility and the untiring care that he displayed in the civil administration of the Empire proved that Nerva's judgment of the man had been correct.

TRAJAN'S ADMINISTRATIVE POLICIES. In Italy, the alimentary institution founded by Nerva was expanded and put under the supervision of the road commissioners, because they were in close touch with the economic conditions of the districts of the peninsula. Provincial affairs were studied attentively. Nerva had been lax in the supervision of his provincial officials, and their carelessness or dishonesty had brought many towns close to economic chaos. Municipalities that were in financial difficulties were sent special curators to help them reestablish fiscal health. Some provinces, such as Bithynia, were bankrupt and received disinterested administrators to review, advise, and reorganize them. Bithynia had been one of the provinces administered by the Senate, but the Senate surrendered it temporarily to the emperor's good offices. Trajan appointed as his governor of Bithynia Pliny the Younger, and we fortunately have much of the correspondence between the emperor and his appointee. No project or problem of which Pliny wrote to Trajan was too petty for the appropriate research and a judicious reply. Where there were precedents, Trajan's file clerks in Rome discovered them, and the emperor directed that they be followed. Where no precedents could be found, Trajan suggested lines of conduct that were sensible and humane. The problems that Pliny faced ranged from the treatment of exposed infants and recalcitrant Christians to canals, collapsing bathhouses, and open sewers. Almost always they pivoted about the economic health of the area and a practical improvement of it.

TRAJAN'S BUILDING PROGRAM. Trajan's interest in the economic health and beautification of the Empire also led him to support an extensive building program. The port at Ostia was greatly improved: a completely safe hexagonal harbor supplemented Claudius' new port and sparked a rapid growth of that city as a great commercial center. The city of Rome itself was adorned with another new forum, this its most magnificent. Connected with it were markets and granaries, and in it stood the famous Column of Trajan, which carried in a spiral a pictorial account of the emperor's conquest of the Dacians. This remarkable frieze could be viewed in its entirety from the balconies of the libraries that Trajan built nearby. Another gift to Rome was a new aqueduct, the Aqua Traiana, which served the poor people that lived across the Tiber. Elsewhere roads and harbors were improved by the government, and private citizens were encouraged to adorn the Empire's cities with new buildings. The early second century A.D. marked the beginning of an era of rich men's generosity to their home towns, and the example set by the emperors stimulated everywhere an unprecedented rise of baths, gymnasia, theaters, aqueducts, temples, and charitable foundations.

TRAJAN'S FOREIGN POLICY: DACIA (101 – 106 A.D.).

As a soldier and a patriot Trajan resented reflections on Roman prestige. The annual subsidy of money and the loan of technicians that Domitian had agreed to furnish Decebalus, the king of Dacia, still rankled with the Romans, and Trajan was resolved to alter this arrangement in Rome's favor. We do not know the details leading up to hostilities, but by 101 A.D. Trajan was at war on the Dacian front. By 102 Trajan's invasion of Dacia had been so successful that Decebalus was forced to relinquish his very favorable position as a subsidized ally, return his Roman technicians, and become a client prince. The Dacian king was dissatisfied with the new arrangement, and there was evidence that he connived with the Parthians, in the hope that they would attack Rome from the East, while he himself was attacking Roman allies across the Danube. By 106, therefore, Trajan was back in Dacia, this time intent on creating a bastion north of the Danube that would ward off further forays into the Balkan provinces by trans-Danubian tribes. The country was overrun; its capital at Sarmizegethusa sacked; the king committed suicide; and the natives were so far extinguished that Roman settlers put a permanent mark on the country, as is shown by the resemblance of modern Roumanian to Italian.

TRAJAN IN THE EAST (114 – 117 A.D.).

From the income of the Dacian gold mines Trajan was able to sustain his many liberalities and his extensive building program. He could also afford to plan with some confidence a reassertion of Roman predominance in the East. Nero's[2] surrender of all but nominal control of Armenia was as offensive to Trajan's nationalism as Domitian's agreement with Decebalus had been. However, the emperor's attempt to apply his aggressive methods in the Orient proved less satisfactory than in Dacia. The policy of the Flavian emperors already had reduced most of Rome's client kingdoms in the East to the status of subjects, and in 105/6 A.D. the governor of Syria carried out Trajan's orders by annexing the lands of

[2]   See above, pp. 394 – 395.

the Nabataean Arabs as well. By this move the rich trade route from the Red Sea to the cities of Syria came completely under Roman control. Such an acquisition undoubtedly increased Roman revenues, but it was only a prelude to a showdown with Parthia. Without consulting Rome, Chosroes of Parthia had recently substituted one Parthian prince for another on the Armenian throne, contrary to the treaty established by Nero. Trajan reacted swiftly. He took the field in person, and in 114 A.D. he easily overran Armenia, which he thereupon turned into a province. Thus he designed to end the threat to Rome's eastern possessions from a Parthian Armenia.

The conquest of Armenia had been easy. At the time Chosroes of Parthia was distracted by dissent within his realm and could offer the Armenians little help. Now it was tempting to Trajan to take advantage of the Parthian's embarrassment and to go farther. In 115, therefore, Trajan's forces swept down through the Tigris and Euphrates valleys without strong opposition, captured the Parthian capital of Ctesiphon, and continued to the head of the Persian Gulf at Spasinu Charax, another important terminus of the trade route by sea from India. Trajan thereupon organized the occupied territory into two new Roman provinces, Assyria and Mesopotamia. However, it soon became clear that the Tigris and Euphrates valleys had merely been overrun, not conquered. Serious disturbances arose to the rear, and the emperor was forced to fight his way back toward Syria and recover lost ground.

Trajan's preoccupation with his Parthian campaign and the pacification of the new provinces afforded the opportunity for a new rebellion by the Jews, discontented since their conquest and dispersion by Titus in 70 A.D. In 115 and 116 A.D. the Jews of Cyrene and Cyprus rose and annihilated their Greek neighbors, Alexandria barely held its own, and even recently crushed Judaea was disaffected. Order was finally restored in 117, partly because Trajan commissioned his capable and uncompromising Moorish general, Lusius Quietus, to stamp out the revolt. By this time, however, the strain of the emperor's many campaigns and constant administrative duties began to tell on his heart. A stroke, complicated by dropsy, finally convinced him that he must return home in the summer of 117 A.D. He left the command in the East in the hands of his relative and nephew by marriage, Aelius Hadrian, but expired on the road in August in the province of Cilicia.

HADRIAN (117–138 A.D.).   Trajan's fairness, candor, hard work, and heroic accomplishments made him a Roman ideal, the *optimus princeps* (best of princes). The very tardiness of his decision to adopt Hadrian as his son and successor until a few days before his death perhaps reflects some uneasiness in his mind. Trajan knew and had proved that Hadrian was a man of great capabilities, yet he also knew that his successor was utterly different from himself, and he felt very uncertain as to how the Empire would fare under this new kind of man. Hadrian was a distant relative of Trajan, was also a Spaniard, and was married to the emperor's grandniece. He had also been Trajan's ward and had been given thorough training in many parts of the Empire by his guardian before his adoption and accession. Hadrian's service under Trajan had given him a good knowledge of Roman affairs and of the Empire's economy. His experience convinced him that Rome did not need and could not afford the policy of conquest and expansion initiated by Trajan. He judged not only that the financial cost was too great, but also that deep involvement with the cultures of the East would present grave dangers to Hellenic culture and its Roman synthesis to which he was deeply committed. Rome, he believed, must turn to internal development, must foster its economy, and must preserve and nourish its own cultural heritage.

The new emperor immediately put his policies to work. Hadrian finished putting down the Jewish insurrection with all severity, for that endangered the welfare of the eastern provinces; but he made it clear that Rome would not waste its substance on the bottomless East. A king was given back to Armenia, the puppet that Trajan had set up in Parthia was withdrawn, and the troops were quietly removed from Trajan's new provinces in the Mesopotamian valley. These were brave acts for a new ruler to dare, for they were bound to be unpopular with the jingoists that had idolized Trajan. His initial tasks were made more difficult than need be because he also had to convince his critics that he had nothing to do with the conviction and execution for treason of four men of consular rank at the very beginning of his reign. Actually the trial and sentence had been the work of the Senate itself before Hadrian's return and without his consent. The condemned men all had been close advisers of Trajan and expansionists who disapproved of Hadrian's pacifistic policy, and they were accused of planning the new emperor's assassination.

Hadrian showed that he could be politic and tactful, however, by returning to Rome to apologize to the senators for having assumed the reins of government before the Senate could be consulted. Once in Rome, he took his seat in the Senate, treated that body with all deference, and swore that during his principate no senator would be tried and condemned for any

428

wrongdoing except by the Senate itself. To show his concern for the poor and unfortunate of the Empire, he cancelled all debts to the treasury and had the records of them burned; and in Italy he extended the alimentary institution.

THE TRAVELS OF HADRIAN.   Hadrian's energy and enthusiasm would not allow him to remain quietly in Rome to administer the Empire from a palace. He felt that he must go to his subjects and talk with them if he were to gauge correctly what the Empire needed. He was absent from Rome on extensive tours of the provinces from 121 to 126 A.D., and again from 129 to 132. Everywhere he was eager to look, listen, advise, and assist. Everything interested him; and wherever he went projects flowered. There were new schools, public buildings, roads, and harbors; oratory flourished; and the public morale reached its highest point in Roman history. He fostered the decoration of the world with some of its most lavish construction, and was himself an amateur architect. In Rome the Temple of Venus and Rome and the Pantheon testify to his competence and daring as a designer; and his great sprawling villa at nearby Tivoli, with its complexes of buildings named for favorite spots enjoyed in his travels, reflects the flamboyance and whimsy of his spirit.

HADRIAN'S MILITARY POLICY.   Hadrian's intent was not merely to preserve the peace, but to insure it by the creation of unmistakable frontiers, ready defenses, and an army with high morale. Walls were constructed along some of the frontiers to delay invaders and discourage infiltration. The most famous of these is the wall between the Tyne and Solway Firth in Britain, but there were others, in Germany for instance. Troops were moved up to the very frontiers from their previous garrisons in the interior, and their officers were encouraged to resort to local recruitment. With this policy Hadrian hoped to increase the enthusiasm and patriotism of the defense, the willingness to serve, and the ease of settlement at the time of discharge. What he contemplated was a truly imperial army to defend its Empire. On his travels he moved from camp to camp, sharing in the soldiers' labors, watching and criticizing maneuvers, and suggesting improvements. Military morale was never higher. Hadrian realized that there was a danger that an army recruited for local service might lapse into being merely a frontier militia. To counteract this tendency he issued orders that the soldiers neither build luxurious quarters nor till the soil; and the vigor of his administration kept the troops in excellent condition. Under less energetic emperors there was a danger that Hadrian's

policies might result in a relaxation of military prepared-
ness, as the domesticity of local troops was allowed to increase. But during his reign Hadrian's military posture was so
much respected that he had to engage in only one serious campaign. This once more was caused by a revolt of the Jews, who
strenuously objected to Hadrian's plan to build a new city,
Aelia Capitolina, on the site of Jerusalem, which had been
destroyed by Titus. The Jews' bitter resistance was increased
by Hadrian's plan to build a Temple of Jove where the Temple
of Jehovah once had been, and by his edict forbidding the
practice of circumcision, which he considered inhumane. The
struggle (132–134 A.D.) was so fanatical and ferocious that the
Jews of Palestine were practically exterminated, and the dispersion begun by Titus was nearly completed.

HADRIAN AND THE LAW.   Since Hadrian was unable to
keep in close touch with the whole Senate during his travels, he
depended to a large degree on the assistance of a small circle of
advisers, his *consilium*, which was able to travel with him.
Hadrian's *consilium* included some of the great jurisprudents of
the day, and to this age belong brilliant advances in Roman civil
law. Hadrian himself favored humane and equitable interpretations of the law. His own legal decisions have a wide range,
from the abatement of taxes in lean years and the establishment
of fair maximum prices in hard times, to the encouragement of
the cultivation of wastelands and the amelioration of the con-
straints placed upon soldiers and slaves. The jurists that accompanied him on his travels were constantly available for advice.
One of them, Salvius Julianus, Hadrian made his praetorian
prefect, and he also gave to him the commission to codify and
standardize the praetors' edicts, which had been handed down,
with modifications, for centuries. Since the praetors' edicts had
itemized the conditions under which a citizen was allowed to
initiate a suit at law, Hadrian's codification ensured a stabilized
legal procedure for all. In Italy he made the receipt of justice
easier by the appointment of four *juridici*, men of consular rank
who would handle legal cases that arose too far from Rome for
the contestants easily to appear in court there.

HADRIAN AND THE SENATE.   While the emperor was revered by most of his subjects, the senators showed an increasing irritation and resentment at a man whom they had never
understood or completely trusted. They felt neglected because
he was so often absent on his tours of inspection of the Empire.
They were jealous of the members of the *consilium*, who could

travel with the prince and participate in his important decisions. Some of the members of the *consilium* were equestrians, and this also annoyed the senators. Hadrian had increased the use of equestrians in the imperial administration, and now they fully replaced the imperial freedmen at the head of the bureaus. Hadrian's policy recognized that the affairs of state were the concern of the people, and not merely of the imperial household; and it further recognized the longstanding reputation of the equestrian businessmen for efficiency. This very efficiency, however, meant further encroachments on the senatorial preserve by the imperial administration. Though the *juridici* of Italy were of consular rank, they were nominated by the emperor; and the Senate was sensitive about this, for the administration of Italy had been considered its own peculiar task. Relations between Hadrian and the senators became worse in his later years, when the emperor suffered from a long and extremely painful illness and tended to become impatient or less tactful in handling senatorial sensitivities. Hadrian's senatorial critics were frustrated by this man who insisted on seeing all, knowing all, touching all, and suffering all, yet whose motives, inner life, and real opinions they could not fathom. They concluded, of course, that he was mad.

Hadrian is indeed not an easy man to understand. He was perhaps the most versatile and most gifted Roman since Caesar. He sought to encompass all things, and yet somehow he remained untouched himself. He loved only once, a Bithynian youth of Greek descent named Antinous. His grief was terrible when the youth committed suicide because he believed that in some magic way he thus ensured the emperor's safety. But normally his detachment from the world of which he was such a responsible and active part, his detachment even from himself, frightened men of a more conventional nature. This attitude of aesthetic aloofness, of a half-playful observation of the world and of himself from a distance, stayed with him to the end, so that on his very deathbed he could compose the famous lines:

> O happy little wandering soul,
> My body's partisan and guest,
> To what far land do you now go,
> Pale and cold and naked so?
> And not a sign of wonted jest!

Throughout his career Hadrian proved himself a servant of the people; but also he was their master, for he was as free of them and their empty vanities as he was of himself.

THE SUCCESSION.   Hadrian first chose as his adopted son
and successor Lucius Ceionius Commodus, whose qualifications certainly were not apparent to others. Critics cited the
choice as a sure sign of the emperor's madness, but that judgment was probably well tinged with disappointed jealousy, for
there is no doubt of the excellence of his second choice after
Commodus' untimely death. Hadrian tried to arrange for the
succession for the next two generations, as Augustus had done
in the case of Tiberius and Germanicus. As his own successor
he adopted Titus Aurelius Antoninus, a wealthy and distinguished member of his *consilium* and a native of Nemausus in
Gaul. He also caused Antoninus to adopt two young men as his
sons and potential successors in the next generation: Lucius
Verus, son of the dead Commodus, and Marcus Annius Verus,
nephew of Antoninus and the youth that eventually became
Emperor Marcus Aurelius.

ANTONINUS PIUS (138–161 A.D.).   Antoninus in the very first
days of his reign earned his sobriquet "Pius" by insisting on the
honors due to Hadrian after his death, despite the bad humor of
the Senate. Further, he continued Hadrian's peaceful policies,
though he did so without Hadrian's vigor; he saved money by
remaining in Italy and trying to supervise the Empire from a
distance. The Senate was mollified by his constant attention to
it and by the withdrawal of the *juridici* from Italy. The administration of the law was everywhere equitable. The frontiers
were further strengthened by the establishment of a number of
advanced positions to create buffer zones, as the Antonine Wall
did in Britain and various advanced fortresses did along the
frontier in Germany. The alimentary institution continued to
expand in Italy; and in Rome, in honor of his wife Faustina, he
established a special fund for poor girls of the city, the *puellae
Faustinianae.* Peace throughout the Empire was but seldom
broken.

However, the inactivity of this good, just, and revered man
meant trouble for his successor. The pacifistic policy of Hadrian
had been successful partly because it had been administered by
an alert establishment; but, when it was followed by the less
energetic Antoninus, there was a temptation for the hard-
pressed or the ambitious across the frontiers to feel that their
time was nearly ripe to feed upon Roman wealth and prosperity. The prestige established among the barbarians by Trajan's
conquests and Hadrian's vigor stood Antoninus in good stead
and during his lifetime held the deluge back—we hear of em-

bassies and deference to him from far and near, even from China—but at his death the dam broke.

MARCUS AURELIUS (161–180 A.D.).   Marcus Aurelius was early marked out as Antoninus' favorite for the succession by the offices that he held, by his marriage, and by his close association with the emperor. In 139 A.D. he was named a Caesar (the title then used to indicate the heir to the throne); in 145 he was given the emperor's daughter, the younger Faustina, in marriage. He held the consulship three times; and he was granted the tribunician power and the *imperium* in 146. He was to need his long apprenticeship.

At the death of Antoninus Pius, Marcus took up the labors of a prince dutifully and reluctantly. At the outset he insisted on associating with himself his adoptive brother, Lucius Verus, as his co-regent and fellow Augustus (the title reserved for reigning princes). This act conformed to Marcus' characteristic self-effacement and affection for his family. It also was prophetic, for it foreshadowed the increasing need for more than one man to carry the burden of government. Had Verus been more capable, he would indeed have been useful in the troubled times ahead; and though Verus actually proved a disappointment, Marcus still tried to use him wherever possible.

Marcus Aurelius had been since his youth a devoted student and a practicing Stoic. His philosophical training appeared everywhere in his public life, in a cheerless sufferance of duty, tasks, folly, and disaster. All were accepted calmly and righteously:

> O World, whatever suits you suits me. Nothing that is seasonable for you can be untimely or out-of-date for me. Whatever, O Nature, you bring, I accept: from you are all things, in you are all things, and all things return to you.
> No harm comes to a stone when it returns to earth after it has been thrown up, nor good in having been thrown up.

THE PARTHIAN WAR (162–166 A.D.) AND THE PLAGUE. Marcus had good need for such comfort as Stoicism afforded, for during his reign disaster followed disaster. Once more a Parthian king nominated his own candidate for the Armenian throne, declared war, and invaded the country. Marcus devised the strategy to repel the attack, but sent his imperial brother Verus with a spate of competent generals to reestablish Roman authority. The eastern legions appear to have been demoralized by their decades of inactivity under Antoninus, and Verus proved to be an indifferent leader; but the generals, especially Avidius Cassius, whipped the troops into shape, recovered Armenia by 163 A.D., and by early 166 the armies had taken the Parthian capital of Ctesiphon.

In 165, however, the Roman soldiers had contracted a plague in Mesopotamia, and this they brought back with them to the West. While the imperial brothers were celebrating their triumph over the Parthians, the people had begun to die like flies, and it is estimated that the provinces lost up to one-third of their populations.

WARS ON THE NORTHERN FRONTIERS. (167–180 A.D.).
While the Roman world reeled for fifteen years under the ravages of the plague, the northern barbarians took advantage of the disaster and poured across the borders. One horde reached Aquileia at the northern end of the Adriatic, another Eleusis in the suburbs of Athens. The two Augusti hurried north, where in 169 A.D. Verus, who for eight years had proved more of a burden than a help, providentially died of apoplexy. The fighting continued almost continuously from 167 to 175 all along the Rhine and Danube, with fresh German tribes probing first here and then there and only slowly being pressed back by the emperor and his generals. Little by little the persistence of the Germans convinced Marcus that Trajan had been right in establishing Dacia as a buffer with excellent frontiers by which the Balkans could be protected. He came to believe that similarly the lands of the Marcomanni and of the Quadi must be added to the Empire as provinces so that the sweep of the Carpathian and Sudeten mountains would make a northern bulwark. Campaign followed campaign against Quadi, Marcomanni, Costoboci, and Sarmatians, and final success seemed close when in 175 A.D. word came of a revolt by Avidius Cassius, the emperor's most successful general in the East.

Cassius had held almost the whole East for the emperor during the years of critical struggle in the North. Now in 175 A.D. it appears that he had been deceived by a false report of Marcus' death. Thereupon he took steps to attain for himself the leadership of the Romans, a position that he believed that he deserved in preference to Marcus' adolescent son and apparent heir, Commodus. As a native Syrian with great power in his own part of the Empire, Cassius at once drew wide support. When it became known that Marcus was indeed still alive, it was too late to draw back. However, the revolt had now lost its point, and Cassius was soon killed by one of his own centurions. Still, the impetus in the drive to the North had been lost, and the emperor felt it necessary to visit the East to restore confidence and harmony there. By 178 A.D., however, renewed unrest in the North had brought Marcus back to the Danube and beyond. Once more he pressed toward the goal of a shorter and improved northern frontier, and by the end of the campaigning season of 179 A.D. success was again nearly in sight — only one more campaign was thought to be needed. But once again the Roman dream of a strong northern frontier, a dream shared by Augustus, Trajan, and Marcus, was foiled, this time by the emperor's death in March 180 A.D. Commodus, his son and successor, abandoned the project.

MARCUS' DOMESTIC POLICIES.   Under Marcus Aurelius the Roman economy was seriously strained by the high costs of war and by the decrease of income from a plague-ridden empire. To finance his northern campaigns Marcus held a public auction of the treasures amassed over centuries by the emperors — art objects, dinnerware, furnishings, even the empress' gold-embroidered gowns·were sold. He plainly told the troops, some of whom sought an increase in pay, that any increase would have to come from the hides of their kinsmen. Slaves, gladiators, and mercenaries were pressed into service for the German wars; and after his victories in the North Marcus transferred whole barbarian peoples to the provinces and even to Italy to replace the losses to the plague, to cultivate abandoned fields, and to furnish future troops. In Italy the pressure of judicial work caused the emperor to increase the number of court days and to reestablish the *juridici*, who had contributed to Hadrian's unpopularity. But through it all he contrived to retain the respect, admiration, and support of the people by his tact, modesty, and the humanity of his measures. In the Senate he disported himself as an ordinary senator, and he referred to that body many high matters of state. The equestrians were treated with care; and the food and entertainment of the people still were provided. Taxes were remitted in hard times; further curators were appointed to assist the municipalities in the improvement of their management of finance; and guardians were assigned to administer, under public scrutiny, the estates of young men between puberty and twenty-five years of age.

THE SUCCESSION.   Marcus' public acts and personal deportment bespeak a just and conscientious man. But it is doubtful that his Stoicism improved his judgment of character as much as it did his sense of justice. His warm and apparently sincere appreciation of the virtues of Lucius Verus, Faustina,

435

and his children as expressed in his *Meditations* does not inspire confidence, for Verus was incompetent, Faustina probably unfaithful, and his children mediocre and worse. Nor are we reassured by his grant of the consulship to his son Commodus, when the youth was only sixteen. True, this honor followed the collapse of Avidius Cassius' revolt, and the move was perhaps dictated by a desire to begin making provisions for the future and to discourage irresponsible ambitions among other generals. Before he was eighteen, however, Commodus was further endowed with the tribunician power and the title "Augustus." As Verus had been, so Commodus now was legally Marcus' co-ruler; but Commodus did not represent, any more than Verus did, that choice of "the best" that had graced and benefited the second century A.D. Marcus' elevation of his son ensured a succession free from internal dispute, but it certainly did nothing to improve that young man's dubious character, nor did it provide for the future happiness of the Roman people.

THE TWO SIDES OF THE SECOND CENTURY A.D.   Of the second century A.D. Edward Gibbon said,

> If a man were called to fix the period in the history of the world, during which the condition of the human race was most happy and prosperous, he would, without hesitation, name that which elapsed from the death of Domitian to the accession of Commodus.

The judgment is famous and the thesis attractive, but already our account of the age shows a need for cautious qualification. Undoubtedly during that era many men lived happy, uneventful, protected lives; that was the explicit ideal of Antoninus Pius for himself and for his people. For the earlier part of the period at least the municipalities generally were prosperous. The rich adorned them with buildings, taxes amounted perhaps to only about one-tenth of income, and the central government was benevolent. There was much pleasant villa life, and the upper and middle classes at least led comfortable existences. The Senate saw its best man chosen to be the leading citizen, and it found itself courted, consulted, and respected. However, all these things had a price. The Senate increasingly reflected the character and policy of the emperor and grew more and more dependent on him, while the officials that he appointed constantly expanded their spheres of authority at the expense of the old republican magistrates. The municipalities found it easy to spend their money foolishly with the expectation that they would be saved from bankruptcy by the central government, and their responsibility was thus eroded. Furthermore, the dependence of the municipalities on the generosity of their own wealthy classes was dangerous, for when hard times came the upper classes would have to seek paid employment with the emperor rather than give their services gratis to their home places, and the towns would find themselves with no reserves. The villas of the countryside were lovely, but there were still the tenement districts in the cities, and their inhabitants became constantly more mongrelized, useless, and parasitic. Even the steps taken by the emperors for the sake of humanity and efficiency—whether providing state guardians for youths or insisting on the registration of birth certificates with the bureaus—constituted an increasing intrusion by the central government into the citizens' privacy. A world directed by a providentially inspired ruler became centralized, standardized, sober, and gray.

INTELLECTUAL LIFE. GREEK LITERATURE.   The material comfort of the second century A.D. had another unhappy companion—a good deal of mental stagnation. We can speak with some authority, for the era has left a large amount of literature in both Greek and Latin. Peace and prosperity had led to much erudition and much dilettantism, but only rarely to genius. The Hellenism of a number of the emperors had encouraged a revival of literary productivity in Greek, most of it in prose and heavily adorned with the rhetoric that plagued all of late Mediterranean culture. The prevalence of the Greek language throughout the Empire is illustrated not only by the large number of Greek literary men that were produced, but also by the language of the Gospels and other documents of the early Christians, and by the fact that Emperor Marcus Aurelius himself wrote his *Meditations,* or *Thoughts to Himself* in Greek.

Aelius Aristides (117?–*ca.* 190 A.D.) composed works on rhetoric in Greek and he has left us fifty-five orations. One of them is an oration on the greatness of Rome. It was delivered in Rome during the principate of Antoninus Pius and glorifies the empire as a condominium of cities under the leadership of Rome. His teacher was the famous orator Herodes Atticus (*ca.* 101–177 A.D.), whose reputation seems to have been due as much to his wealth and public benefactions as to his genius. An older contemporary, Dio Chrysostom (*ca.* 50–115 A.D.), an intimate of Nerva and Trajan, has left a collection of orations in the styles of Plato and Demosthenes which are really little essays on moral and political issues.

Plutarch (*ca.* 46–*ca.* 120 A.D.) was a remarkable man from

Chaeronea in Greece who produced an enormous amount of literature, mostly designed to help men become good. He had been one of Hadrian's teachers, and Trajan awarded him consular rank. He chose thereafter to retire to his native town and participate in local affairs while devoting himself to his writing. His most famous work is his *Parallel Lives of Noble Greeks and Romans*. These lives are conceived not so much as biography as lessons to his readers on proper and improper conduct. But they are lively and sympathetic and they often fill sizable gaps in our historical information. They have been favorite reading for centuries. His other works are essays on the most diverse subjects: about half have to do with moral issues, but many are concerned with philosophical, literary, religious, and antiquarian matters.

Pausanias took Herodotus as his model in an *Itinerary of Greece* in ten books. The work is a mine of information on the art and architecture of Greece, and it is marked by numerous digressions on cults, myths, and folklore. A contemporary historian was Arrian of Bithynia (*ca.* 95–175 A.D.), who modelled his works on Xenophon. He has left us our best account of Alexander the Great, for he found his materials in such excellent sources as Aristobulus and Ptolemy. However, he falls far short of his model, Xenophon, in charm. He also wrote a useful account of the coasts of the Black Sea, and he collected the discourses and sayings of Epictetus, a Stoic philosopher and ex-slave who lived from the time of Nero to Antoninus Pius. Such sermons by Stoics and Cynics continued to be popular, for they satisfied some of the emotional needs and needs for guidance that are served in the modern Western world by its evangelists and syndicated columns in the press. Another second-century A.D. historian was an Egyptian, Appian of Alexandria (*ca.* 90–160 A.D.), who became a civil servant in Rome. He thoroughly appreciated the advantages of life under the emperors as compared to the dangers and uncertainties of the Republic. His *Roman History* was an account of the wars of the Roman people that led to the unification of the Mediterranean world, and his account of the wars is for the most part arranged by the various peoples that the Romans conquered (*The Spanish Wars, Illyrian Wars, Carthaginian Wars*, etc.). One section, *The Civil Wars*, is particularly important, for Appian's antipathy for the Republic led him to use historical sources that otherwise have not survived and that give us an unorthodox and often superior view of the Late Republic.

One very bright spot in this catalogue of uninspired competence is furnished by Lucian of Samosata (*ca.* 120–180 A.D.).

438

His satirical sketches, mostly in dialogue form, poke fun at the pomposities, follies, addled thinking, and frauds of his age. Whether he is toying with theological fuzziness or the pretentiousness of historians, he is fresh and lively, though his cynical wit seldom offers constructive alternatives to the shortcomings that he mocks.

The two outstanding scientists of the day, Ptolemy of Alexandria and Galen of Pergamum (129–199 A.D.), also were Greek. Ptolemy's *Geography* was a work on scientific map-making that reveals the immense advances in that field by the Greeks; his *Astronomy*, though geocentric, continued to be the best description of observed astral movements until the researches of the Renaissance; and his work in spherical trigonometry remains the basis of the modern discipline. Galen's competence as a physician and physiologist called him to Rome and to Marcus Aurelius' service. While a busy practitioner, he also found time to dissect, experiment, observe, and report. His work in medicine and physiology remained authoritative until the Renaissance and the work of Harvey, which demonstrated Galen's errors in regard to the circulation of the blood. Some of his errors were due to the analogies that he drew from the use of monkeys and other animals for dissection rather than humans. Despite a remarkably busy public career, Galen somehow found time to write nearly one hundred volumes, not only on anatomy, physiology, and therapy, but also on a wide variety of philosophical and cultural subjects.

LATIN AUTHORS.   Latin literature had less to offer than the Greek, though one of its figures, Cornelius Tacitus (*ca.* 54–117 A.D.), stands head and shoulders above all others. Tacitus had the normal rhetorical education, but he made rhetoric his servant, not his master. His *Annals* and *Histories* (though each now is fragmented) covered Roman history from the death of Augustus to that of Domitian. His purpose was moral, his material largely political, but his artistry was so great that the reader's interest never flags through a parade of iniquities by princes and of martyrdoms by the Senate. The anti-monarchial color of his work apparently stems from the Stoic opposition under the Flavians, during whose rule he was an official, even though he composed his work in the happier days of Nerva and Trajan. His claims of fairness toward the Julio-Claudians must therefore be treated with some care—it is due to his magnificent but distorted portrait of Tiberius that the excellence of that emperor's reign went long unrecognized.

Almost equally important is the satirist Juvenal (*ca.*

47–127 A.D.). While his rhetorical training was even more pervasive than that of Tacitus, the fire of his indignation (whether real or feigned) at the corruption of contemporary Rome, at the perils of city life, at the tyranny of Domitian, the wiles of womenfolk and foreigners—whether Greek, Syrian, or Egyptian—and at the whole hodge-podge of human iniquity and folly has made him favorite reading. He was the very model of satire for Augustan England.

The Lives of the Caesars by Suetonius Tranquillus are gossipy and uninhibited and have been a ready source of anecdotes. He was a secretary of state for a while under Hadrian with access to the archives, and he was therefore able to preserve and report primary sources of great interest. Another stockpile of information of all sorts is furnished by the *Attic Nights* of Aulus Gellius (*ca.* 123–169 A.D.). Gellius acquired the habit of taking notes while a university student in Athens, and he never lost it. Throughout his life he diligently jotted down interesting extracts from at least 275 ancient authors, many of whom otherwise would have been lost. His notes contain material on subjects as diverse as the meaning of ancient words and rites, and the size of Hercules' feet. This muddle of exotic and undigested facts perhaps reflects as well as anything does the shallow glitter and fashionable chitchat of the age that Gellius represented.

The second century A.D. produced two famous letter-writers, Pliny the Younger and Marcus Cornelius Fronto. Pliny was Trajan's fussy but conscientious governor of Bithynia, whose endless appeals to the emperor for advice have told us so much about provincial administration and imperial paternalism. Pliny was self-consciously writing his letters with an eye to publication, in emulation of the great Cicero. The letters reveal the better side of a cultured and humane society, and their Latin is clear and honest. Fronto was the tutor of Lucius Verus and Marcus Aurelius. His love of archaisms and of quaint effects led him to borrow some of his language from writers of the Early Republic, but his letters, which are filled with platitudes and concern for the health of the imperial family, are not impressive.

Fronto was an African, and from Africa also came a greater and more original writer, Lucius Apuleius (*ca.* 130 A.D.–?). He belongs with the select group of Petronius and Lucian, whose works were based on the present and looked to the future rather than glorifying or aping the past. Apuleius' Latin was florid and sometimes difficult, but it was the Latin that was rising from the speech of soldiers and provincials and the Latin that was to create the vulgar tongues of Europe. His principal work, *The Metamorphoses*, more commonly called *The Golden Ass*, is chiefly concerned with the odyssey of a young man named Lucius, who was turned into the shape of an ass after some ill-advised experiments in magic. He ultimately was returned to human shape through the intercession of the goddess Isis, of whom he became a devotee. The work contains all the astonishing wealth of folklore, magic, religion, bawdry, and unaffected wonder that permeated the masses, but were unknown to Apuleius' contemporaries of the civilized court in Rome.

SIGNS OF ADVANCED CIVILIZATION. Educational opportunities all over the Empire were increased under the adoptive emperors. Pliny testifies to the prevalence of public schools in many places as well as of private endowments for that purpose. And the emperors of the second century A.D. followed Vespasian's example in the increase of endowed professorial chairs in the great cities. Benefits for teachers also seem, at least by the time of Hadrian, to have included exemption from all taxes. The erection of libraries in many towns also increased the opportunities for self-education. More inhabitants of the Roman world than ever before, then, received some education. However, the urge to reach more and more people, no matter how insensible or unprepared they might be, made for standardization and popularization rather than for first-rate literary work.

The same tendencies appeared in the art and architecture of the period. There the worship of ancient art forms, which ordinary people could understand and with which they felt comfortable, led to almost as many archaisms as were found in the studied imitations of the past in the writings of Pliny, Arrian, Fronto, or Pausanias. Only now and then is there a glimpse of a fresh approach, as in the Column of Trajan, or of a feeling for mass, space, and function, as in some of the work of Hadrian. But even in the days of as imaginative a man as Hadrian, work in art and architecture was standardized, reflecting the Graeco-Roman synthesis, and the buildings tended to be large rather than creative. There is a megalomania that is characteristic of advanced civilizations, which leads its participants to repeat their previously successful forms of architecture simply on a larger and larger scale and to boast of size and quantity rather than of excellence and quality. This characteristic was now beginning to appear in Rome: Trajan built the biggest forum, Hadrian the biggest temple. And the standardization of art forms, when it reached the frontier provinces, was copied and vulgarized by the new and poorly assimilated provincials both in their buildings and in their humbler expressions of taste, in pots and pans and headstones. Little by little, as Graeco-Roman culture sifted downward, the barbaric began to show through the thin Hellenic veneer that popular education had given the Mediterranean world.

REGULARIZATION OF THE LAW.   The passion for organization and standardization found its way also into the field of law. The prince, as any other official might, long had issued edicts because he had the *imperium*. By the second century A.D. not only his edicts, but also his instructions to officials, his replies to queries, and his letters were carefully catalogued and used with the force of law in later decisions. Further, although decrees of the Senate now also had the force of laws, they were really but another mask for the emperor's power; for he discussed matters with his *consilium* and reported to the Senate, which ratified his wishes without protest. This development, whereby the prince became a source of law, was defended on the ground that at his accession he was delegated by the people to exercise their power. The same reasoning explained his appearance as the final court of appeal, replacing the ancient appeal to the people in the now moribund assemblies. The emperor's powers of appeal, his general powers to supervise the courts, and his appointment of outstanding jurists to his *consilium* slowly gathered together the judicial processes of the Empire and centralized them in the emperor. The desire for judicial orderliness had led Hadrian to authorize Julian's codification of the praetors' edicts, so that thereafter the principles of civil law would be interpreted by specialists rather than handled by cultured amateurs, which the praetors had been. Similar forces during the second century A.D. led to the replacement of the criminal courts instituted by Sulla, with their large juries of ordinary citizens, by extraordinary courts headed at first by the emperor and later by his delegates, who had specialized training. It is also a matter of note that during this century one of the world's greatest textbooks, *The Institutes of Roman Law* by the lawyer Gaius, presented the essentials of civil law in a methodical and lucid manner.

TENDENCIES AND DEVELOPMENTS IN RELIGION.   The civilization and the imperial government of the second century A.D. provided the people with benefits and security undreamed of before. There was an institution to care for poor children, education for young and old, good roads, frequent festivals and holidays, and fair taxation. One could be sure to find roughly the same facilities for bathing, exercise, and entertainment in any town from Britain to Cyrene; and the standardized justice of the emperor was dispensed with equal hand from Spain to Bithynia. There were strong defensive forces on the frontiers; and few of the cities of the interior could as yet imagine any real peril from the barbarians now stirring on the other side of those frontiers. This world seemed to be secure; but what of the next? As the imperial government shouldered more and more social responsibility, and almost every phase of life and culture became stereotyped and organized, more men began to worry about themselves, about their immortal souls. They turned in ever greater numbers to the Oriental cults that offered them individual attention, even to individual immortality. The three creeds that drew the most energetic and dedicated followers were Christianity, the Cult of Isis, and Mithraism.

Mithraism, which was based on the worship of the God of Light, was of Persian origin and had at first been largely confined to the eastern provinces. With the second century A.D., however, the Mithraia, or special chapels of the followers of Mithras, began to appear in quantities in the West. According to his followers, in prehistoric times Mithras had been a heroic contestant with the powers of darkness. Not only did he create for humanity most of man's material blessings, but he also became an intercessor for man before the great God of Light, Ahuramazda. After his death Mithras still served as a friend of men, acting as a judge of their souls. Man's soul was believed to have descended from heaven at birth and to have acquired impurities as it descended. Mithraism offered its devotees seven stages of initiation which assisted the souls to return expeditiously to heaven after death. Mithraism was essentially a strenuous and masculine faith and was especially attractive to soldiers, who spread it all over the world.

More emotional, perhaps, was the Cult of Isis. Isis was the sister of Osiris, who had been killed by the wicked Set, and she had assisted in his resurrection. It was she who helped Lucius, in *The Golden Ass*, to resume human shape, and Apuleius gives us an attractive account of some of the cult's practices and pageantry. The followers of Isis believed that, if they were initiated in her cult and received the prescribed baptism of water, they would spend eternity in a heavenly paradise where Osiris ruled.

Both Mithraism and the Cult of Isis lent some of their practices and rites to the Christians, who also were beginning to expand rapidly, especially among the poor and the Orientals.[3] Since Nero's day this sect had been suspect, not on religious grounds, for the Romans were tolerant there, but on political ones. This was because the Christians evaded the formal religious act of burning incense before the emperor's statue, an act that accompanied public activity and signified loyalty to the regime; and this evasion was considered subversive and dangerous. While most of the emperors during the second century A.D. did not specifically seek the Christians out, and they discouraged anonymous informers—Trajan wrote to Pliny that the use of such informers was "contrary to the spirit of the age"—still, willful disobedience was punished. The community of interest and of danger that the government's policy brought to all Christians tended to force the hitherto scattered and independent churches into a more highly organized and authoritarian structure. Their earlier almost communistic government gave way to the development of a specialized clergy. The congregations were led by presbyters, who in turn were supervised by bishops; and the bishops submitted to the authority of metropolitans, who were prelates generally residing in the most important cities. While the development of this hierarchical structure was giving the Church solidity and discipline on a national scale, the Christians' apologists were learning to use the language of Hellenic philosophy so that they could make their message more intelligible and more palatable to men with the Graeco-Roman heritage.

The task of the Christians was made easier by the intellectual tolerance of the day. The followers of the various philosophical sects borrowed so freely from one another that some of them were hardly distinguishable—even the Stoic Marcus Aurelius asked for a copy of the Epicurean Lucretius so that he could "uplift his spirit." And religious sectarians were equally eager to identify the various national gods as but manifestations of a universal deity. These syncretic tendencies, combined with the mass hunger for eternal life, during the second century A.D. were paving the way for the general acceptance of some evangelical and monotheistic doctrine.

[3] For a more detailed account of Mithraism, the Cult of Isis, and Christianity, see below, Chapter 43.

Chapter 36

THE RISE OF THE MILITARY MONARCHY: THE SEVERI

For slightly more than a half century (180–235 A.D.) after the death of Marcus Aurelius the Roman Empire maintained its integrity and beat off serious challenges from the peoples outside its borders. It presented an appearance that was only slightly shabbier than the high civilization under Hadrian, and a way of life that was just a little more rigorous. Roman organized society showed traces of diminished freedom for the individual here and there, but it still was a stupendous fabric. Its troubles lay in the texture of its heritage; the Romans seemed almost to insist on magnifying and developing the mistakes and failures of the adoptive emperors, rather than building upon their successes. The disastrous consequences suffered in this epoch are a pointed and poignant reminder to historians of the neglected adage that, when the fathers have eaten sour grapes, the children's teeth are set on edge. The significant features of the period were a gradual worsening of the economic health, the rapid development of despotic ideals and practices in the leadership, and a deference to the soldiers and their whims until they arrogantly swamped the commonwealth.

COMMODUS (180–192 A.D.).   The first steps toward military despotism may be blamed on the defects in personality of Commodus, Marcus' son and successor, and on his father's bad judgment in promoting him. Commodus was not only an incompetent and voluptuary; he was also a coward. He lacked the talent and the character to maintain his position of eminence through the authority that comes from excellence, but he was willing to buy it. Marcus may have hoped that responsibilities would steady the young man and that his own old friends and counsellors could guide and restrain him. But despite his father's express request, Commodus at once made peace with the

445

Quadi and Marcomanni. He exacted from them some troops for his army, some grain, and the promise that they would not occupy the lands along the Danube—though these terms were slowly relaxed in later years. Fortunately for the Romans, Marcus had done his work on the Danubian front so thoroughly that it was some time before there was serious trouble again in that particular area.

In Rome Commodus surrendered himself to the pleasures of the boudoir and the arena, in each of which he showed considerable skill. He kept a harem of concubines and pretty boys, and he liked to display his talents as a marksman by shooting animals in the arena. The Senate, however, was adequately awed by this scion of five generations of gods that it remained docile. Even though the emperor was much distracted by his private pursuits, there continued a sufficient tradition of good government and of personal initiative in the empire that municipalities and governors seem to have performed reasonably well, and the frontiers were everywhere maintained. Somehow appeals from the oppressed still received a sympathetic hearing in Rome. We have the emperor's signature on a document that confirms the maximum amount of labor that supervisors might exact from tenants on imperial estates; and Commodus' governors tried to curb the evils of military billeting in provincial cities. However, during Commodus' reign armed banditry in Spain and Gaul sometimes reached the proportions of a real rebellion, and its appearance seems to indicate widespread economic dissatisfactions. Many of the army deserters and peasants found among the bandits probably were the victims of the strains and burdens resulting from the plague and from the long wars under Marcus Aurelius. There is evidence that Commodus' generals suppressed the unrest, but none that the emperor suggested corrective measures.

Commodus had personal problems. His sister Lucilla, the widow of Lucius Verus, now was married to an old friend of his father, Claudius Pompeianus. While married to Verus, Lucilla had ranked, of course, as an empress. She resented her demotion from that position in her present marriage, and therefore in 182 or 183 A.D. she headed a conspiracy that made an attempt to assassinate the emperor. But her stepson, who was commissioned to perform the act, took the time before he aimed the blow to shout, "The Senate sends you this dagger!" and thereby he completely missed. Though saved by his guards, Commodus was struck by the assassin's words and from then on saw conspiracy everywhere. To his mind safety now lay only with the praetorian guard and its prefects. The former he kept loyal by frequent donatives and favors. He now ruled through a whole series of prefects of the guard, men who were frequently changed because Commodus freely sacrificed them when their excesses in his service made them unpopular with the mob. He seems also to have sought to ensure the support of the army by raising the pay of the legionaries toward the end of his principate. While Commodus left to his prefects most of the administrative duties of his post, he appears to have fancied for himself the role of a second Hercules. Statues of the emperor equipped with Hercules' characteristic club and lion skin began to appear, and his feats of strength and skill increased in number and extravagance. Financial difficulties that attended his expenditures were repeatedly resolved by the judicial murders of rich citizens that he suspected of conspiracy against him. Finally, disgust and fear did create a successful plot, which was led by his virtuous concubine Marcia, his prefect Laetus, and his chamberlain Eclectus. He was strangled by his wrestling partner on New Year's Eve, 192 A.D., just in time to prevent his inauguration the next day as consul—while dressed in the garb of a gladiator.

PERTINAX (193 A.D.).   The conspirators had ready a candidate for the throne, Helvius Pertinax, an aged senator who had been a competent administrator and was reputed to be a disciplinarian. Pertinax set to work to restore the economy of the Empire by planning to return wastelands to cultivation, to reduce customs duties, and to retrench spending. These were long-range policies, however, and Pertinax' time was short. He was sixty-six years of age when he came to the throne, and he did not at once appoint a strong co-adjutor and successor. The delay was fatal. The praetorians and the staff of the palace were irked by his economy and discipline, and after only eighty-seven days of rule the praetorians marched on the palace and cut off the emperor's head.

AUCTION OF THE EMPIRE. DIDIUS JULIANUS (193 A.D.).
The praetorians thereupon made very clear their pretensions to ultimate authority; they auctioned off the empire to the highest bidder. The winner, who offered the members of the guard 25,000 sesterces apiece, was a senator with more money than sense, one Didius Julianus. His imperial career was as short as its inception was inglorious. He lived in Rome, despised by the senators and pelted even by the venal mob, until the fate of empire was decided by the legions. No more now than in 69 A.D. did the legions intend to resign the throne to the whims of

the praetorians. Jealousies among armies and the hope for suitable rewards from grateful commanders evoked three nominations: Clodius Albinus in Britain, who had three legions; Pescennius Niger in Syria, who had nine; and Septimius Severus in Pannonia, who had twelve. Septimius was the closest to Rome and he acted with speed and decision. He assumed the cognomen "Pertinax," to indicate that he came as the emperor's avenger, and moved rapidly into northern Italy. By June 193 A.D. Didius had been killed in the palace and Septimius had ridden into Rome at the head of his elated troops.

CIVIL WARS; SEPTIMIUS SEVERUS (193–211 A.D.).
Septimius realized that his possession of Rome by no means assured him of the Empire, and while still in the capital he took precautions to maintain its allegiance during the inevitable struggle that lay ahead with his rivals. He wooed the Senate by taking the oath that the Antonines had taken: that no senator would be condemned and executed unless tried by his own peers. He disbanded the pampered Italian praetorian guard and substituted for it a guard of 15,000 troops chosen from his victorious Danubian legions. Many of these men were local recruits with little regard for Roman culture, but with great devotion for their general. To protect his rear while he contended with his more formidable rival, Pescennius Niger, Septimius appointed his other rival, Albinus, his "Caesar," a term that had come to indicate the successor-designate to the throne. Then he hurried through the Balkans to the East, bypassed Byzantium, which had gone over to Niger, and by the spring of 194 A.D. had routed his opponent's forces. While he was in the East, it seemed proper to him also to assert his position in respect to Parthia. The Parthian king had offered assistance to Niger, some of Niger's supporters now had fled to the Parthian court and service, and the client state of Osrhoene had renounced its Roman allegiance. In 194 and 195 A.D. Septimius overran Osrhoene and Upper Mesopotamia, where he established a colony at Nisibis.

Septimius seemed well on his way to repeating the exploits of Trajan in the Orient, when disturbing news from the West led to his return. For a while Albinus had remained acquiescent in his position as Caesar. Little by little, however, he was made suspicious of the true designs of Septimius, who had two sons of his own and an ambitious wife. A number of senators also urged that Albinus take precautions against double-dealing by Septimius, for many of them found him a more sympathetic person than Septimius. Therefore, when Albinus believed that Septimius had instigated an attempt to assassinate him, he proclaimed himself Augustus and moved from Britain to the mainland. Albinus set up headquarters at Lugdunum (Lyons) and began to seek support. However, Septimius hurried west, outmaneuvered his rival, and finally defeated him near Lyons in February 197 A.D. That city was then turned over to the victorious troops for plunder, a sack from which it never recovered in antiquity.

Throughout this civil war it had been clear that communities had sided with one aspirant or another for purely local and selfish reasons, and Septimius' punishment for those that had guessed wrongly was sufficiently severe to be long remembered. Famous cities, such as Antioch, were humiliated by being attached to more astute rivals; and Byzantium, which had held out until 196 A.D., had its walls razed and its magistrates and defenders killed. The emperor now revealed his true sentiments toward the Senate. Twenty-nine of those senators that had favored Albinus were put to death. An immense amount of property came to the emperor from the confiscated estates of these men; and to administer the income from this windfall he organized a new treasury, the *res privata,* which was to be completely at the emperor's personal disposal.

ANTECEDENTS OF SEPTIMIUS AND HIS DYNASTY. Now that the new emperor was firmly established on the throne by his legions, the Romans slowly realized that Septimius' antecedents, education, and family connections did not presage a sympathetic return to the principles of government sustained by the adoptive emperors. By birth Septimius was an African from Leptis Magna. Born of equestrian rank, he had been raised to the Senate by Marcus Aurelius and had pursued the traditional *cursus honorum;* but he still spoke Latin with a Punic accent, and some of his family could scarcely speak it at all. Here indeed, after nearly 400 years, was the avenger of Hannibal and of Carthage. Furthermore, his wife, Julia Domna, was a Syrian, a member of a priestly family of Emesa. In this pair was fulfilled the growing tendency of Rome's Empire to dominate its Italian heartland. Romanized provincials had indeed held the principate for nearly a century, but those men had been of Italian stock and in most cases had been more devoted to Roman tradition than the Romans themselves were. But this African clearly had little of the Roman tradition distilled in him that the Spaniards had had. He did realize, however, the importance of the Antonines' prestige, and before he returned

449

from his struggle with Pescennius Niger he announced that he had been adopted into the Antonine family as the son of Marcus Aurelius. Later the same prestige was promoted by his insistence that the Senate deify his "brother" Commodus. His elder son Bassianus, who is commonly called Caracalla because of a Gallic cloak that he affected, was renamed Marcus Aurelius Antoninus. It appears that this fictional adoption did have considerable value as propaganda in the provinces, and that it made very little difference to most men whether the adoption came before or after the adopter's death. Augustus had legitimatized his regime by constantly asserting his devotion to the revered republican constitution; Septimius did the same for his dynasty by insisting upon his connection to the equally revered family of adoptive emperors. Little wonder that the family of a ruler that traced his authority through so long a line of deified mortals should now regularly be termed the *domus divina*, the holy household.

POLICY TOWARD ITALY.   For the provincial Septimius, the preferred position that Italy had long enjoyed in the Empire was a privilege that he had no desire to maintain. During his principate Italy was brought closer to the condition of the provinces in two ways: some actions directly depressed its condition, while others raised the provinces to a status closer to its own. A legion of soldiers now was stationed on Italian soil, and service in the favored praetorian guard was no longer a prerogative of Italians. On the other hand, many provincial areas, especially in Africa and Sicily, were given the *ius Italicum*, whereby their soil was given the legal status of Italian soil and thus enjoyed legal privileges once reserved for Italy alone. The influence of the Senate was minimal. Septimius packed it with his partisans, and the Italians now numbered no more than one third of the body. It met to hear the decisions that the emperor had made, and then it was allowed to ratify them.

ARMY POLICY.   The troops were unequivocally recognized as the source of imperial power. Septimius announced projects or policies to them before he did to the Senate. He granted the legionaries a substantial raise in pay, which assured their loyalty to him and to his house while compensating them for an apparent rise in prices under Commodus. Centurions became eligible for rapid advancement in careers of the civil service, and veterans of the army were given exemptions from public duties when they were discharged and had settled down. Now at length legionaries were allowed legally to marry native

450

women during their period of service, and they were encouraged to till the soil in the areas where they were stationed. Here Septimius appears to have been extending but distorting the ideas of Hadrian, and to be creating a militarized peasantry along the frontiers that would defend its homes and be disinclined to irresponsible adventures. There is evidence of militarized agricultural colonies close to the frontiers in Germany, Thrace, and Africa. Septimius also expanded the army from thirty to thirty-three legions.

THE PRAETORIAN PREFECTS AND THE LAW.   The post of prefect of the praetorian guard rapidly became more important during Septimius' principate. This trend received impetus from the eminence of the emperor's fellow African and close friend, Plautianus. Plautianus was sole prefect, and at the same time he held a seat in the Senate. He had been consul and he had arranged for the marriage of his daughter to the emperor's son. Under him the *Annona* (administration of the important grain supply) came to the prefect's general supervision. In Italy all cases in civil law that arose more than one hundred miles from Rome came under his jurisdiction (the city prefect tried cases in the environs of Rome); and he was often the emperor's delegate to hear appeals from the provinces. It was at this time also that the use of the old jury-courts for criminal cases completely ceased, and their work too fell to the prefects. Plautianus, however, incurred the hatred both of Empress Julia Domna and of his son-in-law, Caracalla, and in 205 A.D. the two engineered an accusation of conspiracy against him and had him killed. Thereafter the emperor generally appointed two praetorian prefects, one of whom was an eminent jurist. The famous Papinian for a long time held the post of a praetorian prefect under Septimius. In the *consilium* of the prince at the same time as Papinian were two other famous jurisconsults, Paul and Ulpian. Both Papinian and Ulpian probably were Syrians and shared in the Hellenistic heritage of the East as well as having received thorough Roman training. The combination brought to the legislation of Severus' epoch a humane approach and an increased care for the protection of the humble. It should be noted, however, that this care for the poor was also related to Septimius' concern for the army; the poor, of course, furnished him his recruits. This cynical observation is given substance when we realize that the period also saw a careful distinction between the upper classes (*honestiores*, which included senators, civil servants, soldiers, and the aristocracy of the municipalities), and the great mass of the people (*humiliores*).

451

The *honestiores* received gentler treatment in court, more dignified sentences upon convicton, and alone retained the right of appeal to the emperor. But they also were held rigorously to their municipal or national duties, especially if they were very rich.

THE GROWTH OF STATISM. The period is characterized by an increasing control of the population by the State, and by a more rigid organization of the government, often along military lines. The bureaus especially became militarized, since the civil servants in them often had received their posts as rewards at the end of successful careers in the army. The jurists of the time began to speak pointedly of the public duties as well as of the rights of the various guilds of tradesmen (the *collegia*), especially those that were in any way connected with the food supply. The councils and leading citizens of the municipalities commenced to be held responsible for the collection of local taxes; and municipal guilds were burdened with special civic duties, such as firefighting, and were carefully supervised. The tendencies toward centralization and imperial supervision which had been apparent for more than a century received great impetus from Septimius' military temperament. And he in turn was impelled to increase his authority by the decreasing vigor of the economy and of initiative on the part of the citizens. There was perhaps some improvement in the economy during the reign, if we can judge from Septimius' ability to raise taxes. But there were also signs of a continued weakness: the emperor had to depreciate the currency; brigandage, fed by deserters and refugees, continued to spread (one Bulla Felix terrified the Italian countryside with a band of 600 men through 206 and 207 A.D.); and tenants on the imperial estates threatened to abandon their farming and take to the hills if they continued to be held liable for civic duties in nearby towns while they were forced to perform their proper tasks as farmers on their leaseholds.

PROVINCIAL AND FOREIGN POLICY. Septimius never felt quite comfortable in the city of Rome and found reasons to be elsewhere frequently. In 197 A.D., after there had been an attack on his colony at Nisibis, he resumed operations against the Parthians. Again the opposition there collapsed, and the emperor was able to effect the capture of Ctesiphon. He reestablished a province of Mesopotamia with Nisibis as its capital, and during this successful campaign he took the opportunity to raise Caracalla to the rank of Augustus, or joint-emperor with himself. The younger Geta became a Caesar. From 199 to 202

A.D. the emperor travelled in the East, visiting Egypt, Asia Minor, and once more the Danubian provinces. Part of the following two years were spent in Africa, where he etablished outposts along the frontiers, raised the status of numerous cities, improved living conditions for the soldiers, and separated Numidia from Africa, making it an independent province. He had already divided Syria into two provinces, and later he did the same for Britain. This policy was probably inspired by a wish to decrease the number of governors that had large armies in their control, a situation that had made possible the recent civil wars. By 208 A.D. the emperor was in Britain. This land had been overrun by the Caledonians, after Albinus withdrew his legions to fight the civil wars. The emperor penetrated far into the highlands, and for a while he held the area between Hadrian's and Antoninus' walls. Ultimately, however, he set the permanent frontier at Hadrian's Wall, which was now manned and repaired. While on this campaign, in 209 A.D., he raised his younger son Geta also to the rank of Augustus; and in 211 A.D. he died at York. Whether or not it is true that his final admonition to his sons was to enrich the soldiers and disregard all others, the anecdote is a just estimate of the direction in which Septimius pointed the Roman world.

CARACALLA (211–217 A.D.) AND GETA (211–212 A.D.). The animosity between the imperial brothers was of long standing, and no efforts of Septimius or of their mother, Julia Domna, made any impression. The situation was made worse because the officials of the court began to choose sides as soon as Septimius was dead. This diversion, however, became pointless when in early 212 A.D. Caracalla had Geta murdered, while the boy cowered in their mother's arms. Caracalla further secured his position by a donative of money to the praetorians, by a raise of pay of fifty percent for the legionaries, and by the wholesale execution of those suspected of favoring his brother. These included his father's eminent judicial adviser, Papinian, and Cornificia, a true daughter of Marcus Aurelius. She had called on Julia Domna to offer her condolences at Geta's death, and this was enough for Caracalla. At her death the lady was brave enough to scoff at the Severi's fictitious claim of adoption by Marcus, when she said, "Depart, little soul, and show that you are *really* Marcus' daughter, whether *they* like it or not."

Caracalla preferred to leave most of the administrative duties to his mother and the *consilium* while he cultivated the troops, for he fancied himself to be Alexander the Great reincarnated. His imitation of his idol was perhaps not simply in the military field, for one of the administrative acts of his reign that has caught the world's imagination bears some resemblance to political ideals attributed to Alexander. This administrative act was the so-called *Constitutio Antoniniana,* or Edict of Caracalla, which was issued in 212 or 213 A.D. By its terms citizenship was given to almost all free residents of the Empire. There seems to have been one exception, the *dediticii;* but the identity of this category is uncertain. *Dediticii* originally was the term used for captured enemies, and it is probable that by the time of Caracalla the word had become the generic name for those persons, such as criminals, who had the legal disabilities that captured enemies had once had. In any case, the edict was the natural culmination of centuries of generally generous treatment of noncitizens by the Romans, and more especially of the policy of the Antonines and Septimius in the past century to raise more provincials to citizenship rapidly. The measure was possibly a further bid for popularity too—its text speaks of a thanksgiving, perhaps for escape from a pretended plot by Geta. A contemporary, Dio Cassius, said that the measure was prompted by financial need: only Roman citizens were liable for the five per cent tax on manumissions and inheritances, and these levies were doubled at this time. Presumably a vast increase in the citizenship would have greatly added to the government's income.

MILITARY EXPLOITS.   Meanwhile, Caracalla both found and created the means to emulate the great military exploits of his ancient Macedonian hero. Across the frontier at the headwaters of the Rhine and Danube a new coalition of German tribes called the Alamanni had arisen, and they now were threatening the frontier. In 213 A.D. an expedition against them headed by the emperor was successful, and he added the title "Germanicus Maximus" to his name. In 213 A.D. he moved through the Balkans toward the East, pausing in Macedonia to enroll a corps of natives so that he could perfect his impersonation of Alexander the Great. However, when he arrived in Syria, he was disappointed to find the Parthians reluctant to pick a quarrel. Instead of campaigning, therefore, he visited Alexandria in Egypt where, with no logical explanation except vexation at the Alexandrians' traditional liberty of speech, he assembled and then massacred the flower of that city's youth. Back in Antioch, he finally found a pretext for war with the Parthians by demanding the hand of the king's daughter in marriage. This request the sovereign wisely refused, for he saw that Caracalla-Alexander thus aimed to unite the two realms, as his hero had done. The year 216 A.D. was spent in feckless demonstrations in Mesopotamia; and when Caracalla returned to the wars in the spring of 217 A.D., at a place near Carrhae, one of his attendants struck him down with a dagger as he dismounted from his horse to relieve himself.

MACRINUS (217–218 A.D.).   Caracalla's assassination had been arranged by one of the praetorian prefects, Ofellius Macrinus, after the prefect had discovered that he himself was marked for slaughter by the emperor. He was only an equestrian in rank, and a Moor in the bargain, but the troops—though they regretted Caracalla—reluctantly proclaimed him prince. Macrinus had been appointed praetorian prefect because of his ability as a jurist, not as a general. His attempts to carry on the campaign in Parthia were feeble and ended with a cash payment to the Parthian king. He also agreed to return to Nero's solution of the Armenian problem, by allowing a Parthian prince to hold the Armenian throne and accord only nominal allegiance to Rome. These inglorious efforts, added to an attempt to curtail the military budget, alienated the troops. To placate them Macrinus arranged for Caracalla's deification; and he further tried to emphasize the orthodoxy of his position by giving the name "Antoninus" to his nine-year-old son, the "Augustus" Diadumenianus. But all in vain: now the troops were prepared to shift their allegiance to an even more remarkable curiosity than the many oddities that this epoch already had seen; and for the last seventeen years of this period the Roman world was to be dominated by a family of Syrian women.

THE SEVERAN WOMEN.   Julia Maesa, the sister of the late Empress Julia Domna, had grown powerful and rich in Rome, but when Macrinus came to the throne he had forced her to return to her native Emesa in Syria. Two widowed daughters of Julia Maesa, Julia Soaemias and Julia Mamaea, also lived in Emesa, and each of these ladies had one young son. Julia Maesa soon learned of Macrinus' unpopularity and she decided to take advantage of it. She proceeded to undermine the loyalty of the troops stationed nearby both with money and with the unblushing assertion that Varius Avitus, the fourteen-year-old son of her daughter Soaemias, had been sired by no other than Caracalla himself and would, therefore, make a splendid successor to Macrinus. The boy Avitus, who was enthusiastically pursuing his trade as the hereditary priest of Emesa's god, Elagabal, was unnaturally handsome, and he caught the soldiers' fancy. Soon

455

Macrinus was faced with a full-scale revolt, and in June of 218 A.D. he was defeated near Antioch by an army urged on by Maesa and Soaemias from their chariots.

ELAGABALUS (218–222 A.D.).   Avitus was now officially known as Marcus Aurelius Antoninus from the official name of his supposed father—we must presume that his "parentage" had the same spurious justification as Septimius' "adoption"—but because of his devotion to his god, Avitus is generally called Elagabalus. Despite the valiant efforts of his grandmother and tutors to prepare him for the Roman public, the lad proved probably to be perverted and certainly to be perverse. When he finally arrived in Rome he set about dispensing offices and honors to his Oriental cronies, and the Senate was astonished to see a woman, Julia Soaemias, participating in its business. In general, however, Elagabalus was content to leave the nation's administration in the willing hands of Julia Maesa, while he tended to the propagation of the true faith, the worship of his conical stone god, Elagabal, which he had brought with him from Syria. His god was given the Punic goddess Tanit for wife, while Elagabalus himself took on a Vestal Virgin. The Romans were thereupon treated to a series of outlandish parades, celebrations, and spectacles that scandalized even that hardened mob. By 221 A.D. Maesa began to realize that the emperor's excesses were endangering the whole family, and she prevailed upon Elagabalus to adopt his cousin Alexianus, Mamaea's son—there was an opportune discovery that he too was a bastard of Caracalla. However, the younger boy was instantly popular, and this so roused Elagabalus' jealousy that he made two attempts to have Alexianus assassinated. The praetorian guard, moved by the danger to a new favorite, finally seized and dispatched both Elagabalus and his mother Soaemias in the spring of 222 A.D.

SEVERUS ALEXANDER (222–235 A.D.). DOMESTIC POLICY. The new emperor, now called Marcus Aurelius Severus Alexander, was a pliant youth of fourteen who seldom gave anyone trouble. Maesa and Mamaea realized that the soldiers had proved too fickle to put their trust in them alone, and they determined to seek prestige and legitimacy by a calculated cultivation of the senators. The ensuing period was looked upon in retrospect as the Senate's happy Indian Summer. Sixteen senators made up the regency, and the *consilium* of the prince also contained many senators, beside the regular contingent of equestrians. Prominent in the government was the famous jurist

Ulpian, who was praetorian prefect from 222 to 228 A.D. But despite all appearances, the authority of the State was really in the hands of Julia Mamaea. Julia Maesa died peacefully in 226 A.D., and thereafter her daughter was completely in control. All of the Syrian women had assumed grandiloquent titles, but Mamaea outdid them all—her inscriptions call her "Augusta, mother of Augustus, and of the camps, and of the Senate, and of the fatherland"! She was an imperious woman who would brook no rival, and she dominated and finally destroyed her son. His wife, of whom she became jealous, she dismissed. Her extreme stinginess with money and her timid military policy brought the administration into disrepute. However, for thirteen years Mamaea was sufficiently adroit, and the world was sufficiently weary of the excesses that had preceded her regime, that she remained in power.

Within the empire there was further social and economic regimentation evoked by serious efforts to recover economic strength. Tradesmen, artisans, and laborers were urged to organize in guilds (*collegia*) in the service of the State. Relief from taxes and from other public duties was given to those workmen that could produce under the State's supervision a sufficient amount of critically needed commodities, such as arms and blankets for the army and vital foodstuffs for the cities. In this development we see the abandonment of the laissez-faire policy that had long characterized Rome's attitude toward manufacturers and tradesmen. A parallel development was the assignment of tax-collecting to the local senators in the municipalities, instead of using officials of the State. This was a particularly burdensome duty, for the collectors were liable to make up from their own pockets any deficits in the annual returns. The government also made grants of land to soldiers in return for hereditary service in the army. Such service was not yet compulsory, but descendants lost the land if they did not perform this service.

All of the regulations during Alexander's regime were not however, repressive. There is evidence that there was an attempt to civilize the population along the frontiers, and that primary schools made their appearance even in the smallest villages. Both Mamaea and Alexander showed an interest in the diverse religious beliefs and practices of their people. The empress-mother summoned to her presence the famous Christian theologian, Origen, to instruct her concerning the doctrines of that sect; and the tendency of the day to merge together all manner of religious notions is demonstrated by Alexander's own chapel, which contained statues of the deified emperors, of

457

the Pythagorean Apollonius of Tyana, of Christ, of Abraham, and of Orpheus.

MILITARY POLICY.   During the early years of Alexander's reign the administration maintained an uneasy truce with the soldiers. But when, in 228 A.D., the praetorians murdered their prefect Ulpian because he was considered too strict a disciplinarian, the weakness of the emperor was made clear, for he was unable to defend his own prefect. Events abroad increased Alexander's perplexities. In 226 the Arsacid kings of the Parthians, weakened by their constant misfortunes at the hands of the Romans, were replaced by a vigorous Persian dynasty, the Sassanids, under Ardashir (or Artaxerxes). As a Persian, Ardashir looked upon himself as the heir of the ancient Persian Empire, and he proceeded to attempt the reclamation of it. Since the Persian Empire had included all Asia Minor and part of Europe, this was a threat to all of Rome's eastern provinces. Alexander and Mamaea raised a large army and worked out an elaborate plan of campaign to combat the Sassanid pretensions. Their strategy called for a three-pronged attack of Mesopotamia with the assistance of the vassal king of Armenia who, as an Arsacid appointee, was hostile to the Sassanids and loyal to Rome. However, Alexander's excessive timidity caused the division that he himself was leading to support the other armies of the invasion insufficiently; and after Ardashir had concentrated upon the right wing and defeated it, the whole expedition withdrew (233 A.D.). Fortunately for the Romans, the Persian forces also had suffered severely in the contest, and the eastern front remained stable for a number of years. While the emperor was still in the East, news reached him that once more trouble had risen with the Alamanni on the northern front. One of the reasons why Alexander thereupon had to abandon any further activity in the East was because such Roman legionaries in his expeditionary force as were normally stationed on the German frontier now demanded that they be allowed to return to the West to defend their homes. In 234 Mamaea and Alexander headed for the northern front, leading an expedition carefully prepared by their general, Julius Verus Maximinus. However, in 235 when the empress persuaded Alexander to begin negotiations with the Germans and to seek peace with them on the basis of promising them a subsidy in cash, the disgusted troops—who would have preferred the money for themselves —elevated their general, the Thracian peasant Maximinus, to the throne, and killed both Alexander and his mother.

THE AGE OF THE SEVERI.   During the next fifty years of anarchy (235–285 A.D.), men often looked back with longing to the days of Alexander Severus as an approximation of their earlier and happier Principate. But actually the Severi and their open dependence on the military forces had so changed the world, that it little resembled the Principate as conceived by Augustus or by the Flavians and adoptive emperors. Princes had repeatedly been chosen by force and by whim. The Senate now consisted of men that reflected the choice and the policy of the individual emperors and had no real independence. Its position was now largely sentimental and decorative. The populace was cowed, harassed, and regimented.

Literature was dumb: one would hardly mention the authors of the period, were it not that both Herodian (*ca.* 170–240 A.D.) and Dio Cassius (155–230 A.D.) were historians of their own day and are invaluable as sources for the Severan Age, for each held posts in the administration. We should also mention the Greek sophist Philostratus. His patroness was Empress Julia Domna, and he wrote lives of Apollonius of Tyana and of the sophists, as well as letters and descriptions of paintings. His work is pleasant and informative. All three of these men wrote in Greek. The poverty of the literature perhaps suggests that the age inspired very little hope in the intellectuals, and that the educational system, which continued to expand, became less profound as it became more diffuse.

On every side were threatening neighbors: the North was stirring once more, and the Sassanids of Persia were strong and ambitious and the more dangerous because they were fanatically devoted to their native religion, Zoroastrianism. And, finally, the soldiers, the arbiters of peace and power for whom the tax mills ground, were becoming as fearsome to the Roman civilians as the barbarians were.

THE CONSEQUENCES OF THE IMPERIAL PAST.   In assessing the Age of the Severi, however, it is important for us to realize that it was built on its predecessors, and that none of its phenomena burst unheralded on the world. The activities and characteristics of this age had their precedents in the earlier decisions, mistakes, or failures of both the leaders and the people. The principle of the adoption of the "best man" had been abandoned by the revered Marcus Aurelius. The principle still commanded respect—as both Septimius' and Julia Maesa's insistence on acquiring the name "Antoninus" showed—but after the reign of Commodus and his deification by Septimius, it could be very cynically applied. The Senate's power was indeed gone, but its primary function as adviser of the prince had long been more ably performed by the smaller compact *consilium* of the prince, which had become very important as early as Hadrian. Even earlier the second prince, Tiberius, had complained that the senators would not show responsible initiative and forced the burdens of empire upon him. That the ruling house assumed pretensions approaching divinity can hardly be wondered at, when its members considered the adulation and worship lavished by the people on their successful predecessors. Even the domineering Syrian ladies of the third century A.D. could point to the considerable influence of Livia, the Agrippinas, and even Trajan's more discreet wife Plotina. The regimentation of society for the service of society had had its small and successful beginnings in the first century A.D., when Claudius had enlisted the interest of the guilds of shipowners to supply the city's stomach; and equally significant for the now disciplined municipalities was the kindly paternalism of Trajan, the best of princes, for it had allowed them to be irresponsible, and finally dependent. The establishment of stationary legions along the frontiers was begun by the conscientious Emperor Hadrian. The experiment, which was designed to foster patriotism and raise morale, had ended in jealousies and in the priority of sectional over national interests, which had forced Alexander Severus to allow the soldiers of his eastern expedition to return to the German frontier. The pecuniary corruption of the troops was not new, but had been given a giant impetus when Claudius confirmed his elevation by a liberal donative to the praetorians. And, finally, the deterioration of literature, the barbarization of taste, and the mongrelization of manners were due not just to the generous grants of citizenship by the emperors in their attempt to create a truly universal state out of the Roman system, but also to the failure of the population of Italy to furnish a sufficient surplus to weld the Empire into a nation. This failure had troubled the Romans as early as the first century A.D., and their concern gave rise to private foundations and finally to the public alimentary institution, which were established to encourage the propagation of Italians. The earlier emperors settled such Italians as they had available in widely spread colonies to promote the homogeneity of the Empire. But the imponderables of disease and of racial suicide confounded their aims, and many Roman citizens from the old cultures of the East or from the barbaric hordes of the North were scarcely touched by those ideals and that outlook that had been Italian.

Chapter 37

THE IMPERIAL ARMY

The imperial policies of Commodus and the Severi were an indication, and the murder of Alexander Severus a confirmation, that the Roman Empire had become a military monarchy and that the troops were in firm political control. This alone would be noteworthy; but the influence of the army was so pervasive — in Roman economy, social structure, administration, culture, and religion — that it requires more than casual attention. The army was the major concern of the imperial budget and a burden to an agricultural economy; yet it stimulated the economy of the areas near its camps, and at the same time improved the Empire's trade routes and protected them. During their years of service the legionaries were often the hated and feared policemen of the central government. The officers and veterans, however, became the gentry of the municipalities, and as such they received very favorable treatment at court, where they often represented their home towns. The early Roman soldier of Italian birth carried his language and culture to the frontiers; but in the Late Empire this trend was completely reversed. As Roman soldiers were recruited more and more from the frontiers, they spread to the very heart of the Empire practices, outlooks, and religions that were completely foreign to the ethos of the Italian people.

ORIGIN OF THE PROFESSIONAL ARMY.   It will be recalled that the Roman professional army originated during the last century of the Republic, when Marius abandoned the ancient policy of universal military service by the propertied classes alone (107 B.C.). He drew his recruits from the proletariat and from those other citizens that lacked responsibilities at home and craved adventure, booty, and improvement in status. To Marius also belongs the characteristic organization of the legion by cohorts, and the creation of the standard or eagle of the legion as the focus of loyalty, pride, and honor. The extended civil wars of the first century B.C. kept legions so long in existence that some of them began to have a permanency of their own, apart from the soldiers that happened to be in them at any one time; the famous Tenth Legion of Julius Caesar and the Fifth Legion Alaudae, made up of Transalpine Gauls, are examples. Experience during this period showed the superiority of the noncommissioned officers (centurions and others), with their long periods of service, over the young men of good family who began their public careers as commissioned officers; and legionary commanders grew to depend more and more on the centurions. In the same way, the legion of professional soldiers with long training and experience had shown itself more efficient than the old militia of citizens called from their civilian employments. Augustus therefore decided to continue to use as his instrument of defense the type of professional army that already had developed in the Roman world. At the end of the civil wars Augustus controlled at least sixty legions, but by 16 B.C. this army had been reduced to twenty-eight legions, some drawn from Augustus' own forces, some from Lepidus' or Antony's. This number continued until 6 A.D. and Varus' disastrous loss of three legions in Germany. At the end of Augustus' principate, then, there were twenty-five legions, already with their own history, traditions, and *esprit de corps*.

ARMY ORGANIZATION.   Theoretically each legion consisted of 6000 men, though usually there were enrolled no more than 5500 at any one time. Each legion consisted of ten cohorts, ideally of 600 men apiece; and the old subdivisions of maniples also were retained. There were three maniples to a cohort, and two centuries (100 men each) to each maniple. In command of each century there was a centurion. There were, therefore, sixty centurions to a legion.

NONCOMMISSIONED OFFICERS.   The centurions of a Roman legion were not all of the same rank. The centurion of the first century of the first maniple of Cohort I (called the *primipilus*) was not only the commander of his cohort, but also was the ranking noncommissioned officer of the whole legion. Further, all the centurions of Cohort I, and the *primipili* of all the other nine cohorts (fifteen men all told), together formed the elite of the legion and were called the *primi ordines* (top rankers), and they were respected and consulted by the commissioned officers. There was regular advancement for the centurions, and length of service was by no means the sole criterion. While men of mediocre talents might rise slowly through the sixty steps in the legion, young men of promise were promoted rapidly to the *primus ordo* and might become *primipili* at an early age. These men were watched, and after discharge they might enjoy a distinguished administrative career, either civil or military, in the equestrian *cursus* of offices. Beside the command that they exercised in war or on maneuvers, centurions were responsible for the assignment of guards and other details, and apparently their income was frequently enhanced by the bribes of foot-soldiers reluctant to perform irksome duties.

The legion also had numerous other noncommissioned officers of lesser rank: each centurion had an understudy (the *optio*), and there were the standardbearer (*aquilifer*), corporal of the watch (*tesserarius*), and a host of armorers, horn-players, doctors, and veterinarians. Important also were the men detached for special duty, such as the *beneficiarii*, who were orderlies to commissioned officers or to officials of the State, and the numerous members of the "orderly-room crowd," who kept the rolls of the soldiers up-to-date and were in charge of the legion's accounts. As the bureaucratic disposition of the Roman government increased, these men became ever more important, and a good deal of our knowledge about the army comes from remains of their interminable paperwork preserved on papyri in the sands of Egypt.

COMMISSIONED OFFICERS.   The commander-in-chief of the legion was called the legate of the emperor (*legatus Augusti*). He was usually a senator of praetorian rank, and in many cases he would have had only the small amount of military training that young men of quality received, one year as tribune on another general's staff. If there was only one legion in a province, the governor of the province (*legatus pro praetore*) was also commander of the legion; if there were more, he was supreme commander, and there was also a subordinate *legatus* for each legion. Under the *legati* were the tribunes. These were the young men of good birth who thus fulfilled their military service before entering a political career. If they were of senatorial families, they did one year of service; if of equestrian birth, they did three years, part of which was spent with auxiliary troops. The tribunes generally performed administrative and judicial tasks during their service; actual military leadership was safer in the hands of the veteran noncommissioned centurions.

There was also an officer with an intermediate status not

unlike that held by warrant officers in the Army of the United States, though he had much more power than warrant officers do. This was the prefect of the camp. He was generally a former *primipilus*, and his post was usually considered the final position in a military career. The prefect of the camp received his appointment directly from the emperor. He not only was in charge of laying out the camp, organizing the transport of supplies, and administering the specialists in the camp, but he also, as the emperor's appointee, could keep a watchful eye for the emperor on the senatorial *legati*. The long military experience of the prefects of the camp was indispensable to the *legati*, who frequently had very little practical training.

AUXILIARY TROOPS.   All legionaries were Roman citizens, but there also were almost as many noncitizens in the imperial military service as well. Some of these were provincials, some the troops of client states, some specialized troops, such as archers or slingers; and the cavalry of the imperial army was almost wholly foreign. They are lumped together under the term "auxiliaries." There were approximately the same number of auxiliaries as legionaries with each legion. They were organized by cohorts or squadrons and served under Roman officers. The need of the members of this polyglot organization to communicate with one another and with their commanders greatly spread the Latin tongue among them and prepared them for citizenship. We do not know as much about their conditions of service as we do about the legionaries', but at discharge they and their descendants, now at least partly Romanized, were given the status of Roman citizens. As early as Hadrian there also were small units of men drawn from the border areas who were called *numeri* and who were allowed to serve under their own commanders and use their own tongues.

THE ROMAN NAVY.   Throughout Roman history the Roman navy enjoyed less prestige than the army, and in the earliest days its sailors were slaves or freedmen. Its commanders until the Flavians also were freedmen, but thereafter the prefects of the navy were equestrians. During the first century A.D. the recruits came to have much the same status as auxiliaries: they were freemen, drawn chiefly from the Balkans, and they received the citizenship after twenty-six years of service. The chief naval bases were at Misenum on the Bay of Naples and at Ravenna on the Adriatic; and there were also lesser flotillas at Forum Julii in southern Gaul, at Alexandria, at Seleucia in Syria, on the Rhine and Danube, and in the Black Sea and

English Channel. There were no real naval wars during the Principate, but the fleets were important for convoy duty, for intercepting movements of barbarians, and for policing the seas against piracy.

SIZE AND COMPOSITION OF THE ARMY.   At the death of Augustus there were twenty-five legions serving with the Roman army. Nero raised the number to twenty-eight, Trajan to thirty, and Septimius Severus to thirty-three. Auxiliaries were increased proportionately, so that the overall number under arms rose from approximately 300,000 men to about 400,000. Since legionaries had to be Roman citizens, in the early Principate they were chiefly drawn from Italy and from the Roman colonies or municipalities of the older provinces. A partial exception was made in the East, where the climate and the prevalence of Greek as the lingua franca made local recruitment desirable. The Galatians and Cappadocians there furnished many soldiers, and apparently they were given the citizenship at enlistment. Auxiliaries were noncitizens and therefore could be drawn from any suitable area. Under the Flavians the army continued to be overwhelmingly Roman in sentiment, but the emperors tended to enlist more men from the municipalities of the Romanized provinces than from the impoverished city population of Italy, which had proved intractable. As the first century A.D. passed, the proportion of Italians in the ranks continued to fall, as Italy's population did not show a healthy increase, and pacifistic sentiments became more pervasive. A further and strong impetus for the provincialization of the army came from Hadrian's policy of recruitment from the areas where the legions were more or less permanently stationed. Now the children of the soldiers' irregular marital alliances in the camp towns became an important source of recruits, and some army rolls in the later years of Hadrian show that a third of the soldiers in certain units were born "in camp." The exigencies of the plague and of the German wars of Marcus Aurelius, and the military policies of the Severi increased the dependence on the more warlike and less Romanized populations; and after the Edict of Caracalla, of course, almost all residents of the Empire were eligible for service, regardless of their cultural qualifications.

PAY.   The pay of the legionary seems low in modern terms, but in view of the low cost of living it allowed to the thrifty soldier some savings above and beyond his expenses. At the death of Augustus (14 A.D.) the legionary received 225 denarii a year.[1] This was raised to 300 by Domitian (81–96 A.D.), to 375 by Commodus (180–192 A.D.), to 500 by Septimius (193–211 A.D.), and to 750 by Caracalla (211–217 A.D.). From this there were stoppages for food, equipment, clothing, burial club, and enforced savings. However, all of these expenses did not recur regularly: for instance, once arms had been bought, they would last for a considerable period, and the army maintained specialists to carry out the occasional repairs that were needed. Food was simple: soup, bread, vegetables, wine or vinegar, and very rarely meat; and a year's supply of the staple, grain, probably could be procured for sixty denarii. The burial club and enforced savings were some insurance against the future. For additional income, there were special grants, donatives from various emperors at their accession or on other happy occasions. And a successful campaign often furnished booty—even from cities within the empire, as unhappy Cremona, Lyons, and many others discovered. Special troops, such as the members of the praetorian guard or of the urban cohorts, received higher pay. The praetorians, for example, received 750 denarii annually under Augustus, and this had risen to 2500 denarii under Caracalla. The pay for the centurions was quite handsome: a regular centurion under Augustus received 3750 denarii, under Domitian 5000; the members of the *primi ordines* 7500 and 10,000 respectively; while *primipili* and prefects of the camp received 15,000 denarii under Augustus and 20,000 under Domitian. We do not have as much information concerning the auxiliaries, but their rate of pay was much lower; under Augustus they appear to have received about half the stipend of legionaries. There was a further recompense for the soldiers in the payment to them at discharge of 3000 denarii, or the equivalent in land, from the military treasury that Augustus had established.

LENGTH OF SERVICE.   Augustus had tried to set the length of service for legionaries to sixteen years of regular service and four more as veterans in a kind of reserve. It developed, however, that the income of the military treasury would not permit such early discharges, and he increased the periods to twenty years with the legions and five in the veterans' reserve. Discontent at the beginning of Tiberius' principate (14 A.D.) led to a brief return to the earlier terms, but he too was unable to re-

[1]   The silver content of 225 denarii would be worth in the mid-twentieth century A.D. only about thirty-six American dollars, but this bears no relation to the purchasing power of this sum in food and services. See Appendix.

solve the financial difficulty and had to revert to Augustus' later solution. By the time of the Flavians (69–96 A.D.) discharges were granted after twenty-five or twenty-six years, all of active service. Twenty-five years also was the normal period of service for the auxiliaries.

MORALE. DECORATIONS.   The Roman command was anxious that its soldiers should be disciplined, efficient, loyal, and proud. Numerous provisions were made to ensure the high morale that this description requires. For feats of bravery on the battlefield there were military decorations appropriate to the event: a civic crown for saving a comrade's life, a mural crown for being the first over an enemy's walls or ramparts, a golden crown for gallantry, and various lesser decorations that took the form of armlets, neckpieces, and embossed disks. For commissioned officers there were, in addition, small silver spearheads and silver-mounted standards. Whole units were also sometimes given citations, and the standards of the group would be decorated with medals and wreaths. A descriptive term, such as *fortis* for great bravery, or *pia fidelis* for loyalty in a time of civil disturbances, might be added to the legion's number and name: there was a II Traiana Fortis under Hadrian, and a II Parthica Pia Fidelis under Elagabalus.

The most common punishment for infractions of the rules was whipping. Dishonorable discharge and death were reserved for the more flagrant crimes. Men with rank, of course, could be demoted as well as promoted. There were only rare uses of the ancient punishment of decimation during the Principate. This entailed the execution of every tenth man in a unit that had disgraced itself, and there are examples of its use under Augustus, Tiberius, and Galba; but it obviously was an unwise choice for commanders who wished to encourage enlistments.

NONMILITARY TASKS.   The Roman army subscribed to the adage that a busy soldier is a happy soldier. Soldiers not only were employed in the construction of walls and roads, which had a clearly military value, but they also were lent out to civilian authorities to assist in all sorts of construction. Preference was given to projects that needed engineering skill, for the army controlled a large number of the available engineers. Clearly the major part of a soldier's career was not spent in combat, and the emperors felt a need to put to constructive use a body that required about half of the annual imperial budget.

Soldiers were encouraged to decrease military expenses by the manufacture of a number of items in their own camps. Men largely drawn from the country or from small towns would have many skills; and we know that tiles, pots, and bricks, for example, were made in such quantities that the surplus could be sold to civilians — perhaps in exchange for provisions. Large factories were connected with a number of camps for the manufacture and repair of arms, and as time went on there was a greater and greater attempt to make the army more self-sufficient. This in part explains the encouragement of farming by soldiers under the Severi, which had been discouraged earlier because it would tend to domesticate the troops.

MANEUVERS.   Military efficiency in times of peace was maintained by forced marches, war games, and maneuvers. Hadrian was present at such an exercise in Africa in July of 128 A.D., and afterward he addressed the troops with a critique of their work. He said, in part:

> Entrenchments which others take many days to prepare, you have accomplished in a single day. You constructed a wall of considerable size and of a quality quite good enough for a permanent winter camp, and you did this in not much longer time than one is normally built of sod. Now this latter type can be built without much trouble, since blocks of turf are cut in equal size and are easy to carry and handle, and they are by their very nature soft and level. But you worked with huge, heavy, unmatched stones, which cannot be lifted up into position unless they are carefully fitted together. You have dug a straight trench through hard and coarse gravel and smoothed its sides so that it has a neat appearance. When you had accomplished this, you hastened back to camp, got rations and arms, and followed the advance guard of horse, supporting with loud cheers those that were starting to fall back. I congratulate your commander because he has chosen for you maneuvers very like true warfare, and for so training you that you all may be congratulated. Your prefect, Cornelianus, has proved very satisfactory in his command. Personally, I do not care very much for open-order tactics, and I have good authority for my opinion. A cavalryman should make use of cover in advancing and should undertake pursuit with caution; for, if he does not look where he is going, or if he is not able to rein in his horse when he wishes, he may well fall into an enemy-prepared trap.

Such a blend of praise and constructive criticism was highly effective. Its success is illustrated by the high morale expressed by the epitaph from the gravestone of a Batavian boy who was stationed on the Danube during Hadrian's principate:

> Once I was called on Pannonian shore
> "Bravest and Best," the Batavian Corps.
> Hadrian watched while I donned all my gear
> And swam the deep Danube to prove I've no peer.
> I shot up an arrow, it hung there amain —
> Then I shot up another that cleft it in twain.
> No Roman or foreigner equals my art
> In hitting the mark with a spear or a dart.
> So here where I lie is a stone with the facts
> Engraved to inspire men to similar acts —
> > While I who leave this tale in stone
> > For model had — myself alone.

ENTERTAINMENT.   Not all of the contributions to the soldiers' morale were quite so strenuous. Even the smallest camp usually had baths attached with all the amenities that went with Roman baths. And outside each permanent camp shacktowns (*canabae*) quickly sprang up with wine-shops and brothels to cater to the tastes and needs of the troops. Until Septimius Severus legionaries were not allowed to marry, but liaisons with local girls were winked at, and before the end of the second century A.D. the offspring of these matches were an important source of recruits. Gaming and hunting were other diversions, and theaters and amphitheaters were frequently constructed close to the camps. There was an effort to isolate troops garrisoned in towns from the civilians, but the soldiers often managed to hang around the town baths and make themselves a nuisance. We also have record at Dura, on the Euphrates frontier, of a troupe of theatrical artists that settled down for nine months in quarters close to those of the garrison. It apparently had been imported to entertain the soldiers at a distant outpost.

FRONTIER DEFENSES.   Augustus had envisioned for the Empire frontiers that approximated prominent geographical features and would be easily defensible: the Atlantic, Rhine, Danube, Black Sea, Syrian Desert and Euphrates, Red Sea, and African Desert. These lines were not held by the legions, however, for many of them were protected by the establishment of client states. Even where there was no such buffer, the legions usually were stationed at some distance back from the actual geographic frontier and could be moved quickly to troubled areas by means of a constantly improved system of roads. In fact, the word for "frontier" *(limites)* originally indicated simply the network of roads leading to and paralleling the lines of defense. As times passed and client states disappeared, the frontiers came to be more distinct and more heavily guarded. Under the Flavians (69–96 A.D.), for instance, auxiliaries were placed along the new lines that were being established between the headwaters of the Rhine and Danube, and the legions could support them, if they were attacked, from their permanent camps to the rear. Succeeding emperors made these *limites* of Germany more and more a defensive line: Hadrian (117–138 A.D.) built a wooden palisade in place of Domitian's earthern ramparts and straightened the line; Antoninus Pius (138–161 A.D.) constructed stone forts along it; and Commodus (180–192 A.D.) and Caracalla (211–217 A.D.) built stone walls to replace the earlier, more perishable materials. Forces were now closely distributed along these lines and, after the conspiracy of Saturninus under Domitian, no more than one legion was in any one camp. This not only made the defenses of the Empire thin, but it also made it more difficult to assemble forces to resist a body of enemy, if one did break through the outer lines. The deep penetration of the Empire by the northern tribes in the principate of Marcus Aurelius illustrates the danger. Further, the policy of Hadrian to recruit from the areas in which the legions were stationed, followed by the Severan policy of granting lands to troops along the frontiers and encouraging their cultivation, by the time of Alexander Severus (222–235 A.D.) had developed a kind of frontier soldiers called the *limitanei*, who were attached to their farms and were practically immobile. It was troops with such ties who forced Alexander Severus to hurry back from the East when they learned that the Alamanni were threatening their home stations.

SOLDIERS AND CIVILIANS.   For Roman civilians the Roman army was one of the most pervasive of institutions. Its influences were much more intimate than the simple financial fact that it commanded half of a man's taxes. There was also a constant effect on many a citizen's eye, mind, morals, comfort, and safety. All over the Empire roads, canals, theaters, arches, baths, and other public buildings met the eye and testified to the constructive uses of the military. The *canabae*, which serviced the soldiers' needs, often developed into handsome and thriving towns and were a stimulus to the development of areas that previously had been quite barren. And wherever the soldiers were stationed, their need for supplies and entertainment stimulated the economy and redistributed the tax money among the

470

taxed. Beside their duty to defend the citizens against foreign enemies, the soldiers were also given police duties within the Empire. Market places and highways were the natural targets of robbers and brigands, and in the larger villages along the routes of trade there were established *stationes* with small detachments of troops called *stationarii* to maintain the peace. Between stations along the highways towers (*burgi*) were built where smaller detachments of *burgarii* protected travellers. These services became especially common from the reign of Commodus. But the police duties of soldiers often were more sinister; they were detached from their units to serve the central government by exacting delinquent taxes, arresting suspects, and serving as political spies. The power that they enjoyed led frequently to extortion, persecution, and bribery, and the very names of these agents — *speculatores, frumentarii, agentes in rebus* — became synonymous with hatred and fear. The exigencies of the national defense also required troops to be stationed in various cities, although the Romans theoretically disapproved on the grounds that city life corrupted soldiers. When permanent quarters were built for the soldiers, there was every effort made to cut the military quarter off from the rest of the town, but often contact with the civilian inhabitants was unavoidable. Where adequate military quarters did not exist, soldiers were simply billeted in private homes, one third of each house being liable for such requisition. In towns so garrisoned the commander of the unit was the most important man in the place, and the temptations of this power must have been considerable.

The soldiers spread their language and tastes among the civilians both by constant contact and by preferring to buy those items that were closest in style and workmanship to what they were accustomed. This was one of the most important ways that Latin and Roman culture were broadcast, but this was not a one-way street: soldiers often found wives, satisfying religious practices, and colorful vocabulary among the civilians with whom they were stationed, and many of these acquisitions were carried back to the heartland of the Empire by the movement of the troops. As the soldiers themselves began to come from the less Latinized areas, their consequent influence on the future of Roman culture, when they were stationed in the Empire's cities, was substantial.

MILITARIZATION.   Even under the best conditions the Roman army was a formidable machine, but by the early third century A.D. there were alarming indications that it might abandon its role as protector and might, instead, feed upon or even swallow the State. Many of the soldiers were now set up along the frontiers as a militarized peasantry, the *limitanei,* and they were losing both the discipline and the mobility that had given the Roman army its superiority. The establishment of home life in the barracks, after the legalization of marriage by Septimius, not only interfered with the strictly military purposes of army camps, but also made troop movements expensive and cumbersome. Already soldiers were used as policemen on the staffs of imperial officials, such as procurators. In time troops actually were detailed to collect the taxes; and their power and arrogance boded ill for the future serenity of taxpayers.

Under the Severi the staffs of provincial governors also were highly militarized. Civilians fell away, and six or seven times more military personnel were employed in bureaucratic positions than had been under the Antonines. The trend penetrated every corner of government; and more and more an honorable discharge from the army was the key to advancement in the high offices of the administration. Those familiar with the tendencies of military training to encourage extreme conservatism of mind, concern for petty detail, and reverence for rank may wonder how healthy a development this was for society. Most ominous was the threat to Roman civilization. Whereas Roman troops once had carried their culture to the frontiers, and foreign troops had been drilled and commanded by Italian centurions, in the third century A.D. the policies of the Severi were changing all that. Italians were practically eliminated from the military roster. Now illiterate peasants and mountaineers as recruits received their training from men who, at the best, were themselves semicivilized. As the Empire waned, more and more would these half-barbarian troops be garrisoned in its cities, while their discharged veterans became the elite of municipal societies. As the power of the army increased, and the government was more thoroughly militarized, the brilliant city life of the Empire was barbarized from within. The citadel of Roman civilization had fallen long before the Gothic hordes overran Italy.

Chapter 38

THE STRUCTURE OF THE EMPIRE: MUNICIPALITIES AND PROVINCES

The Romans of the second century A.D. viewed the Roman Empire as a great aggregate of city-states under the leadership of the preeminent state Rome and of its leading citizen, the emperor. "A democratic commonwealth has been established, organized and led by the best citizen," said Aelius Aristides in his famous encomium of Rome, "and it is just as though we all could assemble in town meeting, for each man gets what is his due." It was a matter of wonder, pride, and satisfaction to the Romans that an estimated one hundred million people lived together in harmony, surrendering a minimum of their national character, and enjoying everywhere the protection of an imperial army and the administration of an imperial bureaucracy, each equally composed of citizens. Even Italy, which had conquered the world, little by little assumed more the role of a partner than that of a mistress.

ACQUISITION OF NEW PROVINCES.   At the death of Augustus there were twenty-eight administrative districts or provinces in the Empire, and these were increased in the next two centuries by about a dozen. Not all of the new provinces were acquired by conquest. Some of them were former client states annexed when the ruling family died out or proved unsatisfactory, or where Roman interests had become paramount in the area. Examples are Cappadocia (17 A.D.), the Cottian Alps, Thrace (46 A.D.), Judaea (6 A.D.), and the Mauretanias (42 A.D.). Conquest accounted for the addition of Britain (44 A.D.), Arabia (105 A.D.), Dacia (106 A.D.), and Mesopotamia (115, 165 A.D.), while others were formed by such administrative measures as the detachment of the Germanys from Gaul by Domitian, or the partition of larger provinces into smaller safer units, as was done by Septimius in Syria, Africa, and Britain.

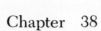

473

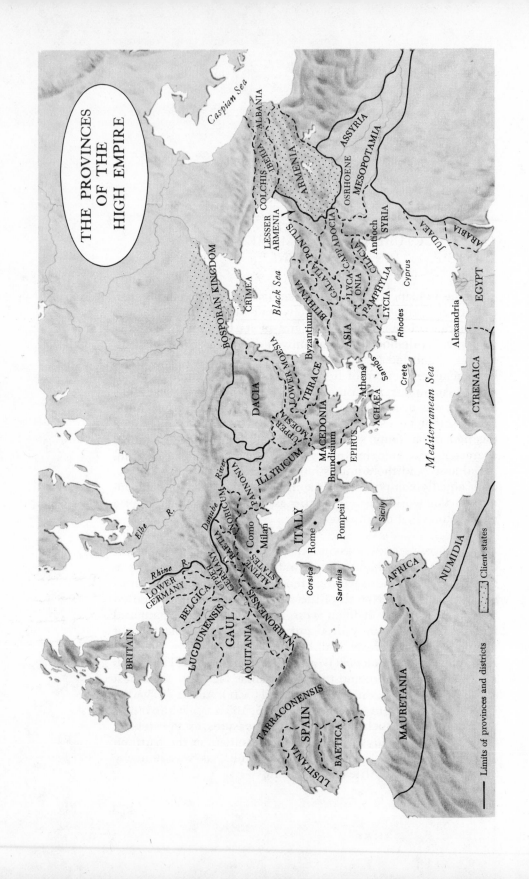

THE PROVINCES
OF THE
HIGH EMPIRE

Caspian Sea

ALBANIA

IBERIA

COLCHIS

ARMENIA

ASSYRIA

OSRHOENE

MESOPOTAMIA

LESSER ARMENIA

PONTUS

CAPPADOCIA

GALATIA

CILICIA

Antioch

SYRIA

ARABIA

JUDAEA

BITHYNIA

PAPHLAGONIA

LYCA-ONIA

PAMPHYLIA

LYCIA

Cyprus

Rhodes

EGYPT

Alexandria

ASIA

CRIMEA

Black Sea

BOSPORAN KINGDOM

Byzantium

THRACE

LOWER MOESIA

UPPER MOESIA

MACEDONIA

Athens

Saronis

ACHAEA

Crete

CYRENAICA

Mediterranean Sea

DACIA

Raea

PANNONIA

EPIRUS

Brundisium

ILLYRICUM

NORICUM

Danube

Elbe R.

RAETIA

ALPINE STATES

Como

Milan

ITALY

Rome

Pompeii

Sicily

Rhine R.

LOWER GERMANY

UPPER GERMANY

BELGICA

GAUL

LUGDUNENSIS

AQUITANIA

NARBONENSIS

Corsica

Sardinia

AFRICA

NUMIDIA

TARRACONENSIS

BRITAIN

SPAIN

LUSITANIA

BAETICA

MAURETANIA

Limits of provinces and districts

Client states

CLASSIFICATION OF PROVINCES.   In accordance with the division of powers inaugurated by Augustus, the older, more highly civilized provinces, such as Asia, Africa, Achaea, and southern Spain, continued to be administered by the Senate, which used the ancient republican machinery. But for the frontier provinces and those requiring the presence of the legions (with the exception of Africa) the emperor took the responsibility. New provinces, however, naturally appeared in areas requiring imperial oversight, so that the original number of twelve imperial and ten senatorial provinces soon showed a greater disproportion in favor of the emperor. The division was not considered a hard and fast one: Achaea and Macedonia, for example, were transferred to the emperor under Tiberius, and back to the Senate under Claudius. Egypt was in a special category. There the emperor was looked upon as the legal successor of the Ptolemies, and in some sense the country was, therefore, his private property. Egypt furnished the city of Rome with one-third of its annual requirement of grain, and its possessor had great power. The danger that would come from its seizure caused the emperors to forbid all persons of senatorial rank access to Egypt without special permission, and they established there a special government under an equestrian prefect.

PROVINCIAL ADMINISTRATIONS.   The senatorial provinces continued to be governed by former consuls and praetors, though all now were called proconsuls. They served for terms of one year, and they were regulated by the old Pompeian Law.[1] They each had as a financial assistant one quaestor, and they also had three lieutenants, who had been approved by the emperor. Governors in the imperial provinces also were drawn from the consular and praetorian ranks, and their title was *legatus Augusti* (lieutenant of the emperor). *Legati* of the emperor had less prestige and dignity than the proconsuls had, but their power was actually far greater, for they often had sizeable bodies of troops under their direction. They remained at their posts at the emperor's pleasure—usually from three to five years—and they received a salary sufficiently large that there was little need or temptation for corrupt practices. Under Tiberius one man was the governor of imperial provinces for twenty-four years, for the emperors tended to leave good men in their posts so that they could thoroughly understand the provincials' problems.

[1]   For the Pompeian Law, see above, p. 289.

475

The fiscal duties in the imperial provinces were performed by procurators, usually of the equestrian class. They not only supervised the collection of taxes and forwarded them to Rome, but they also superintended the constantly increasing private property of the emperors. Under this guise procurators of the emperors also were found in senatorial provinces, but in the early Principate their duties were strictly private. The emperor found it convenient, however, to have these personal agents in both the imperial and senatorial provinces, for they could report to him on any irregularities that they observed wherever they occurred. Since the emperor was legally endowed with proconsular power and *maius imperium,* which set him above all other proconsuls, he was in a position to initiate improvements and correct abuses, even in the senatorial provinces.

There were a number of areas in which imperial interests needed protection, yet which were not sufficiently large or important to warrant a *legatus Augusti* and a full complement of troops. In these places procurators sufficed to care for the financial interests of the central government and to carry out such other administrative duties as arose. The districts with procurators as governors generally had a small detachment of troops allotted to them to keep order. The administrative procurators of such districts were under the general supervision of the governor of a nearby larger province, as the procurator of Judaea was under the governor of Syria and, in the early Principate, Cappadocia was under Galatia.

The large number of provinces required a large number of governors, and the emperors almost without exception were determined that these should be trustworthy men. Since the governors were drawn from the ex-magistrates of Rome, the emperors had to be sure that only qualified men rose through the *cursus honorum.* This is the reason why Augustus and his successors felt compelled more and more to control the candidacies and the machinery of election to the higher magistracies. Such control frustrated the expectations of some Romans, whose sole claim to office was their high birth, and their frustration explains some of the resentment felt by the senatorial class toward the princes in the early Principate. At the same time, the imperial interference in elections accounts for the growing dependence of ambitious men on the good will of the emperor.

The strength of the central government and its unflagging interest in the good health of the provinces led the governors to show far less independence and initiative than they had in republican days; and the development of an efficient public post (*cursus publicus*) meant that inquiries and requests for guidance could be forwarded to Rome with a minimum of difficulty or delay. A governor's tasks were largely supervisory: to provide for the safety and tranquillity of the area in his care; to assume judicial supervision where important principles or the rights of Roman citizens were at stake; and to see to it that provincials discharged their obligations to the State. His work was greatly simplified by the almost complete responsibility that the local governments within the provinces assumed for purely local affairs. In the early Principate the smaller units, whether they were city-states or tribes, did indeed govern themselves; and the average citizen had small contact with the higher representatives of Rome.

TAXATION.   From the viewpoint of the central government the most important duty of its representatives in the provinces was the efficient and equitable collection of the taxes; and even in this task a great deal of the work was done by the local authorities. The chief tax was that on the land (*tributum soli*), which was based on the productivity of each piece of property taxed. There was also a personal tax (*tributum capitis*), which generally was not a poll tax, but was a tax on the members of the trades and professions. There was also the *annona*, a tax in kind, levied to furnish grain and other staples for the troops and officials in a province. A duty on legacies applied only to Roman citizens and was used for the payments of a bonus to army veterans at discharge. The most important indirect tax was the customs duty. This applied not only to imports from outside the Empire, but also to goods moving between one customs district and another within the Empire. The customs charges varied from two to five percent of the value of the goods taxed, but two and one-half percent seems to have been most common. While the imperial procurators supervised the collection of all these taxes in the imperial provinces, and in the early Principate quaestors did so in the senatorial provinces, the actual collection of the direct taxes was generally performed by the municipalities. By the second century A.D. ten leading citizens (*decem primi* in the West, the *dekaprotoi* in the East) were appointed to perform that task as an unpaid public service (a liturgy). Tax-farmers continued to be used for the indirect taxes until the end of the second century A.D., when they were replaced by procurators.

THE NATIONAL CENSUS.   To assure a fair distribution of the burden of taxes, a complete survey of the Empire's resources was needed. Such a survey was begun by Julius Caesar, though

477

the first complete census was not finished until late in the principate of Augustus. A new survey was taken thereafter periodically. In the East, at least, the government attempted to take a census every fourteen years. The survey furnished a careful analysis of the character and quality of the land. The surveys of the land required the work of professionals, but the data of the popular census was collected by local officials and forwarded to the provincial censor, who compiled the statistics and forwarded them to Rome. The organization at the local level would differ from place to place: in colonies or *municipia* every fifth year the chief magistrates of the municipalities were called *quinquennales*, instead of the ordinary *duoviri* or *quattuorviri*, to indicate that they were authorized in their year of office to take the census. The censor not only compiled a list of citizens, but he also gave an account of their wealth and trades. By all these means a fair distribution of the burden of government could be made among and within provinces, for the emperor in Rome could use the material from the survey and from a census to create a compendium of the Empire's resources.

LITURGIES.   Most of the taxes could be foreseen and were largely based on the ability to pay. But there was another type, the liturgy, which became more burdensome as the Empire progressed. This was basically an ancient form of taxation on the wealthy, both in Greece and Rome, whereby they were called upon to perform certain tasks for the State without remuneration, and the device is still in use. In republican Rome the magistrates themselves performed a kind of liturgy, for they were obliged to provide games and shows at their own expense. (Similarly, in America today the obligation of employers to withhold income taxes from the pay of employees is a liturgy.) In the Empire the liturgies, such as the duty to remit to the government the full assessed tax of a town, or the requisition of draught animals for army transport or the public post, could be disastrous. In the first case, the collector might be forced into bankruptcy if a sufficient number of citizens evaded the payment of their taxes; and in the second, the requisition of farm animals might come at the most critical times for a farmer. True, there might be financial remuneration for articles requisitioned, but the money often would not easily replace a horse or an ox when it was desperately needed at planting time.

IMPERIAL CONTROL OF PROVINCIAL ADMINISTRATORS.
There were indeed numerous laws and directives against the captious abuse of the right to requisition or to billet, but laws

against misgovernment were not enough. There had to be some kind of an arrangement whereby the complaints and appeals of provincials could reach the central government. The governors and procurators generally were pleased to report to the emperors about each other's activities, and this could be a powerful restraint on misconduct, unless there were collusion. Embassies to Rome from the separate municipalities were frequent, and if any members were veterans of the legions they got an extremely sympathetic hearing from the emperor. Many towns also elected powerful residents of Rome as their patrons, and in return for this honor it was the duty of these patrons to represent the town's interests with the central government.

An institution of increasing importance for the airing of provincial grievances was the provincial assemblies (*concilia*). These consisted of representatives of the various towns of a province who gathered annually in the chief town to elect a high priest and to conduct the rites connected with the worship of Rome and Augustus. After the religious ceremonies were completed, it was natural for mutual secular problems to be discussed, and it became customary for the delegates either to commend the administration of the governor, or to forward a delegation to Rome with a complaint. This custom was encouraged by the emperors, who corresponded directly with the assemblies and made them the prosecutors in cases of malfeasance of office. Such cases normally were heard before the Senate. These provincial assemblies were developing toward true representative government, when the civil disturbances of the third century A.D. ended all progress. But they furnished the model for the deliberative gatherings or synods of Christian prelates, and they thus have had a continuing influence in the Western world.

TYPES OF LOCAL GOVERNMENT IN THE EMPIRE.
The Roman emperors of the first two centuries of the Principate and their administrations took much thought for the protection and well-being of the Empire. To the ordinary man, however, Rome was very grand but very remote; to him the government that had constant importance and interest was the government of his own home town. Here indeed the greatest volume of the Empire's political activity was carried on, for the Early Empire did not have either the staff or the experience to undertake the vast responsibility of government at the bottommost level. To expedite local self-government, the Romans generally encouraged the organization of the provinces into city-states and in most areas urbanization was rapid. Hither Spain, for example, had

179 towns and 114 cantons (or country districts) under Augustus; but by the time of Antoninus Pius there were 248 towns and only 27 cantons. The sole exceptions to rapid urbanization were Egypt and large parts of Gaul. Gaul had been given a tribal organization based on its historical peoples. This accorded well with the agricultural character of the province and therefore cities appeared there more slowly except in southern, or Narbonese, Gaul. In fact, Rome made little effort anywhere to standardize or to "Romanize." The *Romanitas* (Roman character) of the Empire was based on the appreciation of men for the benefits that came from their joint enterprise, rather than from any conscious effort by the Romans to impose language, religion, or culture on others. All over the Empire, however, municipalities tended to move away from the more democratic type of city government that had been developed by the Greeks, and to adopt a more oligarchic system that was similar to the government of early Rome.

The cities of the Empire differed in their forms of government and in their legal status according to their past history and geographic location. Some of them were not legally subjects of the Empire at all. These, the *civitates foederatae* (allied states) had signed a treaty as legal equals with Rome, often during the wars that preceded the acquisition of a province. They were essentially independent enclaves, within a province, but not of it. They were not taxed and they were not under the governor's jurisdiction, though they could not, of course, pursue an independent foreign policy. Also tax-exempt were the *civitates liberae et immunes* (free and immune states), but their legal status was more precarious, for their freedom had been granted unilaterally by the Senate, and it could be revoked at the government's pleasure. The largest category, however, was the *civitates stipendiariae*. Towns of this order paid tribute and were fully under the governor's jurisdiction, though they too were accorded much freedom in local government. There were also in the provinces an increasing number of communities of Roman citizens. These were either Roman colonies, founded in great numbers by the earlier emperors, or *municipia*, ancient cities that had been granted the Roman citizenship. These places, unlike Roman towns in Italy, had to pay taxes on their land unless they had been granted the *ius Italicum*—the right to be treated as if they were Italian. This right was given only rarely, however, and was reserved for areas where settlement needed encouragement or where the emperors had sentimental attachments. Some places were granted "Latin rights," that is, they had the political status that ancient Latin cities in Italy once had. Their magistrates automatically became Roman citizens (after Hadrian the members of the town councils also did), and the position was considered a halfway house to complete citizenship.

As time went on there was a tendency for the variety of local governments within the Empire to decrease. Apparently under financial pressure Vespasian revoked the freedom of Achaea, Byzantium, Lycia, Rhodes, and Samos. Under Trajan we find cities willingly abandoning their special status. Meanwhile, more and more areas were acquiring a higher citizenship status. Nero gave Latin rights to the Cottian and Maritime Alps. Galba and Otho conferred Roman citizenship on peoples of central and eastern Gaul; Vitellius gave Latin rights to many in Spain and Africa; and Vespasian gave Latin rights to all the towns of the Spanish peninsula that did not already have them. The trend reached its final and full expression, of course, in the grant of universal citizenship by Caracalla (212 or 213 A.D.), and in the acquisition of equal rights by all the communities of the Empire.

THE ANCIENT TOWN: THE SETTING.   Each municipality was set in the middle of a territory of varying size which it administered. This might include a number of villages and marketplaces as well as agricultural property. A visitor to such an ancient town could learn a great deal about the character, economy, and inhabitants of the place even before he reached its gates. The surrounding countryside—whether it was pastureland, vineyards, olive groves, wheatlands, or dotted with the evidences of mining and smelting—would tell him something of the chief industries of the inhabitants. Some distance from a town the roads would pass through the farms and truck gardens that supplied it. Lack of refrigeration and the high cost of transport meant that most places were largely supplied with food grown in the immediate area. The suburbs were, therefore, verdant with vegetables and fruit trees, and the air was alive with the gush of irrigation ditches and with the sounds of the fowl and small animals that supplied the town's meat markets. Just before the town's entrance, the roads were lined with the sepulchres and graveyards of the inhabitants. The tombs often were large and they were graced with sculptures and inscriptions giving details concerning the family and achievements of the deceased.

Inside the town the streets were paved, in Italy often with black basalt. In an old village the streets would be narrow and crooked, but in the colonies civil engineers laid out wide streets

481

at right angles to one another, with every fifth street an avenue of unusual breadth. In the residential areas the streets were lined with blank walls broken only by an occasional door or a shuttered second story window, for Roman houses looked inward to a central court instead of onto the street. The business sections, however, were alive with all the color, bustle, and odors of the bazaars of the modern Near East. The shops opened directly onto the streets and often were the exterior rooms of a block which contained private residences in its interior. These stores in many cases included the workshops as well as the salesrooms of the tradesmen. This indicates that business was in the hands of small entrepreneurs; and baking, fine jewelwork, and leatherwork were done on the premises under the interested eyes of the prospective purchasers.

The focal point of the town was the forum—the agora in the East—for this was the public square of the ancient city, and it was flanked by its most pretentious buildings: the *curia* where the town council met, the basilica where the judges sat, the offices of the local officials that performed such useful services as the inspection of the weights and measures used by the tradesmen, the meeting places of the associations of the most important trades, and temples. In western towns particularly there probably would be a capitol, which was set on a high podium or hillock and which contained a temple to Jupiter Capitolinus in the Roman fashion. The forum also served, as it still often does, as an open-air market for the display and sale of fruits, vegetables, and small animals raised on nearby farms. Most towns also would have baths (gymnasia and palaestrae, if they were in the East), theaters for pageants and plays on festival days, and possibly also an amphitheater for gladiatorial combats and athletic contests.

THE INHABITANTS.   The inhabitants of the typical municipality were a cross-section of Roman life and of the social and economic factors that dominated it. The local aristocrats tended to be of two sorts. There were the owners of estates in the vicinity, who resided in the town, lived on the profits of their olive groves, vineyards, or ranches, and served as magistrates, and benefactors of their native places. Most of them were wealthy enough to be counted as members of the equestrian class (with a patrimony of at least 400,000 sesterces). In the same category we must place the army veterans, particularly those that had risen through the ranks to the higher grades of the centurionate. They not only received at discharge a considerable bonus, but they often also were raised to equestrian rank

482

by the emperor. They frequently invested in land when they settled down and became prominent in local affairs.

Just down the scale from these rural aristocrats, or decurions as they were called if they sat in the town council, were persons of wealth but of low birth: freedmen or freedmen's sons, who had made money in the trades or by canny investments. They generally were not considered worthy of the local magistracies or of service in the local senate or *curia*, but they did stand for election to the boards of Augustales, men selected to carry on the cult of the emperor. As such, they were able to realize positions of dignity worthy of their wealth, and they tended in their gratitude to repay the municipality with monuments, buildings, entertainments, and endowments.

ECONOMIC LIFE.   In the first and second centuries A.D. the trades at the local level seem to have flourished. Almost every town had guilds or associations of smiths, fullers, bakers, clothiers, leatherworkers, carpenters, and others. More specialized groups were found in towns with special features; a seaport like Ostia, for instance, had numerous bodies of men that specialized in just one of the many aspects of loading and unloading cargo. There were several different kinds of boatmen and stevedores, and even the divers, who recovered goods dropped in the harbor, were organized in a guild. Freemen, freedmen, and slaves all might participate in this kind of labor. The existence of a large class of poor, free, and often unemployed residents of the municipalities, as well as of Rome, is indicated by the public alimentary institution inaugurated by Nerva to support and educate the children of the poor in Italian towns, and by the appearance of private endowments for the same purpose in the provinces. In addition to all these classes of people, there were, of course, the small farmers or the tenant farmers of the municipality's property, who brought their produce to town to exchange for the manufactured necessities that the place had to offer. There also were numbers of slaves, not simply those owned by the well-to-do, but also public slaves, owned by the municipalities and detailed to furnish the menial labor needed to operate many of the public services.

ENTERTAINMENT.   Life in the Roman town was not as dull as one might expect, or as the residents of the capital at Rome liked to pretend. Almost all towns were equipped with public baths; and these, with their pleasant colonnades and porches, their exercise rooms and ball courts, were natural gathering places. More elaborate entertainment was furnished at frequent

483

intervals by the rich. The townsfolk celebrated comings-of-age, marriages, funerals, and elections with games, shows, banquets, and handouts that might go on for days. In the reign of Augustus one Aulus Clodius Flaccus, upon being elected a magistrate of Pompeii, between July 6th and 13th presented a procession, a bullfight, Greek and Roman boxing matches, a performance of music and ballet in the theater, thirty pairs of athletes and five pairs of gladiators; and then later, with his colleague, thirty-five pairs of gladiators, and a baiting of wild beasts, including bulls, boars, bears, and other animals. The popularity of the arena over the theater may be seen by noting that the two theaters of Pompeii seated 4000 and 1500 respectively, while the amphitheater accomodated from 13,000 to 20,000. A comparison of the number of theaters and the size of the stadia in the cities of the Western world indicates that the Romans were not inferior to the moderns in the taste for wildly emotional mass spectacles. Most towns also were provided with brothels. These consisted of rows of small cubicles with suggestive and erotic pictures over the doors. They generally were run by male panderers, and the girls were slaves. Some limited precautions against infectious disease were prescribed through regulations for washing and bathing. At Pompeii, a backdoor to private bathing rooms in the Baths opened discreetly close to a famous brothel. Owners of inns and cookshops often kept singers and dancers as well.

EDUCATIONAL FACILITIES. Even the smaller towns had elementary schools where reading, writing, figuring, and some knowledge of the law could be acquired. These schools were privately owned and the government did not assume responsibility for them. Public-spirited citizens, however, often did, and they might band together to furnish suitable masters. Pliny the Younger, for instance, though childless himself, was concerned that his native town of Como had no advanced training in literature and rhetoric. He offered to foot one-third of the bill, if the other townspeople would put up the remainder, to import a qualified teacher from Rome. Qualified teachers were not always easy to find, if we can judge from the experiences of Aulus Gellius. He was present at the interview of a candidate for a teaching position in Brundisium, and he was amused at the wonderfully botched-up interpretation of the *Aeneid* that the prospective schoolmaster presented. Boys who wanted the highest training in law, literature, philosophy, oratory, and the arts spent the last years of their studies in one of the great university cities, such as Rome, Athens, Alexandria, or Antioch.

Opportunities for adult education were not lacking in the municipalities, and we have notices of the establishment and endowment of libraries in quite small towns.

RELIGION.   Public religion in the municipalities, as in Rome, was dominated by ceremonies performed for the town by the magistrates, and the people were spectators rather than participants. Gods of the regular Roman pantheon were worshipped, but often the town would have some special deity of its own. Some of these local gods were derived from the localized spirits that men had sensed since prehistoric time, and to whom they ultimately had given names and human form. The feasts of these municipal gods were celebrated with much pageantry, processions, and spectacles and attracted many visitors for the show. However, the hearts of the people belonged to, and their religious sensibilities were stirred by, the spirits of the field, family, and home. These were the familiar and homely Lares, Penates, and garden gods, whose interest and help still were needed and still were felt by the country-folk. The emperor-cult also was early adopted in the municipalities, as the existence of the freedman Augustales in most towns implies. In fact, to many townspeople Rome must have seemed as magnificent and remote as Olympus itself, and surely the benefits of the imperial government were more rational and more dependable than the activities of the Olympians ever had been. In some places the cult of the emperor's genius largely replaced, in public documents at least, the older deities that the local priests once served.

MUNICIPAL GOVERNMENT.   Julius Caesar drew up a model municipal constitution, and this was copied for centuries, though the charters of the western municipalities nevertheless showed some variations. There sometimes was only one college of magistrates, or sometimes as many as three. At the head of the municipal government there might be a single dictator, as in some Latin cities, or a committee of two, four, or even five persons. But the majority of western communities had three colleges of magistrates. The typical western municipality has as its highest magistrates a two-man board called duumvirs, who were the chief administrative and judicial officials of the town. Every fifth year the duumvirs were called the *quinquennales*, and during that year of office they took the census and forwarded their findings to the appropriate national officials. At the same time they also revised the list of the local senators or decurions. In the normal town there also would be a board of aediles

485

charged with the care of public works and services, and a board of quaestors in charge of financial affairs. All these magistrates were elected by an assembly of the free citizens of the municipality organized by wards or *curiae*. Aside from the election of magistrates, the western Roman-type assemblies appear to have had very little to do, unlike their more powerful and democratic Greek counterparts, which often had traditional legislative and judicial functions until the Greek municipalities fell under the influence of the Roman model.

In the western or Roman type of municipality, the ruling power was largely in the hands of a strongly aristocratic body, the *curia* or local senate. This council was made up of one hundred municipal magnates, who were commonly called decurions or curiales. The members held their seats in the *curia* for life, and replacements were made every five years by the *quinquennales*. Ex-magistrates were appointed *ex officio*, and some distinguished and especially honored families held what amounted to hereditary seats. The young sons of such families were allowed to attend sessions, as they once had been in early Rome, to learn procedure, but they did not become voting members until the age of twenty-five. Except for the actual election of the local magistrates, this local and aristocratic senate governed the municipality under the leadership of the equally aristocratic magistrates, though the latter had indeed been subjected to popular election.

MUNICIPAL FINANCES.   Roman municipalities did not have the large fiscal responsibilities that modern cities do. However, they did need to construct or maintain public buildings, public grounds and institutions, streets, and roads; and they were expected to arrange for public entertainments, and provide for the sale of flour and oil to the citizens, for Roman towns ordinarily did not leave the distribution of these two staples to the vagaries of a fluctuating market. It was the job of the local aediles to see to it that there was a steady supply of necessary foodstuffs at stable and reasonable prices, even in times of general scarcity. To meet these rather limited obligations the towns had several sources of regular income. Most of them received rentals from their landed properties — some of which were in the immediate environs, some far distant (Capua, for instance, owned lands on Crete). Some towns also owned shops, stores, baths, and even hotels, and these were exploited for the local treasuries. In many places there was a charge for the use of water from the municipal aqueduct, and there might

be a tollgate fee on commercial traffic. There also was an assessment on officials, for the magistrates, far from being paid,
usually paid a set fee to the town upon entering office, and so
did many decurions upon receiving their seats in the *curia*.
Finally, the towns often had permanent capital which they
invested; some of this capital resulted from the legalization of
bequests and legacies to the municipalities at the end of the
first century A.D. Such benefactions were recorded on stone and
thus the benefactors ensured their own immortality. The erection of buildings and the outlay of gifts of money were looked
upon by Roman townspeople as the virtuous occupations of the
rich man; but inscriptions show that individuals of only moderate means also bore their share in effecting the beautification
and comfort of their home places.

MUNICIPAL ELECTIONS.   Unlike the proletariat of Rome,
which early lost all interest — and then all rights — in regard to
elections, the people of the municipalities engaged for generations on spirited contests for the magistracies. When Pompeii
was destroyed in 79 A.D., sixty-five years after the Senate at
Rome became responsible for the election of Roman magistrates, the populace still was exhibiting the liveliest interest in
the outcome of the political contests for the magistracies of that
small Campanian town. Much of the campaigning was done by
means of election posters painted on the blank outer walls that
lined Pompeian streets. In preparation for the application of
campaign slogans, the walls were whitewashed, and then the
notices were painted in large red letters. The candidates were
urged to run by friends, neighbors, and members of local guilds
or clubs. Once the candidacy was declared, there were references to the virtues of the candidates: "Modestus will save the
treasury"; "Polybius will see to it that we get decent bread";
"The ball-players want Firmus."

THE CONSEQUENCES OF FISCAL IRRESPONSIBILITY.   Despite
the municipal enthusiasm for self-government, little by little
independence of action disappeared. This was partly due to the
irresponsibility of the municipalities themselves. Repeatedly
their anxiety to outdo their neighbors in the beauty of their
public buildings and in the lavishness of their entertainments
led townspeople into financial difficulties. In part their careless
waste of income seems to have been due to the realization that
a beneficent central government existed for real crises. In the
early second century A.D. the letters of Pliny to Emperor Trajan

again and again illustrate the fiscal follies of the towns, as well as the interest and concern of the emperor. By the time of Hadrian the emperor was appointing with greater and greater frequency an extraordinary official, a *curator rei publicae,* to straighten out municipal finances that had become dangerously tangled. And by the time of the Severi, these curators of municipal finances had become regular imperial officials, instead of representing an extraordinary favor extended only occasionally. Parallel to the *curatores rei publicae* were the equally extraordinary *curatores kalendarii,* who were appointed by the emperors to survey municipal accounts and to see to it that monies owed to the towns were promptly and properly collected.

The efforts of these disinterested bureaucrats, who were intent on balancing local budgets, of course resulted in higher taxes, greater burdens, and fewer privileges for the local decurions and magistrates. To receive the extended services that municipal irresponsibility evoked, communities had to face a constant rise in the cost of government and in the centralization and standardization of the administration. The emperors were forced to expand the civil service to meet the increased demands made upon the central government, at the very time when the bureaucracy itself was being militarized both in organization and in personnel. As the prosperity of the Empire declined in the late second and the third century A.D., there was a great temptation for leading citizens of the municipalities to seek employment in this civil service. Salaries for public servants were good, and bureaucrats enjoyed many exemptions from the burdensome liturgies. Many members of the municipal equestrian class therefore began to seek the security of a government job. This development was a disaster for the municipalities, for the equestrians had once furnished their services to their home places gratis. It was the defection of these local aristocrats that, by the end of the second century A.D., led the government to fill the municipal senates with persons having the required property valuation regardless of their own wishes. By the end of the third century A.D. the situation had further deteriorated to cause service in the local senates to become a hereditary obligation. And by the fourth century A.D., the local senates had become a kind of penal institution, in which a citizen might be placed as punishment for some offense. In the third and fourth centuries A.D. also, as life within the empire became more precarious and the exaction of taxes and liturgies more difficult, detachments of soldiers more and more took over the police duties that the municipalities once performed for themselves; and the people, harassed by military police and

488

militarized bureaucrats, found their once lovely cities become prisons that only inspired flight.

The policy of decentralization followed by imperial Rome under the early Principate kept alive a healthy interest in self-government for generations in the towns of Italy and the provinces, long after the national government had lost all semblance of popular control. However, to retain that independence, the citizens had to be determinedly self-reliant, the economy strong, and the central government laissez-faire. In fact, the people did lean upon the central government, the economy did weaken in the late second century A.D., and the emperors were concerned for the welfare of the towns of the Empire. It is rather disheartening to reflect that the very interest of the central government in the happiness and well-being of those towns led to a paternalistic bureaucracy that ultimately inundated the sense of municipal responsibility and pride in local traditions and emasculated their vigor.

Chapter 39

ROMAN BUREAUCRACY

The great families of republican Rome that acquired the Roman Empire were a society of amateurs, who not only had no civil service, but were suspicious of the professionalism that the term implies. But it is one thing to win an empire, and another to administer it; and the problems that imperial administration presented ultimately developed one of the most elaborate and pervasive bureaucracies that man has seen. It is not that paperwork and petty detail were unknown to the republicans, but it was part of the duty of wealthy Roman magistrates during their terms of office to furnish from their own households (their educated slaves and freedmen) much of their secretariat. In addition, there was available in Rome a class of accountants, clerks, and menials, often freedmen, who were hired by the government to assist the various elected officials.

489

AUGUSTUS' ADAPTATIONS OF REPUBLICAN PROCEDURE.

After the Senate and Augustus had divided the superintendence of the Roman world between them, it was clearly impossible for Augustus to supervise personally all the provinces and armies that were in his care, as well as to exercise the leadership in Rome that his position as *princeps* demanded. Augustus tried, however, to follow the example of the Roman republican magnates as far as he possibly could. His legates were his personal representatives with the legions, and they were appointed for the administration of the frontier provinces. He followed here the precedent of Pompey, the Republic's champion. For his financial responsibilities a separate treasury (*fiscus*) was set up in each province, and procurators were sent out to handle income and disbursements. Procurators also cared for the emperors' constantly increasing personal estates, some of which were in senatorial as well as imperial provinces. Augustus normally made use of equestrians for the procuratorships, for the years of experience that they had had in business affairs made them very useful, and they did not have the traditions of personal dignity which the senators had and which inhibited them from serving under a man that they considered their peer. In Rome Augustus endeavored to handle the mass of business that came to hand as any other Roman noble would, by means of his own household of slaves and freedmen. These men he supervised closely, and he, in consultation with his friends, was responsible for each decision made in his house.

Augustus was responsible for a number of services in Rome and Italy, an area which was considered the Senate's sphere of administration, and he needed considerable time and tact in making proper arrangements. A *praefectus urbi* (supervisor of the city) was appointed several times during Augustus' principate, but the office became permanent only toward the end of his life. This official had three urban cohorts at his command to maintain order in the city, but the emperor saw to it that the prefect was always a senator of consular rank, in deference to the Senate's sensitivities in this area. The three curators in charge of the aqueducts also were senators. On the other hand, equestrians were appointed to the posts of prefect of the grain supply (*Annona*) and prefect of the praetorian guard. The latter arrangement is easy to understand, for the praetorian prefect commanded the emperor's personal bodyguard, and such a position would be considered undignified for a senator. Later, when in 22 B.C. Augustus was given the care of the grain supply, for similar reasons it seemed quite natural for him to have an equestrian as his executive officer. A prefect of the

Watch, established in 6 A.D. to command seven cohorts of firemen, also was an equestrian. This move followed a number of disastrous fires when the service had been left in the hands of the elected republican aediles. Of course, the emperor's representative in Egypt, the prefect of Egypt, was a knight, for the strategic importance of that realm had led Augustus to close it to all senators without special imperial permission.

RISE OF IMPERIAL FREEDMEN.   Augustus ran his household with a firm hand, and Tiberius was inclined to follow his example. But Tiberius' long absence on Capri left some initiative to his servants; and under the easygoing and sometimes gullible Claudius the imperial freedmen (*liberti*) attained great power. The rise of the imperial freedmen to importance was partly due to the pliancy or weakness of Claudius, but it was also partly due to their efficiency and breadth of experience. These former slaves of the emperor, who had been freed as a reward for competence, served as his confidential secretaries. Most of them were Orientals of Greek birth or breeding, and they were far better educated than most Roman knights or senators. Into their hands came reports and requests from all over the Empire, and they had to process and prepare these for the emperor's eyes. Moreover, the personal estates of the emperors grew prodigiously year by year, thanks to the complimentary legacies that the emperors received and to the acquisition of at least some of the estates of condemned persons. Soon the freedmen, who handled all these details, had an unparalleled knowledge of imperial affairs.

CLAUDIUS FORMALIZES THE BUREAUS.   Under previous emperors there had been some specialization by the various palace assistants, but Claudius formalized his household service into a number of bureaus, each with a trusted freedman at its head. The *libertus ab epistulis* was in charge of the flood of correspondence that came to the emperor from his provinces, from his legions, and from his procurators. The *libertus a rationibus* was in charge of the revenues from the imperial provinces. It was probably at this time that the individual provincial fiscs were concentrated in one central *fiscus* in Rome. To the *fiscus* also came a tax on manumission and on some of the profits from the imperial domains. The *libertus a libellis* received petitions to the emperor, to which a brief reply and the emperor's signature were to be affixed. The *libertus a cognitionibus* investigated the legal aspects of cases in which the emperor was interested and advised him before he took action. Later there was added a bureau *a memoria*, which was in charge of the records necessary for the proper preparation of imperial decisions. From the days of Claudius through the principate of Domitian some of these freedmen exerted great influence in the government. Freedmen began to appear even among the procurators (emperor's financial agents) in the provinces; and, since some of the lesser provinces received procurators as their chief magistrates, we occasionally find freedmen even in those positions (as Felix was in Judaea in the days of St. Paul). In spite of the freedmen's occasional misuse of their position to gain great wealth, and despite the hatred or scorn with which they were regarded by those Romans that dared, their industry and intelligence and their sympathy for the provinces, from which they came, gave the provincials every reason to prefer the government of the Principate to that of the Republic.

One other palace functionary should be mentioned, though he was not strictly a part of the bureaucracy. This was the chamberlain (*cubicularius*). Chamberlains were in close association with the person of the prince and controlled access to him. Such a position could be, and often was, abused. The right to see the emperor was sold; reports on the emperor's purposes or even on his moods were sold (the Romans called this "selling smoke"); and weak emperors often were greatly swayed by these freedmen in making decisions. Cleander, Commodus' chamberlain, is said to have appointed twenty-five consuls in a single year! Freedmen continued to hold this domestic post long after they had disappeared from the bureaus of the civil service.

EQUESTRIANS IN THE BUREAUCRACY. When it was realized that the service of the emperor brought great personal power, men of better birth began to forget that the bureaus had originated among the prince's personal servants, and they too became anxious to take service in them. From the beginning equestrians had dominated the prefectures and the procuratorships, and in 69 A.D. under the rather unexpected leadership of Otho and Vitellius (they otherwise showed no great administrative acumen), equestrians began to be used as the heads of the great bureaus. Otho had a rhetorician as his secretary *ab epistulis,* and Vitellius apparently gave all the secretariats to knights. Knights and freedmen were used together by the Flavians and Trajan: Domitian had an equestrian *ab epistulis* and Trajan an equestrian *a rationibus.*

The tendency to raise the social status of the imperial secretaries, which had appeared under the Flavians and Trajan,

was given formal organization by Hadrian. He wished a dignified as well as an efficient civil service, and he saw that the
senators had failed to provide one, while the emperors' freedmen had raised antagonisms. Now the knights were placed in
almost all the important posts of the bureaus in Rome and in the
procuratorships overseas, and the appearance of a freedman in
them thereafter is exceptional. Hadrian built up a regular *cursus
honorum* in the civil service for the equestrians, and its steps
were distinguished by definite and rather handsome salaries:
60,000, 100,000, 200,000, and 300,000 sesterces annually. Many
men started in the army in the regular equestrian service, and
then rose through graduated steps to the highest offices, even to
the prefectures. An example can be found in one Gaius Junius
Flavianus, who started as a military tribune in the Seventh
Legion. He then served in a subordinate position in the office
that handled the tax on inheritances in Rome (this tax went to
the *aerarium militare*, which cared for discharged soldiers).
After this, he served as the emperor's procurator in three different areas of ascending importance: the Maritime Alps, Hither
Spain, and then Lugdunum and Aquitania in Gaul. In these
positions he became well acquainted with the emperor's financial interests outside Italy. Then he returned to Rome, first as
the head of the office handling inheritance taxes, where he had
started as a subordinate, next in charge of all finances (*a rationibus*), and finally he was prefect of the grain supply (*Annona*),
one of the civil service's top jobs.

Hadrian was anxious to enlist the most capable men, even
when they were not disposed to submit to the preliminary requirement of military service, which had been customary since
the days of Augustus. By waiving the military requirement
Hadrian meant to encourage all men of talent and efficiency to
assist in the imperial administration; but this policy meant that
later, in a time of national stress, the men that controlled the
military forces and the men that kept the administrative machine running were strangers to one another. Hadrian's passion
for efficient organization also led to bureaucratic expansion. He
centralized the direction of the public post, which had been
started by Augustus, in an office in Rome under an equestrian
prefect; and he appointed *advocati* to defend the interests of
the *fiscus* by pursuing delinquent taxpayers and representing
the government in suits that involved financial claims.

MILITARIZATION OF THE BUREAUCRACY.   Hadrian's love
for organization and efficiency was more than matched by Septimius' devotion to the military forces. With his regime, the staff

493

of the bureaus was thrown open not only to the equestrians from the municipalities, but also to professional soldiers that had risen to the higher steps of the centurionate. This might at first be thought to be a reversion to the pre-Hadrianic requirement for some military training for public officials; but there was a great deal of difference between young men of birth who had merely spent one or two years on a legate's staff, and the hardened veterans of twenty-five years' service in the army. These men brought to the bureaucracy the hierarchical notions of the army, and the dead weight of the "chain of command" and multiplication of paperwork. The civil service now came to resemble a great military organization, with the emperor and his chief-of-staff, the praetorian prefect, at the summit, and the staffs of the various bureaus, arranged in careful gradations of rank and responsibility, below them. Ex-centurions brought, also, their experience in exacting tribute in one way or another from their subordinates; and the Roman taxpayer could expect little more mercy from these men in civilian garb than they had received when they were in uniform. Further, the military policy of the Severi had led to the recruitment of men from the less civilized portions of the Empire; and thus men of barbaric habits and tastes, whose training in things Roman was largely confined to military life, were settled after discharge in critical civilian posts in the very heart of the Empire.

FINANCIAL ADMINISTRATION.   The financial management of the emperor's vast domains, both public and private, was one of the first and most important reasons why an organization of imperial financial officers was needed. There were, from the beginning, four separate treasuries, for three of which the emperor was directly responsible. The old *aerarium* of the Senate continued for some time to receive the direct taxes from the provinces that were under senatorial supervision and a tax on the sale of slaves. This treasury was under the Senate's direction. But there were also three other treasuries: the *fiscus*, which received the direct taxes from the provinces under imperial supervision, duties on manumissions, customs duties, and some income from imperial domains; the *patrimonium*, which represented the private property of the emperor and also received some of the income from imperial property; and the *aerarium militare*, established by Augustus to furnish severance allowances to soldiers. While the *fiscus* and the *patrimonium* were at first separate, they seem to have been run on about the same lines. With the Flavians, however, the Julio-Claudians'

494

patrimonium was converted to public property and was therefore administered by the officials of the *fiscus*. The personal
property of the Flavian emperors was known as the *patrimonium privatum*. At the head of the *fiscus* was the secretary *a
rationibus* in Rome, the most important financial agent in the
Empire. Funds and reports from all manner of sources poured
into his office. It was his duty not only to handle all the incom-
ing funds, but also to coordinate income with expenses. He had
to make the estimates on probable income and determine the
expenses for army and navy, transport, and the public works
projects that the emperor contemplated.

Procurators collected the public revenues in the imperial
provinces and the income from imperial estates in the senatorial
provinces, and they also supervised the collection of those
indirect taxes that still were in the hands of tax farmers or other
contractors. As tax-farming became less attractive, because
under governmental supervision there were fewer opportunities for enormous profit, imperial procurators also were appointed for the collection of indirect taxes. The procurator of an
imperial province was its chief financial officer and, as the *fiscus*
slowly arrogated to itself the duties of the *aerarium*, he came to
hold the same position in all the provinces. In some of the
smaller provinces, such as Judaea, Noricum, or Raetia, which
did not require imperial officials of the highest rank, the procurator was at the head of the province's administration. As special imperial appointees, the procurators were useful to the
emperor as independent informants on the activities of the
provincial governors; and as early as 53 A.D. their value to the
State was recognized by the grant to them of jurisdiction in the
trial and decision of cases where the *fiscus* had an interest.

State properties, such as mines and quarries, might be run
directly by their specially appointed procurators, who used
hired freemen, slaves, convicts, or even military labor; but the
State's resources often were leased to capitalists for exploitation. The great agricultural estates presented special problems,
particularly in Africa, where large tracts had come into Nero's
hands by confiscation. In Africa, either an imperial official ran a
tract (*saltus*) partly with slaves and partly with tenant farmers
(*coloni*); or a lease was taken by a financier (*conductor*), who
worked the areas with slaves and tenants. Tenants on such
estates were expected to contribute a specified amount of free
labor to the *conductores* or to the imperial supervisors on the
lands that their landlords themselves cultivated. In Africa, the
saltus were grouped together in great tracts or regions, each of

which had an imperial official as a supervisory procurator, and over these regional procurators was the provincial procurator in Carthage.

Besides all the regular sources of revenue, the imperial wealth was constantly increased by war, by confiscations of the property of condemned criminals, by the property of those that died without heirs, and by inheritances. By the late second century A.D. all these sources of income required special bureaus, with procurators in charge of each one of them. In fact, the bureaus connected with finance had to expand very rapidly under the Antonines, for the numerous grants of Roman citizenship during that period required a great expansion of the office that handled inheritance taxes, since those taxes were levied only on citizens. This was especially true after the Edict of Caracalla, which granted citizenship to almost all the residents of the Empire. Another bureau set up by Septimius Severus was the *res privata,* which administered his own private fortune, the nucleus of which was the estates confiscated from the supporters of Niger and Albinus. Although the *res privata* was theoretically Septimius' private property, he used much of it for public purposes, such as the increased pay for the soldiers. The use by Septimius of a public official, a procurator, to administer his private estate, a use which paralleled in detail the organization of the *fiscus,* indicates the monarchical tendencies of the Severi: their property and the public property were to be looked upon and treated as identical.

DEPARTMENT OF STATE.   Even more powerful than the secretary *a rationibus* was the general secretary of state, the secretary *ab epistulis.* He had to receive and digest the mass of reports and queries that came to the emperor from all over the world, direct negotiations with client states, transmit the emperor's orders to the various bureaus, and keep an eye on the capabilities of the men that were rising through the ranks of the army and the civil service. This post was made a great office under Narcissus, a freedman of Claudius, but by the end of the first century A.D. it was normally held by a knight. The pressure of business in the second century A.D. was so great that the office was divided between two men, and there was a secretary for Greek correspondence, the lingua franca of the East, and another for the Latin correspondence in the West.

SPECIALIZED BUREAUS.   A number of bureaus were more specialized. The prefecture of the *Annona* (grain supply) was administered by knights. The prefects of the *Annona* employed and supervised procurators in Ostia to control the receipt of grain there, and agents in the great grain- and oil-producing areas to arrange for an orderly supply to the Roman market. A *praefectus vehiculorum* was a knight in charge of the public post. Both of these offices needed to be in constant touch with the ministers *ab epistulis* and *a rationibus* for coordination of efforts and for budgetary allowances. In the second century A.D. there were equestrian procurators of the mint, who operated establishments close to areas of military concentration in order to facilitate the payment of troops. There were two bureaus connected with the water supply of Rome: the old senatorial commission, run by curators, kept the aqueducts repaired and furnished a plentiful supply for the city. An imperial bureau, under a procurator, supervised the distribution of water within the city by a system of pipelines, and granted licenses to private customers.

PERSONNEL.   All of the imperial bureaus enjoyed a generous supply of personnel. The press of business forced the emperors to create assistant prefects of the Watch and of the *Annona* during the second century A.D. In each of the bureaus there was a complement of clerks, accountants, paymasters, and treasurers. Some of these employees were descendants of the government clerks that had found employment in the Late Republic, but more were imperial slaves and freedmen. Freedmen and slaves tended to be more tractable than those born free and they were willing to handle steadily and responsibly the masses of routine work that the machinery of government required. With Septimius Severus many of these lesser bureaucratic posts were opened to veterans of the armies, but some freedmen and slaves continued to be used, at least through the third century A.D.

INFLATION AND MULTIPLICATION OF BUREAUS.
Year by year the bureaucratic structure of the offices of public service became larger and more complex. The paternalistic bent of early emperors encouraged throngs of embassies, petitions, appeals, and thank offerings from the provincials to the emperor's household, and this stream of communication brought countless problems that required imperial decision. To cope with the flood, the emperors had to acquire a large and trained staff to handle and classify the various requests for assistance and to do the research necessary for just and adequate decisions. The more effective the central government's service was, the more temptation for local authorities to shirk responsibility

and to increase further the duties of the Roman bureaucrats. Yet, the blame does not lie with the provincials alone, for there is within bureaucratic structures themselves a natural tendency toward immoderate growth: the bureaucrat's love of classification and of specialization in the name of efficiency swiftly leads to a morass of supernumeraries relentlessly multiplying tasks of an ever more petty nature. The militarization of the offices after Septimius Severus aggravated the situation. Conservatism is bred into soldiers by the nature of their dangerous occupation — deviations from tested procedures can be fatal — but this rigid dependence on precedents also can be stultifying. Furthermore, the soldier's conservatism is combined with a devotion to station that is comical, when it does not frustrate all improvement. Men become rigidly classified in a hierarchy of ranks. It was under the influence of such a militarized bureaucracy that sonorous titles became attached to Rome's higher officials: senators were *viri clarissimi*, prefects and imperial secretaries were *perfectissimi*, procurators *egregii*, and the praetorian prefect *eminentissimus*. This was not simply an example of military influence, however; it is a characteristic of weakened societies to bolster their morale in this boastful fashion, and we shall see a parallel inflation in the imperial titles during the later Empire.

The bureaucrats' routine kept many imperial services running even when incompetents sat on the throne or civil war rent the State. For this Roman citizens could be grateful. But ultimately the enormous size of the bureaucracy became an unbearable financial burden. The emperors did not leave us records of their annual budgets, but in the early fourth century A.D. the Christian Lactantius could complain that in his day the civil servants outnumbered the taxpayers. The consequent distress of the ordinary citizens — the farmers, manufacturers, and tradesmen — led them more and more to evade civic responsibilities. However, evasion by the ordinary citizens increased further the work of the bureaucrats, for they were bound to see to it that the goods and services that the people, army, and officials needed were provided, whether the people were willing or not. By the middle of the third century A.D. the Roman world had developed a political and economic situation and had created the appropriate instruments for a rigorously regimented and bureaucratized society.

Chapter 40

DEVELOPMENTS IN ROMAN IMPERIAL ECONOMY

Despite the highly urbanized appearance of much of the Roman Empire by the second century A.D., its economy was basically agricultural. The chief items of produce in almost every province or district were the fruits of the land: the oils, flax, and minerals of Spain; the grain and vines of Gaul and Germany; the grain and herds of Britain; the mines, forests, and pastures of Raetia and Noricum; the iron of the Balkan provinces; the wools of Asia; linen and grain of Egypt; grain, oil, and fruits of Africa. Even such old provinces as Sicily or Sardinia were largely devoted to grain or grazing, and impoverished Greece still had some wine and oil. Along the frontiers the troops, drawn increasingly from the peasantry, were invited by the Severi to take up the hoe in their spare time and renew their ancient occupation.

The emperors had set up city governments everywhere— Septimius even did so in highly agricultural Egypt—and they had two reasons for doing so. Municipal governments were expected to make the administration of the Empire easier for the central government, and the cities themselves were thought effective in spreading Graeco-Roman culture and its ideals in backward areas. There are disturbing indications, however, that in much of the world the cityfolk dwelt with a minimum of effect on the rural masses that surrounded them. Everywhere we find evidence that old languages and religions survived. When the cities had finally decayed and the peasants were called to man the armies and rule the world, local religions, languages, and practices that had been eclipsed by the brilliant town life broke through the Graeco-Roman veneer and reasserted themselves.

DECLINE OF ITALIAN AGRICULTURE. In the face of the increased agricultural productivity of the provinces by the second century A.D., the farms of Italy were not as prosperous as they had once been. The scientific cultivation of the vine and the olive, which had created so much wealth and such lovely villas in Italy during the first century A.D., now had to face competition from first-rate, even superior, products from the provinces. The result was that many of the well-to-do in the Italian municipalities, who had owned and managed estates of moderate size in the immediate neighborhood of their home towns, now felt an economic depression. There was a marked overproduction of wine at the end of the first century A.D., and the consequent decline in financial return forced many of the municipal proprietors to sell all or part of their estates. The result was a new increase in larger estates or *latifundia* in Italy. The men who bought up these decaying farms of Italy were generally not local residents, but were men like Pliny the Younger, who was part of the new imperial aristocracy of service, or they were merchants, bankers, and freedmen, who now lived in Rome on the proceeds of respectable and safe investments in the land. This meant that the new owners were satisfied by a lower rate of income per unit of land, since the great size of their acquisitions made up for the decreased productivity of each part. This development, however, was an economic disaster for the Italian towns nearby these new *latifundia*. In the past, the income from the surrounding estates was enjoyed and spent by residents of the town. Now the proceeds of the land went to absentee landlords who lived and spent their money in Rome. The deterioration of Italian municipal economies, which so much depended on the generosity of the local rich, was rapid and marked. The productivity of the land also declined further, because the tenants had little incentive to improve their methods of farming and they lacked the stimulus of interested and constant supervision that the local landowners once gave. The central government recognized the growing tendency toward absentee ownership and the dangerous consequences of this for local Italian economies, and some efforts were made to stem them. For example, Nero and Vespasian tried to revive some of the declining cities with infusions of veterans; Nerva bought lands on which to settle proletarians as cultivators of smaller plots; and Domitian tried to curb vineyards in the provinces in order to protect the Italian investment in the production of wine.

THE ALIMENTARY INSTITUTION: SOCIAL PURPOSES.
The most ambitious scheme to cope with the decline in the Italian economy was the alimentary institution. The imperial plan

followed the example of private foundations, engendered in the first century A.D. by a real alarm at the increased poverty and the ominous decline of the birthrate in the municipalities of Italy. More than one thoughtful magnate realized that a decline in the birthrate not only threatened the future vitality of Italy, but that it also would soon dry up the surplus Italian population needed to Romanize the Empire. Private funds set up by individuals generally took the form of investments that would ensure a regular income for the rearing of the poor children of a given town and perhaps also provide a small nestegg when each child came of age. Nerva inaugurated a parallel state-supported program, and all the adoptive emperors expanded and fostered it vigorously. The public program, however, had a wider purpose than the private ones had had, for it was carefully calculated to invigorate the declining Italian estates of medium size, and thus to bolster municipal economies, as well as to assist the poor of the municipalities directly.

THE ADMINISTRATION OF THE ALIMENTARY SYSTEM.
For administrative purposes Italy was divided into nine districts: large ones in the Po Valley and the extreme south, while in central Italy there were seven smaller ones, named after the great Roman roads that passed through them. In most cases the director of the program in each of these districts was also the road commissioner. In him the emperor found the person that probably had the best first-hand knowledge of the financial health of the districts. In each community a study was made to discover the number of children that needed aid for their support and education, and how much money was required. The needs were reviewed and redetermined periodically so that new allotments could be made when necessary. The administration then determined how much principal must be invested at five percent annually to yield enough interest to satisfy the requirements. Imperial agents then made loans at five percent annual interest to landowners of the community concerned, and the landowners put up their real estate as security. At this point the imperial agents stepped out of the picture: the interest was collected in semiannual installments by local officials with the title of quaestor, and these same men generally were responsible for the distribution of the funds to the poor children that were eligible. Ordinarily there was little reason for the State to call in the loans, and it did so only if the mortgagee was in arrears in the payment of interest. Normally the mortgagees were allowed by the program to mortgage their property only up to ten percent of its value, and there was, therefore, little

temptation for them to allow foreclosure. Wasteful litigation was thereby kept at a minimum. The whole program was devised to run with as little administrative machinery as possible: most of the routine work was done by interested local officials, while the small hierarchy of regional and national officials was needed only to transmit complaints and petitions to Rome, supervise new allotments, represent the treasury in litigation, replace old borrowers, and arrange settlements when mortgaged properties changed hands.

ECONOMIC PURPOSES OF THE ALIMENTARY INSTITUTION.
The effect of the alimentary institution as a weapon to encourage an increase in population is problematical. But its attractiveness on the economic side, as an attempt to improve the competitive position of municipal landowners in Italy, is unmistakable. We can infer something of the institution's agricultural purposes from the size and location of its administrative districts. The Po Valley comprised one very large district, for it consisted of rich farm lands, and cases of extreme poverty were exceptional there. It was close to the frontiers, where the army furnished a ready market, and it thus kept more prosperous than the rest of Italy. On the other hand, a very large district comprising all southern Italy was warranted because the area had been so thoroughly devastated and depopulated during and after the Hannibalic War that it was mostly barren ranches, where population was sparse and the countryside beyond reclaim. But the area between these extremes needed smaller and more carefully supervised districts. In these the land was still productive, but it was being allowed to slip away to absentee landlords and their less diligent tenant farmers, because the municipal owners did not have the ready cash to adjust their crops to changing markets. What the emperors hoped was that, in each district where the poverty was testified to by the numbers of poor children, landowners would be found who would borrow money and use it to improve the economic health of their local area by adapting their estates to the changing economy. And it seems that the landowners found the emperor's offer reasonable and profitable, for in one town alone, between the first and second letting of funds by the State, there was a rise of nearly 800 percent in the number of proprietors that wished to participate in the program.

The emperors used the immediate return from their loans (the five percent interest paid by the landowners) to improve the economic health of poverty-stricken areas by paying for the food and education of the poor children of the areas. They also

502

hoped that the landowners would use the principal lent in a wise manner that would bring additional benefits to the local economy. For example, the introduction of new crops or more intensive cultivation would involve the employment of local labor, the fathers and brothers of the same impoverished children that enjoyed the interest from the loans. By the injection of the principal into the local economy, jobs could be created for the local labor market, and at the same time the profits for the owners per unit of land could be increased. Thus the whole area might show an improvement that would ultimately decrease the need for the program. The alimentary institution was, then, quite remarkable for its administrative expediency, since it used competent and interested officials already at hand; in its psychological acuteness, since it invested its funds with people that had a sense of responsibility for their own towns; and in its economic practicality, since the needy communities could reap all the benefits of an increased economic activity and might in time be freed from a need for further aid. There are steady but unspectacular references to this program well into the last third of the third century A.D.; and we must suppose, therefore, that it proved a self-perpetuating financial success which ended only when military disorders and runaway inflation made all such investments worthless.

THE GROWTH OF LATIFUNDIA THROUGHOUT THE EMPIRE.
There was indeed a natural trend to larger estates in Italy, and in the provinces the trend was irresistible. The expansion of the emperor's property overseas alone accounted for enormous tracts under single ownership; and the nobles, imperial favorites, and millionaires followed the emperor's lead. Such vast areas could not receive individual supervision, and they generally were cultivated by tenant farmers who, at least in the case of the imperial estates, rented land from contractors, who were themselves under the supervision of imperial procurators. The tenants paid a share of their crops to the contractors, and they also owed free labor at the times of sowing and reaping to those contractors that tilled part of the estates on their own behalf. Tenants, however, made indifferent farmers, and there were constant complaints that contractors attempted to elicit from them more than the legal share of crops and of free work. During the second and early third centuries A.D. there are also frequent references to abandoned lands. Throughout the second century A.D. the emperors encouraged the reclamation of abandoned properties and were willing to grant very favorable terms to those that brought them back to cultivation; and they also repeatedly

forbade exactions of extra work from the tenants. But, as the needs of the army and of the bureaucracy increased and productivity fell off, there was a temptation for bureaucrats to be increasingly demanding. This was especially true because the emperors and their servants had before them the peculiar example of Egypt, whose rulers for centuries had exacted from the peasants whatever services they needed.

THE EXAMPLE OF EGYPT.   The annual floods in Egypt and the requirements for cooperative efforts to carry out frequent surveys and to construct the drainage ditches and canals had led that country at an early date to become a highly bureaucratized despotism. The land of Egypt had been for millennia the property of the pharaohs, and later of the Ptolemies; and the peasants of Egypt were rigorously organized tenants of imperial estates who performed whatever tasks were assigned to them. Cleopatra was the last of the Ptolemies, and the Roman emperors continued the same exploitation of the Egyptians that they found already operative. It is true that some private ownership did develop in Egypt under the Romans, but this was a privilege for a few imperial favorites, for veterans, and for those that wished to reclaim marginal lands above the flood levels, which lands required special care and artificial irrigation. The Roman emperors found the methods used in Egypt wonderfully efficient, whatever the cost to individual liberty, and therefore the Egyptian system served as a model for much of the Roman bureaucracy, and its methods molded Roman policy all over the Empire. The second and early third centuries A.D. saw short-term tenancies everywhere run into long-term leases, and even into lifetime ones. Also the pressures brought to bear on leaseholders and municipal officials to collect the required levies on behalf of the government, or to risk in forfeit their own personal fortunes, led to even more rigorous treatment of the peasants and encouraged many of them to abandon their lands altogether and flee. The dilemma presented by this turn of events caused the central government and the local officials to develop even harsher measures for the peasants, and these were prophetic of future serfdom.

PROVINCIAL COMPETITION WITH ITALIAN MANUFACTURES.
Italy was not only at a disadvantage in competitive agriculture; it also suffered eclipse in the field of manufacturing. In the Augustan era there had been a ready market for the products of Campanian and Etruscan factories, for the Empire was expanding, and the areas into which it penetrated either were undeveloped

or had been disorganized by long and costly wars and welcomed Italian manufactured goods. However, with the long era
of peace in the first and second centuries A.D., the provinces
began to manufacture most of the goods that Italy did. No patent laws kept provincials from copying, even counterfeiting,
Italian products. And the high cost of transportation, especially
overland, meant that cheap or heavy items had to be produced
close to their markets. The low purchasing power of the ordinary citizen, which seems steadily to have declined all over the
Empire, also dictated the mass production of local wares of
inferior quality. Gallic factories for pottery and metals soon
captured most of the northern market from Italy, and even in
Gaul the decentralization continued, and the earlier manufacturers of southern Gaul gave way to the manufacturers on the
Rhenish frontier. As a result, the famous Augustan Arretine
ware, which once was found from Britain to India, was replaced
by the end of the first century A.D. by inferior Gallic manufactures. In Africa the fine Italian lamps of the early Principate
were first replaced by those of Carthaginian manufacture, and
then by those of purely local origin. Northern Italy still held its
own as a manufacturing center because of the importance of
Aquileia in command of the trade routes to central Europe. But
elsewhere by the second century A.D. Italy had only its own
market. The change is dramatized by the replacement of Puteoli
by Ostia as the favorite port of call for freighters. Formerly
Puteoli was preferred by shipowners, despite its greater distance from Rome, because their ships could pick up the desirable Campanian manufactures, which Ostia lacked, for the return
trip to the provinces or to the Orient. But in the second century
A.D. this advantage ceased to exist. The mass production of
superior articles might have been the answer, but private individuals found it difficult to finance large-scale ventures in manufacturing. For one thing, Roman law stood in the way: except
for the public contractors, such as the tax-farming companies,
joint-stock companies were not permitted, and business ventures had to depend on private initiative or, at the best, on
partnerships of unlimited liability.

The goods produced in the provinces of the Roman Empire during the first two centuries A.D. did not differ materially
from those of the Augustan Age, but their places of manufacture
were consistently decentralized, and the products consistently
showed a decline of artistic merit, since they were produced by
less skilled workers for more impecunious clients. Only the
areas that had goods that were difficult to copy escaped the
trend toward regional or local self-sufficiency: Egypt had a

monopoly of papyrus, Syria and Asia had their inimitable dyed wools, and it was almost impossible for other provinces to equal the steel products of Spain or of Noricum and the glass of the East and of Alexandria.

CONSTRUCTION AND ENGINEERING.   The cause of the deterioration in the manufactures of the Empire cannot be found in any decline in technical skills and engineering. These continued to be superb. The system of roads was constantly expanded. The older roads were kept in repair, and the whole transportation system was a wonder of durability. Ideally, Roman roads were constructed of four separate layers of durable materials placed over a prepared foundation, the whole following the shortest route possible. The construction of these highways sometimes is criticized by modern engineers on the grounds that it is too rigid. However, travel on these roads still is frequently practicable, which is a sufficient rejoinder to the critics in the light of the rapid deterioration of abandoned strips of modern macadam or concrete. Aqueducts continued to be built during the first and second centuries A.D. The newer ones were increased in height in order to furnish greater pressure for the lofty tenement houses and for more efficient distribution throughout the towns. The last major aqueduct built for Rome was constructed by Alexander Severus. Irrigation systems were multiplied, and the one designed for Africa was especially wonderful, for it turned a desert into one of the Empire's most prosperous areas until the Africans suffered the invasion of the Vandals (429–533 A.D.) and later the rule of the Arabs. The buildings and temples became progressively larger, making full use of vaults and domes of solid concrete; and the magnificent Baths of Caracalla, one notable product of the early third century A.D., exemplify the successful enclosure of enormous space.

The mines of the Empire continued to be exploited effectively. A few were owned by private citizens and paid the government a percentage of the output. Some publicly owned ones were leased to capitalists; but there seems to have been a preference for small entrepreneurs, who worked single claims leased from the government. These lessees worked under the general supervision of an imperial procurator. Rules were set up for safety and efficiency, and model communities run by state-licensed monopolists were established for the workers.

COMMERCE.   Commerce continued to prosper in the early Principate, though the profits differed widely, ranging from

506

one-hundredfold returns in some foreign ventures to margins so small in the heavier domestic traffic that the State felt compelled to offer incentives to shipmasters to engage in the grain trade. Nevertheless, some really spectacular fortunes appear to have been made through commercial ventures; and in this respect commerce was to the Principate what moneylending to provincials had been in the Late Republic. The lucrative Indian trade appears to have been largely in the hands of Near Easterners, who in this field reasserted their superiority over Italians as merchants as they already had in business ventures in the western Mediterranean. In like manner, the Gauls and Germans came to dominate the northern trade routes during the second century A.D., though Italians still clung to one line northward through Aquileia. One internal economic measure of some of the emperors, the depreciation of coinage, had an especially interesting effect in foreign trade. Both the Germans and the Orientals prized Roman coins for their intrinsic value, and these are discovered in quantities in their hoards and treasures. However, after the debasement of the coinage was begun under Nero, very few such collections are found. Apparently, after Nero foreigners insisted on giving most of these fiduciary coins back to the Romans in payment for unadulterated goods.

The greatest amount of trade, however, was within the Empire; and the biggest customer was the government, since it had to provide both for the foodstuffs of Rome and for the far-flung armies. There also was a great demand for provisions by many of the large cities of the East, whose environs were not sufficiently fertile to raise enough grain. Hence, much of the trade within the Empire was in essentials: Egypt furnished glass, grain, linen, and paper; Syria, linen, glass, and dyed wool; the best oil was from Spain and the cheapest from Africa; the best wines were from Asia Minor, Greece, Gaul, and Italy. Greece, Asia Minor, and the eastern armies received a good deal of grain from the Crimea and the Ukraine, while Egypt, Africa, Sicily, and Sardinia-Corsica sent theirs to Italy. The opportunities for commerce were furthered by the open seas, by improved harbors and canals, and by the system of roads, which facilitated the transport of lighter goods. An empire-wide system of banking also contributed to the ease of exchange. Banks accepted money on deposit and paid interest on at least some of the deposits. Credit could be transferred from one account to another without an actual transfer of cash, and these transfers of credit were especially useful in a world where there always was a scarcity of coinage. The bankers also filled an important need in providing for the exchange of money. Much of the coinage

used within the Empire was standardized, but the central government was unable to mint enough copper to serve all the
needs of the trade. Hence, many local mints continued their
ancient issues, and the banks were able to provide to itinerant
merchants their requirements in local coinage at a rate of exchange regulated by the government.

TOWN AND VILLA ECONOMY.   The tendencies toward decentralization mentioned earlier, however, acted against a continuing expansion in national commerce. Even at its highest
point of development, probably one half of the Empire's economy was what one could call a town economy: that is, half the
needs of each town was satisfied by its own artisans and by the
farmers in its immediate vicinity. The growth of enormous
private or imperial domains accelerated the tendency to self-
sufficiency. It was Antoninus Pius' stated wish to live a simple
life that was afforded all its physical necessities by his own
farmlands, and many Romans agreed with his ideal. To live in
this manner in the second century A.D. was, perhaps, a tour de
force for wealthy romantics; but by the third century A.D. some of
the great estates found it economical and even necessary to
provide most of their own foods, apparel, services, and even
their own markets. A continued rise in taxation, in the cost of
living, and in the uncertainties of life caused many men to make
local products do, no matter how inferior they might be, in
place of imports from other parts of the Empire. Thus the stage
was set for a movement from the national and town economies
of the High Empire to the town and villa economies of the Late
Empire.[1]

TRADES ORGANIZATIONS.   The preoccupation with agriculture in the Roman Empire should not obscure the large number
of trades and services that were performed by the little people
of the municipalities. Our best information for these comes from
the numerous inscriptions of their associations or guilds—the
Romans' most common name for them was "colleges" (*collegia*).
Some of the guilds had been formed in the earliest days of
Roman history and had led relatively innocuous existences
until, in the first century B.C., Clodius organized some of them
as political action groups. The riots that thereafter rent the city
led Julius Caesar, and later Augustus, to suppress them; but in 7
B.C. Augustus allowed those trades associations that proved
themselves harmless and useful to the State to be licensed,

[1]   For the development of the villa economy of the Late Empire, see pp.
567–568.

either by himself or by the Senate. There was thereafter, in the first two centuries of the Principate, a proliferation of these associations, some with specific approval, many probably only receiving tacit consent because of their obscurity. They generally were composed of men engaged in the same or similar trades, who gathered together to worship a common patron god and to enjoy the fraternity of those that had common interests. The participants were from the humblest orders—poor freemen, freedmen, and slaves. They sought in the *collegia* a refuge from the dull anonymity of their existence; and they enjoyed a feeling of comradeship and of importance in the company of others just as lonely as themselves and just as ignored by the exclusive elite that ran the Roman world. The number in any one guild was very small. The average was perhaps around 150 members, and the largest colleges boasted no more than from 1000 to 1500. The guilds could not, therefore, exert the immense pressures or have the economic aims that modern unions do; they did not even have the professional aims of the medieval guilds to improve production. Their activity centered around the worship of their patron god, their dinners and entertainments, and the provision of a decent funeral and burial place for the members. Occasionally, however, their numbers gave them a certain strength to resist encroachment on their rights by officials, and this was especially true if they enjoyed the services of an influential patron. All of the colleges sought wealthy patrons for themselves, who could represent the guild's interests with the government in Rome, and these benefactors might be men of the highest rank. Often, however, the patrons were wealthy members of the lower classes, who themselves had a passion for importance and immortality, and who achieved both by the liberal entertainments that they furnished the guildsmen, and by deathless memorials and endowments that they lavished on the corporations that had elected them.

The constitutions of the *collegia* were modelled on municipal and on military government. Each guild had chief magistrates elected for five years, aediles in charge of finance, a common treasury, patrons, and an assembly. They not only received gifts from patrons and others, but there also were initiation fees, donations by the elected officials, and fines for the infraction of the rules. It is to be observed that the feeling for caste in the ancient world remained strong even among these humble folk, and at banquets or distribution of largesse the patrons and magistrates received larger portions than came to the lay members.

The deep desire for a dignified exit from life was the driving force behind many of the colleges and, in recognition of this, as early as the reign of Claudius a blanket approval was given by a decree of the Senate to guilds formed for this specific purpose. These were the funerary guilds, *collegia tenuiorum,* literally, "associations of the very humble." Undoubtedly a good many groups whose aims were more worldly justified their formation by pretending also to be funerary guilds. However, by the reign of Marcus Aurelius (161–180 A.D.) the guilds acquired still greater strength by receiving the right, as corporate bodies, to accept legacies just as municipalities could. From this time on many of them acquired a good deal of property.

TENDENCIES TOWARD STATE SOCIALISM.   Once the colleges had been formed and approved, the State at first interfered but little in their activities, as long as they were not secret or conspiratorial. There was, however, one exception: from the earliest days of the Principate, three guilds—the carpenters, tarpaulin makers, and men somehow connected with lumber or trees (*dendrophoroi*)—were charged with the task of firefighting in the various towns. When these guildsmen were engaged in that particular public service they appear to have been led by a prefect appointed by the government, and members of those guilds were granted certain exemptions and immunities from other public burdens. At first view that would appear to be an innocent use of citizens. Even more innocent were the earliest relations of the State with the shipmasters. Under Claudius the office of the *Annona* approached individual shipmasters and prevailed upon them to engage for at least part of the sailing season in the transport of grain to Rome from Egypt, Africa, Spain, or the Islands. Again, those that accepted were allowed certain privileges in respect to civic responsibilities, taxes, or customs duties; or they were given the "right of three children" (*ius trium liberorum*).[2] In the beginning the guilds had nothing to do with these government contracts, which were concluded with individual shipmasters. However, inevitably the shipmasters that were engaged, for example, in the African grain trade formed a guild. As the decades passed, such guilds, their members, and the rights and duties of the government contracts with the guild members became inextricably connected in the public's mind. By the time of Septimius Severus it was plainly stated in law that the guilds of shipmasters had certain privileges, and that these privileges were enjoyed because the

---

[2]   For the privileges of persons that had three children, or who were treated as though they had three children, see above, p. 366.

guildsmen had undertaken certain burdensome tasks (*munera*) for the State. Those conscious of the prevalence of liturgies— compulsory public services—in antiquity[3] find the use of this language pregnant with future demands that would be made by the State on the shipmasters and their association. It remained for Alexander Severus (222–235 A.D.) to recognize the great utility for the State in a careful exploitation of the guilds as instruments of bureaucratic administration. He was the first emperor to take the initiative in organizing all the crafts and trades in colleges under public protection and surveillance. Early in the third century A.D., therefore, in the trades as well as in agriculture, commerce, and in municipal government, the stage was set for the appearance of a society organized for and dedicated to the needs of the State. Egypt had known that kind of an order for centuries; now the Empire as a whole needed only a crisis and a despot to impose the same fatality on the whole Mediterranean world.

---

[3]   For liturgies, see above, p. 478.

PART
Eight

Anarchy And Dominate

Chapter 41

THE PROBLEMS OF UNDISCIPLINED FORCE

THE DESTRUCTION OF THE HIGH EMPIRE. The century from the accession of Vespasian to the death of Marcus Aurelius (69–180 A.D.) is sometimes called the High Empire, for it was marked by handsome buildings, a genteel and responsible society, and a parade of learned and competent scholars. Fifty-five years later, by the end of the Severan dynasty, the Roman world was much changed, though it still was an imposing structure. It continued to give an appearance of a universal state ruled by law, in which free men were protected in the pursuit of their livelihoods both at home and abroad. Perhaps the arts and literature did not equal in brilliance those of the earlier days of the Principate, but there was widespread literacy, fine and imposing buildings still were built everywhere, trade was extensive, the frontiers were intact, and the cities still boasted an active and prosperous bourgeoisie. However, the assassination of Alexander Severus was followed by fifty years·(235–284 A.D.) of such madness, disaster, and misery that they brought to an end the calculable and comfortable world of the early Principate—the world of the kindly Pliny and of Antoninus Pius, of Petronius and his rascally scholar-beggars in the *Satyricon*, of Galen's famous medical research, and of the hopefully perpetual endowments and ambitious financial investments for the young of Italy. All these disappeared. The fifty years of anarchy that followed the assassination of Alexander brought a new social and economic structure, a new military disposition, and a new theory of government that was just beginning to take form when Diocletian ascended the throne in 284 A.D.

THE MUTINY OF THE ARMIES. The source of madness was the army, which created over and over the anarchy that briefly though frightfully had rent the State in 68–9 A.D. after Nero, and again in 193–7 A.D. after Commodus. During this period of fifty years twenty-five Augusti were duly recognized by the Senate. Most of them were elevated by the troops, and a majority died by the same hands; a death from natural causes is attested for only one or two of them. And these twenty-five were the successful ones. There were probably twice as many pretenders, who did not receive sufficient support to force senatorial recognition—Gallienus (259–268 A.D.) alone had to deal with eighteen. The following catalogue of the recognized Augusti, with their dates and fate is eloquent testimony that the army's embrace was now a sentence of death.

THE MILITARY EMPERORS (235–284 A.D.).   It will be recalled that Alexander Severus (222–235 A.D.) was killed by his own troops because he parleyed with the Germans and was deferential to his mother and to the Senate. Maximinus (235–238 A.D.) was raised by his fellow troops, doubled their pay, and was slain by them before the city of Aquileia, which was making a determined stand against the emperor in behalf of a senatorial revolt. Meanwhile, in Africa resistance of landowners against the confiscatory taxes of Maximinus raised the governor of Africa, Gordian I (238 A.D.), and his son Gordian II (238 A.D.) to the purple, and they were recognized by the Senate. But the troops of Numidia were true to Maximinus and slew Gordian II, whereupon his father committed suicide. The Senate, now thoroughly compromised, raised two of its own members, Balbinus and Pupienus (238 A.D.), who outlived Maximinus but fell victims to the praetorian guard, because the emperors had preferred a German honor guard to it. The praetorians next raised a grandson of Gordian I, Gordian III (238–244 A.D.). He was murdered by his troops at the instigation of his praetorian prefect, Philip the Arab, while he was on a campaign in the East.

Philip (244–249 A.D.) met his fate at the hands of one of his successful generals, Decius. Decius (249–251 A.D.) was proclaimed emperor by his troops much against his will, and he tried to come to an understanding with Philip; but negotiations were in vain and Decius' troops slew Philip. Decius and his son and colleague Herennius Etruscus were slain by the Goths near the lower Danube, and a second son and Augustus, Hostilianus, succumbed to the plague. The troops of Lower Moesia raised their legate, Trebonianus Gallus (251–253 A.D.), to the throne, and he associated with himself as Augustus his son Volusianus, but they were killed by their own troops when challenged by the Rhenish legions of one of Gallus' generals, Licinius Valerian.

516

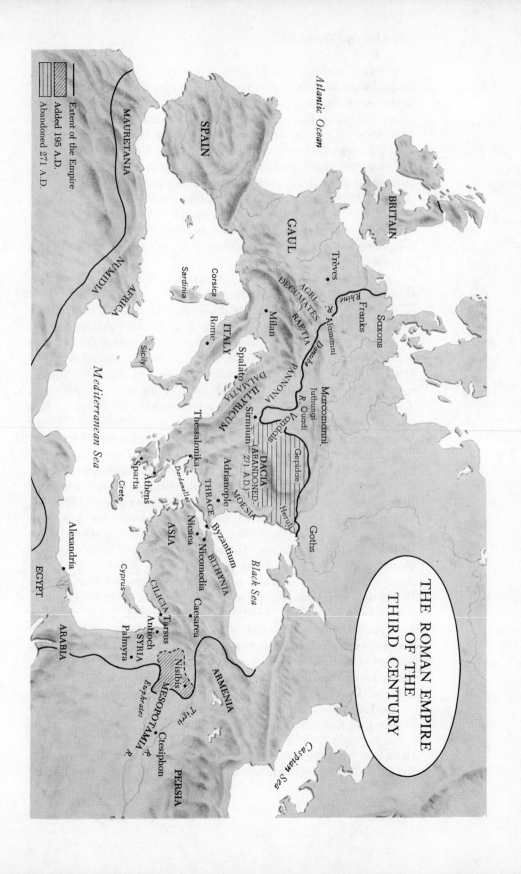

THE ROMAN EMPIRE
OF THE
THIRD CENTURY

Extent of the Empire
Added 195 A.D.
Abandoned 271 A.D.

Atlantic Ocean

BRITAIN

Saxons

Franks

R. Rhine

GAUL

Trèves

AGRI DECUMATES

R. Alamanni

RAETIA

Danube

PANNONIA

Juthungi

Marcomanni

R. Quadi

Vandals

Gepidae

Heruli

Goths

SPAIN

MAURETANIA

NUMIDIA

AFRICA

Sardinia

Corsica

Rome

ITALY

Milan

Spalato

DALMATIA

ILLYRICUM

Sirmium

DACIA
(ABANDONED
271 A.D.)

Sicily

Mediterranean Sea

Thessalonika

Adrianople

THRACE

MOESIA

Dardanelles

Byzantium

Nicaea

BITHYNIA

Nicomedia

Caesarea

Black Sea

Crete

Sparta

Athens

ASIA

Alexandria

EGYPT

Cyprus

CILICIA Tarsus

Antioch

SYRIA

Palmyra

ARABIA

Nisibis

MESOPOTAMIA

Euphrates R.

Tigris R.

Ctesiphon

ARMENIA

Caspian Sea

PERSIA

Valerian's reign (253–259 A.D.) was a series of disasters from Gothic invasions and Persian successes, which culminated in the emperor's capture by the Persian Shapur I. Valerian died a foreign slave. His son Gallienus (259–268 A.D.), despite his strenuous efforts against a score of pretenders and his intelligent attempts to bring about economic and administrative improvements, was assassinated by his own entourage on the grounds that he was too effeminate. His successor, Claudius II (268–270 A.D.), was one of the ringleaders. He earned the title "Gothicus" from his military successes in the Balkans, where he fell victim to the plague. His brother Quintillus (270 A.D.) committed suicide when abandoned by his troops at the revolt of Aurelian.

Aurelian (270–275 A.D.) reasserted the integrity of the Empire by defeating the Palmyrenes in the East and the Gauls in the West, both of whom had seceded from the Empire, but he fell victim to assassination by a group of soldiers falsely informed that the emperor intended to execute them. The discovery of the hoax for once, but only briefly, raised feelings of penitence in the army, and it demanded that the Senate nominate a successor to Aurelian. The senators fixed upon Tacitus (275–276 A.D.), a seventy-five-year-old worthy, who within seven months sank into death under the insults and outrages of the unappreciative soldiery. His brother Florianus (276 A.D.) lasted about three months and then was dispatched by his troops at the approach of the successful general Probus.

Probus (276–282 A.D.) cleared the Empire of new waves of barbarians, but he also tried to use the expensive military establishment in times of peace to clear and restore the Empire's growing wastelands, and this led to his undoing, for a work detail of soldiers resented this useful labor and murdered the emperor. His prefect of the guard, Carus (282–283 A.D.) was then pressed into service, but after a successful invasion of Persia he was assassinated at the instigation of his own praetorian prefect, Aper. The same fate soon befell his younger son, Numerianus (283–284 A.D.), who had been with him on the expedition. The elder son, Carinus (283–285 A.D.), had remained in the West. There he fell victim to a cuckolded husband, just after he had earned a military success against a rival general, Diocles, who already had been recognized as emperor in the East. Thereupon the troops all went over to Diocles, and he became Emperor Diocletian (284–305 A.D.).

DECLINE OF MILITARY EXCELLENCE.   The armies' reasons for elevating and casting aside emperors with such bewildering speed were not very honorable. Sometimes the soldiers found the emperor too gentle, sometimes too stern; frequently one army was jealous of another; and too often the change was prompted by nothing but elemental greed, the hope that the new candidate, if successful, would reward his supporters handsomely. The increasing enlistment of troops from the less civilized sections of the Mediterranean world also had something to do with their lack of concern, or even their hostility, for the more cultured areas.

BARBARIANS ON THE OFFENSIVE. THE WESTERN FRONT. The mad folly of the army led it often to neglect its primary function, to guard the frontiers. During the third century A.D. hordes of barbarians were gathering in central Europe in search of new homes. Some were pressed forward by the expansion of Asiatic peoples to their rear. Some needed wider pastures for their animals during a period when rainfall had been disastrously light. These peoples found their raids or invasions of the desirable South made all the easier by Rome's fratricidal distractions. During this period the piratical Saxons of the North Sea began to make attacks on the shores of Britain and Gaul. The league of Franks across the lower Rhine launched attacks on the Roman frontier as early as 231 A.D., and after 253 their forays were frequent and serious. Some of them in 258 even penetrated the Empire as far as Spain and then crossed to Mauretania. Farther up the Rhine the Alamanni made repeated inroads. Their pressure on Raetia was continuous. One group in 258 or 259 not only devastated Gaul, but also northern Italy, and one detachment made its way to the very environs of Rome. The dangers of the times led the residents of Gaul to a separate government for that province from 260 to 273 A.D. This action put the armies on the Rhine and the Danube in opposition to one another, and the areas between the headwaters of the two rivers (the *Agri Decumates*) as well as Raetia became especially vulnerable to outside attack. Even after Gaul was reunited with the Empire, under Probus (276–282 A.D.) sixty Gallic cities had to be cleared of barbarian invaders. On the upper Danube old and new names appear among the invaders: the Marcomanni and Quadi renewed their attacks, and they were joined by the Juthungi, Gepidae, and Vandals. The Juthungi, for example, invaded Italy twice in the early years of Aurelian's principate (270–275 A.D.), and the difficulties and dangers met in driving them out led that emperor to initiate the construction of a wall around the city of Rome (begun in 271 A.D.), the first time that such defense had been needed since the days of Hannibal.

q

*middle
to 2nd
part of
3rd century.*

THE DANUBIAN FRONT.   The most urgent dangers were on the lower Danube, where the Goths, abetted by the Heruli, made repeated inroads, and the Roman armies suffered stunning defeats. The Goths were originally a Scandinavian people that now had settled in the Ukraine. They were men of immense stature and great daring, and for a long time the Roman defenses against them were particularly ineffective. After the defeat and death of Emperor Decius at their hands (251 A.D.), their depredations went on almost unchecked for nearly two decades. Not only did they overrun Moesia and Thrace by crossing the Danube, but with the Heruli they also took to ships and, via the Black Sea and Dardanelles, descended upon Asia Minor and the cities near the Aegean. Many old and famous places were sacked and destroyed in raids of 253, 254, 256, 267, and 268 A.D. The last expedition took Athens and penetrated as far as Sparta; but this time, as the barbarians headed overland homeward, they were intercepted by Emperor Gallienus and severely defeated. The succeeding emperor, Claudius II (268–270 A.D.), was also victorious over the Goths, and this checked their inroads for some time.

One result of the Gothic raids was the Roman withdrawal from Dacia, carried out by Aurelian around 271. This province had long been a battered outpost beyond the Danube in a sea of barbarians and no longer could justify the expense of maintenance. Those inhabitants that wished were transferred to the southern bank of the river where they strengthened the Empire's defenses. Their old homes were occupied by the branch of the Goths known as the Visigoths.

THE EASTERN FRONT.   In the East Shapur I came to the Persian throne in 242 A.D. and immediately launched an attack on Syria that carried almost to Antioch. Gordian III recovered Mesopotamia in 243; but the Roman position was even more seriously endangered in 252. At that time Shapur succeeded in putting a satellite on the Armenian throne. He now was free to attack Syria without running the risk of a flank attack from the north. Thereupon repeated frontal attacks were made on Roman positions, and Nisibis, Rome's stronghold on the Euphrates, was captured in 254. In 256 Valerian arrived in Antioch to direct the defense, but his army was weakened by the plague, and his attention was divided between the Persians and the Gothic raids on Asia Minor. His expedition ended with his capture by the Persian king, and the seizure by the Persians of Antioch and other cities as far away as Tarsus in Cilicia and Caesarea in Cappadocia. However, a champion of the Roman cause appeared in the person of Odenathus of Palmyra, a Roman ally, and he effectively drove back the Persians, even reaching the gates of Ctesiphon by early 267. Aurelian during his short reign (270–275 A.D.) reunited the Empire, but was assassinated before he could come to grips with the Persians; and Probus (276–282 A.D.) suffered the same fate while marshalling his forces to go to the East. It remained for his successor Carus (282–283 A.D.) to recover all Mesopotamia for the Empire, and he was in the vicinity of Ctesiphon when he was struck down by assassins.

THE AFRICAN FRONT. Not even Africa escaped unscathed. There were incursions from the south on Egypt by the Blemmyes under Aurelian and Probus; and in 260 A.D. Numidia was attacked by Moorish tribesmen, who ultimately were repulsed. We have already mentioned the Frankish wanderers who in 258 A.D. reached Mauretania on ships that they had seized in raids on the ports of Spain.

PARTITION OF THE EMPIRE THREATENED: GAUL. The need for self-defense in the face of the constant incursions of barbarians and of a distracted central government led to a certain amount of separatism during this period. In 260 A.D. the Rhenish armies rose under a usurper, Latinius Postumus, who in effect established an independent Gallic state with its own senate and consuls. This structure at least served the purpose of holding the barbarian invasions in check, and for a while both Britain and Spain adhered to it. But the malady of the times operated even within this restricted area, and the rulers of Gaul had to contend with rivals and civil wars within civil wars. Postumus himself was killed by his troops (268 A.D.) when he refused to allow them to sack Mainz, where a rival had taken refuge. He was followed on the Gallic throne by three successors, the last of whom, Tetricus, connived with Emperor Aurelian in 274 A.D. for the return of the western provinces to the Empire.

PALMYRA. The separatist movement in the East was more dangerous, for it arose among a Hellenized Semitic people with a smaller commitment to Rome. Odenathus, prince of Palmyra, had won the gratitude of Emperor Gallienus for his defense of the East against the Persians after the defeat of Valerian (260 A.D.). His continued services and increasing importance had gained for him in his own country the title "king of kings," and Gallienus accorded him the position of *corrector totius Orientis*

521

her husband
was ruler of east as noted
by Gallienus

(co-ruler of the whole East). After Odenathus' assassination in 267 A.D., his beautiful and ambitious widow, Zenobia, carried on the government in the name of her son, who was a minor. The Palmyrene army continued to dominate the Orient and to defend the eastern frontier; but at the death of Claudius II, Zenobia refused to recognize his immediate successor, Quintillus, and rapidly took over the government of Syria, Egypt, Arabia, and parts of Asia Minor. A lightning campaign against her by Aurelian in 271 and 272 A.D. was successful, partly because Aurelian had learned to emphasize the use of cavalry and thus could fight on equal terms with the Orientals, who were particularly adept in the use of mounted troops. Zenobia and Tetricus, former emperor of Gaul, both walked in the triumph that Aurelian celebrated after he had reunited Palmyra and Gaul to the Empire, and the emperor allowed both ex-monarchs to live thereafter in Italy, where they were treated with honor and respect. Palmyra, however, soon rose again against the governors that Aurelian had left for it, and the city was recaptured and destroyed.

THE DILEMMA OF THE EMPERORS.   By 274 A.D. Aurelian had restored unity to the Roman world. This task had been easier for him than it would be for later emperors, because the world state was still the ideal of government for most of the residents of the Empire. The final dismemberment of the Empire was still nearly two centuries away. Yet the growing attachment of the legions to the localities in which they were stationed, the need of imperial administrators to spend much time in cities of great strategic value, such as Antioch, Sirmium, Nicomedia, Trèves, and Milan, instead of in Rome, and the increasing intensity of the barbarian assault—all were prophetic of the coming fragmentation of the Roman world.

The emperors of this period were mostly prisoners of their own troops. Many of them were very reluctant candidates for the Roman throne; but once elevated they struggled heroically to hold the world together while appeasing their masters, the soldiers. The appetite of the armies forced the emperors constantly to increase the demands on the civilian population in taxes, requisitions, and personal services. Unfortunately these demands came at a time in which we have already noticed a slow regression in economic health.

THE DECLINE OF THE CITIES.   To procure the money and goods that they needed, the emperors had to turn to the cities. But the cities were feeling both the general decline in commercial activity and a decrease in population. Cities have never maintained a steady population without immigration from the country, and in the third century A.D. war and pestilence were cutting off from the municipalities that overflow of country folk that nourished them. The cities themselves suffered even worse from epidemics than the country did, and another violent plague swept the Empire between 250 and 270. Despite their hastily raised defenses, many cities were sacked by the barbarian raids; and the itinerant Roman armies, ever intent on some new civil war, were scarcely more merciful. Archaeological evidence shows that cities in many parts of the Empire at the end of this period were only a fraction of their size before 235 A.D. Everywhere the urban middle and upper classes were refusing to raise children. Under these conditions the demands of the central government fell upon fewer and fewer persons. The demands had to be shouldered by individuals, for Maximinus (235–238 A.D.) appears to have confiscated the treasuries of many of the municipalities in order to satisfy the demands of his troops for money; and thereafter there are few references to the establishment of endowments, which the well-to-do once delighted in lavishing on their home towns. The position of magistrate or decurion in a municipality once had been a great honor for the local nobility; but during the third century A.D. municipal office became a burden to be avoided if possible. The signs of the times are found in the willingness of some men to renounce their property because it would not support the demands made upon it. Other persons of property simply disappeared as fugitives, while magistrates were forced to sentence returning exiles to serve as decurions in local senates.

THE CRISIS IN AGRICULTURE.   While the country people perhaps did not suffer as severely from the plague as the city people did, they were hit harder by the raiding barbarians, against whom they had no protection. Their animals were driven away, their buildings destroyed, and they themselves often ended up as slaves. The steady production of agriculture, upon which the Roman economy largely depended, fell alarmingly. Great territories became abandoned wastelands. Following the example set by Marcus Aurelius in the second century A.D., a number of emperors settled barbarians on the abandoned lands. The amount of land available for the barbarians must have been of considerable extent, for Probus alone is credited with settlements in Britain, Gaul, Italy, Moesia, and Thrace, and it is said that he gave 100,000 Bastarnae homes in the last province. By these means the emperors undoubtedly hoped both to raise agricultural production and also to furnish recruiting grounds for future armies. But the steadily increasing demands upon the farmers and the inability of the central government to prevent its own soldiers and officials from making irregular and illegal requisitions vitiated the emperors' good intentions.

The inflated prices that accompanied the debased currency of the period forced the emperors not only to raise the soldiers' pay, but to put more emphasis on the tax in kind, the *annona*, whereby the country people were required to furnish quantities of provisions for the military. This once had been a measure reserved for emergencies, and such requisitions were supposed to be paid for. Now the *annona* was a regular levy as an additional tax, and decurions of each municipality were liable for the collection and delivery of the agricultural goods exacted from their territory. The collectors had to make up any shortages, and this policy resulted in bankruptcies and in desertions of their posts both by farmers and by decurions. Where the emperors could not persuade the citizens to compliance, they tried compulsion. Abandoned lands were assigned to towns or to landowners by a system called *epibolé*, and a stated amount of produce from these was required for the government's use. The very rich, of course, could often bribe their way out of such duties so that the assignments often fell on those least able to bear them. Attempts by the humbler citizens to renounce their property because of its excessive burdens often ended in corporal punishment. It is to this period, then, that we must assign the first impulse toward serfdom, toward a hereditary attachment to the land, a system which was to be taken for granted in the fourth century A.D.

An ancient Egyptian custom had allowed the peasants to take refuge in the temples (*anachoresis*) when the burdens put upon them by the State became unbearable. But by the third century A.D. the rights of asylum for Egyptian peasants had been withdrawn. Now the fugitives from civic life had to seek their refuge in the hills or the swamps, rather than in the temples, and there they constituted roving bands of robbers and brigands. This increase in refugees from society created a new liturgy for those that remained in the towns, robber-hunting; and the denunciatory communications from the government to these vigilantes show that the hunters had as little stomach as they had training for their task.

DECLINE IN COMMERCE AND INDUSTRY.   The military anarchy of the third century A.D. had equally disastrous effects on trade, commerce, and industry. The depreciation of the currency ultimately led bankers to refuse to handle the government's fiduciary issues of coinage. Trade with India practically disappeared, probably because of the worthless "silver" coinage offered. That with the North was cut off because the lands along the Rhine and Danube had been repeatedly devastated, and the trade routes were interrupted by wandering hordes of barbarians. Within the Empire poverty forced district after district to fend for itself and to make local products, however inferior, suffice. This meant a shortage of readily available manufactured goods for the needs of the State's army and bureaucracy. The result was that certain guildsmen in critical industries were given quotas of manufactured goods to fill, and their freedom of movement began to be seriously curtailed. Like the decurions and the peasants, artisans and laborers slowly began to serve the needs of the State regardless of economic practicability or personal preference. The desperate therefore joined the many peasants and decurions to swell the population of fugitives.

ATTEMPTED REFORMS: ARMY COMMAND.   Despite the critical nature of the empire's malady, the will to survive was still strong among the Romans. During the first half of the period of anarchy (235–259 A.D.), it is true, the situation steadily worsened. Maximinus (235–238 A.D.) purposefully robbed the bourgeoisie; Decius (249–251 A.D.) indulged in the most savage religious persecutions; and a series of disastrous invasions under Valerian (253–259 A.D.) culminated in that monarch's capture by the Persians. But slowly it was becoming clear to Roman leaders that there must be a reform both of the army and of the throne, in order to save even a remnant of Roman civilization and the integrity of the Empire. Emperor Gallienus (259–268 A.D.) seems the first to have recognized fully the need for change and to have taken action. Although he himself was an aristocrat, he forbade the future use of senatorials in army commands, for their inexperience had made them ineffectual soldiers and they were dangerously ambitious commanders. Instead, men with a military background were allowed to rise through the ranks to important commands. Septimius had given his under-officers equestrian rank; Gallienus bestowed it on his centurions' sons at birth. He thus created a military aristocracy that undoubtedly was more efficient in war, though it also was probably less Latin, since generation after generation it was drawn from frontiersmen.

MODERNIZED ARMY ORGANIZATION.   Another change effected by the later military emperors was in the organization of the army itself. In the second century A.D. detachments (*vexillationes*) from the more or less stationary legions had often been moved from place to place as they were needed. In the late third century A.D. use of these more mobile *vexillationes* was apparently regularized by Gallienus. While the militarized peasants, *limitanei*, frequently reinforced by barbarian settlers, continued to man the frontiers, defense in depth was achieved by placing the mobile units at strategic centers to the rear. From their interior stations they could be swiftly dispatched to cope with any breakthrough. Their mobility was enhanced by equiping them with lighter arms and armor than the legionaries had carried. In addition, the new army made greater use of mounted troops. There were specialized cavalry units, such as the Moorish javelin-men or the Oriental archers, and very important were the *cataphractarii*, which were heavy cavalry equipped with armor and long spears. Repeated defeats at the hands of Gothic and Oriental cavalry had ultimately proved to the Romans that their dependence on the infantry was out-of-date, and in the later third century A.D. the cavalry became the more important branch of the Roman army. This emphasis, which seems to have been inaugurated by Gallienus, was further developed by Aurelian, who was himself a cavalryman.

CHANGES IN ARMY RECRUITMENT.   Although the right of conscription never had been surrendered by the government, the emperors of the third century A.D. found it advisable to depend more and more on mercenaries. Instead of performing service in the army, the civilians substituted a payment of money called the *aurum tironicum* with which the emperors could hire Romans from less civilized areas, or even barbarians. The emperors often preferred to do this, for men drawn from such sources proved to have strong loyalty for their imperial commanders, since their own futures would rise and fall with the prince. From the third century A.D. on, Roman soldiers consisted chiefly of the sons of former soldiers and of these mercenaries. It is clear that this policy did increase the loyalty of the troops, but it also widened the differences between the civilians and the military in race, traditions, and even speech, and it further separated the civilians from the government, which was reserved for the elite of the military machine.

THE EMPEROR AS THE SYMBOL OF THE STATE.
The emperors of the later third century A.D. realized that the throne could be used as a focus to develop unity and loyalty in the State, and they recognized the importance of religion in bolstering the imperial authority. The emperor-cult went back to the

principate of Augustus, and for a long time attempts to evade at least formal observance of it were considered treasonable. Citizens were expected to burn a little incense before a statue of the emperor on public occasions to indicate their loyalty to him as head of the State and to the system for which he stood. It was not a concern for the pagan gods, therefore, but a concern for the unity of the State that animated the violent persecution of the Christians by Decius (249–251 A.D.) and by Valerian (253–259 A.D.), for the Christians rejected this act as a worship of false gods. Decius and Valerian saw in the growing body of the Christians a state within the State whose aims and practices might increase the disunity of the Roman people, a disunity that was already very painful and that threatened to dismember the Empire. If the emperors knew enough of early Roman history to reflect upon the fatal effects of another internal organization, that of the plebeians, on the Republic, they had reason to be alarmed, for that state within the State ultimately had dominated the republican government and had been instrumental in its downfall. Further, it was convenient to blame the "godless" Christians for the world's increasing misfortunes and thus to divert public discontent at the world's worsening economic and political conditions.

Some of the later third-century emperors followed the lead of Decius and Valerian, but a more constructive attitude was taken by Gallienus (259–268 A.D.) and Aurelian (270–275 A.D.). Gallienus was a highly cultured man, and he surrounded himself with a coterie of scholars, a number of whom were developing the system called Neoplatonism, which fused the work of Plato with elements from Aristotle, the Stoics, and the mystical speculations of the East. Gallienus was tolerant of the Christians and allowed them free use of their church properties, perhaps because he believed that Neoplatonism would wean people of all temperaments away from such superstitions as Christianity. Aurelian attempted to encourage unity by fostering the worship of the Sun-God, Sol Invictus. The emperor felt that the Graeco-Romans, the Orientals, and indeed many of the devotees of the mystical cults could find common ground in devotion to this deity. Aurelian seems to have considered himself the god's vice-regent on earth, and he hoped that he could thus become the figure around which all the diverse elements within the Empire could rally. This policy marked a distinct step toward the establishment of a military autocracy based on the divine right of kings.

ACHIEVEMENT OF THE ILLYRIAN EMPERORS.   Most of the vigorous efforts to turn the tide against the forces that threatened to destroy the Empire came in the last two decades of the period of anarchy. The emperors that sparked those efforts were largely energetic, though still short-lived, men of Illyrian descent. Indeed, in the third century A.D. Illyria furnished some of Rome's best troops as well as the emperors that saved the Empire. It retained enough of its originally wild character to breed men of vigor and stamina, yet it had long enough been a part of the Empire that its sons wished to preserve the Roman world. It is not mere chance, then, that Claudius II, who beat back the Goths, Aurelian, who restored the Empire's unity both in the East and in the West, Probus, who tried to invigorate the economy, and Carus, who reasserted Roman prestige against Persia, were all Illyrians.

THE TREND TOWARD BARBARISM.   The Illyrian emperors did indeed reunite the Empire, but that structure little resembled the Empire of the early Principate. Now the troops were frankly acknowledged to be the basis of power. This was a reversion to the political situation of the primitive Republic, when the centuries of the republican army made themselves sovereign through the *comitia centuriata*. Yet the situations are not really parallel, for there was a great difference between the soldiers of the Early Republic, and those of the third century A.D. The ancient Roman soldiers were a homogeneous group of men who for most of the year were civilian farmers, and they organized themselves into a disciplined legislative assembly; but the heterogeneous armies of the third century lent themselves to no formal or legalized position within the State. Their power was exercised incalculably and irrationally, and only slowly did their personal loyalty to a divinely approved autocrat bring about some control of their blind and brutal power. The Roman Senate no longer had national significance. It now amounted to little more than the esteemed town council of the city of Rome. At the end of this period Carus had merely informed it that he had been elevated to the throne by the troops. The citizens were shackled to their stations and trades by the all-pervading need to maintain the State intact, and many of them were but recently settled barbarians, only one step removed from their brothers across the frontiers. Over the whole presided a general who was also a precarious autocrat, ruling with the aid of divine favor and a host of bureaucrats, soldiers, and spies.

In a world ground down by danger and oppression, it is no wonder that the chief literature of the period consists of the otherworldliness of the Neoplatonist Plotinus (204–270 A.D.), who believed in mystic revelation and tried to reconcile the philosophy of Plato with ideas of Oriental religion; the theological fulminations of the Fathers of the Church against the pagans and against each other; and the works of Porphyry (*ca.* 232–304 A.D.), the special antagonist of the Christians and the editor of Plotinus. These men all were forced by the deterioration of the world around them to seek solace elsewhere, in unity with the God of the Christians or the Absolute of the Neoplatonists. There was also much tedious and superstitious nonsense written by Iamblichus (*ca.* 250–? A.D.), who assembled a great hodgepodge of Greek and Oriental rites, gods, imagery, and magical practices with which to combat the spread of Christianity. In his own day Iamblichus was greatly revered.

One great literary masterpiece alone probably belongs to this period, the *Pervigilium Veneris* (The Night-long Vigil of Venus). Not only is this little work a final evocation of the pagan world, but it also heralds by its cadences and refrain the new Western civilization that was in embryo. And, with all its delicacy and beauty, there is in it a savor of the hopelessness that had settled over the world:

May love find him that ne'er has loved, and lovers love tomorrow—
For spring is young, and spring is song, and spring's the world's renewal.
In spring all loves sweet concord know; in spring the birds are mated;
And trees let down their tresses green 'neath showers generative.
May love find him that ne'er has loved, and lovers love tomorrow.

          ❉ ❉ ❉

Now loud-voiced swans make pools resound with raucous trumpeting,
And nightingales in poplar shade the tale of Tereus sing—
You'd think the song a song of love, so wildly sweet the note,
And not complaint of barb'rous king from violated throat.
May love find him that ne'er has loved, and lovers love tomorrow.

They sing; but we are silent still: for me is there no spring?
When will my voice at length be freed and, as the swallow, sing?
I've stayed so mute my muse has fled, Apollo's turned away—
Thus storied Sparta, mighty once, learned Death in Silence lay.
May love find him that ne'er has loved, and lovers love tomorrow.

Chapter 42

THE REASSERTION OF AUTHORITY: DIOCLETIAN

THE FOUNDATION OF THE DOMINATE.   While the unity of the Empire and, for the most part, the integrity of its boundaries had been regained through the efforts of the Illyrian emperors, the assassination of Carus and of Numerianus, the revolt led by Diocles, and the murder of Carinus showed that there still was no improvement in the basic problem of the Empire, the problem of undisciplined force. Furthermore, there continued to be invaders from outside the Empire, and there were inflation and discontent within. Diocles, who assumed the name of Diocletian when he came to the throne, appears to have given much thought to the Empire's problems before his elevation — at least he initiated a number of corrective measures almost immediately. Diocletian's appraisal of the needs of the Empire and of the priorities to be followed in satisfying them made him the founder of a new form of government. Like Augustus, Diocletian sought a stable government after a long period of constitutional anarchy. Augustus came to terms with the Republic by creating the Principate, in which he was the first citizen (*princeps*) among republican peers. Diocletian's solution for the military anarchy of the third century A.D. was the Dominate (from *dominus*, master), in which he was the devoted ruler, but also the complete autocrat, chosen and inspired by the gods.

DIVISION OF AUTHORITY: MAXIMIAN CO-EMPEROR.   Diocletian's first indication of a change of policy was his choice in 285 A.D. of an old army comrade, Maximian, as his Caesar, and the rapid promotion of Maximian to the rank of Augustus, or co-emperor, in 286. By this move Diocletian recognized that the problems of empire were too widespread for one man and that it was better to associate with oneself a capable and loyal coadjutant. Such an action had a precedent during the second century A.D. in Marcus Aurelius' sentimental and rather unsuccessful

530

experiment with Lucius Verus. In the third century A.D. a number of emperors had associated their sons with themselves for administrative and dynastic purposes; most recently Carus had left his elder son, Carinus, to administer the West while he and Numerianus were campaigning in the Orient. Diocletian's aim, however, was to establish this procedure as a regular feature of the government. Moreover, Diocletian indicated that an emperor ought to choose his associate because he was "the most suitable man," the criterion that had animated most of the adoptions in the second century A.D.

The wisdom of the policy was at once demonstrated. Maximian suppressed a rebellion of farmers in Gaul in 285 A.D. and successfully campaigned against the Alamanni (286–287), Franks (288), and Moors (289–290), although he could not prevent the establishment in 286 of an independent British emperor, Carausius, because he lacked sufficient sea power. Meanwhile, in the East Diocletian was busy on the Danubian frontier in 286, and again in 289 and 292. In 288 he prevailed upon the Persians to recognize Roman sovereignty in Mesopotamia, and he put his own candidate on the Armenian throne, while in 290 he had to meet an Arabian attack on Syria and in 291 a revolt in Egypt.

THE TETRARCHY: CO-OPTATION OF TWO CAESARS.
This simple list of the emperors' activities suggests that military pressures could absorb most of the attention of even two rulers. Diocletian saw in this circumstance a need both for a further division of responsibility and for some provision for the succession—a need which Augustus had never successfully met, and which the adoptive emperors had sometimes postponed until they were under dangerous pressures. In 293 A.D., therefore, Diocletian appointed two Caesars, Constantius Chlorus to be Maximian's aide and deputy in the West, and Galerius to be his own in the East. While the device of adoption had been used before, Diocletian doubled and formalized it. The Caesars were bound to their Augusti by marriage to daughters of the Augusti; and they now proceeded to practice the arts of leadership and administration under the direction of their elders. They thus could receive adequate preparation for their own future careers as Augusti. Maximian assumed the general supervision of the West, with his headquarters at Milan, while Constantius had special responsibility for Gaul and Britain, with his center of operations at Trier (Trèves). Galerius guarded the Balkans and part of Asia from Sirmium, while Diocletian was in general control of all the East from his headquarters at Nicomedia in

Bithynia. Laws were issued in the name of all the members of the Tetrarchy (rule of four) and each could pass freely through the territories for which the others were responsible. Diocletian maintained a guiding hand over the other three rulers, both through his seniority and greater authority, and through the genuine respect in which he was held by his junior colleagues.

The Tetrarchy proved a success, both because of the wisdom of Diocletian and because the men that he had chosen were capable and loyal. Constantius finally returned the independent British Empire to Roman control in 296; Maximian overcame a revolt in Mauretania in 297; Galerius campaigned on the Danubian frontier from 294 to 297; and Diocletian himself was involved in suppressing an insurrection in Alexandria between 295 and 297.

DEFEAT OF THE PERSIANS.   One of the most brilliant military successes of the Tetrarchy came against the Persians, whose new king, Narses I (293–302 A.D.), was energetic and ambitious. He invaded Syria in 296 and inflicted a severe defeat on Galerius, whom Diocletian had called up to meet the threat. But Galerius soon recovered. He invaded the Persian realm through Armenia and drove to Ctesiphon, where he captured the wives and children of the Persian king. In the settlement that followed, Rome not only recovered full control of Mesopotamia, but it also was ceded some new districts across the Tigris, was conceded its right to a protectorate over Armenia, and was granted control of the overland routes to the East. So sweeping was the Roman victory that more than fifty years passed before the Persians again gave trouble. The victory also gave Galerius considerable prestige and more weight in the councils of the Tetrarchy than Constantius had.

ORIENTALIZATION OF THE IMPERIAL COURT.   The firm control of foreign enemies and of internal discontent by the tetrarchs allowed Diocletian the time to initiate and to make fully operative a number of new policies and reforms. As in the formation of the Tetrarchy itself, many of Diocletian's innovations were suggested by the experiments or temporary makeshifts of the past, which now were developed in a purposeful and systematic manner. The existence of four rulers discouraged uprisings by ambitious generals and unruly troops, but Diocletian went farther. He had spent much time in the East— it is significant that he chose to reside there throughout most of his reign—and he had noted that Oriental monarchs, who were secluded and aloof, seldom suffered the indignities that the

Roman emperors often did from their "fellow soldiers." Therefore, though a man of simple tastes, he surrounded the throne with the trappings of Oriental monarchy. He seldom appeared in public, and when he did, he was displayed with diadem, scepter, throne, and the royal purple, embroidered with gold. Everything about the imperial person and his household was referred to as "sacred" (*sacer*) until the word finally became synonymous with "imperial." Even the highest officials knelt and kissed the hem of his garments (*proskynesis*) when the emperor received them, and the Council of State was called the Consistory (from *consistere*, to stand with) because the ministers had to stand in the imperial presence.

These formalities, many of which had appeared in embryonic form under earlier emperors, were reinforced by the claim that the emperors especially enjoyed the favor of the gods. The king of the gods spoke through Diocletian, who assumed the epithet "Jovius" (the representative of Jupiter), while his faithful Maximian became "Herculius" (the representative of Hercules, Jupiter's industrious son and helper). So closely were these gods identified with the emperors that it was now common for inscriptions to refer to the emperor as *dominus noster*, "our master." In the fourth century A.D. the lives of the emperors still were not perfectly secure, but this aura of divine protection that had been invoked by Diocletian continued to furnish to his successors far greater stability than the emperors of the third century A.D. had known.

REORGANIZATION OF PROVINCIAL ADMINISTRATION.
Governors of some of the larger provinces, since they were bound to have several legions under their command, had repeatedly proved dangerous to the reigning prince. This source of potential rivals now was eliminated by the simple expedient of breaking up the larger provinces into smaller ones. Septimius had done this to certain provinces that had proved dangerous to him, but now the number of provinces rose from probably less than fifty to well over one hundred. No longer were there senatorial and imperial provinces—all were held by imperial appointees—although some were reserved for senators, others for equestrians. The provinces were grouped into twelve dioceses, in charge of each of which was a deputy (vicar) of the praetorian prefect. Both the vicars and the governors, who now were generally termed *praesides* (presidents) or *judices* (judges), were purely civilian officials charged with administrative and judicial tasks. Armies in the provinces enjoyed a completely separate government under commanders called *duces* (dukes, leaders).

The provincial armies depended for their commissariat, however, on the civil administration. By effectively separating the civil and military functions in the provinces, yet not allowing either to be completely independent of the other, Diocletian largely eliminated the danger of provincial conspiracy. The smaller size of the provinces also enabled the governors to carry out their administrative and judicial duties in person and with greater care than heretofore.

The reorganization of the provinces may have improved the Empire's stability, but it also greatly increased the burden of the imperial government. The two praetorian prefects, who headed the civil service, the twelve vicars, and the multitude of governors and commanders all required adequate office staffs, and these increased enormously the weight and expense of the bureaucratic machines.

THE ARMY.   Diocletian's organization of the army followed the trends that had begun under Gallienus and Aurelian. The army was increased in size to perhaps 500,000 men. Along the frontiers the *limitanei* now regularly tilled the soil and sustained the first shock of attack, while new mobile legions were normally stationed in garrison cities from which they could be dispatched to points attacked. These new legions were far smaller than the old standard legions of 6000 men. They had developed out of the mobile detachments (*vexillationes*), and they contained between 1000 and 1500 men. The importance of mounted troops continued to develop, and there is evidence for the beginnings of special crack troops who were called the *comitatenses*, the friends of the emperor. A new unit to serve as the imperial bodyguard was indeed needed, for the long and evil history of the praetorian guard was near its end. It no longer guarded the emperor, but was left in Rome by Diocletian to serve as a garrison there.

THE TAX STRUCTURE.   Diocletian undertook an ambitious building program and encouraged his colleagues to do the same. Some of the work, such as the enormous Baths of Diocletian at Rome or the palace that Diocletian built for his retirement at Spalato in Dalmatia, were largely ornamental. Others, such as a great highway from Damascus to the Euphrates, had considerable military value. Useful or not, the public works of the tetrarchs seriously increased the demands on the imperial finances, already strained by an enlarged army, a multiplied provincial administration and bureaucracy, and the maintenance of four courts. To meet the financial needs of the government a complete reform of the tax structure was needed, for the system of indirect taxes and slapdash requisitions had brought the Empire to financial anarchy. A new survey of the resources of the Empire was made; and a new tax system was based on the establishment of units of approximately equal value. The system by which tax estimates could be made was called *jugatio* and *capitatio*, because the unit of land was called a *jugum*, and that of living things a *caput*. A *jugum* consisted of different kinds and amounts of land: twenty acres of first-class plowland, or forty acres of second-class, or sixty of third-class, or five acres of vineyard, or 225 olive trees. The value of the produce of each of these units was about the same. A *caput* could be the value of the labor of one man, or of two women, or the sale value of a given number of sheep or cattle. Each year the emperor and his advisers determined the national budget, and the praetorian prefects would then determine the tax rate per *jugum* and per *caput*. At first the nation's resources were reviewed every five years, but after 312 A.D. the assets of the empire were redetermined every fifteen years. This cycle of fifteen years was called an indiction, and for a long time it was used as a method of dating.

Much of the tax assessment was collected in kind, though in the fourth and fifth centuries A.D. there existed a rate by which the tax in kind could be commuted to money, at least for the *capita*. The ability to pay the taxes in produce was a benefit to most people who, in a world of shrinking trade, had found it difficult to sell surplus products in order to get the money with which to pay taxes. The collectors of taxes were selected from the *curiales* of local senates, and they were liable to make up from their own property any shortages assessed to their district. Italy, which had been divided into a number of provinces just as the rest of the Empire had been, now also paid the same taxes. Thus the heartland of the Empire at length attained the same position as the outlying provinces.

REFORM OF THE CURRENCY.   The anarchy of the third century A.D. had forced the military emperors to debase the coinage repeatedly in order to pay their armies, and by the accession of Diocletian the silver coins were simply bronze with a silver tinge. The emperor therefore instituted a sweeping reform of currency near the end of the third century A.D. All the old provincial mints ceased the production of local issues, and the imperial mints turned out uniform coinage for the whole Empire. A standard gold coin, a coin of pure silver, and three smaller pieces in an alloy of copper and silver were issued. The relation of this reform in the currency to a runaway inflation that occurred at the same time is not thoroughly understood. Probably the central government found it impossible immediately to replace the masses of worthless coinage that had flooded the Empire during previous reigns; and when the news of a projected replacement of old currency with new was broadcast, it hastened frantic attempts to turn older currency into goods, with a consequent astronomical rise in prices.

PRICE CONTROLS.   The runaway inflation of the late third century A.D. greatly disturbed the emperor, for it endangered the livelihood of his soldiers and clerks, who were on fixed salaries. In 301 A.D., therefore, Diocletian issued an edict setting maximum prices for all the goods and services of the Empire—from onions and radishes to haircuts, and from coarse woolen cloaks to Chinese silk. The penalty for infringement of the law by either buyer or seller was death—a penalty that could be avoided easily, Diocletian's preamble to the edict disarmingly asserts, by simple obedience. It is frequently stated by modern economists that the outraged public forced the withdrawal of the edict. Actually, price-fixing became unnecessary as soon as the new currency had completely replaced the older issues. But the edict long served as the standard for the government in reckoning the pecuniary value of taxes paid in kind; and a study of the prices on the list not only informs us of the relative value of various goods and services, but also suggests certain changes that had taken place in the economy since the late Republic and Early Principate. Wheat was somewhat more expensive; but meat was cheaper; while clothes, wages, and metals were higher. These facts indicate that there had been an increase in the amount of grazing land since Augustus, a decrease in the competition of slavery with free labor, and a decline in the productivity of the Empire's mines.

PERSECUTION OF THE CHRISTIANS.   One group that appeared to some Roman citizens to be uncooperative in the revitalization of the Empire was the Christians. Those who honestly believed in the divine authorization of Diocletian's government, and in the importance of the state-religion as a critical factor in binding the citizens together, viewed the schismatic activities of the Christians with distaste. One of the critics of the Christians was the Caesar Galerius, whose prestige and influence in imperial councils had been high since his rout of the Persians. In the winter of 302/3 A.D. Galerius pressed his views on the aging emperor, who had pursued a policy of tolerance for the Christians for nearly twenty years. Diocletian insisted that there should be no bloodshed, but finally in 303 he issued an edict banning Christian churches, assemblies, and sacred books. This was followed by three more edicts, each progressively more severe: one directed the imprisonment of the Christian leaders and clergy; another ordered that they be forced to perform the conventional sacrifice to the imperial gods and then be released; and the last commanded all to sacrifice or face the death penalty. The severity of these measures is partly explained by two mysterious fires that broke out in the emperor's palace at Nicomedia after the first edict. The Christians had been involved in incendiarism from the earliest times, both in their alleged connection with Rome's great fire in the days of Nero and in their notorious expectation of an early and fiery end to the world. The last and harshest edict was perhaps the work of Galerius alone after Diocletian had suffered a severe illness, probably a stroke, in early 304. In any case, the edicts were observed in a very uneven fashion: Galerius executed them rigorously; but in the West Constantius apparently only gave effect to the first edict, and the tolerant pagans all over the Empire connived with the Christians to shield them from the rigors of the law.

ABDICATION OF DIOCLETIAN (305 A.D.). After his illness in 304 Diocletian decided that his new system of government had had sufficient time to prove itself, and on May 1, 305, he abdicated at Nicomedia. By prearrangement Maximian performed the same act at Milan on the same day. Galerius and Constantius now were elevated to the rank of Augusti, and two new Caesars were appointed, Severus for the West and Maximin Daia for the East. Both Constantine, the son of Constantius, and Maxentius, the son of Maximian, had been passed by. Constantius was declared the senior Augustus, but both of the new Caesars were favorites of Galerius.

CIVIL WARS OF DIOCLETIAN'S SUCCESSORS (306–324 A.D.)
The Tetrarchy foundered almost at once. Constantius died suddenly in 306 A.D., and his troops elevated his son Constantine without regard for formality or imperial consultation. Galerius accepted the *fait accompli*, however, and Severus was raised to the rank of Augustus, with Constantine and Daia serving as Caesars. Next, Maxentius, son of Maximian, insisted that he had as much right to the throne as anyone, called his father from retirement to assist him, and rallied Italy to his cause. This he did the more easily because he promised to return the peninsula to

its ancient and preferred status in the Empire and to restore the praetorian guard to its former eminence. Africa also went over to him. There followed a whole series of usurpations, intrigues, conferences, dynastic marriages, and armed clashes between the various Augusti and Caesars that were more bewildering than significant. Diocletian, however, firmly refused to leave his retirement at Spalato to set the world aright. Fortunately for the world, his previous work had been sufficiently effective that a few years of idiocy were possible without irreparable harm to the Romans either from within or without the Empire. From 307 to 311 A.D. five men claimed the rank of Augustus — Galerius, Maxentius, Daia, Licinius (who had replaced Severus), and Constantine. Galerius died of a loathsome disease in 311; Maxentius perished in a battle fought against the forces of Constantine at the Milvian Bridge over the Tiber in 312; and Daia died in 313 after a defeat at the hands of Licinius. From that time until 324 the Empire was divided between Constantine and Licinius, who had married Constantine's sister.

Just before Galerius died, he had a change of heart concerning the Christians and issued an edict of tolerance. However, the chief beneficiary of the new policy was Constantine, for he received the credit for the milder view toward the dissident religion. Constantine was clever and ambitious, and he kept his army in excellent shape while he was co-emperor with Licinius by making frequent excursions against the Germans. He also cultivated the Christians, whose God he insisted had helped him in his defeat of Maxentius in 312. In 323, during a foray against Gothic invaders, Constantine's army trespassed on areas administered by Licinius. Altercations ensued between the two emperors, and were followed by military action. In 324 Licinius was defeated and subsequently executed, and the Empire once more was reunited in the hands of one man.

THE ACCOMPLISHMENT OF DIOCLETIAN.   Diocletian died at Spalato in 316 A.D., where for more than ten years he had tended a garden, raised cabbages, and watched his Tetrarchy being destroyed. The old man felt, no doubt, that his efforts had failed. In fact, his reforms set the tone and methods of the next century and were to be perfected in an even more elaborate system by Constantine. Future emperors saw, as Diocletian had seen, that the responsibility of government had to be shared, and they would act upon this idea. The generally authoritarian nature of the government and the Oriental color of the court also continued; and Diocletian's military, administrative, fiscal, and monetary policies all were retained or further developed. The needs of empire that kept Diocletian and his colleagues at Nicomedia, Sirmium, Milan, and Trèves had started a decentralization in imperial administration that continued. Rome was no longer the great administrative capital of the Empire, and the term *Romanitas* had become only an abstraction. It stood for the great past and for an ideal of world empire, not for the fashions and practices that were found in the metropolis on the Tiber.

Diocletian's reorganization of the tax structure had one effect that was almost immediate and that did much to determine the nature of future society. The duty imposed upon the *curiales* to collect taxes and to put up their own property as guarantee prompted many of the municipal nobility to evade the obligation. By the time of Constantine, therefore, the duties imposed upon local officials would become obligatory and hereditary. In the same way, many a tenant found it difficult to raise on his land as much produce as Diocletian's agents estimated was possible, and therefore attempted to change his residence or employment. But once the number of productive units (*juga* or *capita*) had been determined, any abandonment of a part of them would have been fatal to the carefully calculated budget. Hence, farmers and their heirs were straightway tied to their occupation and places of origin just as the local nobles were, and they were destined to sink into that form of serfdom that distinguished the Late Empire and is called the Colonate. Tradesmen, artisans, and soldiers were not far behind the farmers and petty nobles in being tied to their trades in order to satisfy the requirements of the central government. The indictions and the system of *capitatio* and *jugatio* inaugurated by Diocletian, then, gave a strong impetus to the change from a regime of free contract, which had prevailed in the society of the Republic and Principate, to a regime of status, in which all men were tied to an inherited trade and location in the interest of a beleaguered State.

Chapter 43

CHRISTIANITY AND THE STATE

ROMAN RELIGIOUS CLIMATE IN THE PRINCIPATE.
The Roman world of the first and second centuries A.D. was a sophisticated world, a world that knew, tolerated, and toyed with a variety of strange doctrines. The pagans found that many of the religious beliefs, practices, and deities in different parts of the world were very similar to each other. This led them to believe that the special names and special forms of worship for the numerous pagan deities must be simply the names and forms favored by the same gods in different localities. In matters of religion there was a good deal of borrowing and reciprocity by the Romans and their subjects, which was leading many men to a belief in a rather vague pantheism, in which the multitudes of deities were but different revelations of the same god or gods.

In such a society the message of Jesus Christ at first made little impression. He had come into the world in the principate of Augustus (23 B.C.–14 A.D.), and he had taught and been crucified under Tiberius (14–37 A.D.). His teachings seemed to most observers just another queer and obscure doctrine from a section of the world that had spawned many strange notions. For a long time his followers were considered merely a dissident sect of the Jews, a race that the Romans had known, tolerated, and despised for centuries; and at first the Christians enjoyed the protection of that tolerance. Christ's message had comfort for the humble and for the spiritually inclined, however, and made considerable progress during the first century A.D. among Orientals, the poor, and slaves.

THE SPREAD OF CHRISTIANITY.   The diffusion of Christian belief was hastened by the early conversion (*ca.* 33 A.D.) of the apostle Paul, a Hellenized Jew of Tarsus, who was also a Roman citizen. He persuaded other earlier followers of Christ that their message was not for Jews alone but for all men, and he

540

embarked on a number of missionary visits to the cities of the Near East. Paul made many conversions, which were facilitated by his ability to communicate with other Hellenized Orientals in the terms of Greek philosophy, with which he was familiar. Congregations were established in a number of cities. Their sense of fellowship and of interdependence led to a correspondence with one another and with the leaders of the movement, and this practice gave a rudimentary basis to the systematic organization of the Church that ultimately evolved.

By the middle of the first century A.D. Christians were sufficiently numerous, their disputes with the Jews sufficiently noisy, and their practices and public deportment sufficiently eccentric that the pagan world had become conscious of them and of their singularity. Therefore, when two-thirds of the city of Rome was destroyed by fire in 64 A.D., and Emperor Nero himself was suspected as an arsonist, there was some plausibility to his accusation of the Christians, who were expecting instantly a second coming of Christ and the destruction of the world by fire. Perhaps the charge of "atheism" made against Flavius Clemens, the cousin of Emperor Domitian (81–96 A.D.) executed toward the end of the century, concealed his sympathy for the Christians. If so, the sect had begun to attract some members of the upper classes at an early date.

EARLY IMPERIAL POLICY TOWARD THE CHRISTIANS.
Despite its occasional notoriety, the Christian sect still was not widely known by the second century A.D. As experienced a lawyer and administrator as Pliny the Younger was apparently ignorant of the Christians' doctrine and uncertain of their legal status during the reign of Trajan (98–117 A.D.). But the reply of Trajan to Pliny's inquiries shows that the administration presumed that membership in the sect implied subversive or conspiratorial tendencies (because Christian gatherings were secret and unlicensed) and hostility to the State (because the rigid monotheism of the Christians precluded the adoration of the gods of the official cult). Trajan's letter directed, however, that the Christians could easily be absolved of their guilt if they simply burned a little incense before the emperor's statue—a kind of salute to the flag—and he discouraged special investigations or witch-hunts. But he instructed Pliny that documented accusations must be tried, and impenitent culprits must be punished. Apparently some of the Christians' fellow citizens did indeed resent them and accuse them. But we do not know whether the pagans' resentment was from patriotic motives, from moral disapproval, or from economic loss—we do know that where

541

Christians abounded the market for small sacrificial beasts fell away because the Christians did not make the sacrifices to their god that the pagans did to theirs. The pagans also widely misinterpreted the exclusive nature of some Christian rites: the Christian emphasis on love and the eating of the flesh and blood of Christ were understood by many non-Christians to cloak sexual licentiousness and cannibalism. Furthermore, some Christians were tempted to make dark insinuations about the morals of other Christians whose orthodoxy was suspect, and these charges and countercharges by Christians themselves lent credence to the pagans' suspicions of the whole sect. Marcus Aurelius (161–180 A.D.) disliked the Christians for their stubbornness, and there are some martyrdoms reported during his reign. Commodus (180–192 A.D.), however, was favorable to the Christians in deference to his favorite concubine, Marcia. The Severi (193–235 A.D.) showed the natural interest of Orientals in the sect. Although Septimius Severus restricted Christian missionary work, Julia Mamaea listened to the learned Origen preach, and Alexander Severus kept a statue of Christ along with other heroes and divinities in his chapel. During the early third century A.D., therefore, the Christian organization had an opportunity to expand and strengthen itself, and it even could indulge in the luxury of a squabble between the churches of Italy and Asia as to the precise date on which Easter should be celebrated.

ORGANIZATION OF THE EARLY CHURCH.   In the earliest days the Christian congregations kept in touch with one another by letters and by occasional visits by leaders of the movement. Gradually the leader of the church in each town assumed the title of bishop (*episcopus*, overseer), and his oversight of the congregation's spiritual welfare often broadened into some supervision of material affairs as well. Copying the annual provincial assemblies of pagan priests, who met to do honor to Rome and Augustus and to discuss affairs of mutual interest,[1] the bishops of a province also began to meet regularly to discuss matters of doctrine and of survival, and the bishops of the leading provincial cities soon exercised a larger authority over less important brethren and began to style themselves metropolitans (or archbishops). Thus the Church had evolved by the middle of the third century A.D. into a formidable and well-knit organization so large and influential that the civil government was forced to assume some positive attitude or policy toward it.

[1]   For the provincial religious *concilia*, see above, pp. 479.

542

The Christians still formed a small minority of the total population of the Empire, but the Church's discipline and the dimensions of its network meant that the emperors were faced with a state within the State that could pose problems not unlike those that the plebeian organization once posed to the patrician state in early Rome.

THE ATTRACTIONS OF ORIENTAL CULTS.   The increasing power of the Christian organization was fostered in part by characteristics that were peculiar to the Christians alone. There also existed, however, a number of purely external factors that did much to attract converts to the Christian Church. These factors were related to the social, economic, political, and intellectual situation that accompanied the rapid urbanization of the Empire during the Principate. Even during the last century of the Republic the primitive and native Roman religion had proved unsatisfactory for many of the city proletariat of Rome. Emigration to the city from distant places and long separation from the farm diminished the vividness, meaning, and suitability of the ancient worship of local spirits of the soil and generation. The philosophic agnosticism of many of the cultured city folk also sifted down to the humbler urban residents and increased their dissatisfactions. To fill the spiritual vacuum thus created, a number of Oriental cults of a more personal, ecstatic, and universal nature than the old cults of field and garden had found their way to the West; and the practices that accompanied them conditioned the Romans to emotions and enthusiasms that were new.

MOTHER GODDESSES.   As early as the Hannibalic War (218–201 B.C.) the Cult of Cybele, the Great Mother goddess from Asia Minor, had been officially imported into Rome. The Romans were impressed by the orgiastic ritual of Cybele's worship and startled by the fanatic devotion of her priests, who castrated themselves as part of their initiation into her service. In such excesses the Romans were introduced to a relation to divinity that was far different from the formal and businesslike arrangements that existed between their ancestors and the ancient Roman deities.

Far more attractive and ultimately more important than the Cult of Cybele was the worship of Egyptian Isis. She had been the sister and wife of the great god Osiris; and when he had been killed and mutilated by his evil brother Set, she had collected his scattered body and effected his resurrection. Thereafter Osiris ruled over and judged the dead, while Isis

543

was the great intercessor for men. In time she became the
model of all womanly and wifely virtues, the mother of god.
Her devotees were baptized in water and took vows of abs-
tinence, and her priests were shaven and tonsured. The high
influence of Isis with Osiris in behalf of her followers after their
deaths seems to have suggested to the early Christians a similar
role for Mary as the intercessor with Christ on behalf of sinners;
and in time it was easy for the Christians to transform the jew-
eled statues of Isis into madonnas.

MITHRAISM.   More masculine than the cults of Cybele and
Isis were many of the sects connected with the worship of the
Sun. Emperor Aurelian (270–275 A.D.) had tried to centralize
men's loyalties to god and Empire by encouraging the worship
of Sol Invictus (the Unconquered Sun), with himself the god's
vice-regent on earth. After Constantine broke with his Hercu-
lian father-in-law, Maximian, he also took the Sun as his sponsor. One of the solar cults, Mithraism, became especially important. According to this sect, the great Lord of Light,
Ahuramazda, was so far above mortals that they could have little
apprehension of him. However, the hero-god of the sect, Mithras, was more accessible to man. He was born in human form
in a cave on December 25th. He was first worshipped by shepherds, and when he grew up he slew a sacred mythical bull by
whose blood all the good things of earth were generated for
men. At length Mithras returned to heaven, but there he continued his interest in men and constantly interceded with the great
god in their behalf. Initiates worshipped him in Mithraea,
which were underground caves in memory of his place of birth.
Part of the initiation included baptism in the blood of a sacred
bull. Seven degrees of initiation signified seven stages in the
purification of the soul in its preparation for an ascent to heaven
after death. The sacred day of worship was Sunday. Mithraism
made no distinctions of race or rank and it was especially popular with soldiers. It appears, however, not to have accepted
women, and this was a distinct competitive weakness in a world
where that sex has been devoted to religious superstitions.

TENDENCIES TOWARD MONOTHEISM.   The universal appeal
of the Oriental religions and the resemblances discovered between their gods, practices, and messages were leading men
closer and closer to a kind of monotheistic belief. This tendency
was furthered by a disposition to concentrate adoration on that
greatest of all earthly benefactors, the emperor. If he was not
one of the gods himself (and few asserted that), he surely was

544

close to them, interceded with them, and might become one of them at his death. The policy of Aurelian and of his successors favored monotheism, for it suggested that men should seek contact with the divine through the emperor as the gods' chosen representative on earth.

The philosophies of the Principate also tended to foster monotheistic beliefs. Stoicism long had taught the essential brotherhood of man, for the Stoics believed that all men partook of a divine spark, and all that divine part of man would one day again be reunited in the great cosmic conflagration or cosmic soul. But Stoicism was an intemperately cold and austere system that appealed largely to a few intellectuals. The Neoplatonism of the third century A.D., however, as conceived by Plotinus and expounded by his pupil Porphyry, went far beyond the ideal world that Plato taught and postulated a World Soul of pure intelligence in whom wise men sought to lose themselves completely in ecstatic contemplation and communion. In other words, not only were the religions of the day moving toward a belief in a single god, but the philosophies were moving from the rational to the ecstatic and spiritual. Even the sophisticated agnosticism of many citizens favored tolerance and the search for some common principle to explain the many manifestations of the divine that man found throughout the Roman world. Further, the deplorable economic and political conditions of the Empire during the third century A.D. turned many men to any system that could promise a happier life hereafter. Any opposition to this otherworldliness that wealthy pagan temples or charitable foundations once could have presented had by now completely disappeared, for the licentious soldiers had devastated and confiscated both religious and secular wealth with an impartial hand.

ATTRACTIONS PECULIAR TO CHRISTIANITY.   The popularity of Oriental cults, the etherealization of philosophy, and the economic depression of the third century A.D. were, so to speak, external factors that prepared men's minds and wishes for the Christian message. There were in addition a number of characteristics peculiar to the Christians, or especially exemplified by them, that were favorable to the spread of their doctrine. These may be termed the internal reasons for their competitive success.

The earliest Christians were social and economic communists and contributed their property to a common fund from which they were supported and charitable activities were financed. This aspect made the sect especially attractive to the humble and to idealists. As the eagerly awaited second coming of Christ was delayed, however, human nature triumphed over this early practice, and Christians once more owned private property. In place of the renunciation of all private property, tithes now were exacted from the communicants, and the income from these continued to aid the afflicted, as well as support the clergy. The charity of the Christians proved so generous that it was praised and copied even by the detractors of the sect.

Further, the Christians were enthusiastic about their creed and sufficiently convinced of their duty toward their fellowmen that they felt obliged to bring their happiness to all others by converting them. This they did with a zeal that was unparalleled by any except, perhaps, the earlier Epicureans. And the simple goodness of their lives and their honesty in dealings with others soon struck a responsive chord in a Roman world where the sanctity of a man's word had once been fundamental and still was idealized. The historicity of the Christians' Saviour, and the miraculous powers that he and his disciples displayed attracted many of the pagans. The unprivileged appreciated the certainty of a happy life after death and the hope of improvement in this world through divine intercession.

Finally, the activities of Christian theologians, philosophers, and apologists and the discipline of the evolving hierarchy of the Church prevented the fragmentation that most of the pagan sects suffered. From the second century A.D. onward a succession of apologists—Tertullian, Justin, Minucius Felix, Clement, Origen, Arnobius, Lactantius—spoke to the world in terms that educated men could understand. Still, these early theologians anchored their arguments so firmly in the Jewish Old Testament and in the Gospels and early epistles of the Church that they curbed the tendency of some of the early Christian converts to indulge in wild flights of philosophic imagination about the relations of God, Christ, and Man. These deviants were known as Gnostics. The Gnostics claimed to be Christians, but their elaborate systems of Godhead and ethereal spirits, and their rational inquiries into whether Christ was really human or divine, were early scandals of the Church that exercised the orthodox apologists. The elimination or control of Gnostic speculation proved the efficiency of the authoritarian hierarchy of bishops and metropolitans, for these worthies excluded the deviant thinkers from their fellowship. There were, however, some important and persistent aberrations from orthodox doctrine. In the second century A.D. the Montanists were puritans and protestants who tried to recall the Christians to their simpler, earlier communistic life and who questioned

546

the increasing power of the bishops, to the great resentment of that ambitious order. In the early fourth century A.D. the followers of Donatus in Africa so reproached the leniency of the Orthodox Church toward penitent apostates that ultimately they excommunicated all the rest of Christendom! In general, however, the apologists and the hierarchy of the orthodox Christians were able to maintan a fairly homogeneous Church as long as all Christians alike were endangered by pagan hostility.

CHURCH AND STATE IN THE THIRD CENTURY A.D.

The constantly increasing Christian congregations and their permeation of Roman society in the third century A.D. attracted more and more imperial attention, and occasionally imperial persecution. Sometimes the object of the persecution was merely loot from the Christians' treasuries, as seems to have been the case with Maximinus Thrax (235–238 A.D.); and sometimes the emperors responded to popular indignation, roused by a superstitous belief that the godless Christians were to blame for the troubled times. Emperor Decius (249–251 A.D.) pursued a policy that deliberately tried to destroy the Church, for he believed that the imperiled Empire required a unanimity of effort on every level, physical and spiritual, and he found the Christians uncooperative. Emperor Valerian (253-259 A.D.) in his later years seems to have reached the same conclusion. Most of the emperors thereafter, however, followed the tolerant or contemptuous attitude of Gallienus (259–268 A.D.), and Christians appeared in the civil service and the army, and at the court itself. The Christians consistently protested that in worldly matters they were loyal to the State and to the emperor; and their years of involvement in the government's service and of peaceable coexistence with pagan neighbors removed much of the suspicion and alarm from the public mind. However, after tolerating the Christians for the first eighteen years of his administration, in 303 Diocletian was convinced by his Caesar Galerius that his new political dispensation, centered on his own position as the vice-regent of Jupiter, would never be fully effective as long as the Christians denied its validity. In his attack on the Christians Galerius was supported by the Neoplatonist philosophers and by the Oracle of Apollo at Miletus, which testified that Christian activities were interfering with the true revelations of Apollo at his shrine. The terms of this last great persecution were severe,[2] and in the East at least they were rigorously enforced; but in 311 Galerius, desperately ill,

[2]   For the edicts of Diocletian on Christianity, see above, pp. 536–537.

recognized the futility of his effort and from his deathbed issued
an edict of toleration and a request for Christian prayers.

CONSTANTINE AND CHRISTIANITY.   Constantius, the father
of Constantine, had been lenient toward the Christians, and
Constantine early showed some interest in them, though political policy dictated that he should proclaim his devotion to the
Unconquered Sun. According to his own account he was instructed by dreams and visions during his campaign against
Maxentius to fight under a Christian sign. The shields of his
troops were therefore emblazoned with a Christian insignia at
the Battle of the Milvian Bridge in 312. Constantine's complete
victory there convinced him that the Christian God was indeed a
militant god, a god of hosts, and from this conviction there
could be no turning back. With this event there began an association of Christian Church and Roman State that was to prove
fatal to them both.

Early in 313 Constantine and his Eastern associate, the
Augustus Licinius, met at Milan and agreed on a policy of
toleration for all faiths throughout the Empire. Constantine
cannily and politically postponed his own baptism as a Christian until his deathbed so that he could continue to serve the
majority of his subjects as their pagan pontifex maximus. His
sons, however, were brought up as Christians, and Constantine
himself was an anxious participant in the theological controversies of the day. He appointed arbiters to settle the Donatist
quarrel in 313, called a council to discuss the subject in 314,
and finally settled it himself in 316. Despite his presumed
neutrality, several pieces of his legislation established special
privileges for Christians and their clergy. He was especially
exercised by the bitter dispute that broke out around 318 concerning the nature of the Trinity. He finally convened an ecu-
menical council at Nicaea in Bithynia in 325 and insisted that a
definitive statement be worked out and subscribed to by all
Christians. The resultant Nicene Creed—that the Father and
the Son are coeternal and of the same substance—has remained
a fundamental of orthodoxy. A large and violent minority, however, followed the opinion of the learned presbyter Arius, who
maintained that the Son was created by the Father and that they
could not be coeternal. Constantine was right to be concerned
about Arianism, for that heresy was destined to split the Christians for centuries. More important for the history of the
Church, however, was the precedent that the emperor set at this
time for imperial leadership and discipline in matters of theological dogma. The example of Constantine in this matter never
was shaken off by the Eastern Orthodox Church.

CONSTANTINOPLE.   Constantine's reign was not without secular activities and triumphs as well as advances in religion. The emperor concluded successful wars against the Goths and settled 300,000 suppliant Sarmatians along the Danubian frontier as a reservoir of farmers and soldiers. But his most notable achievement was the construction of a new capital, a new Rome, for the Empire. On the shores of the Bosphorus at the site of ancient Byzantium between 324 and 330 A.D. there arose Constantinople. The harbor was magnificent, the place was easily defensible, and strategically it was more or less equidistant from the dangerous Danubian and Persian frontiers. And though Constantine ransacked the pagan world for treasures with which to adorn his city, this was to be the Christian capital, the city untainted by pagan sacrifice. However, the abandonment of Rome was a prelude to the abandonment of the West, and the new holy city of Constantinople became the heart of an empire, a culture, a religion, an outlook, and a society in which there soon would be nothing Roman except the name.

THE DYNASTY OF CONSTANTINE.   The conversion of Constantine to Christianity did not seriously change the autocratic tendencies of the administration or of the court, where the Oriental pomp introduced by Diocletian was furthered. The emperor now had a heavenly example in God Almighty upon which to pattern his earthly kingdom, where all men should accept their position, rank, and lot with happy submission. Neither did Christianity change the ruthless suspicions and ambitions of Constantine and his sons, whose histories are neither fraternal nor inspiring. In 326 Constantine jealously executed his popular eldest son, Crispus, his empress, Fausta, and his nephew, Licinianus. He thereupon established as administrative Caesars his remaining sons, Constantine II in the West, Constantius in the East, and Constans in Italy, Illyricum, and Africa, while two nephews, Delmatius and Annabalianus, were given districts in the Balkans and Armenia to administer. He treated the Empire as his personal property to be distributed among his relatives and descendants as he saw fit.

When Constantine died, a baptized Christian, in 337 A.D. the army was inspired to murder all of his nephews except two very young ones, Gallus and Julian, and the Empire fell to Constantine's three surviving sons. But Constans defeated and killed his brother Constantine II in 340, and himself fell a victim to a usurper, Magnentius, in 350. By 353 Constantius found himself master of an empire where the need to share the administrative and military responsibilities had been repeatedly shown. He first tried to use his cousin Gallus (351–354 A.D.)

as his aide, but years of confinement had made Gallus a brutal lout, and the experiment ended in his being beheaded. In 355 Constantius elevated his remaining cousin, Julian, to the rank of Caesar, gave him his daughter Helena in marriage, and sent him to Gaul to stem an invasion of Franks and Alamanni. Julian was so successful a commander that his troops proclaimed him Augustus in 360, and a trial of arms with his cousin Constantius was at hand when the latter died of a fever in 361. Despite, or perhaps because of, his experiences as a Christian Julian (360–363 A.D.) underwent a revulsion of feeling and returned to paganism (hence his sobriquet, "the Apostate"), and was followed by many of his men with the same alacrity with which they had earlier embraced Christianity. But Julian soon died of wounds received in battle on the Persian frontier, and the new church that he tried to create based on Neoplatonist philosophy perished with him.

THE DYNASTY OF VALENTINIAN. THEODOSIUS I.   With the death of Julian, the house of Constantine was extinct, and the choice of the generals fell on a minor military tribune named Jovian (363–364 A.D.), who returned at once to the Christian faith and made a sudden and unfavorable settlement with the Persians so that he could hasten to the West to confirm his elevation. He died, however, before he had left Asia Minor; and the leaders of the army and of the administration elected in his place Valentinian I (364–375 A.D.). Valentinian straightway associated with himself his brother Valens (364–378 A.D.), and both princes were steadily involved in the defense of the Rhenish and Danubian frontiers. Valentinian repeatedly repulsed the Germans along the Rhine, while his general Theodosius the Elder cleared Britain of its invaders and then suppressed a Moorish rebellion in Mauretania and Numidia. Valentinian died of an apoplectic stroke while berating some penitent German ambassadors; but Valens perished more heroically in an utter rout at the hands of the Goths in 378. Here, at the Battle of Adrianople, the superiority of Gothic cavalry over the footsoldiers of the Roman legions was finally and unequivocally demonstrated, but the demonstration came at a time when the Empire's financial resources could ill afford a strong and thorough reform of the military arm. Valentinian's young son, Gratian (375–383 A.D.), succeeded his father in the West and associated with himself his infant brother, Valentinian II (375–392 A.D.), while he appointed the son of the general Theodosius the Elder, Theodosius I (379–395 A.D.), to act as junior Augustus in the East. In the Balkans Theodosius reached an agreement with the Goths, who settled there in large numbers as federate allies of the Romans. In the West Gratian had been killed by the army of a usurper, Magnus Maximus, in 383, but he was finally avenged in 388 by Theodosius, and the West was restored to Valentinian II. He too fell to a plot, this one engineered by his general Arbogast in 392, and a pagan usurper, Eugenius, held power in the West until 394, when the Empire was once more briefly reunited by Theodosius. However, Theodosius died in Milan early in 395, and the Empire was thereupon finally divided between his two sons, Arcadius in the East (395–408 A.D.) and Honorius in the West (395–423 A.D.).

ORTHODOXY AND ARIANISM.   Despite the Nicene Creed adopted in 325 A.D. at the insistence of Constantine I, the unitarian arguments of the Arians — that God was One, and that his Son and the Holy Spirit were separate beings — was intellectually too attractive for immediate defeat. Slowly Arians or semi-Arians returned to power and found much support for another variant doctrine, that Christ was of a similar, but not the same, substance as God. Indeed, Constantine I himself was baptized by an Arian bishop, and Constantius and Valens both favored Arian doctrine and churchmen. But orthodoxy prevailed in the West, and Gratian and then Thedosius I used their secular power to reimpose the Trinity upon the world.

AMBROSE OF MILAN (334–397 A.D.).   Both Gratian and Theodosius I were greatly under the influence of Ambrose, Bishop of Milan (334–397 A.D.). The nature of the power of that prelate and of his organization may be inferred from two experiences of Theodosius while he was resident in Milan. In 388 A.D. the monks of a small town in the Near East incited a Christian mob to destroy the local synagogue. The emperor ordered the guilty parties to restore the building or make reparation; but Ambrose considered this kind of justice persecution, and he refused the rites of the Church to the emperor until he granted immunity to the offenders. Again, in 390 a mob in Thessalonika murdered the emperor's resident general and part of his staff in that city because the general had imprisoned the town's favorite charioteer for seducing a handsome boy. The emperor's enraged reaction was to order a massacre of the city's guilty citizens. The order was later revoked, but the countermand arrived too late. This time Ambrose imposed months of public penance on Theodosius before he could again enjoy the Church's fellowship. In 392 Theodosius forbade pagans to make sacrifices or to perform their ordinary rites of worship on the grounds that these were acts of treason; and Christian monks and mobs recognized this order as a signal to pillage and destroy the ancient temples, while the civil authorities stood idly by.

EFFECTS OF THE CHURCH TRIUMPHANT ON THE STATE.
It is sometimes reported that the last words of Emperor Julian on his deathbed were, "Thou hast conquered, pale Galilaean"; but subsequent events impose cautious qualification on the accuracy of the Apostate's judgment. The Christian triumph was far from thorough and its consequences for the State were not invariably beneficial. Freedom from the bonds of persecution allowed the Christians to give full vent to bitter theological argument, and their interminable squabbles rent the State and set province against province, brother against brother. From being the persecuted, the Christians became the persecutors, both of heretics and of pagans; and in their persecutions they showed a fanatic and self-righteous zeal that was more bloody and more dreadful than what they had suffered at the hands of the more indulgent pagans. Further, the Christian missionaries to the barbarians were mostly heretical Arians. This meant that when the Goths and Germans crossed the frontiers and inundated the West to set up the successor states there, the rulers were Arian heretics and their subjects orthodox Catholics. Relations between rulers and ruled, therefore, were especially embittered by the most violent of prejudices—those arising from the intolerance of doctrinaires and zealots. We must add, however, that when, by the seventh century A.D., the problems of Christology had been fairly well worked out, Christianity healed that spiritual breach that had divided and plagued the intelligentsia and masses of the Roman world for centuries, and the peoples of Western Europe generally enjoyed a common religious endowment. However, the civilizations that focussed upon the Church at that time were no longer Roman but new, derivative cultures, Byzantine and Western European.

EFFECTS OF THE CHURCH TRIUMPHANT ON CHRISTIANITY.
The early triumph of the Church was far more fatal to Christianity than it was to the State, for the triumph was followed by a spectacular loss of spiritual power. Church and State combined to use force instead of persuasion to enlist new recruits, though this was in utter contempt of the example of Christ. Multitudes of countryfolk (the *pagani*), torn from their ancestral devotion to spirits of field and pasture, transferred wholesale their superstitious veneration, practices, and prayers from their ancient pagan

552

deities to saints and martyrs, real or imaginary. Regardless of the casuistic apologies and explanations made by their spiritual superiors, the Mediterranean peasants have continued to the present to worship their local deities, camouflaged though they may be by Christian titles and fables. Moreover, the Church modelled its hierarchical structure on the authoritarian government of the Late Empire; and the enormous power gained by the prelates of the Church too often led to a presumption and arrogance that alienated the truly spiritual. The seriously devout often could find solace only by withdrawing from the world as monks or hermits, and this they did in great quantities, to the detriment of productive society. In brief, the Church became worldly, and mankind dumbly suffered for centuries the consequent ambitions, corruptions, and irresponsibilities of its spiritual leadership. At length, in the periods of the Renaissance and Reformation, disgust and reason were destined to generate new schisms within the Church. And the religious wars that were consequent to the worldliness of the Church and the schisms within it were to rend its Master far more viciously than the puzzled Romans of the Principate ever did.

PART
Nine

The Old And The New

Chapter 44

SOCIAL AND ECONOMIC PETRIFICATION
IN THE LATE EMPIRE

Just as Augustus had appeared after a century of civil war
that destroyed the Republic (133–31 B.C.) and used the lessons
taught by Rome's suicidal conflicts and political compromises to
create a system of government acceptable to a world that craved
peace, so Diocletian and Constantine contrived for the Romans
a system based on the experiences of the anarchy in the third
century A.D. Circumstances in the third century, however, were
not the same as those at the end of the Republic. In the third
and fourth centuries A.D. the pressures of barbarian peoples
from outside the Empire were more insistent than they had
been at the time of Christ; and the economy, wealth, and
morale of the citizen population were now far weaker. Once
again, however, the desire for peace and stability was paramount, and the development of a highly centralized government during the three centuries between Augustus and Diocletian suggested that the emperors of the fourth century A.D.
could try patterns of authoritarian government that Augustus
never would have dared to try.

When Diocletian came to the throne the state of the Empire was desperate. At the time of his accession the countryside
had been devastated by civil strife, by the requisitions of emperors and usurpers, by barbarian raids, and by terrible plagues.
Meanwhile, the cities had been so decimated by disease, pillaged by armies, and milked by tax collectors that the surplus of
consumers upon whom commercial prosperity depended had
disappeared. A desperate situation seemed to call for desperate
measures. Diocletian's solution had included an enlarged army
to cope with foreign dangers; reformed currency and a new
system of taxation for the economy; an expanded bureaucracy
and multiplied administrative units to increase internal security
and efficiency; and an appeal to Jupiter and Hercules to bol-

ster imperial authority. The solution did achieve some stability, but pressures from without and weaknesses within still remained: civil wars were not yet completely brought to an end; and it was Constantine's own experiences with the conflicts of rival emperors between 306 and 324 A.D. that forced him further to refine and reform the system that Diocletian had inaugurated. To this task Constantine was able to bring the vitality of the young and authoritarian religion of the Christians. In his hands and in those of his successors the result was a totalitarian state—on earth as it was in heaven.

THE TRANSFORMATION OF THE ROMAN ARMY.   Diocletian had begun the creation of a mobile army poised in various strategic centers to back up the frontier troops (*limitanei*) wherever a breakthrough threatened. Constantine elaborated this system. He pulled the best troops out of the frontier legions to increase the efficiency of the field army, and under him and his successors the *limitanei* sank closer and closer to the status of ineffective militarized peasants. This development had significance for the national economy, for it created an auxiliary source of farm produce to supply the army at a time when civilian agriculture was weakening. The emperors of the fourth century A.D. also reconciled themselves to a constant increase in the barbarian content of the army. Roman recruits were now at a premium; the manpower of the Balkans and Pannonia, which had been a mainstay of the army, had been decimated by years of recruiting and by the repeated barbarian invasions. It is true that the Roman government had never surrendered its right of universal conscription, but the waning population was now barely able to sustain the burdens of civilian government. For a while the emperors tried to divide the Empire into units of agricultural land, each of which was required to furnish one recruit for the army each year. It was calculated that 75,000 to 100,000 such recruits were needed each year as replacements for soldiers that had been lost or discharged. However, landowners tended to submit to the army recruits with such poor qualifications that the emperors instead decided to exact from the landowners a sum of money (the *aurum tironicum*) with which competent mercenaries could be hired. The one fertile and trustworthy source of citizen soldiers came from the sons of soldiers and of veterans. However, these men were in diminishing supply, and this led the emperors to take more and more of a calculated risk with barbarians. Some barbarians outside the frontiers were subsidized to countercheck others and thus to divert them from attacks on the Empire; others the emperors

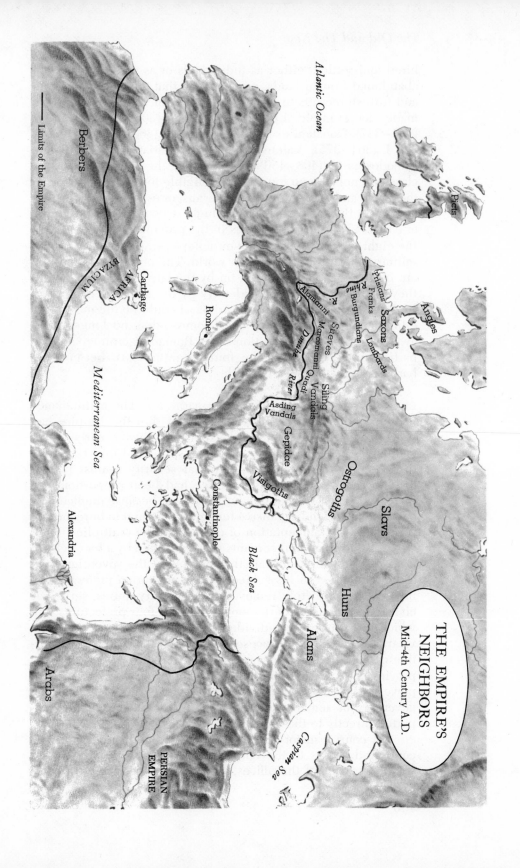

THE EMPIRE'S
NEIGHBORS
Mid-4th Century A.D.

Limits of the Empire

Atlantic Ocean

Berbers

BYZACIUM

AFRICA

Carthage

Rome

Mediterranean Sea

Alexandria

Picts

Angles

Frisians
Saxons
Franks
Rhine R.
Burgundians
Lombards
Alamanni
Sueves
Marcomanni
Quadi
Siling
Vandals
Asding
Vandals
Gepidae
Danube River
Visigoths

Constantinople

Black Sea

Ostrogoths

Slavs

Huns

Alans

Caspian Sea

PERSIAN
EMPIRE

Arabs

hired and settled, either as individuals or as whole groups, on abandoned Roman lands, on condition that they cultivate them and furnish recruits to the Roman army. Such settlements were made, for example, by Diocletian (284–305), Constantine I (307–337), Constantius (337–361), Julian (360–363), Valentinian I (364–375), Valens (364–378), Gratian (367–383), and Theodosius II (408–450). Members of the Roman senatorial class and nobility no longer were eligible for high command in the army, and leaders of the barbarians, or especially competent men from the ranks, rose to the highest positions as the *duces* or *comites*, who led the armies in the provinces, or even one of the eight great masters of foot or of horse, who now directed the military fortunes of the Roman world. The origins of these men are betrayed by their names, for by the late fourth century A.D. they scorned to hide their identity by the adoption of Romanized names, and a Stilicho or Arbogast could be the most powerful man in the Empire. Such commanders no longer were awed by the Roman tradition or by Roman discipline, and the barbarian mercenary of the fourth century A.D. became the barbarian kingmaker of the fifth.

ELABORATION OF THE ADMINISTRATION.   The maintenance of the central government's authority within the Empire had proved equally important and expensive. By the early fourth century A.D. the provinces had been splintered into 120 small districts in order to ensure imperial security against powerful governors, and the civil service had been proportionately increased. This was not the end, however, because inefficiency, corruption, and the expansive tendencies natural to bureaucracy increased the fragmentation of duties and the multiplication of posts. An army of civil servants was controlled by a hierarchy of ministers and high officials that prevented the sovereign from actual contact with his subjects. Four praetorian prefects, who now were completely removed from military duties, served as civil representatives of the emperor in the four prefectures into which the Empire was divided. Below them in rank were the vicars of the thirteen dioceses into which the Empire was further carved. Below the vicars, in turn, were the governors of the provinces. To reduce a somewhat dangerous concentration of power in the hands of the prefects, however, the vicars and the governors of some ancient and more important provinces reported directly to the emperor.

At court a major official was the grand chamberlain, who controlled access to the emperor's person. Equally important was the master of the offices, who headed the four bureaus in charge of memorials, petitions, epistles, and directives. These offices alone employed 148 secretaries, most of them skilled in the law. A count (*comes*) of the sacred largesses was the treasurer-general of the Empire, and he supervised the collection of revenue, exploitation of mines, issues of the mints, foreign trade, and the factories that now manufactured weapons and clothing for the army and court. There was also a count in charge of the emperor's vast estates, and two counts of the domestics, who commanded the 3500 troops that guarded the emperor.

INFLATION OF NOMENCLATURE.   All the persons connected with the imperial administration were arranged in an elaborate order of precedence. Members of the senatorial class were ranked as *clarissimi* (the most honorable). Above them were the *spectabiles* (the admirable), which rank included the vicars of the dioceses, the heads of the four bureaus, and the governors of Achaea, Asia, and Africa. At the top were the *illustres* (the illustrious). Members of this last class included the annual consuls, whose only duties now consisted of giving their names to the year and presiding at the New Year's festival, the prefects, the masters-general of the army, and the patricians. "Patrician" was a title revived by Constantine and bestowed on court favorites and old and distinguished ministers, and it was a personal and not an hereditary distinction. The growing extravagance of these mighty titles parallels and reflects the decrease in actual power of the recipients, just as the enormous size of some of their buildings reflects the bankruptcy of artistic ability in the Late Empire. The world was ransacked of its treasures as the only way to find the proper adornment for contemporary structures; the Arch of Constantine, for example, was decked with the sculptures of earlier and more productive epochs rather than with contemporary work. The emperors' titles also became more and more formidable and more unrealistic. The simplicity of an imperial letter of 6 B.C., which begins "Emperor Caesar Augustus . . . greetings" is in sharp contrast to a rescript of 333/7 A.D., "Emperor Caesar Flavius Constantine Maximus Germanicus Sarmaticus Maximus Gothicus Victor Triumphator Augustus . . ."; and the last feeble emperor of the West, who was contemptuously pensioned off by a barbarian king, was called Romulus Augustus (475–476 A.D.), an ironical reminiscence of perished glory.

INCREASED EXPENSE OF IMPERIAL GOVERNMENT.   The need to pay the army and the mercenaries, support the bureaucracy, subsidize the greedy barbarians, and build the new Christian capital at Constantinople, while maintaining roads, fortifications, and other structures, required increased resources in money, men, and materials. This was at a time when all three were seriously depleted. The emperors were convinced, however, that the Roman world must be held together, whatever the cost, and few citizens would have challenged that aim. To them the Roman Empire was so old and venerable a parent that they could not imagine its decease. Even most of the barbarians thought of themselves as participants in the Empire (though they proved intractable ones), rather than successors to it. Moreover, the Roman idea of liberty was not so much an anarchic concept of personal freedom as an insistence on political status and civil rights in the courts of justice under established law. From the earliest Republic, the citizens had esteemed the State and its needs as being far above personal considerations, but now the Romans pushed this ideal to its extreme, until the price proved too great for the benefits attained.

THE CURIALES AND TAX-COLLECTING.   Early victims of the State's increased and urgent claims were the members of the class of municipal senators (*curiales*), who formed the Empire's bourgeoisie. As early as Septimius Severus the administration had ceased to promote the interests of this class. Instead, the municipal governments had been forced to serve as convenient sources of money and labor for the central government, while their local independence of action evaporated. The property taxes of the Empire were now largely collected in produce, and this entailed considerable supervisory labor. Of course, many of the provinces had from the earliest days paid their tribute in grain or other goods, but at that time the collectors had been contractors who generally managed to elicit an adequate recompense for their efforts. During the fourth and fifth centuries A.D. the collection had descended as a duty upon the *curiales*. By the collection of goods as taxes and by the distribution of the goods to the State's employees, men on fixed salaries were granted some relief from the suffering that came from inflation.

The crisis in agriculture and in manpower, however, increased the problems for the *curiales*. Repeated reports of arrears in payment of taxes, particularly in the late fourth and early fifth centuries A.D., indicate their difficulties. As farmers had been unable to meet their quotas, or had experienced especially bad years, they had begun to desert their farms and disappear. But the government's requirements were set by the central bureaus at the beginning of each year regardless of local

562

conditions, and the productivity of an area was reviewed no oftener than once each fifteen years (the indiction period). The central government, therefore, held the *curiales* responsible for the amounts allocated to their municipal districts. The drain upon private fortunes, already suffering from the economic regression of the towns, increasingly led men to avoid the municipal offices that they once had gladly sought. No substitutes for these men could easily be found, however, and they rapidly deteriorated into the status of involuntary and unpaid government employees. They were expected to allocate, collect, and transport local taxes, whether in kind or in money, provide for the public post, and see to the supplies for military detachments passing through their areas. And their own property was surety for the proper and full execution of these duties. They were the sinews of the State, and 192 laws regulating their lives and duties, issued between 313 and 436, testify to their importance. The earliest measures (313, 325 A.D.) show that individual *curiales* were bound to their position regardless of their own desires; and slightly later (320, 331 A.D.) we find that their status was become hereditary. Every avenue of escape — to the army, church, or trades — was closed. Fugitives were hauled back to their towns, lands, and duties, and the bourgeoisie of the municipalities was slowly ground down, debased, and ruined.

SERFDOM FOR FARMERS. THE COLONATE.   Heavy as the burden placed on the *curiales* was, they did not bear that burden alone, for the government readily recognized that the municipal officials could not collect produce from untilled lands; the peasants too could not shirk their duties toward the State. Since the tenant farmers of imperial and other estates (*coloni*) were necessary for continued production, they soon were forbidden to leave their tax-districts, and were threatened with reduction to slavery if they did so (332 A.D.). Their freedom of movement and of contract was at an end, and soon they were bound to their estates and passed from owner to owner along with the land, not slaves, but serfs. In Roman history this condition is generally referred to as the Colonate, from *coloni*, the Latin for tenant farmers. It was not long before the free hired laborers suffered the same fate, and they were permanently attached to the estates where they had worked.

The tone of the edicts emphasizing the duties of the *coloni* increased in severity during the fourth and fifth centuries A.D., and the penalties for disobedience became more pitiless; but still the farmers ran away and the amount of abandoned land increased. In 422 it was reported that one third of the imperial domains in old Africa were untilled, and more than half of those in the African district of Byzacium. In 395 Honorius removed over 350,000 acres from the tax rolls of Campania, and this was the most fertile district of peninsular Italy. Everywhere there are indications of increased sheep-raising, a sure sign that the fields were being abandoned; and there was never a lack of land to be distributed to the barbarians who were repeatedly admitted and settled during the fourth and fifth centuries A.D. In an attempt to counter the reduced production of goods, the government resorted to the practice known as *epibolé*: deserted lands were assigned to the *curiales* or to all the possessors of a given municipality, and they were ordered to cultivate them and undertake the payment of taxes on them. The burdens so imposed brought further ruin upon the *curiales*, the municipal landowners, and the distracted peasantry.

THE PROFESSIONS BECOME HEREDITARY.   The members of the trades and professions found themselves equally involved in the service of the fatherland. The commitment to maintain the markets of the Empire, and to supply the proletariat of Rome (and later of Constantinople) long had involved the ship-masters with government contracts and had earned for them exemptions from various municipal and legal duties for which other citizens of comparable wealth had always been liable. Alexander Severus (222–235 A.D.) had recognized the convenience of such guilds and encouraged their formation for many of the trades. Soon the emperors found it advantageous to deal directly with these guilds instead of with their individual members. Contracts for government work could be made with the guilds, and the guilds were made liable for the tax in gold and silver (the *chrysargyrium*) that artisans and tradesmen paid. Now in the fourth and fifth centuries A.D. the decline in the economy made many of the trades far less attractive. The cities, upon which a healthy economic life depended, were decaying and shrinking. Trade routes were dangerous and markets were reduced. Many of the very rich provided for their own needs on their extensive estates and demanded only a few luxury items from the cities, and the poverty-stricken masses could afford only the cheapest manufactures. The Empire's failing man-power further thinned the ranks, and the government found itself faced with a reduced labor force to perform the tasks necessary for its continued existence.

By 314 the edicts of Constantine indicate that the ship-masters were compelled to remain in their jobs; and the position soon became hereditary. It appears that at first the government merely forbade investors to transfer their capital from one business to another—investments in shipping could not be transferred to manufacturing—but in time the burdens were so great and the returns so small that many were willing to abandon their capital investments altogether in order to seek a living elsewhere. However, durable investments such as ships were obviously useless without men to run them, and the State thus was forced to the next steps of making membership in the guilds of shipmasters compulsory, and then hereditary, as the only possible solution. Other vital services soon suffered the same fate—bakers, millers, miners, and the workers in the State factories that had been established for weapons and clothing. Even the acrobats, actors, and charioteers finally fell victim to public demand, and they and their children were tied to their professions. However, the opportunities of manufacture and trade continued to decline as Graeco-Roman urban culture gave way to the rural self-sufficiency of medieval civilization, and poverty forced more men to use any subterfuge in seeking more profitable employment. Finally, by the end of the fourth century A.D., the State resorted to the branding of some workers who fled their vital but unprofitable tasks so that they could be recognized and returned.

THE ARMY.   Even the soldiers, for whose support so many men were bound to their professions, became a caste, and their regimentation reflects the desperate shortage of recruits. Sons of soldiers and veterans were branded on the arm and destined to future service. The *limitanei* along the frontiers were tied both to the cultivation and defense of their allotments. Attempts were even made to regiment the immigrant barbarians. They often proved refractory, but they were given their lands on condition that they would perform hereditary military service. When whole peoples were admitted and settled within the Empire, they were treated as corporations that owed a quota of recruits to the government annually. Despite the relatively favorable treatment of soldiers—they enjoyed special military courts; they did not need to perform municipal services; and they had many tax exemptions—there was much shirking and dissatisfaction, as twenty-two laws between 319 and 398 relating to the duties of soldiers' sons indicate. If the soldiers were unhappy in their status, however, we can imagine the greater misery of guildsmen, *coloni*, and *curiales*, all of whom tried to escape their fate by seeking clandestinely to enlist in the army. Repeated imperial edicts provided for the apprehension and branding of such culprits and their return to their inherited tasks.

FROM REGIME OF CONTRACT TO REGIME OF STATUS.

The economic, social, and political forces of the Late Republic and of the Principate finally had led in the fourth and fifth centuries A.D. to a totalitarian state. This was not at all because the Romans were dedicated to or approved of state socialism; but resulted from some of the ancient experiences of the Romans that even predated Augustus and also from the desperate efforts of Roman culture to save itself when it was faced with extinction. The Romans had freely accepted the paramount claims of the State upon themselves in the Early Republic, and this attitude invited an expansion of authoritarianism as the needs of the State increased. The legal constitution of the Principate made it easy to steer the naturally patriotic disposition of the earlier Romans toward an acceptance of autocracy. It is true that the *lex de imperio,* which conferred sweeping powers on the prince, specified that he should use his powers in the State's interests; but he was the judge as to what those interests were. Under these conditions, there was a steady but slow reaction against the individualism and anarchy of the Late Republic and a growing willingness to recognize the need for individuals to accept increasing social responsibility. The crises of the late third century A.D., however, forced into sudden and deadly flower the assertion of the State's full authority over its citizens, and its concentration in the hands of the emperor. The political and intellectual heritage of the Romans apparently made this the only solution that men could conceive. Such a solution, however, did not command unsupervised obedience, and the price of the massive machine that kept the Empire running was too great. The armies of bureaucrats became as oppressive and as corrupt as the governors and tax-farmers of the Republic had been. Their very number protected them as they connived with one another to fleece the taxpayers and to fool the emperor. The efforts of the emperors to control these malpractices were futile: their edicts were evaded or disregarded; and the use of official spies, the *agentes in rebus* (agents for affairs), led to even greater abuses. The *agentes* became the greatest nuisances of all, for they not only spied upon and reported illegal or treasonable activities, real or imagined, but they themselves also became experts in corruption, selling without conscience their complicity in wrongdoing or their silence. Despair fell upon the citizens tied from birth to their places of origin, their professions, and their status. The ambitious had no hope for improvement, the humble no relief from indigent servitude; and no one was free to move from his inherited tasks to new or imaginative ventures that might have revitalized the economy. Mankind was frozen into a regime of status; and in their dull hopelessness many Romans ran away to become brigands or conspired with the barbarians to bring a breath of freedom to a servile world.

THE NOBLES AND VILLA ECONOMY.   In one rank of society, however, there was a strong and successful reaction against the totalitarian state. Individualism reared its head in the speedy development of the great estates or villas of the mighty. The members of the very rich senatorial class, the *clarissimi*, now were drawn from all over the Empire. As *honestiores* (the better people) they enjoyed special privileges in the eyes of the law; but no longer did they need attend sessions of the Senate, and most of them retired to their country estates. In their country seats the nobles replaced the civilized practices that once had characterized Graeco-Roman society with rural pleasures and pastimes. Their villas were fortified against brigands, marauding barbarians, and ultimately against the tax-collectors themselves. These nobles of the Late Empire grew fat on the misery pervading society, just as the great landowners after the Hannibalic War did. Enormous tracts were bought, appropriated from public or abandoned lands, or merely stolen. Much of this land was made sufficiently lucrative by turning it to pasture. The great estates began to display that self-sufficiency that the Roman noble had always held as an ideal: they raised their own food, made clothing and wines, and they even undertook the manufacture of many articles, such as bricks, pottery, and household utensils. Only articles of luxury still needed the expert hand of urban artisans, and the growth of villa economy was one of the factors in the economic decay of the cities.

The independence and insolence of the great nobles had a certain amount of justification. In the Late Empire they often were forced to raise private armies to protect themselves and their tenants and slaves from brigands and barbarians when the government was dilatory or helpless. They defied excessive claims by the central government both by the use of force and by their influence with the government's own high officials, who shared their economic ideals and social status. The ancient Roman system of patronage and clientship seemed once more to emerge in the relations of these powerful nobles and the humbler citizens that sought their protection. This time, however, the dependent clients readily fell into the status of serfs instead of exhibiting the fierce resistance that characterized the plebeians of the free Republic. The patronage of the nobles included not just their tenants and slaves; freeholders and even whole villages surrendered their freedom in return for protection against barbarians and bureaucracy alike.

The emergence of the great estates of the late Roman world, with their fortified villas, private armies, prisons, chapels, and manufactures, and with their bands of serfs and dependents subject to the jurisdiction and protection of their noble owners, heralds the social system of medieval Europe. When the Germanic invaders settled down within the bounds of the old Roman Empire, they found much in this Roman system that was attractive, for the Germans lived in a society of fighting men bound by oaths of loyalty to a chief, and one in which the manual labor was performed by serfs, women, and slaves. The villa economy of the late Romans, therefore, was widely adopted by the barbarian lords of the successor states and, somewhat modified by Germanic traditions and practices, it generated a social and economic system that survived in western Europe for over a thousand years.

Chapter 45

THE DISMEMBERMENT OF THE WEST

In the fifth century A.D. the consequences of ancient prejudices, policies, and errors of the Roman people, some of which had silently festered during the Principate and Early Dominate, came to a violent focus on the Mediterranean world. In eighty-two years the Western Roman Empire, which still was geographically intact at the death of Theodosius I (395 A.D.), had almost completely disappeared. The causes for this sudden collapse were largely internal; the decisions that we have seen the Romans taking in the conduct of their affairs far back in the Republic and Principate led inexorably to disaster. But there were also some external contingencies that had staggering consequences—the ravages of epidemic disease and the attack of the barbarians on almost all fronts. It happened that at the very time when Rome's internal problems were most troubling, her barbarian neighbors also were hard pressed by forces at their backs that made them desperate for new homes; and so at the moment of Rome's last illness hordes from the North were at hand to deliver the *coup de grâce*.

FINAL DIVISION OF THE EMPIRE.   Theodosius the Great at his death divided the Roman Empire between his sons, Arcadius and Honorius, and the division was final. Such partition long had been heralded, in the second century A.D. by the experiments of Marcus Aurelius with Verus and Commodus, in the third century A.D. by various emperors with their sons, and finally by the tetrarchy of Diocletian, and by the voluntary association of Valentinian I and Gratian with colleagues. But now there was no longer a pretense of unity between East and West. Edicts issued in one realm were operative in the other only if submitted to and ratified by the other emperor. At the death of the emperor of one half of the Empire the thrones were not reunited; rather, a successor for the vacant spot was often sought without reference to the wishes of the other court. Most of the Western emperors after the division of 395 A.D. were recluses and incompetents, if not worse. They served largely as a kind of monstrous, invisible fetish worshipped by the court and the bureaucrats, and thus imperial policy carried to the extreme the Oriental seclusion that had been introduced by Diocletian. For many of the fifth-century emperors such retirement not only created a proper public image, but also hid their native weakness and cowardice. For us these emperors are scarcely worth more than a listing.

THE LAST EMPERORS OF THE WEST (395–476 A.D.).
Honorius (395–423 A.D.) was an indolent weakling. Large portions of his long reign were spent in the care of his yard of poultry. In 408 A.D., however, he did spare the time and effort to arrange the murder of his talented master-general, guardian, and father-in-law, Stilicho, who was of Vandal extraction and was unpopular with the favorites at the court. It was Honorius' timidity in the days when Alaric the Goth threatened the invasion of Italy that led to the establishment of the royal residence at Ravenna (*ca.* 404 A.D.), where the imperial coward could be protected from hostile armies by canals and morasses, and from invasions by sea by the shallow waters around his new capital. His nephew, Valentinian III (423–455 A.D.), was his uncle's equal in cowardice and was a blackguard in the bargain. At the approach of

569

Attila the Hun in 452 he fled even from the safety of Ravenna to Rome, whence an easier flight from Italy could be arranged. After this danger had receded, the emperor lingered in the ancient capital long enough to be known and thoroughly detested by his subjects. In 454 he stabbed with his own hand his master-general Aëtius, who had turned Attila back at Châlons in 451 and had repeatedly saved the Empire. In the next year the emperor raped the wife of a distinguished senator, Petronius Maximus, a circumstance that soon led to his own assassination. Maximus (455 A.D.) proved a good husband but utterly improvident prince, and he was killed by the soldiers and the city mob when Genseric, the Vandal king of Africa, used the assassination of Valentinian as an excuse to capture and plunder the city of Rome. His successor, Avitus (455–456 A.D.), was the nominee of the Visigothic king Theodoric II, whose people were now settled in Spain and southern France; but Avitus was soon deposed by the master-general Ricimer. Ricimer was of Suevic and Gothic parentage and was the actual ruler of the western Roman world from 456 A.D. to his death in 472. His first nominee, Majorian (457–461 A.D.), was the only fifth-century emperor worthy of his post. He set about to correct many administrative and fiscal abuses, but he thus won the hatred of the bureaucrats and the fear of Ricimer, who had the example of Stilicho and Aëtius before him, and who felt obliged to depose his emperor to ensure his own safety. Thereupon Ricimer elevated a complete nonentity, Libius Severus (461–465 A.D.), and at his decease the master-general did not bother for two years to appoint anyone as emperor.

The incessant raids of the Vandals on Italian shores, however, finally induced Ricimer to request the military assistance of the Eastern emperor Leo I, and incidentally he also asked Leo to make an imperial nominee for the West. Leo named Anthemius (467–472 A.D.), and the new emperor became Ricimer's father-in-law; but they were soon at odds, and at length Anthemius was dispatched in the streets of Rome and was replaced by a new selection of Ricimer, Olybrius (472 A.D.). Both Ricimer and Olybrius expired of natural causes in 472 A.D., and Ricimer's nephew and successor as master-general, Gundobald, proposed one Glycerius as emperor (473–474 A.D.); but the arrival of a new candidate from the East, Julius Nepos (474–475 A.D.), who was already the ruler of Dalmatia and was a nephew by marriage of the Eastern empress, caused Glycerius to prefer a bishopric to the throne. Nepos soon returned to his Dalmatian realm after sedition had arisen among the mercenaries in Italy who were under the command of the master-general Orestes. Orestes thereupon raised to the throne his own son, Romulus, whose full name, Romulus Augustus, has been derisively transformed into the diminutive Romulus Augustulus (475–476 A.D.). This handsome and inoffensive youth, whose name ironically recalls so many glories of Roman history, was the last phantom emperor of the West, and he was ultimately pensioned off to a Campanian estate by the German general Odoacer, who was elected king of his people at that time.

TOWN AND COUNTRY.   The expedient of barbarian mercenaries, which had seemed reasonable and efficient in the fourth century A.D., had made the emperors of the fifth century the mercenaries' prisoners and playthings. And the frantic measures taken by the emperors of the fourth century to tie Roman civilians to the financial support of this army had ended by the fifth century in serfdom for the countryfolk and rigid economic castes for the townspeople. The farmers or *coloni*, now bound to the soil, were sullen, indifferent to political change, and helpless in the face of it. Repeated imperial enactments of the fifth century A.D. governing them and the reclamation of abandoned lands indicate that they continued to seek any escape possible from the land right up to the collapse of the Empire, and that, if all else failed, they simply refused to bring up children. The guildsmen and merchants of the towns continued to be burdened by the duty to furnish manufactured goods and to collect the sales taxes, duties which they strenuously tried to avoid. A sufficient black market was established in this period to diminish revenues from the sales taxes noticeably and to evoke indignant imperial protests and threats. The *curiales* were distracted by the government's continued insistence that they be responsible for all arrears in the property taxes, which they collected without remuneration. The caste fell on such evil days that many members sought sanctuary as day laborers on the great estates and married their daughters off to *coloni* or even to slaves. Majorian in an edict of 458 A.D. was specific about these attempted evasions of duty, and he did try to improve the lot of the *curiales* by making them liable only for an accounting of the arrears in taxes in their districts instead of actually having to pay them. It is clear from the anxious enactments published in the *Theodosian Code* (issued in 438 A.D.) and from those subsequently added until 468 A.D. that these three castes in the population—the *coloni*, guildsmen, and *curiales*—were disappearing with a speed that promised bankruptcy to an economy that depended on them. As for the urban proletariat—and many a town beside Rome and Constantinople had one—it was interested only in its stomach, games, shows, and Christian theology. No one had ever dared curtail its doles and its amusements, and the increasing barbarity of its entertainment reflected its taste for brutality and lust; the barbarians surprised the citizens of more than one town in the amphitheater gloating over the spilled blood of tortured animals.

INTELLECTUAL LIFE.   The noble senatorials long had been excluded from any real participation in civil affairs, and since Gallienus (259–268 A.D.) they also had been denied military careers. Most of these educated and wealthy men from all over the Empire, therefore, retired to their estates, which they tried to make safe and self-sufficient. There they endeavored to lead the lives of country gentlemen, with some pretense of cultural interests. The literature that they cultivated consisted of the ancient classics, or of punctilious echoes written in a language no longer in current usage. The Latin fathers of the Church were prolific, but the lively fulminations of the earlier apologists gave way to sterile theological dispute, dreary exegesis, and sermons adorned with involved and foolish imagery. Of the whole lot only the *Confessions* and *The City of God* of St. Augustine (354–430 A.D.) are still widely read.

SPREAD OF EXTORTION.   The civil and military administrators, both at court and in the field, outdid themselves in dishonesty. They produced false and highly complicated tax bills to confuse the citizens, and used military detachments and torture to extort their unjust claims. Bribes were accepted to drop illegal demands; payment in ancient and rare coinage was required, and failure to find such pieces of money resulted in punitive fines in the current coin. Coinage was pared by the officials through whose hands it passed; and a large portion of the exactions, legal or illegal, never found its way to the imperial treasury. It appears that in 450 A.D., for example, almost none of the revenues of Sardinia ever reached the proper officials. Extortion and demands for gratuities by various officials were everywhere. The emperors' legal advisers issued ordinances that thundered against these practices; but at length in despair they bowed to this new source of revenue for imperial bureaucrats. The emperors thereupon set stated amounts that officials could exact from their subordinates at promotions, on holidays, and on other joyous occasions, just as in many places in the Western world the blackmail of tipping has been regularized.

THE BARBARIAN COMMANDERS.   The really capable men of
the fifth century A.D. were the masters-general of the troops:
Stilicho and Constantius, who served Honorius; Aëtius and
Boniface, who commanded under Valentinian III; Ricimer, who
dominated the last two decades of the Western Empire; and
Orestes, who was in command at its dissolution. Stilicho was a
Vandal, Ricimer a Goth; Aëtius had been a hostage of the Huns
and had many connections with them; and Orestes had been for
a time a subject of and ambassador for Attila. It is clear that the
need to use non-Romans in the national defense dictated that
the military commanders be men with backgrounds and capabilities appropriate for the management of foreign soldiers. As
early as 394 A.D., when Theodosius I battled with the Western
usurper Eugenius, the contest was really one between an army
of Goths, Alans, Iberians, and Huns (including Stilicho and
Alaric the Goth) under Theodosius and the army of Franks and
Alamanni of Eugenius. The great generals of the fifth century
were much admired and were reasonably loyal to the Roman
throne; but in the first half of that century they were the constant targets of the jealousy and malice of a corrupt court, and
they lived in considerable personal danger. This circumstance
therefore led the later masters-general, Ricimer and Orestes, to
insist while they were in power that there be tractable and
complaisant occupants of the throne. The masters-general suffered many drawbacks. Their armies were of limited size, and
the revenues with which to pay them were declining. They
were under contradictory demands from the many fronts under
attack by barbarian invaders. And they were subjected to re-
lentless slander and suspicion because most of them had
adopted the unorthodox version of Christianity called Arianism
and because they found it wise to maintain the familiar contacts
that they had with their relatives in the enemies' camps. With
their scanty means, however, the barbarian commanders managed the defense and foreign policy of the country with a skill
that delayed, though it could not prevent, the final collapse.

THE SETTLEMENT OF THE FOEDERATI.   The paucity of
men of Roman tradition, culture, and heritage, both in quantity
and in quality, spelled the doom of the Roman system. More
and more barbarians were admitted or called in to imperial
territory to occupy the deserted or waste lands and to furnish
troops. District after district was taken over and ruled by them
under their own native kings as federates (*foederati*, allies) of
the emperor. Finally, in 476, Italy also became a federated
kingdom under the German king Odoacer, and this event phys-

ically marked the end of a Roman Empire in the West. We see in this eventuality too the culmination of policies and practices that we have followed at least from the second century A.D. when Marcus Aurelius (161 – 180 A.D.) settled barbarians within the Empire to recompense the losses of the great plague. And for this act Marcus well could have pleaded that from the earliest Republic the Romans had traditionally been tolerant of new citizens of diverse race. His example had frequently been followed during the third and fourth centuries, and each time the exigencies of the case dictated the acceptance of a people a little less ready to assume the name and responsibilities of Roman citizens. There had indeed been an attempt to segregate some of the least assimilable, the so-called *laeti*, into separate cantons where they were bound to the soil, administered by prefects, given the hereditary duty to furnish troops, and forbidden intermarriage with Romans. With the late fourth century A.D., however, there had been no attempt to segregate or absorb; whole peoples were allowed to settle on Roman lands as federates while preserving their own languages, customs, and kings. At first, however, they were merely an intrusion that did not displace the civil government of the Roman citizens in their midst. Early examples were the Salian Franks, whom Julian allowed in 358 to settle on the left bank of the Rhine in Belgium. In 376 Asding Vandals, Ostrogoths, and Visigoths as federate allies had been allowed sanctuary south of the Danube from the oncoming Huns, and some of them were so goaded by rapacious Roman officials that they struck out against their hosts and inflicted the stunning defeat on Valens at Adrianople in 378 A.D.[1]

STILICHO IN COMMAND.   Upon the Empire of the early fifth century A.D., already weakened by the infiltration of barbarians and establishment of federate states, there fell a series of crises. The restless Visigoths of Moesia had gone on a rampage in the Balkans after the death of Theodosius in 395. After this people had created widespread havoc, Alaric, the leader of the Visigoths, had extorted the title of master of the soldiers from the Eastern emperor and a new homeland for his people in Epirus. In 401 and 403 Alaric, now also elected the king of the federate Visigoths, attempted invasions of Italy. These were foiled by the strategy of the Western master-general, Stilicho; but to protect Italy Stilicho was forced to run the risk of attack on the Western provinces from the North by calling home some

[1]   See above, p. 550.

574

MOVEMENTS:
——— Visigoths
– – – Germans, Alans, Vandals
—†— Vandals, Alans, Sueves

Picts
Scots.
Irish
Jutes
(POST 410)
Angles
WALES
CORNWALL Britons
Saxons
Slavs
BRITTANY
Seine R.
Rhine R.
Salian Franks (358)
Ripuarian Franks
GAUL
(407-9)
Alamanni
Siling Vandals
AQUITANIA
Sueves
Danube
Huns
Sueves and Asding Vandals
AUVERGNE
(406)
Asding Vandals
Ostrogoths R.
Alans
PROVENCE
SPAIN
Florence
Aquileia
Ravenna
DALMATIA
(401-10)
Siling Vandals
Balearic Is.
Corsica
Rome
ITALY
Visigoths (375-396)
Tangiers
Gibraltar
Sardinia
EPIRUS (398-401)
Constantinople
Berbers
Carthage
AFRICA
Sicily
Mediterranean Sea
THE WESTERN EMPIRE AND THE INVADERS
410 A.D.
TRIPOLIS

of the troops from the Rhine and from Britain to defend Italy. Then, in 406, before these troops could be returned to their posts, a huge and motley horde of Germans, Alans, Vandals, and Ostrogoths, said to number more than 200,000 pushed over the Alps into northern Italy. There, in the vicinity of Florence, Stilicho managed to surround and starve the invaders into submission, though he had only 30,000 men. Stilicho had to attain his victory by a time-consuming series of tactical maneuvers, for he knew that the safety of the Roman world rested on these few and he dared not risk his men in a face-to-face confrontation on the battlefield. While the Roman master-general was thus engaged, however, he could not prevent in 407 a flood of barbarians—Vandals, Alans, and Sueves—from sweeping into Gaul and through it to Spain.

THE LOSS OF BRITAIN.   The sufferings of Gaul and the desertion of Britain by the central government once more led to separatist tendencies in the West as had happened in the third century A.D. Britain furnished three usurpers in rapid succession; and the last of them, who styled himself Constantine III, took what troops still remained on the island and landed in Gaul to assert his claims. He survived for some months of 407 A.D. After his ultimate defeat, however, his troops never returned to Britain, and that province was left to the mercy of the neighboring Irish, Scots, and Picts, and of the Angles, Saxons, and Jutes, who raided the island from across the North Sea. The Romanized Celts of Britain appealed to Honorius for help in 410, but his government testily replied that the Britons must look after themselves. Thus the westernmost province was lost; and the rest of its history is one of stubborn resistance and slow withdrawal to Cornwall and the mountains of Wales, while the Britons' barbarian successors obliterated the cultural advances of three centuries.

WANDERINGS OF ALARIC AND THE VISIGOTHS.   In 408 the savior of Italy, Stilicho, fell a victim to palace intrigues, and Alaric and his Visigoths seized the opportunity. Demands were made upon Emperor Honorius which he, from his swampy lair in Ravenna, refused. The Goths' revenge was the capture and sack of the city of Rome in 410. At Alaric's death a few months later, his successor, Ataulf (Adolphus), reached an agreement with the government in Ravenna. He used his Visigoths in the service of Rome to relieve Honorius of yet another Gallic usurper (413) and then to attack the Vandals, Alans, and Sueves, who had settled down in Spain, nominally as federates of the Empire. Ataulf's successor, Wallia, in 416 exterminated the Alans and Siling Vandals in Spain. Thereupon the current master-general of the Romans, Constantius, in fear of the growing power of the Visigoths, recalled them from Spain to Gaul, where they were given a home in Aquitania. The Sueves and Asding Vandals were allowed to remain as federates in central and northwestern Spain.

THE VANDALS IN AFRICA.   The reign of Valentinian III (423–455 A.D.) held even bloodier reverses for the Western Romans than that of his uncle Honorius. The jealous rivalry of two of his generals, Aëtius and Boniface, led Boniface, who held command in Africa and believed that his life was in danger, to invite the Asding Vandals to move from Spain to Africa in 429. In ten years they overran much of rural Africa and were accorded the status of federates there. Their rapid advance owed as much to the exasperation of the native Christians, who still defended the view of Donatus[2] against the orthodox church of Italy, and to the semi-civilized Berbers, who hovered menacingly in the mountains of the hinterland, as it did to Vandal prowess. In 439 the Vandal king Genseric broke his treaty with Rome and captured Carthage, and in 442 his realm was recognized as an independent kingdom. Genseric soon used his native skills and materials to build a fleet, and as a pirate became the scourge of the Mediterranean. In 455, following the assassination of his professed ally, Valentinian III, Genseric landed in Italy and pillaged Rome so thoroughly and pitilessly that in contrast the sack of the city by Alaric appeared a mere pilgrimage. By the time of Genseric's death in 477 his kingdom included most of the African coast from Tangiers to Tripoli, Sardinia, Corsica, the Balearic Isles, and western Sicily. Meanwhile, some of the hard-pressed Britons crossed over to the Gallic coast and appropriated the peninsula thereafter known as Brittany; while the Burgundians of the Rhineland, terribly slaughtered by a branch of the oncoming Huns (436), were finally granted an area in the vicinity of Geneva as federates.

INVASION OF THE HUNS.   The Huns, a nomadic people from central Asia, with bewildering rapidity had spread across the Ukraine and central Europe as far south as the Rhine-Danube line. Finally, under their greatest king, Attila (434–453), they held all the Germans as vassals except the Frisians and the Salian Franks. The Eastern Roman emperor paid the Huns tribute, and in 451 Attila resolved to add the West to his dominions. During his first invasion, Attila was met near Châlons in Gaul by a combined force of Romans, Salian Franks, Burgundians, and Visigoths under the master-general Aëtius and King Theodoric I of the Visigoths, and he was forced to turn back. In 452 Attila invaded Italy, totally destroying a number of towns, the most notable of which was the rich and famous Adriatic port of Aquileia, which never rose again. He was, however, turned back from Rome itself by bribes and by the authority of Leo, Bishop of Rome. His death of a hemorrhage in 453 during one of his frequent wedding nights was swiftly followed by the disintegration of his empire. One lasting conse-

[2]   See above, pp. 547, 548.

577

THE
WESTERN EMPIRE
450 A.D.

Areas lost by 450 A.D.

quence of his invasion of Italy was a gathering of refugees from
the mainland on the low islands at the head of the Adriatic, and
these men formed the nucleus for the future republic of Venice.

ESTABLISHMENT OF THE SUCCESSOR STATES.   The players
in the final act of Western Roman history were now all at hand
and the denouement was rapid. The Visigoths expanded rapidly
into Spain (469–478 A.D.), leaving only a Suevic kingdom and
the Basques in the northwest of the peninsula. In Gaul the
Visigoths were conceded Auvergne in 475 by Julius Nepos, and
in 477 they extended their control over Provence to the Alps.

THE
SUCCESSOR STATES
480 A.D.

Altogether the Visigothic kingdom was the most impressive of
the successor states. The Burgundians dominated the central
Rhone Valley, while the Salian Franks had pushed south to the
Somme; the Ripuarian Franks held the central Rhine and the
Moselle; and the Alamanni controlled the upper Rhine. Only
the kingdom of Soissons in the valley of the Seine still was
Roman, and this was in the hands of a rebellious Roman
general. Surrounded by these practically independent states,
the German troops stationed in Italy desired a similar federate
state for themselves; and when in 476 the master-general Orestes refused them one third of the peninsula for this object,

579

they rose under their leader Odoacer, murdered Orestes, deposed the last emperor, and established their German kingdom. Julius Nepos lingered on in his principality of Dalmatia as a shadowy Western emperor for four more years, but at his death in 480 this area also was added to Odoacer's realm. The process of imperial disintegration was now essentially complete: the federate German state, invented in the fourth century A.D. as a temporary expedient in the Empire's battle for survival, in the fifth century became the conventional arrangement for the Western world and replaced a system that had become no more than a glorious name.

A SUMMARY.   The Western Romans' idealization of agriculture and land tenure as the only dignified way of life went deep into the historic past, and they never lost this devotion. Their view was not shared by the Easterners, and this fact has something to do with the continued productive vigor of the East long after the West had sunk into a primitive slumber. The Western Romans had an ill-concealed contempt for trades, and their cities were, therefore, artificial things — actually glorified marketplaces. They contained a few artisans who were often of servile or foreign extraction, and their economies were very largely dependent on the productivity of the surrounding land. The love of the land repeatedly led the Roman upper classes to invest almost exclusively in it, and their acquisitions forced the peasantry either to the towns, where they became a semi-idle proletariat lacking the opportunities of an expanding factory system, or ultimately to the unproductive and inferior status of tenant farmers. There was a consequent decline in numbers and in moral stamina in both the upper and lower classes. The decrease in population was partly due to urbanization and an increased standard of living, in which environment populations repeatedly show a decline. The change in moral stamina was to a large extent a result of the loss of independence, self-respect, and civic responsibility; but it was partially because the cityfolk were deprived of the comforts of their ancestral religion and were subjected to a parasitic society and economy. The unfortunate effects of these changes were compounded in the second century A.D. by a devastating plague, and in the third century by yet another plague and the ravages of an alienated army. The army no longer reflected the ideals and opinions of the civilians because the reduced population of the more civilized interior could no longer find the necessary recruits for it and the emperors had been forced to turn for recruits to more virile but less Romanized areas. Further, in the third century A.D. well-

580

founded imperial fears of rivals had removed the Roman nobility from its traditional army commands. The ancient Romanizing function of military service was thereby the more diminished.

The disorders of the third century A.D. sealed the Empire's fate, for it started a spiral of social and economic movements that paralyzed Roman society with a caste system, which had been imposed on most Romans as early as the fourth century A.D. On the structure thus weakened and demoralized there were exerted new external pressures, for the barbarians of the North also were subject to new forces propelling them from the rear. The expedients found by the emperors to buttress the failing fabric of the State—mercenary armies, the settlement of barbarian federates, the dependence on vigorous barbarian generals—assured its end. But the period in which these barbarians were associated with the Romans in one capacity or another and their widespread adoption of Christianity, although in the heretical Arian form, did much to soften the Empire's fall. Indeed, the fall finally amounted to little more than a change of masters, and possibly the lightening of the load for some of the taxpayers. The average resident of the Western Empire had little reason to regret or even to note the date 476 A.D.

Chapter 46

THE TRANSFIGURATION OF THE ROMAN EMPIRE

Rome, which had begun its career on the fringes of Hellenic civilization, ended by creating a world state that engulfed its cultural parent. But Rome's great sprawling Empire never attained true homogeneity in language, religion, or taste. It is true that the educated Roman could speak Greek as well as his native Latin, and that the Eastern administrator carried on the government's business in Latin despite his Hellenic background, but these people were exceptional. The Hellenic culture of Greece and Asia Minor was ancient and deep-rooted, but in the West Latin culture did not have such roots. In some districts of the West the Latinity was certainly shallow; the British peasants under the pressure of the Germanic invasions lapsed quickly back into being Celts, despite their 300 years of Roman rule.

The western part of the Empire extended so awkwardly around the Mediterranean that it required a defensive system too elaborate to be supported by the manpower and income of an economy that was largely agricultural. The transfer of the capital to Constantinople was a half-conscious recognition that it was unrealistic to mass the Empire's meager resources in the defense of the West. The use of the barbarian federates to defend the West was a shoddy device that quickly ended in the fragmentation of the Western world.

There were, nevertheless, cohesive forces within the Roman Empire that made it endure so long. Men of all backgrounds learned to appreciate lives enjoyed in security and equity, and they shared the consequent devotion to the ideal "Rome and Augustus," with which they identified a stable and calculable world. And from the subsequent wreckage of the Empire there emerged with uneven pace three new cultures, Byzantine, Arabic, and Western, all of which were products of a synthesis of Roman and native genius, and which showed the unmistakable marks of the Roman parent.

THE BYZANTINE EMPIRE.   The Eastern Empire survived in unbroken line until the capture of Constantinople by the Turks in 1453. In the fifth century A.D., however, there was a danger that it might share the fate of the West. The emperors were weak, or ignorant, or both, and the court was corrupt and beset with intrigue. Corps of foreign guards sometimes dominated the imperial government so effectively that the emperors could get rid of them only by having them massacred (Goths in 400, Alans in 471 A.D.). The capital and the provinces alike were distracted by passionate controversies about the nature of Christ, controversies that ultimately alienated Syria and Egypt from the Eastern Empire.

In the later part of the fifth century A.D., however, the Isaurian troops of Asia Minor proved loyal to the imperial government, and the Huns spared the East and turned their attacks on the West. Anastasius I (491–518 A.D.) created a better climate for economic development and well-being by cancelling the old gold and silver tax on the trades (the *chrysargyrium*) and by lifting the responsibility from the *curiales* for the arrears in taxes in their districts.

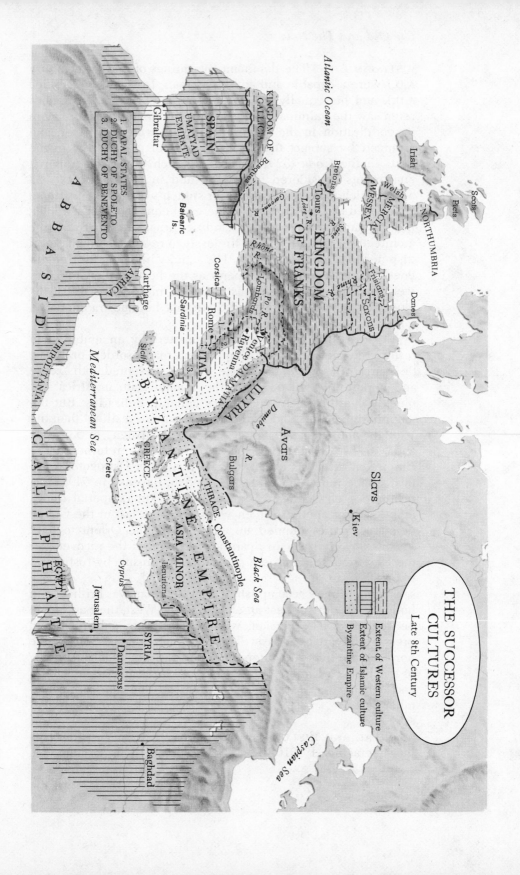

THE SUCCESSOR
CULTURES
Late 8th Century

···· Extent of Western culture

||| Extent of Islamic culture

≡ Byzantine Empire

1. PAPAL STATES
2. DUCHY OF SPOLETO
3. DUCHY OF BENEVENTO

Atlantic Ocean

KINGDOM OF
GALLICIA

SPAIN

UMAYYAD
EMIRATE

Gibraltar

Balearic
Is.

Corsica

Sardinia

A B B A S I D

AFRICA

Carthage

TRIPOLITANIA

Mediterranean Sea

Sicily

Rome
ITALY

Ravenna

Venice

DALMATIA

ILLYRIA

B Y Z A N T I N E   E M P I R E

GREECE

Crete

THRACE

Constantinople

ASIA MINOR

Iscurians.

Cyprus

Jerusalem

SYRIA

Damascus

EGYPT

C A L I P H A T E

Baghdad

KINGDOM
OF FRANKS

Bretons

Tours

Loire R.

Garonne R.

Rhône R.

Po R.

Rhine R.

Seine R.

Lombards

Basques

Frisians

Saxons

Danes

Welsh
(WESSEX)

MERCIA

NORTHUMBRIA

Picts

Scots

Irish

Danube R.

Avars

Bulgars

Slavs

Kiev

Black Sea

Caspian Sea

JUSTINIAN I.   The dominant Byzantines of the sixth century A.D.) were a capable and ambitious man, Justinian I (527–565 A.D.), and his equally capable empress, Theodora. Justinian's reign saw the culmination of the development of Roman law in its codification in the *Digest* (533 A.D.), which collected and arranged by subject the legal opinions of great jurists of the past; in the *Code* (529, 534 A.D.), which preserved imperial enactments considered still valid; and in the *Institutes* (533 A.D.), which formed a textbook for students of the law. Justinian supervised the construction of the great church of Hagia Sophia in Constantinople, the outstanding ornament of Byzantine architecture; and he labored tirelessly to resolve the theological disputes that rent his country. His activity in that field strengthened the position of the emperor as the head of the Church as well as of the State; and Justinian did much to establish the close relations of Church and State that became traditional in Greek Orthodox countries.

Above all, Justinian was dominated by an ambition to restore the ancient Roman Empire. Internal disorders or dynastic quarrels in some of the Western states presented both excuse and opportunity. In 533–534 the Vandal state in Africa was quickly overthrown by Justinian's general, Belisarius. But the neighboring Moors and Berbers proved more resilient than the Vandals, and their subjection required campaigns in 535–539 and 546–548. By the time that Africa had been returned to the Empire, it also was exhausted. Italy and the Ostrogoths were next. Rome fell to the Easterners in 536, Ravenna in 540; but a resurgence of Gothic resistance in Italy kept imperial troops employed for another fifteen years until the last of the Gothic defenders were rounded up and sent to the Orient to fight Persians. A civil war in Spain also expedited the recovery for the Empire of the southern part of that peninsula by Justinian's troops (554 A.D.).

The military accomplishment of Justinian was brilliant and hollow. To pour so great an effort into the West, the East had to be neglected. The Persians were bought off by subsidies from pressing the attack in Asia. The Slavs and Bulgars pierced the northern frontiers and entered the Balkans. The whole economy of the Eastern Empire was so severely taxed that for a century and a half after Justinian it experienced one defeat after another.

SURVIVAL AND INFLUENCE OF THE BYZANTINES.   It is true that Heraclius I (610–641 A.D.) inflicted a mortal blow on the Persians and recovered from them Syria and Egypt; but this victory was almost immediately followed by the violent appearance of the Arabs, whose forces spread so swiftly and successfully that they even besieged Constantinople by 678, while the Bulgars were carving out a kingdom for themselves in the Balkans (679 A.D.). This time the Empire was saved by an Isaurian, Leo III (717–740 A.D.), who raised a native army and drove the Moslems out of Asia Minor. In the eighth century A.D. the Eastern Empire consisted of Asia Minor, Thrace, Greece, Crete, the Dalmatian Coast, Sicily, and a toehold in Italy. Much more compact than in the old days, it also was more homogeneous. The Byzantines were strengthened by a new dependence on the peasantry as the backbone of their army, and the emperors were the chief defenders of the small farmers against the constant ambitions of great landowners. Herein lay one of the strengths that preserved the Eastern Empire. Another lay in the loss of Syria and Egypt to the Arabs; these provinces long had been at odds with the capital in the bitter theological disputes of the day, and their constant bickering had weakened the structure of the State. Further, an enlightened treatment of artisans and tradesmen resulted in a prosperity that made Constantinople the most brilliant metropolis in the world.

The Easterners continued to call themselves "Romans," but through the centuries a new culture was forged in Constantinople out of Roman, Greek, and Persian antecedents. The language was a modified Greek, the art was largely religious—icons with their strong spiritual appeal, and mosaics richly studded with black and gold. The architecture combined the engineering of Rome with the religious spirit of the Orient—Omar Khayyam's phrase, "That great inverted bowl we call the sky," aptly describes the dome of Justinian's Hagia Sophia, which was a triumph of late Roman engineering. Literary studies flourished around the university at Constantinople, and histories and memoirs appeared. Church and State were closely intertwined. The Byzantine missionaries among the heathens taught respect for the emperor, God's representative and champion on earth. The Bulgars were converted to Christianity in 864, the prince of Kiev in 988 or 989; and though the Empire made little effort to assert political authority over these Slavic princes, the satellites of the north were irresistibly drawn to Byzantium by religion, art, and learning. This source of radiant energy and attraction is called Byzantine culture; and its political aspect, the Byzantine throne, is perhaps the most nearly perfect example of absolutism that the world has ever seen.

THE RISE OF ISLAM.   On the southern and eastern shores
of the Mediterranean in the seventh and eighth centuries A.D.
the Arab followers of Mohammed (*ca.* 570–632 A.D.), the prophet of Islam, spread with incredible speed. They brought a
monotheistic religion, which in its puritanical simplicity was a
refreshing contrast to the theological squabbling of the Christians; and they brought the specific instructions of their founder
to wage a holy war on unbelievers. The Persian Empire,
weakened by recent defeats at the hands of Heraclius I, swiftly
fell to the Arabs (637–649 A.D.). Syria and Egypt, estranged from
the Empire by theological dispute, were easy conquests (636–
638, 640–642 A.D.). Tripolitania was taken in 642; the rest of
North Africa was in Moslem hands by 696; and most of Spain fell
in 711 with the defeat of the Visigoths. But the Moslems' naval
attack on Constantinople in 718 was checked, and the Byzantines slowly pushed them out of Asia Minor, while in 732 the
Frankish noble Charles Martel stopped their advance near
Tours in France. By the eighth century A.D. the Moslem Empire
had expanded until it stretched from the Pyrenees to India.
There ensued for it a long period of comparative stability during which there was an opportunity for striking developments
in government, economy, and the arts.

THE UMAYYADS.   Mohammed had founded a theocratic
state, but under the caliphs of the Umayyad dynasty (661–749
A.D.) the government took on a secular tone. The capital was the
great commercial city of Damascus, and the Umayyads turned
to the model of Roman bureaucratic government to administer
their extensive domains. The Arab yoke was comparatively
light—the Arabs were tolerant of Jews, Zoroastrians, Christians,
Christian heretics—yet there were massive conversions among
all these people to Islam. This was due to the attraction of this
religion's straightforward theology and code of personal conduct. The Arabic language spread nearly as rapidly as the Moslems' religion, for there was a reluctance to translate Islam's
sacred book, the Koran, into other tongues. A knowledge of the
Koran was important for every Moslem, for it was the authority
for each individual's conduct. Islam did not develop the hierarchy of spiritual guides and autocrats that the Christians did,
and therefore the individual Moslem had to read and interpret
Mohammed's words for himself. The Umayyad period is notable for a beautiful flowering of religious architecture, exemplified by the Dome of the Rock in Jerusalem. It was also a period
of integration, of sorting, studying, and experimenting with the

remains of Roman and Persian cultures and seeking to adapt them to the needs of a new religion and culture.

THE ABBASIDS (750–847 A.D.).   The Abbasid successors of the Umayyads established a new capital at Baghdad, and their court and imperial organization assumed a distinctly Persian tinge. Court life was elaborately ceremonial. Viziers of great power directed bureaus of the administration, and princely emirs governed large areas from courts that vied in splendor with that of the capital. During this period there was a large increase in material prosperity. Both trade and agriculture were encouraged. Moslem manufactures were of a superior quality, and great technical progress was made in animal husbandry and the cultivation of new agricultural produce. What is more, the literary and scientific treasures of the Greeks, Romans, Persians, and Indians, to which the Arabs had fallen heir, were collected and translated into Arabic in scholarly centers. Works on literature, philosophy, medicine, astronomy, mathematics, chemistry, geography, law — all were studied and became the stimuli for further advances. The Arabic contributions in mathematics (they invented algebra and our system of numbers), metallurgy, and medicine are famous. And although the system of emirates ultimately split Islam into a number of largely independent states, the community of religion and language, and the brilliant culture that flowered under the early Abbasids provided the bond that still gave unity to the Moslem world. More important, Arabic culture preserved, enhanced, and transmitted to the modern world treasures of the Graeco-Roman mind that the more immediate heirs of the Roman Empire had neglected or lost.

THE WESTERN SUCCESSORS. THE OSTROGOTHS.
The new Germanic masters of the West had not come in large numbers, and they did not come with the intention of destroying the Roman world. Rather, most of them had expected to participate in and enjoy the fruits of Mediterranean civilization. However, their previous semi-nomadic existence, loose political organization, and devotion to warfare and hunting must at times have made prospects for a survival of any Roman culture at all in the West seem very slight.

Perhaps the people with the greatest potentiality for cultural advancement were the Ostrogoths of Italy. This branch of the Goths had settled in Pannonia and Illyria after the Hunnish invasions, where they were frequently at odds with the

Eastern emperors. In 488 Emperor Zeno, who was at the time on bad terms with Odoacer, the German king in Italy, gave at least his tacit blessing to an invasion of Italy by the Ostrogoths under their hero Theodoric. Zeno thus got his revenge on Odoacer and at the same time got rid of some troublesome federates. The struggle between the Goths and Germans was difficult, but by 493 Theodoric was master of Italy, and was elected king of the Goths (493–526 A.D.).

Technically Theodoric was considered the Eastern emperor's representative in Italy, though in fact he was a completely independent monarch. Theodoric proved a capable and respected ruler. He maintained the Roman civil administration under Roman functionaries, protected the provisioning of Rome, repaired the water system of the city, and maintained a strong foreign policy, in which he posed as an arbiter of quarrels and a protector of the weak. But dynastic difficulties that followed upon the death of Theodoric's grandson and successor (534 A.D.) gave the Eastern emperor, Justinian, his chance to foster his ambitious policies and interfere.[1] The consequent war of twenty years not only devastated the countryside, but eliminated a people that had proved itself capable of husbanding and defending Italy.

THE LOMBARDS.   In 568 the Lombards, whom Justinian had used as mercenaries against the Ostrogoths, descended upon Italy in quantities. They pillaged and butchered with a free hand. The exarchs at Ravenna, who were the viceroys of the emperor at Constantinople, received little aid from an exhausted East, and the Lombards whittled away at the Byzantine holdings in Italy until by the middle of the eighth century A.D. they held it all except Venice, the toe of the Italian boot, and an area around Rome controlled by the pope. The years of strife and the petty bickerings of Lombard nobles, who established semi-independent duchies up and down the peninsula, left the country a desolate waste and Rome a small decaying town. Italy's future for centuries was ruined.

THE CATHOLIC CHURCH.   A firmer prop for Italy, and ultimately for the whole West, was the Church. The bishops of Rome long had asserted their spiritual precedence because they occupied the see of St. Peter. This claim received only grudging assent, however, from the patriarchs of Alexandria, Antioch, Jerusalem, and Constantinople. Rome's bishop, the pope, had

[1]   See above, p. 584.

long taken the lead in the West to protect his city and communicants from Hun, Goth, Vandal, and Lombard alike. Under
Justinian the popes had been forced to follow the imperial will;
but in the disasters to the Empire that followed, their independence was reasserted. The loss of Alexandria, Jerusalem,
and Antioch to the Moslems left the patriarch of Constantinople
the pope's only spiritual rival; and the see of Constantinople was
at a disadvantage, for it could not boast an apostle as its founder
as Rome could. Further, as the area and authority of the exarchs
at Ravenna narrowed, the pope became the sole Roman official
still operative in Italy. His influence softened the laws issued
by the Germans, his educated subordinates were often called
upon to assist in the government of the successor states, and his
missionaries penetrated northern Europe and the islands.
Gregory the Great, pope from 590 to 604, did much to make the
papacy a political force. The Church alone fully retained the
Roman tradition in the form of its organization, in its hierarchy,
in its territory, which was divided into provinces, dioceses and
cities, and in the careful husbanding and administration of the
Church's property. The permeation of the Church's influence
was further strengthened by the spread of monasticism in the
West from the sixth century A.D. onward. The monks, following
the rule established by St. Benedict (480–543 A.D.), were
pledged to poverty, chastity, and obedience; and they became
the teachers, both spiritual and technical, of the ignorant of the
West.

The independence of the Western Church took a giant
stride in the eighth century A.D. A great coolness had risen
between the religious leaders of Rome and of Constantinople
because the Eastern emperors had forbidden the preservation
of icons and other religious symbols on the grounds that they
were idolatrous. The Lombards pretended adherence to the
Eastern emperor's views and used this religious quarrel as an
excellent opportunity to attack the extensive papal territories in
Italy. The papacy thereupon arranged an alliance of its own
with the Frankish noble Pepin the Short, which resulted in
Pepin's election as King of the Franks, and his solemn anoint-
ment and ordination as king by the papal legate. The Church's
new ally thereupon sent expeditions into Italy in 755 and 756,
which curbed the Lombards. Pepin also confirmed the right of
the popes to certain lands between Ravenna and Rome, and this
confirmation later became a basis for the popes' claim to temporal authority over the so-called Papal States. The papal-Frankish
entente also resulted in cooperation to reform the Frankish
clergy, which had become notoriously debauched and worldly

under the Merovingians; and the alliance culminated in the coronation of the Frankish king, Charles the Great (Charlemagne), by Pope Leo III in 800 as Roman emperor. It is true that after the death of Charlemagne (814 A.D.) dark days lay ahead both for his empire and for the papacy, which fell into the hands of ambitious and worldly Italian nobles. But the seeds had been sown for a new culture stimulated by and united by the ideals of a universal Roman Church.

THE VISIGOTHS.   The Visigoths of Spain displayed the tolerant temper and civic responsibility that the Ostrogoths of Italy had shown. Under their great king Euric (466–483 A.D.) their empire stretched from the Loire in central France to Gibraltar and from the Atlantic to the Rhone, and it appeared the strongest Western power. Even after the defeat of Alaric II by Clovis the Frank in 507 and the almost complete expulsion of the Visigoths from France, their kingdom in Spain presented an impressive appearance. After King Recared became a Catholic convert in 589, the native Romans and the Visigoths intermarried freely. In 654 a Latin code was published which applied to all Spanish citizens, Visigoths and Romans alike, and which superseded the practice that was common elsewhere, by which Romans lived by Roman law and the invaders by their own primitive codes. The clergy of Spain was noted for its sobriety and responsibility, characteristics quite contrary to those that distinguished their fellow churchmen in the Frankish north; and the king, nobles, and clergy met regularly in synods to discuss problems, establish policy, and hear the oppressed. However, the Visigothic monarchy was greatly weakened by the independence and ambition of the Spanish bishops and Visigothic nobles. After the extinction of the ancient Gothic royal line in 531, no incumbent of the throne could establish a stable dynasty in the face of the powerful nobles' jealousy. Justinian took advantage of the divisions within the Visigothic state to reestablish imperial control of southern Spain in 554; and although that territory was all recovered by the Visigoths by 631, the ambitions of the nobles reduced the kingship to an elective office by 636. The kings naturally resisted the encroachments of the nobles, and the clergy favored first one side and then the other. In the atmosphere of mutual suspicion and lowered morale that resulted among the rulers of Spain, the Moslem Berbers had no difficulty in 711 in ending the Visigothic kingdom by a single battle.

THE VANDALS.   The Vandals, who had preceded the Visigoths in Spain, carved out a new state for themselves in North

590

Africa between 429 and 477. They themselves appropriated most of the land in the old province of Africa, but left the ancient Roman residents to exploit most of the rest of the territory that they controlled. The Vandals maintained the Roman administrative and fiscal machinery, and the people seemed to find them no more oppressive than the imperial officials of Rome had been. In the Vandal kingdom Vandals and Romans were each subject to their own traditional laws, though the Vandal king had general supervision of all his subjects regardless of their origins. In the two or three generations that the Vandal kingdom survived, however, it is clear that the Vandals were being assimilated to Roman custom and culture. As with the Ostrogoths of Italy, a stock thus reinvigorated might have created a strong state. But, as in Italy, the ambitions of Justinian of Byzantium laid a baneful hand on the country, and after more than ten years of campaigns in Africa (533–548 A.D.), the area was so weakened that it never recovered, and it soon fell an easy victim to the westward sweep of the Arab conquerors.

THE BURGUNDIANS.   The kingdom of the Burgundians was the most precarious of all the successor states. The kings of Burgundy recognized their own military weakness and long clung to their legal status as federates of Rome, so that they could signify their dependence on and their loyalty to imperial policy. Intermarriage between Romans and Burgundians was permitted, and a legal code for both races was issued in the Latin language. At length their kings sought popularity with their Roman subjects by renouncing their Arian Christianity and accepting the orthodox version preferred by the Roman Catholics.[2] But all was in vain; the implacable ambition of the Frankish kings ended the royal line of the Burgundians and their independent status in 534.

THE FRANKS.   The Franks formed the most vigorous and enduring and, in many respects, the least constructive of the successor states. In one generation Clovis, the king of the Salian Franks (481–511 A.D.), by means of arms, trickery, assassinations, and religion, conquered the larger part of ancient Gaul. Since France was to become the heartland of the new Western culture, it has a special importance in a survey of the successor states. The Franks had been settled as federates in the vicinity of Belgium as early as Emperor Julian (360–363 A.D.), but after the dismemberment of the Empire their expansion was ruthless and rapid. In 486 Clovis overturned that remnant of Rome in

[2]   For these two versions of Christian doctrine, see above, pp. 548, 551.

the Seine Valley, the kingdom of Soissons. In 496 or 497 the Alamanni became his subjects. In 500 he defeated, though he could not annex, the Burgundians. In 507 the Visigoths were driven out of most of their possessions in southern France; and before his death Clovis had asserted his hegemony over his kinsmen, the Ripuarian Franks. Under the influence of his queen, Clotilda, Clovis had been converted to the Christian faith, and to the orthodox Catholic version, which was favored by the old Roman residents of the provinces, rather than to the Arian creed, which was supported by the Gothic and Burgundian invaders. It was widely supposed that this circumstance gained Clovis considerable treasonable support among the Roman subjects in the states of his Gothic and Burgundian rivals.

The Franks appropriated for their own use a part of the lands that they had conquered, but the remainder was left to the Gallo-Roman natives to exploit as they had before the conquest. The Roman bureaucratic machinery was maintained as far as possible to administer the country; and the same tolls and taxes were levied upon the trades, commerce, and land. The Franks retained the Roman standards of coinage; and trade with the rest of the Mediterranean continued for some time unabated. But the Merovingians (the house of Clovis and his descendants) looked upon their kingdom as their private property, to be wasted, disposed of to favorites, or divided among offspring as the owners saw fit. There was no sense of responsibility to their land or people — only a right to self-satisfaction. In such an atmosphere the education and training necessary to furnish administrators and to keep the taxes in line with the actual condition of the land were completely ignored. Soon the Frankish kings had to depend completely on the income of their private estates and upon tolls on highway traffic, which still could be levied as long as roads and bridges could be barred. The nobles were swashbuckling hunters and murderers, the clergy little better, and the successors of Clovis generally died at an early age from dissipation. While the Merovingians lived, they fought with their relatives, parried with the Frankish nobles, and conspired against their neighbors.

Ultimately this degenerate line was replaced by one founded by a hereditary feudal servant of the Frankish court, the mayor of the palace. This functionary was a kind of finance minister in charge of the king's estates, and he gained great power. Charles Martel, who defeated the Moslems near Tours in 732, was mayor of the palace; and his son, Pepin the Short, who became mayor in 741, deposed the Merovingians in 751 and assumed the crown. The first three members of this dynasty (the Carolingians) worked vigorously to expand the frontiers, improve the administration, and effect a revival of arts and letters. The great success of Pepin's son, Charlemagne (768– 814 A.D.), led to his coronation in 800 as Western Roman emperor by Pope Leo III, an old Frankish ally. Charlemagne labored sincerely in cooperation with the Roman Church to reform and improve the Frankish clergy. He, and his successor Louis the Pious (814–840 A.D.), continued their family's policy in encouraging the work of missionaries and insisting that all new subjects be straightway converted to Christianity.

The pressures of tradition and of German feudalism, however, were too much for the Carolingians, and their empire soon disintegrated into the smaller states of France, Germany, Lorraine, Lombardy, Burgundy, and others—and all these were further fragmented into the quarrelsome principalities of the Middle Ages. It was not just in the political field that fragmentation and particularism were triumphant. The Frankish nobles, both lay and ecclesiastical, had built their great demesnes on the foundations and on the model of the late Roman *latifundia* or villas. In the ninth century A.D. we find this system fully matured, a world dotted with little self-sufficient worlds—an economy of consumption substituted for an economy of exchange.

BRITAIN.   Britain had been the first of the western provinces to leave the Roman Empire, and it was the last to return to the family of Western Europe. While its Anglo-Saxon kingdoms had been converted to Christianity by missionary effort, it had remained a chaos of rival states until the ninth century A.D. Then, however, under the stimulus of the Scandinavians, which people ravaged the world far and wide, Alfred of Wessex (871–899 A.D.) was roused to throw the invaders back. By the end of the tenth century A.D. he and his successors had created a kingdom of England that approximated the territory of the ancient Roman province and that became a participant in the newly emerging Western culture.

When compared with Byzantium and Islam, the West seemed discouragingly tardy. But with the Carolingians in France there were signs that the interplay of a classical tradition and of German creativity was slowly having effect. The Roman

Church had established itself as the focus for ideals and conduct and the model for administrative government. The ubiquitous monks had preserved much of classical thought and literature, which would in time water the burgeoning seed of Western civilization. Roman law had left its mark everywhere—either through direct influence on the Germanic codes or through the law of the Church, which also was Roman. And the heavily vaulted church, the painted mural, the medieval hymn, the occasional lyric—all were prophetic that much of Rome that had long lain fallow would emerge transformed in the culture of Western Europe, the latest and most vigorous of Rome's offspring.

Simplified Stemma of The Julio-Claudian Family

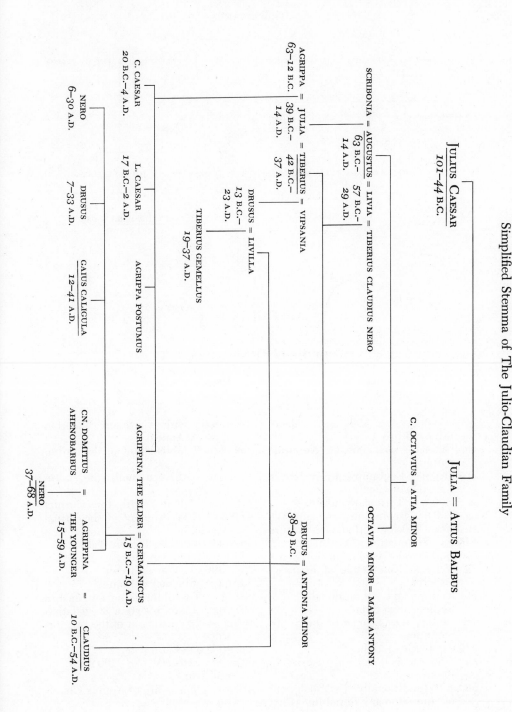

Stemma of The Severi

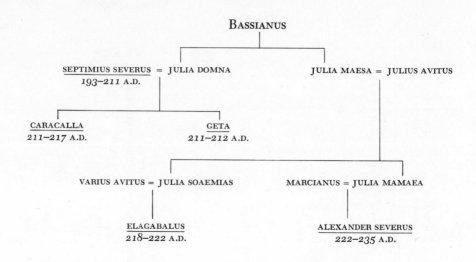

BASSIANUS

SEPTIMIUS SEVERUS = JULIA DOMNA
193–211 A.D.

JULIA MAESA = JULIUS AVITUS

CARACALLA
211–217 A.D.

GETA
211–212 A.D.

VARIUS AVITUS = JULIA SOAEMIAS

MARCIANUS = JULIA MAMAEA

ELAGABALUS
218–222 A.D.

ALEXANDER SEVERUS
222–235 A.D.

APPENDIX 2

CHRONOLOGICAL TABLE

500,000 B.C.?–*ca.* 5000 B.C. Palaeo-lithic culture

ca. 5000 B.C.–*post* 2000 B.C. Neolithic culture

ca. 2000 B.C. Beginning of Bronze Age Lake-Dweller culture

ca. 1500 B.C. Terramara culture

ca. 1000 B.C. Beginning of the Iron Age

ca. 1000–750 B.C. Villanovan culture

814 B.C. Foundation of Carthage

775 B.C. Greek colony at Pithecusa

ca. 750 B.C. Emergence of Etruscan culture

8th century B.C. (traditionally 753) Settlement at Rome

7th century B.C. League of the Septi-montium

540 B.C. Battle of Alalia

ca. 550–*ca.* 500 B.C. Etruscans in Rome

509 B.C. (traditionally) Establishment of the Roman Republic. First treaty with Carthage. Valerian Law on Appeal

494 B.C. Establishment of the Tribunate

493 B.C. Alliance with the Latin League

486 B.C. Alliance with the Hernici

471 B.C. Establishment of the Tribal Assembly

451–449 B.C. The Twelve Tables

445 B.C. Canuleian Law

405–396 B.C. War with Veii

390 B.C. Gallic sack of Rome

381 B.C. Tusculum given citizenship

367 B.C. Licinio-Sextian Legislation

366 B.C. Establishment of the praetorship

340–338 B.C. Latin War

325–321, 316–304, 298–290 B.C. Samnite Wars

312 B.C. Censorship of Appius Claudius

300 B.C. Ogulnian Law

290 B.C. Annexation of the Sabines

287 B.C. Hortensian Law

281-272 B.C. War with Tarentines and King Pyrrhus

268 B.C. Sabines given citizenship

264-241 B.C. First Punic War

256-255 B.C. Regulus' expedition to Africa

241-238 B.C. Revolt of Carthaginian mercenaries

241 B.C. Sack of Falerii

241 B.C. Tribes reach 35 in number

post 241 B.C. Reform of Centuriate Assembly

237 B.C. Annexation of Sardinia and Corsica

232 B.C. Distribution of the *Ager Gallicus*

228 B.C. Defeat of Teuta and the Illyrians

227 B.C. Sicily and Sardinia-Corsica organized as provinces

226 B.C. Ebro River established as demarcation line in Spain

225 B.C. Defeat of Gauls at Telamon

219 B.C. Defeat of Demetrius of Pharos

218-202 B.C. Second Punic War

217 B.C. Battle of Lake Trasimene

216 B.C. Battle of Cannae

215-205 B.C. First Macedonian War

214 B.C. Defection of Syracuse

214-210 B.C. Recovery of Sicily

211 B.C. Fall of Capua

210-206 B.C. Scipio captures Spain

209 B.C. Recovery of Tarentum

205 B.C. Cult of Cybele imported to Rome

202 B.C. Battle of Zama

200-196 B.C. Second Macedonian War

197-191 B.C. Recovery of Cisalpine Gaul

197-178 B.C. Campaigns in Spain

192-189 B.C. War with Antiochus the Great

181-163 B.C. Campaigns in Sardinia and Corsica

181-154 B.C. Campaigns in Liguria

171-167 B.C. Third Macedonian War

154-140 B.C. Campaigns in Spain

149-148 B.C. Fourth Macedonian War

149-146 B.C. Third Punic War

146 B.C. Achaean War; destruction of Corinth

143-133 B.C. Numantine War

135-132 B.C. First Sicilian Slave War

133 B.C. Tribunate of Tiberius Gracchus. Kingdom of Pergamum left to Rome

129 B.C. Asia organized as a province

125 B.C. Revolt of Fregellae

123-122 B.C. Tribunate of Gaius Gracchus

118 B.C. Foundation of Narbo

111-105 B.C. Jugurthine War

107, 104-100 B.C. Six consulships of Marius

102-101 B.C. Defeat of Cimbri and Teutons

104-99 B.C. Second Sicilian Slave War

91 B.C. Tribunate of Livius Drusus the Younger

90-88 B.C. Social War

89-84 B.C. First war with Mithridates

88 B.C. Sulla captures Rome

86 B.C. Marius' seventh consulship

82 B.C. Sulla captures Rome second time

82-79 B.C. Dictatorship of Sulla

81-72 B.C. Revolt of Sertorius in Spain

78-77 B.C. Revolt of Aemilius Lepidus

74-63 B.C. Second war with Mithridates

73-71 B.C. Revolt of Spartacus

70 B.C. First consulship of Crassus and Pompey. Trial of Gaius Verres

67 B.C. The Gabinian Law

66 B.C. The Manilian Law

65 B.C. First Catilinarian conspiracy

63 B.C. Second Catilinarian conspiracy

59 B.C. Formation of the First Triumvirate

58-51 B.C. Conquest of Gaul

56 B.C. Conference at Luca

53 B.C. Defeat of Crassus at Carrhae

52 B.C. Pompey sole consul

48 B.C. Battle of Pharsalus

48-47 B.C. Alexandrine War

47 B.C. Battle of Zela

46 B.C. Battle of Thapsus

45 B.C. Battle of Munda

44 B.C. Assassination of Julius Caesar

43 B.C. Formation of the Second Triumvirate

42 B.C. Battle of Philippi

40 B.C. Peace of Brundisium

39-36 B.C. War with Sextus Pompey

36 B.C. Antony's Parthian expedition

35-33 B.C. Illyrian campaigns of Octavian

34 B.C. Donations of Alexandria

31 B.C. Battle of Actium

27 B.C. Octavian given title "Augustus"

23 B.C. Establishment of the Principate

23 B.C. – 14 A.D. Augustus

18 B.C. Julian Laws on marriage

17 B.C. Secular games

9 A.D. Papian-Poppaean Law on marriage. Disaster of Varus in Germany

14 – 37 A.D. Tiberius

27 A.D. Tiberius retires to Capri

31 A.D. Fall of Sejanus

37 – 41 A.D. Gaius Caligula

41 – 54 A.D. Claudius

42 A.D. Mauretania added to the Empire

43 – 47 A.D. Britain added to the Empire

46 A.D. Thrace added to the Empire

54 – 68 A.D. Nero

61 A.D. Rebellion of Boudicca in Britain

64 A.D. Great fire in Rome

66 A.D. Tiridates of Armenia crowned in Rome

66 – 70 A.D. Jewish rebellion

68 A.D. Rebellion of Julius Vindex

68 – 69 A.D. Galba

69 A.D. Otho
Vitellius

69 – 70 A.D. Revolt of Civilis

69 – 79 A.D. Vespasian

79 – 81 A.D. Titus

79 A.D. Destruction of Pompeii and Herculaneum

81 – 96 A.D. Domitian

96 – 98 A.D. Nerva

98 – 117 A.D. Trajan

101 – 106 A.D. Dacian Wars

105/6 A.D. Annexation of Nabataean Arabs

114 – 117 A.D. Parthian Wars

115 – 117 A.D. Revolt of the Jews

117 – 138 A.D. Hadrian

ca. 129 A.D. Codification of the Praetor's Edict

132 – 134 A.D. Jewish rebellion

138 – 161 A.D. Antoninus Pius

161 – 180 A.D. Marcus Aurelius

161 – 169 A.D. Lucius Verus

162 – 166 A.D. Parthian War

165 – 180 A.D. The Great Plague

167 – 175, 178 – 180 A.D. German Wars

180 – 192 A.D. Commodus

193 A.D. Pertinax

Didius Julianus

193 – 197 A.D. Civil wars

193 – 211 A.D. Septimius Severus

211 – 217 A.D. Caracalla

211 – 212 A.D. Geta

212 or 213 A.D. *Constitutio Antoniniana*

217 – 218 A.D. Macrinus

218 – 222 A.D. Elagabalus

222 – 235 A.D. Severus Alexander

226 A.D. Sassanid dynasty assumes Persian throne

235 – 238 A.D. Maximinus

238 A.D. Gordian I, Gordian II
Balbinus and Pupienus

238 – 244 A.D. Gordian III

244 – 249 A.D. Philip the Arab

249 – 251 A.D. Decius, Herennius Etruscus, Hostilianus

251 – 253 A.D. Trebonianus Gallus, Volusianus

253 – 259 A.D. Valerian

259 – 268 A.D. Gallienus

260 – 270 A.D. Secession of Gaul

268 – 270 A.D. Claudius II

270 A.D. Quintillus

270 – 272 A.D. Secession of Palmyra

270 – 275 A.D. Aurelian

271 A.D. Aurelian's Wall around Rome begun. Abandonment of Dacia

275 – 276 A.D. Tacitus

276 A.D. Florianus

276 – 282 A.D. Probus

282 – 283 A.D. Carus

283 – 284 A.D. Numerianus

283 – 285 A.D. Carinus

284 – 305 A.D. Diocletian

286 A.D. Maximian, co-emperor

293 A.D. Establishment of the Tetrarchy

296 A.D. Galerius defeats the Persians

301 A.D. Edict of Prices

303 – 304 A.D. Edicts against Christians

305 A.D. Galerius and Constantius

306 A.D. Galerius and Severus

307 – 311 A.D. Galerius, Maxentius, Daia, Licinius, Constantine I

311 A.D. Death of Galerius

312 A.D. Battle of Milvian Bridge; death of Maxentius

313 A.D. Death of Daia
Edict of Religious Toleration

313 – 324 A.D. Constantine I and Licinius

316 A.D. Death of Diocletian

324–337 A.D. Constantine I
324–330 A.D. Construction of Constantinople
325 A.D. Council of Nicaea
337–340 A.D. Constantine II
337–350 A.D. Constans
337–361 A.D. Constantius
360–363 A.D. Julian the Apostate
363–364 A.D. Jovian
364–375 A.D. Valentinian I
364–378 A.D. Valens
375–383 A.D. Gratian
375–392 A.D. Valentinian II
378 A.D. Battle of Adrianople
379–395 A.D. Theodosius I
390 A.D. Massacre at Thessalonica; penance of Theodosius I
392 A.D. Official suppression of the pagans
395 A.D. Final division of the Empire into East and West
395–423 A.D. Honorius, Western emperor
ca. 404 A.D. Ravenna becomes Western imperial residence
406–410 A.D. Abandonment of Britain
410 A.D. Alaric the Goth captures Rome
418 A.D. Visigothic kingdom established in Aquitania
423–455 A.D. Valentinian III
439 A.D. Vandals capture Carthage
442 A.D. Vandal kingdom established in Africa
443 A.D. Burgundian kingdom established in Savoy
451 A.D. Attila the Hun defeated at Châlons
452 A.D. Attila invades Italy
455 A.D. Petronius Maximus

Vandal sack of Rome
455–456 A.D. Avitus
457–461 A.D. Majorian
461–465 A.D. Libius Severus
466–483 A.D. Euric king of Visigoths
467–472 A.D. Anthemius
472 A.D. Olybrius
473–474 A.D. Glycerius
474–475 A.D. Julius Nepos
475–476 A.D. Romulus Augustus
476 A.D. Odoacer, German king of Italy
480 A.D. Dalmatia added to Italy
481–511 A.D. Clovis king of the Franks
491–518 A.D. Anastasius I, Eastern emperor
493–526 A.D. Theodoric king of the Ostrogoths
507 A.D. Clovis defeats Alaric II, the Visigoth
527–565 A.D. Justinian I, Eastern emperor
529–534 A.D. Codification of Roman law
534 A.D. Franks capture Burgundy
570–632 A.D. Mohammed the Prophet
654 A.D. Visigothic Code published
661–749 A.D. The Umayyad dynasty
711 A.D. Visigoths defeated by the Moslems
732 A.D. Charles Martel defeats Moslems at Tours
750–847 A.D. The Abbasid dynasty
751 A.D. Pepin king of Franks
768–814 A.D. Charlemagne
800 A.D. Charlemagne, Western Roman emperor
871–899 A.D. Alfred of Wessex
1453 A.D. Capture of Constantinople by the Moslems

APPENDIX 3

ROMAN COINAGE, VALUES, AND PRICES

The expression of ancient values in terms of modern currency presents problems to the historian because it is impossible to find any firm standard of comparison between the two economies. If the intrinsic value of the metals in the coinage is used, the computations are complicated by the constant changes in the costs of the metals and by the wide use and manipulation of fiduciary currency in the Western world. If the price of a basic commodity, such as wheat, is used, we establish quite different values from those established if the average daily wage of a laborer or the cost of metals is used.

The problem is made more difficult by the scantiness of the ancient evidence on prices. A selection of the few that are available is here given for three periods of Roman history: The Early Republic, Later Republic and Principate, and Later Empire (from Diocletian's Edict of Prices). Most of these prices are cited in *An Economic Survey of Ancient Rome* (six volumes; ed. Tenney Frank; Baltimore, 1933–40). The author has felt free, however, to quote the ancient weights and measures in their *approximate* modern American equivalents (*e.g.* one modius = one peck; one jugerum = 2/3 acre). A list of approximate equivalents appears below. Also, in many cases the quantities and prices are given in larger amounts or prices (*e.g.* bushels instead of pecks, denarii instead of sesterces) than in the ancient sources so that the reader may find it easier to make comparisons with modern prices and with other ancient prices.

WEIGHTS AND MEASURES

Roman foot = .296 meters = 11.64 inches
Roman mile = 1480 meters = 4856 feet = .92 mile
jugerum = .622 acres

sextarius = .53 liters = 1.12 pints
amphora = 48 sextarii = 25.5 liters = 27.9 quarts = 6.7 gallons
modius = 8.49 liters = .96 pecks
Greek medimnus = about 6 modii

Roman pound (*libra*) = 12 ounces (*unciae*) = 326 grams = .719 pounds
    (327.45 grams, .722 pounds for coins)

CURRENCY

1 talent = 6000 drachmas = 6000 denarii (a Greek drachma was slightly heavier than a Roman denarius, but they were generally exchanged at equal value).
1 denarius = 4 sesterces
1 sesterce = 4 asses

THE EARLY REPUBLIC

While barter was the earliest method of exchange used by the Romans, by the beginning of the Republic the Romans also were using rough lumps of bronze, which had to be weighed in scales at each commercial transaction. By the early third century B.C. they had developed a heavy cast coin of bronze weighing one pound (the libral *aes grave*, or libral as). The following prices from the early Republic have been converted to that standard, though the ancient texts often express prices in later and lighter coins. The Roman pound weighed 327.45 grams, but early asses are found ranging in weight from 276 to 340 grams, and by the fourth century B.C. they were often closer to ten ounces than twelve.

To get some idea of the value of the metal, in 1956 a pound of copper of 453.59 grams sold for about forty cents. Thus, the value of the metal in an as of the early Republic (the libral *aes grave*) would in the twentieth century A.D. be less than thirty cents. However, it should be observed that, if in the mid-twentieth century A.D. a beef animal costs about $100, a sheep about $15, and a bushel of wheat about $2, then the purchasing power of a libral as equalled or exceeded $1.

DATE	ARTICLE	PRICE	COMMENT
430 B.C.	1 ox	100 libral asses	The Julio-Papirian Law established pecuniary
	1 sheep	10 libral asses	equivalents for the old fines that were levied in animals.
400 B.C.	Minimum wealth of a citizen of the first *classis*	10,000 libral asses	The following prices were given by the ancient authors in terms of the
	Minimum wealth of a citizen of the fifth *classis*	1,250 libral asses	one-ounce as (2nd cen. B.C.) and have to be divided by 10 to approxi-
	1 jugerum (⅔ acre) land	500 libral asses	mate the earlier libral as.
	1 horse	500 libral asses	
	1 bushel barley	1½ libral asses	63 bushels to feed a horse for one year cost 100 asses.
	1 bushel wheat	3 libral asses	Wheat was normally double the price of barley in antiquity.

LATER REPUBLIC AND PRINCIPATE

During the third century B.C. the weight of the bronze as was rapidly reduced until by the middle of the second century B.C. it weighed only one ounce. A law of 98 B.C. further reduced it to one-half ounce. Meanwhile, in the mid-third century B.C. the use of silver was rapidly developed by the Romans. During the early second century B.C. the denarius became the favorite silver coin and its weight ultimately was standardized at 1/84 of a Roman pound (3.9 grams) and remained at that weight until the time of Nero. Sometime during the Gracchan era the denarius was tariffed as the equivalent of sixteen asses. The denarius is a coin about midway in weight between an American dime (2.5 grams) and an American quarter dollar (6 grams). Its silver content in 1965 A.D. would be valued at about sixteen cents. Most Roman prices are given in denarii, in the bronze as, or in the brass sesterce (abbreviated HS), which was tariffed at ¼ denarius.

The denarius was reduced to 1/96 pound by Nero, but this was perhaps merely a recognition of a rise in the price of silver. However, the amount of base metal in the silver coins was rapidly increased in the second century A.D. until it amounted to fifty percent by the beginning and to seventy or eighty percent by the middle of the third century A.D.

The Romans often expressed very large sums in talents. The ancient talent varied greatly in weight and value, but the silver talent is generally reckoned at about 6000 denarii. In other words, as bullion the talent was worth roughly $1000.

In summary:
1 talent = approximately 6000 denarii
1 denarius = 4 sesterces
1 sesterce = 4 asses

DATE	ARTICLE	PRICE	COMMENT
2nd and 1st cen. B.C.	wheat	3 den. per bushel	This is common opinion based on prices given below. Price in mid-20th-century America, *ca.* $2 per bushel.
210 B.C.		2½ den. per peck	War conditions.
203–201 B.C.		1 den. per bushel	Glut after 2nd Punic War.
196 B.C.		½ den. per bushel	Glut after 2nd Macedonian War.
123 B.C.		1½ den. per bushel (6⅓ asses per modius)	Government wheat sold by Gaius Gracchus at fixed price (cost?).
73–70 B.C.		2–4 den. per bushel	Prices fluctuated for grain procured in Sicily.
Late 1st cen. A.D.		2 den. per bushel	Price in Asia
1st cen. A.D.	refined wheat flour	*ca.* 13 den. per hundredweight	Wheat flour in America has wholesaled *ca.* $5.50 per hundredweight.
	1 loaf bread	*ca.* 3 asses	A loaf of bread retails in America *ca.* 25¢.

In the Po Valley and in Spain during the Republic the price of wheat was ¹/₇ to ¼ the Roman price.

In respect to the staple, wheat, the buying power of a denarius equals about 50 cents (American), but the cheapness of labor made its buying power for some processed foods even higher.

DATE	ARTICLE	PRICE	COMMENT
2nd cen. B.C.	olive oil	½ HS per pound (app. ⅜ den. per qt.)	Retails in America *ca.* $1.25 per qt.
Late 2nd cen. B.C.	native vintage wine	25 den. per amphora	27.9 qts.
89 B.C.	imported wines	96 den. per amphora	
mid-1st cen. A.D.	vin ordinaire	3¾ den. per amphora	wholesale.
1st. cen. A.D.	wine at retail	1 to 4 asses per pint	According to grade in Pompeian taverns.
2nd cen. B.C.	100 lb. hog	5 den.	Price in Spain and
”	600 lb. ox	10 den.	Gaul.
180 B.C.	600 lb. ox for sacrifice	80–100 den.	Delos
130/160 A.D.	carcass of cattle	50 den.	
202 A.D.	horse	400 den.	Estimated from a
”	mule	400 den.	customs list in
”	ass	133⅓ den.	Africa. In mid-
”	cow	133⅓ den.	20th cen. America
”	pig	66⅔ den.	av. value per head
”	sheep, goat	66⅔ den.	of cattle $100, of
”	kid, lamb	33⅓ den.	hogs $25, of sheep $15, of horses and mules $75.
Late 1st cen. B.C.	3 lbs. dried meat plus 1 lb. salt fish	1¼ den.	

Although there are variations from animal to animal, it appears that when buying meat a Roman denarius would buy approximately 50 cents' worth.

204 B.C.	salt	⅙ as per pound	Set by government.
1st cen. A.D.	black pepper	4 den. per pound	In America pepper retails at app. $1.30 per Roman pound.
”	ginger	6 den. per pound	App. $1.80 per Roman pound.
202 A.D.	dates, figs	20 den. for 100 lbs.	Estimated from customs list in Africa.
2nd cen. B.C.	outfit of clothing for Cato (toga, tunic, shoes)	100 den.	Cato was extremely frugal.
1st cen. A.D.	wool	25 den. for 100 lbs.	*Ca.* $14 in America
202 A.D.	blanket	25 den.	
Early 1st cen. A.D.	land	300 den. per jugerum (.622 acre)	Land bought for veterans.
2nd cen. A.D.	”	250 den. per jugerum	Land to plant vines.
2nd cen. B.C	farmhouse	1000 den.	40′ × 40′
125 B.C.	rental of town house	1500 den.	Considered too high.
92 B.C.	town house of Crassus the orator	1,500,000 den.	
2nd cen. B.C.	plowman slave	300 den.	
”	skilled slave	1500 den.	
1st cen. B.C.	able bodied slave	500 den.	
202 A.D.	”	500 den.	
2nd cen. B.C.	cost to maintain one slave for one year	100–125 den.	Includes original cost and depreciation.
”	wages for hired out slave	½ den. per day	
2nd cen. B.C.	minimum cost of maintenance for a laboring couple	300 den. per year	Estimated by T. Frank in *ESAR*, 1.189.
1st cen. A.D.	worker in vineyard	1 den. per day	In Palestine.
137 A.D.	fee for prostitute	6 asses to 1 den.	In Palmyra.
2nd. cen. B.C.	est. profit from 200 jugera (120 acres) of olives	400 den.	Estimated by T. Frank (*ESAR*, 1.171), based on Cato and Pliny. 12,500 gross income; 12,100 expenses (includes interest on investment and depreciation).
2nd cen. A.D.	est. profit from 7 jugera (4⅓ acres) vineyard	1075 den.	Estimated by T. Frank (*ESAR* 5.150), based on Columella. 1,575 gross income. Interest on investment (including a slave vintner) 500 den.
1st cen. B.C.	Income of a gentleman	150,000 den. per year	Based on Cicero.
”	Income of a *very* wealthy gentleman	1,000,000 den. per year	Based on the career of Crassus.
1st cen. A.D.	Minimum requirement of equestrian census of 100,000 den. yields		An income of 6000 den. per year.
”	Minimum requirement of senatorial census of 250,000 den. yields		An income of 15,000 den. per year.

THE EDICT OF DIOCLETIAN

After the half century of chaos, both political and financial, from 235–284 A.D., Diocletian tried to put Roman coinage once again on a solid basis. In 301 A.D. he issued a silver coin worth 1/1000 of a pound of gold and weighing 1/96 of a pound of silver. This coin (often called a miliarense) was of the same weight as the silver denarius of Nero.

Apparently the appearance (or the rumor) of a new system of coinage brought about fantastically inflated prices in terms of the old debased denarii of the third century A.D., which still were in large circulation. Diocletian therefore sought to alleviate the suffering among those persons on a fixed salary by issuing an edict in 301 A.D. which set maximum prices for goods and services in terms of the old currency. If we are to take seriously the statement in the edict that the cost of one pound of gold was 50,000 denarii, then the debased denarii of the list must be reckoned as worth 1/50 of the denarius of the Principate, and all the prices of the edict should be divided by fifty in order to compare them with those of the Principate.

As new coinage replaced the old, the need for a control of prices of course disappeared. But the listed prices in the following selection are a useful check on the comparative values of the day and (after being divided by 50) reveal so large an agreement with the prices for the same articles in the Principate that it is perhaps permissible for us to suppose that prices for articles and services on this list for which we have no earlier evidence would not have been far different in the days of the Republic and Principate.

ARTICLE	QUANTITY	PRICE
wheat	1 bushel	400 den.
dried kidney beans	”	”
rice	”	800 den.
Falernian wine	1 pint	30 den.
one-year-old wine	”	24 den.
(first quality)		
(second quality)	”	16 den.
(ordinaire)	”	8 den.
beer	”	2 – 4 den.
ordinary olive oil	”	12 den.
best honey	”	40 den.
pork	1 pound	12 den.
beef	”	8 den.
goat and mutton	”	8 den.
lamb	”	12 den.
best liver	”	16 den.
salt pork	”	16 den.
ham	”	20 den.
rabbit	one	40 den.
butter	1 pound	16 den.
best sea fish	1 pound	24 den.
best river fish	”	12 den.
oysters	100	100 den.
dried cheese	1 pound	12 den.
best endive	10	10 den.
lettuce	5	2 – 4 den.
cabbage	5	2 – 4 den.
beets	5	2 – 4 den.
dried onions	1 bushel	200 den.
garlic	1 peck	60 den.
eggs	1	1 den.
apples	10	2 – 4 den.
table grapes	1 pound	1 den.
olives in brine	40	4 den.
fresh cheese	1 pound	8 den.
cinnamon	1 pound	125 den.
dry ginger	”	250 den.
farm laborer	per day with maintenance	25 den.

604

carpenter	"	50 den.
camel-, ass-, muledriver per day with maintenance		25 den.
shepherd	"	20 den.
barber	per customer	2 den.
shearer	per sheep	2 den.
scribe, best writing	per 100 lines	25 den.
gymnastic instructor	per student per month	50 den.
elementary teacher	"	50 den.
arithmetic teacher	"	75 den.
teacher of Latin, Greek, literature, geometry	"	200 den.
advocate for pleading a case		1000 den.
heavy boots (farmers and soldiers)		100 – 120 den.
shoes		70 – 150 den.
good freightwagon without ironware		6000 den.
passenger wagon	"	3000 den.
freight charge 1200 pound wagon load per mile		20 den.
purple silk	"	150,000 den.
wool (acc. to quality)	"	25 – 200 den.
linen yarn "	"	72 – 1200 den.
gold	"	50,000 den.

APPENDIX 4

BIBLIOGRAPHY; ENGLISH TRANSLATIONS OF THE ANCIENT SOURCES

The following bibliographies for each of the Parts of this History include *most* of the important ancient sources for each epoch. Their purpose is to provide detailed and first-hand information to supplement, qualify, and illuminate the modern text. In choosing the editions to be included an important consideration has been expense, and paperbound volumes (and occasionally abridged ones) have been given preference. Where no paperbound versions exist, the availability of that particular work in the Loeb Classical Library is indicated. The failure to indicate Loeb editions elsewhere does not mean that they do not exist, but that there are less expensive alternatives. Modern works have occasionally been included when the work is very famous and easily available, or where there is a lack of suitable ancient literature, as for Parts I and IX.

With the advent of paperbound editions, there is a bewildering appearance and disappearance of a good many useful titles. However, each year one issue of *The Classical World* (published by The Classical Association of the Atlantic States) includes a list of most of the inexpensive books available for the study of the Classics, and that journal can therefore be used to keep this bibliography up-to-date.

1. PRE-ROMAN ITALY

BOARDMAN, JOHN, *The Greeks Overseas* (Pelican). CHILDE, V. GORDON, *The Dawn of European Civilization* (Vintage Books). CHILDE, V. GORDON, *What Happened in History* (Pelican). DIO CASSIUS COCCEIANUS, *Roman History* I, II (Loeb; tr. Cary). DIODORUS SICULUS, *Library of History* VI-X (Loeb; tr. Old-father). DIONYSIUS OF HALICARNASSUS, *Roman Antiquities* I-IV (Loeb; tr. Cary). HARDEN, DONALD, *The Phoenicians* (Praeger). HUS, A., *The Etruscans* (Ever-green Books). JAMES, E. O., *Prehistoric Religion* (University Paperbacks). LIVY, *From the Founding of the City* I (*Early History of Rome*, Livy I-V, Penguin; tr. de Selincourt). PALLOTTINO, M. *The Etruscans* (Pelican). PLUTARCH, *Lives* of Romulus, Numa (Modern Library; tr. Dryden). WARMINGTON, B.H., *Carthage* (Pelican).

2. SURVIVAL AND UNIFICATION (509–265 B.C.)

APPIAN, *Roman History: Samnitica, Celtica, Italica* (Loeb 2; tr. White). CICERO, *On the Commonwealth* (Liberal Arts Press; tr. Sabine and Smith). DIO CASSIUS COCCEIANUS, *Roman History* III-X (Loeb; tr. Cary). DIODORUS SICULUS, *Library of History* XI-XXII (Loeb; tr. Oldfather, Sherman, Welles, Greer, Walton). DIONYSIUS OF HALICARNASSUS, *Roman Antiquities* V-XX (Loeb; tr. Foster). LIVY, *From the Founding of the City* II-X, *Epitome* XI-XV (Loeb; tr. Foster). PLUTARCH, *Lives* of Publicola, Camillus, Coriolanus, Pyrrhus (Modern Library; tr. Dryden). POLYBIUS, *Histories* I (Loeb; tr. Paton). *Remains of Old Latin* III: *Twelve Tables* (Loeb; tr. Warmington).

3. THE GREAT RIVALRY (264–201 B.C.)

APPIAN, *Roman History: Sicula, Hannibal, Libyca, Iberica* (Loeb; tr. White). CORNELIUS NEPOS, *Lives* of Hamilcar, Hannibal (Loeb; tr. Rolfe). DIO CASSIUS COCCEIANUS, *Roman History* XI-XVII (Loeb; tr. Cary). DIODORUS SICULUS, *Library of History* XXIII-XXVII (Loeb; tr. Walton). FLORUS, *Epitome of Roman History* (Loeb; tr. Forster). LIVY, *From the Founding of the City* XXI-XXX; *Epitome* XVI-XX (Loeb; tr. Foster, Moore). PLUTARCH, *Lives* of Fabius, Marcellus (Modern Library; tr. Dryden). POLYBIUS, *Histories* I-III, VI-XI, XIV-XV (Loeb; tr. Paton). *Remains of Old Latin* II: Livius Andronicus, Naevius (Loeb; tr. Warmington). VELLEIUS PATERCULUS, *Compendium of Roman History* (Loeb; tr. Shipley). WARMINGTON, B. H., *Carthage* (Pelican).

4. THE WAGES OF SUCCESS (201–133 B.C.)

APPIAN, *Roman History: Syriaca, Macedonica, Illyrica, Mithradatica, Iberica, Bellum Civile* (Loeb; tr. White). CATO, *On Agriculture* (Loeb; tr. Hooper). DIO CASSIUS COCCEIANUS, *Roman History* XVIII-XXIII (Loeb; tr. Cary). DIODORUS SICULUS, *Library of History* XXVIII-XXXII (Loeb; tr. Walton). FLORUS, *Epitome of Roman History* (Loeb; tr. Forster). LIVY, *From the Founding of the City* XXXI-XLV, *Epitome* XLVI-LVII (Loeb; tr. Sage, Schlesinger, Geer). PLUTARCH, *Lives* of Aemilius Paulus, Marcus Cato, Flamininus (Modern Library; tr. Dryden). POLYBIUS, *Histories* XV-XXXIX (Loeb; tr. Paton). *Remains of Old Latin* I, II: Ennius, Caecilius, Pacuvius (Loeb; tr. Warmington). *Roman Comedies:* Plautus, Terence (Modern Library; ed. Duckworth). VELLEIUS PATERCULUS, *Compendium of Roman History* (Loeb; tr. Shipley).

5. THE DISINTEGRATION OF THE REPUBLIC (133–31 B.C.)

APPIAN, *Bellum Civile* (Loeb; tr. White). CAESAR, *War Commentaries* (Mentor; tr. Warner and Everyman; tr. Warrington). CATULLUS, *Complete Poetry* (Ann Arbor Paperbacks; tr. Copley). CICERO, *Basic Works* (Modern Library; ed. Hadas); *Selected Works* (Penguin; tr. Grant); *On the Commonwealth* (Liberal Arts Press; tr. Sabine and Smith). CORNELIUS NEPOS, *Life* of Atticus (Loeb; tr. Rolfe). DIO CASSIUS COCCEIANUS, *Roman History* XXIV-L (Loeb; tr. Cary). FLORUS, *Epitome of Roman History* (Loeb; tr. Forster). FRONTINUS, *Stratagems and Aqueducts* (Loeb; tr. Bennett and McElwain). LIVY, *Epitome* LVIII-CXXXIII (Loeb; tr. Schlesinger, Geer). LUCAN, *Civil War* (Loeb; tr. Duff). LUCRETIUS, *Nature of the Universe* (Penguin; tr. Latham). PLUTARCH, *Lives* of Marius, Sulla, Lucullus, Crassus, Sertorius, M. Brutus, Pompey, Caesar, Cato the Younger, the Gracchi, Cicero, Antony (Modern Library; tr. Dryden).

Remains of Old Latin II, III: Accius, Lucilius (Loeb; tr. Warmington). SALLUST, *Jugurthine War* and *Conspiracy of Catiline* (Penguin; tr. Handford). SUETONIUS, *Lives of the Twelve Caesars* (Modern Library; tr. Gavorse); *The Twelve Caesars* (Penguin L-72; tr. Graves). TAYLOR, LILY ROSS, *Party Politics in the Age of Caesar* (Univ. of California Press Paperbound). VARRO, *On Agriculture* (Loeb; tr. Hooper); *On the Latin Language* (Loeb; tr. Kent). VELLEIUS PATERCULUS, *Compendium of Roman History* (Loeb; tr. Shipley).

6. THE AUGUSTAN DISPENSATION (31 B.C. – 14 A.D.)

AUGUSTUS, *Res Gestae Divi Augusti* (Loeb; tr. Shipley). DIO CASSIUS COCCEIANUS, *Roman History* LI-LVI (Loeb; tr. Cary). FLORUS, *Epitome of Roman History* (Loeb; tr. Forster). HORACE, *Odes and Epodes* (Phoenix; tr. Clancy); *Satires and Epistles* (Phoenix; tr. Bovie). JOSEPHUS, *Jewish War* (Penguin; tr. Williamson). *The Latin Poets* (Modern Library; ed. Godolphin). LIVY, *Epitome* CXXXIV-CXLV (Loeb; tr. Schlesinger, Geer). NICOLAUS OF DAMASCUS, *Life of Augustus* (Smith College Classical Studies; tr. Hall). OVID, *Art of Love* (Midland Books; tr. Humphries); *Metamorphoses* (Midland Books; tr. Humphries). STRABO, *Geography* (Loeb; tr. Jones). SUETONIUS, *Lives of the Twelve Caesars* (Modern Library; tr. Gavorse); *The Twelve Caesars* (Penguin; tr. Graves). SYME, R., *The Roman Revolution* (Oxford Paperback). VELLEIUS PATERCULUS, *Compendium of Roman History* (Loeb; tr. Shipley). VERGIL, *The Aeneid* (Scribner Library; tr. Humphries); *Eclogues and Georgics* (Anchor; tr. Lewis). Vitruvius, *The Ten Books of Architecture* (Dover; tr. Morgan).

7. THE PRINCIPATE: TIBERIUS THROUGH THE SEVERI (14 – 235 A.D.)

APULEIUS, *Golden Ass* (Midland Books; tr. Lindsay). ARISTIDES, *The Ruling Power* (American Philosophical Society; tr. Oliver). AULUS GELLIUS, *Attic Nights* (Loeb; tr. Rolfe). AURELIUS, MARCUS, *Meditations* (Penguin; tr. Staniforth). AURELIUS VICTOR, *Brief Imperial Lives* (tr. Echols). COLUMELLA, *On Agriculture* (Loeb; tr. Ash, Forster, Heffner). DIO CASSIUS COCCEIANUS, *Roman History* LVII-LXXX (Loeb; tr. Cary). DIO CHRYSOSTOM, *Discourses* (Loeb; tr. Cohoon, Crosby). EPICTETUS, *Moral Discourses* (Washington Square Press; tr. Carter, Higginson). FRONTINUS, *Stratagems and Aqueducts* (Loeb; tr. Bennett and McElwain). FRONTO, *Correspondence* (Loeb; tr. Haines). GAIUS, *Institutes* (Oxford Univ. Press; tr. de Zulueta). GALEN, *On the Natural Faculties* (Loeb; tr. Brock). HERODIAN, *History of the Roman Empire* (U. of California Press; tr. Echols). JOSEPHUS, *Jewish War* (Penguin; tr. Williamson). JUVENAL, *Satires* (Midland Books; tr. Humphries). LUCAN, *Civil War* (Loeb; tr. Duff). LUCIAN, *Selected Satires* (Liberal Arts Press; tr. Reardon). MARTIAL *Selected Epigrams* (Midland Books; tr. Humphries). MINUCIUS FELIX, *Octavius* (Loeb; tr. Rendall). PERSIUS, *Satires* (Indiana U. Press; tr. Merwin). PETRONIUS, *Satiricon* (Mentor; tr. Arrowsmith). PLINY THE ELDER, *Natural History*, selections (Frederick Ungar Publ. Co.; ed. Haberly). PLINY THE YOUNGER, *Letters* (Penguin; tr. Radice). PLUTARCH, *Lives* of Galba, Otho (Modern Library; tr. Dryden). QUINTILLIAN, *Institutio Oratoria* (Loeb; tr. Butler). *Scriptores Historiae Augustae* I, II (Loeb; tr. Magie). SENECA, *The Stoic Philosophy of Seneca* (Anchor; tr. Hadas); *An Anthology of Roman Drama* (Rinehart; ed. Harsh). SILIUS ITALICUS, *Punica* (Loeb; tr. Duff). STATIUS, *Silvae, Thebaid, Achilleid* (Loeb; tr. Mozley). SUETONIUS, *Lives of the Twelve Caesars* (Modern Library; tr. Gavorse); *The Twelve Caesars* (Penguin; tr. Graves). TACITUS, *Complete Works* (Modern Library Paperbacks; tr. Church and Broadribb). TERTULLIAN, *Apology, De Spectaculis* (Loeb; tr. Glover). VELLEIUS PATERCULUS, *Compendium of Roman History* (Loeb; tr. Shipley).

8. ANARCHY AND DOMINATE (235–395 A.D.)

AMMIANUS MARCELLINUS, *History* (Loeb; tr. Rolfe). AURELIUS VICTOR, *Brief Imperial Lives* tr. Echols). CUMONT, F., *Oriental Religions in Roman Paganism* (Dover). EUSEBIUS, *History of the Church* (Penguin; tr. Williamson). HERODIAN, *History of the Roman Empire* (U. of California Press; tr. Echols). JULIAN THE APOSTATE, *Works* (Loeb; tr. Wright). PLOTINUS, *The Essential Plotinus* (Mentor; tr. O'Brien). *Scriptores Historiae Augustae* II, III (Loeb; tr. Magie). *Theodosian Code* (Princeton U. Press; tr. Pharr).

9. THE OLD AND THE NEW

ST. AUGUSTINE, *City of God* (Modern Library; tr. Dods and Merton); *Confessions* (Modern Library; tr. Pusey). BURY, J.B., *A History of the Later Roman Empire* (Dover). *Decline and Fall of the Roman Empire: Why Did It Collapse?*, ed., D. Kagan (D.C. Heath & Co.) GIBBON, E., *Decline and Fall of the Roman Empire* (Dell; ed. Bourne). GUILLAUME, A., *Islam* (Pelican). JUSTINIAN, *Institutes* (Oxford U. Press; tr. Moyle). LAING, G., *Survivals of Roman Religion* (Cooper Square Publishers). LOT, F., *The End of the Ancient World and the Beginnings of the Middle Ages* (Torchbook; ed. Downey). PROCOPIUS, *Secret History* (Ann Arbor Paperbacks; tr. Atwater). RUNCIMAN, S., *Byzantine Civilization* (Meridian). *Theodosian Code* (Princeton U. Press; tr. Pharr).

GENERAL

Ancient Roman Statutes (U. of Texas Press; tr. Johnson, Coleman-Norton, Bourne). BARROW, R., *The Romans* (Pelican). *A History of Rome*, ed., M. Hadas (Anchor; selection of sources). Harsh, P. (ed.), *An Anthology of Roman Drama* (Rinehart; selections from Plautus, Terence, Seneca). Robinson, C. A. (ed.), *Selections from Greek and Roman Historians* (Rinehart). Sinnigen, W. (ed.), *Rome* (Free Press; selection of sources) Wheeler, M., *Roman Art and Architecture* (Praeger).

Index

Roman persons are generally indexed under their gentile names (*nomina*) preceded by an abbreviation indicating the *praenomen*. However, persons usually known by their family names (*cognomina*) are so entered here, with the *praenomen* and *nomen* indicated in parentheses. Emperors and famous authors are entered under the common anglicized form of their names, but their full Latin names are given in parentheses. The more important places and peoples are listed with the page number of at least one map where they can be located. More than one map entry generally indicates additional information as to status or location.

Arnobius, 546

Arpinum, 37, 239. *See also* map, 36

Arretium, 129, 324; manufactures, 324, 357, 360–61, 505. *See also* maps, 112, 347

Arrian (Flavius Arrianus), 438

Asculum, 253, 255, 327; Battle of, 71, 99. *See also* maps, 60, 250

Asia, 154, 155, 157, 287; administration of, 188, 227, 246–47, 260–61, 263–64, 277, 313, 317, 327, 475; Arab invasion of, 585; becomes province, 183, 222, 224; economy of, 358, 499, 506, 507; Gothic raids on, 520; Mithridates in, 256. *See also* maps, 149, 260

C. Asinius Pollio, 371, 397

Assyria, 427, 428. *See also* map, 423

Ataulf the Visigoth, 576

Atellan Farce, 323

Atestine Culture, 14, 17

Athens, 150, 152, 181, 219, 260, 327, 434, 484, 520. *See also* maps, 148, 423

Atintanes, 124, 136, 166. *See also* map, 123

Attalids, 150, 161

Attalus I of Pergamum, 135

Attalus III of Pergamum, 161, 221, 224, 227

Atticus (T. Pomponius), 293, 326

Attila the Hun, 570, 577

P. Attius Varus, 295, 297

auctoritas, 341

augurs, 101

Augustales, 368, 370, 399, 483, 485

Augustine, 330, 572

Augustus (C. Julius Caesar Octavianus), emperor, 373–75, 403, 409, 410; administrative and foreign policies, 303, 339–43, 344–45, 348–54, 355, 379, 380, 388, 389, 396, 414, 432, 435, 450, 469, 473, 475, 476, 478, 490, 491, 508, 530, 557; and the army, 326, 343–44, 462, 465, 466, 467; economic policies, 355, 356, 362; and Pompey, 294; and religion, 330, 368–70, 399; rise of, 309–11, 334–35; and second triumvirate, 311–21; social and cultural policies, 364–68, 370–75, 400

Aurelian (L. Domitius Aurelianus), emperor: abandons Dacia, 520; army reforms of, 526, 534; religious policy of, 527, 544–45; wars of, 518, 519, 521, 522, 528

C. Aurelius Cotta, 276

aurum tironicum, 526, 558

auxiliary troops, 410, 464

Aventine Hill, 38, 229. *See also* map, 44

Avidius Cassius, 434, 436

Avitus (Flavius Eparchus Avitus), emperor, 570

Bacchus, 197, 329

Baecula, Battle of, 138. *See also* map, 112

Balbinus (D. Caelius Calvinus Balbinus),

emperor, 516

Balearic Isles, 224, 234, 577. *See also* maps, 148, 240, 579

bankers, banking, 179–80, 181, 188, 277, 325, 500, 507–8, 525

barbarians, settlement in the Empire, 435, 523–24, 526, 528, 551, 558–60, 565, 573–74, 578–80, 581, 582

Barcids, 115, 117, 143, 155, 166. *See also* Hamilcar; Hannibal; Hasdrubal Barca; Hasdrubal Gisgo; Mago Barca

Basques, 578. *See also* map, 579

Batavians, 407, 469. *See also* map, 422

Belisarius, 584

St. Benedict, 589

Beneventum, 71, 99, *See also* map, 75

Berbers, 577, 584, 590. *See also* maps, 559, 579

Berytus, 19. *See also* map, 20

Bestia, (L. Calpurnius), 237, 238

Bibulus (M. Calpurnius), 283, 285, 288

billetting, 471, 478

bishops, 444, 542, 546, 547

bishops of Rome, 588–90

Bithynia: administration of, 425, 440; client state, 256; organized as province, 279, wars in, 277, 278; willed to Rome, 277. *See also* map, 260.

Blossius of Cumae, 218, 224

Bocchus of Mauretania, 241

Bocchus II of Mauretania, 298

Boii, 122–23. *See also* map, 123

Bolsena, 26. *See also* map, 28

Boniface, 573, 576–77

Bononia, 154. *See also* map, 148

Bosporan Kingdom (Crimea), 349, 360, 390. *See also* map, 347

Boudicca, queen of Britons, 394

Boulogne, 388, 390. *See also* map, 422

bribery, 206, 208, 209, 228, 237, 324, 325

Britain, Britons: abandonment, by Romans, 575–77; becomes England, 593; Caesar's expeditions into, 287; conquest of, 390–91, 473; defense of, 417, 453, 519, 531, 532; economy of, 499, 523; revolt of Boudicca, 394; trade with, 357, 360, 388. *See also* maps, 284, 361, 422

Britannicus (Ti. Claudius Caesar), 391, 393

Brittany, 577. *See also* map, 578

Bronze Age, 12–14

Brundisium, 262, 315, 318, 484. *See also* map, 250

Bruttii, Bruttium, 67, 70, 72, 131, 133, 135. *See also* map, 60

Bulgars, 584, 585. *See also* map, 583

Bulla Felix, 452

bureaucracy: description of bureaus, 491–92, 494–97; formalized by Claudius, 389, 491–92; influence of, 463, 492, 497–98, 504, 534, 560, 566, 568, 572, 592; origins of, 353,

612

Diophanes, teacher of the Gracchi, 218
Dolabella (P. Cornelius), 297
domesticated animals, 8, 11–13
Domitia, 416
Domitian (T. Flavius Domitianus), emperor: administrative policies of, 414–16, 418–19, 421, 440, 492, 500; early career of, 411, 414; military policies of, 416–18, 466, 470
Cn. Domitius Ahenobarbus, 273
Cn. Domitius Ahenobarbus, husband of Agrippina II, 391, 392
L. Domitius Ahenobarbus, consul (54 B.C.), 292
Cn. Domitius Calvinus, 296
Donatus (Aelius), 547, 548, 577
Drepana, 114. *See also* map, 112
Drusilla, sister of Caligula, 388
Drusus the Elder (Nero Claudius Drusus), 350, 352, 374, 380
Drusus the Younger (Drusus Julius), son of Emperor Tiberius, 380, 381, 382, 386
Drusus Caesar, son of Germanicus, 382–83, 386
duces, 533, 560
C. Duilius, 113
duoviri, quattuorviri, 478, 485
duoviri perduellionis, 94
Dyrrachium, 293. *See also* map, 284

Ebro River, 125, 126, 137. *See also* map, 112
edict: praetor's, 186, 430, 442; provincial, 186
Edict of Caracalla, see *Constitutio Antoniniana*
education, Roman, 194–95, 368, 397, 412, 420, 441, 457, 459, 484–85
M. Egnatius Rufus, 344
Egypt, Egyptians: administration and defense of, 381, 475, 504, 511, 521; Antony and, 318–21; Caesar and, 295–96; economy of, 358, 363, 480, 499, 504, 505–6, 507; kingdom of, 150, 151, 155, 161–62, 191, 280; loss of, 582, 585, 586; prefect of, 354, 475, 491; as property of emperor, 348, 381, 475
Elagabalus (Varius Avitus Bassianus), emperor, 455–56
Elba, 6, 21, 30, 357. *See also* map, 28
emancipation, 223
Emesa, 449, 455. *See also* map, 423
Enna, 133, 216. *See also* map, 112
Q. Ennius, 195–96, 369
epibolé, 524, 564
Epictetus, 438
Epicureanism, Epicurus, 198, 270–71, 283, 304, 305, 330–31, 398, 546
Epirus, 161, 164, 167, 205, 293, 326. *See also* map, 148
equestrian class (*equites*): in the army,

463; as businessmen, 178, 189, 227, 234, 235, 242, 253, 256, 278, 325, 373; in civil service, 353–54, 368, 373, 418–19, 431, 435, 488, 490, 492–94; as jurors, 189, 228, 242, 244, 276; in the municipalities, 482–83, 488; origin of, 62, 83–84, 96, 367; in politics, 92, 227, 234, 235, 236–37, 239, 244, 245–46, 248, 257, 264, 267, 278, 343; proscribed, 265, 312
erosion of land, 172
Ethiopia, 348. *See also* map, 361
Etruria, Etruscans, 23–32; art of, 30–31; Civil Wars and, 259, 263, 272–73; conquest by Romans, 64, 69, 79–80, 96, 98; decline of, 29–31, 63, 81–82; early history of, 21, 38–39; economy of, 29, 173, 176, 219, 324, 356, 357, 504; government of, 26–27, 217; influence on Romans, 23, 31–32, 42–50, 79–80, 102, 177; language of, 24; religion of, 25–26, 32; in Rome, 42–50, 102; during Social War, 253, 254; source of, 11, 24. *See also* map, 28
Euboea, 22. *See also* map, 20
Eugenius (Flavius Eugenius), 551, 573
Euhemerus, 196, 369
Eumenes of Pergamum, 157, 160–61
Euric the Visigoth, 590
exarchs, 588, 589
extortion, extortion courts, 188–89, 227–28, 232, 234, 242, 244, 247–48, 324–25

Q. Fabius Maximus Cunctator, 129–30, 133, 136, 140, 143, 201
Fabius Valens, 404
Falerii, Faliscans, 35, 36, 42, 59, 60, 64, 97, 119. *See also* maps, 36, 61
familia, 102
C. Fannius, 228, 251–52
fasces, 27
Fausta the empress, 549
Faustina the Elder, 432
Faustina the Younger, 433, 435–36
federates (*foederati*), 573–74, 577, 578–80, 581
federation of Italy, 73–80, 117, 128, 176
Felix (Claudius Felix), 492
Felsina, 29. *See also* map, 28
Fidenae, 39, 42, 59. *See also* map, 36
Fimbria (Flavius Fimbria), 259, 260
fiscus, 356, 490, 491, 493, 494–95
flamen Dialis, 259, 368
flamines, 101
Flamininus (T. Quinctius), 152–53, 156–57, 191, 200, 208
C. Flaminius, 121–22, 123, 129, 143, 201, 204, 331
C. Flavius Clemens, 416, 541
Flavius Sabinus, 406
Florianus (M. Annius Florianus), emp., 518

615

foedus Cassianum, 50, 76, 96
fora, 79
Fortuna-Felicitas, 270–71
Forum, Roman, 39–40, 45, 46. *See also* map, 44
Forum Julii, 464. *See also* map, 422
Franks, 519, 521, 531, 550, 573, 579, 591–93; Salian, 574, 577, 579, 591–93. *See also* map, 517, 575, 579, 583
Fratres Arvales, 368, 399
freedmen (*liberti*), 174, 208, 216, 329, 365, 367–68, 483, 500; as businessmen, 354–55, 483, 500; Cornelii, 267; in government service, 389, 391, 431, 490, 491–93; numbers limited, 366–67
Fregellae, 68, 69, 98, 173, 224, 225, 229, 247. *See also* map, 75
Frisians, 577. *See also* map, 559, 578
frontiers, defense of, 305, 348–51, 412, 417–18, 426–27, 429–30, 432, 433–35, 458, 469–70, 519–22, 531–32, 549, 550, 558–60, 573, 574–78, 582
Frontinus (Sex, Julius), 418
Fronto (C. Caristanius), 418
Fronto (M. Cornelius), 440, 441
frumentarii, 471
Q. Fufius Calenus, 314
Fulvia, 314–15, 318
M. Fulvius Flaccus, 224, 251
Fundi, 37, 78, 97. *See also* map, 36
fundus (plantation), 171–72

Gabii, 39, 42. *See also* map, 36
A. Gabinius, 278
Gades, 21, 139. *See also* map, 20
Gaius, jurist, 442
Galatia, Galatians, 157, 348, 465, 476. *See also* map, 474
Galba (P. Sulpicius Galba), emperor, 395, 403–4, 424, 467, 481
Galen of Pergamum, 439, 515
Galerius (Galerius Valerius Maximianus), emperor, 531, 532, 536–37, 538, 547–48
Gallienus (P. Licinius Gallienus), emperor, 516, 518, 547; army reforms of, 525, 526, 534; defenses by, 520, 521; religion, 527, 547
Gallus (Constantius Gallus), 549–50
Gauda, 241
Gaul, Cisalpine, 30, 154, 173, 263, 280, 285, 290; organized as province, 269. *See also* map, 346
Gaul, Transalpine: administration of, 355, 480, 481; barbarian attacks on, 519; conquest and organization, 183, 285, 286, 287, 327; economy of, 359, 363, 385, 390, 499, 505, 507, 523; revolts in, 385, 402–3, 407, 519, 521, 531, 576. *See also* Franks; Gauls; map, 148, 474

Gauls: conquest by Rome, 150, 154, 158, 170; invasions of Italy by, 30, 69, 96, 122–23, 128, 132, 134–35; sack Rome, 2, 62–64, 84, 96; settle in Po Valley, 107, 125. *See also* Gaul, Cisalpine
A. Gellius, 440, 484
Genoa, 122, 135. *See also* map, 240
Genseric the Vandal, 570, 577
Gepidae, 519. *See also* maps, 559, 579
Germanicus (Nero Claudius Drusus), 380–82, 386, 432
Germans, Germany, 241–43, 350–51, 381, 403, 417, 434–35, 589. *See also* maps, 284, 346
Germany, Upper and Lower: organized, 417, 473; products of, 499. *See also* map, 422
Geta (P. Septimius Geta), emperor, 452–53
Gibbon, Edward, 436
Glaucia (C. Servilius), 244–46
Glycerius the emperor, 570
Gnosticism, Gnostics, 546
Gordian I (M. Antonius Gordianus), emperor, 516
Gordian II (M. Antonius Gordianus), emperor, 516
Gordian III (M. Antonius Gordianus), emperor, 516, 520
Goths, 516, 518, 520, 549, 550, 551, 552, 573, 582, 589. *See also* Ostrogoths; Visigoths; map, 517
governors, provincial, 185–87, 204–5, 463
Gracchus (C. Sempronius), 188, 215, 224–31, 234, 247, 251, 303, 306, 328
Gracchus (P. Sempronius), 218
Gracchus (Ti. Sempronius), the Elder, 158, 218
Gracchus (Ti. Sempronius), tribune, 165, 199, 200, 215, 216, 218–26, 230–31, 269, 272, 306
grain, distribution of, 225–26, 244–45, 247, 266, 285, 301, 324, 345. *See also* Annona; *Lex Livia frumentaria; Lex Sempronia frumentaria*
Gratian (Flavius Gratianus), emperor, 550–51, 560, 569
Greece, Greeks, 22–23, 147, 152, 164, 176, 179, 327, 358, 394, 411, 499, 507, 585; Greek culture and the Romans, 147, 193–201, 581; language, 179, 193, 581, 585. *See also* colonies, Greek; map, 20
guilds. *See collegia*
Gundobald, 570

Hadrian (P. Aelius Hadrianus), emperor; administrative policies of, 428–29, 430–31, 432, 460, 481, 488, 493; character of, 431, 438, 441; early career of, 427; foreign policy of, 428; and the law, 430, 442; military policy of, 429–30, 465, 468–69, 470

Masinissa of Numidia, 139, 140, 141, 163, 235
Massilia, 70, 125, 159, 190, 191, 224, 292. *See also* map, 148
Massiva, 237
Mastarna. *See* Servius Tullius
master-general of the army, 561, 573
master of the horse, 94
master of the offices, 560–61
Mauretania, 182, 349, 388, 390, 417, 473, 519, 521, 532, 550. *See also* maps, 148, 422
Maxentius (M. Aurelius Valerius Maxentius), emperor, 537, 538
Maximian (M. Aurelius Valerius Maximianus), emperor, 530–31, 532, 537
Maximin Daia (Galerius Valerius Maximinus), emperor, 537, 538
Maximinus (C. Julius Verus Maximinus), emperor, 458, 516, 523, 525, 547
meddix, 67
C. Memmius, 237
mercenary soldiers, 526, 558, 571, 581. *See also* Carthage, army of
Merovingians, 590, 592
Merula (L. Cornelius), 259
Mesopotamia, 427, 428, 448, 452, 455, 458, 473, 520, 521, 531, 532. *See also* map, 423
Messallina, 391
Messana, 110–11, 119. *See also* map, 112
Messapia, Messapians, 10, 72, 99. *See also* map, 60
Metaurus River, Battle of, 135. *See also* map, 112
Metellus (Q. Caecilius), censor (131 B.C.), 217
Metellus Creticus (Q. Caecilius), 278
Metellus Numidicus (Q. Caecilius), 238–39, 245, 246
Metellus Pius (Q. Caecilius), 262, 263, 274, 275
Metellus Pius Scipio Nasica (Q. Caecilius), 288, 295, 297, 298
metropolitans (archbishops), 444, 542, 546
Micipsa, 235
Milan (Melpum), 62, 96, 123, 522, 531, 539; Edict of, 548. *See also* map, 123
military tribunate with consular power, 82, 84, 87, 96
military tribunes, 88, 463
Milo (T. Annius), 286, 288
Milvian Bridge, Battle of, 538, 548
mimes, 323
mines, 506
Minturnae, 37, 216. *See also* map, 36
M. Minucius Felix, 546
M. Minucius Rufus, 129–30, 143, 204
Misenum, 315, 318, 343, 359, 464. *See also* map, 347
Mithraism, Mithras, 443, 544
Mithridates of Armenia, 386, 388
Mithridates of Pergamum, 296

Mithridates of Pontus, 256, 260, 264, 274, 277–79
Mithridatic War I, 256, 260–61, 277
Mithridatic War II, 277–79
Moesia, 350, 418, 520, 523. *See also* map, 347
Mohammed, 586
monasticism, 553, 589, 594
money, value of Roman, 176, 178, 466, Appendix
Montanists, 546–47
Moors, 531, 550, 584. *See also* Mauretania
mos maiorum, 56
Motya, 21. *See also* map, 20
Mt. Algidus, Battle of, 59, 96. *See also* map, 61
L. Mummius, 200
Munda, Battle of, 299. *See also* map, 284
municipia: decline of, 500, 522–23, 562–63, 564; description of, 481–85; government of, 302, 334, 425, 435, 436–37, 452, 461, 477, 479–81, 485–89, 499, 562–63, 564; origins of, 78–79, 261
Mutina, 154, 310. *See also* map, 148
Mycenaean Culture, 14
Mylae, Battle of, 113. *See also* map, 112
Myos Hormos, 363. *See also* map, 361

Nabis, 152–54, 156
Cn. Naevius, 122, 195
Naples, 67, 68, 70, 98. *See also* map, 61
Narbo, 234. *See also* map, 240
Narcissus, 496
Narses I, 532
navy, Roman, 464–65
Neolithic Age, 6–9, 11, 35, 100
Neoplatonism, 527, 528–29, 545, 550
Neo-Pythagoreans, 399
neoteroi, 332
Nepet, 60, 64, 97. *See also* map, 61
Nero (Ti. Claudius Drusus Germanicus Caesar), emperor, 391, 392–95, 396, 398, 402, 403, 405, 408, 411, 426, 465, 481, 500, 507, 541
Nero Caesar, son of Germanicus, 382, 386
Nerva (M. Cocceius Nerva), emperor, 416, 421–24, 425, 439, 483, 500, 501
New Carthage, 138. *See also* map, 112
nexum, 85–86
Nicaea, Council of, 548, 551
Nicolaus of Damascus, 371
Nicomedes of Bithynia, 256
Nicomedia, 522, 531, 537, 539. *See also* map, 517
Niger (C. Pescennius), 448
Nisibis, 448, 452, 520. *See also* map, 517
nobility, 82, 86, 178, 190, 207, 231, 236, 340, 357, 369, 373. *See also* patricians; senators
Nola, 67, 68, 69, 98, 257, 259, 373, 375. *See also* map, 61
C. Norbanus, 262

93, 96, 97

plebiscites, 55, 93; on Caesar's candidacy, 289

Q. Pleminius, 139–40

Pleuratus the Illyrian, 136

Pliny the Elder (C. Plinius Secundus), 360, 399

Pliny the Younger (C. Plinius Caecilius Secundus), 418, 425, 440, 441, 444, 484, 487–88, 500, 515, 541

Plotina, 460

Plotinus, 528–29, 545

Plutarch, 1, 437–38

Po River, 5, 363; Valley, 357, 502. *See also* maps, 123, 422

Polybius, 95, 192, 194, 217, 330

Pompeia, 281

Pompeii, 177, 253, 357, 414, 420, 487. *See also* map, 347

Cn. Pompeius, 298–99

Q. Pompeius, 165

Sex. Pompeius, 299, 312–13, 314–16

Q. Pompeius Rufus, 258

Cn. Pompeius Strabo, 255, 258, 259, 263, 273

Pompey the Great (Cn. Pompeius Magnus), 263, 269, 272, 273–76, 278–94, 295, 298, 299, 326, 327, 328, 340, 490

pontiffs, Roman, 2, 101, 370

Pontine Plains, 65, 304. *See also* map, 61

Pontus, 256, 260, 264, 277, 278, 279, 296, 348, 388. *See also* maps, 260, 423

popes. *See* bishops of Rome

C. Popillius Laenas, consul (172 B.C.), 162

M. Popillius Laenas, consul (139 B.C.), 165

M. Popillius Laenas, consul (173 B.C.), 202, 210

P. Popillius Laenas, consul (132 B.C.), 222, 225, 234

Poppaea, 393, 395, 405

popular party (*populares*), 129, 207, 240, 272, 276, 278–80, 297, 302, 303

population problems, 168–70, 215, 250, 301, 364–67, 409, 460, 501, 523, 564, 580

Populonia, 176. *See also* map, 28

Porphyry, 529, 545

A. Postumius Albinus, 238

Sp. Postumius Albinus, 237–38

Postumus of Gaul (M. Cassianius Latinius Postumus), 521

praefecti (circuit judges), 79

praefectus vehiculorum, 497

Praeneste, 29, 37, 39, 42–43, 64, 65, 177, 263. *See also* map, 36

praesides, 533

praetorian guard, 345, 382, 389, 404, 405, 410, 446–48, 456, 458, 466, 534, 538; prefect of, 354, 451, 490, 498, 534, 535, 560–61

praetors, praetorship: duties of, 89, 93–94, 267, 268; early Latin title, 37, 53;

established as judicial officers, 85, 88, 97; as governors, 121; peregrine, 120–21, 333–34; rank of, 103

prefect of the camp, 464

Prefectures, 560

presbyters, 444

price controls, 536

primipilus, 462–63

primus ordo, 462–63

princeps, principate, 288, 341, 372, 373, 379, 387, 396, 407–8, 419, 490, 530

Probus (M. Aurelius Probus), emperor, 518, 519, 521, 528

procurators, 353–54, 476, 477, 479, 490, 492, 495, 496, 498

proletariat: in the army, 410; as colonists, 283, 302, 328–29; economic and social status, 173–74, 210, 216, 301, 329, 345, 373, 483, 564, 571–72; origins of, 86, 215, 219; in politics, 92–93, 206, 210, 228, 231, 234–35, 237, 239, 244, 246, 247–48, 253, 264, 266, 272, 308–9, 487; religion of, 197, 329–30, 369, 543, 580

promagistracy, 137, 143, 185–86, 204–5, 269, 475

propaganda: Augustan, 316, 319–20; Roman, 156, 157, 166

Sex. Propertius, 371, 372

proscriptions, 265, 292, 312–13, 322

protectorates. *See* client states

provinces, 183–89, 475–78, 533–34, 560; acquisition of, 473; administration of, 121, 180, 183–89, 268–69, 303–4, 324–25, 327, 373, 384–85, 394–95, 408, 415, 425, 429, 440, 446, 475–79, 533–34, 560; assemblies, *see concilia*, provincial; classification of, 475; patrons of, 189, 479

provocatio. *See appeal*, right of

Ptolemy I, general of Alexander, 150

Ptolemy V, 155

Ptolemy XI Auletes, 295

Ptolemy XII, 294, 295–96

Ptolemy XIII, 296

Ptolemy XIV Caesarion, 319, 321

Ptolemy of Alexandria, 439

Ptolemy of Mauretania, 388

publicani, 187, 188

public lands, 171, 172, 220–21, 222–24, 226, 233–34, 251, 411, 415. *See also* common lands

public post. *See cursus publicus*

public works, 46–47, 174, 177, 266, 304, 328, 362–63, 370, 385, 388, 390, 410, 411–12, 413, 414–15, 425–26, 429, 441, 467, 534

Punic War I, 111–17

Punic War II, 126–44, 147, 169, 170, 186, 502

Punic War III, 163–64

Pupienus (M. Clodius Pupienus), emperor, 516

Puteoli, 177, 324, 357, 359, 388, 505. *See also* map, 347

Pydna, Battle of, 160. *See also* map, 148

Pyrrhus, 70–72, 80, 99, 109

Quadi, 418, 434, 446, 519. *See also* map, 422

quaestors, quaestorship, 54, 83, 87, 90, 94, 96, 103, 120, 186, 267, 475, 477; municipal, 486, 501

P. Quinctilius Varus, 351, 352, 462

quinquennales, 478, 485

Quintilian (M. Fabius Quintilianus), 419

Quintillus (M. Aurelius Claudius Quintillus), emperor, 518, 522

Raetia, Raetians, 10, 12, 16, 350, 495, 499, 519. *See also* maps, 15, 474

rate of interest, 85–86, 97, 180, 266, 277, 354

Ravenna, 343, 359, 464, 569, 584. *See also* map, 575

Recared the Visigoth, 590

regimentation, economic and social, 457, 460, 472, 528, 539, 562–67, 571, 581

Regulus (M. Atilius), 113–14

religion: Christian, 32; Etruscan, 25–26, 32; Italic, 18; Latin, 41–42; Neolithic, 9; Roman, 45, 101, 196–97, 235, 244, 285, 301, 329–31, 368–70, 399–400, 401, 413, 420, 443–44, 457–58, 479, 485, 499, 526–27, 533, 536–37, 540–48, 551–53, 557–58, 580, 584, 585; terramara, 14. *See also* Christianity, imperial cult, Isis, Mithraism

res privata, 449

revenues, government, 169, 175–76, 282, 452, 496; of the *municipia*, 486–87

rex (king), 41, 46

Rhegium, 22, 111. *See also* map, 112

rhetoric, 396–97, 412, 437

Rhodes, 150–52, 157, 161, 166, 181, 411, 481. *See also* map, 149

Ricimer, 570, 573

di Rienze, Cola, 408

roads, Roman, 74, 183, 234, 334, 362–63, 385, 388, 392, 413, 414, 417, 506, 534; *Via Appia*, 87, 98; *Via Domitia*, 234

Roma, the goddess, 369, 479

Romanitas, 480, 539, 582

Rome, city of: capture of, 63, 258–59, 263, 576–77, 584; decline in importance, 539, 549; defense, 63, 97, 519; disorders in, 287–88, 405, 570; under Etruscans, 29, 43–49; fire in, 392, 393; foundation of, 38–42, 100; prefect of, 345, 451, 490; public works and services of, 174, 304, 344–45, 388, 390, 392, 425, 484, 588; residences in, 174; slum population of, 215, 572. *See also* map, 44

Romulus Augustus, emperor, 561, 571, 580

Romulus and Remus, 38, 369

L. Roscius Otho, 278

Rubicon River, 269, 292, 299. *See also* map, 250

P. Rupilius, 216, 222, 225

P. Rutilius Rufus, 238, 243, 246–47, 252

Sabellian, Sabellians, 10, 17–18, 66–67, 70. *See also* map, 15

Sabines, 18, 39, 42, 45, 49, 51, 69, 72, 78, 96, 98–99, 121. *See also* maps, 15, 51

sacrifice, human, 122–23, 132, 235

Sacriportus, 263

Saguntum, 125–27, 137, 166. *See also* map, 112

Sallust (C. Sallustius Crispus), 211, 332

salt, 6

saltus (ranches), 171–72

Salvius Julianus, 430, 442

Samnite Wars, 67–70, 98, 185

Samnites, Samnium, 30, 65, 66–70, 71, 97–98, 130–31, 159, 170, 173, 253, 255, 261, 263, 265. *See also* maps, 60, 75, 112, 250

Samos, 411, 481. *See also* map, 474

Sampsiceramus, 294

Sardinia, 5, 14, 27, 117, 118, 120, 159, 183, 224, 263; economy of, 358, 499, 507, 572; organized as province, 121, 184; under Vandals, 577. *See also* map, 148

Sarmatians, 418, 434, 549. *See also* map, 423

Sarmizegethusa, 426. *See also* map, 423

satire, 203, 323

Saturninus (L. Appuleius), 244–46

Saxons, 519, 576. *See also* maps, 517, 575, 579

Scaevola (P. Mucius), 199, 217

Scaevola (Q. Mucius), 246–47, 330, 334

Scipio (Cn. Cornelius), 127–28, 136–37

Scipio (L. Cornelius), 157, 218

Scipio (P. Cornelius), 127–28, 136–37

Scipio Aemilianus (P. Cornelius), 163–64, 165, 194–95, 211, 217, 218–19, 223, 236, 251

Scipio Africanus (P. Cornelius), 138–41, 143, 157, 183, 201, 208, 218, 331

Scipio Asiaticus (L. Cornelius), 262

Scipio Nasica (P. Cornelius), 209–10, 222, 223

Scolacium, 227. *See also* map, 250

Scots, 576. *See also* map, 575

Scribonia, 315, 316

secession: to Sacred Mount, 55; to Janiculum, 86, 88. *See also* maps, 44, 51

secret ballot, 209, 217, 223, 324

Segeda, 162. *See also* map, 148

Sejanus (L. Aelius), 382–84, 386, 388, 396

A. Sempronius Asellio, 256

C. Sempronius Tuditanus, 223

Sena, 70, 99. *See also* map, 60

Senate, senators: composition of, 90, 95, 103, 205, 207–9, 248, 267, 305, 341–42, 368, 390, 450, 459; decline of, 389–90, 396, 414, 430–31, 436, 442, 446, 449–50, 459–60, 476, 528,

623

Tyre, 19, 21. *See also* map, 20

Ulpian (Domitius Ulpianus), 451, 457, 458
Umayyads, 586–87
Umbria, Umbrians, 69, 173, 253, 254, 259, 357. *See also* maps, 15, 250
urban cohorts, 345, 466, 490
urbanization, 173–74, 216, 479–80
Utica, 21, 118, 239, 298. *See also* map, 20

Vaccaei, 162–63. *See also* map, 148
Valens (Flavius Valens), emperor, 550, 551, 560, 574
Valentinian I (Flavius Valentinianus), emperor, 550, 560, 569
Valentinian II (Flavius Valentinianus), emperor, 550–51
Valentinian III (Flavius Placidus Valentinianus), emperor, 569–70, 576–77
Valerian (P. Licinius Valerianus), emperor, 516, 518, 520, 525, 527, 547
Valerius Flaccus, 419
L. Valerius Flaccus, consul (86 B.C.), 259
L. Valerius Flaccus, *interrex* (82 B.C.), 264
M. Valerius Laevinus, 134
M. Valerius Messalla, 371
Q. Valerius Orca, 292
Vandals, 506, 519, 570, 575, 576; Asding, 574, 576–77, 584, 589, 590–91; Siling, 576. *See also* map, 559, 575, 578, 579
Varius Hybrida, 253, 255
Varro (M. Terentius), 49, 95, 276, 292, 304, 334, 368
P. Vatinius, 285
Veii, 30, 52, 59–62, 77, 83–84, 96, 116. *See also* map, 28
Velitrae, 65, 66, 339. *See also* map, 61
M. Velleius Paterculus, 397
Venetia, Venetians, 10, 13, 17, 62, 578, 588. *See also* map, 15
P. Ventidius Bassus, 317
Venus, 271
Venusia, 253. *See also* map, 75
Vercellae, Battle of, 243, 245. *See also* map, 240
Vergil (P. Vergilius Maro), 32, 196, 371–72
L. Verginius Rufus, 395, 403, 404
C. Verres, 276, 324
ver sacrum, 18

L. Verus (L. Aurelius Verus), emperor, 432–34, 435, 436, 440, 446, 531, 569
Vespasian (T. Flavius Vespasianus), emperor, 402, 406–8, 409–13, 414, 416, 417, 481, 500
Vestal Virgins, 235, 320, 415, 456
Vestini, 18, 68, 253. *See also* map, 15
Vesuvius, 414
veterans, 244, 245, 265–66, 270, 272, 280, 282, 283, 297, 302, 308, 310, 314, 479, 482, 565
veto, right of, 95
vexillationes, 526, 534
Vibenna, brothers, 29, 43–44
C. Vibius Pansa, 310, 311
vicars, 533, 560, 561
vicomagister, 345, 367, 369
Vicus Tuscus, 47, 176. *See also* map, 44
villa economy, 508, 567–68, 593
Villanovan Culture, 14–17, 24, 37
vineyards, 171, 415
M. Vinicius, 350
Viriathus, 162, 165, 167
Visigoths, 520, 570, 574, 576, 577, 578–79, 586, 590, 592. *See also* Goths; maps, 559, 575, 578, 579
Vitellius (A. Vitellius), emperor, 404, 405–6, 481, 492
M. Vitruvius Pollio, 358
Volscians, 18, 29, 49, 51, 59, 63, 65, 66, 96. *See also* map, 15
Voltumna, 26
Volusianus (C. Vibius Gallus Volusianus), emperor, 516

Wales, 417, 576. *See also* map, 578
Wallia, 576
Watch, Prefecture of, 345, 491, 497
Western Culture, 529, 552, 593–94
women, place in society of, 31–32, 333
writing, introduction of, 2

Xanthippus, 114

Zama, Battle of, 141. *See also* map, 112
Zela, Battle of, 296–97. *See also* map, 284
Zeno (Flavius Zeno), emperor, 588
Zeno, king of Armenia, 386
Zenobia, 522
zilath, 26–27
Zoroastrianism, Zoroastrians, 459, 586

3456789